BY THE SAME AUTHOR

STRAVINSKY

SELECTED CORRESPONDENCE

ALFRED A. KNOPF   NEW YORK   1985

STRAVINSKY

SELECTED CORRESPONDENCE
VOLUME III

EDITED AND
WITH COMMENTARIES BY
ROBERT CRAFT

This is a Borzoi Book published by Alfred A. Knopf, Inc.

Copyright © 1985 by Robert Craft

All rights reserved under International and Pan-American Copyright Conventions.

Published in the United States by Alfred A. Knopf, Inc., New York.

Distributed by Random House, Inc., New York.

Letters and other copyright material
from the Stravinsky Archives are published
by kind permission of the Paul Sacher Foundation.

Library of Congress Cataloging in Publication Data

(Revised for volume 3)

Stravinsky, Igor, 1882–1971.   Stravinsky, selected correspondence.

Includes bibliographical references and indexes.

1. Stravinsky, Igor, 1882–1971.   2. Composers—
Correspondence.   I. Craft, Robert.   II. Title.

ML410.S932A395   1982   780'.92'4   [B]   81-47495

ISBN 0-394-51870-5 (v. 1)

ISBN 0-394-52813-1 (v. 2)

ISBN 0-394-54220-7 (v. 3)

Manufactured in the United States of America

First American Edition

To the memory of

VERA ARTUROVNA STRAVINSKY

non enim posthac alia caleba femina
HORACE

Tant je l'aimais
qu'en elle encore je vis
SCÈVE

The most beautiful union between Russia and the West is the work of Stravinsky, which summarizes the whole thousand-year history of Western music and at the same time remains in its musical imagination deeply Russian. (Milan Kundera)

CONTENTS

III

ACKNOWLEDGMENTS

The letters from Jacques Handschin were translated from the Russian by Lucia Davidova. The Russian letters in the Boosey & Hawkes chapter were translated by Helen and Franklin Reeve. Mrs. Reeve also translated the German letters in the B. Schotts Söhne chapter. The rest of the letters were translated from the French by myself, Eva Resnikova, and Kristin Crawford.

The second and third sections of Appendix D appeared, in somewhat different form, in *The Times Literary Supplement,* October 1984, and *The Musical Times,* November 1984, respectively.

I am indebted to Eva Resnikova, Phyllis Crawford, Elbert Lenrow, Lawrence Morton, and Robert Gottlieb for valuable suggestions and improvements in the manuscript. I would also like to express my appreciation to Betty Anderson, whose attractive and lucid design has enhanced all three volumes.

I

CORRESPONDENCE WITH

1912 ✑ 1918

CLAUDE & EMMA DEBUSSY

CLAUDE DEBUSSY TO STRAVINSKY

80, avenue du Bois de Boulogne
Paris
April 10, 1912[1]

Dear friend,

Thanks to you I spent an exquisite Easter holiday in the company of Petrushka, the terrible Moor, and the delicious ballerina. I imagine that you have spent incomparable moments with these dolls . . . and I do not know of many things as precious as the conjuring trick [*"tour de Passe-Passe"*], as you call it, with its mysterious transformation of mechanical spirits into human beings at the hands of a sorcerer. . . . There is a sonorous magic here, of which, until now, I believe you are the unique inventor, and an orchestral infallibility that I have encountered only in *Parsifal*—you understand what I mean, I am sure! You will go much further than *Petrushka,* no doubt, but you can already be proud of what that work represents.

You must excuse me for having taken so long to thank you for your score [*Zvezdoliki*], whose dedication attributes to me a much too exalted role in the mastery of music, which we both serve with the same zeal and selflessness. . . . Unfortunately, I have had sick people around me lately! My wife in particular, who has been suffering for many days. . . . I have even had to play house-husband; and let me say right away that I have no talent for the job.

I hope soon to have the joy of seeing you, since [someone has had] the fine idea of playing your music again. . . . Please remember the street where we live, where everyone will be delighted to see you.

Affectionately yours,   Claude Debussy

DEBUSSY TO STRAVINSKY

80, avenue du Bois de Boulogne
November 8, 1912

Clarens

Don't faint, dear friend, it is only I! Just think, by the time we would have endeavored, you to understand and I to explain, why I have not written, our hair would have fallen out! And then, one admirable thing does happen here: you are spoken of at least once a day. Your friend Chouchou[2] has composed a fantasy about *Petrushka* that would make tigers roar, and though I have threat-

---

[1] Stravinsky had written to Debussy on November 4, 1911.

[2] Debussy's daughter.

ened her with every torture, she continues to claim that "you would find it very good." So how can one be expected not to think of you?

I still remember the performance of *Le Sacre du printemps* at Laloy's[3]. . . . It haunts me like a good nightmare, and I try in vain to recover the impression. For this reason I await the performance like a gluttonous child to whom sweets have been promised.

As soon as I have a decent set of proofs of *Jeux,* I will send it to you. . . . I would like to have your opinion of the three-way banter! You were stunned by the title *Jeux,* and preferred *Le Parc!* Take my word for it, *Jeux* is better: first, it is clearer; second, it is an apt description of the "horrors" experienced by the three characters.

When are you coming to Paris [so that]—finally!—some real music can be presented?

Fond regards from the three of us to your wife and yourself!

Your old friend,   Claude Debussy

DEBUSSY TO STRAVINSKY

Clarens

Paris
January 1, 1913[4]
[Telegram]

Best wishes to you and yours. Letter follows.   Debussy

STRAVINSKY TO DEBUSSY

80, avenue du Bois de Boulogne
Paris

Clarens
[January 1, 1913]
[Draft of a telegram]

Best wishes for the New Year and above all good health for all of you and all of us. Affectionately,   Stravinsky

DEBUSSY TO STRAVINSKY

Hôtel Splendide
avenue Carnot

[Paris]
May, 15, 1913
[Hand-delivered note]

Dear friend,

My telephone is out of order, and I fear that you may have attempted to reach me without success. If you have seen Nijinsky and he has [signed] the papers, would you please give them to my chauffeur, since it is urgent that they be at the Société des Auteurs before five o'clock? Thank you. . . .

Your old   Claude Debussy

---

[3] Louis Laloy (1873–1944), French musicologist and critic, author of a study of Debussy (1909).

[4] Stravinsky had written a postcard to Debussy on December 13, 1912 (text in the Alfred Dupont Collection, Paris).

DEBUSSY TO STRAVINSKY   *[Paris]*
                                                    May 31, 1913
Hôtel Splendide   *[Pneumatique]*
avenue Carnot

Dear Stravinsky,

I tried in vain to telephone you (perhaps there was someone behind all this?),
to find out when you and your wife will honor us by coming to dinner, since
good traditions should not be lost.

    So reply as soon as possible, and be assured that I am, as always,

                      your devoted old   Claude Debussy

EMMA DEBUSSY TO CATHERINE STRAVINSKY   *80, avenue du Bois de Boulogne*
                                                            Paris
Hôtel Splendide   *June 11, 1913*[5]
[Forwarded to 29, boulevard
Victory Hugo, Neuilly]

Dear madame,

Not having heard from your husband, and not knowing . . . where to find you,
we are very worried. We were informed that you left the hotel. If you have a
minute, please drop me a line. All my devoted fond wishes,

                            Emma Debussy

E. DEBUSSY TO C. STRAVINSKY   *Thursday [June 1913]*

What you are going through is terribly sad, Madame, the more so because you
are surrounded by affectionate people who can do nothing but wait for that
wretched fever to pass, powerless to speed the recovery!

    Please do not hesitate to ask me for whatever you may need; the automo-
bile [facilitates matters], and I could send a package off to you immediately.
You must be tired, despite your remarkable energy, and I would like to diminish
your torment as much as possible.

    I await news about your poor sick one.

    With all of our fond wishes and sympathy, dear Madame, I send you my
best regards.

                        Emma Cl. Debussy

---

[5] Evidently, Debussy had not received the 4-hand score of the *Sacre* that Stravinsky
had mailed two days before: "To my very dear friend Claude Debussy, in memory of
the battle of May 29, 1913, [from] his Igor Stravinsky, Paris, June 9, 1913."

DEBUSSY TO STRAVINSKY   *[Paris]*
                                                August 18, 1913
[Ustilug]

Dear old Stravinsky,

Excuse my delay in thanking you for the package, made precious by its dedication, among its other qualities.

I was just overtaken by expulsive gingivitis. . . . It is villainous and menacing, since one could wake up one morning to find that all one's teeth have fallen out! After that there's not much left to do but have them made into a necklace! Perhaps that is no consolation?

The music for *Le Roi des étoiles*[6] is extraordinary. It is probably "the harmony of the spheres" of which Plato speaks (don't ask me the page number!). I cannot foresee a possible performance of this "cantata for planets," except maybe on Sirius or Aldebaran. As for our more modest Earth, I dare say that a performance would be lost in the abyss. I hope that you have completely recovered. You must, because music needs you so much.

Would you give my respects to your charming mother, and my best wishes to your wife?

Your devoted old   Claude Debussy

E. DEBUSSY TO C. STRAVINSKY   *Wednesday morning [October 1913]*

What must you think of me, dear friend? If I had to describe all of the mishaps that have not ceased to befall us since our departure, you would have a small tome. I shall abridge as much as possible:

My mother-in-law, very ill—
My mother, ill—
My husband, ill—
And your devoted friend, also ill, anxious, and crazy.

We have spent these long and insipid days trying to restore ourselves, except that the two poor old mothers are too aged to recover completely. . . .

Do you forgive me for having remained silent for so long?

How I envy you the tranquility of Clarens. Calm is the friend of work. . . .

Life here is the same, a bit of a mess [illegible], but there is no recourse. To change things we would have to go away, and at present only one departure is on the horizon: that of my husband for Moscow and St. Petersburg. He seems quite sad about it, but I think it is almost harder for me than for him, because those who are almost "old" don't like to separate often.

I would very much like to have news of you all. It would be very kind of you to write to me.

---

[6] The printed vocal score of *Zvezdoliki* with Stravinsky's autograph inscription to Debussy is in the British Museum.

We attended a wonderful performance of *Boris,* though, alas, Boris himself . . . !, the only one, was in St. Petersburg. The other singers were truly superb, but then: nothing more! It is a real pity and a real disaster.

How I would like to see you. Won't you come here someday?

With my respectful regards to your mother-in-law, I send my sincere fond regards to you and your husband.

> Your friend,   Emma Claude Debussy

Chouchou embraces you, of course. My husband sends you his devoted respects.

DEBUSSY TO STRAVINSKY   *Paris*
                                                           November 9, 1913

Dear Stravinsky,

Because one still believes in certain traditions, one wonders why one's letter is not answered. But the music I have just received [from you] is worth more, for the affirmation and victory it contains! Naturally your growing mastery makes certain people uncomfortable, and if you are not already dead, it is no fault of theirs. They did not fail to let forth the most discordant protestations; I have never believed anything in the gossip columns—need I tell you? No! . . . Nor do I need to tell you that I enjoyed seeing my name associated with such a beautiful thing, whose beauty will increase with time.

For someone like me, who is on his way down the other side of the hill but still in possession of an ardent passion for music, there is a special satisfaction in declaring how much you have enlarged the boundaries of the permissible in the Empire of Sound. Pardon these rather grandiloquent words, but they express my thought precisely!

You have probably learned of the lamentable fate of the Théâtre des Champs-Elysées. It is really a pity that the one place in Paris that was devoted to the honest presentation of music did not succeed. May I ask you, dear friend, what you plan to do about it? I saw Diaghilev at *Boris Godunov,* the only performance, and he said nothing to me. . . . If you can give me a hint without being indiscreet, do not hesitate. In any case, will you be coming to Paris?

What a lot of questions, you will say. If you do not feel like answering . . .

Your postcard arrived this very moment. So, dear friend, you did not receive my letter? That is too bad for me, since you must be holding this against me. Did I bungle your address? And, then, Ustilug is so far away. . . . I will not be going to Lausanne, for rather complex reasons, which, in any case, are of no interest. That is one more reason for you to come to Paris, to afford me the joy of seeing you again. . . .

Agreed that I shall leave for Moscow on December 1. I sense that you will not be there! You know that my trip will be more arduous [without you]. I wrote to Koussevitzky on this subject, requesting some indispensable information, but he has not replied!

For the Société de la Musique Actuelle, I want only to be amenable and to thank them for the honor they wish to bestow upon me. But I do not yet know whether I will have enough time to stay for their concert!

My wife and Chouchou send their fond regards to you and your wife.

Your devoted old friend, as always,   Claude Debussy

THE DEBUSSYS TO THE STRAVINSKYS

Paris
December 30, 1913
[Telegram]

Touched by your remembrance. We send fond wishes for the New Year. Emma Claude Debussy

DEBUSSY TO STRAVINSKY

[Paris]
October 24, 1915[7]

First, I am overjoyed at long last to have news of you, very dear friend, through your friends, who, for I know not what reason, left me in the dark as to your health and place of residence.

We are doing almost well, or, rather, as well as most French people. As is natural, we have had our share of sorrows, and of personal and domestic difficulties. Now that the need to participate in this tragic "concert" consumes Europe and the rest of the world, one wonders why the inhabitants of the planet Mars don't join in the game. As you put it, "they won't drive us crazy." Nevertheless, there is something higher than the brute force that "closes the window" on beauty and destroys the true meaning of life. But we will have to open our eyes and ears when the necessary noise of the cannon makes way for other sounds! The world will have to be cleansed of this bad seed. We will have to kill the microbe of false pride and organized ugliness that we have not always perceived for what it is: simple weakness.

You are definitely one of those who can wage a victorious fight against these "gases," as deadly as the others, for which we have no masks.

Dear Stravinsky, you are a great artist! Be a great Russian artist in all ways! It is a wonderful thing to be of one's country, attached to one's soil, like the humble peasant! And when the foreigner treads upon it, how bitter are the jokes about internationalism.

In these last years, when I felt the Austro-German miasma extending into the arts, I would have liked to have more authority, in order to cry out in distress and warn of the danger confronting us . . . !

How did we fail to see that these people were attempting to destroy our art, as they prepared the destruction of our countries? And especially [with] that old racial hatred, which will end only with the end of the Germans! Will there

---

[7] Stravinsky had written to Debussy on October 11, saying that the Germans were cold-bloodedly aiming at the destruction of the morale of the Allies (text in the Alfred Dupont Collection, Paris).

ever be a last German? I remain convinced that German soldiers beget German soldiers.

For the Nocturnes, [Gustave] Doret, the Swiss composer, is right: I made a lot of changes. Unfortunately, I have broken off relations with the publisher (Fromont, rue du Colisée). The other annoyance is that, at the moment, there are no copyists capable of doing delicate work! I shall continue searching and endeavor to satisfy Ansermet.

I must admit that music is in a sad state here. . . . Its ends are strictly charitable. But surely music itself is not to blame. I myself was not able to compose for a year, and only in these last three months, spent at the seashore with friends, have I recovered the faculty of musical thinking. The state of war, although we play no direct part in it, is contrary to thought. Only that Olympian egotist Goethe managed to work, apparently on the very day that the French entered Weimar. . . . We also have Pythagoras, who was killed by a soldier at the moment he was about to resolve God knows what problem. Moreover, I have only written pure music, 12 Etudes for piano, and two sonatas for various instruments—in our old form, which, mercifully, did not impose tetralogical auditory efforts.

And you, dear friend, what have you done? Be assured that you can send me [promises] on that question, which contains no base curiosity, only a continuation of my affection for you.

And your wife? And your children? Did you have worries about them?

My wife's eyes have been very bad, and she had intolerable [rheumatoid arthritis]. Chouchou has a head cold, which she transforms into something monstrous for the attention of those who regard her little person.

One terrible problem is not to know when we will see each other again and to have only the feeble resources of "words." Finally, be assured that I am your loyal old

Claude Debussy

All of our fond thoughts for all of you.

I received a notice from the Société des Auteurs that you chose me as your sponsor for membership in that organization. I thank you.

STRAVINSKY TO EMMA DEBUSSY   *Morges*
                                                        March 28, 1918
80, avenue du Bois de Boulogne   *[Telegram]*

We have learned of the great unhappiness that has just befallen you. Dear Madame and friend, know that we share your grief with all our heart.   Stravinsky

CORRESPONDENCE WITH

<hr>

1 9 1 2 ~~ *1 9 2 3*

<hr>

E R I K   S A T I E

STRAVINSKY TO ERIK SATIE

May 18, 1912
[Calling card]

Dear M. Satie,

I beg you to give me the pleasure of your presence at the Châtelet Thursday at nine o'clock for the dress rehearsal of *Petrushka*. Do not neglect to bring our friend [Roland-] Manuel. I want that very much.

> Yours truly,   Igor Stravinsky

SATIE TO STRAVINSKY

Arcueil-Cachan
June 14, 1913

Hôtel Splendide
Paris
[Forwarded to 29, boulevard Victor Hugo, Neuilly]

My dear friend,

I heard that you are ill with disagreeable stomach troubles. It is not serious, is it? I plan to come and console you in two or three days.

> Fondly,   Erik Satie

SATIE TO STRAVINSKY

Arcueil-Cachan
July 3, 1922

Maison Pleyel
Paris
[Forwarded to Villa des Rochers, Biarritz]

My dear Stravinsky,

Hello, dear friend. How are you? You have certainly had some *"emmerdements"!* Fortunately, you are [sturdy].

    I deeply regret having missed *Mavra:* I could not come for many reasons. I am very sorry. Poulenc wrote an article about your work, which is due to appear in *Les Feuilles Libres,* along with my article. So much the better.

    I must ask you an enormous favor. Here it is: a big American magazine requested that I write an article about you. I hope you do not have any objections. This article should be "easy and light" for the reader, while serious at heart.

Would you be so kind as to send me your:

Christian surnames;
place of birth;
date of same;
teachers (in order);
a chronological list of your works (dates, places performed, publishers);
an indication of the principal booklets and most important articles written about you.

I will follow your instructions, and ask you to suggest what in particular you would like me to say about you, if anything.

Send it to me as soon as possible, dear friend, I implore you.

Derain told me that you went to see him. . . . I wish I had been there.

I do not know whether you know that [Florent] Schmitt* is a *"con"*? And a big one! . . . What an "ass"!—if I do say so myself.

In the end, we can do nothing.

Amicably yours,   Erik Satie

* He calls himself Schmitt in order to shock us.

SATIE TO STRAVINSKY

Arceuil-Cachan
August 9, 1922

Villa des Rochers
Biarritz

My dear and illustrious friend,

It is nice of you to have written me such a friendly little note.

I have not forgotten you, since I have been working on your article.

I do not permit myself to judge you, for I am not a pawn like those I would rather not mention: they are too stupid, the poor things. Besides, this is not surprising, and on top of this, they are idiots.

My dear friend, I do not judge you. I admire you and speak only of the beautiful "light" that is you: for me to confuse you with the "damp fools"— who are as familiar to you as they are to me—would be impossible. What sad clods! Yes.

I plan to send you *Parade*. Please greet Madame for me and present my respects.

Best to you, I am   ES

SATIE TO STRAVINSKY

Villa des Rochers
Biarritz

Dear great friend,

I am rather shamed by your thanks. Well!

When are you coming to Paris? I will give you *Parade* in person.

I just wrote my article about Debussy. Hm! . . . I brought up a small "question"—very small. The Debussyist asses tend to forget certain things. I remind them, simply and very politely. This is my privilege.

Your article will appear shortly. You will receive it and will be able to read it: you speak *"l'english,"* I think. You will see how much I admire you.

My respects to Madame Stravinsky, please.

Best to you,   Erik Satie

SATIE TO STRAVINSKY

Maison Pleyel
Paris

Dear illustrious friend,

I am writing another article about you, this time for *Les Feuilles Libres*. Raval (not Ravel) asked me if you might perhaps have a [manuscript] page to send them for reproduction.

I would like to discuss your "mechanical" [pianola] works. A few measures of your choice would enrich my article.

Would you please address them to 81, avenue Victor Hugo, office of *Les Feuilles Libres*?

My respects to Madame Stravinsky, please.

Your old friend,   ES

P.S. When will we see you? The "return" is rudely and poorly announced.

SATIE TO STRAVINSKY

Maison Pleyel
Paris

Dear Stravinsky,

Thank you for the charming letter. I just submitted the article about you to *Les Feuilles Libres*. I discuss the stupid prejudice that *artists* (?) have against all mechanical interpretation, and I point out all that we owe to you in this respect. I present one of your recent "aspects," which testifies to your perpetual transformation. Please send the example* you wish us to use to M. Marcel Raval, Director of *Feuilles Libres,* 81, avenue Victor Hugo. Again and always, thank you, my dear Stravinsky; please do not forget to present my respects to Madame Stravinsky.

Amicably yours,   ES

* Just a few measures.

SATIE TO STRAVINSKY

Arcueil-Cachan
December 26, 1922

Maison Pleyel
Paris

Dear great friend,

A villainous cold (a glass of *rhume*[1]) prevents me from attending your concert tonight.

I am very sorry!

You do not owe me any thanks for the *Feuilles Libres* article: it is a tiny little note about nothing at all. The big, beautiful one, in *Vanity Fair,* has not yet appeared, though I have already been paid both for this one and the one about Debussy.

Regards to Ansermet, please.

My respects to Madame Stravinsky, please.

Best to you,   ES

SATIE TO STRAVINSKY

Arcueil-Cachan
September 15, 1923

Paris
[Forwarded to Villa des Rochers, Biarritz]

Dear illustrious friend,

How is your health? Here, nothing new. I am working for our dear director [Diaghilev]. I have just finished the second act of *Le Médecin malgré lui.* I imitate Gounod—which can't be more foolish than imitating Ravel. Perhaps it would be better to write like Schmitt—yes.

For that the piano part would have to be written on eight staves. Alas! I cannot: I am not intelligent enough.

You, I adore you; are you not the great Stravinsky?

I am but the little

ES

---

[1] A pun on the words *"rhume"* (cold) and *"rhum"* (rum).

SATIE TO STRAVINSKY   *[No date]*

M. Stravinsky—dear friend,

Are you all right? Come by to say hello. Would like to see you.

Fondly,   Erik Satie

CORRESPONDENCE WITH

1913 ~ *1923*

MAURICE RAVEL

MAURICE RAVEL TO STRAVINSKY

Villa des Fleurs
Clarens

4, *avenue Carnot*
Paris
January 19, 1913[1]

Old friend,

From the three of us to all of you, sincere best wishes. These are belated, but I have not yet finished correcting the proofs of *Daphnis,* in which I discovered things that would make Astruc's hair stand on end. I had news of you through Delage, who was looking to the *Sacre du printemps* for the antidote that his own harmonies need. When one thinks that M. d'Indy, whose *Fervaal* I heard the other day, is in good health! There is no justice.

Have you heard that [Manuel?] intended to divorce, and that he asked the Abbé Petit's opinion on this project?

I have been assured that Nijinsky never wants to hear about dance again. Well, this seems fine to me. I guess M. Poincaré will have to try his hand at choreography. *A bientôt.*

Affectionately,   MR

RAVEL TO STRAVINSKY

Clarens

4, *avenue Carnot*
Paris
March 15, 1913

Old friend,

Would you please telegraph the name of the hotel you reserved for us? This is absolutely essential! I am already sending a lady's dressing gown[2] in your name.

We arrive [on the] *Monday night* ([arriving] 8:oo a.m.) train.

Fondly,   Maurice Ravel

---

[1] The correspondence seems to have begun in 1912, but Stravinsky's side of it has not yet come to light.

[2] For Ravel's mother, who accompanied her son to Clarens, where he and Stravinsky prepared a version of *Khovanshchina* together.

RAVEL TO STRAVINSKY   *Monday [May 1913]*

Old friend,

First, admire the paper—checks are the thing this season—and, second, my memory: in the midst of such pleasures—as you see, I am at the bistro, escaping the heat—the thought of the errands you have entrusted to me comes to mind.

I asked for the rates at the Hôtel Splendide: two rooms, one large with two twin beds, the other smaller but adequate (all connected) = 25 francs, with an additional 2 francs for an extra bed in the second room. This looks out on the avenue Carnot. I could leap into your apartment from my balcony, though I would not take advantage of this possibility. From morning on—around 12:30—we could exchange flatteries in our pajamas.

No way to obtain a reduction. . . . The price list is attached. But you must decide right away. Write to me by return mail, or, if you prefer, directly to the hotel.

The weather is splendid, what I had hoped for at Lago Maggiore.[3] Tomorrow I go to the S.M.I. [Société Musicale Indépendante] to pester them about your membership.

Upon my arrival I saw Delage, who is flourishing and working.

Madame C [asella?] has been completely drained and stuffed with absorbent cotton. She is doing very well.

As for Madame S [chmitt?], the operation was successful, but the chloroform caused an [intestinal inflammation]. Fortunately, it is not serious.

Thank you for the fragment of the chorus [from *Khovanshchina*], without which I would not be able to elaborate No. 2 . . . and other things. But do not send me more.

It seems that the Théâtre Astruc [Théâtre des Champs-Elysées] is beyond everything . . . only, as [José-Maria] Sert assures us, *this must not be said*.

Last night I was supposed to go to *Benvenuto*, but I lost heart at the last moment.

And that nose-picking? Did it go well? I am thrilled to learn that everyone is doing well. I touch my muzzle, which is made of wood.

Tomorrow I go to see that unfortunate Isadora Duncan. I tremble at the thought. It is really too awful, too unjust.

A bientôt, old friend. My respects to Madame Stravinsky, and to Madame Beliankin, if she is still in Clarens. Give the children a hug from Madame Ravel, and Monsieur, and be assured of the affection of your devoted

Maurice Ravel

---

[3] Stravinsky and Ravel had journeyed to Varese together in April.

RAVEL TO STRAVINSKY   4, *avenue Carnot*
                                                              Paris
Hôtel du Châtelard   *May 5, 1913*
Clarens

Dear Igor,

We are delighted to learn that little Nini [Soulima] is recovering from the operation, but we regret the augmentation of your nose—especially my brother,
who will no longer receive the congratulations that were destined for you.

 At the same time that I received your letter, I heard the good news about
the ruling that Monsieur and Madame Miquel Alzieu must pay you the
10,000 francs.[4] You will finally be able to have the car and yacht that you want.
So will I, I think, having just had a visit from M. Enckell-Bronkowsky, who
came on behalf of the Sanine [Free] Theatre to ask me about the orchestration
of [Mussorgsky's] *Marriage.* I did not conceal the truth from him, which is that
I would be obliged to devote my three months of vacation to that task. M. Enck-
ell . . . etc. told me that I will soon receive confirmation of the commission from
Berlin, and that, with my reply, these gentlemen would consider themselves
obligated to me. I await this letter with curiosity, since money was not the issue.
I am somewhat perplexed as to the attitude I should take vis-à-vis Bessel. To
what extent may I impose conditions on the subject of a work to be released by
this publisher? I hope that you will be in Paris when I receive the letter from
Berlin, and will give me the cooperation of those Northern Lights so praised by
Voltaire.

 Do not worry: the acoustics of the Théâtre des Champs-Elysées are so perfect that even the subtlety of Berlioz's harmonies can be perceived. Less perfect
are the performance, the decor, the audience, Van Dyck, and Gabriel [Astruc]
himself. Serge [Diaghilev] and he parted at loggerheads yesterday. Everything
was off. Five minutes later, all was mended again.

 I sent the letter to *Muzyka:* we shall see what comes of it.

 Pardon me: I completely forgot the valise. I will have it delivered to you,
according to your wish.

 Contrary to common belief, the Countess G [reffuhle] still intends to present her international avant-garde concerts. What do you foresee from the Russian school? Do you have something besides your *[Le Roi des étoiles]*?
Wouldn't Scriabin's *Prometheus* take the place of two concerts? And if you see
something interesting in the foreign schools, in Germany, for instance, send a
note to alert me.

---

[4] Stravinsky had sued Madame Alzieu, a pianist who had borrowed 3,000 rubles from
him and had not repaid the loan. See *S.S.C.* II, p. 276.

A bientôt, my old friend. My respects to Madame Stravinsky, embrace the children, and be assured of the affection of your

Maurice Ravel

The [hotel] rooms have been reserved for May 13.[5]

RAVEL TO STRAVINSKY

Ustilug

23, rue Sopite
St.-Jean-de-Luz
August 28, 1913

I do not reproach you in any way, old friend: I believe that you sing the *Nightingale*'s song day and night. Myself, I loom from the ridge, and, as our colleague Tcherepnin says, I leap. I just finished the third Mallarmé poem. I will now look at the second again, and then go on to the *Zazpiacbat.* I allow myself a day of respite, but devote it to some two dozen letters. Think of the poor people, waiting more than two months for a reply by return mail. I need your assistance with one of these letters: I need the address of the [Ballets] Russes. Since June those poor devils have been waiting for a letter from me, in order to send me money (author's rights for a fourth performance [of *Daphnis et Chloé*]). That is for Svetlov. I must also write to Diaghilev again so that he does not count on me for the Scarlatti ballet. I really have better things to do.

Thus, reply by return mail, but not in my way. No need for literature: address of the Russes, news about the family, be assured, etc., signature.

For you and those around you, the affectionate regards of your devoted

Maurice Ravel

And then if you have a moment, write to me at length.

RAVEL TO STRAVINSKY

Hôtel des Crêtes
Clarens

Comarques
Thorpe-le-Soken
December 13, 1913
[Postcard]

Old friend,

A while has passed since I have had sensational news of your health. About three weeks ago I heard of your sudden death, but since I had received a letter from you that very morning, I was not shaken. Delage was supposed to tell you that your *Japanese [Lyrics]* will be performed on January 14 together with his *Hindu* and my "Mallarméian." We are counting on your presence. In three days I will be in London, where I hope to hear some talk of the *Sacre.*

Will the *Nightingale* soon sing? My respects to Madame Stravinsky. Embrace the children and be assured of the affection of your devoted

Maurice Ravel

---

[5] Stravinsky arrived in Paris on May 13 to attend the rehearsals and performance of *Le Sacre du printemps.*

RAVEL TO STRAVINSKY

41, *rue Gambetta*
St.-Jean-de-Luz
February 14, 1914

Clarens
[Forwarded to Leysin]

Dear Igor,

I learned from Madame Casella that Madame Stravinsky left for Leysin. I hope that this is only a precautionary step. Please console me with a note.

I have taken refuge in my native region in order to work, which had become impossible in Paris.

Embrace the children for me, present my respects to Madame Stravinsky, and be assured of the affection of your devoted

Maurice Ravel

RAVEL TO STRAVINSKY

23, *rue Sopite*
St. Jean-de-Luz
September 26, 1914
[Postcard]

Salvan
[Forwarded to La Pervenche, Clarens]

Send news, my old friend. How are you doing in the midst of all this? Edouard[6] has enlisted as a driver. Myself, I do not have such luck. They did not want me. In the next examination I hope to be deemed unfit for service. . . . The thought of being drafted made me finish five months' work in five weeks. I completed my trio. But I had to finish the works that I was planning to finish this winter: *La Cloche engloutie!!* And a symphonic poem: *Wien!!!*[7]

That was pointless. How are your wife and the little ones? Write to me quickly, my old friend. If you knew how hard it is to remain so removed from the world! Affectionate regards to everyone.

Maurice Ravel

RAVEL TO STRAVINSKY

4, *avenue Carnot*
Paris
November 14, 1914
[Postcard]

La Pervenche
Clarens

Dear old friend,

Here I am, back in Paris . . . and things are not going well. I have a greater desire to leave than ever before. I can no longer work, and Mama has been confined to bed since our arrival. Now she is up, but she is supposed to follow an albuminose diet. The causes of her condition, of course, are her age and anxi-

---

[6] Ravel's brother.

[7] *La Valse.* According to Francis Poulenc (*Moi et mes amis*), when Ravel played *La Valse* for Diaghilev and Stravinsky, the latter made no comment at all.

eties. No news from Edouard since October 28. And before then we hadn't heard from him in a month.

Delage is in Fontainebleau. He leaves to go on missions now and then. Schmitt, who is bored to death in Toul, managed to obtain permission to go to the front. I have not seen Misia yet.

All of our fond regards to yours, dear old friend. Write soon, I beg you, and believe in the fraternal friendship of your

Maurice Ravel

RAVEL TO STRAVINSKY
4, *avenue Carnot*
Paris
December 19, 1914
[Postcard]

La Pervenche
Clarens

Old friend,

So it is understood: you would not sleep well in the lumber room that served as my brother's bedroom, and which, for your sake, was transformed into a Persian chamber. But come quickly, or else you will not find me here. I am enlisting as a driver. This is the only way left for me to remain in this capital, where I must see *Daphnis et Chloé*. You say nothing about your brother [Gury]. I hope that he is completely recovered.

So try to come sooner. Our best regards to you all.

Your   Maurice Ravel

RAVEL TO STRAVINSKY
4, *avenue Carnot*
Paris
January 2, 1915[8]

Clarens
[Forwarded to the Hôtel Victoria,
Château d'Oex]

Well, old friend, everything was prepared to receive our ally in a worthy fashion: A Persian chamber with Genoese veils, Japanese prints, Chinese toys; a synthesis of the Ballets Russes, what more? Everything but a mechanical nightingale. And now you are not coming. . . . Ah! the Slavic fantasy! Is it to Slavic fantasy that I owe the reception of a note from Szanto, expressing his delight at learning that I will be arriving in Switzerland at the end of January? As I wrote to you, I will be leaving soon, but I strongly doubt that I will be traveling in your direction.

---

[8] On December 27, 1914, Ravel had written to Jacques Rouché, director of the Paris Opéra: "I had hoped that the military authorities would make it possible for me to accept your kind invitation [to the concert of the 29th]. That hope has just been taken from me. I was nevertheless very happy to see you and dear Stravinsky again. Would you do me the favor of telling him that I will be at home tonight after 5:30? Thank you in advance."

I await news about your brother and your whole family. In the meantime, find here all of our best wishes for the New Year (New Style).

Your devoted   Maurice Ravel

RAVEL TO STRAVINSKY

7, avenue Léonie
St.-Cloud
2, Place St. Louis   *September 16, 1919*
Morges

Dear Igor,

I am heart-broken not to have been able to see you.[9] Why didn't you telephone Durand's?[10] They would have given you my address and telephone number (St.-Cloud 2-33). Well, I hope we will see each other soon, perhaps even in Morges, because I am going to try to go and visit my uncle before the end of autumn.

I continue to do[11] nothing and am probably barren.

Send news soon, and if you come to Paris again, try to extricate yourself more effectively.

To all of you, the fond memory of your

Maurice Ravel

RAVEL TO STRAVINSKY

Le Belvédère
Montfort-l'Amaury
c/o Pleyela   *June 26, 1923*
avenue de l'Opéra
Paris

Dear Igor,

How marvelous your *Noces!* And how sorry I am not to have heard—and seen—it more frequently! But even to have come the other night was apparently not prudent of me: my foot was terribly swollen, and I have to stay off of it again until next Sunday at least.

Thank you, my old friend, and affectionately yours,

Maurice Ravel

---

[9] Stravinsky had been in Paris for a week to discuss *Pulcinella* with Diaghilev and to receive the "Pergolesi" manuscripts from him.

[10] Durand & Cie, Ravel's publisher.

[11] Ravel writes "f . . . ." (*"faire"*? *"foutre"*?).

[June 1923]
[On the calling card of Lucien Garban]

RAVEL TO STRAVINSKY

Old friend, could you arrange for the admission tomorrow of Garban and his wife, or for as many as possible, [but] at least a seat for this one person? Many thanks in advance,

MR

STRAVINSKY TO RAVEL   *Les Rochers*
Biarritz
My dear Ravel,   *July 14, 1923*[12]

I was very touched by your kind letter, and I am very happy, too, that you liked . . . my *Noces.* Pity that you did not hear the first performance, when it was so well done. How is the foot doing now? You would be very kind to send news and to write (in general) a little more often to your old friend

Igor Stravinsky

On December 29, 1937, L'Intransigeant published an obituary of Ravel by Stravinsky.

> The death of Ravel did not surprise me. I had known for some time that his illness was serious and the cause of grave anxieties. I also knew that the sudden halt in his musical production was directly attributable to the nature of his illness.
>
> For me he was an old friend. I had known him since the time of my debut in Paris with *Firebird,* and I recall that it was at that time that he let me hear fragments of *Daphnis et Chloé,* which he was then in the process of composing.
>
> With his death, France has lost one of its great musicians, whose prestige is recognized worldwide. It will be left to history to guarantee him a glorious position in the realm of music, which he conquered with great courage and conviction.

The following day, Stravinsky attended the funeral service at Levallois.

---

[12] A year later, Stravinsky and Mengelberg's secretary, Salomon Bottenheim, the Dutch musicologist, who had come to Biarritz to sign a contract with the composer to conduct the New York Philharmonic, drove to St.-Jean-de-Luz to see Ravel. (The visit probably took place on August 22 or 23, since Bottenheim departed on the 24th.) Bottenheim left a description of the occasion in his essay "Maurice Ravel: Souvenirs personnels": "It was a pleasant chat. Stravinsky was very witty, often strongly opinionated, but always courteous." Bottenheim also describes Ravel at the Paris premiere of the *Symphony of Psalms,* conducted by Stravinsky, in February 1931.

II

CORRESPONDENCE WITH

1 9 1 5   ⮜⮞   1 9 3 7

C . - F .   R A M U Z

On January 27, 1955, Madame Berthe Bouchet-Ramuz, daughter of Charles-Ferdinand Ramuz,[1] wrote to Stravinsky asking for her father's letters to the composer for publication in a book. On February 19 Stravinsky promised to comply with the request in mid-May, after his return from a concert tour, but to Madame Bouchet-Ramuz's reminder at the beginning of June, he answered in the negative: "I have examined the file of my correspondence with Ramuz, but my feeling is that the letters should not be published during my lifetime: the contents are too personal and too close to me." (June 15) Ramuz's daughter wrote again, expressing her understanding of the composer's decision but promising that only the letters relating to "the heroic period of Histoire du soldat*" would be published. She already had six from René Auberjonois,[2] but, of course, those to Stravinsky were more important. On July 16 he agreed to make a selection, explaining, however, that he needed some weeks for this, "because I am terribly busy and already behind in my work." On September 26 he wrote to say that he had chosen twelve letters covering the period February–August 1918, and the next day he sent the originals of these by registered surface mail.*

Another communication from Madame Bouchet-Ramuz, January 29, 1959, requesting letters from her father written between 1920 and 1934, evidently prompted Stravinsky's immediate response, since on February 23 he asked for acknowledgment of their receipt. On March 5 he wrote again, to say that a packet of letters that he had recently sent to someone else had not reached its destination, making him fear that the one to Madame Bouchet-Ramuz might also have been lost.

During the creation of Histoire du soldat, *Ramuz rarely dated his letters and notes to Stravinsky, no doubt because the two collaborators were neighbors who saw each other often and also talked on the telephone. Postmarks are significant, therefore, but unfortunately most of the surviving envelopes have been philatelically mutilated. Stravinsky himself labored to establish the chronology of the letters, and his order is followed here. Internal evidence is generally of little assistance in respect to dates, although a letter discussing ticket prices, for example, and marked "Thursday morning" undoubtedly belongs to the final period of the planning, since neither the hall (Théâtre Municipal, Lau-*

---

[1] Charles-Ferdinand Ramuz (1878–1947), the eminent Swiss novelist and essayist.
[2] René Auberjonois (1872–1956), Swiss painter who designed the set and costumes for the original *Histoire du soldat*.

sanne) nor the date had been fixed very long before the premiere (September 28, 1918). Another letter, marked simply "Thursday," is unquestionably from September, since Ramuz encourages Stravinsky to dance the last piece himself, which the composer had volunteered to do on the 4th of that month. Regrettably, the correspondence is incomplete, and at least thirty exchanges are missing, partly because Ramuz's were vaguely marked and could not be related chronologically. Moreover, Stravinsky's communications were unobtainable, and at the time of Histoire *he did not own a typewriter and kept copies only of business letters. Yet the friendship is brought to light here for the first time, in the words of both men.*

Histoire du soldat *can be described with justice as the principal event of Ramuz's artistic life, but he seems not to have understood that his and Stravinsky's contributions to the piece were of unequal value. This was cruelly spelled out after the Paris stage premiere (Théâtre des Champs-Elysées, April 24, 1924), when Gabriel Marcel, the philosopher, wrote that the text should be dropped completely, while another critic said that Stravinsky's "passion for a Ramuz has made me lose all confidence in the composer's literary taste," and a third remarked that "the music is one of Stravinsky's greatest masterpieces, but the effort of going back and forth from the music to Ramuz is too much."[3]* (Nouvelles Littéraires, *May 30, 1924)*

When Stravinsky moved from Switzerland to France, in June 1920, and continued to develop powers whose universality was increasingly evident, Ramuz was left behind in every sense. He felt acute disappointment that the composer, traveling rapidly on to new works, did not devote more time to the promotion of the Soldat. *Ramuz had also hoped for an income from it,[4] and he became bitter because the work was a popular success only in Germany, which is to say in translation. Yet his constant rewriting is evidence that he perceived the weaknesses in diction and dramatic construction. The most serious of the latter is that the larger musical numbers are crowded together near the end, and that after forty minutes of nearly uninterrupted dramatic dialogue, the audience almost forgets that music is one of the elements. Many reviewers,*

---

[3]Ramuz did not attend the Paris performances but went instead to the three in Zürich and one in Winterthur taking place at the same time.

[4] Aside from Ramuz's frequent supplications to Stravinsky for money, much of the correspondence reveals the writer's exaggerated concern with the *Soldat's* financial potential. For example, Stravinsky wrote to Henry Kling of J. & W. Chester, September 14, 1932: "I think that Ramuz will be content with a guaranteed minimum. In any case, tell him that it is useless to dream of a larger one in the present bad state of the theatre." Kling replied, September 17, that if Ramuz insisted on this minimum, a sold-out house in, for instance, the Dresden State Theatre would come to 2.1 billion marks, yet still not cover even the authors' rights: "I propose to fix the minimum for Germany and Austria at £2 sterling for each of you." Three days later, Kling wrote that "for Germany the minimum will be £1 sterling, but we will ask for a guarantee of ten performances."

including Comoedia's, *observed that the music is disproportionately short.*

    Stravinsky would tolerate no criticism of Ramuz's libretto (or of Auber-jonois's set and costumes), and when Ramuz described the results of the Paris performance as "disastrous," Stravinsky in turn wrote to Otto Kling[5] that "the Soldat *at the Champs-Elysées was a very great success" (April 29), which indeed was true of the music. Nevertheless, Stravinsky's discontentment with some of Ramuz's concepts and with his lack of theatrical expertise at the time of the composition is evinced in the correspondence.*

    The composer's letters of the 1920s betray an irritation at Ramuz's obsession with Histoire *and his apparent inability to move on to other work. The two men drifted apart rapidly as Stravinsky became more religious-minded. On August 13, 1936, Catherine Stravinsky wrote to her husband:*

> I am reading the Ramuz book [*Questions*], and I agree with your marginal notes.[6] . . . He does not find the main answer and discusses everything according to some kind of semi-religious plan. How sorry I am for him, and how I want him to be enlightened. . . . Why does he like these stylistic diversions so much; I don't like them. . . . I am reading the *Dobrotolyubiya* every day and comparing how these people with great souls and faith, who lived only in God and for God, talked and measured and thought about life. How simple and clear everything was to them.

A week later, Catherine wrote again: "I finished Ramuz's little book, and my overall impression is one of sadness."

---

[5] Otto Marius Kling was director of J. & W. Chester Ltd., London. During a 1915 trip to Russia, he secured exclusive representation abroad for Stravinsky's works from his Russian publishers. In the summer of 1916, Kling's brother Aimé, a resident of Geneva, called on Stravinsky, explaining that Chester had become the chief Western depot for Russian music and wanted to publish Stravinsky's new works. Negotiations were complicated because of Stravinsky's exclusive contract with Diaghilev for *Les Noces* and because the Russian Revolution and the Bern Convention deprived the composer of copyrights in some countries. Stravinsky's relationship with Otto Kling was not smooth, but that with his son, Henry, who succeeded his father in 1924, was so stormy that on March 5, 1927, the composer severed all personal connection with Chester and entrusted his business with the company to G. G. Païchadze of the Edition Russe de Musique. In this missive, Stravinsky says: "In all that concerns M. Ramuz, you must deal with him directly. His rights do not concern me, but only my proprietary rights in all stage performances of *Histoire*."

[6] A typical one says: "Not very comforting, all this! Moreover, I always knew it and noted with regret this [illegible] condition of Ramuz's."

C.-F. RAMUZ TO STRAVINSKY   *Treytorrens*
                                                         August 9, 1915[7]

Villa Rogivue
Morges

I know that Chavannes[8] is with you this afternoon, for which reason I did not
telephone. . . . I think about you a great deal. . . . See you within the next few
days.

AUGUST 12, 1915. *Ramuz sends a satirical poem,* Von Bosh *(i.e.,* boche), *in
    which French place-names are spelled as Germans might pronounce them
    (e.g., the "Moulin Rouche").*
JANUARY 7, 1916. *Ramuz sends New Year greetings.*
FEBRUARY 5, 1916. *Ramuz informs the composer of his new address: L'Acacia,
    Cour Lausanne.*[9]
APRIL 6, 1916. *Ramuz invites Stravinsky to dinner for Monday, April 10.*

RAMUZ TO STRAVINSKY   *July 20, 1916*

I asked Gilliard[10] to tell you what happened. Diagnosis: weak nerves; treatment:
mountains. This is the only plan I have on earth for the remainder of the summer; a move is involved, so there will be expenses. This note is therefore to beg
you to advance me the sum—we will arrange the matter later, when we see

---

[7] It has only recently been established that the true account of the first meeting between Ramuz and Stravinsky is that of Adrien Bovy, first published in Pierre-Paul
Clement's preface to the 1979 edition of Ramuz's *Souvenirs sur Igor Stravinsky.* (This
version contradicts Ansermet's.) Bovy says that in the autumn of 1915, he, Stravinsky,
Ansermet, and Alexandre Cingria (brother of Charles-Albert) went by car to Ramuz's
home, at his invitation. But the season must have been early summer.

[8] Fernand Chavannes (1868–1936), professor of German and a contributor to the *Cahiers Vaudois.* The composer preserved Chavannes's postcards sent to him on October
11, November 20, and December 28, 1918, and March 16, 1919. In the one of November 20, Chavannes remarks that, after the end of the war, "an impressive silence has
fallen over everything, but we must not forget: The Germans are pigs!" On March 20,
1936, Catherine Stravinsky wrote to her husband: "I was very grieved by the news of
the sudden death of our kind friend Chavannes. I, too, sincerely loved him, and it was
somehow always very nice to see him, especially here [in Paris]. In fact, the last time
that I was with him, just before my departure from Paris, he seemed such a healthy old
fellow. No doubt the sclerosis was very advanced. And where did he die, in Spain? God
rest his soul." Another close friend of Stravinsky, also a member of the *Cahiers Vaudois,* was René Morax. Stravinsky wrote to his elder son, January 23, 1963: "God bless
this dear, kind friend. . . . I always remember René Morax with love and tenderness."

[9] Unless otherwise specified, all of Stravinsky's subsequent letters were sent to this address.

[10] Edmond Gilliard, professor of French literature, founded the *Cahiers Vaudois* in
1914.

each other. . . . I knew that you came to Lausanne. Is the studio suitable for you? The blind soldier is touching.

OCTOBER 17, 1916. Ramuz sends the composer a receipt:

Received from M. Stravinsky the sum of 200 francs for 4 *Berceuses [du chat]* and 4 *Pribaoutki,* in exchange for which I agree to renounce my publication rights in America.

Lausanne, October 17, 1916
C.-F. Ramuz

NOVEMBER 12, 1916. Ramuz acknowledges the receipt of 500 francs for his French translation of Renard.[11]

---

[11] The Princesse de Polignac, intending to present *Renard* in French in her salon, had offered to pay for the translation. Stravinsky wrote to her, October 5, 1916: "Very dear Madame, Enclosed is the finished translation of *Renard,* which M. C.-F. Ramuz made at my request. . . . This [translation] was a considerable task, much more difficult than I had thought it would be; I insisted that the French text preserve the flavor of the original, without [sounding] translated. . . . Moreover, the question of accents complicated everything. . . . I think that we have been successful in this task, which we did together (of course, I participated only when musical questions arose), and I hope that it will please you. The translated work will be particularly valuable for future presentations, since Russian is hardly spoken and even more rarely sung outside of Russia; also, the [translation] . . . will facilitate your performances. Let me assure you, besides, that Ramuz's translation is not only the best that I know but is very close to the original as well. . . .

"If you recall, you agreed to pay 300 francs for the author's honorarium. I now realize (and this was my fault) that this sum would be totally disproportionate to the amount of time that M. Ramuz devoted to the task. I would be ashamed not to offer him more than this. What is your opinion, dear Madame? I thought that I would state the case to you candidly, since I am so happy that the work is finally completed, and better done than I would have dared to hope. Thus I allow myself to assert that 1,000 francs seems to me the minimum for this author, whom I esteem highly and whose name alone merits such an adjustment. You have simply to send a check to M. C.-F. Ramuz . . . through the Bankverein [?] Suisse, as you have always done for me.

"One other thing. I just submitted the piano and voice reduction of our *Renard* to the copyist with the French text. I will do everything possible to guarantee that you have this, along with the full score, before the end of the month.

"I seize this opportunity to thank you for the 3,000 francs, which I received without complication. Be assured, dear Princesse, of my sincere admiration.   Igor Stravinsky

"P.S. Have you managed to find a copyist to do the remainder of the orchestra score of *Renard?*

"P.P.S. When will you be in Switzerland? Dare I ask you to bring the orchestra score of my *Scherzo fantastique* (which M. Rouché has) and the parts of my [Three Pieces for String] Quartet, which M. Delgrange (the gentleman to whom I introduced you in Morges) will deliver to you soon?" [Jacques Rouché was director of the Paris Opéra; Félix Delgrange was a French conductor and cellist.]

RAMUZ TO STRAVINSKY   *November 21, 1916*

As I told you yesterday evening, to discuss business matters with you greatly embarrasses me, so I am writing them down instead. I think that the best solution is for you to pay me a lump sum, after which I would have no further involvement either with the accounting or with your representatives. The 1,000 francs that you propose to give me does not include my rights in the edition of *Renard* (1,000 francs for the piano score and 200 francs for the orchestra score). It is understood that my performance rights are reserved separately. You offer to pay me 100 francs each month. My objection to this is that 1,000 francs would be much more useful to me right now, especially since the future is so uncertain.[12]

JANUARY 1, 1917. *Ramuz sends a New Year's greeting: "Thanks for Rasputin. . . ."*[13]

RAMUZ TO STRAVINSKY   *January 13, 1917*

I heard about the complications you have had recently, and I only want to say that I share them with you from a distance.

                                                        January 30, 1917
RAMUZ TO STRAVINSKY   *[Postcard]*

One can subscribe to the *Russkoii Slovo* in Lausanne for 8 francs and something a month, *if nothing has changed.* I am writing to you because I may not be able to come tomorrow; my central heater just exploded, and who knows what will have to be done. If I cannot come, I will telephone you.

RAMUZ TO STRAVINSKY   *July 9, 1917*

I forgot that I have a dinner tomorrow with Gilliard; hence I am not free. Let me know if you have a spare moment on Wednesday.

RAMUZ TO STRAVINSKY   *July 22, 1917*

Thank you for the check, received this morning. . . . I asked Gilliard if there was somewhere to stay in Les Diablerets, but after what he told me, I have changed my mind. Perhaps we will go to Rougemont, where my brother lives. Are you making progress with your work?

---

[12] On November 23, Stravinsky's Geneva lawyer, Philippe Dunant, sent a contract to the composer and to Ramuz.

[13] Rasputin had been assassinated a few days before.

RAMUZ TO STRAVINSKY   *July 26, 1917*

Alas, dear friend, everything is much too expensive, and I am very poor. Gilliard described the chalet to me, and I will answer him, through you, that I cannot even dream of it. If we go away—which is not definite—we will go to Rouge-mont, where my brother has found us something quite nice and exceptionally inexpensive. . . . I am happy to know that you are working; so am I. Specifically, I am undoing everything I did in order to do it again, but all in good humor and quite peacefully.

RAMUZ TO STRAVINSKY   *August 4, 1917*
                                                        [Postcard]

Dear Stravinsky,

Not a drop of the Stephens ink to be had; I have been in six shops and found an abundance of various inks, which I have taken upon myself to send to you. This afternoon I will send you some blotting paper. For the time being I will not be coming up—I will write and tell you why. Good-bye Stravinsky. From behind bars, the prisoner extends his hand to all of you.[14]

                                        Rumet
                                        Professor of Diction

RAMUZ TO STRAVINSKY   *August 14, 1917*

Enclosed is the contract that we drew up the other day. I have two more questions to discuss. First, what would the arrangement be if you were to sell not only the performance rights but also the publication rights in America? In that case I would have nothing to do with the premieres, and I would have to place my claim for the rest with the publisher. Thus it would be worthwhile to establish the respective importance [of performance and publication rights].

     Second, it must be agreed that the French texts will never be published without the music, or at least not without my consent. You know that a translator is a slave, first to the original, then to the musician's intentions: the translator's work is of value only in relation to the pre-existing work, and to isolate a translation is to falsify its meaning.

RAMUZ TO STRAVINSKY   *August 16, 1917*

My stipulations about publishing the libretto with the music are not financially motivated, and you cannot possibly disagree with the reasons I gave. Of course it goes without saying that I do not object to the publication of the text in pro-

---

[14] The postcard is a photograph of Ramuz behind a barred window, with his daughter in the foreground.

grams for concerts or stage productions. Thank you for the precise details about how my rights would be affected if you were to relinquish yours outright. Complete and return the contract,[15] if you deem it acceptable. You are so much better at these things than I am.

RAMUZ TO STRAVINSKY   *August 27, 1917*

I will arrive [in Les Diablerets] the day after tomorrow at 12:05. Reserve a comfortable, modern suite. My best wishes to all. If something comes up, I will cable.

STRAVINSKY TO RAMUZ   *Janaury 1, 1918*

Let these few words that I send on the first day of the new year testify to my great admiration for you, a testimony absolutely distinct from that of the last day of the past year.

　　Little does it matter that you will receive this testimony on the third day of the new year; what is important is that the statement be made on this very day.

                                                        Your   Stravinsky

RAMUZ TO STRAVINSKY   *[January 24, 1918]*

This still is not going well, and I will have to cancel my visit with you this afternoon and my trip to Sion[16] with you on Thursday. I have written to Muret[17] asking him to be in Sion, but without stating the exact number of visitors. I attach the songs to this letter: I think that "L'Ours"[18] should be included. Please examine Mika's [song], and we will look at it again together. As far as I can tell from reading your music, there will not be too many difficulties. If it would not make you too angry, please deposit the sum for me. That would be a great help, since I have no more money. We had agreed that "L'Ours" would count as 2; $2 + 3 = 5$; $5 \times 25 = 125$. My compliments to you and yours.

                                                               Ramuz

---

[15] Also drafted by Philippe Dunant, this contract gives Stravinsky three-quarters and Ramuz one-quarter of performance rights for all of Stravinsky's works using Ramuz's translations.

[16] The site of Werner Reinhart's Château de Muzot. See n. 1 on p. 139.

[17] Albert Muret, painter.

[18] The published version of "L'Ours" ("The Bear") does not indicate whether only one verse is to be sung and two of them recited, but the manuscript shows that all three are sung.

I did not think that things could be sent by express mail today; otherwise I would have done so.

[*At the bottom of the letter, in Stravinsky's hand*] 1918. Translation of the text of "L'Ours" and of the little song dedicated to Mika, which I decided not to publish.

RAMUZ TO STRAVINSKY   *January 25, 1918*

I do not think that we will leave tomorrow, not in this dreadful weather. I shall therefore wait until Monday to make the trip, if the weather has improved, unless you advise me otherwise.

RAMUZ TO STRAVINSKY   *February 28, 1918*

Impossible to work with you tomorrow: I am behind on a multitude of tasks, and I want to unburden myself of them at all costs before undertaking something new. I have put a lot of thought into *Histoire,* which I hope is evolving in your mind, too. At the end, the Devil will lead the Soldier away to The Soldier's March (as in the beginning). Have you seen or telephoned Auberjonois?

Many fond regards.

Ramuz

If I am able to come, I will call you early.

RAMUZ TO STRAVINSKY   *Monday [February 28, 1918]*

Dear one,

My wife has announced that there will be some "ladies" visiting at my house tomorrow, so I hesitate no longer: this afternoon I will do errands, and tomorrow I will visit you. I am sending this note by express mail, along with the rough draft of the letter to Reinhart. Tomorrow you can tell me if you agree. Auberjonois has left for Sion.

Many fond regards, dear friend.

R.

RAMUZ TO STRAVINSKY   *March 10, 1918*[19]

Dear friend,

Heard from Reinhart.[20] His reply was very kind and simple, assuring us of his complete support in our enterprise. He is also determined to arouse the interest of all the *"amateurs d'art"* of Winterthur and Zürich. Reinhart himself will put 3,000 francs at our disposal immediately. I have a very favorable impression of him. I will show you his letter. He says that for some time now he has wanted to introduce the people in his circle to your music, and that this seems an excellent occasion.

Many fond regards,   R.

---

[19] Stravinsky was preoccupied at this time by a proposal from the Cercle des Beaux Arts in Madrid to conduct six concerts: three in Madrid (two of symphonic music and one of chamber music), two in Barcelona, and one in Lisbon. Six million francs was offered, as well as travel expenses for the composer and his wife from Lausanne to Lisbon and back. The concerts were to have taken place in March and April. Stravinsky immediately began to enter thoughts for programs and financial calculations in one of his notebooks ("How will payment be made?"; "Refusal of wife's ticket and consequent payment of my living expenses"; etc.) and then answered the letter, carefully itemizing his many questions. The most important issue was whether or not he would be permitted to pass through France, and, if he could, whether he would have to go by way of Paris and Irun rather than Lyon and Barcelona. Since the beginning of the Russian Revolution a few months before, former tsarist nationals were unable to obtain visas. Among other conditions, he stipulated that he could not carry the music himself, since he would certainly not be allowed to cross the French border with it, and hence the scores and parts would have to be taken in a Spanish diplomatic pouch.

Stravinsky's letter contains much information about the state of his music at the time. First, he says that it exists in unique copies, for the reason that it is being engraved in Germany and the French censor will not allow it through. He advises the Spanish Minister of Foreign Affairs that concerning *Firebird* and *Petrushka,* it would be more practical to address himself to Diaghilev, who is in Madrid and has the scores and parts: "The suite [from *Petrushka*] comes from the complete ballet." Stravinsky also explains other problems with obtaining scores and parts. The parts of the Symphony in E flat, for example, were purchased by the Kursaal in Montreux, the administration of which has informed Stravinsky that it is willing to sell these, but for 500 francs. The parts of *Scherzo fantastique,* on the other hand, are in Paris at the Opéra. Most surprising of all, Stravinsky seems to propose *Renard* for the chamber-music concert, since his "repertory of chamber music is too small"; the manuscript of the orchestra score is complete, he states, but not the vocal score.

To finish the story of this aborted Iberian concert tour, Stravinsky received another note from Bern on March 16, asking for an immediate reply, since the courier for Madrid was to leave the following morning. Mysteriously, the composer received a registered letter on May 22, together with a check for 5,000 francs, which may have been an advance for this or another proposed set of concerts.

[20] Reinhart sent a postcard to Stravinsky on March 19: "Ramuz hinted that you may

RAMUZ TO STRAVINSKY   *April 11, 1918*

Dear Stravinsky,

First, here is a draft for the letter to Madame Roussy.[21] Look at it, correct it, change it, copy it, and send it. I considered the matter, and I think that only you should sign the letter, not me.

Now think about telephoning M. Odescalchi—if you have not already done so—and proceed with this matter, which is amusing, if nothing else, but could also be productive. O. is putting strong, personal pressure on B.[22] and the B. girls.

Finally, I am sending you a copy of the *Petit Blond* for Madame Stravinsky. It is a model of style. See how Joffre is naturally induced, between the medium and the pastel.

I wish many things for you. I am working.

                                                              Ramuz

This letter was written before my telephone call. Since then I have received a letter from Brandenbourg,[23] giving me two new addresses. He seems to be interested in the project.

RAMUZ TO STRAVINSKY   *April 21, 1918*

Dear friend,

Here is the plan:

1. Check the lengths of the pieces, and then I will try to adhere to your timings.

2. I think I have an idea for the narrative following the scene of the drunken Devil and preceding the dance of the Princess. You recall that the first

---

accompany him on his visit here. To have you here with me at Chandolin for a few days would give me great pleasure, and I eagerly await a telegram announcing your arrival."

[21] On April 18, Stravinsky sent this letter to Madame Auguste Roussy, in La Tour de Peilz, Vevey, asking her to underwrite the project for 15,000 francs, "either as capital or as guarantee." In return, he promised that he and his collaborators would give her their manuscripts, sketches, and *maquettes*. Madame Roussy answered this first letter, but apparently not the second one.

[22] Bugnion, a banker.

[23] Auguste Brandenbourg, director of the Banque Brandenbourg and of the Union des Banques Suisses, Lausanne. One of the addresses was that of Aurèle Sandoz, to whom Stravinsky wrote on April 18: "I just learned from M. Brandenbourg that you are interested in supporting our enterprise, and I wish to express our warm thanks to you myself. Would you give me the pleasure of dining with me one evening? I will invite M. Ramuz and M. Brandenbourg, too, and through the intermediary of the latter I will let you know the time and place of our little gathering."

of these two scenes ends with the Narrator's comments, which continue throughout the next scene; instead of stating events in this narration, the music should be translated into words: I envisage trousers and ties, dressing the boy up in his Sunday best. . . .[24]

3. I received a letter from Reinhart, who will arrive on Wednesday. He asked to see me on Thursday. I discussed it right away with Auberjonois, whom I saw.

Auberjonois would like the three of us to have dinner at his house on Thursday evening, which I think is a good idea. I will have Reinhart meet me at my house, then we will proceed to Auberjonois's, where you will join us, and we will dine together. *Keep this Thursday evening free.* Reinhart would also like to have a separate meeting with you, preferably on Sunday. . . . We will settle the details on Thursday.

4. I have no ticket for tomorrow's concert.[25] Must I purchase one? My little sister is certain that the hall is already sold out.

We eagerly await the arrival of Madame Stravinsky and yourself.

Many fond regards.

Ramuz

RAMUZ TO STRAVINSKY
Monday morning
[May or June 1918]

Dear,

Could Madame Stravinsky locate without too much difficulty the *Petit Blond* pastel that I sent to her? I would like to insert it in my text. Did things go well last night? I made out well: now I have returned, and I am working this morning.

Best wishes,   R.

RAMUZ TO STRAVINSKY
July 7, 1918

Dear friend,

Please see if this paper is the same size as yours (I have R.'s[26] manuscript paper in mind, and I think that I could find more like his, at God knows what price!).

Another thing: I have just received notice from Brandenbourg that the 12,000 francs has been deposited. Write a short note expressing your feelings about this. I will write at greater length, not having done so the other day.

Do you think that each of us should withdraw 1,000 francs immediately? Without taking too large a slice out of the capital, this would at least allow *us* to

---

[24] For a discussion of the libretto, see Appendix A.

[25] The premiere of the Eight Easy Pieces, at the Lausanne Conservatoire.

[26] Gabriel Rosset, who played the part of the Soldier, and who later, under the name Birel, joined the Georges Pitoëff Company.

get started while we wait for the various items of the budget to become more definite.

I received a letter from the Soldier: among his comrades he found a possible Devil, and along with the Devil would come a dancer. In my opinion, the best idea would be to have everyone meet together someday soon. Telephone Nicati[27] to ask for and reserve the hall (Salle Rouilly).

I have the impression that there will be three times as many buyers as we need, which will permit us to choose.

Finally, I enclose Perrin's estimate. We should obtain a second opinion from another shipper for comparison.

Best wishes, dear friend.

R.

RAMUZ TO STRAVINSKY   *July 15, 1918*

Dear friend,

I spent the whole of yesterday afternoon with M. Rosset. I read the story to him and explained it carefully: he would like to take the part of the Devil.[28] He would play it with an eye to the cinema, and I feel that he could do the role well. I have therefore written to D. asking him to play the part of the King instead. I await his reply. Furthermore, M. Rosset has suggested a possible Princess, a young *café-concert* actress. One of these days I must meet her, and if she is suitable, I will ask you to give her an audition. Meanwhile, I will not write to her, since that would create one more obligation.

Good-bye. Do you want me to come? On Wednesday I rewrote all of the narratives, and the story reads much more smoothly now.

In the beginning passage where I state our intentions, I have omitted the sentence: "This is not a play, it is a story." These intentions should not be explained but rather demonstrated, asserted.

Kisses to the children. I am quite ill.

Your   Ramuz

What did Nicati say about the hall? We begin rehearsals at the end of the week.

P.S. I just received your letter, and I am in complete agreement with you, as you have already gathered. Until Wednesday, unless you change your mind. Regarding Madame Pitoëff, do not take any action until then.

---

[27] Jules Nicati, director of the Lausanne Conservatoire.

[28] The part of the Devil-violinist was played by Jean Villard, who became a famous actor. A letter from Jacques Copeau to Stravinsky, October 31, 1919, reveals that the composer and Ramuz had recommended Villard for a position in Copeau's company at the Théâtre du Vieux-Colombier.

RAMUZ TO STRAVINSKY   *July 19, 1918*

Dear,

It was impossible to telephone you: ten people had signed up ahead of me.

I wanted to inform you of the following: (1) Rosset has the flu, and tomorrow's rehearsal is canceled; (2) I forgot to ask you the other day what you have arranged with Nicati, and whether we can use the hall; (3) I have rewritten *everything,* and shortly I will submit to you several ideas for the second part.

Many fond regards.

R.

Reinhart has written to me asking if we would object to meeting him at his house instead: he is not certain whether he will be able to return home via Lausanne. We will have to discuss this again.

RAMUZ TO STRAVINSKY   *July 20, 1918*

Dear,

It was impossible to reach you, so I am writing to say that I saw Auberjonois last night on the way back from Morges. He told me that you intend to accompany him to Geneva on Monday and to see Madame Pitoëff, and he asked me if I would go along. I thought it wiser to come to a conclusion beforehand about whether she is suited for the role. I sent a note to her requesting a meeting and describing what would be expected of her. If she likes the project, she is supposed to reply by return mail—thus I should receive her answer by tomorrow morning. I will let you know through A., and I will be waiting when the boat docks. Otherwise, A. will make inquiries in Geneva on Monday as to the possibilities of finding someone else, and we will decide afterward.

I am working: I have four plans for the beginning of the second part. When we see each other I will tell you about the one that I think is the best, so that you may keep in mind the impression I seek to create. This plan would allow for a new scene in place of that of the King.

Fondly,   R.

RAMUZ TO STRAVINSKY   *Sunday*
                                                        July 28, 1918
Dear friend,

Gadon[29] is better, thank you. We were frightened. I am feeling awful but will be at Auberjonois's on Monday, regardless.

Many fond regards until then.

R.

---

[29] One of Ramuz's daughters; later Madame Gadon Olivieri Ramuz, wife of the commercial attaché to the Italian Embassy in Mexico City.

RAMUZ TO STRAVINSKY   *August 1, 1918*[30]

Dear friend,

I began writing to Rosset and had to break off in the middle of it. It is useless to ask him these questions until we know what our limitations will be, particularly regarding the musicians. Try to be in touch with Ansermet, and tell me the outcome of your conversation on Saturday. Rosset should be on his way to Winterthur, where I intend to write to him immediately.

   Best wishes, dear friend.

                                            R.

RAMUZ TO STRAVINSKY   *Sunday morning*
                                       [August 4 or 11, 1918]
Dear,

This afternoon I will take the manuscript to the printer. And tomorrow I will come to your house with Gagnebin,[31] who is very nice.

                          Best wishes,   R.

RAMUZ TO STRAVINSKY   *[Before August 17, 1918]*

Dear,

I am writing:

   1. To Auberjonois.
   2. To Chavannes, inviting him to be the Narrator; I will see him tomorrow.
   3. To Rosset, to announce our . . . decision; I will not send you a copy, because it would be pointless.
   4. To Robert, as you find here attached. Please add a few lines. For example:

Dear M. Robert,

I want you to know that M. Ramuz is speaking for us both in expressing his gratitude for the devotion that you have shown our enterprise. We made this decision together and with deep regret. Both of us would very much have liked to continue working with you. Rest assured that it is not a question of you, or of us, but only of the best interests of the work, and of your role in particular. We concluded that, despite appearances, he does not *know* you. We evidently did not realize the extent to which an intimate

---

[30] On the following Wednesday, August 7, Stravinsky wrote to the Queen of Spain, asking for her patronage.

[31] Elie Gagnebin (1891–1949), professor of paleontology at the University of Lausanne.

rapport is essential, and neither did you. Perhaps you will think that we ought to have thought of this sooner; in fact, we did foresee it, but we had hoped to surmount the problem through working together. Only yesterday did we conclude that it was insurmountable. I am quite certain, dear M. Robert, that you will understand, and please be assured nonetheless of my feelings of sincere respect. . . .

Please write this out, attach it to my letter, and send it by express mail to M. Paul Robert, Villa les Pléiades, Vevey.

You see that I enclose the check for the agreed amount. He could ask for a severance fee, which is not included; since Robert did not rehearse until the end, though, I think that it balances out.

Unless you advise me otherwise, I will come on the nine o'clock train. I would like to see Auberjonois, and we will have more time than if we arrive in the afternoon. Meet me at the station; I will be in one of the last cars.

I rehearse with Gagnebin on Monday night.

Your   R.

Kisses to the children, and my fond regards to Madame Stravinsky.

RAMUZ TO STRAVINSKY   *August 18, 1918*

Dear Stravinsky,

I asked Rosset to give you a call as soon as he gets home to let you know that there will be no rehearsal tomorrow because *I do not have my manuscript.* I just received a letter from the copyist stating that the manuscript will be ready by Friday. I think that it would be easiest, therefore, to skip tomorrow's rehearsal and to hold the next one on Saturday at eleven o'clock in the theatre, as planned; then we will have an extra rehearsal next week. On the other hand, I would not mind seeing you beforehand to discuss actors, which we have not yet done. The boat arrives in Ouchy at 9:55; I will wait for you there to have a chat.

Rosset has proposed a very modest fee for his functions as impresario. Remind me to talk to you about this too.

These boys are extremely excited by your music. Good-bye, dear friend. Send me a note saying whether I can count on you for Sunday.

RAMUZ TO STRAVINSKY   *August 23, 1918*

Dear,

I was very encouraged by last night's rehearsal with Gagnebin as the Narrator. I would like to see you before the rehearsal tomorrow (Saturday).[32] I will wait

---

[32] In a letter dated simply "Thursday," Ramuz informs Gagnebin that "we will rehearse the day after tomorrow . . . at about four o'clock. . . . Stravinsky will be there,

for you at the dock at 9:55. If you will not be on that boat but plan to come by train instead, let me know. I am writing to Brandenbourg. Thank you for your letter. What should we do? We will have to consent to their bottom price, since that is the only one the budget can bear.

Best wishes.

R.

Gilliard (who is in the country) writes that he is giving an exhibition of his *Images*.[33] You are included on the guest list, so you should receive an invitation soon.

RAMUZ TO STRAVINSKY   *Sunday [August 25, 1918]*

Dear,

Enclosed are:

1. A letter from Komarax:[34] his proposals seem acceptable; tell me what you think of them on Wednesday, and I will write to him.
2. A letter from Reinhart. Please show it to Auberjonois, at the Hotel Victoria, along with the *little design* which I attach. It will probably be necessary to ask Reinhart if we could put a curtain in front of the podium;[35] then that part will be ready.

Best wishes.

R.

Until Wednesday at eleven o'clock, in front of the Café du Théâtre.

Come and fetch me, if you can.

I am sending the manuscript to Madame Pitoëff.

---

and since the narration is closely connected to the music, I would be happy for you two to see each other." (August 22 or 29) This would seem to imply that Stravinsky had not yet met Gagnebin, so perhaps the meeting Ramuz proposed earlier did not take place.

[33] *Quatre Images*, original woodcuts in color by Henri Bischoff, published by the Editions des Cahiers Vaudois.

[34] Director of the Zürich marionette theatre; Reinhart had recommended him as manager of the *Soldat* touring company.

[35] In a letter to David Oppenheim of Columbia Records, November 4, 1954, Stravinsky describes Auberjonois's original curtain as "representing a whaling episode on the high seas" and as having "no apparent connection with the *Soldat*. The idea is the same as in circus shows or small popular theatres, where a striking effect is more important than a relation to the plot."

RAMUZ TO STRAVINSKY   *Sunday [September 1, 1918]*

Dear friend,

Considering all of yesterday's issues, I conclude that the more *abstract* the
mask, the stronger the effect. I wonder if a canvas mask, without any detail, and
perfectly clean-shaven (like the one we had yesterday), would be the most effective, and truly *diabolical*.[36] This fleeting character would be distinguished
by:

1. his bearing
2. his costume
3. the back of the head: no wig in this scene, I think.

I will write to Auberjonois immediately, so that he can start looking for
someone; I will keep my eyes open in this vicinity, too.

One other thing: can we really expect to present *Histoire* in Lausanne on
the 28th? I am very discouraged about the actors. The musicians (and the
music) and the sets will be perfect; but the rest is a blank. For now, I cannot
even find my manuscript. . . . Nevertheless, there are many things of which I
am certain,[37] but unfortunately they are not of great consequence.

Give it some thought, dear friend, and if necessary we will reconsider the
whole matter.

Best wishes.

R.

I will speak to Auberjonois about the costumes. A stifling rigidity would yield
some beautiful effects. The Devil should be wooden.

Could you bring your music next Wednesday? Gagnebin will be present, and I
would like to clarify some of the Narrator's actions and gestures.

RAMUZ TO STRAVINSKY   *Thursday [September 5, 1918]*

Dear,

Bring all of your music with you next Saturday. Only by playing it will we have a
clear picture of the general effect. Also, the music is the best stimulus for the
actors and helps them to understand their roles.

While I have it in mind, do you think that we should try doing the Devil's
monologue in front of the curtain during the Royal March? I think that perhaps

---

[36] Here Stravinsky penciled in the margin, partly in French and partly in Russian: "To
admit this principle would take us too far from our magic-lantern idea. All of these
changes are simply proof of the author's uncertainty about the theatrical aspects of the
piece. And I, with my practical sense, know that the fault is usually the author's."
[37] Stravinsky wrote in the margin: "Which things are those?"

the music and the text alternate in a little too uniform a fashion. We should avoid superimposing music and "poetic" text, but there would be no risk of that kind here. Text and music are both created from unrestrained fantasy, and we might accidentally end up with some unwanted effects.

For example, I envisage the music ending when the Devil says: "He will do away with himself." The next phrase ("but to proceed elegantly") and the reflections that follow would be spoken by the Devil from offstage, without music. The Devil would appear at the Reprise of the March, animating that whole section. Think about it. And then consider the end of the first part of the music, which occurs there: I think that the effect would be powerful and justified, if we conceive of [the Devil] as having arrived there on his own. The little curtain comes down, the concert continues, and the big curtain is lowered during the end of the concert. And then you dance the last scene yourself: you will liven it rhythmically and save everything.

Your   R.

RAMUZ TO STRAVINSKY   *[September 1918]*

I am annoyed to have missed you this morning, dear, but when you left I was in the midst of dressing. . . . I came down too late to catch you in the hallway; he who eats sleeps.*

I sent the curtain to Auberjonois.

R.

* "He who sleeps eats," but one of the attributes of a proverb is its reversibility.

RAMUZ TO STRAVINSKY   *Thursday morning*
                                               [September 1918]

Dear friend,

Am I too late to ask you to speak to Auberjonois tomorrow about admission prices? This matter must be resolved soon. Take the seating plan of the theatre and Brandenbourg's scale of ticket prices. Show them to Auberjonois and consider our project realistically (seats too expensive in my opinion). Brandenbourg tells me that even with the "opera" prices, he is not sure that we will fill the house.

Our calculations were based on a full house and may therefore be completely askew. Discuss it with Auberjonois over your dinner. He has plenty of sense and is familiar with the right people here.

Many fond regards, and I will see you at the boat on Saturday. I spend my days writing letters: this is my sixth of the morning.

R.

SEPTEMBER *14 [?], 1918.*[38] *Ramuz receives the proofs of the program from the printer, La Concorde. They reveal that Rosset played the Soldier, Jean Villard played the Devil, Georges Pitoëff performed the Devil's dances, and the musicians were Closset (violin), Fricke (contrabass), Allegra (clarinet), de Bier (bassoon), Schöldlin (cornet-à-pistons), Miene (trombone), and Jacobi (percussion). On the reverse of the program, Ramuz wrote a note to Stravinsky:*

. . . Here are the proofs. I just gave the fair copy to be printed. It will come out better than this copy. . . .

As for the *timbre:* sheer nonsense, if the price is 15 francs! We would be better off having invitations made: The Messrs . . . have the honor of inviting you to attend the dress rehearsal of *Histoire du soldat,* which will take place, etc. This invitation would then serve also as a ticket. The seats are not reserved.

Who do you think [should be invited]? Send me a note by tomorrow morning, so that I can take care of this. For one hundred copies the cost will be approximately 15 francs.

RAMUZ TO STRAVINSKY   *[September 1918]*[39]

I am writing to B. to inform him that Rosset, who has the seating plan of the theatre, will cross off the reserved seats before the tickets are put up for sale to the general public. The tickets will be sent to those with reserved seats now.

I received the masks. Tell Brandenbourg that those who hold reserved seats are invited to attend the dress rehearsal.

SEPTEMBER *27, 1918 (FRIDAY).*[40] *Dress rehearsal.*

STRAVINSKY TO RAMUZ   *October 8, 1918*

Enclosed is a second letter from Allegra.[41] Note the few lines that I have scribbled on the back.[42]

---

[38] According to a letter from Ramuz to Rosset dated "Friday," Ramuz was to pick up the program the following day, Saturday, which would almost certainly have been either the 7th or the 14th.

[39] Ramuz's note to Stravinsky is written on a letter from Brandenbourg concerning the premiere on the 28th. Brandenbourg's letter is dated simply "Wednesday."

[40] As late as September 26, Stravinsky made a note to tell Gagnebin to begin reading "immediately after the end of the first march."

[41] Edmond Allegra, the Zürich clarinetist, was to play in the first performance of Stravinsky's Three Pieces for Clarinet Solo.

[42] Stravinsky's note says that *Histoire* is eagerly awaited in Zürich and that the performance date there has been fixed for October 28. Since some members of the cast and ensemble had Spanish influenza, Ramuz went alone and read the play.

Hello, Ramuz. Today I feel much better. I just read in today's *Gazette* that the Orchestre de la Suisse Romande has begun its rehearsals: finally Ansermet has recovered! Write a note telling him that I am extremely vexed that he has forgotten us (me in particular). Also tell him that there is no alternative: he must come to conduct the *Soldat* in Zürich and Winterthur. Otherwise we will have to start over again, and he himself knows how much effort went into one week of work. Furthermore, I (you, too) counted on his word. We agreed to do a tour, not one or two performances in Lausanne or Geneva. Correct? I hope that you will tell him this. I embrace you.

> Your   Stravinsky

Please send me all of my music immediately.

RAMUZ TO STRAVINSKY   *October 9, 1918*

I received your letter and am sending you the music.

Chavannes, after speaking to you on the telephone, told me that you are feeling better, so I will take advantage of this moment to let you know where we stand.

1. Budget for the performance: The last bills are still trickling in. Rosset is to bring me all of these, and as soon as I have them, I will finish figuring the accounts. We will get something back from him, although very little.

2. Budget for the preparations: I told you that I owe Mermod[43] 466 francs, 35 centimes for construction of the little theatre. Now the last bills have just arrived through Auberjonois. The dressmaker from Geneva wants 289 francs, 50 centimes, which is reasonable. The hairdresser: 77 francs, 40 centimes, reasonable enough. The disaster is the Pitoëff costumes: . . . 545 francs (of which 100 have already been paid by Auberjonois, leaving 445)! This is insane. What should we do? Refuse payment?[44] I would have liked to see Auberjonois, but

---

[43] H.-L. Mermod, the publisher, a friend of Stravinsky.

[44] On October 19, Georges Pitoëff wrote to Stravinsky: "Why are we all being punished by influenza? We were very upset to hear that you and your family were ill. Thank God all that is over for now. The cancellation of the Geneva performance saddened us, but you will eventually give the *Soldat* under more propitious conditions. . . . Since Rosset may present the *Soldat* in Zürich on the 28th, I am leaving this date free and hope to have the performance here on the 30th. Now I must ask you for a favor. . . . The delay in our season and the delay with *Histoire du soldat* have put our finances in a very sorry state. Could you give us an advance of 300 francs? It would rescue us. If you and Ramuz find this possible, the money will go for the next performance of *Soldat*. I imagine how many financial problems you must have, so I apologize and repeat that I would not permit myself to ask this of you if it were not an absolute necessity. Life, already hard enough, is now a disaster with this flu epidemic. . . . But the Germans will surrender soon and the war will end, after which the Bolsheviks will be cleaned out. Perhaps Lyudmila and I are stupid optimists, but we believe that this nightmare is almost over.

he has left Lausanne. In the end, I deposited 198.50 for him. . . . Here are my figures:

77.40
289.50
445.00
20.00 bouquet
198.50 Auberjonois
1,030.40!

This is nearly 500 francs more than what I had expected. About 1,800 francs remains for us.

3. Zürich performance: Bodmer bombards me with letters. I enclose the most recent one: please return it to me. I told him that you have not yet recovered, but that he must nevertheless take steps to provide for the eventual success of the presentation. You will notice the innumerable demands he makes of me: in the margin you will find my replies, all negative. A financial guarantee would put an end to all that: they ask everything and offer nothing. Answer quickly, telling me what you think.

I have millions of things to tell you about the work itself,* about the performance and the conclusions I have drawn, but I will save all this until we see each other.

Extremely nice letter from Reinhart, whom I shall keep up-to-date on developments.

Good-bye, dear friend. My best wishes and regards to all. I am not at all well. I have a cough, and I cannot sleep. I have a terrible headache, which is becoming chronic.

* A small audience is *enchanted* and wants to see it again, but a *small* and *poor* group. The rich people are annoyed. Madame Cartel wrote to Auberjonois that she fears that the Genevans may be vexed. A very Genevan nuance.

It is necessary either to stand firm now or to mount it again in different circumstances.

Gilliard has sent me the proposals for publication. I will discuss them with you.

We will be so glad to see you again. Even Nadia remembers 'Tari, Tari' and occasionally starts dancing. Monsieur 'Tari, Tari' is you." On the 30th, he wrote again: "I have just received the 250 francs, for which many thanks from me and from Lyudmila. . . . We were completely without money. Rosset became ill two days ago, but not too dangerously, according to the latest news." And on November 1, he wrote: "I have written to Ramuz thanking him for the advance. When I see him in person I will thank him again for his generous response to our difficult situation. Do you expect to give the *Soldat* here in the near future? The Geneva theatres are open and well filled, and Rosset is well and beginning to rehearse with us."

RAMUZ TO STRAVINSKY   *Saturday, October 26, 1918*

Please see if this is all right. If so, please put the enclosed envelope in the mail.
If not, return it to me with your comments.

I wrote to Reinhart and sent him the bills.

I wrote to Villard.

I wrote to Gagnebin.

I have written all morning . . .

I hope that everything is finished. I will not write anymore.

RAMUZ TO STRAVINSKY   *November 9, 1918*

1. I have three packets of envelopes for you, half of what remained after
the complimentary tickets for the *Soldat* were sent out.

2. I owe you 3 francs for one of the two candlesticks that Auberjonois purchased and that were not used. I have asked Auberjonois to send you this
amount.

3. *I still have heard nothing from Reinhart,* not even an acknowledgment
that he has received the invoices. I am beginning to worry. Are you sure that he
did not misunderstand your telephone conversation? In any event, it seems difficult to go on to the next step (concerning which Auberjonois and I are in agreement) so long as the expenses for the other matter have not been recovered.

4. Sauvin[45] consents to our conditions (1,500—1,000—1,000) and is willing to handle the job. Now the *Cahiers* [*Vaudois*] could arrange the finances
with him. That should be decided sometime next week, I think. Until then, it is
only a proposal.

Good news from Berlin and elsewhere?

RAMUZ TO STRAVINSKY   *November 19, 1918*
                                       [Postcard]

Excuse the soiled postcard. I am writing this in the post office to inform you
that I have withdrawn the money and sent the check to H., and that everything
is in order. Also, I want you to know that I find 15,000 [francs] to be too expensive, in retrospect. 12,000 would be better, no? But will this note reach you in
time?

RAMUZ TO STRAVINSKY   *Saturday afternoon*
                                       [Autumn 1918]
Dear friend,

I just tried to call you, but in vain, for the telephone was in a state of ruination. I
had wanted to inquire about Madame Stravinsky's condition and to ask your

---

[45] Sauvin's transport company was later to move Stravinsky's possessions from Morges
to France. See *Stravinsky in Pictures and Documents* (New York: Simon & Schuster,
1978), pp. 626–7, fns. 5 and 6 (hereafter referred to as *S.P.D.*).

forgiveness for not having done so sooner. I had no idea of what had happened, since I have been away recently (in Basel). Through Chavannes and Ansermet I learned of the distress that you have suffered, and also that your anxieties are already somewhat relieved. I hope that by today they are completely over. Even if that is the case, please communicate our best wishes and regards to Madame Stravinsky, and pardon this involuntary tardiness.

Your   Ramuz

RAMUZ TO STRAVINSKY   *December 31, 1918*

Best wishes to you, to Madame Stravinsky, to the children, and to all of yours.

My mother is slightly better. I have been completely at a loss for the past two weeks: I have seen no one. I hope to see you soon: I will be in touch.

No news from Zürich (concerning what we sent), and I am writing to Reinhart.

I received the bill from Michoud (the costume designer): 10 francs, which I will pay.

You do not say in your letter, for which I thank you, what question it is that you wish to discuss with me. Nothing pressing, I guess; nothing bad, I hope.

Auberjonois and I ran into each other, and he told me that everyone is well.

RAMUZ TO STRAVINSKY   *February 2, 1919*[46]

Is your financial situation sufficiently stable for you to advance me 500 francs for the business matters that we are handling together? I am drowning in bills. Soon the coal bill will arrive, and [I have] nothing with which to pay it. Please see if this can be arranged. I would like very much to see you. Will you be coming to Lausanne? If not, I will go to Morges. Did Mika arrive safely?

---

[46] Stravinsky had written to Otto Kling on January 17: "Perhaps you have heard something about *Histoire du soldat*, presented at the Théâtre de Lausanne last autumn, and which I composed in collaboration with C.-F. Ramuz (author of the text). The tale is spoken, played, and danced (with a little portable theatre), with marches, dances, arias, preludes, intermezzi, etc., for an ensemble of seven musicians: clarinet, bassoon, cornet-à-piston, trombone, violin, c-bass, and percussion. The original ensemble would be suitable for a chamber-music concert (soon to be presented under Ansermet in Lausanne, Geneva, and several other Swiss cities). Numerous requests have been addressed to me for a piano-and-violin reduction (in which the violin would have the more substantial role), so I have decided to arrange a little suite of the work, employing a clarinet along with these two instruments. I would like the suite to be presented in London this season. It would consist of the following numbers: (1) Soldier's March, (2) Soldier's Violin (Soldier at the Brook), (3) Little Concert, (4) Dance of the Devil. The conditions for performance would be the same as those for the Quartet."

Two drawings of Ramuz by Stravinsky, made at the time of Histoire du soldat.

RAMUZ TO STRAVINSKY   *March 11, 1919*

Dear friend,

Since we were not able to conclude yesterday's conversation about R. de C., and I did not provide enough information for you to make up your mind, I am sending you his prospectus. . . . Will you see R. de C. soon? I think that he has a telephone. If our "overtures" are well received, we could meet, as you had proposed.

    In any event, do not lose sight of this matter, because even the (minor) steps in these negotiations lead somewhere: only by increasing the number of threads can one catch anything in the net.

    Many fond regards in the meantime.

                                           R.

RAMUZ TO STRAVINSKY   *April 23, 1919*[47]

I have not yet worked on your songs [*Podblyudnye*]: when will I be able to? I am surrounded by bothersome uncertainties and petty concerns that hinder me from applying myself to anything. Tell me if those women really have arranged to sing for you, and when. I would hate for you to miss that opportunity on my account, but I also would not like to make halfhearted translations. That is how the matter stands.

---

[47] On April 6, Jacques Rivière, editor of the *Nouvelle Revue Française,* had written to Stravinsky asking him to "relay my best regards to Ramuz and Auberjonois."

RAMUZ TO STRAVINSKY   *June 6, 1919*

Please be so kind as to send a postcard by return mail telling me M. Pečič's first name, and also how to spell his last name in French.[48] This is in order to print his name on a subscription copy.

I am drowning in chores, but these do not thwart my desire to see you soon.

As for the *Soldat,* it is almost ready.[49]

RAMUZ TO STRAVINSKY   *July 11, 1919*[50]

We leave tomorrow, on the noon train, and will bring the notes and the translations with us.

RAMUZ TO STRAVINSKY   *July 31, 1919*

I was unable to meet you at the railway station because I did not see your telegram until my return home, at around 7:00 p.m. I was running around all day yesterday, and I am very annoyed at having missed you. Tomorrow, between trains, I am going to the Pechitches' to pick up the translation—will I see you?

RAMUZ TO STRAVINSKY   *August 8, 1919*

I wanted to telephone you, but I could not get through.

This was to ask you if, by chance, I left the texts of the last songs I translated at your house: I cannot find them. I was considering publishing two of the songs, with your permission, in the *Revue [Romande]*.

I also wanted to ask you if you have heard anything from Ansermet. Apparently he has returned, and I would like to see him.

I hardly leave the printer's these days. . . .

Please note the *timbre.*

---

[48] Bela Pechitch (Ansermet's spelling) was the husband of Maja Strozzi-Pečič, the Croatian soprano to whom Stravinsky dedicated his *Quatre Chants russes.*

[49] This refers to the publication of the libretto.

[50] Stravinsky wrote to an unidentified person that summer: "I thank you for your (second) letter without replying to it, because I hope to be able to answer you shortly in person. If circumstances are favorable, I am planning to go very soon to Paris, where I would like to be able to mount *Histoire du soldat* myself in the autumn or winter. I henceforth consider myself completely free from any obligation to Diaghilev. I would be happy to try for once to realize a completely new work, one that seems interesting to me, as long as my intentions would be followed faithfully (on condition that the delays not be too long). But it is impossible to accomplish anything at a distance. Ramuz and I should therefore be [in Paris] very soon, in about three weeks. Do you see any way in which to find the sum for us beforehand (2 to 3,000 francs), since neither of us, at the moment, has the money to pay the expenses for the trip?"

RAMUZ TO STRAVINSKY   *October 22, 1919*

Do you think that the Kl [ing] business could be settled soon?[51] If so, it would
be helpful (there is an avalanche of urgent bills, purchases for the winter). But
if nothing can be expected to happen on this front for the next eleven days or
so, could you possibly advance me 300 francs (I think that you will be able to)?
I would pay you back as soon as the accounts are set straight. You would do me
a great service. . . . I need this money before the end of the month.

RAMUZ TO STRAVINSKY   *November 24, 1919*[52]

The undersigned declares to have received the following amounts from M. Igor
Stravinsky for the publication rights (performance rights reserved) of the following works, which I translated into French:

1.	*Renard*	1,000 francs
2.	*Berceuses du chat*	100 francs
3.	*Pribaoutki*	100 francs
4.	*[Quatre] Chants russes*	100 francs
5.	*Les Noces villageoises*	1,500 francs

C.-F. Ramuz

---

[51]Stravinsky wrote to Otto Kling on October 28: "I hope that your trip was not too ex-
hausting and that negotiations for *Histoire du soldat* in Brussels went well"; and again
on November 14: "Did you receive my cable concerning the *Soldat* in Brussels? The
same conditions apply for two performances as for one: thus 4,700 Swiss francs for two
performances. If this [performance] is to take place, we must know as quickly as possible."

[52] Stravinsky wrote to Otto Kling that same day: "Today I am sending you just a few
lines to express my regret that the Brussels performances of the *Soldat* will not take
place. I am, however, very surprised to learn that you attribute the failure of the negotiations to my excessive demands. Do not think that I am angry. I only want you to understand that in reproaching me for the high fees (4,250 francs), you are forgetting
that my share of that sum is minimal—250 francs—the same amount that you yourself wanted to charge for the rental of the parts, which you own. Permit me to remind
you of the breakdown of the remaining 4,000 francs: (1) payment for Ansermet
(everything included), 1,500 francs; (2) Gagnebin (everything included), 1,000
francs; (3) rental of the sets and costumes, 1,000 francs (which cost us 10,000 in
Lausanne); (4) fees of Ramuz and Auberjonois, 250 each. What, then, is so excessive,
I ask you? Or perhaps these [Belgian] gentlemen supposed that everything would be
taken care of (consequently Ramuz and I would be the ones to pay for the whole
thing) simply because they declared that the performances would be given for purely
artistic reasons. But the artistic goal of the enterprise does not necessarily imply that
material matters will be renounced. I *always* compose with artistic goals in mind, but
no one can blame me for wanting to earn a living by my work. I think that if you reflect
upon this for a moment, you will see that I am right."
    Stravinsky wrote to Kling again on November 28: "I sent you the list of instru-

RAMUZ TO STRAVINSKY   *December 11, 1919*

Have you authorized *Littérateur* to publish the *Berceuses* and *Pribaoutki*? If so, only one problem remains: all of the texts have been printed the wrong way, rendering them unrecognizable.

RAMUZ TO STRAVINSKY   *Monday, December 16, 1919*[53]

Enclosed are the texts that I received from M. Pečič, corrected and rewritten in part. I did my best, and it was not easy. Would you please return them to him, as soon as possible, since I do not have his address? I wrote him a brief letter and slipped it into the middle of the package: please be sure that it does not get

---

mental parts, piano, voice, etc., to be attached to the document, in order to conclude our contract more quickly. Let me explain: by the present contract, you will acquire, for example, not only the music of *Histoire du soldat* in its original form (full score) but also a small supplementary work that I made: (1) Suite of four [later five] numbers for clarinet, violin, and piano; (2) the piano reduction." And the following day, Stravinsky wrote: "In regard to *Histoire,* as I see it, [the Brussels gentlemen] were more frightened by Ansermet than by the fees."

[53] Stravinsky wrote to Otto Kling that same day: "Since I jealously guard my reputation as a man of good faith, and since that discourteous letter from the Brussels gentleman that you forwarded to me was not accompanied by any note from you, it is difficult for me to determine your point of view. Do you share this man's opinion, or do you agree with my reasoning about the prices for mounting *Histoire* in Brussels, as presented in my letter of November 24? If my letter convinced you, it seems to me that you would be [eager?] to explain to the gentlemen from Brussels that these Swiss gentlemen had no intention of making a profit from the artistic endeavor, but, on the contrary, took all measures to facilitate the success of that endeavor by: (1) asking very modest fees;* (2) attempting to render a truly artistic performance by inviting M. Ansermet to conduct and M. Gagnebin to be the Narrator. These two men know the work profoundly and would have represented an artistic guarantee. That their end was an artistic and disinterested one was demonstrated all the more after Brussels declined to pay the travel expenses of one Swiss gentleman—your amiable servant—deeming his trip to be less valuable to the enterprise (since it would increase the expenses) than that of Ansermet and Gagnebin.

"These Brussels gentlemen must finally be made aware of what everyone knows, that a truly *artistic* performance is more costly than a run-of-the-mill one. Nevertheless, there is one recourse: to give several rehearsals before a paying audience and thus make the money back. Perhaps it will be said that when the public must pay, the endeavor is not [purely] artistic, but how else are those who work only for Art to survive? No, my dear M. Kling, I will be frank about my understanding of the matter. These Brussels gentlemen wanted to mount the *Soldat,* and when they realized that it would be expensive* * (beyond what they had envisioned), they decided that the most elegant way to withdraw from the project would be to accuse the Swiss gentlemen of a lack of [artistic] concern. Why all of this? Would it not have been a thousand times

lost. I would like to have the proofs, those of *your* songs, if nothing else. When will I see you again? I do not know. I am seldom at home anymore. We are becoming increasingly anxious about my mother's condition.

RAMUZ TO STRAVINSKY   *Tuesday, January 27, 1920*

Dear friend,

I am writing to you at the Hôtel Meurice,[54] in the hope that you will be there.

G. just deposited 12,000 francs. What should be done?

Since you are in Paris, and particularly well situated to carry out this plan, I would like very much for you to keep your eyes open for interesting collaborators. Take advantage of your circumstances.

Music: you are not in need of any guidance.
Painting: ask your friends Picasso and Derain.
Literature: undoubtedly you will be seeing some of this set.

We already discussed this, if you recall. The idea is to establish a small, independent branch with the prospect of reaching a new audience.

Chavannes informs me that the Gogol is ready—so much the better. Also, see Charles-Albert Cingria and speak with him about the plan.

I send you my best wishes for everything to go according to your design, and I am entirely at your disposal, if you need me.

Best from all of us, and my fond regards.

Ramuz

---

simpler to have admitted that they were obliged to cancel the performances because they would be too expensive?

"I am sending a copy of this letter to M. Chaumont and send you my best wishes. Devotedly

"*Surely they cannot find 250 francs for each of us—you, Ramuz, Auberjonois, and myself—to be exorbitant.

"* * Especially now, given the Swiss rate, because these Swiss gentlemen living in Switzerland and spending their money in Switzerland have no reason to count on Belgian money."

On January 16, 1920, Stravinsky wrote to Henry Kling: "In his last letter (of January 13) your father asked me to send him copies of the Suite from *Histoire du soldat,* the [*Piano-*] *Rag Music,* and the Three Pieces for Clarinet, if by chance I have any copies left. The only one of which I still have copies is the Three Pieces. . . . You should have in your possession two copies of the *Soldat* Suite with score parts."

[54] Stravinsky was in Paris for the premiere of his ballet *Le Chant du rossignol* at the Opéra on February 2, but he was staying at the Hôtel Continental.

RAMUZ TO STRAVINSKY   *June 16, 1920*

Carantec

Thank you for the tobacco. I have more than a little bit of the Russian variety left, and I smoke as much as possible, blending it with the Vaudois tobacco. This note is to inform you that I am sending your copy of the *Soldat* by the same mail.[55] Send me a few lines to acknowledge its receipt: this mailing is the first attempt. How was your trip? How are you? Regards, best wishes from us to all of you and your friends.

                                                            Ramuz

I am proud to have an address as long as yours.

RAMUZ TO STRAVINSKY   *June 30, 1920*

Received, corrected, and returned the proofs to Kling.[56]

RAMUZ TO STRAVINSKY   *   *July 29, 1920*

Indeed, I owe you all sorts of apologies. I would have addressed these lines to you much sooner, had I perceived my own error, but you are the one who has pointed it out to me. . . . What happened? I am not sure. In any case, I am entirely to blame, or, at least, I am solely responsible. I should have told you this immediately, in the hope that my confession would merit your pardon. I am well aware of the gravity of my negligence. But keep in mind that this limited edition of the tale almost did not appear, and that I forbade them to send it to Paris or to release press copies.

    I say all this in an attempt to reassure you. . . .

---

[55] Stravinsky wrote to Otto Kling on June 21: "The proofs of the *Soldat* Suite will be corrected immediately." He wrote again on July 12: "Along with these lines I am sending you . . . the proofs of the *Soldat* Suite (for piano, clarinet, violin), the piano score with clarinet and violin, and the two scores for violin and clarinet. Please tell the printer to make corrections according to the violin and clarinet scores. The lines for these two instruments are found in the full score (which is to say the piano, violin, clarinet score). I did not review them again after correcting the score for piano, clarinet, and violin, in order not to keep you waiting. In short, you may consider the following as completely corrected: (1) the piano; (2) the separate scores of a. violin and b. clarinet. . . . M. Desbaillets [J. & W. Chester's Geneva representative] writes that you intend to print the full score (for seven instruments) of the *Soldat*. If this is so, please wait until the revisions are complete. Unfortunately, I have absolutely no time to finish them before the new year. . . . As with the other editions, please send me that little *Soldat* Suite directly off the press. I am sending the copy of the Suite with the violin and clarinet scores to Ansermet so that he may examine the numerous revisions."

[56] On August 3, Otto Kling in Geneva wrote to Stravinsky in Paris acknowledging that

STRAVINSKY TO RAMUZ   *Carantec*[57]
                                                                 Finistère
My dear Ramuz,   *August 23, 1920*

I received your letter in Paris; I just spent ten days there hunting for an apartment, but for the time being I have returned empty-handed. In three weeks we
will all leave Carantec for Garches, where a friend of mine[58] has offered to lend
me her villa until I find something suitable of my own (and God knows when
that will be!). My address after September 12 or 13 will be: Villa Bel Respiro,
avenue Alphonse de Neuville, Garches (Seine-et-Oise).

After my return to Carantec I suffered a bad case of indigestion, which explains why it is only now that I take up the pen to write to you on this cheap
paper.

Indeed, the mistakes in the list of instruments of my orchestra are annoying, to put it mildly. But in your letter you neglect even to mention the credits
page,[59] about which I wrote to you, stressing the specific character it should
convey. In its present form, the page implies that our collaboration was of an
entirely different nature from what it was in reality. My role in *Histoire du soldat* was not confined to composing music for a pre-existing play. Yet from reading your credits page, one would deduce that the *Soldat* could be readily performed with different music—as it could be, for example, with different sets
(which goes without saying). Is this what you believe, Ramuz? I think not,
since you are all too well aware of the part that I played in the development of
the scenario; and had we not collaborated on it, the *"histoire"* of the *"soldat"*
simply would not be what it is. Do not misconstrue this as pretension on my
part: I do not intend to have my name figure next to yours when the text is
published *separately*. As I wrote to you, I propose simply to substitute the program from the *Soldat* premiere, which would suffice to indicate to the reader
that an intimate collaboration existed between us on your and my *Soldat,* in
place of this erroneous credits page. I hold firmly to my argument, dear Ramuz,
and it would deeply sadden me to learn that you were the one who composed
that unfortunate page, knowingly and with an ulterior motive. . . .

I do not mention Auberjonois, because his collaboration with the two of us

---

the composer would receive 250 Swiss francs for each performance of *Histoire* with
Ramuz's libretto. Kling also promised to write to Ramuz and ask for his terms and for
the use of the sets.

[57] When Stravinsky left Switzerland he moved for three months to Carantec, on the
northern coast of Brittany, at the suggestion of Misia Sert. A letter from her niece,
Mimi Godebska Blaque-Belair, sent from Morocco, March 8, 1939, contains the exclamation: "Ah! I think about Carantec, where we were all together."

[58] Gabrielle ("Coco") Chanel. Her villa served Stravinsky as a temporary residence
until the spring of 1921, when he moved his family to Biarritz and rented a two-room
studio at the Maison Pleyel, in Paris.

[59] Published by the Editions des Cahiers Vaudois in 1920, *Histoire du soldat* bore only
Ramuz's name on the cover, and the roster of instruments included a flute and omitted the clarinet and trombone.

was limited to the pictorial, theatrical dimension of the *Soldat,* and he was in no way involved in the realization of the musical work.

All of the above issues are of an ethical order. Questions of a material order exist too, and here they are:

Father Kling is preparing to publish the full score of the *Soldat.* Before he does so, I need to clarify with you the question of the sections of text that are an integral part of the music. How am I to regard the role of those indispensable fragments at certain points in my music, which will be published in the orchestra score and which the stage manager, Narrator, and players will employ in future stagings of the work? The published musical text and published literary text must correspond exactly, and verbal fragments must be entered in the score at crucial spots (for example, at the marches, the Little Concert, the Devil's Couplets), or, in other words, at all points where my music begins or is punctuated. I hope that you will not object to my regulating the music with the verbal text according to the way I hear it. The published score, which will be used in the eventual performances of our *Soldat,* would be incomplete without this, rendering the stage manager's job very bothersome.*

I hope for a prompt reply from you on this subject.

Enough of that! I am sick of it. How are you? Myself, I feel bad most of the time and only occasionally good: one never knows why, but what I do know is that the number of days on which I feel good is small. People (certain acquaintances in Paris) annoy me. And furthermore, I can't say that Brittany enchants me (as the Vaudois countryside did!). To begin with, the weather is consistently terrible, and that, in my opinion, is not French, but chiefly British.

Granted, the peasants are decent enough, but peasants everywhere are decent, even in *Bochie!* Conventional little French types come here, lacking the means to go to Deauville (not amusing at all); these are people who start singing in front of our windows when we are on our way to bed, and more loudly than is called for in the street, since they think that being on vacation justifies a lack of restraint.

I hardly sleep, and I am composing music. I miss you terribly. I embrace you very affectionately.

Your   Stravinsky

* In concert form, the various numbers in the *Soldat* Suite will be done without words, of course. Moreover, I think that coherent verses will be needed only for The Soldier's March; the rest is comprehensible only with your complete text, and fragments would merely be confusing.

RAMUZ TO STRAVINSKY   *August 27, 1920*

I am replying to you immediately. Please believe that my intention was never to deny the part that you played in developing the *Soldat.* Consider, on the other hand, the position in which you left me, with your departure for Paris, and when you announced in so many words that you wanted to withdraw your

music and use it elsewhere.[60] A certain contradiction exists in desiring to consider our version of the *Soldat* a definitive work while at the same time planning
another version, as was the case. To insist upon your collaboration was in some
degree to isolate you (from the public), and you know me well enough to realize that I was and am far from doing that. What my part in this demonstrates is
a kind of *caution,* and that is all, I assure you; and I thank you for having given
me the opportunity to say so. I beg your forgiveness if my caution still seems
exaggerated to you; I insist upon using that word to describe my action because
the nuance is essential. And I must remind you that I published this libretto
much less for readers, or for bookstores, than to unburden myself of it as soon
as the means were presented to me. There you have my clear and frank explanation; are you satisfied with it? If so, let us not speak of it again, and forget the
little difference of opinion.

In regard to the publication of the fragments of text that would be helpful
with the music, you are free to employ them according to your understanding.
You have only to excerpt them from the "ordinary" copy, which I am sending in
this mail, and to advise M. Kling, who bombards me with letters asking my conditions, the rental fee for the sets and costumes, etc., etc. I told him to address
himself to you; he replies that you told him to address himself to me: in the end,
we agreed to a minimum of 250 francs (each) for the authors' rights (total
amount fixed by you), and the same sum divided by two, or 125 francs each, for
the rental of the sets and costumes.

So much for business. As for the rest, my situation is very confused, and
consists of the following: a magnificent summer, three weeks in a beautiful
area near Germany, which left me with a desire to live there, but no houses
were available (as everywhere); a great disgust for towns that are not towns,
like Lausanne; your absence; the feeling of being at a turning point, but with
the turn not yet taken; a great dispersion of direction and energy, which is to

---

[60] That Ramuz was offended by Stravinsky's use of the *Soldat* music in concert suites
seems unreasonable, especially since precedents existed in the suites from *Firebird*
and *Petrushka*. From the first, Stravinsky's intention had been to compose a work that
could serve both as incidental music for a play and, with no changes aside from the
omission of certain numbers, as a concert suite (in two different instrumental forms
and a piano solo). Stravinsky wrote to Edwin Evans, November 19, 1918: "A piano reduction, or one for piano and a different instrumental combination with a few numbers—marches, arias, pieces for violin and piano, dances, etc.—could be extracted
from the larger suite to make a smaller one." Hans Reinhart, brother of Werner and
translator of the German libretto, wrote to J. & W. Chester in April 1932 suggesting
that the publisher encourage the composer to transcribe all of the *Soldat* music for the
piano, violin, and clarinet combination in order to make the work available to a theatre
company, the Hass-Berkow Truppe, which wanted to take the piece on tour. Stravinsky answered (though his son Theodore signed the letter), May 3, 1932, to the effect that a trio version of the complete opus would compete against the original version
and that the percussion part at the end could not be transcribed but would require a
fourth player.

say the universal whirling of the conditions of existence and events; the feeling that we are in a period of transition; the need for something definitive (which could be routed into the flow of the pen, mind you); the horror of the Polish cliché: a young, gallant, and not at all Jewish Bolshevik general; academics everywhere, nothing else; not much love, either, I think, for the Bretons, among whom one vacations. I am just back from Morges, your apartment is closed, a north wind was blowing, the lake was Prussian blue, I followed the main street from one end to the other and had a great desire for some aluminum household goods, which, nevertheless, I did not buy.

You must let me know how everyone is. You seem terribly rushed. Remember us to Madame Stravinsky and your relatives. Embrace the children, if they remember me. I embrace you.

Ramuz

I spent two days with Ansermet in Bière. He gave me news of you. He is well: eating fondues in the mountains and cooking chickens in the woods. We drank an enormous amount of Dezaley. *A bientôt!* I recommend [that we see each other soon], but is it always necessary to recommend?

M. Maurice Muret has a boat, which he calls the *Exquisite Hour* and which has the same tone as those gentlemen who sing under windows.

RAMUZ TO STRAVINSKY   *September 2, 1920*

I am in the process of surrendering myself to luxury* literature (understand me well), so how can I be expected to add to that luxury the luxury of moving to an apartment (if one can be found) for 1,000 francs? My idea for today is that my way of life should be that of a craftsman-gardener, . . . with a little concrete house and rabbits (which one slaughters oneself) for Sundays. Such a situation sounds refreshing to me. Do you intend to carry out a similar reform in Garches? A question: surely this is what is missing down your way, with those gentlemen under your windows. I know, besides, that the situation can be found (the house, the rabbits, the workbench) only with good tools [by constructing them oneself]; otherwise it will never be found. Everything is a matter of finances!

* A treatise on applied theology

RAMUZ TO STRAVINSKY   *October 3, 1920*

Did you receive my letter thanking you for the package?* Since I have not heard from you, and mistrust the mails, and since I also may have given the wrong address, I am slightly worried that my package did not reach you. Send a note telling me whether this is the correct address. We would all be very pleased to know how Madame Stravinsky is feeling and how the children like their new home.

* The [*Quatre*] *Chants* [*russes*]

RAMUZ TO STRAVINSKY   [*October 1920*]

Greetings, Stravinsky family, and welcome to the new residence at Garches (Seine-et-Oise).

My idea of becoming an artisan is not at all an aesthetic one, but rather a financial one. I am considering the fact that . . . in the future I could have a lot of trouble earning as much money as the artisan in question. So why perpetuate the costly, deceitful, and useless front of a "liberal career," with the rent, clothing, domesticity . . . that it presupposes? If the artisan lives in a certain manner, it is because he is forced to do so, spending exactly what he can afford to spend. I confess that my views fall into the category of anti-poetry. The only miracle that I await is a *pecuniary* reform (without which, as Gagnebin says, they have you hanging by a hook). I only wonder if this is possible. Alas! we are "classified." We belong to an era in which things happen only in a series, by chain reaction. Moreover, you are correct: this is the baggage that we must lug around, and, in the end, I allow things to happen. What enchants me is your phrase ". . . when the anti-poetic, by means that are independent of us, becomes true, great* poetry. The essential thing is to have a good starting point: the rest is beyond you."

* Perhaps even great enough that I would not cross it out.

RAMUZ TO STRAVINSKY   [*October 1920*]

Dear,

I was saddened at having to return the . . . notebook to you (it was sent out yesterday); but what would I not do for you?

Your   R.

RAMUZ TO STRAVINSKY   *November 22, 1920*

Would you do me a favor? Recently things have been very difficult here: change—protectionism—"reaction"—financial crisis, etc. Several friends are attempting to establish a small "fund" for me that would allow me to print my books myself. Already some pledges have been made. You see the freedom that this would provide me. . . . I considered [asking] Reinhart [for help], and I do not think that he would refuse. He has written several times on this subject, asking how the project is coming along, and I have promised to submit a plan to him. It is ticklish for me to ask him myself to underwrite the project; but the other people who are interested in it have no relationship with him. Would you undertake to do this? Once an in-principle agreement is acquired from him, I would step in and give him all of the necessary information. Thus you would have only to make the overture. I am writing this in great haste. Send a note, please, as soon as possible. . . .

P.S. Please do not mention this matter to anyone. You are the only one who is to know about it. And as yet it is nothing more than a project, but I must find some means to extricate myself from these difficulties.

RAMUZ TO STRAVINSKY   *January 8, 1921*

Dear Stravinsky,

Has something happened, or are you still too busy to write? I am waiting for your reply. Try to find a moment and tell me where the matter stands. This course of action is of great importance to me at present because *everything has stopped,* and prudent people (nowadays everyone is prudent) will not take risks for just anything. Hence one can count only on oneself, and I have some plans brewing.

Please thank Madame Stravinsky for the letters; my wife intends to write back soon.

How are the children? How are you?

I have not yet seen Ansermet, who, it seems, is ill, but I have no details. My respects, kind regards, and best wishes to everyone.

Your   R.

I continue to find everything very beautiful here.

RAMUZ TO STRAVINSKY   *August 10, 1921*

We have not heard from you and yours in a very long while. My wife and daughter of ten inquire about Madame Stravinsky, but I am unable to reply. I do not know much about what *you* are doing, either, apart from the events of your public life, which is not at all what interests me. . . . I live here in complete solitude. Some days are very beautiful; other days, less so. My situation would suppose the intervention of grace (if you believe in it) or of inspiration (but that is a poetic word), for in this dead land without resources, everything must be extracted from within. A few very good friends still live here, but I feel that they too are paralyzed by the surroundings. They always ask about you and miss you.

STRAVINSKY TO RAMUZ   *Anglet*
                                               August 18, 1921

Ramuz,

Thank you for the letter. I was very happy to hear from you finally! And, at last, I too shall send you news of me. I live here in tranquility while composing an opera with four characters, based on a short Pushkin novel.[61] A young Russian poet[62] is doing the Russian text, and he composes the verses quite well. The music is *very simple,* even more so than that of *Histoire du soldat.* I am satisfied at the way in which the work is unfolding, with arias, duos, and trios, and all "very melodious"—as Bakst said of the Good Friday music in *Parsifal.*

I too find that there are days when everything goes well and gives me pleasure, even during the most sinister rain. On other days I look only for the chance to slam doors and scold people, particularly tram conductors and post office workers, really despicable types.

My dear Ramuz, I would like to see you too, and I miss you very, very much. True, we are far apart, but I assure you that neither the thousand kilometers nor the entire year that has passed has changed my feelings toward you. I remain the same, eager to see you, to talk to you, to hear you talk, and, as always, enormously interested in your work.

You know that I plan to settle here in Biarritz, where I have found a very good house with a small separate structure next to it that will serve as my studio. Both are very inexpensive and can easily be sublet in the summer for a nice profit. Unfortunately they are furnished, but I will keep only the pieces that I like, enough for two rooms, and in the meantime have my own furniture sent from Paris. That I cannot live and work in Paris with any fruitfulness is axiomatic: Paris is not for me. From time to time I am obliged to visit, but I could not live there. As you know, I have a studio in the Maison Pleyel, where I prepare the pianola versions of all of my published works. This mechanization interests me a great deal, and I have invented some splendid tricks.

In my new abode there will be enough room to put you up very comfortably, and should you decide to tear yourself away from Cour for a while (which would do you an *enormous* amount of good), to have you among us would give me and all of us great joy. I assure you that the trip would not be expensive: it is the equivalent of one night in Paris, that is, 108 francs, in second class. Life here would not cost you a sou. . . .

After a three-month separation from my family,[63] I found everyone in good health. My wife: good appearance and humor; my children: all grown bigger. Theodore is very tall (bigger than I am, which, in the end, is not so difficult); he is doing magnificent paintings on the walls of a huge room in the house of an old friend of mine who adores Theodore and his painting. The boy is much

---

[61] *Mavra,* based on *The Little House at Kolomna.*

[62] Boris Kochno. When Stravinsky wanted the libretto translated into French, he asked Ansermet to do it, then Cocteau, then Larmanjat, but conspicuously not Ramuz.

[63] Stravinsky had been in Spain in April and May, England in June, and Paris in July.

changed—very happy and constantly gay. Nini is becoming a handsome boy, but he is still the same, though he has stopped drawing to concentrate on playing the piano. He is rewriting the same waltz that he composed in Garches. Two days in a row he sat before a piece of music paper with a calligraphic title, "Petit Valse," followed by nothing. Mika thinks only of housewifery and of having a farm with chickens, cows, etc., when she gets married. And Milene, not yet having any clearly pronounced desires, contents herself with desiring the same thing as Mika. That is the word on my family, old friend. As for the Beliankins,[64] they have opened a restaurant in Biarritz and the business is prosperous enough, except that their substantial debts (particularly to us, who are once again in a pretty tight situation) do not permit them any perceptible profits. No space is left on the page, so I sign off by embracing you and begging you to decide to come and visit me. Despite my willingness, I cannot visit you in Switzerland, since a 2,000-franc deposit is required to cross the border. All best regards to your wife and to Madame Gadon.

Your   Stravinsky

RAMUZ TO STRAVINSKY   *October 9, 1921*

Dear friend,

I would have written to you a long time ago had Ansermet not told me upon his arrival that you had already deserted Anglet for the *anglais* (if you will allow me that) or for Paris. In the meantime, this is a business letter, and urgent, for which reason I will send it to rue Rochechouart and have them forward it. I received a note from Hébertot,[65] who mentions "having dealt" with you regarding the *Soldat,* which will be presented in February. He asks me to send him the text, which I have already done. Finally, he wants to know if he can borrow the sets that we have here. I will not answer until you tell me what arrangements you have made with him. In particular, would the sets be rented or lent to Hébertot? What other conditions would there be? Auberjonois, whom I just saw, will allow his sets to be used, but he refuses to have his name on the program or posters. I have a million things to tell you. This is the main point, though, and I repeat: What have you arranged with H.? How shall I reply on the subject of the sets? If they are to be rented, what price would you set?

I thank you, dear friend, for your letter, which gave me great pleasure, and I send you my best wishes.

Ramuz

---

[64] Grigory Beliankin had married Stravinsky's wife's sister, Lyudmila. See the correspondence with G. P. Beliankin in *S.S.C.* II.

[65] Jacques Hébertot, director of the Théâtre des Champs-Elysées.

P.S. Auberjonois insists that the sets were not designed for a hall the size of the Champs-Elysées. . . . There are no costumes. —Good-bye—

STRAVINSKY TO RAMUZ *Anglet*
October 15, 1921

Dear Ramuz,

Just back from Paris. Please excuse these lines, written in such great haste, but I am in the process of moving, there are thirty-six letters and replies per day, I am doing the instrumentation for some numbers of a Tchaikovsky ballet [*The Sleeping Beauty*] that Diaghilev is mounting in London on October 29, and I am about to depart for London myself (October 24 or 25), etc.

With regard to the *Soldat,* I have stated all of our conditions to Hébertot. It is up to you to demand a fee for the rental of the sets, and then all that will remain to be done is for him to sign a receipt with you at rue Henner. Some of the conditions were impossible because the authors' rights will be paid automatically. I think that we can ask Hébertot to pay and also to arrange for the round-trip transportation of the sets. The rental could be on a nightly basis or a set fee. The nightly arrangement might be less advantageous, because we do not know how many times he plans to perform the *Soldat.* At least with a set fee a sum can be pocketed, and who gives a damn about the rest. Ask Hébertot for 3,000 Swiss francs, which will give each of us about 4,500 French francs.[66] I must warn you, my dear friend, that I will have absolutely no time to devote to this matter, for my entire season is as crammed as my trunk when I leave for a trip. I feel confident about my music, since it is in Ansermet's hands. So attend to the text and reach an agreement with Hébertot about the stage manager and the Narrator. I think that Hébertot is willing to reimburse you for the travel expenses, and perhaps for your stay in Paris, so suggest this to him. He wants *very much* to present the *Soldat:* of that I am certain. Write to me at Chalet des Rochers, rue la Frégate, Biarritz, until October 24, then at the Savoy Hotel, London, then, after two weeks, in Biarritz again.

Your   Stravinsky

René Auberjonois is a testy old codger.

RAMUZ TO STRAVINSKY *October 17, 1921*

Dear friend,

All that is very nice, but what do you suggest that I do from this distance, not knowing Hébertot or anything about him: what kind of man he is, sympathetic or not, his resources, his intentions, in short, *nothing.* I was counting on seeing

---

[66] Stravinsky's files contain a calling card from Ramuz advising the composer to accept Hébertot's offer of 4,500 French francs.

Ansermet today, but he did not come. You say that your music is in good hands; my text (and the whole work), however, risks falling into very bad hands. In any case, I think (from far away and all alone) that 3,000 Swiss francs is *too much*. H. could have a new set painted for that price. I am finding it difficult to write to him (he has been waiting two weeks for my reply). I will let him know, moreover, that you are in agreement with me about renting the sets to him out-right. I will ask his conditions and keep you up-to-date.

(If the amount seems too small to us, we will stress that there are advan-tages for *him* in dealing with us, and that we have already made certain expen-ditures.)

I will be very sad if you divorce yourself from the enterprise, which inter-ests me only if you are involved.

You are in Biarritz, no? Best regards on behalf of my wife and myself, and please present my respects to Madame Stravinsky. Embrace the children, if they remember who I am.

Your   R.

I am in desperate need of some French francs. If the performances go well, I plan to rework the third narration and the third scene of Part One (these are the weak spots). If not, I won't bother. How would this affect the authors' rights? In any event, what percentage?

RAMUZ TO STRAVINSKY   *October 27, 1921*

Dear friend,

I have written to Hébertot requesting that he suggest a rental fee for the sets. Meanwhile, I saw Ansermet, who is under the impression that H. expects the sets to be lent to him. 3,000 Swiss francs, in any case, seems an impossible sum to obtain. I would have liked to have some background on Hébertot. But he is slippery. Once again, he is asking me to set a fee (and to send him some photo-graphs, which don't exist). I will reply that I must come to an agreement with you, which is actually the reason for this note. Will it reach you? I hope so. If so, either write to me immediately stating your *minimum* fee, or go to see Hébertot when you are in Paris and settle it directly with him. The latter course is prefer-able, because you have more influence than I do.

I will come to Paris a month in advance, if everything works out.

How are you? How is your life going?

All kind regards,   R.

A very English envelope, and I am not at all English. And you?

STRAVINSKY TO RAMUZ   *Savoy Hotel*
                                                 London
Dear Ramuz,   *October 30, 1921*

Having received your note here in London, I hasten to send you a note in response: First, I am not English and have no desire to be. Second, you must at
least try for 3,000 francs for Hébertot. What can you lose? If he intends to present the *Soldat* at all costs, he will find some solution. . . . We will just have to
let him *se démerder*. We could ask *his* terms, of course, but he certainly has the
right to ask to see photographs of the sets that he will be renting. And then
what should be done? I do not know if I will have time to see him in Paris on my
way home (in a week), because I am going directly to Biarritz. We will see how
he answers your last letter.

My dear, do not think, of all things, that I am indifferent. On the contrary,
I am unhappy not to be able to devote myself with my usual ardor to this work,
which is so close to my heart. I really do not know how I will manage to complete my opera and the instrumentation of *Noces*, which are enormous projects
for the little time that remains. We will perform both at the Opéra (what a disaster!) at the end of May.

I am overjoyed at the thought of seeing you again, my dear Ramuz.

                                 I embrace you,   Stravinsky

The Tchaikovsky ballet, *The Sleeping Princess,* gave me great pleasure, as did
its music, which is extraordinarily fresh! I wrote a long letter to Diaghilev about
it and will send a copy of the French version to you. The letter appeared in *The
Times* [October 18]. Everyone here loves you as before and sends you best
wishes.

RAMUZ TO STRAVINSKY   *November 19, 1921*

Dear friend,

I am extremely worried because of Reinhart, whom I asked for Auberjonois's
drawings and *maquettes,* and who seemed delighted that the sets would finally
be recalled from retirement.

You understand that this is really the issue. I share your opinion on everything else, as you know. But this question is especially delicate for me, since I
am here. The sets belong to us only theoretically. I had to convey your conditions to H., although I disagree with you on this subject. In my opinion, to lend
them would be a gesture of goodwill. If, as is possible, the question arises again,
would you allow me to make this proposal personally? You would not have to be
involved. . . . I feel that I must not forget the one who, after all, is responsible
for our having these materials.

Good-bye, dear friend . . .

                                 Your very devoted   Ramuz

RAMUZ TO STRAVINSKY   *November 23, 1921*

Dear friend,

I am sending this document back in the next mail (because I am an excellent correspondent). I have simply signed it, without filling it in, as I understood I was supposed to do—is that correct?

I thank you—I plan to write to Hébertot . . . in my own name—I would like to have a clear conscience about this. I will inform you of his response. Of course, he will cover the transportation costs.

I would very much like to see you; in the meantime, I hope to *hear* you on Saturday in Geneva. Ansermet (who is sad) loves your "Debussy Symphony" [Symphonies of Wind Instruments], and I am very happy because of the throngs of "music lovers" in (French) printing houses who attempt to bore you to death with your past. Past = passive, for everyone; it is very tragic, very beautiful, and very just.

Good-bye, dear friend—give my best to everyone. I have a little commerce going in books. . . .

                                              Your   R.

General inertia—If you say something is very beautiful, it means it *should be* very beautiful.

P.S. You had said you would be sending me a "letter to Diaghilev."

RAMUZ TO STRAVINSKY   *December 16, 1921*

Dear friend,

I did not write to you sooner because I was waiting for Hébertot's reply. I relayed the proposal to him . . . as well as your letter (this in my own name, in order not to make it seem as though you were behind it). Until now, I have heard nothing, not a word, not the least sign of life. In the meantime, I have learned:

1. that Pitoëff was going to do a "season" in [Hébertot's] theatre, including Hamlet, dressed all in black velvet;
2. that Morax was going to play *Le Roi David* there, with music by Honegger . . .

So perhaps it is better that I have not heard anything [from Hébertot] . . . . But then, there is always the chance that I therefore will not see you—maybe never again—which saddens me.

Thank you for the letter to Diaghilev, which I return to you, enclosed. I will not broach this subject with you now, because it would require all afternoon and twenty pages of this yellow paper. That would be a good excuse to see you again, but Biarritz is some 1,000 kilometers from here: too bad [you] chose to settle so far away from me, though at the threshold of all elegance.

                        Respects, remembrances . . .   Ramuz

RAMUZ TO STRAVINSKY   *February 23, 1922*
                                                              [Postcard]

Dear friend,

Your letter awaited me upon my return from a short trip. This note is to thank
you and to ask you to send me the proofs without delay. The more quickly I
begin working on them, the better, though I am already swamped with my own
proofs. Instruct me as to your wishes. I would very much like to see you, but it
certainly looks as though I will never see you again. Perhaps in Paradise, if I
make it—you will, naturally; composing good music, one definitely goes to
Heaven. . . .

                                                        Your   R.

RAMUZ TO STRAVINSKY   *March 2, 1922*
                                                              [Postcard]

Dear friend,

I received your package only this evening (Tuesday). You see that the mail
does not necessarily move quickly; nonetheless, it does move. I will now start
correcting, and then I will send the package to Chester. The task will be tricky,
so far as I can tell, because of the music (and my incompetence in that
field). . . . I think that you will be receiving a third set of proofs. I am very sick. I
hope that you and yours are not. . . .

                                                        Your   R.

                                                           March 3, 1922
RAMUZ TO STRAVINSKY   *[Postcard]*

I sent the package to Kling by registered mail. I made my corrections in pencil
so as to avoid confusion with yours. Mainly, the mistakes were orthographi-
cal—that the printers are English is evident. Punctuation—nonexistent; but I
like that and made no changes. At any rate, please rest assured that the corrections were made very carefully. I would be pleased if this French text were not
too much of a mess. I would also like to attend the premiere—when?

    Fond regards.

                                                        Your   R.

RAMUZ TO STRAVINSKY   *March 6, 1922*
                                                              [Postcard]

Dear one,

Just received second package of proofs. Will begin correcting and send them to
London as soon as they are ready, as with the first package. You should have
received my letters, which crossed with yours in the mail.

    Everything is in order.

                                                        Your   R.

Dear friend,

I was very happy to hear from you. For a long time now I have not seen anyone or heard anything from you. Ansermet has vanished: someone told me that he is ill, and I just wrote to him. No news about your Paris "season," nor about anything else. But *I understand you very well.* Writing letters is impossible. You begin to philosophize, and then stop yourself, because that would demand twenty pages. . . . And neither you nor I will ever again embark on a twenty-page letter (we did that about eighteen years ago). So just think of me, and I will tell myself that you are thinking of me. That is not entirely enough . . . but you use the distance between us as an excuse, while I become poorer and poorer, of which I am quite proud, but which precludes trips. It seems to me that you are just playing on one end of the keyboard. Myself, I play both extremes more and more, and exclusively the extremes:

The sublime	the ignoble
the angelic	the diabolic.

. . . Is this a mistake? At any rate, I believe that I am in the realm of truth, I am in . . . my nature; and this is reality, alternating between perfect happiness and perfect misery. When I die I will not know what I was, but I will certainly not regret having lived.

PHILOSOPHY

The bad thing is that I live among people who never venture to play anywhere but in the middle of the keyboard, without even realizing that the keyboard has two extremes. Thus it gave me pleasure to hear you touch those low notes (beneath which there are no high notes).

We would all like to have news of Madame Stravinsky and the children.

We have a nine-year-old daughter who absolutely refuses to learn to read, but she knows the story of Adam and Eve very well, and that explains everything.

Dear friend,

A business note. I just had a visit from Ansermet, who said that you had entrusted him to tell me something, but that he no longer remembers what it was. The question was that of my author's rights for *Renard.* Apparently, I cannot collect these directly, since I am not a member of the "Société" [des Auteurs et Compositeurs Dramatiques]. If that is true, please collect the sum for me and send it on: it would be most welcome. And if this information is not accurate, please send me a note of explanation.

RAMUZ TO STRAVINSKY

November 3, 1922
[Postcard]

Dear friend,

No reply from you; did you not receive my letter? If I am to collect that money, I would very much like to do so before the franc hits zero. Regards to everyone.

Your   R.

STRAVINSKY TO RAMUZ

Biarritz
December 7, 1922

My dear Ramuz,

I beg your pardon for not having answered your letter; it was delivered promptly, but I have only just read it. I have been far, far away, in Stettin and Berlin, fetching my mother, who is now here with us in Biarritz.

I owe you 452 French francs and 10 centimes, minus the 13 francs (3 percent) that the Société keeps. Since all of the authors' rights were sent to me, and since you are not a member of the Société, I will figure the accounts with you directly, according to our agreement. . . . Thus for every French-language performance of *Renard* employing your translation, you should receive 12 percent of my author's rights for the text, amounting to one-third of my total rights: two-thirds of mine are composer's rights. In other words, you receive one-sixth of my total rights. I received 2,612 francs, 20 centimes; therefore 452 francs, 10 centimes, one-sixth of that sum, is yours. As I said before, 3 percent, or 13 francs, 55 centimes, must be subtracted from this, leaving 438 francs and 55 centimes. I beg you, my dear Ramuz, to excuse the delay, and I am certain that you will when you hear that my affairs (again, alas) are going very, very badly. I reproach myself, but I am often late in answering my friends' letters. I enclose herewith 438 francs and 55 centimes, requesting that you acknowledge their receipt by return mail.

I embrace you.

Faithfully yours,   Igor Stravinsky

RAMUZ TO STRAVINSKY

December 11, 1922

Dear friend,

I did not know that you had collected that money; Ansermet did not tell me that. I thought that the Société had kept it and that, given the fall of the franc, it was not good for me to leave the money much longer. Thus my insistence: excuse me. I only hope that having to attend to this small sum (which became large as soon as it crossed the Jura) has not annoyed you. I received a check for 159.75 Swiss francs, the receipt for which you will find attached. But none of that matters. I am very sad to hear nothing about you or what you are doing. I always run into M. Venizelos and not you; I live next door to M. Tchitcherine and not you. I would like to go to Paris to see you along with a great many of your Lausanne friends, but you have the bad habit of scheduling your concerts for Christmas day, which will impede the realization of my plan. Thus I must content myself with giving you my best regards, to be relayed to all of you, and my respects to Madame Stravinsky, and with confirming a friendship which, as far as I am concerned, will be taken to the grave. . . .

Received from M. Igor Stravinsky in Biarritz the sum of 159.75 Swiss francs for my author's rights for six performances of *Renard* given at the Opéra in the summer of 1922.

C.-F. Ramuz, Lausanne, December 10, 1922

RAMUZ TO STRAVINSKY   *September 16, 1923*[67]

My dear Stravinsky,

This envelope is out-of-date, having spent six months on my desk awaiting word from you. I was not able to go to Paris for *Les Noces* because I was too poor.[68] Today I must discuss business. Upon my return from the Haute-Savoie (where we spent the summer), I found a letter from M. Kling requesting the use of my libretto in the unabridged edition of *Soldat* that he intends to publish.[69] We agreed on terms, and he finally proposed to give me a percentage of the performance rights. Today he sent me a contract with a section that concerns you: "I have not stipulated a minimum sum for the performance rights because, given the upheaval in the world today, we will be obliged to determine the best

---

[67] In August, Stravinsky had attended a performance of *Histoire du soldat* at the Bauhaus in Weimar (see Stravinsky's letter to Ansermet of September 9, 1923, in *S.S.C.* I, p. 170). According to a letter from Gustel Jansen Scherchen to Vera Stravinsky, August 16, 1979, the cast at the Bauhaus performance was made up of members of the Schauspielhaus in Frankfurt, where the work had received its first German performance, on June 20, 1923. In Frankfurt the sets and designs were Auberjonois's originals, lent by Werner Reinhart, whose brother Hans sent Stravinsky a detailed description of the Frankfurt staging, saying that "the performance of *Geschichte vom Soldaten* at the center of the music festival was its high point, together with a *ganz herrlichen* a cappella chorus by Schoenberg performed last night." (June 25) Hindemith played the violin part, and Carl Ebert, who twenty-eight years later would direct the premiere of *The Rake's Progress*, was the Narrator.

[68] Stravinsky had written to Ansermet on July 29: "Send me news about . . . M. C.-F. Ramuz, who finds it amusing not to come to Paris when *Les Noces* or *Renard* is played."

[69] O. M. Kling had written to Stravinsky on September 11: "Being in touch with M. Ramuz about the rights to his text for the new edition, I proposed that he allow us to collect his performance rights, for a small commission. But he raised an objection, because his rights and yours are to be shared equally. Since we are the owners of the parts, perhaps you should allow us to do the same, for a 10 percent commission."

conditions according to the individual situation, taking each country into account separately. A long time ago M. Stravinsky talked about a possible 500 Swiss francs per performance—250 francs for the composer, 250 francs for the author—and then 100 francs for the rental of the parts per performance. Add to that the sets, the actors, the orchestra, the rental of the hall, and you will see that this amount is no longer feasible, and even less so if the same conditions must be rigidly imposed in France, Italy, Belgium, and elsewhere. In England, we will never be able to ask 600 Swiss francs (about £25) just for the right to mount *Histoire du soldat*. Perhaps you could come to a definite understanding with M. Stravinsky on this subject!"

Myself, I have no opinion. What is yours? First question.

I told you that I was dealing with Kling regarding the *Soldat* text, and on that occasion I rewrote part of it.[70] I was able to evaluate it, in retrospect—and, as though it were not mine, I deemed it quite good. This encouraged me to busy myself (as I had been asked to do) with arranging a series of performances, scheduled to take place in February in Zürich, Winterthur, and probably Lausanne and Geneva. Reinhart invited me to take the part of the Narrator, and I accepted. The Soldier and the Devil remain to be found, which is impossible here. Now, I am too poor to go to Paris. You, on the other hand, will be there soon, and you know the work. It is in your interest as well as in mine that the piece at last be staged. Would you undertake to find the actors? I thought of Jouvet[71] for the Soldier, since he has the right character, more or less, but I cannot think of anyone for the Devil. You will be in a position to do something, and you could make inquiries at that time. So there you have my second question.

Please remember me, and *us;* and please present our fond regards to Madame Stravinsky; embrace the children . . . as I embrace you.

R.

I just received another letter from Chester asking for "our conditions. . . ." I will have him address himself to Reinhart.

I am totally ruined by the currency exchange; the money I receive from Paris is decreased more than three times, life is horribly expensive here: stamps—120 French francs (40 Swiss); newspapers—50 centimes (15 Swiss).

I would very much like to see you, and for this reason I would go to Paris, or even to Biarritz.

---

[70] O. M. Kling had written to Stravinsky on September 6: "I have decided to publish the complete piano score after all. I am in touch with M. Ramuz, since I intend to print the complete text in this new edition. According to his letter, M. Ramuz is revising the text, but will his revision affect the music in any way?" Kling wrote to the composer again on September 20: "I received the manuscript of M. Ramuz's new version, for which we have acquired the rights, including those for translation."

[71] Louis Jouvet, stage and screen actor, who at one time courted Stravinsky's niece Ira Belline.

RAMUZ TO STRAVINSKY   *Saturday, September 29, 1923*

Dear one,

I am very discouraged. I asked this favor of you because you will be in Paris and I will not. You can well imagine that it is not possible to find *anything* here. What is to be done? As for me, I recognize my own helplessness and deplore it, because, as you say, "it would not have been worth the trouble." I am in agreement about the rest of the matter, but the rest of it is not my concern.

Your   Ramuz

RAMUZ TO STRAVINSKY   *November 5, 1923*

Dear Stravinsky,

I just found a long letter from you of the period when we used to write to each other—I think that time is over; we now limit ourselves to business letters. As for the "means of existence" that you claim to seek, I would have you know that I too am forever in the process of looking for it, always without finding it, which is not very amusing. [I have planned] an impossible trip to Paris (unless you will not be there around the end of the month), . . . because of an idea that occurred to me after a discussion with Auberjonois about the performances of the *Soldat.* I receive letters from Zürich, where they are urging me to conclude the matter, and I assure you that to do so is not easy here. So I wondered if the simplest way would not be to approach the Pitoëffs, asking them to work with Jouvet, who is already performing with them at the Champs-Elysées. Pitoëff—Devil; Madame Pitoëff—Princess; Jouvet—Soldier. Meanwhile, I do not want to take any action without your advice, which I beg you to give to me as soon as possible. Moreover, it is not yet definite that the Pitoëffs will be able to undertake the venture: everything depends upon the season and their contract with Hébertot. I only want to know if you think that this is a feasible step to take. If you say yes, I will attempt it; if not, no. But then I will be embarrassed and will stay always hidden behind my bars, with a view of the first chrysanthemums and a big wall covered with dirt. Our compliments to everyone and best regards to Madame Stravinsky. Embrace the children.

I embrace you,   R.

RAMUZ TO STRAVINSKY   *November 25, 1923*

Dear one,

The little slip of paper arrived after some delay, which is now imputable. Ansermet had it in his pocket and just sent it to me.

In regard to your agreement with Chester (since we are always talking business), what I do not understand is whether the price of the rental of the sets is included in the £½, or £1½, or whether, in that case, the work would be done with the theatre's own sets. But where would you find sets?

I did not go to Paris.

I am trying to get out of the mess of these Swiss performances, which are drawing near. I wrote to Pitoëff, who does not reply. If the Pitoëff scheme fails, I cannot envision anyone or anything else.

What are you doing in the near future?

And are you now in Biarritz, where I am writing to you?

Ansermet should be in London—perhaps you saw him when he passed through Paris.

Please remember us to your family. We are starting to toboggan here—if you know what it means to toboggan. The Word is the thing.

Embrace the children. My regards to Madame Stravinsky. Be assured that I remain

your   R.

I am *always very* nice.

Over, please.

Received a reply from Pitoëff just as I closed this letter. He says that Hébertot, upon whom they are dependent, only wants to let them come to Switzerland on condition that the *Soldat* could be mounted in Paris. "So evidently," Pitoëff adds, "it will be possible to do four or five performances in Switzerland."

Then you will remember our previous negotiations with the aforementioned Hébertot and their conclusion.

What should be done?

Send a note quickly on this subject, please. In the meantime, I will content myself with informing Pitoëff (who probably already knows) of what happened with Hébertot. Again,

your   R.

STRAVINSKY TO RAMUZ   *Biarritz*
                                                November 29, 1923
My dear poet,

The ££££ that I mentioned, whether £½, £1, or £1½, constitute the minimum fee that each of us is supposed to receive through the intermediary of J. & W. Chester, and of course the eventual price for the rental of the sets is not included in this.

You ask where we will find sets in the event that Auberjonois's cannot be rented. But, my dear, it is up to the theatre that stages the work to commission a painter. Never again can you or I, except in extraordinary cases, concern ourselves with such matters, or take the same pains that we did in Lausanne in 1918. Alas! Our child must leave our tutelage and dirty himself in life like the rest of us. Suppose, on the other hand, that a theatre wanted to mount our *Sol-*

dat specifically with Auberjonois's sets—so much the better; if they were free at that time, we would rent them to the theatre by common agreement between us, or between us and Reinhart.

I am delighted by the Pitoëff-Switzerland, Pitoëff-Hébertot scheme. Hébertot, in Paris, must come to an understanding with Reinhart, who is supposed to be back in Switzerland any day (if he is not already there) after his trip to India. I refuse to see that dangerous pederast Hébertot, for which reason please give Pitoëff an energetic push so that he will do everything necessary to persuade the director of the Champs-Elysées.

I am here until January and await your next letter with growing impatience.

I embrace you.

RAMUZ TO STRAVINSKY   *December 11, 1923*

Dear Maestro,

1. See the enclosed. (I was not able to write to you sooner, because this just arrived.) What should be done?

In order not to waste time, I will tell Hébertot that everything will be ready by January (sets, actors, and text), but without committing myself.

These conditions remain: I ask that he propose a sum to us for the rental of the sets, since our other rights would be collected automatically.

Is that all right? Type out the details; with my pen I am sure to be imprecise.

2. Ansermet talks about a projected presentation of the *Soldat* in America, but it would be necessary to adapt the piece to the tastes of that audience. I would like to make a reduction of the text for the régisseur with scenes in pantomime. Then a good translator and a régisseur would have to be found, one with a sense of the material and, at the same time, a familiarity with his audience.

3. I just received the text from Chester:[72] I still find it to be good (although a little long; however, certain cuts are possible). But will the audience understand its *tone*? In any case, I would very much like you not to abandon me. If Hébertot consented to give me a small amount of money for travel expenses I would gladly come to Paris.

Good-bye—or until the next time, dear friend, and send a note quickly, please. With all compliments, all kind regards, and all fond memories,

C.-F. Ramuz

---

[72] O. M. Kling had written to Stravinsky on November 20: "I am sorry to torment you with this *Histoire* engraving, but before final submission of the score and parts, it is essential that the two correspond. . . . Did you know that Ramuz made a revision, which you will find in the score that I am sending to you? Is he authorized to make changes in the rhythmically notated part of the narrative?"

STRAVINSKY TO RAMUZ

My dear friend,

Received your letter, and here is my opinion. Things must be facilitated for Hébertot with respect to the *Soldat;* otherwise he will not let the Pitoëffs do it [in Switzerland]. By "facilitate" I mean that you should rent the sets to him for practically nothing; for this reason I regret that he has been asked to propose a rental price to us. I think that he will reject the idea, since he himself is generally paid by the companies; he will propose (again!) to pay only for the transportation of the sets. My advice arrives too late, alas, and we now have no recourse but to await his reply.

One other thing. If your trip to Paris is dependent upon the travel expenses you hope to receive from Hébertot, I strongly doubt that we will see each other this time, either. Furthermore, I do not understand why you mention travel expenses in your letter but say nothing about your fee as Narrator. You will take this role, won't you? I attach Hébertot's letter (as you may need it) to this one, along with my faithful friendship.

RAMUZ TO STRAVINSKY

Sehr lieber Igor Stravinsky,

Man liest im Berliner Tagblatt *unter Signatur von Herrn Dr. Aber: "Das radikale Spiel der drei zu seltener Einheit verbundenen Künstler erlebte seine Erstaufführung mit einem Publikumserfolg, dessen Stärke fast verfliessen musste"*—on that subject (because I definitely have no intention of continuing in German), I received a telegram from Reinhart asking if the sets could be sent to Berlin for a series of twelve performances. I said yes, on the condition that they take place during the first half of January. In any case, this is a pity.

You, you don't care; me, I am easily fooled in German.

In regard to Hébertot, he now says that he will allow the Pitoëffs to come to Switzerland only if we make less stringent conditions.

I replied at once, in accordance with your letter, that after having discussed it with you, I am willing to *lend* him the sets.

But a new difficulty has arisen. Ansermet informs me that he will not be able to conduct in Paris in January or February, and probably not before April, because of his prior engagements here.

He must write to Hébertot and find out what his conditions are.

How to get out of this mess? And, in any event, it would be disagreeable for Reinhart if, thanks to Paris, the performances could not take place here.

What do you think of all this? Send a note quickly, please. I am writing thousands of business letters, and they bore me to death. Acknowledge that it is complicated.

We all embrace you.

R.

[*In the margin*] I made my first trip to hear the *Sacre* in Geneva. I would like to be able to tell you about it. . . . The people in Geneva are a funny sight. Gagnebin made a dreadful scandal.

Are we going to receive at least a little bit of money for the German performances?

STRAVINSKY TO RAMUZ   *Biarritz*
                                                                    December 22, 1923

My dear friend,

Dankend erhalten Ihr wertes Schreiben von 20 dezember und mit das . . .

It gave me great pleasure to learn of the *Soldat*'s success in Berlin. In short, I do not give a damn about Berlin or other cities in the Reich, the Empire, the Kaiserthum. I care as little about the Germans in their misery as in their prosperity; what pleased me is not this single triumph but the continuing series of triumphs of which this last is only one further confirmation.

The *Soldat* enjoys real success everywhere, and since I am enormously fond of this work, I will rejoice for you and for myself if it is staged in Paris. Do not worry about a conductor: one can always be found, and this is not a catastrophe. Now you see that I was right about Hébertot! What annoys me most is that we must give in to that pig, in view of the performances in Zürich and Winterthur; without these we would resist him firmly.

In England the possibilities are numerous. I go to Paris on Wednesday and will probably see an important English director who is very interested in the *Soldat*. I will keep you posted.

I am very happy that you heard the *Sacre;* evidently it was a beautiful performance.

But, Ramuz, is it impossible for us to see each other? Must we chat only by letter? I am very sad. Yes, and I say *merde*.

Useless to go on. I am, as always,

                                            your faithful   Igor Stravinsky

RAMUZ TO STRAVINSKY   *January 16, 1924*

Dear friend,

If you are in Paris, please find out what is happening. Ansermet is the one who was supposed to follow up on the negotiations with Hébertot (at A.'s own insistence, since he had personal matters to arrange with H.). Now Ansermet informs me that the performances were "postponed" and that Hébertot refuses to "lend" the Pitoëffs in February. Therefore, the Zürich performances will fall through. I am very annoyed, not for myself, but for Reinhart, who had already arranged everything (the parts have even been distributed to the musicians!). Also, it would seem that I allowed this to happen, which is not the case. The truth is that I can do nothing useful from this distance. And you, since you are there, couldn't you find out and then let me know?

I just received an English translation from Kling,[73] conceived, as Ansermet says, in the spirit of the sentimental moralizing that, as you know, characterizes Anglo-Saxon expressions of feeling. I am writing to Kling and trying to get myself out of this mess, but I will not be able to do so without you. Thank you for your letter. It is true that we never see each other, and also true that I am not writing anything of importance; I do not know what to do. The situation here is impossible. The franc is at 25 centimes. Send me a short note, please.

I embrace you.

Your   R.

RAMUZ TO STRAVINSKY   *March 12, 1924*

Dear Stravinsky,

I received a letter from Madame Picabia[74] in which several things greatly astonish me. I have answered Madame Picabia, but before I sign anything, I would like to see you. I can be in Paris toward the middle of next week. Where will you

---

[73] Stravinsky had written to Henry Kling on January 1: "Unfortunately, I have neither the complete score nor the piano reduction with me. Also, since M. Ramuz has changed his text many times, I do not know if *these* changes affect the verses to which you refer. I leave for Belgium tomorrow, so I suggest that you write to M. Ansermet, who knows the music as well as I do and can confer with M. Ramuz, who lives in Lausanne." Kling replied on January 15: "Ramuz's text was in order, and we made an English version and are waiting for M. Reinhart's German translation." Stravinsky was in Spain in March, and on the 17th, at the Hotel Ritz in Barcelona, he received a letter from O. M. Kling: "In a few days I will send you the proofs of the piano score, which M. Ramuz has already checked."

[74] Gabrielle Picabia sent a copy of her letter to Stravinsky, as well as the original of Ramuz's answer. She had written to Ramuz on March 11, offering him 5,000 francs—Stravinsky was to receive 10,000—for the rights to *Histoire du soldat* for the Paris production. Any receipts over 15,000 francs were to be shared equally among herself and the authors. She claimed to have two offers from France, one of which would include sets by Picasso, the pantomime performed by Massine, and Lydia Lopokova as the Princess; but the text would have to be "altered." She proposed to come to Lausanne to discuss the matter the following week, if Ramuz showed any interest. In fact, she went to Lausanne on the 19th, not only to see Ramuz—who, in his letter, rejected the one-third share—but also to obtain the sets, since the Picasso proposal had fallen through in the meantime.

Hearing of this, the wealthy singer-cum-impresario Marguerite Beriza proposed to present the *Soldat* on April 24, 25, and 27 at the Théâtre des Champs-Elysées on a double bill with a short opera by Lord Berners. The Pitoëffs would be in charge of the staging, and Auberjonois's sets and costumes could be remade according to the surviving *maquettes*. (Stravinsky always claimed that he liked these sets and costumes. On March 27, Auberjonois wrote to the composer, saying how unhappy *he* was with

be? Can you come? The trip to Bayonne is a little long, and I am poor. Will this letter reach you in time? Ansermet told me that you are in Barcelona. In any case, let me know what you need, and give me your advice. As for the question of "alterations in the text" and "pantomimic interpretation"—although the latter would be interesting, I intend to reserve the rights for myself.

RAMUZ TO STRAVINSKY   *Sunday, May 4, 1924*

Dear one,

I expect to be in Paris on the 9th or 10th. I would like very much to see you on this trip. Also, when is your concerto? Two questions. A word in reply before my departure, please.

  Be assured that I remain

              your C.-F. Ramuz

RAMUZ TO STRAVINSKY   *Paris*
                    Saturday morning
Dear,   *May 10, 1924*

Would it be possible to see you? Where? When? How? Tonight, for example. Send a pneumatique, please, to my hotel: Hôtel du Pas-de-Calais, 59, rue des Saints-Pères, VI.

RAMUZ TO STRAVINSKY   *May 16, 1924*

Dear one,

Alas, Wednesday night was impossible! I was before the *ministers,* and by ten o'clock the speeches had hardly begun.

  I like music better, nevertheless.

  I leave Monday morning. When will we see each other? I am busy at noon and this evening. This has accidentally come out in rhyme. This afternoon, per-

---

both, but particularly with the costumes; the Paris press was as brutal to Auberjonois's work as it was to Ramuz's.)

  Madame Picabia had written to Stravinsky on March 19 trying to persuade him to conduct the last of the three Paris performances. His fee was too large for the budget, but she agreed to renounce her commission and said that Ansermet would do all of the rehearsing. Stravinsky replied through Madame Vera Sudeikina, with whom Madame Picabia shared an apartment, that he had no time for conducting the performance and, in any case, had no desire to do so. Madame Picabia then proposed to give him the 10,-000 francs for his share of the contract, but as a personal transaction and without informing Ramuz, as well as 2,000 francs in return for his presence ("which would permit us to make use of your great name"). On April 6, Madame Picabia, Ramuz, and Stravinsky drew up an official contract (different from the private one).

haps, or tomorrow: you decide, send a definitive reply on a scrap of paper. All of the other people bore me. . . .

Send a pneumatique to the Hôtel du Pas-de-Calais, 59, rue des Saints-Pères, Paris VI.

RAMUZ TO STRAVINSKY   *May 20, 1924*

Dear,

[The only consolation of my trip was] to have seen you again. You know very well that I am not working, and back here I am faced with the truth. The misery, so far as I am concerned, is that I have been in a completely scatterbrained state these past few days, of the sort in which one finds oneself when *one is not working.* The skeleton *falls to pieces,* like the dead. And these pieces are not instantly reassembled, except thanks to you. The rest of the time I walk them around in the sack of my skin, where they make unpleasant noises. So it is necessary for us to see each other again. When? How? The franc fell to 30 today. Kling is sending me £2 (and to you also, I think). Tell Madame Sudeikina that I have not forgotten the chocolate, and I send her my regards. I returned by foot the other night, walking very fast, while you were walking in the opposite direction, which was unpleasant to contemplate. For the moment, my wish is for you to earn piles of dollars . . . Danish crowns, marks, etc.; you know that I have a good nose for this sort of thing. You will see how well you make out. For want of money, I carry with me the equally valuable memories of our visit to [the Eglise des] Saints-Pères and of our walk on Sunday. I had a very nice trip. I include a note for Madame Stravinsky, expressing my regrets at having missed her; please deliver it to her yourself, since I do not have her address.

I embrace you again.

Ramuz

STRAVINSKY TO RAMUZ[75]   22–24, *rue Rochechouart*
                                                              Paris
My dear Ramuz,   *May 23, 1924*

You cannot imagine the pleasure I had in reading your letter, which arrived just as I was catching a taxi at the stand to go to the Opéra[76] or to hell.

Luckily my fears were unfounded, for it went very well and I had a great

---

[75] This letter contains a note from Catherine Stravinsky: "Dear friend, By way of these few words, allow me to thank you for your touching letter and to tell you how sorry I was to learn that you are no longer in Paris, and not to have seen you, as I had hoped to. Igor talks about you a lot. Give my best regards to Madame Ramuz on my behalf and embrace Gadon, who will have grown so big that I would never recognize her. Good-bye, dear Ramuz. I shake your hand cordially. Catherine Stravinsky."

[76] To play the first performance of his Piano Concerto.

success. I thought of what you said the other day about my being a natural-born interpreter (you said "conductor," but I say "interpreter").

It gave me great joy to have the opportunity to verify for myself that the pleasure I have always had from your presence has only augmented. I hope that the black cloud that took shape upon your departure will not last long, and my wish is to see you again soon and for a long time, and then to see you frequently.

I embrace you very affectionately.

Your   Stravinsky

RAMUZ TO STRAVINSKY   *June 9, 1924*

You must let me know where you are and what you are doing, where you will be and what you will be doing. Send a note from time to time. Otherwise, it will hardly have been worth the trouble of finding each other again, if we proceed to lose each other so soon. Will you really move to Nice? My best regards to Madame Sudeikina. Did she receive the chocolate?

STRAVINSKY TO RAMUZ   *June 26, 1924*

My dear Ramuz,

Your letter gave me immense pleasure. As you say, it is not worth the effort of finding each other again only to lose touch anew. Continue to write to me *here*; my mail will always be forwarded, and I will send news as often as possible.

Right now I am in the middle of "business," a tour contract: Holland and Switzerland in October; Germany in December; America in mid-January, February, and half of March. This should earn enough money to pay for the growing needs of my very large family and for my own also increasing needs (alas, or fortunately?—hard to answer, but easy to prove).

At the beginning of July I go to Copenhagen to play my concerto, and around the middle of July I stop in Paris, on the way back to my family in Biarritz. Then, after nineteen days, I depart for Nice with Catherine to look for a future residence. Nice is closer to Cour than is Biarritz—closer, my dear, and much more convenient. What do you say? The contrary, of course!

Evenings here in Paris are spent with Vera at the Ballets Russes or the "Cigale" ("Palais Beaumont").[77] Everywhere we encounter the wicked snob-

---

[77] The Soirées de Paris of Count Etienne de Beaumont (1883–1956) gave one season, at the Théâtre de la Cigale. André Chameix, a reporter for the *Journal Littéraire*, described the weirdness of the place and its audience: "I do not know if the Cigale constitutes an appropriate setting for an artistic ceremony patronized by the Chief of State, the Ambassadors, the Prefect of Police, and the Parisian aristocracy. The regulars at the bar made a tremendous racket. The audience was an odd combination of

bery of vile people who flutter about restlessly and serve no purpose in life (fortunately), princesses who do nothing but ask you to dinner, upstanding bourgeoises who mistake *L'Education manquée*, Chabrier's comic opera, for *Le Sacre du printemps*, because they came to the Ballets Russes performance at which Chabrier's piece was played between the *Sacre* and Auric's *Les Fâcheux*.

Is there something amusing about that? Yes, but in the long run one is overcome by disgust and risks becoming a pessimist, which is what I fear most in the world.

I will see Madame Picabia, who will be back from the Midi in a few days, and explain the authors' rights to her. Now I will close this incoherent, messy letter—please forgive me. Write to me, and be assured that I love you very much.

Vera is very appreciative of your fond regards and sends her best wishes.

Your   IStr

P.S. Why don't you see Auberjonois anymore? Have you had a falling-out?

The chocolate was devoured—a long time ago.

RAMUZ TO STRAVINSKY *July 8, 1924*

Dear,

I wanted to write to you on your return from Copenhagen, and, indeed, I am writing to you, but strictly on business. I saw Giovanna[78] (from the orchestra), who told me that your Lausanne concert will not take place, thanks to the committee. Then I saw Gagnebin, and we concluded that if the committee is not involved, so much the better, as long as the concert takes place anyway. Gagnebin plans to raise the necessary sums: he will rent the hall, hire the orchestra, and provide your fee (1,000)—so that after all of those official concerts, you will have YOUR OWN CONCERT. In other words, you will choose the program and arrange the whole evening according to your wishes.

The only limitation (not such a terrible one) is that, for reasons of economy, you will have only a concerto orchestra at your disposal (forty musicians, I think).

As for me, I think that it would be absolutely fitting for your Vaudois friends to be allowed to receive you in a personal fashion: What do you think? Would you like that?

Montmartre, Montparnasse, and worldly and intellectual types. Boulevard Rochechouart is perhaps not entirely congenial to demonstrations in severe and somewhat haughty style, like the ballet in which Massine dances." (May 22, 1924) From the Ballets Russes program: "We thank M. Diaghilev, who returns in loyal friendship to present the Stravinsky cycle for us (without *Firebird*, alas)." (*Ibid.*, June 21, 1924)
[78] Ernest Giovanna, secretary of the Orchestre de la Suisse Romande.

I would be delighted, as would Gagnebin. The concert would be given at the Théâtre [de Lausanne] on December 1.

Think about this and reply. If you like the idea, consider a program. Couldn't we give another Stravinsky work, too: the Octet, for example? Would you conduct it?

You understand that I am so full of proposals because your tour would be finished, and here you could make music for your own pleasure.

Since Giovanna is supposed to see you, I am writing this letter in great haste, so that you will have it beforehand.

> I embrace you,   R.

RAMUZ TO STRAVINSKY   *July 20, 1924*

Dear,

Everything has been arranged. A group exists here called the "Soirées de Lausanne"; Brandenbourg was one of their members. Last winter I did some work for them, and they promised to take care of everything.* They will pay your fee (1,000, as agreed), rent the hall, and hire the orchestra. It is understood that if there were any profit—highly improbable, given the small number of seats—it would go to the musicians. I will put Giovanna in touch with these ladies and gentlemen of the Soirées committee; thus you will have simply to reach an agreement with him. I have stressed two points, that (1) the concert must be done entirely according to your taste, and (2) you must be made to feel at home here (since this is, in fact, your home). I think that the Concerto and the Octet would make a perfect second half. Play what you want in the first. Giovanna will arrange everything, so you are in good hands. In effect, the Ansermets cannot be reached at the moment (six weeks coming and going), but Giovanna is perfectly up-to-date on everything. Personally, I would very much like you to give the Octet; this would be a special gratification for your friends here and would add to the intimate character of the evening. We will present the plan to Ansermet in its true light—I think that Gagnebin has written to him, in any case. But all of that can be arranged later. This note is just to assure you that Lausanne can be included on the list of towns where you will stop. . . .

I am still contemplating a move, and the idea of returning to Paris rears its head more and more often. Alas! . . . I must earn a living no matter where I am. Meanwhile, I encountered M. Lyon[79] in his motorcar and spoke to him for a minute. He had two little girls in the back seat and his wife in the front. I signed the document, and I don't know where you are.

> I embrace you,   R.

I am sending this to Pleyel, as per your instructions.

* Complete financial security with full guarantees

---

[79] Robert Lyon, who was director of Pleyel & Cie, and in charge of Stravinsky's business affairs.

STRAVINSKY TO RAMUZ   *July 23, 1924*

Dear Ramuz,

I have returned from Copenhagen, where I was very well received and played my concerto well enough.

I am about to leave for Biarritz but must wait until [Salomon Bottenheim], due any moment, arrives from Amsterdam.[80]

I thank you wholeheartedly for all you say in your letter, which awaited me on my table. Giovanna was here before my departure for Copenhagen, and I discussed the Lausanne date with him. November 30 is the only possible time because I must be in Germany—I do not know exactly where—for rehearsals on December 3.

As for the Lausanne program, the first part will consist of Bach (Ansermet's choice), my Symphonies of Wind Instruments, and more Bach. In the second part, I will play my concerto and conduct my Octet. Ansermet will conduct the first part of the program and my concerto. If, for some reason, the Symphonies cannot be given, Ansermet will easily find a way of substituting another of my so-called classical works. The crucial thing is to arrange the concert for November 30.

My dear, I beg you to take steps, I no longer know through whom, so that I may obtain a visa for several months (two would suffice) from your consulate in Paris. The visa must allow me freedom of passage to come, go, and stay in Switzerland for as long as my concerts require. I must inform you that on November 1, I will probably play my concerto in Basel. I have had an offer to do some symphonic concerts, to be conducted by Suter.[81] Look around you, my friend, for someone who might be able to arrange this matter, since filling out forms and answering idiotic questions (color of my father's and mother's hair, etc. . . .) is intolerable, especially the way I leap from city to city and from country to country! The Germans have given me a similar visa for half a year, and naturally those pigs made me pay through the nose: 200 francs!! But what does it matter, if one is spared the stupidities and the waste of time.

I count on you. I embrace you. I love you. Write to me in Biarritz.

                                        Your   Stravigor

RAMUZ TO STRAVINSKY   *July 30, 1924*

Dear,

The program that you propose is perfect. I would already have sent it to Giovanna, but it occurred to me that if you were to do this yourself, the proposal would have more authority, and you could give him some useful technical explanations, too. There is no rush.

---

[80] See n. 12 on p. 22.

[81] Hermann Suter (1870–1926), Swiss composer and conductor.

Thus the questions of the date and the visa remain.

I wrote immediately to Gagnebin regarding the visa so that he could give me some tips. As you know, I live here in complete isolation, with no official connections of any kind, and for me to find an official "someone" would be very difficult. But surely Gagnebin will have an idea. At any rate, rest assured that we are attending to the matter.

Unfortunately, the 30th is not a good date, because it falls on a Sunday, a rehearsal day at the theatre. The 1st, on the other hand, would be ideal. I think that even if you do a concert on the 1st, you will have time to arrive in Germany by the 3rd (twenty-four hours from here to Berlin). Ask for the precise dates in Germany, warn them that you must be here on the 1st, and surely they will accommodate you by making an adjustment.

Madame Picabia is in the mountains, not far from here. She has written to me about possible performances of the *Soldat* in Prague and Leningrad. I plan to see her soon.

I would like to write you a long letter, and I would do so were I not in a horribly agitated state at the moment because of certain decisions that I must make by the 27th! I find it increasingly onerous to make any decision at all and recoil from it more and more. Please decide for me. When you have a free moment, consider me and my situation and tell me what to do. You possess all of the elements necessary to determine what should be done: should I stay here or settle in Paris? I would almost prefer to yield to economic circumstances than to aesthetic considerations.

Good-bye.

P.S. I was delayed in mailing this letter, but in the meantime I have seen Gagnebin, who was in Bern (concerning your passport). The reply should arrive soon. We are taking care of you. Sleep peacefully.

STRAVINSKY TO RAMUZ   *Biarritz*
                                                  August 6, 1924

Very dear one,

Deeply touched by your kind lines, I hasten to reply with an affectionate "thank you."

Pardon me for writing to you so infrequently. In spite of the vacation, I work like a slave and am buried in jobs: composing, endless proofs, endless letters, etc. . . .

I enclose a copy of the letter that I wrote yesterday to Giovanna. Please try to arrange the Lausanne concert for November 28, since this is the best date for me.

As for your plan of moving to Paris, I really do not know whether that would be better or worse for you. Certainly I understand the pecuniary factors that oblige you to do so, but life in Paris is also expensive . . . ; furthermore, moving expenses in themselves are exorbitant. And to find a good, pleasant place in which to live that will not cost an arm and a leg is yet another obstacle. If I seem pessimistic about your idea, my dear Ramuz, blame the expenses! As soon as one ventures to move, these become overwhelming. I have just returned from Nice, where my wife and I spent last week searching for a place. We found one, but at such a price that I do not dare even to type it, and this at a time when my dollar is disintegrating (which may be to your advantage, since the French franc is rising everywhere).

I must finish my letter, for it is 10:30 and I still have many things to do. I retire early in order to be fresh in the morning. Keep writing to me. I embrace you affectionately.

RAMUZ TO STRAVINSKY   *September 2, 1924*

Dear,

I wanted to wait for everything to be in order before writing to you; everything is still far from being in order, but I must bring you up-to-date anyway.

Switzerland is at war with Russia. . . . Russia boycotted Switzerland, which in turn is boycotting Russia. The move is intended as an attack against the *youpins,* but the true Russians bear the brunt of it in the end, of course. Now Russians, especially authentic ones, can no longer return to Switzerland. The border is absolutely sealed. Gagnebin and I approached M. [Daniel] Secretan, who works in Foreign Affairs in Bern. To obtain permission is extraordinarily difficult; in the past ten months, only two Russians have been admitted: an archbishop and a gentleman with a *boche* name who came all the way from Moscow to observe Mars from the top of the Jungfrau!

An exception will probably be made for you as well: what an honor! They have not yet told us yes or no, but only that we must try again on September 15 (why September 15?), by petition to the Minister of Police, letter to the President of the Confederation, etc., etc. Finally, a cable will be sent to the Legation in Paris with a special order to examine your passport; but you must come through Paris in any case. I just saw M. Secretan, who gave me some new details. This is not at all amusing, and I am powerless. . . . I will send the document to Paris quickly. . . . M. Secretan says that the matter could be settled by the end of September. The annoying thing is that Gagnebin happens to be on a trip just now, and businessmen are all on vacation, whereas in the month of November it is cold, there is snow at 1,000 meters, and by then most people are interested only in all kinds of nonsense and not in anything worthwhile. I will write to you again soon. Tell me what you think. I have had a request for the *Soldat* from Lithuania. I would provide Madame Picabia's address, but I do not know where she is. . . .

I embrace you.

R.

STRAVINSKY TO RAMUZ   *September 12, 1924*

My dear Ramuz,

Excuse my silence. I have been in Paris for a week and have not had a single free moment in which to write to you.

When I went to the Swiss Consulate, I was very moved by the pains you have taken in my behalf. Letters about me had already arrived from Secretan and also from the foreign department of the Federal Police, expressing the hope that everything would be arranged for me. M. de Weck, the chargé d'affaires, received me very cordially. I asked him to obtain a similar visa for my wife, who will come to Switzerland for my concerts.

Giovanna writes that Bern wants me to do a concert on December 8–9, but this is impossible because of Germany, where I must perform at precisely the same time. Could the [Bern] dates be changed, perhaps?[82]

I will be here for another week, then in Biarritz for a few days, then I move to Nice, and I plan not to budge from there for a month. I tell you this so that you will be up-to-date on my addresses, and, if necessary, able to transmit urgent messages to me.

I embrace you very affectionately.

                                                    Café des Deux Magots
                                                                  Paris
RAMUZ TO STRAVINSKY   *May 20, 1925*

I arrived in Paris thinking that I would find you here, but you were nowhere to be found. Then Madame Picabia told me that Madame Stravinsky had been ill and that I should have written long ago to inquire about her and to send my best wishes for a speedy recovery. Alas! The days fly by here in an idiotic fashion. Already a whole *histoire* surrounds our *Histoire du soldat,* and encumbered with a very Parisian humor, which is not at all becoming to the work. I walk 50 kilometers a day, I see people, and I attempt to make money.

Today I have a short respite, and I am taking advantage of it, as you see. I hope that your worries are over.

I will be at the Hôtel du Grand Condé (2, rue St.-Sulpice, Paris VI) for a few days more, . . . and if all goes well, I will remain in Paris until July, so I hope to see you. A small apartment is available to me, and I will send for my wife and daughter. . . . There is a young conductor who is very intelligent: his name is Desormière.[83] He is nice, with black eyes, calm, politic, drives a little Citroën, and loves your music.

---

[82] The Bern concert did not, in fact, take place.

[83] Roger Desormière (1898–1963) later replaced Ansermet as chief conductor of the Ballets Russes.

RAMUZ TO STRAVINSKY   *[End of May 1925]*

Where are you? No news. As for me, I have moved. You will find my address below.

    I send you my best wishes.

C.-F. Ramuz
3, rue Joseph-Bara
Paris VI

RAMUZ TO STRAVINSKY   *[Beginning of June 1925]*

Of course I would like to see you; in fact, I would like nothing better. . . . But my family had scarcely arrived when Gadon had an angina attack. I am still quite worried, and it is impossible to budge from here, since my wife is alone with her. This apartment is much too small, and all the devils with whom you are familiar have come along, too (and I have no one to chase them away, alas!). As soon as this situation improves, I will come to see you. Please explain to Madame Picabia why I will not be there tonight. I have taken the necessary steps concerning her piano.

    Many fond regards.

R.

RAMUZ TO STRAVINSKY   *[After June 18, 1925]*

Dear,

This is utterly sad and annoying. I went out yesterday with my family just before your message arrived, and we did not return until after you had already come by. I did not know where to catch up with you. In short, we missed each other.

    Look me up some other time, but notify me a little bit in advance; I will do the same.

    I send you all of my best wishes (though slightly belated) for your birthday. The real way to celebrate it would have been to open a bottle together. We will save that for next year.

    Things are not going very well here; we are horribly cramped; I am not accustomed to this and am too old to endure it. I plan to leave at the end of the month.

    A bientôt . . . best wishes to everyone. I embrace you.

R.

RAMUZ TO STRAVINSKY   *[Before June 22, 1925]*

Dear,

What has become of you? I no longer see you. You missed me the other day; I
would like to miss you, in turn, and I am sad not even to have the chance. . . .

 I expect that you will have a little more free time now that your concerts
are over.

 I received £3 from Chester for three performances in Wiesbaden. . . . You
must explain these accounts to me once and for all, because the Devil would
have us support ourselves and our children without money, and we must not let
ourselves be had by him. . . .

 I embrace you.

R.

RAMUZ TO STRAVINSKY   *June 22, 1925*

Dear friend,

I have just suffered the sudden loss of my mother.

 I plan to return to Paris in two or three days. I hope to see you there again.

 I embrace you.

R.

RAMUZ TO STRAVINSKY   *Paris*
                                                       June 30, 1925
Dear,   *[Pneumatique]*

I have returned, but I leave again tomorrow. I will do everything possible to be
able to see you, and if all goes well I will be at your house around 7:30. If I am
not there by 8:00, do not wait any longer.

 Many fond regards.

Your R.

RAMUZ TO STRAVINSKY   *July 13, 1925*

Dear,

Please excuse me for not thanking you, in Paris, for your telegram, but I had
not yet received it. Instead of forwarding it, the postman put it in the mailbox,
where I found it two weeks hence, upon our return [to Lausanne]. Permit me
to tell you, though a little late, how touched I was by your kind thoughts. You
must not have understood my silence: here is the explanation. I suppose that by
now you are somewhere between Valence and Nice, and I wish you a good stay

there. Better than ours, but that would be easy. We have found a rotten house in a desert. The only pleasing elements are the breeze and the water, hearing the lake sounds and watching the trees sway. There are no humans anymore. Please remember me to Madame Stravinsky. . . . I embrace you.

R.

STRAVINSKY TO RAMUZ   *July 29, 1925*

My dear Ramuz,

I was very happy to receive your kind lines. . . .

I am back in Nice again. . . . Every day I go out in my automobile with my chauffeur. I have a chauffeur who, for the time being, is very nice, very expensive, and constantly introduces me to his chauffeur-colleagues: one became the proprietor of a bistro, the other a bicycle merchant, etc. He presents me by saying: "Here is my new boss." He is fortyish, an old Paris-chauffeur type, but he has been here in Nice for seven years already, so he knows the area well.

Let me remind you that you promised to send me your most recent books, which my wife, Theodore, and I are eager to read.

Besides going for drives in the automobile, I compose regularly every morning, take a dip every morning in the sea (before composing), and in the afternoon I write letters, prepare my next season, and practice the piano (in order not to lose the technique that I have acquired in the past year).

This letter, which is accurate enough, seems to me very boring to read, for which reason I must bring it to a close.

I embrace you, my dear Ramuz, and I send you and yours fond regards.

Igor Stravinsky

RAMUZ TO STRAVINSKY   *[May 1926]*
                                       [Postcard]
Dear friend,

Are you in Paris? I am writing to you in Nice to find out. I have a telephone (Gobelins 72-81), but I don't know how to use it. Embrace those big boys and girls. My respects to Madame Stravinsky. How are you? I don't hear anything from anyone anymore. I just walked 2,500 kilometers. . . .

Here is my address: 15, rue de Cluny, Paris V.

In full middle age, I embrace you.

Ramuz

RAMUZ TO STRAVINSKY   *May 29, 1926*

Dear friend,

This is a letter. I remember the beginning of the conversation we had the other day (at the restaurant at the Porte Maillot), concerning a letter I wrote to you about two or three years ago, in which I proposed a project that interested you. I would very much like to be able to remember what it was. At this moment it would be particularly useful for me to hit upon a theme, one that would not be far from my heart, and that would not be purely "literary" or arbitrarily chosen for literary purposes. Precisely what you told me about the subject in question convinced me that it would have been perfect, at least as a point of departure in this new enterprise. But I unfortunately have no memory. . . . Thus I must once again have recourse to you so that we might continue our interrupted conversation.

But where? And how? I have tried in vain to reach you on the telephone every day. On behalf of Chavannes, I wanted to invite you to dine in a very pretty country house he has near Chatenay. At Pleyel they claim not to know you; at Acacias, you are always "out." Thus I return to this conventional method, which I hope will be effective. Send me a quick note in reply. Meanwhile, I send you all of my friendship.

R.

RAMUZ TO STRAVINSKY   *September 25, 1926*

Dear,

Two things and one page (in place of the fifty that I would like to write):

1. The Roman d'Or has asked me to submit something for its next issue of *Chroniques.* I have nothing, but they are insisting. I thought of the French text of *Noces*, which must already have appeared once in a review. What do you say? If yes, send me the libretto (I don't have a copy) with your instructions for the staging.

2. The Soirées de Lausanne is going to ask you if you would do a concert here next winter. Proposed terms: 1,000 [Swiss] francs (6,800 [French] francs). Chamber music, your pieces for solo piano, and you. Perhaps in conjunction with a trio (that of the *Soldat*) or some vocal pieces. You would have to be free on a Wednesday (the theatre is booked for all other days). Say when. And above all, say yes. All of your friends await you. And particularly the one who signs below and asks you to present his devoted respects to Madame Stravinsky and the children.

R.

Please reply before October 5 (so that the Théâtre [de Lausanne] may be reserved).

RAMUZ TO STRAVINSKY   *June 2, 1927*

Dear Stravinsky,

I too can type. . . . This note is to inform you right away how sorry I am not to
have been able to come and spend a few days in your neighborhood in Paris, but
circumstances were against it. I just had news through that nice Gagnebin, still
inebriated with music, who told me, specifically, that you are at Pleyel. For this
reason I am writing to you immediately, since this note is almost guaranteed to
reach you, extraordinary as that may seem. . . .

   All of my best wishes to Theodore (for his exhibition).[84]

RAMUZ TO STRAVINSKY   *July 15, 1927*

Dear Stravinsky,

Are you in Nice? I received a letter from Chester telling me, in effect, that the
contract with Madame Picabia expired on March 31 and that "since that date
[Chester] is again responsible to us for the portion of the rights that belongs to
us." [Chester] proposed a new agreement between Chester, *le Maître* Stravinsky . . . and myself. Ten percent commission, as before. What should be
done? I await word from you before replying. It seems that *Histoire du soldat*
was just given in London. . . .

   I would be very happy, dear friend, to have news from you: I have not
heard from you in so long. I was hoping to see you in Paris, and then that plan
was thwarted. How are all of you? . . . I was and will be ever yours.

                                                      C.-F. Ramuz

STRAVINSKY TO RAMUZ   *Nice*
                                                      July 28, 1927
My dear Ramuz,

I had hardly returned from Paris (three weeks ago) when my wife fell ill with
pleurisy, which explains my silence: I am very sad. Now the fluid is being reab-
sorbed and her temperature is beginning to go down, though very slowly. If all
goes well, I will take her to the mountains around August 15 to give her a
change of air: it is dreadfully hot here. I write in great haste, although my let-
tering is quite neat, is it not?

   Until another time, when perhaps I will have a chance to tell you something more amusing. I embrace you, my old Ramuz.

---

[84]See S.S.C. I, pp. 107–12.

RAMUZ TO STRAVINSKY   *July 30, 1927*

Dear friend,

Your letter arrived and I do not want to leave for the mountains, where I will join my family—in Diablerets, do you remember?—without replying. Pardon me for having sent you that ridiculous business letter, particularly at such a difficult moment for you, but I was ignorant of your circumstances. . . . Please give [Madame Stravinsky] all of my best wishes . . . for a complete recovery. Great pity that these mountains cannot go to you, since you will not make the trip. That would give us a chance for a leisurely visit, which is impossible (and ever more impossible) in Paris. Did I tell you how sorry I was (and still not enough) not to have seen you there in June? I expect . . . that everything will go better and better. I too live in terror of illness (not my own). And you, how are you?

                              To you in all friendship,   R.

RAMUZ TO STRAVINSKY   *May 19, 1928*

Dear Stravinsky,

I waited for your return to Paris before writing, to be certain that my letter would reach you at rue Rochechouart (which is a good old French name, instead of these unreadable, unpronounceable English names, which intimidate me). All this to inform you that the *Souvenirs* will not appear in a review, but in a series of pamphlets, which I intend to write myself for immediate publication. From that alone you will ascertain their character; it is precisely the intimacy of the enterprise that has tempted me to undertake it. The subject will be your Morges period, our excursions in the country, the *Soldat,* certain events, big and small, that we experienced together and that I still remember with pleasure. The few sentences excerpted from your letters should serve as illustrations, and at the same time they make you a collaborator. I send you these excerpts; tell me what you think. . . . Would you happen to have a photograph of a page of the *Soldat* manuscript? But for all of this we will have to see each other and talk; I am enraged because, despite my persistence, I always make mistakes in typing (now another one).

I send you my fond regards. Gagnebin eagerly turned on the radio Saturday night [to hear your concert] but heard nothing except a vague rattling of plates.

STRAVINSKY TO RAMUZ   *May 29, 1928*

Dear Ramuz,

Received your letter, and I am in complete agreement about the publication of the excerpts from my letters that you have sent.[85]

Regarding the *Soldat,* the project has become less feasible in view of the fact that I have nothing either with me or at home, if I recall correctly. Besides, I could get into trouble with Chester, with whom I have had no contact in months, because [Henry Kling] is a real bastard, as everyone knows except himself.

I await you and will be very happy if you do not disappoint us but come as promised.

This is my last month here at old rue Rochechouart. I will soon be moved to the new Pleyel office on the rue du Faubourg St.-Honoré. This is something different, alas!

I embrace you wholeheartedly.

Igor Stravinsky

STRAVINSKY TO RAMUZ

Chalet des Echarvines
Talloires
Haute-Savoie

Dear Ramuz,

August 11, 1928

What a pity not to have seen you! We arrived at that sad casino in Thonon exactly at noon. Only Auberjonois was there awaiting us, with a white Muller [?] bag that he immediately gave to me because I liked it so much.

He discussed a planned trip in Mermod's Buick and promised to come and see us. You should all come together. I will be away for a week or ten days beginning August 31. Before then, if you would come around 6:00 p.m., I could devote the entire evening and even the night to you. Unfortunately, all morning and afternoon I must work on an urgent task which has to be finished by August 31.[86] Thus I am depriving myself of even such natural activities as visiting with friends whom, like you, I do not often see. So, *à bientôt,* my dear Ramuz.

Very affectionately,

---

[85] On the basis of this authorization, Ramuz included several passages of this correspondence in his *Souvenirs sur Igor Stravinsky* (Lausanne: Editions Mermod, 1928), but in editing the text he destroyed Stravinsky's spontaneity and introduced numerous errors. See Stravinsky's letter to Ramuz of December 16, 1928.

[86] Stravinsky had promised to deliver half of the score of *Le Baiser de la fée* by then.

RAMUZ TO STRAVINSKY   *[August 1928]*

Dear Stravinsky,

This has not worked out well: your note arrived here the day we were supposed
to meet. You should follow the [mountain] passes (good exercise for the boys)
and come to see us here in this magnificent country (much more beautiful
than that of Lake Annecy), especially this year: not a rainy day in two months,
38 degrees in the shade. If not, we will try to see you in Talloires with Auberjonois and Mermod (big Buick), but until when will you be there? We plan to
be here until about the 20th. A note before then, please. I too would be very
pleased to see you, after having missed you in Paris. . . .

   I embrace you.

                                                                  Ramuz

RAMUZ TO STRAVINSKY   *September 12, 1928*

Dear Stravinsky,

The Buick broke down. Until when are you in Talloires? That is what you neglected to tell me.

   But *above all* send me a page of the [*Soldat*] manuscript. If it is impossible
to have one from the *Soldat,* please send one from *Noces.*

   Friendly greetings, fond regards to everyone and to you.

                                                                  Ramuz

We could perhaps come to see you now.

STRAVINSKY TO RAMUZ   *Nice*
                                                          October 25, 1928
My dear Ramuz,

It is more than a month since I received your letter. . . . Do not suppose that
this is my reply. . . . Mine will be in person, since I plan to be in Switzerland
and, I hope, will see you on November 5. I have a concert in Zürich on the 6th
and would like to be there in the evening. Unless I am mistaken, my train arrives in Lausanne at one-something in the afternoon, allowing me a few hours
with you there. Look for me at the station: it is the train from Grenoble, Aix-les-
Bains, and Geneva. But do not mention my visit to anyone. I fear that my wife's
relatives, M. and Madame Schwartz, might find out, and I have too little time to
share it with all of my Lausanne acquaintances, especially such uninteresting
ones. But I would be very pleased if I could see Auberjonois at your house, and I
think that by one o'clock I will be hungry and would not object if you were to
offer me a good or even a bad meal.

   A bientôt, my old friend.

RAMUZ TO STRAVINSKY   *October 27, 1928*

Dear Stravinsky,

This is utterly comical: I myself have a concert (vocal) on November 6, and
right next to Zürich, in St. Gall. Unless you are on a special train, we could
make the trip together, and we could even return together: everything will depend on your plans. In any case, I will go to the station and wait for you, and will
alert Auberjonois; just try to find out the time of your arrival. And don't forget to
bring me a page of the *Noces* manuscript; you have millions, and one would be
of use to me. . . .

                                                      C.-F. Ramuz

STRAVINSKY TO RAMUZ   *October 29, 1928*

My dear Ramuz,

What an odd coincidence: I would be thrilled to go to Zürich with you. Why not
spend the night together in Zürich, then? The next morning I will go to my
rehearsal, and you to St. Gall. As for the rest, we can decide that at the
time. My train is due in Lausanne at 1:30, and I will not get off, as planned, but
will continue on to Zürich. Meet me on the train, and we will make the trip
together, then determine whether we could return together, too, you to
Lausanne, I to Paris. I will be happy to shake Auberjonois's hand at the station,
if he really wants to take the trouble to come and see me. From Geneva to
Zürich I will be in second class. Quick, send a reply by return mail that all
is settled.

                                                      I embrace you.

RAMUZ TO STRAVINSKY   *October 31, 1928*

Dear Stravinsky,

There is a train that arrives at 1:35, but it does not continue directly to Zürich.
You must wait until 3:00. This is not enough time to go down to the house
for lunch, and too much time to spend sadly in a train station. But I see
that there is another train from Marseille, arriving at 11:45 and continuing
on directly to Zürich: wouldn't you prefer to take that one? A note in reply,
please. I will tell Auberjonois. If I hear nothing, I will wait for you at the
station. . . .

                                                      Your   Ramuz

RAMUZ TO STRAVINSKY   *November 8, 1928*

Dear Stravinsky,

Please find the enclosed:
1. My thanks for the manuscript, which arrived safely from Zürich;
2. My regrets for having been obliged to leave you so early;
3. All of my best wishes for a good stay in Paris;
4. My respects and best wishes to Madame Sudeikina;
5. Three copies of the second volume [of the *Souvenirs*], containing a beautiful picture made especially for you;
6. A copy of your drawing, which I ask you to autograph for Mermod, who is very nice and would very much like to have this memento of you.

That already makes quite a few things, to which I attach many other thoughts too long to express in writing. . . .

                                                        C.-F. Ramuz

Don't forget to return the drawing for Mermod. Thank you in advance.

RAMUZ TO STRAVINSKY   *December 10, 1928*

Dear Stravinsky,

By the same mail, I am sending you four copies of the third volume [of the *Souvenirs*], with my fond regards.

Did you return to Nice, and safely? You told me that you would have some spare time there. If that is the case, I must propose a project to you.

I could make an edition, apart from these *Souvenirs,* of about eighty pages, in which I would include several photographic plates: a view of the Café de la Crochettaz, another of the vineyard of Lavaux. That would be completely documentary. And to complete the documentation, I would ask you to consent to attach some notes indicating your personal reactions: "This is false," "This is true," "I do not share this opinion," and, in a few words, explain why. From time to time you could even add one of your own reminiscences. . . . I think that this would add spontaneity, sincerity, and a quality of unusualness, and would of course increase the value of these *Souvenirs.* . . .

Say yes. And embrace everyone and yourself.

                                                        C.-F. Ramuz

STRAVINSKY TO RAMUZ   *December 16, 1928*

Dear Ramuz,

My heartfelt thanks for your *Souvenirs,* of which the third volume is in no way inferior to the preceding ones.

These *Souvenirs* have deeply touched me. Once deposited, the residuum of the past begins its geological life, carefully covered over by new strata in formation; this residuum, no less potent than those that we have drunk together many times in three gulps (your three volumes), has gone to my already reeling head; I turn toward you in gratitude for having guarded these memories, dear to us both, in so safe a place.*

But the eyes in my head now open wide, astonished at your proposal to attach my personal reactions to your text in the form of "notes."

Of course I have reactions, my dear Ramuz; but when I am asked, as you have just done, to formulate them into commentaries, I recoil like a snail into its shell, fearing to expose myself in my nakedness. Let me explain: intelligent things must be said in these cases, you will surely agree. Everyone, myself included, can make intelligent remarks; but if I am asked to write them down, to fix them, an uneasiness suddenly overtakes me, for I lack the competence to express them. Writing is a skill, as you well know, and I must admit that I have no training in it. Furthermore, I confess that I was born slightly lazy.

What must satisfy you are my comments in the postscript. Here they are:

1. Gogol did not burn the second part of his *Dead Souls* by direct order from God, but upon the advice of his religious mentor (Father Rjevski), a man of eminent spiritual value.

2. I have never lived in Candebec-sur-Mer and consequently would never have written to you from this place, which is not to be found even in Larousse. I do find Carantec listed, however, and I wonder if perhaps you received my letter from there (in 1920, not 1921).

3. Several more errors may exist, but they are not worth mentioning.[87]

In the hope that you will not be too irritated by this rather evasive reply, I limit myself, wretched thing that I am, to sending you only my best *"souvenirs."*

> Your   Igor Stravinsky

P.S. See the comments above.

* Your bottle, which still seems to bear a label with three bells, was delivered to me, and, in fact, was uncorked by my sons, as you had predicted.[88]

RAMUZ TO STRAVINSKY   *June 7, 1929*

Dear,

Are you in Nice? Reports about you turn up in London, Berlin, Budapest. . . . This note is to tell you that the *Souvenirs* will appear this autumn . . . with a revised and augmented text, in the *N* [*ouvelle*] *R* [*evue*] *F* [*rançaise*]. I want to

---

[87] Ramuz incorporated Stravinsky's corrections into the Gallimard edition of the book.

[88] At the end of the *Souvenirs*, Ramuz imagines his manuscript, rolled up in a bottle, cast into the Rhône, and arriving in Nice with the help of "a kind wind." He had written to Stravinsky: "If you do not find it yourself, one of your sons will, one day while swimming, and thus it will be delivered to you."

ask you for an unpublished photograph to complement the text; for example, the one you sent to Auberjonois in which you resemble Ramses XXXXVI, with a cane. . . .

I also need to know the name of the Russian folklorist who is the author of the two big volumes you had in Morges in which the story of the *Soldat* appears.

I must also announce that I am currently homeless, having been chased out of Cour, and I don't know where to go. . . .

Send the photograph and the information to my old address; they will be forwarded. For the time being I live in hotels, and switch to a new one on a daily basis. . . .

Respects, fond regards, remembrances.

Ramuz

RAMUZ TO STRAVINSKY   *Ouchy*
September 18, 1929

Dear Stravinsky,

There are three steps in the [Swiss] naturalization process:
1. Request addressed to the Federal Council in Bern (there is a form to fill out);
2. In case of a favorable predisposition, acquisition of a bourgeoisie [*sic*] . . . (to exemplify the rules for admission to the bourgeoisie of Lausanne);
3. The definitive ratification (or decree of naturalization) from the Grand Council (that of the Canton of Vaud, in this case), determined by majority vote.

Thus the Confederation, the Commune, and the State intervene one after the other, but, in short, everything depends on a favorable predisposition on the part of the Federal authorities, following which the various offices proceed with their investigation.

You should authorize me to broach the subject by introducing your name to certain influential persons, who will attend to it. That would be a first "official" step and would guarantee that you would not fail in the end.

Please come to a definite, in-principle, decision . . . so that negotiations can begin, though they will still remain completely confidential.

I await a word in reply before taking any step, of course, and I send you our fond regards.

C.-F. Ramuz

RAMUZ TO STRAVINSKY   *September 30, 1929*

Dear Stravinsky,

I wrote to Daniel Secretan, who replied with the nicest letter, placing himself entirely at our service.

Here are the *Federal* conditions:

1. A total of six years' residence during the past twelve years;
2. Two years of uninterrupted residence prior to the presentation of the request;
3. Favorable reports* . . .

Secretan adds that the only difficulty he sees in your case is that you have not lived in Switzerland for these past two years; yet he feels certain that you will succeed in the end. He offered to pay an official visit to the Minister of Justice and Police but will not do so without confirmation from you. Please let me know whether you agree. Of course this visit (though confidential) would bind you "ethically."

At the moment Secretan is away (in Rome) for two weeks or so, but he will see to this on his return.

The other information I gave you is correct. After the solicitation, the Federal Police will deliver (or not) a decree of naturalization, following which the Commune and the Canton enter the picture. The Federal authorization in no way binds the Commune and the Canton. The fee for the Federal formalities is 20 francs. You must expect these measures to take a year.

Many fond regards,   Ramuz

* Politics! (good) Finances! (good) "Worthy of assimilation," etc.

RAMUZ TO STRAVINSKY   *October 31, 1929*

Dear Stravinsky,

It failed. The visit took place, but it seems that there is no recourse, thanks to the clause . . . stipulating a two-year residence [just prior to the demand] . Otherwise, there would have been no obstacle—but this one suffices, alas! Forgive me, but I fear that I have done all I can, as has Secretan, and he was particularly well situated to carry out the plan, had it been possible. . . .

RAMUZ TO STRAVINSKY   *September 15, 1930*[89]

Dear Stravinsky,

Where are you? The most contradictory news is circulating. Word has it that you are in Poland—is this true? I am addressing this to you in Nice, in the hope that you will perchance pass through there one day. Please present my respects to Madame Stravinsky and place my family (a woman, a child, and myself) at the feet of your family. I am and will remain

your   R.

---

[89] In 1930, an "Association du Prix Romand" was formed by Werner Reinhart, Chavannes, and Henri-Louis Mermod. Elie Gagnebin wrote to Stravinsky asking him to

RAMUZ TO STRAVINSKY

Voreppe

[1931]

Dear friend,

I just had a visit from Gino Severini,[90] who saw you recently and gave me some very good news about you. . . .

Would you be disposed to cede your rights to *Histoire du soldat* for a still-vague project involving a cinematographic adaptation? It would be done by your young Flemish (Netherlandish) friends, who just sent me a beautifully illustrated edition. They propose to give you 10,000 Swiss francs, with the rights to be negotiated. I am writing to M. Stols, editor of *Maestricht*.

Take "effervescent calcium": * I was given it for my arms, and it made my soul feel like new. Colitis is a disease of the soul.** Your children are ridiculous and serve no purpose but to weaken you. I will send news about the *Soldat* as soon as I hear something myself.

* Effervescent calcium, twelve tablets, Fabrique de Produits Cliniques Sandoz, Basel, Switzerland

** As are feruncles

STRAVINSKY TO RAMUZ   *January 1, 1932*

A very long letter to Ramuz, written in Voreppe (Isère)

I write to you on very handsome paper—manufactured here in Rives, not far from our home—to inform you that if the "vague project" of the *Soldat*'s cinematographicization (God that's long!) for my "young Flemish (Netherlandish) friends" were to become a certainty in the near future, the new year (I received your news on January 1) would not be off to such a bad start.

You say that you are writing to Stols, editor of *Maestricht*. What does he have to do with it? To whom am I supposed to write, not having received any proposal, either from him or from my "young Flemish (Netherlandish) friends"? Moreover, if I may be indiscreet, what have you told them? Who proposed this "vague project," which, however, is not lacking in certain exactitudes, since you seem already to be familiar with the sum that would be offered to me ("10,000 Swiss francs and negotiable rights," as you say)? Send a few more lines on the subject so that I may envision it more clearly.

Thank you.

---

become a subscriber and identifying Ramuz as the first recipient. Stravinsky's name appears as one of eleven signatories of the declaration accompanying the prize when it was presented to Ramuz. (This document begins, strangely, with the claim that Ramuz's work is the most considerable ever written "on the soil of this country." More than that of J.-J. Rousseau?)

[90] Gino Severini (1883–1966), Italian painter, first a Cubist, later a Futurist.

For the third day in a row, my four children are in the snow, skiing (*schi* in German—a pretty word, *nein?*). They leave at eight o'clock every morning and come home at 6:00 p.m., burned by the sun and contorted with muscular pains. As for me, this is the third day of a fast, prescribed by my Russian doctor. For a week (seven days and not five, as it is with the communists, whom you so admire and who detest you, good Christian)—a whole week, you understand—I must eat a little porridge and half an apple in the morning, at noon some mashed potatoes, an egg, and half an apple, at 6:00 p.m. half a glass of water, and at 8:00 a little mashed potato and vegetables. That is all for the twenty-four-hour period. I think that it would be simpler not to eat at all than to follow such a regimen, which makes one suffer terribly. I know that you will laugh, but this is not funny to me. Nevertheless, it is the only way to put a stop to my colitis, which I have not managed to overcome since last June. Above all, it is idiotic to detain *you* with this. Excuse me. What is happening in my colon or another of the organs of my body, or of our bodies, is not serious: what matters is what is happening outside our bodies, and then being passed to and among them. Pretty philosophy? But that would be more easily and quickly elaborated in person. "In person" is easy to say, but when? Still, I do not despair of hopping over to see you in Pully, because Pully is so much closer to Voreppe for me than Voreppe from Pully for you.[91]

I embrace you,   IStr

RAMUZ TO STRAVINSKY

January 14, 1933
[Postcard]

Best wishes to all of you from all of us, and thanks for your [best wishes], which are much needed by this poor, *sick* one, who sends you his regards. . . .

R.

RAMUZ TO STRAVINSKY[92]

July 10, 1933

Most nobly born,

Your two other letters will have been forwarded, and I am sending the first one back to you. Please greet your progeny, which spring from such extraordinary blood, with a friendly handshake.

C.-F. Ramuz

---

[91] Stravinsky was to see Ramuz that April. A photograph of the two men, together with the publisher Mermod and others, was taken in Ouchy at Mermod's home on the 4th.

[92] German is the original language of this letter. This and its sarcastic tone would seem to indicate that Stravinsky had either told Ramuz about or sent him a copy of the genealogical declaration made to Willy Strecker of B. Schotts Söhne. See Stravinsky's letter to Willy Strecker of April 14, 1933, in the present volume.

RAMUZ TO STRAVINSKY   *December 19, 1933*

Were you not [even] considering mounting the *Soldat* with [Ida] Rubinstein next season? Your friend Gide tells me that you would have all of the necessary components, including an excellent Narrator and régisseur (Jacques Copeau).

I was thinking of coming to Paris for two or three months, but first I must rent my house here, which is not easily done.

Fifteen degrees below zero, a little snow, not much. And infrequent news from you.

From faraway we send you our best wishes for Christmas and the new year. Please present my respects to your mother and to Madame Stravinsky. Our best regards to you great gentlemen and ladies. Be assured of my feelings of loyalty toward you and of my loyal attachment.

                                             C.-F. Ramuz

RAMUZ TO STRAVINSKY   *June 25, 1934*[93]

Very happy to learn that you have recovered completely. Sent a letter to your house. Letter returned to sender. "It is the life in us that believes in life and the part that is [already] dying that believes in death." (Claudel) Do you think that this is true? I would like the *Soldat* to be done well once again.[94] I am writing a metaphysical treatise entitled *The Need for Grandeur*. Come to see me.

Best wishes, respects, and fond regards.

                                             R.

RAMUZ TO STRAVINSKY   *June 28, 1935*

Dear Stravinsky,

How are you? Did you have a good trip? And America? Since I never see you, I will never know anything.

But thank you for the note and the book.[95] It is very good. I am not indulgent, I am veracious. It is clear and well structured. And it reads easily (which is essential). And, of course, I like very much what you say about music that

---

[93] Earlier that month, Ramuz had sent a copy of his *Taille de l'homme* to Stravinsky, inscribing it at length but somewhat coldly, and asking the composer to send news from time to time.

[94] In fact, a memorable performance was to take place at the Théâtre de Genève on December 15 of that year, with Cocteau as the Narrator. In an interview in the Lausanne newspaper *Le Radio*, November 9, 1934, Cocteau says that he had met Hermann Scherchen in Winterthur and that the conductor had invited him to participate in the Geneva performance.

[95] The first volume of Stravinsky's *Chroniques de ma vie*, published in Paris by Denoël & Steele, had appeared in March. The second volume followed in December.

must be *seen*. And many other things (you know which). (Wagner—but I like Wagner.)

I have heard nothing from Madame Stravinsky, and I am to blame. I wanted to write to her but did not have her address. I have a seventeen-year-old daughter who spent the spring in Rome and saw Nini there. Nini was supposed to send me the address in question but of course did not do so. Would you like to send it to me instead? In any case, give my regards and best wishes to your sick one. . . .

I embrace you, if you will permit me.

R.

And please send a large score with a large dedication (everything becomes large) for the little children of Pully: we give them bread and chocolate and have arranged a lottery for their benefit.

STRAVINSKY TO RAMUZ *June 29, 1935*

My dear Ramuz,

Very happy to hear from you: I will come to visit you, and you *will* see me, though you are convinced of the contrary. Thank you for the kind comments on my book. I doubt that you like Wagner. What I do not like about him are his tomb and his theatre, both in Bayreuth.

I am working terribly hard right now on two things: (1) a concerto for two pianos, which I will play with Nini at the end of November in Paris; and (2) a second volume of my *Chroniques,* which Denoël & Steele wants by the autumn.

Along with this note, I will send a score of *Perséphone,* with your friend Gide's text, Theodore's cover, and a dedication.

Affectionately, your   I. Stravinsky

P.S. All that I have on hand is a score of *Le Baiser de la fée,* which I will send to you instead.

RAMUZ TO STRAVINSKY *July 6, 1935 (Already!)*

Thank you, dear Stravinsky, for the fine package, with the lion inside and the dedication in the book. It will make people happy (one adult, a millionaire, I think, and many chocolate-loving children, which is more worthwhile). Thank you for the

LETTER

as well. You say that we will see each other; I hope so, but you do not say how, and you have now expanded into two realms, the literary and the musical.

The weather is beautiful, the lake is beautiful, the mountains are beautiful.

I am writing to Madame Stravinsky, though you gave me only half an address. . . . I have a vague recollection of the [doctor's?] name but no longer remember whether it begins with a "J" or a "T."

Is everything else still the same?

I embrace you,   R.

RAMUZ TO STRAVINSKY   *July 20, 1935*

[Postcard]

Sancellemoz

Respects, regards, friendly greetings.

R.

RAMUZ TO STRAVINSKY   *[March 20?, 1936]*

I thank you for the hospitality that you showed the little girl. I beg you above all to present my respects to your mother and to express my appreciation for the attention that she paid to my daughter, indulging her in her whims. She arrived last night and told us all about her experience, which left her deeply touched. And now I must give you some very sad news: F. Chavannes just died (suddenly, I think). He was one of my oldest friends, and I know that you saw him quite frequently. You become the perfect traveler, and I the perfect anti-traveler. Embrace all those around you (the big boys and the big girls), and please believe, dear friend, that I am your loyally devoted

R.

P.S. I know nothing about the circumstances of Chavannes's death; I was informed of it by a phone call; his family had already left for Paris. Perhaps, being there yourself, you will find out more. He had a great deal of talent.

RAMUZ TO STRAVINSKY   *July 7, 1936*

Dear one,

I have the papers (1,450 pages) here and have put them in an envelope for you. B. mentioned a "family foundation," of which you would be the director, based in Switzerland and with a branch in England. This seems an elegant solution to the problem.

Respects and best wishes to all.

I embrace you,   C.-F. Ramuz

RAMUZ TO STRAVINSKY   *September 18, 1936*

Dear one,

I received a note from these gentlemen in Zürich, asking me to participate in a
little supplementary exhibit they plan to organize for [November] 8, on the occasion of your concert, I think. They have invited me to speak. What do you
think? I have given an in-principle acceptance and await clarification from
them. But this would be an opportunity for us to see each other.

What has become of the dancer?

What is Theodore's address? I would like to write to him but have no idea
where he is.

Respects, remembrances, fond regards.

C.-F. Ramuz

RAMUZ TO STRAVINSKY   *September 25, 1936*

Dear one,

To continue with last night's telephone conversation: I must now write to the
actors and find out whether they will be free on the dates you set. Then I must
outline the financial plan for the enterprise, since it could easily cost more than
I had thought ([thanks to] the dancer and *her mother*). In particular, I must
write to the various theatres asking their terms. Will you conduct? When? In
any case, you will have a replacement. I have Lausanne, Geneva, Neuchâtel,
Bern, Basel, and Zürich in mind. Do you think that your impresario could take
charge of these initial steps? A request always makes much more of an impression when it comes from Paris.

You too must see this little girl dance. Do you have photographs of her?
And you must reach an agreement with Madame [Bronislava] Nijinska about
her fees. All of that is not impossible, but very complicated.

And finally, you must consider that first part of the performance, about
which I spoke to you.

I have: the actors, the orchestra, the sets. Only the costumes and the
money are missing.

Send word, please.

Fond regards,   R.

STRAVINSKY TO RAMUZ   *Paris*
                                                      September 28, 1936
My dear Ramuz,

I see that the project cannot be executed for the simple reason that you point
out: lack of money (and of costumes), without which we clearly cannot undertake anything at all. How is it that this did not occur to you until now? You say

that it will be very complicated, but not impossible. No more complicated than any other business, whose first condition is that one must have money (who will pay for the costumes, the publicity, and all of the necessary advances?) and someone to take charge of the organization of the project.

I have likewise misunderstood your questions: "Will you conduct? When?"—since I had already fixed the dates for you by telephone, saying that I could participate in the performances between November 12 and 23.

As for the dance, we have the prima ballerina of the Ballet de Monte Carlo, who just left that very good company for personal reasons. She is still very young, and there might be a question of paying her mother.

So I ask, as you did, what are we going to do?

I embrace you, your

RAMUZ TO STRAVINSKY   *October 1, 1936*

Dear one,

You are wicked (I had doubted this until now), and I find it very painful.

I have already seen the orchestra. They are very cooperative and will be all prepared when you arrive. They ask 12 francs for each three-hour rehearsal.

The actors (also very enthusiastic) will rehearse for nothing. They plan to begin their own negotiations with Neuchâtel and Bern. I fixed the sum of 2,000 outright for each performance and will have their reply in a few days.

I must see Gagnebin soon and have him set the Théâtre de Lausanne in motion. I am going to write to Zürich.

If we have six guaranteed performances, meaning about 12,000 francs, I think that we could go ahead.

Naturally I would be the Narrator when you conduct.

Please ask the dancer to wait a few days longer for the definitive decision. And please warn M. Soulima that I will soon have the honor of writing to him.

I do not embrace you,   R.

P.S. I wonder if something could be arranged in Geneva, where one performance has already taken place (Scherchen).

STRAVINSKY TO RAMUZ   *October 2, 1936*

Fairly dear one,

Everyone except you knows that I am good, and I can do nothing about it. You trouble yourself excessively, and, as always, you exaggerate. Thus I say that an honorarium of 2,000 francs per performance for your two actors is a hyperbolic figure, with one zero too many. Am I right? Probably so, because otherwise the budget of 12,000 francs, which you consider satisfactory, would not suffice.

Another thing. I foresee difficulties in, if not the utter impossibility of, staging the work in Zürich, since I am giving a concert there, whose sponsors certainly will not tolerate posters announcing my appearance in the *Soldat* only a week away.

You do not breathe a word about costumes. Have you resolved that question? If you recall, there are eight: two for the Soldier, one for the dancer, and five for the Devil. Perhaps we could borrow the ones used in Geneva last year.

If you are handling Lausanne and Bern, do you think that my agent (Madame Bouchonnet) should write to Basel, Geneva, and elsewhere, if Zürich is impossible?

Why do you not embrace me?[96]

RAMUZ TO STRAVINSKY

October 5, 1936
[Telegram]

[Received] letter [from] Schulthess. Interested in shows. I ask guarantee of 2,500 per performance.   Ramuz

RAMUZ TO STRAVINSKY

October 15, 1936

I did not write to you sooner because I had no news (except from Lausanne, and that was very bad news, since the theatre will not be free one single night while you are here). Thus I have not written to Geneva. Nothing is certain except Neuchâtel, which offers 2,000.

I have forwarded your proposal to Schulthess, but you would have done better to send it yourself, since we are losing three days in the process, and time is crucial.

I will let you know how I am making out. Would you mind asking Nini how long his concert lasts, so that I can calculate how much time to allot for my lecture?

Ergebenster,   CFR

RAMUZ TO STRAVINSKY

October 16, 1936

I wanted to telephone you just now but could not, because I do not have your number. You included it in your last telegram, but I no longer have that telegram. I send you this note hastily to say that it would be infinitely preferable to

---

[96]By this time the two men were less than intimate friends, having gone very different ways in their ideologies. Simone Hauert observed them dining together in the Restaurant du Central, Lausanne: "Three men around a table: Stravinsky, Ramuz, Auberjonois. . . . Stravinsky is dressed in light gray. . . . His eyes, his large mouth, and his whole being take part in his talk. 'Freud . . . dream interpretation . . . these things do not interest me.' He has no need to fill in the gaps with intellectual constructions: he believes, he has Faith! Abruptly he stops talking. . . . His large hand hides the lower

broach the subject with Geneva from Paris (people are more impressed by that here). Remember that Gagnebin went to see Henn on your behalf last year as well. Everything hinges on the reply from German Switzerland, to whom I have written. They must hurry, though: I fear we will not have enough time. I will write to you as soon as I hear anything, but perhaps you will know before I do.

Best wishes,   CFR

Don't forget to ask Nini about the duration of his concert.

STRAVINSKY TO RAMUZ   *July 2, 1937*

Hello, my dear Ramuz, I would like to hear from you. Here are our plans. We, the whole family, meaning grandmother, parents, children, grandchildren, are going to a *pension* in the country, Château de Monthoux, near Annemasse. We will leave around July 13. I will be on a very strict diet until September. How pleasant! Two scarred ulcers have been discovered, one in my stomach, the other in my intestine. These continue to plague me and to make life impossible.

Madame N. Bouchonnet, who is dealing with Schulthess in Zürich about the *Soldat* (a tour is still planned), would like to know *if you have received a letter* from him concerning the cost of the actors and the musicians. His silence on this subject surprises Madame Bouchonnet, who had requested that he write to you. A note in reply, my dear Ramuz.

I embrace you.

Your   Stravinsky

RAMUZ TO STRAVINSKY   *July 3, 1937*

Dear Stravinsky,

We are all full of healed ulcers. Do not think about it: forget the diet. I just wanted to tell you that Auberjonois underwent an operation for a stomach ulcer this morning. Write him a little note: Clinique Cécil, Montbenon, Lausanne.

---

part of his face, and his clear, scrutinizing eyes search far into the distance. The power of Mussolini comes to mind! The encounter between those two men was something magnificent; such rapport eludes human measure. They create the Revolution! . . . Ramuz . . . contradicts [Stravinsky] . Defensive, reserved, he does not want to surrender anything. He denies psychoanalysis and metaphysics but confesses an interest in Trotsky. An admission from Ramuz is just another concealment; he is the picture of pride. Auberjonois listens, with his acutely sarcastic smile. . . . Nothing escapes him, he has an aloof air but follows the conversation without missing a single gesture or intonation. . . .''

I have also replied to S. (about ten days ago), saying that we charge 2,000 per performance, with a minimum of seven performances.

I look forward to seeing you again. Our best regards to all. My respects to Madame Stravinsky.

A bientôt,   R.

RAMUZ TO STRAVINSKY   *September 28, 1937*

My dear Stravinsky,

Here is the letter that I received from Schulthess: I understand precisely none of it. What do you think of his proposals? So far as I can tell, we are the ones running the risks, since S.'s "guarantees" would not even cover the expenses. Shall we continue with these proceedings, and, if so, could you find a ballerina (impossible to find one here)? Moreover, there would be no question of giving it in the Maison du Peuple in Lausanne (which is much too small); we would have to do it in the Théâtre [de Lausanne] (1,200 seats). Geneva? Neuchâtel? Maybe Fribourg.*

A word in reply, please. I embrace you.

R.

* Rome, where Madame Pecci-Blunt has a theatre, is a possibility.

Ramuz died on May 23, 1947,[97] *and Stravinsky sent a cable to the family that arrived just as the funeral was beginning. Later, the composer replied to a request from the* Suisse Contemporaine *for a statement:*

Do not ask me to write. . . . These things must be done in cold blood, otherwise one risks altering one's memories and being unfair to the past. Facts reconstructed by memory are deformed if invoked during a state of grief. That grief is still fresh and too precious for me to renounce at will. In this mood it is impossible for me to write memories or to formulate thoughts worthy to pay homage.

---

[97]Elie Gagnebin wrote to Stravinsky on June 6: "He was very pessimistic, convinced that because of his sclerosis, his body could not stand the shock of the operation. He survived it, though, and the surgeon seemed quite satisfied. . . . [Then he] suffered an internal hemorrhage and went into a coma."

Throughout the war years, Gagnebin had kept Stravinsky informed about performances of his music in Switzerland, writing on March 15, 1942, for example, about a concert of his works in Winterthur eleven days earlier. In the same letter, Gagnebin mentions seeing Ramuz, Auberjonois, and Charles-Albert Cingria frequently. In 1949, when Gagnebin was himself near death after the removal of his cancerous left lung, he wrote to Stravinsky: "I hope that one lung will give me enough breath to fulfill my role as the Narrator in *Histoire du soldat.*"

Shortly thereafter, Stravinsky wrote to Auberjonois:

Just a word to tell you that I was very touched not only by your "epitaph" about poor Faravel[98] but by the very fact that you thought to write it.

For this humble disappearance to pass unnoticed, eclipsed by the event of Ramuz's death, would be unjust—and you have spoken. [June 15, 1947]

---

[98] Gaston Faravel, of Morges, died eight days after Ramuz. The son of a circus acrobat, Faravel studied painting under Auberjonois and decorated a number of Swiss churches. According to the obituary by Auberjonois, Stravinsky and Faravel were good friends during the composer's years in Morges.

CORRESPONDENCE WITH

1 9 1 7 ～ 1 9 5 2

C.-A. CINGRIA

CHARLES-ALBERT CINGRIA[1] TO STRAVINSKY   [1917]

Dear friend,

What a beautiful memory I have of our trip to Rolle.[2] I am still transported. Haunted like the wood of a guitar by your myriad and ferocious rhythms and your harmonies,[3] [or] like a belfry in a village high in the mountains, on a gray [river] near Mukden. I feel as though I had visited the land of the poem that Rimbaud did not have the courage to finish in verse and described thus in prose:

> *La cascade sonne derrière les huttes d'opéra-comique. Des girandoles se prolongent, dans les vergers et les allées voisins du Méandre,—les verts et les rouges du couchant. Nymphes d'Horace coiffées au Premier Empire,— Rondes Sibériennes, Chinoises de Boucher.*

Yes, that is it, is it not?

And Kibalchich[4] was there. I needed him to be there, with his brick-shaped head and wonderful gold glasses. He was the chorus, not an individual, but a race: the whole of sacerdotal and administrative Russia. The piano, the enormous piano with the nude dolls, their legs far apart (the archetypical world, the gods!), and Madame Stravinsky sitting straight up, attentive and sweet, saying of your projects, "That's good," like the wife of a great chef, keen and comfortable. . . . She was at one end of the piano and completed the lovely composition of this tableau. Thank you for everything you gave us that day. . . . An imbecile, Lanzon (French, of course), just wrote a book to say that if the Germans are

---

[1] Charles-Albert Cingria (1883–1954) was one of Stravinsky's closest friends, as well as a writer whose views on art, literature, and religion exerted a strong influence on the composer. The two men had first met in Paris in May 1914.

[2] On Lake Geneva, Canton de Vaud. Frédéric-César de La Harpe, the tutor of Tsar Alexander I, was born here in 1754.

[3] Stravinsky had played *Les Noces* for Cingria.

[4] Vasily Kibalchich, choral conductor. Stravinsky met him in Château-d'Oex in 1915 and attended some of his concerts in Geneva and Lausanne. He formed a Russian chorus in Paris after World War I, and the group was used for Diaghilev's performances of *Les Noces*. Kibalchich emigrated to America and occasionally saw Stravinsky there.

forceful, . . . the Russians are humanitarian *par excellence.* And he is right. In my estimation, you are an extraordinarily good man with unlimited generosity.

Because nothing moves me like goodness, and nothing is more rare these days, I extend my hand to you and say good-bye and *à bientôt.*

P.S. By accident I left two letters on your desk. . . . Please be so kind as to send them to me. . . .

CINGRIA TO STRAVINSKY   *[1919]*
                                                          [Postcard][5]

Morges

Dear Igor,

The little streams in the countryside around Geneva have a lot of charm. Here it is wilder and better. One would go mad having to live with these committeemen and see only them. Already the arteries of the Big Rhythm throb for you. Come! Come!

                                                          C. Cingria

I have also found a good little wine.

CINGRIA TO STRAVINSKY   *Paris*
                                                          [April 1919]

Morges

Happy Easter!

               Your friend who embraces you,   Charles-Albert Cingria

Give my best to Ramuz and [Henri] Bischoff.

CINGRIA TO STRAVINSKY   *Basel*
                                                          January 10, 1931

Dear friend,

Mermod delivered your note, but only after a long delay. He was in Arons, having a secret conference with the squirrels on the snow.

Thank you for your kind wishes; accept mine in return. This I say to you just as you say it to me, with the perfect verticality of shooting stars in July. These are the little things I do. I am obliged to express myself with reduced armaments. What did you expect?

I love Basel, one of those cities that say nothing at first. Then, little by little, one discovers, and it is crazy! . . .

I shake your hand affectionately.

                                                          Ch.-Albert Cingria

---

[5] Picture postcard of the battleship *Justice.*

CINGRIA TO STRAVINSKY   *[After December 17, 1931]*

Dear friend,

I am very happy to have attended this perfect performance of Ragtime and to have heard *Firebird* done as never before: under you, your will and presence obliging comprehension and purity.[6] Thank you for having thought of me. The misunderstood instructions at the box office deprived me of the Violin Concerto. I was able to enter [the Salle Pleyel] only at intermission. But I am deeply curious about your current phase. Will they not perhaps repeat the program shortly? If not in Paris, I will do my best to hear it elsewhere, because, thank God, I am moving around a bit. I may even pass through Grenoble.

I shake your hand with rapture.

C.-A. Cingria

[December 14, 1932]
CINGRIA TO STRAVINSKY   *[Postcard]*[7]

Only in the adagio,[8] the [illegible] which can be hurled at full speed from the dust of diamonds. It is Petrarch. You [deserve] this equivalence. Do another Petrarch, in the manner of Duo concertant. Perhaps this title would make them understand. How good it [is]; I am in it entirely. The trees are red on the snow.

Pétrarque[9] has appeared and will be sent to you from Lausanne.

Voreppe
December 28, 1932
STRAVINSKY TO CINGRIA   *[Draft of a letter]*

What a beautiful book, your *Pétrarque*. I took great joy in reading it. Not a moment's pause! I like that. Thank you, dear friend, for having sent it to me, and with such a flattering dedication. Thank you as well for the very kind words after my concert—I was deeply touched.

I send you many, many good wishes for the New Year. Please be assured of my firm admiration.

Your   IStr

---

[6] On December 17, Stravinsky conducted the Paris premiere of his Violin Concerto, with Dushkin and the Orchestre Symphonique de Paris. *Apollo, Ragtime,* and the *Firebird* Suite (original version) were also on the program.

[7] Picture postcard of the rapids at Fontaine de Vaucluse.

[8] Of the Duo concertant, which Cingria had heard at its first Paris performance, December 8, 1932.

[9] Published by the Cahiers Romands, Librairies Payot & Cie, 1932. Cingria inscribed Stravinsky's copy: "To the author of Duo concertant, which goes so well with Petrarch, from the [author] of this book, which [seeks to] justify nothing in the deafness of our era. C.-A. Cingria."

Your comment on lyricism (page 46) is perfectly on target, so much so that one is tempted to turn it into a generalization to be applied to all art forms:

> *Oui, l'art, . . . bien que divin parce que soumis aux cordes, doit être astu-cieux et difficile.*[10]

Magnificent, my dear!

CINGRIA TO STRAVINSKY   *[1933]*

Dear friend,

Thank you for the kind lines. I needed some consolation. No one has said anything about this book, which gave me a hard time last summer. . . . [In the room] next to mine was an Armenian who snored and did not pay. I was the only one in the whole house who did pay. Mermod requested the *Pages sur Rome,* and I was obliged to do it. These are sinister memories. Let us not discuss them. Let us talk about the present instead.

I am exactly in the center of France at a cafe [alongside] a canal . . . with billions of shiny leaves. The breezes serve only to circulate the heat. From time to time men arrive and cathedrals pass. This is the slow traffic from Arons to Lisbon. I have followed the flock, spending the long weekend, Saturday–Tuesday, in the country. This evening I will already be in Paris, the life-giving capital.

I was very happy to see Theodore again this winter, at Pecci-Blunt's, among other exhibition places, and I greatly admired his exhibition. . . .

I hope that your collaboration with Gide is fruitful. . . . While he is converting to communism, I am going in the opposite direction. Communism itself is not out of the question, but the ideology of Judeo-Germano-Slavic academicism disgusts me. . . .

With all my soul,   C.-A. Cingria

CINGRIA TO STRAVINSKY   *August 23, 1933*
                                                                  [Postcard]
Voreppe

Dear friend,

Thank you for your very nice card . . . greetings to everyone around you. If D [omenico] de' Paoli is in Voreppe, tell him that the article about his book (thus about you) did not appear in the *N[ouve]lle Revue Française.* This I just discovered, upon receipt of the issue. . . . Instead, there was a long review of Markevitch by [Boris de] Schloezer. Eventually, my article will be published— I have already been paid for it and corrected the proofs—but not immediately. I

---

[10] Stravinsky underlined this and the preceding paragraph in his copy.

proclaim that the most exciting and interesting period (in respect to innovation) is the present, thereby contradicting the din of Sauguet-Picabia-Noailles, who seek to limit the public's attention to old productions. I discuss [*Symphony of*] *Psalms* (citing the dedication to God, which must have angered them) and the Petrarchan style in your most recent adagios (Violin Concerto, etc.). Gide certainly has nothing to gain by chaining his review to the Noailles crew. We will see. In the meantime, not another word on the subject. . . .

A *bientôt,* perhaps. . . .

C.-A. Cingria

CINGRIA TO STRAVINSKY   *August 27, 1933*

Dear friend,

In your last letter, you claimed to be envious of me. You have reason, indeed, for this Tessin is poignant and mysterious and tender. And astute. And timid.

The cacti hum on the fissured rocks. The bells of five villages sound softly, blending together. This I prefer to Grenoble, despite the imperturbable mountains whose gray features are silhouetted on the sullen three-story houses and on the despair of a bachelor.

Let us not think about Paris. My last letter was meant to deceive you. The point was simply to produce. Which you do. Personally, I am defective in that I still allow stupidity to exasperate me.

Find enclosed one virgin [the Madonna del Sasso], of a violent sanctity and beauty, and two other little photographs: the descent from the cross, which is 200 meters from my house [in the Franciscan convent of the Madonna del Sasso], and . . . the Pedrazzini fountain, a modern monument that they commissioned from a sculptor (there should be more like him), inspired by a healthy pride to adorn their city—Locarno—with a perpetual memory of their name. These are the noble *tessinois,* grafted from Venezuelans, whose blondness and laughter spatter the old walls.

That is all. I have finished.

But no. Here is another photograph (but for Theodore): the work of the Duchesse de Zèle, with a commentary by a friend.

Auberjonois's letters give me great consolation. I shake your hand tenderly . . .

Charles-Albert Cingria

P.S. In contrast to what I told you, nothing of significance happened at the *N.R.F.* The writers simply took advantage of Paulhan's[11] vacation and put their own wishes into action. I am going to reassure Domenico de' Paoli. But to hell

---

[11] Jean Paulhan, editor of the *Nouvelle Revue Française,* was a friend of Stravinsky.

with all that. Many other things exist between heaven and earth, as the English say.

Di nuova,   C.-A.

Dear friend,

I chose an unfortunate word. Evidently there is no longer a "collaboration" or a possibility of a "collaboration" between Gide and yourself, no more than there was between the author of the libretto of *Fidelio* (quite amusing when read in four languages at once) and that of its music.

All you needed were syllables and someone to compile them. Gide, rather than Cocteau or someone else. What you create will involve only you and Persephone. Oh, but I am very eager to hear it.

That Paulhan writes nicely . . . is all too well known. The Noailles seek to impose their living Buddha on the universe at any cost. The completely enslaved Schloezer and the *N.R.F.* are the real authors of that filth I pointed out to you. Claudel—who is also in Isère—informed me: "I wrote to Paulhan, who replied with a very friendly letter, but Gide and Schloezer are fearfully hostile."

You see, everything is done by decree. Talent and the need for meaningfulness no longer count. The question is to please Gide, to please the Noailles gang, to listen respectfully to the wails of their living Buddha. We have to content ourselves with writing for God and the Philadelphia Orchestra.[12]

What things here, what beauty, spectacles, scents! Sunday I was in a kind of triangular Portuguese spot in the heart of a valley. . . . There were worldly ladies seated in lawn chairs; a bronze automobile, getting extremely hot in the sun, laughter, ice cream, exquisite *politesse.* I was shown a door with angels armed with long, thin plaster trumpets. Yes, architecture surrounded this stable of the ancient Lord's dogs. The moment any displeasure was detected, as a result of the appearance of vagabonds in the region, the doors were simply opened, and a dozen dogs sufficed.

After that, I went up high into the mountains with them in a Balilla (Fiat), along footpaths from Chamois, in search of other places of stone, other palaces with little chambers and tiny windows, passionately plain and regular, and respectful people, and beasts, and raspberries, coleoptera, snow. The next day the cows and goats descend and pass through the village. People jump to give them salt. This is an infernal scrimmage, a tradition, and [the animals] recognize it. You must approach judiciously, without fear, and train them. If you hesitate— as I did—they push you and pursue you all the way to the staircases.

---

[12] The *Symphony of Psalms* had been "composed for the glory of God and dedicated to the Boston Symphony Orchestra."

But I have forgotten the crucial matter: that dreadful cold which has you strapped to the bed. I hope it has passed. I have done plenty of groaning now. I have a kind of tonsilitis in two spots, which will undoubtedly spread to the ears and perhaps to the brain. I am waiting for this to go away. I may have had too much sun; it did not come from the cold.

Ramuz should be advised to read Claudel's stunningly beautiful pamphlet, *Sur la présence de Dieu. . . .*

Good-bye. See you soon, perhaps, if I go through the Savoie and France. But I know nothing. Never have I been such a pawn in the hands of circumstance as this year. It is as though I were [in] an icon, with the pavilions and apple trees under the white sword. . . .

Your very affectionate   C.-A. Cingria

CINGRIA TO STRAVINSKY   *[April 30, 1934]*

Dear friend,

The flu has had a savage grip on me for five days now, and I cannot go on. But I had someone fetch me a copy of *Excelsior,* so I saw the way the little text we compiled together was used. The company in which you appear was an unpleasant surprise[13] and could not have been anticipated. Oh well, too bad and so much the better. What does Ansermet think?

I appealed to the *Nouvelle Revue Française,* but in vain. Not a centimeter of space left, and furthermore the issue appears tomorrow morning. I shall attempt to publish the review I had intended for [the *N.R.F.*] in one of the daily papers.

I hope everything goes well tonight.[14] I will attend Wednesday or the last night. I think I will have recovered by then. In the meantime, I send you this note.

Very affectionately,   C.-A. Cingria

CINGRIA TO STRAVINSKY   *[May 1935]*

Dear friend,

In regard to what we discussed, I obtained the sum of 5,000 [francs], but we will have to wait at least ten days for a definitive reply and to settle the details.

I wanted to telephone you, but I guess you are in Sancellemoz. So, until your return.

---

[13] Articles by Arthur Honegger, Jacques Ibert, and Florent Schmitt were printed on the same page.

[14] The premiere of *Perséphone,* at the Paris Opéra.

I hope that you are well. I am breathing—I have slightly less work—and Provence and the beautiful rhythms and rhymes resume.

A bientôt. I shake your hand affectionately.

C.-A. Cingria

CINGRIA TO STRAVINSKY

Paris

Arcueil-Cachan
June 3, 1935
[Postcard] [15]

Dear friend,

I have done an article of sorts for the *N.R.F.* anthology (June 1 issue). [16] My allusion to Ramuz's "little Latinity" is in response to an abuse of the same order that I suffered at his hands. Opportunities for revenge must never be missed. . . .

Perséphone in Rome? [17] The choruses? Was the performance good, if not better?

I call this the most dislocated landscape on earth.

CINGRIA TO STRAVINSKY

Dear friend,

Café des Platanes
Vétraz-Monthoux
Haute-Savoie
June 17, 1935

I myself am in the Haute-Savoie. What a pity that I do not know how to keep track of you! Thanks for your charming note. I attempted to teach them a lesson with that *[N.R.F.]* article, they who consistently display meager virtuosity. But when will we see each other again? At Ramuz's? Hmm . . . I do not have what could be called wonderful memories [of him]. True, this is my fault. . . . But I was overjoyed to see the Chekovs [18] (Loiret) again. The day of my departure I ran into all of them on the Boulogne train. . . . [We] reminisced about very old things: M. Godet, Dr. Weber, route de Chêne. [19] I like it here. I am in a combination café–telephone booth–*pension,* under five plane trees. Tonight I plan to help a neighbor anesthetize the bees, and then we play with them, like [toy] soldiers. Gide was disgraceful; perhaps you heard? He treated me condescendingly, as though shocked that in a Review belonging to him—he inserts

---

[15] Picture postcard of a retirement home, Cousin de Méricourt, in Cachan, with a Roman aqueduct in the background.

[16] A review of *Chroniques de ma vie.*

[17] On May 29, 1935, in Rome, Stravinsky had conducted Debussy's *Nuages* and *Fêtes,* Dukas's *Sorcerer's Apprentice,* a suite from *Petrushka,* and the 1919 *Firebird* Suite at the Augusteo (*Perséphone* was canceled because Ida Rubinstein was ill). On the 27th Stravinsky attended a concert at the Sala Borromini, and on the 30th he was received by Mussolini at the Palazzo Venezia.

[18] Stravinsky was the godfather of Alexis Chekov.

[19] The street on which Auberjonois lived.

capital letters—someone would dare to express opinions that are not [Gide's] . I have not yet answered him directly, but that will not take long. All best wishes and see you soon, God willing.

C.-A. Cingria

CINGRIA TO STRAVINSKY

Paris

St.-Jean-de-Chevelu
Haute-Savoie
[1935]
[Postcard]

Dear friend,

I had told you I was not going anywhere, but suddenly some money arrived, and I had to leave. Stage One: St.-Jean-de-Chevelu, near Culoz, in a château where I have a room like the Place de la Concorde, whose armchairs have absorbed the impressions of some very exalted individuals. . . . And street corners like [the] one [pictured here]. If Hayger replies, I gave my concierge an address in the Savoie. All best to you.

Sincerely,   Cingria.

I will go by Rey Millet's house within the next few days.

CINGRIA TO STRAVINSKY

Dear friend,

Rustic Hôtel
Guillard
Haute-Savoie
August 6, 1935

Please excuse me for not having shown the slightest sign of life in such a long time. I think of you often. Alexandre[20] sends his regards. I am staying along the Arne, half in Geneva (a charred, deserted city). I will be here until the beginning of winter. Auberjonois ventured into my territory yesterday, magnificently escorted.

See you soon, God willing. Best regards to those around you.

Charles-Albert Cingria

---

[20] Cingria's brother Alexandre (1879–1945) was also a friend of Stravinsky. Two early notes from Alexandre survive in the composer's archives, one conveying best wishes for the New Year (December 30, 1918), and the other for Easter (April 20, 1919). Twenty years later, upon the death of Stravinsky's wife, Alexandre expressed his sympathy in a letter: "Dear friend, This second loss, of which Borg informed me, has caused me great sorrow. I remember the kindness that you and your wife showed me when I underwent a similar trial many years ago. The distance that separates us today prevents me from surrounding you with my friendship, as you did for me when my wife died. [But] I surround you with my thoughts and shake your hand firmly. Alexandre Cingria." (March 20, 1939)

CINGRIA TO STRAVINSKY   *December 27, 1935*
                                                                    [Postcard]

Paris

Dear friend,

I have underlined all of the important passages [of the second volume of *Chroniques de ma vie*]. I plan to review it, but for February. In any case, I will be the first to write about it. This second volume was essential. The Concerto was really an event for me the other night, increased by my joy at seeing you again. Thanks doubly for having invited me. I was and am going through a bad period. It will pass. Working like mad. I hope that you will have good news from Passy [and] Chamonix. Best to Theodore, Milenka, Nini, and Lyudmila Mandelstamm. I will telephone to arrange a meeting, if you have time. And Merry Christmas.

                                                            C.-A. Cingria

CINGRIA TO STRAVINSKY   *Sunday*
                                                                  11 o'clock
Dear friend,   *[January 25, 1936]*

I did not sleep all night, and by the time I pulled myself together this morning it was too late to join you at the radio. I hope that you will pardon me. Tonight I will go to see them on my own, and tomorrow or the day after I will telephone you to find out what has been decided (Luxembourg and Paris).

I have not forgotten that you leave for Echarvines on the 26th. The Glinka was good. We should organize some concerts as propaganda for this music, which is much more Russian than that of those intent on [proving their Russianness]. Received proofs of my notice (*N.R.F.*) concerning your book. . . .

                                    Best wishes to all,   C.-A. Cingria

CINGRIA TO STRAVINSKY   *[April 10, 1936]*

Dear friend,

You leave tonight: *bon voyage!* We did not manage to see each other; it was impossible. Too much work, and on top of that I am not well. But I will see you soon, for at our age one neither leaves nor returns: one oscillates and [lives vicariously] on the whole earth. I must go to Switzerland for a while, then to Portugal (then to the Azores). I will find you again in the great heat of Corpus Christi, when the immense tapestries of garnet-colored velvet with white [bees?] will be displayed at the Madeleine . . . and when a dense peace pervades Paris. Thank you for those fortifying evenings, Glinka, and all you explained about yourself. I hope that Masson[21] will outdo himself. . . . Saturday at

---

[21] Pierre Masson, music critic.

5:00 p.m. you will be sailing, while in the cathedrals, surrounded by cacti and tufa, and aflame with prophecies, there will be singing. Here is Baruch: *"Les enfants d'Agar qui recherchent cette prudence qui n'est que de la terre, les négociateurs de Mertha et de Thêman, ces littérateurs et inventeurs de prudence et d'intelligence qui ont ignoré la voie de la sagesse ('fabulatores et exquisitores prudentiae et intelligentiae')...."*

A bientôt . . . bon voyage to you and to Mika.[22]

Ch.-A. Cingria

Have Mika send me a letter from the funicular in Rio.

CINGRIA TO STRAVINSKY   *July 5, 1937*

Dear friend,

Here it is,[23] though extremely late. And I fear that these little verses may be too long. . . . I will not arrive until August 2 or 3, thanks to complications, but also

---

[22] Cingria had thought that Stravinsky's elder daughter was accompanying her father to Brazil.

[23] When invited to compose a short piece for C.-F. Ramuz's sixtieth birthday (September 24, 1938), Stravinsky asked Cingria to provide verses suitable for music. The draft he submitted to the composer contains three additional stanzas but otherwise differs only slightly from the published version. From Cingria's forty lines, Stravinsky chose three quatrains to be sung as refrains, thereby dividing and relieving the recitation of the spoken rhymes. The structural principle of the unaccompanied melody is the same as that in *The Five Fingers,* but in this case Stravinsky uses eight pitches within the range of an octave. Melodic patterns are repeated from one stanza to another, with variations in rhythm, melodic succession, and inversion of interval direction. Furthermore, each stanza begins with close intervals and gradually, if inconsistently, moves toward wider ones. The *Petit Ramusianum harmonique,* though as economical as possible, is subtly formed. The composer's pencil sketch differs from the published score only in that the former is measured in three-fours and four-fours, the latter in three-fours and two-fours, and, in the published score, each stanza is typeset in four lines.

After some correspondence with the Neuchâtel publisher Richard Heyd in September 1937, Stravinsky completed the tiny composition in Paris on October 11, almost a year before Ramuz's birthday. When the Stravinskys returned to the Château de Monthoux in the summer of 1938, Heyd called on the composer, requesting his permission to include the musical greeting in *Hommage à Ramuz,* a garland of testimonials by Claudel, Cocteau, Maritain, Valéry, Thomas Mann, Stefan Zweig, and others. Heyd explained that the authors would not be compensated, because the edition, to be published by the Librairie Centrale et Universitaire, V. Porchet et Cie, Lausanne, was limited to eight hundred copies. He promised Stravinsky that his singing telegram would be given first place in the volume.

On August 8, Porchet sent a letter of agreement to Stravinsky, defining his role as that of an unpaid collaborator and donor of his manuscript, and stating that the costs of photographic reproduction of the music, in facsimile, would be assumed by the pub-

because Paris is not at all disagreeable in this tolerable heat. I hope that you are in good health. Best wishes to all. . . .

PETIT RAMUSIANUM HARMONIQUE

—Bonjour monsieur Ramuz.
—Entrez donc, mais entrez.
—Nous sommes tous accourus
  Petits et grands
  Vous dire en termes émus
  Not' compliment.
—Entrez donc, mais entrez.

Ce q'vous avez écrit sur l'eau,
  Le ciel,
  La faux,
  Le sel,
  La vigne,
Décèle un talent sublime;
  Et même sans rime,
  Avez su dire des mots
Eprouvés à la lime.

Les Fleuves de Provence:
Rhône, Garonne, Durance.
Les rivières de France
Ont de vous souvenance.

Vous êtes féroce en
  Dialectique
  Scolastique

---

lisher. The composer replied angrily, after obtaining Cingria's signature in support of his own, that the contributions were the property of the authors, that the copyright for the music belonged to him, that its use, gratis, was limited, and that the publication costs did not concern him (letter of August 11, 1938). Heyd wrote back on August 23: "With regard to the letter that you wrote to M. Porchet, the matter is, quite simply, a misunderstanding, the fault of editorial gibberish. Also, certain people have circulated a rumor to the effect that I will be making a profit from this edition. . . . It must be understood, however, that the collaborators want to make gifts of their contributions yet retain the copyrights in the event of future publication. . . . For your protection, and that of M. Cingria, I have asked M. Porchet for a written confirmation of this. . . . Confidentially, the publisher will not even cover his costs until the six hundred and fiftieth copy has been sold. . . ." H.-L. Mermod invited Stravinsky to a lunch for Ramuz at the Pavillon, Lavaux, on September 25, 1938, but the composer did not accept, because Ansermet was certain to be present. Cingria did attend. (See his letter of October 24, 1938.)

Infatigable en diagnostique
Pulvérisateur
Epouvantable, un gnostique
Et en moustiques.

Monsieur Auberjonois
Plein de meutes aux abois
Du fond de son carquois
Tire le pinceau adroit
De l'histoire du soldat

La blonde rose enfant
En turban vert et blanc
Dit
Merci
Pour tant ce que vous avez fait pour
Le pays.

Adieu monsieur Ramuz
Il est fini vot' compliment;
Nous vous sommes tous reconnaissants
De nous avoir si bien reçus.

—Voulez-vous boire que'q' chose?
—Mais oui, mais certain'ment.
—Entrez dans ce pressoir grandiose.

STRAVINSKY TO CINGRIA   *Château de Monthoux*
                                          July 28, 1937

My dear Charles-Albert,

Thank you for the precious parcel and for your kind lines. I am in a hurry to see you, not only in order to compliment you on the verses, but to break open a bottle of Côtes du Rhône, particularly pleasing in these beautiful surroundings. Things here are not good, unfortunately. My wife's lungs are worse again. I am worried. . . .

    I embrace you.

                              Your   I. Stravinsky

CINGRIA TO STRAVINSKY   *[March 4, 1938]*

Dear friend,

Such a triumph is . . . overwhelming![24] I embrace you and shake your hand affectionately.

---

[24] Stravinsky had conducted *Jeu de cartes* and *Symphony of Psalms* in a radio broadcast with the Orchestre National at the Salle Gaveau. The first half of the program,

Pardon me for having disappeared. I feared that I would never be able to return; one must be very careful, for the springtime tests us. . . . *A bientôt*, and pay no attention to the critics. Laudatory or not, reviews, after an evening like this, can only be idiotic. The Ravel at least had the honor of serving to set you off. You represent sane music, and the public understands, or seems to understand.

A bientôt and thank you. I shake your hand.

C.-A. Cingria.

CINGRIA TO STRAVINSKY   *[August 15, 1938]*

Dear friend,

How nice of you to have thought of me. Yesterday I would have liked to come to the rehearsal;[25] to watch all of the phases in a fine-tuning is interesting and leads to a good understanding. But I had already left to take a plunge in the Oïse, a desperate step . . . prompted by a desire to find again this element deprived of which I am devastated. But here I am, back home. So, until tomorrow. Although lately I have not telephoned with much frequency, I was anxious about Milene's health, and glad to see Nini, who reassured me. Thus I have been relieved of a great worry about you, and I hope that from here on in the best will clearly emerge.

I await tomorrow feverishly. I am intrigued by the beautiful arrangement of the program. The audience must be guided and gratified. . . .

Good-bye. Thank you again. Until tomorrow, my respects to [you and] yours.

C.-A. Cingria

CINGRIA TO STRAVINSKY   *October 24, 1938*

Dear friend,

I saw many people at [Ramuz's] sixtieth-birthday dinner, . . . but Auberjonois did not attend: he stayed in bed. Ansermet was gossiping as never before, although very cautiously in my presence. The homage volume did not materialize, then; you must have received it only recently. What an idea to have put that hand *"J'exprime"* on the cover![26] And then Cézanne[27] . . . As for our contribution: no facsimile, in spite of our request. I was happy to find your note-design just as you played it for me before leaving—a good lesson in syllabification for

---

conducted by D.-E. Inghelbrecht, was devoted to Ravel: *Rapsodie espagnole*, Introduction and Allegro for Harp, and *Daphnis et Chloé*.

[25] A radio performance of *Le Sacre du printemps* conducted by Manuel Rosenthal.

[26] A picture of a hand squeezing a cluster of grapes, with the caption, "I express!"

[27] An essay by Ramuz. Stravinsky did not even cut these pages in his copy of the book.

Buenos Aires. Adrien Bovy, page 69, is excellent, and though the [portrait of Ramuz by] Alexandre [Blanchet] is a little patriarchal, the image is fresh and solid.

Did you see the good, short article about you by Muller in the *Cahiers du Sud,* Marseille, the issue before last (August–September)? If not, I will bring it to you. Everything that comes out of Marseille is sympathetic . . . and very good. . . .

It was thrilling to hear Mika's voice over the telephone yesterday. . . . I learned with sorrow that you have had much anxiety,[28] but that your mother is now completely recovered. . . . I want to see you and talk to you before you leave for Transylvania.[29] A *bientôt* . . . until one of these evenings. . . .

CINGRIA TO STRAVINSKY   *[December 1938]*

Dear friend,

You are often in my thoughts, and I wonder how you are. Your tribulations trouble me deeply and accompany me in my own worries in these sad, cold days before Christmas. Of course work is one escape—indeed, there is nothing but work. I pity those who do not have this refuge.

The Ocampo affair[30] is going nowhere, and after the very cutting remark she made yesterday, I have lost my enthusiasm for South America. What idiotic cliques must exist down there! And what an entourage she has in Paris! How insane that she takes her opinions from such people! Someone should have guided her, but it is too late [now]. . . . Sad, for she is a good woman at heart. She has [Suvchinsky's] manuscript and has paid for it in part—which is a good point. Yesterday she informed me that while you are justified in detesting Debussy and Ravel, I do not have the right to do so, and that I am not competent to express myself on a subject of this nature. . . . I think I was wrong to have been so friendly at the beginning, and perhaps I made the additional mistake of not being esteemed in official literary circles. . . . (Who knows—I may even have been wrong not to [reprimand] her sufficiently. She says to herself: So, finally, who is this boy and what right has he to toss out assertions?) She asked me to write an article about [G. K.] Chesterton. The people she sees draw exactly the opposite conclusions.

---

[28] On October 3, Stravinsky wrote to W. Strecker: "Forgive my silence. My wife and my daughter Mika are both in bed, and I am taking care of them. My wife has had pneumonia for two weeks, and Mika is undergoing a crisis right now. My life this year is enough to drive anyone crazy!"

[29] I.e., some remote place.

[30] Victoria Ocampo, C.-A. Cingria, Roland-Manuel, and Stravinsky had dined at Vera Sudeikina's Paris apartment on November 8.

CINGRIA TO STRAVINSKY   *Bern*
                                                January 5, 1939

Paris

Dear friend,

I hope that you will not already have left Turin.[31] It is so cold in Italy and so hideous everywhere. The day that I left, I received a very kind note from Suvchinsky inviting me for dinner. I answered from the Lyon railroad station, in time, I hope. His article, which I would like to see, is probably very well documented. Mine will appear without much delay, I hope, and without Sch [loezer]'s having been informed in any capacity other than that of the ordinary *N.R.F.* reader. I think [the *N.R.F.*]—because of Ocampo—has a desire to improve itself, which is always possible. I believe that Auberjonois is in Paris. I am certain that you have fondness for the creature, as I am that you would prevent him from lacerating me. I do not know what is wrong with him. I plan to give him a good lashing myself, but not immediately. And sanity, my dear, and courage after the terrible trial [of Mika's death]. . . . I hope all is well. I think often of you, of her, of all of you, with all my heart.

Bern is a little lugubrious after the thaw (a filthy, obstinate beast with its damp feet on the arcades) but . . . the nights are full of ferocious bears in armor. Best wishes for Russian Christmas and the New Year.

Yours with all my heart,   Cingria

CINGRIA TO STRAVINSKY   *Paris*
                                                April 12, 1939

Sancellemoz

Dear friend, and disputant of the century,

How gratifying it is to find what one is searching for! In the Vulgate, I, 20: *"Ubi sapiens? ubi scriba? ubi conquisitor hujus saeculi?"* He who has never had any ambition other than to conquer the century. The man of the pen *par excellence*. But Saint Paul wrote that in Greek, and I would like to have the Greek. Where? Do research? Never. The mere thought of a [public] library gives me a headache. The pretty house in the Norman bourgeois style is in Lisieux: that of Saint Teresa's parents. I hope that you are better.

All best to you,   C.-A. Cingria

---

[31] After conducting in Rome on November 27, Stravinsky was to give a concert in Turin, but upon arrival at the Turin railroad station he telephoned Paris, learned of his daughter's death, canceled the concert, and returned immediately to France. He made up the Turin concert on December 29.

CINGRIA TO STRAVINSKY

59, *rue Bonaparte*
Paris
[Early May 1939]
[Postcard] [32]

Sancellemoz

Dear friend,

Places like this are lovely. Excavations probably; but of Hellenism, at any rate, . . . on a beautiful blue terrain. . . . Nothing eventful here. I hasten to leave, but I fear the cold. And your health? Much better, I have been told. So patience and courage! As for Stravinsky and Roland-Manuel, the articles were printed.

Best to everyone. I look forward to hearing the Turin radio broadcast.[33]

With all my heart,   C.-A. Cingria

CINGRIA TO STRAVINSKY   *[May 1939]*

Dear friend,

The attached letter has been left undelivered for a month. . . . I hope that you were happy with the performers and the audiences in Florence. Thank you for the letter in which [Bruno?] Barilli's name appears like letters in a procession. He is one creature for whom I have great fondness. We heard Sauguet's opera[34] with Nini and Suvchinsky. The orchestration is remarkable, and consistent from beginning to end, with no weak moments, no lack of imagination, as is the case with [his] other works. Then I reread *Chartreuse.* Of course there is no connection [with the opera], but [Stendhal] is magnificent. After this I will no longer be able to appreciate literature that lacks *éclat* (as one thinks of a dog or horse having *éclat*). The French are lucky just to have *this one author.* I never liked him before. How one changes!

I hope that your health is stable and good, always better. Best to Milene, Denise, and Theodore. I shake your hand affectionately. See you soon, perhaps.

C.-A. Cingria

CINGRIA TO STRAVINSKY   *[June 1939]*

Dear friend,

Thank you for your last postcard. Suvchinsky visited me, and through him I heard the sad news of the passing of your dear, worthy, valiant, and saintly mother. I pray for her and sympathize deeply.

---

[32] Picture postcard of a monument in the Chersonesus, Taurica, Crimea.

[33] Stravinsky conducted in Milan on May 12 and in Florence on the 16th.

[34] *La Chartreuse de Parme.*

May God improve your health. Good care and the climate will help you toward that end.

Here it is terrible, the struggle against the elements and fools. I hope that the *Revue Musicale* will appear shortly, as well as my article about pure music in the *N.R.F.*

See you soon, I hope. Best to Theodore, Denise, and dear Milene. Love to the Savoie.

Alexandre is here. He is a great consolation through all of these traumas. The Swiss do not have even an embryo of that organ called the heart. They think that playing the villain takes care of everything.

I shake your hand and embrace you.

C.-A. Cingria

CINGRIA TO STRAVINSKY

Paris
May 30, 1947

1260 North Wetherly Drive
Hollywood

Dear friend,

Hideous paper, but hello!

I think of you continually. I have so many things to tell you and don't know where to begin, and so I shall not say anything. Above all, I want you to know how much I think of you, and with constant affection; a thousand times I have thought of writing and have not done so until now.

But now it is urgent. Alexandre is gone, Ramuz is gone. We no longer have anyone with whom to converse—it is necessary to converse in this world, to have testimony to thought—and here before us the earth is opening up, and those on whom we were counting . . . slip away. Only the stars remain in these magnificent nights . . . and then letters that communicate only half of what we wish to say.

I am still at 59, rue Bonaparte. Every day I resuscitate myself and contemplate the fullness of my agenda: fifty things to do at once. Writing, writing, writing, writing, and not as I would like it, at full speed. And it is so dreadful that imagination enters the battle, . . . making me a ferryman, for example, on a powerful river in India, in order to see many people and no longer to know anyone.

Dear Nini told me that you read the article about Auberjonois in *Formes et Couleurs*. This made me happy, because writing it gave me great joy. Soon I will take steps to have it sent to you. Do not doubt me; I have my heart set on this. What I write is for you and for a very few other people, and soon the language and languages will change, and we do not know what we will become, but the heart will remain, and with an access—I hope, I believe—of the excellent things we have formulated (especially you!), and that the abstraction made in all vanity will not be destroyed. That will continue for a long time, like the signs of the zodiac: the Chais [?], Arcturus [Sobinsky's?], shield, etc.

The local rags printed disastrous reviews. I would have liked to reply to them, but one cannot repeat the same thing a hundred thousand times.

Good-bye. I will write to you again.

I embrace you,   Charles-Albert Cingria

CINGRIA TO STRAVINSKY   *[July 12, 1947]*

Dear Igor—the only one in our time in this world.[35]

I don't think you have this book. When it appears again—pretty soon—I will call it *Le Vizir de verre*. That's better. And then I will also send you the book you requested: *Pages sur Rome* (but since it is from Gallimard, the paper is lousy and the printing miserable).

A bientôt. Many possibilities of meeting again present themselves at the crossroads of your victory.

Tutto suo,   C.-A. Cingria

CINGRIA TO STRAVINSKY   *Geneva**
                                                        December 12, 1947

Dear, dear! . . .

I received your last letter, full of important points essential to a healthy understanding of the world, especially that of the aversion to showcase existentialism and the riffraff who mouth it.

I am sending you my most recent work, *La Reine Berthe et sa famille,* with a dedication. . . . Auberjonois wrote to say that he is enchanted by the illustrations. (He just had all of his teeth extracted, to replace them with an apparatus of which we should [all] avail ourselves from a young age.) In fact, I must confess that I have virtually written the book around them. Charlemagne in particular, and the glorious father of Pépin [*sic*]—whom the Venetians ignored—and Constantine VII Porphyrogenite, who was a verbose writer, a great chatterbox of the pen, precisely at the time of Queen Berthe (Verte). . . .

The Kyrie and Gloria of your Mass are finished, it seems. I await their performance with great impatience,[36] as well as their continuation: the Sanctus and the Agnus. This will be a great European and transatlantic event.

---

[35] This is the dedication in Cingria's *Le Bey de Pergame,* published by Mermod in 1947.
[36] These two parts of the Mass were first performed in February 1947 at Sanders Theatre, Cambridge, Massachusetts, with Irving Fine conducting a chorus and two pianos.

In great affection I shake your hand. . . . Let us remember and pray inces-
santly for Alexandre and Ramuz.

C.-A. Cingria

* But in three, four, five, six days—alas! how I love Switzerland— [I return to]
59, rue Bonaparte, VI.

CINGRIA TO STRAVINSKY   *Aix-en-Provence*
                                                    [September 15, 1948]

Dear Igor,

Please forward this letter to Françoise.[37] I am in Aix and think of you often. No
news from the civilized world anymore. Every time I risk walking past the Café
des Deux Garçons, I cross the street . . . to avoid the Oxford dilettante and the
slender Parisian. But the moon is beautiful when it comes up, like tonight,
crackling white on the rooftops.

What will happen? What will become of us? I dare not think about this.
Our dearest ones are dead. I ponder it at night while gathering my thoughts. If I
read one author, it is Saint Paul. It is necessary to have lived a lot to approach
such mastery.

Until someday, I hope. I have heard excellent things about you from those
who have seen you.

Very affectionately,   C.-A. Cingria

P.S. If you write back, do so within a month, at the old address: 59, rue Bonaparte, Paris.

Saw the Botkins (Chekov), who are doing very well. Had news from Auberjonois. He is desolate at having lost his apartment on Grand Chêne and cannot
get used to the house that he had built in Pully. But he is . . . behaving himself.
We pray for Alexandre and Ramuz. Ansermet is the most deceitful creature on
earth.

Will we have war? I do not think so.

Di nuovo,   C.-A. Cingria

CINGRIA TO STRAVINSKY   *Albergo Unione*
                                                            via Guidone
                                                             Ravenna
Dear friend,   *September 16, 1951*

What a great joy it was for me to hear the *Carriera d'un libertino*[38] and how
marvelous to recapture you—to see you and converse; alas, just for an instant—to find you agile and increased tenfold, textual nonetheless. It would

---

[37] Soulima Stravinsky's wife, living in Hollywood near Stravinsky at the time.

[38] *The Rake's Progress.* Cingria had attended the premiere in Venice on September 11.

have been nice to stir up the past a bit: that will happen, but not until you come to Switzerland. I was reluctant to bother you, even by telephone (especially by telephone). And then I could not tolerate Venice any longer: that too-slow vaporetto, that uncertainty in the streets, the indiscretion (a real torture) of the people with whom I was lodging, who made fun of me, of my hat, and rummaged through everything in my absence, etc. I soon left for Ravenna, where I expected to find water, air, and basilicas in divine grass. Nothing [of the sort], but still it is marvelous; though noisy and overpopulated, the mosaics, the towers, the round bell towers, and the soldiers are no disappointment; Eridan[us] and the sea, tepid, fine, and gray. And the wine! And the faces!

A bientôt. . . .   C.-A. Cingria

P.S. Since you initiated me, I have had only Cinar (at cocktail hour).[39] This morning I plucked a laurel branch—for sauces—to the [delight] of Galla Placidia.

CINGRIA TO STRAVINSKY   *Paris*
                                                              [May 1952]
Dear Igor,

Thank you for those wonderful performances, and for having facilitated my access to you. . . . Now every note of *Oedipus* is secured in my ear with the correct timing—the formidable incision—and sonority. And that I shall carry with me for weeks and months. When great music haunts me, I become like Aristotle's savage god—*aut fera aut deus*. Ah yes, but the orchestra and timbres are essential. A piano reduction barely serves as a reminder. The inventiveness you lavished, which gave pure satisfaction, is mad: yes, your poise was absolute and infallible at that time, and though I cannot say more, it is at least as much so now. . . . The audience-Cocteau incident should not be magnified. Nothing went better than that Hellenist conception; the great Cretan in the hall simply demonstrated that the bandwagoners of yesteryear still exist. They wanted repertory Hellenism or German Hellenism. Or Duncan perhaps. I understand that you were overwhelmed by sorrow and had to leave the hall.[40] But I saw you finally, and, so much the better, in Venice. Thank you. Several articles will follow: I will send you copies.

Your very affectionate   C.-A. Cingria

Give my regards and warmest sympathy to Jean; I will write to him.

---

[39] Stravinsky's doctors in Naples and Milan had obliged him to forgo Scotch whiskey before dinner and to drink Cinar, a beverage made from artichokes, supposedly a tonic for the liver.

[40] No. When a part of the audience booed Cocteau—Hans Rosbaud was conducting and Cocteau narrating—Stravinsky, sitting next to the present writer in a box, said, "I'm going to the hotel and wait there; I know my way out of this theatre" (Théâtre des Champs-Elysées). He was not upset, and not greatly surprised.

CINGRIA TO STRAVINSKY

Paris
[May 27, 1952]
[Postcard]

Palace Hôtel
Brussels

Charles-Albert congratulates himself on having been so lucky in the last few minutes before the train pulled out.[41] Very fast, to listen to the Symphony in C . . . poetry. *La musica è poesia pur se stesso,* as Orazio Vecchi says. The Oxford lecture is superb.

Toto carde et animo,   C.-A.

---

[41] Cingria came to the Gare du Nord to see the Stravinskys and the present writer before they left for a tour in Belgium and Holland.

LETTERS FROM

1931 ~ 1933

JACQUES HANDSCHIN

JACQUES HANDSCHIN TO STRAVINSKY[1]

18 Schlüsselgasse
Zürich
February 20, 1931

La Vironnière
Voreppe[2]

Dear Igor Fyodorovich,

For a long time I could not say for certain whether or not I would be able to go to Paris on the 23rd;[3] I waited and waited, and now it turns out that, after all, I cannot come. I have a long article to rewrite before the 26th; also, I must give a decision here on a dissertation. Then too, I am obliged to attend an "important funeral" on the 23rd. And there is still another little matter to consider; but

---

[1] Jacques Handschin (1886–1955), musicologist and organist, was the only Russian contemporary and friend of Stravinsky to have exerted an influence on him in later life. In the early 1930s, Handschin stimulated the composer's growing interest in medieval music, and Stravinsky read his writings on the schools of Saint Martial and Notre Dame, early English polyphony, Byzantine music, and Bach.

The two musicians first met in St. Petersburg in 1909; one of Handschin's letters reflects this long-standing relationship and also provides the only support so far to appear in print for the belief that, before the Russian Revolution, Stravinsky may have been "leftist"-minded. Handschin also seems to have been the only friend of Stravinsky to have brought to his attention a question of mistranslation in the Vulgate text used in the *Symphony of Psalms*.

That Stravinsky gave Handschin suggestions for his booklet *Igor Stravinsky: Versuch einer Einführung* (Zürich, 1933) is remarkable because of the emphasis that this work places on the Stravinsky-Schoenberg polarity, and because of the inclusion of the text of Schoenberg's verse satire *Der kleine Modernsky*. But, ignoring this, Stravinsky even sent his old friend a page of the full-score manuscript of the *Psalms* symphony.

The present writer has not succeeded in tracing Stravinsky's side of the correspondence. Nor is Handschin's side complete as printed here, communications dated September 22, 1930, September 25, 1930, and December 19, 1932, having been omitted owing to their illegibility. But perhaps the publication of this small selection of even one side of the correspondence will encourage scholars to renew the search.

[2] All of the letters in this chapter were sent from Handschin's Zürich address to Stravinsky in Voreppe. At the time of these letters, Handschin was a professor at Basel University and organist at St. Peter's in Zürich.

[3] To hear the composer conduct his *Symphony of Psalms*.

enough of this. So, dear Igor Fyodorovich, my plans have been thwarted, and I will not be hearing your *Symphony of Psalms* this time. I am certain that it would have filled me with the same joy and excitement as did the two piano concertos and the Sonata. (I will not mention the last two ballets, since joy predominated over excitement in them.) I will be thinking of you on that evening and wishing you success, but more in the sense that the Parisian public, which I happen to respect, will understand that this is really a serious and important work. I remember a composition that was somewhat similar to your trilogy,[4] Roger-Ducasse's three motets (with organ), programmed by Siloti (of course) in St. Petersburg. The music consisted of echoes of soft impressionism, for which reason I think that this composer is silent now: the genre, though pleasant enough, is no longer contemporary. And then, to be sure, his talent itself was not great.

I often think back on our exchanges of ideas. Is it not true that the reason why you are more *rightist* now than I am is that in the early years you were more *leftist?* One thing is certain: in some questions it is impossible to be too conservative. And as for current politics, I am inclined to leave things up to the professionals.

Once, while I was employed as a translator, I had the opportunity to work on an article by Glebov [Boris Asafiev] on Muss[orgsky] (*Die Musik, XXI*), an article that he gave to me in the form of a rough draft! I hope to have the opportunity to do the same with his book on you—which would have to be updated to include your latest compositions. That would be very interesting. It is true that at the moment I am fully occupied with another task. And my dilemma is always the same: on the one side I am an axe, clearing the way for science (impersonally, but with enthusiasm!), and on the other side I get caught up in these matters of the heart and the imagination—precisely for that reason, of course.

Regards to Ekaterina Gavrilovna, to your daughter, and to Arthur [Lourié], from Elena and me, and, most important, to you, from

> your devoted   J. Handschin

HANDSCHIN TO STRAVINSKY   *November 20, 1932*

Dear Igor Fyodorovich,

Would you be good enough to send me—which is to say, lend me—a picture of yourself and a page from the *Psalms* score before the end of November, or at least let me know where to write in order to obtain them?[5] I have been commissioned to put together a booklet about you. The size of the pages is quite large,

---

[4] The three Psalms that Stravinsky set, numbers 38, 39, and 150.
[5] Stravinsky sent a photograph by Lipnitzki and the next-to-last page of the second movement.

but there are not many of them. Also, please let me know how you are doing and when you think you might come to Switzerland again.

I thought the Zürich performance of your *Psalms* much too bland. Besides, the conductor made almost no pause between sections, as if he were afraid that they were unable to stand by themselves. Sacher[6] is preparing *Les Noces* and the *Psalms.* As is the custom in Basel (one of which I do not approve), I have received an invitation to read a more or less "prepared" lecture, and I have consented if only to prevent any of their "cripples" from getting the chance.

It is possible that I will move to Basel in the spring to take the place of the organist there, but the university would have to reimburse me. Thanks to a certain power in the Department of Philosophy here, a professor of philosophy, we will probably not be able to establish a music department at the university during his lifetime. Are you pleased with your move to Grenoble? How is your health and that of Ekaterina Gerasimovna [*sic*]? Warm regards to you from

your devoted   J. Handschin

HANDSCHIN TO STRAVINSKY   *[November]* 1932

Dear Igor Fyodorovich,

Thank you! I will be very happy to keep both, especially because of the inscription, but I doubt whether I can keep the page from *Psalms,* since it might be desirable someday to have the entire manuscript in one place; and so I will keep it, shall we say, until you need it. I think that two or three words are missing from the first movement after *"Remitte mihi"*—*"peccata mea,"* or something like that?[7] I noticed this when I was reading through the text, and then I remembered that Sacher had also said something about this. What kind of composer are you, then, that you do not have enough inspiration for the last couple of words?

I am glad to have your Swiss dates in advance and will, of course, lay an ambush for you.

Devotedly yours,   J. Handschin

HANDSCHIN TO STRAVINSKY   *December 29, 1932*

Dear Igor Fyodorovich,

I will be glad to translate the booklet, though I am not convinced that it is worth doing. Also, I do not know if the translation will be clear to a Russian reader

---

[6] Paul Sacher, conductor of the Basler Kammerorchester.

[7] The words *"ut refrigerer"* do not appear in the soprano and bass parts but only in the alto and tenor.

(and for which one, a Soviet or an émigré?), and whether one would like to say this or that a little differently.

I must tell you about a thought that I have had for quite some time: would you consider composing a concerto for two flutes and orchestra? I imagine one of the solo parts requiring a real virtuoso, the other a flutist in the orchestra. The first flute part would have more movement, the second *plutôt des tenues*. That way the piece would be easier to rehearse. Forgive me for expressing my thoughts, which may be stupid, and accept my gratitude for your instructions for the booklet. Heartfelt greetings from your devoted Handschin, and Happy New Year and new optimism—though I do not mean that the concerto for two flutes must sound optimistic!

HANDSCHIN TO STRAVINSKY   *January 21, 1933*

Dear Igor Fyodorovich,

Last night I gave my lecture in Basel. Sacher's chorus performed the first tableau of *Les Noces* afterward . . . and *Psalms*. Even though the orchestra had only one piano, the work sounded powerful and inspiring, especially as the auditorium was small. The performance was not nearly so pale as the one with "Andriushka,"[8] . . .

As for my talk, I think I was successful in putting the question on a wider, and at the same time a more solid, footing than I was able to do in the booklet, because of the deadline. I remarked on "Russian simplicity," too. Now I can return with pleasure to my "real work," digging through materials of the Middle Ages. I mentioned in my lecture that the nonsense said about modern music is not important, such criticism in itself being a kind of recommendation. Nevertheless, if I am to have an opportunity to return to the booklet, these new ideas will have to be included. I found the *Psalm* measures (the end of the 38th, beginning of the 39th, and almost all of the 150th). In the first of these there are indeed no wrong words, but here the Latin version of the Bible is not correct.

                    Warmly and devotedly yours,   J. Handschin

HANDSCHIN TO STRAVINSKY   *February 22, 1933*

Dear Igor Fyodorovich,

I am very grateful that you continue to give your attention to my booklet, but I am very sorry to say that I was not able to incorporate your latest comments because it had already been printed. This is particularly disappointing because of

---

[8] Volkmar Andreae (1879–1962), Swiss conductor and composer, director of the Zürich conservatory 1914–39.

the two choral compositions;[9] these would certainly be of great interest here, where choral music is so popular. Perhaps we might mention them in a newspaper article; if you do not say anything further about them to me, I will assume that they are for unaccompanied mixed chorus. It seems that [André] Schaeffner cannot be relied upon either. I know that I did not give up any ground to him on the question of biographical facts. The one comfort is that the publication is a local one and cannot be expected to have a wide circulation. This means, too, that a popular price for it is not possible; it costs nearly 4 Swiss francs. In keeping with an old tradition, the firm is planning to send you a copy, asking you to accept it as a token of . . . etc. . . .

I plan to spend about ten days in Paris sometime during the first half of February. I am called there periodically to examine treasures at the Bibliothèque Nationale. Well, warm regards from

your devoted   J. Handschin

P.S. I did not want to ask you to hurry, but rather thought that you would notice from the title page that this was the New Year's issue.

HANDSCHIN TO STRAVINSKY   *April 1, 1933*

Dear Igor Fyodorovich,

I look back on and remember your concert with great pleasure. Did you know that there is a center for Gregorian singing where you are, Abbaye St. Waudville? No, let me correct that: they merely publish their paper in Grenoble; they themselves are in the Seine-Inférieure.

Did you see the *Revue Musicale* Bach issue that came out in December? Let me send a few clippings. The Bach article, of course, does not do justice to the man's greatness (but perhaps that was not the intent . . . ?). I send you all best wishes, and please convey the same and our regards to Ekaterina Gavrilovna.

Devotedly yours,   J. Handschin

Another correction: I see that, evidently, I already sent you the Bach article.

HANDSCHIN TO STRAVINSKY   *September 18, 1933*

Dear Igor Fyodorovich,

Unfortunately, the Zürich event happened without me, since I returned from England only yesterday. I believe that the initiative of interpretation belongs to the composer and conductor, not to the chorus. Since the piece was performed in the theatre, ballet was added. That the performance occurred so early in the

---

[9] Pater Noster, Credo.

season may be attributed to the comparative unimportance of the chorus in concert life there: the chorus was in a hurry to try to attract the attention of the public before the season's "stellar" events. Nevertheless, concerts in September have become quite frequent in recent years. It is said that plans are afoot for a third performance, in which case I hope to be of more use to you as a reporter.

I had a marvelous time in Cambridge and Oxford, spending most of it, of course, in the libraries. I like the English very much and think that we on the Continent do not know them sufficiently. Forgive the dullness of the material that I am sending to you. They say that Mr. Gyson's review was less favorable, but, luckily, that is unimportant even from a practical point of view. I kiss the hand of Ekaterina Gerasimovna [sic]. Greetings to you from

your devoted   Handschin

P.S. As I now see, the article by Mr. Gyson is even indecent, but I enclose it to complete the picture.

HANDSCHIN TO STRAVINSKY   *October 1, 1933*

Dear Igor Fyodorovich,

And so the repeat—which is to say the third performance [of *Oedipus Rex*] — was given for the benefit of those members of the public who returned again. The third performance was said to be not quite up to the second in quality. What bothered me was that the soloists behaved like opera singers, except that they were not walking around. The chorus looked like several rows of light spots in semi-darkness. The first act was over by the time that we became oriented to this, but afterward, with the appearance of Jocasta, the greatness of the music dominated everything. She sang very well, and Oedipus, when he joined her, outdid himself. Again I was pleased to realize what a mighty work is *Firebird*.

Handschin

P.S. Please take a look at the examples of medieval melodies that I am sending to you. Do you by chance know Vicar-General Ginon and Canon Grospellier? But perhaps they may no longer be among the living.

CORRESPONDENCE WITH

1918 ～ 1938

WERNER REINHART

Stravinsky's correspondence with Werner Reinhart[1] reveals the composer as a master diplomat. In 1923, he calculated that the minimum number of concerts for a profitable tour in Switzerland was three. But since his music was scarcely known there, except in Geneva and Lausanne, and since few Swiss orchestras were capable of performing it, the chances of finding three engagements within a short period were slight. Therefore, after signing contracts for concerts in Geneva and Winterthur, Stravinsky explained his terms to Reinhart in a way that induced him to pay the composer for a third concert even though it did not take place. By 1925, Stravinsky had increased his minimum requirement to four concerts and made Reinhart responsible for obtaining three of them in addition to paying for the nonexistent fourth. Moreover, Stravinsky successfully presented these and his other victories as concessions on his part.

When Reinhart showed an interest in the violin and piano suite from Pulcinella as a vehicle for Alma Moodie,[2] Stravinsky answered that the piece had already been promised to Paul Kochanski.[3] Then, when Reinhart let it be known that Miss Moodie was a good friend of his, Stravinsky discovered that he had no legal commitment to Kochanski after all. Soon thereafter, Reinhart was paying for an exclusivity of eight months during which his protégée could play the suite in Europe. Soon, too, the not-always-so accommodating Stravinsky was including the suite on his programs and performing it himself with Reinhart's friend.

From the early 1930s, it becomes evident from Stravinsky's letters that he deplored Hermann Scherchen's influence on Reinhart. In any case, the correspondence was not resumed after World War II, except that Reinhart signed a group postcard after a performance of Les Noces in Lausanne on May 26, 1950,

---

[1] Werner Reinhart (1884–1951) inherited his mother's family business, Volkart Brothers, which enabled him to become a patron of the arts. He is remembered chiefly for having underwritten the first production of Histoire du soldat and for placing his Château de Muzot at the disposal of Rainer Maria Rilke in the poet's final years. Thanks to Reinhart, the principal manuscripts of Histoire du soldat, Les Noces, and the Three Pieces for Clarinet Solo (Reinhart was an amateur clarinetist) are now in the Rychenberg Stiftung in Winterthur, together with the originals of Stravinsky's letters, including those for the years 1918–23, which are unavailable.

[2] Australian violinist (1900–43). She gave the first performance, with Stravinsky at the piano, of the suite from Pulcinella, in Frankfurt, November 25, 1925.

[3] Paul Kochanski (1887–1934), Polish violinist.

and that he informed Stravinsky of his intentions to attend the premiere of
The Rake's Progress *in Venice—but died shortly before the event.*

WERNER REINHART TO STRAVINSKY

Dear sir,

It is a little late for me to be thanking you for your kind lines of March 14. As I
wrote to your friend Ramuz, I look forward with the greatest pleasure to having
the opportunity, on one of my next trips to Lausanne, to discuss your project
with you and M. Ramuz and to give an answer to your interesting proposal. I
expect to spend some days with one of my uncles [in Geneva?] in the latter half
of this month, and I will be more than delighted to spend some hours with you
in that beautiful corner of Morges that M. [René] Morax showed me not long
ago. I am delighted to be able to make your acquaintance and that of Madame
Stravinsky, and I look forward with great joy to being initiated by you and your
friends into the "secrets" of your new work. Then I can form a precise conception of the piece, and it will be easier for me to interest other people here in your
project. I will inform you of the day and time of my visit. Meanwhile, please believe, dear sir, in my sincere and devoted interest.

Werner Reinhart

REINHART TO STRAVINSKY

Very dear sir,

Yesterday, returning to my office for a few moments, I found your little packet
enclosing, to my great surprise, the superb painting on glass that I so much admired in your home. It is really far too nice of you to offer this to me, and you
have deeply touched me by this new gesture of sympathy toward me. I thank
you with all my heart.

    As you see, I am in Zürich. I came for a few days with those good people,
Morax and [Henri] Bischoff, to observe the final preparations of the marionette
theatre. I have been so absorbed by what I have seen that I have been unable to
write to you, and I fear that you will think me ungrateful not to have sent a note
since I saw you.

    Let me tell you today how delighted I was by the charming reception that
you and Madame Stravinsky so kindly prepared for me. On departing, I took
with me the most exquisite memories of that afternoon in your ravishing home
and of our dinner together at "La Couronne." But apart from all the beautiful
things that you showed me there, I was impressed above all with what you revealed to me, and let me hear of, your works, so full of charm and spirit and so
passionately alive. At the present time, in which, unfortunately, the arts often

tend to become purely intellectual manifestations, to encounter an artist like you, dear sir, is a real pleasure. You tap music's profound and eternal sources.

Our friend Morax tells me that, for the moment, the Lausanne concert you had planned cannot be arranged. I regret this very much but hope that it can take place in the autumn and that I can be there to hear it. I will also inquire as to whether we can arrange a performance of some of your works for voice and instruments during our next season in Winterthur. I will write to you on this matter as soon as we discuss our programs for the winter in our Musikkollegium.

M. Isler, editor of the *Schweizer Musikzeitung*, told me that he received your compositions from Henn.[4] Isler has promised me to write about them in his paper, and I will send you the issue in which his article appears. I hope that M. Isler will understand your music even though he comes from the camp of Reger. I am going out with Morax in a moment and must end this letter. Please present my respects to Madame Stravinsky, and believe me, dear sir, to be

your cordially devoted   Werner Reinhart

P.S.   I return home tomorrow.

REINHART TO STRAVINSKY

Winterthur
June 10, 1918

Dear sir,

I very much regret having been away in the country when you tried to telephone me last Saturday. According to what my brother Oscar[5] told me, it seems that Her Royal Highness the Infanta Beatrice of Spain is very interested in the composition on which you are working with your friends Ramuz and Auberjonois, and she has graciously offered to find people in Zürich ready to contribute part of the sums necessary to enable you to carry out your project. If I understood correctly, Her Royal Highness wanted to speak to me on this subject, and since I was not going to Zürich, I gave Her Royal Highness the information she asked for by telephone.

I believe you know from your friend Ramuz that the matter rests for the moment with the Zürich lecture agent Hottingen, who is very interested in your work and who will no doubt decide to present it to his subscribers next autumn or winter. He would like to have an approximation of the financial involvement of the enterprise. The Lecture Society usually engages authors and

---

[4] Adolphe Henn, Geneva, was the original publisher of *Pribaoutki, Berceuses du chat,* the Three Easy Pieces, and the Five Easy Pieces.

[5] On August 11, 1922, Ansermet wrote to Stravinsky: "Prince Argutinsky wrote to me that he spent a good day with the Reinharts and that he sold the Rembrandt to Oscar for 40,000 French francs."

artists for fees established in advance, and M. [Hans] Bodmer, the president, thinks that this arrangement is also preferable for the two parties in the case of the *Soldat*. I understand, however, that to prepare a budget is very difficult, if not impossible, for you. Perhaps a satisfactory solution can be reached when we see each other at the end of this week. I will be in Geneva on Thursday (Hôtel de l'Eau) and come to Morges Friday at 5:00 to spend the evening with our mutual friend René Morax. My time will be taken, since I must go to Lausanne on Saturday morning, but perhaps we can meet between the Tonkünstler concerts. I will see Mademoiselle Brandenbourg[6] and hope to interest some people in Zürich in contributing both moral and material support. Hottingen himself will not give us any financial help toward the preliminary expenses.[7]

I look forward to the pleasure of seeing you again soon. Please present my respects to Madame Stravinsky and believe, dear sir, in my cordial and devoted feelings.

Werner Reinhart

REINHART TO STRAVINSKY   *Winterthur*
                                                          June 27, 1918
Very dear sir,

Only a note to tell you that you understood correctly. The 15,000 francs will be guaranteed to you and to Ramuz by me personally and independently. For the rest, I have renewed the discussions with the groups interested in your work and expect to be able to give you more precise information soon. Meanwhile, you could tell me as nearly as possible the costs of one performance so that I can disclose this amount to other people. Perhaps the simplest course would be to tell me if you have a bank where I could deposit a sum now as an advance against copying the parts as well as for your work.

This would greatly facilitate my efforts for St. Gall and Basel. Is it possible that Ansermet could tell me the cost of the concerts? I send this note to you in haste between rehearsals for *Sainte Chagrin*. Please give my respects to Madame Stravinsky, and believe, dear sir, in my best wishes.

Your   Werner Reinhart

---

[6] Daughter of the banker Auguste Brandenbourg.

[7] The 1918–19 prospectus for the Lesezirkel Hottingen, Gemeindestrasse 4, Zürich, lists *Histoire du soldat* as the opening event (October 28), Rilke reading his poems as the third event (November 25), Heinrich Wölfflin lecturing on Rembrandt as the sixth event (February 10), and Gerhart Hauptmann reading from his works as the eighth event (March 10).

REINHART TO STRAVINSKY

Very dear sir,

Thank you very much for your friendly letter, for your and M. Ramuz's so generous offer to give me your manuscripts, and for offering me a choice of the
sketches of your friend Auberjonois. This new token of friendship is a bit overwhelming. But I want very much to accept it because this will be something
very precious to me, not only the work that I am going to hear but much more
in those delicious hours that have united me with you and your friends at
Morges, Cour, and Lausanne and to which I owe the birth of your beautiful
work. As for my very modest part in the realization of your enterprise, believe
me, dear sir, I already felt more than recompensed on the day when I had the
great pleasure of seeing and hearing your work in your home. Following your
instructions, I will deposit money for the preparations, which is to say 12,000
francs, at Brandenbourg and Company, Lausanne.

As for the cost of the performances, I have examined your detailed and
precise calculations, and I see that the expenses for each evening will come to
about 3,000 francs. I told this to M. Bodmer, who will preside next Sunday at
the meeting of the Lecture Society, where he promised me to speak of your
work.

I have also seen M. Robert Hérold, president of the Museum Society of St.
Gall. He will examine the possibilities of a performance in that city. After the
meeting, knowing where we stand in the different cities,[8] we can draw up the
itinerary and fix the dates of the performances. For Winterthur, I have September 24 in view.

It interests me to know whether Ansermet has succeeded in assembling
the musicians that you need. M. Komarax, the assistant director of our marionette theatre, will be free after September 15 and would accept with great pleasure the position of régisseur to accompany the tour of the *Soldat*. It will be necessary to decide on this and also on the honorarium before the end of this
month. I leave for my vacation on the 8th, and my address will be Hôtel Chandolin, near Sierre (Valais). Please believe, dear sir, in my very sincere wishes.

Werner Reinhart

And please present my best regards to Madame Stravinsky and also to your
friends Ramuz and Auberjonois.

---

[8] Notes in Stravinsky's hand on the envelope of this letter indicate that the tour was to
have included Zürich, Winterthur, St. Gall, and Basel.

REINHART TO STRAVINSKY

Hôtel Chandolin
August 19, 1918
[Postcard]

Very dear sir,

Many thanks for your kind letter. Excuse the postcard: it is so beautiful here
that one is out of doors the whole day. Ramuz promised to come for a visit together with you. I have just written to him that it would be a great pleasure to
have you for some days as my guest at the Chandolin, and I only await your telegram announcing your arrival. I send you and Madame Stravinsky my best regards.

Werner Reinhart

REINHART TO STRAVINSKY

Winterthur
March 10, 1919

Dear friend,

Please excuse the haste with which I must write to you concerning what has
happened in Bern, but I have so much to do that I really do not know how to
complete all that must be done before our departure for India. It gave me great
pleasure to see you at Bern, if only for a moment. I was very upset to learn how
much material deprivation the war has caused you, but I also admire the courage with which you know how to endure all of these trials. I regret that it is not
possible to reply exactly to your request, but I think that you understand the
reason I gave you. I hope that before my long voyage I will once again have the
pleasure of shaking your hand, and I leave with you my greetings to Madame
Stravinsky and all my friends.

REINHART[9] TO STRAVINSKY

London
May 4, 1919
[Postcard]

Place St. Louis
Morges

Friendly greetings from Werner Reinhart. Enchanted by your *Petrushka*,
which I will go to hear again tomorrow.

REINHART TO STRAVINSKY

Winterthur
December 26, 1919

Dear friend,

Until now, the many cares and occupations of the end of the year have kept me
from writing to thank you for the superb volume on African sculpture that you
so thoughtfully wanted to give me. I know from this book how perfectly you
have divined my taste, because if something is more alive, stronger, and more
magnificent in sculpture than these heads and figures, I do not know what it is.

---

[9] The card is signed by Ansermet and René Morax as well as by Reinhart.

My brother George (who was in London during your visit here) bought a superb specimen in Paris of this still almost unknown art. If you are in Paris at the moment (I do not know), go to see the beautiful collection in the possession of the art dealer Hesselle. My brother has talked to me about him.

I often think of your visit, of the unforgettable concert in Zürich,[10] and of *Renard,* as you played it for us here. I would have liked to attend the premiere of the "symphonic" *Nightingale* in Geneva. I think that the reactions of a certain segment of the audience did not really upset you. The most beautiful victories are always those that have been won against our adversaries. I do not know when I will again be in French Switzerland and see you. To you, dear friend, and to Madame Stravinsky and to all your family, my best wishes for the New Year.

Very cordially, your   Werner Reinhart

REINHART TO STRAVINSKY

Positano
July 13, 1920
[Postcard]

Carantec
France

Dear friend,

From this beautiful place I send you my best regards and my regrets not to find you here. Many thanks for your postcard. All the best to you and my respects to Madame Stravinsky.

Your cordially devoted   Werner Reinhart

REINHART TO STRAVINSKY

Winterthur
May 25, 1923

My dear friend,

A year has already slipped by since I had the pleasure of seeing you on that memorable evening of *Mavra.* I greatly regretted not being able to come to see you in Biarritz on my return from Spain, as you so kindly invited me, but I was in a great hurry to return to my work. I hope that all is well with you and with your family. From time to time I have indirect news of you through Ansermet, and I understand that you have done a great deal of work this winter and made beautiful new things for us.

Today I would like to discuss a project with you that concerns one of my friends, M. Hermann Scherchen, a young conductor of great talent who has done much for modern music in Germany. This artist came to Zürich this month to serve on the jury of the Société Internationale (of which you are one of the honorary presidents). He spoke to Ansermet and to me about a project to stage *Histoire du soldat* in Frankfurt with the full text—after obtaining autho-

---

[10] A concert of Stravinsky's chamber music was presented in Zürich in October 1919.

rization for the translation. To spare you the correspondence, I have written directly to Chester to find out the terms for renting the orchestra parts. Chester telegraphed today that you control all theatrical rights to the work. The point of this letter is simply to ask if you will agree to the performance of *Histoire du soldat* in Frankfurt, in the same form as in Lausanne. I can guarantee that the performance of the music, under the baton of Scherchen, will be excellent. He has studied the score during his stay here with me, and he understands perfectly the spirit of your music. As for the visual side, Auberjonois has agreed to let us use his designs. The actors will be chosen in Frankfurt. I also hope that Pitoëff will give Scherchen all the necessary instructions, or, better still, come himself to Frankfurt for the stage direction. The performance must take place around June 20. You would be most kind to send me a note or telegram as quickly as possible if you are in agreement and also to give instructions to Chester to send the music to M. Scherchen, whose address is Hainstrasse 18, Cronberg, near Frankfurt.

Concerning your author's rights for this single performance, please name the sum, and I will arrange this directly with you. Please excuse these hastily written lines. With my respects to Madame Stravinsky, I send you, dear friend, my cordial and devoted greetings.

Werner Reinhart

(Copy of the letter that I sent to you today at Biarritz)

REINHART TO STRAVINSKY   *Winterthur*
                                                         June 6, 1923
My dear friend,

Thank you very much for your kind note and for having so agreeably consented to the performance of the *Soldat* in Frankfurt. I am touched by all that you tell me on this subject, and I hope that the Frankfurt performance will do justice to the work. My brother [Hans] and I finished the translation some time ago. Only in the course of our work did we realize how difficult it is to preserve in translation something of the very particular savor and force of Ramuz's style. I hope that our translation will not be thought too bad. The essential thing for me was to be able both to realize the project of my friend Scherchen and to acquaint the German public with a score that, in my opinion, is not only one of the most masterful and most characteristic by its author, but is also one that, so it seems to me, marks an important point of departure in your work and in music in general. My greatest satisfaction in hearing *Mavra* last summer was the way in which you courageously followed your voice, not listening to what was said around you but obeying your interior voice only. This strength has been a quality of all the great creators.

I was distressed to learn from Ansermet about the failure of your American project and how much this restricts you in your present situation. It is painful for me to know that you are overburdened by material worries at the moment when you should be free to work.

Would you, using an actor's diction, try out certain places [in the narration]? Not much will have to be changed. I believe I told you that not all of the costumes were found in Lausanne. There too, certain details must be worked out, but you will see that Scherchen and his troupe are inspired by the best intentions. The music, the most important element, seemed to me very well done. One must not forget that Scherchen had an extremely difficult task, since neither Ramuz's libretto nor the parts sent by Chester contain any indication as to the staging. It seems to me essential to establish a kind of régisseur's prompt book for future performances. This will help us for the performances in Winterthur and Zürich, which are to take place in February with Ansermet.

I hope that these lines reach you before your departure.

Our postcard from Salzburg will have told you about the triumphant success there of your Three Pieces and Concertino. The Pro Arte Quartet played them wonderfully! There was truly no comparison to what I heard played by the Flonzaley Quartet. We have had some extremely interesting days, but I will tell you about all that when I have a little leisure. Can't you come to see us on your return [from Weimar]?[11] How delightful that would be.

In haste and very cordially,

your devoted   Werner Reinhart

REINHART TO STRAVINSKY

Hôtel d'Angleterre
Copenhagen
June 26, 1923

Maison Pleyel
24, rue Rochechouart
Paris

My dear friend,

Excuse me for not having answered your kind letter before now, but it arrived just at the moment when I was leaving for Frankfurt and the north. First, let me thank you with all my heart for the exquisite [sketch] score of *Les Noces*. You cannot imagine the pleasure you have brought me with the gift of this very precious manuscript, and I am both touched and proud of this new proof of your friendship. It is always a special joy to see a masterpiece in its first state and to find all the freshness of the inspiration of the first few moments. I also

---

[11] On returning to Paris from Weimar, Stravinsky and Madame Sudeikina went with Alexandre Benois, on August 26, to visit Prince Argutinsky at his home in Magny-en-Vexin. Stravinsky then returned to Biarritz, and Madame Sudeikina went to Enghien-les-Bains, where, on September 28, Stravinsky sent her a gift of his first sketchbook for *Mavra* (still with the title *The Little House at Kolomna* on the cover).

thank you, dear friend, for all that you say in your letter. I am happy to know you, and I hope that everything will work out for you.

I was very sad not to be able to come to the premiere of *Les Noces,* but I can tell you that I was extremely pleased to have been present at the tremendous success of the *Soldat* in Frankfurt. The public was enthralled from the moment the curtain went up. The music was beautifully rendered by Scherchen, and the players were excellent, above all the composer Paul Hindemith, who played the violin in a spirit that would have delighted you. The performance of the actors was truly good. Scherchen plans to give the work again in Berlin and Leipzig. I will write to you on this subject when I have something more definite to say. In the event that you wish to say something to Scherchen, who deserves the credit for this so meticulously prepared presentation of the *Soldat,* his address is: Kapellmeister Hermann Scherchen, Hainstrasse 18, Cronberg (Taunus), Germany. You can write to him in Russian; he knows the language perfectly. He told me that he wants to play everything that you have written. Can he present *Les Noces* in translation? What do you think?

I am here in this charming city of Copenhagen, where surely the delights of the Tivoli have won your admiration. The people have something of the naive spirit of the eighteenth century. I have been to a ravishing pantomime theatre and have seen marionettes in an unforgettable comedy. I leave tomorrow for Sweden and expect to be home about July 7. I hope that all is well with you and that I will have the pleasure of seeing you again this year. Please present my respects to Madame Stravinsky, and please believe me to be

your devoted   Werner Reinhart

REINHART TO STRAVINSKY[12]

Winterthur
July 28, 1923

Dear friend,

I assume that my letter, sent from Copenhagen at the end of June, has reached you. How I regret not to have heard *Les Noces.* People tell me about it with the greatest enthusiasm. What do you think of Scherchen's proposal to translate it into German and present it at Frankfurt? His small chorus is excellent. I heard it in an enormously difficult piece by Schoenberg [*Friede auf Erden*], and the performance was perfect. Scherchen wants to stage the piece. Would this be possible, or does Diaghilev have exclusivity for his Ballets Russes?

You would be giving a great treat to Scherchen and to all of your admirers in Weimar if you would go there for August 19. Unfortunately, I cannot go my-

---

[12] This letter is found on the last page of a much longer one from Scherchen to Stravinsky, describing the forthcoming Weimar performances. Kandinsky will be in charge, Scherchen says, and the program of August 18 will consist of Hindemith's

self, but in February we will finally mount the *Soldat* in Zürich and Winterthur, with the collaboration of Ramuz and Pitoëff and under the baton of "the good God Ansermet." You must not miss this.

REINHART TO STRAVINSKY   *Winterthur*
                                              August 10, 1923
My dear friend,

Thank you very much for your letter, which has reached me after a considerable delay because of my trip to Salzburg. I telegraphed you this morning at Biarritz that the rehearsals of the *Soldat* at the Bauhaus in Weimar will begin on the 16th. The performance will take place on Sunday the 19th. On receiving your wire this afternoon, I repeated the contents of my telegram to your Paris address.

I am truly upset at not being able to go to Weimar myself while you are there; but having just been away from my work, I cannot absent myself again so soon. I am very happy that you will make the effort to go to Weimar, because it is essential that everything be settled according to your instructions for the performances that will follow in Berlin and Leipzig in September. When I arrived in Frankfurt on the day of the premiere, it was too late to offer certain observations to my friend Scherchen concerning the staging. Most important, the dancer needs instruction concerning your intentions. The Devil, on the other hand, seemed excellent. His role is played by [Hermann] Schramm of [the] Frankfurt [Opera], one of the best buffo tenors in Germany. The Narrator, [Carl] Ebert, naturally has a style that is different from Ramuz's but nevertheless delivered the text with such artistry that he made a very strong impression on the audience.

I think that in spite of the manner of presentation, you can accept the contents of this letter,[13] which I offer in all good faith. Believe me, dear friend, I do this with the greatest pleasure, happy to be able to assist you a little and not dreaming of any return. If, however, you are induced to accept my gesture as I intend it, I will tell you that I am nevertheless proud to possess the magnificent score of the *Soldat,* and if you have in your drawer another small score that you judge me worthy to possess, it will evidently be a great pleasure for me to add this to the other. But, as I tell you, I do not make it my condition.

I am devastated not to have been able to come to the premiere of *Les Noces villageoises,* as I had planned, but it was necessary for me to stay here for the moment. I will be happy to be able to leave in time for the performance in Frankfurt, which takes place on the 20th, and I will go from there directly to Sweden for a two-week vacation. I also strongly regret having to miss the whole

---

Marienleben and Busoni's Piano Pieces; that of the 19th, Krenek's Concerto Grosso and Stravinsky's *Soldat.* Hans Reinhart also added a paragraph to the letter.

[13] Reinhart had evidently enclosed a check.

Paris season of the Ballets Russes, but I hope to be able to come to see you on another occasion.

Meanwhile, please present my respects to Madame Stravinsky, and believe me, dear friend, to be

your cordially devoted   Werner Reinhart

REINHART TO STRAVINSKY

Port Said
Egypt
November 20, 1923

Dear friend,

[Postcard]

Returning from India, where I made a very brief trip, I send my best regards to you and yours. Will you come to Switzerland for the performances of the *Soldat?* I strongly hope so. With friendly greetings,

your devoted   Werner Reinhart

REINHART TO STRAVINSKY

Winterthur
June 18, 1924

My dear friend,

It seems to me that an eternity has passed since I gave you news of me and, above all, since our last meeting—too soon, unfortunately, after the premiere of *Mavra.* I had still hoped to return to Paris, or, better yet, to come to see you in Biarritz. But my work has always taken me in other directions and, among others, once again to the Orient. I very sincerely regret not having been able to come and applaud *Les Noces* and the Concerto.

It is on the subject of the latter composition that I would like to speak to you. Ansermet and other friends have talked to me with such enthusiasm of this new work, and of the incomparable manner in which you have achieved it, that our committee (Musikkollegium) has decided to act quickly and to invite you, by the intermediary of Geneva, to come and perform the Concerto at Winterthur in one of the subscription concerts. This would occur on Wednesday, November 26, under the direction of Volkmar Andreae, the very capable conductor of the Tonhalle in Zürich. Perhaps you will object that we should have chosen Ansermet as conductor, but prior reasons obliged us to take this decision and specifically for this concert. The administration of the Orchestre [de la Suisse] Romande writes to us that you are prepared to come to Switzerland for [not fewer than] three concerts for a sum of 1,000 Swiss francs for each one. Two of these concerts, Winterthur on November 26 and Geneva on November 29, are set. For the third we have tried to find a city that can give the piece, but all of them say that they already have other commitments. You understand that I do not want the idea to fall through, and it is for this reason that I am asking you if you would accept my guarantee to pay you the difference myself—which is to say that you would permit me to make up the difference when you come here in whatever way is most convenient for you. (Believe me, dear friend, I will be delighted to see you and to receive you at Rychenberg, and to listen to your magnificent concert.) Andreae looks forward with equal joy to having the pleasure and the honor of accompanying you with his orchestra. He does this very well, having a superb sense of rhythm and much technique and life in his baton. Our orchestra will also be at the height of its form, since we have just found some very good wind players.

I hope that you and yours are well and that you can soon give me a definitive reply. Kindly present my respects to Madame Stravinsky, and believe me, my dear, to be

your cordially devoted   Werner Reinhart

STRAVINSKY TO REINHART

Paris
June 21, 1924

Winterthur

Very dear friend,

I thank you very warmly for your new testimony of friendship for me. I am profoundly touched, believe me.

I will certainly be happy with a minimum of two concerts (Winterthur and Geneva), not wanting in any case to abuse your inexhaustible generosity.

Please believe, my dear friend, it is a great joy for me to come to your home and to see again your good, very good, country, where I spent some very happy years of my life. I send you all my faithful and friendly greetings.

REINHART TO STRAVINSKY

Winterthur
July 18, 1924

My dear friend,

Thank you very much again for your letter, in which you so kindly made me understand your acceptance to come and play your Concerto with us on November 26. Geneva informed us that you were afraid of not being able to arrive in time after your Amsterdam concert on November 23, but I have looked at the train schedules and can tell you that by leaving Amsterdam on the 24th at 8:43 in the morning, you will arrive in Basel (by way of Frankfurt) on the 25th at 5:50 a.m. and at Winterthur at 10:50 in the morning. I assume that two rehearsals with the orchestra will be sufficient for you. One of these is set for the 25th at 8:00 in the evening, the other for the day of the concert (26th) at 1:30 in the afternoon. This last (dress rehearsal) is public, but it is not in the nature of a concert, which is to say that the conductor and the soloist can stop and repeat as they wish. It would be rather difficult for us to postpone the date of the concert to the 27th, but if you are afraid of being tired by the trip, please tell me, and we will see what can be done.

Quite probably Basel will also invite you to come and play your Concerto there. M. Suter spoke to me about it recently.

I hope that you are well, and I ask you to present my best wishes to your family. Please believe me, dear friend, to be

your cordially devoted   Werner Reinhart

STRAVINSKY TO REINHART   22, 24, *rue Rochechouart*
                                                          Paris
Winterthur   *July 22, 1924*

Very dear friend,

I have just returned from Copenhagen (where I played my concerto at Tivoli on July 18 with great success) and found your kind letter of the same date (18th) on my desk. What you write suits me very well, the trains, rehearsals, etc.

I also received a letter from the Allgemeine Musikgesellschaft in Basel inviting me to come and play my concerto there next winter, giving me the dates and proposing a fee of 800 francs. I have just answered that the only convenient date for me is November 1 and that, as an "honorarium," I cannot accept less than 1,000 Swiss francs, the fee that I receive in Winterthur and Geneva. In addition, I told them that for the rental of the parts of the Concerto they must write to M. Ernest Oeberg (22, rue d'Anjou, Paris), to whom I also directed M. Giovanna of Geneva and to whom I also ask you to direct the administration of the Winterthur concerts.

Tomorrow or the day after I will go to Biarritz, where I will be happy to have news of you. I am, I remain, and I will always remain

your inalterable friend,   I. Str.

STRAVINSKY TO REINHART   167 *blvd. Carnot*
                                                          Nice
Winterthur   *October 20, 1924*

My dear friend,

Perhaps you have not yet returned, in which case this letter will await you at Winterthur.

During your absence I received some letters from the Musikkollegium replying for you to the questions that I had asked you, not knowing that you were far away.

Happily, we, my wife and myself, have obtained Swiss visas. I will come to Winterthur on November 25 (probably in the morning) directly from Amsterdam, and I think that two rehearsals will be sufficient for me.

My wife will join me at Winterthur, coming from Lausanne, where she will stop for a day en route from Nice, where we now live. I would be much obliged to you if you could meet her at the station; she will telegraph you the day and hour of her arrival.

For the parts of my concerto, which is still at the printer's, it is necessary to write directly to Mr. E. Oeberg, 22, rue d'Anjou, Paris 8. As a last resort, I could perhaps bring them myself from Amsterdam, but I cannot say so definitely at this moment. In any case, M. Oeberg can send the orchestra score of the piece to the conductor before my arrival.

Here I end my letter in sending you, dear friend, my faithful devotion.

I. Stravinsky

P.S.   I will stay here until October 29, the date of my departure for Warsaw, where I begin my tour for this year.

REINHART TO STRAVINSKY

Winterthur
October 27, 1924

Nice

Dear friend,

I hope that this letter reaches you before you leave for Warsaw. I must excuse myself concerning your letter, but I was traveling, and on my return I was bedridden for nearly three weeks with a grippe from which I am only just now recovering.

I am very pleased that the passport questions are settled, and I am very happy that Madame Stravinsky will give us the great pleasure of coming to Winterthur. I was sorry that you had had so many nuisances with the visas and that you were the victim of these restrictions. But, happily, our position and the personal intervention at Bern of M. Andreae overcame the difficulties.

Oeberg wrote to me that we can count on receiving the parts of your concerto in time, and I trust that you will be satisfied with our orchestra. Above all, the brass this year is very good.

What infinite pleasure I had hearing your Octet in Salzburg, admirably played by musicians from Frankfurt under Scherchen's baton.[14] We will perform the piece here in February with our players, also with Scherchen, then repeat it in Zürich on March 19 in the Tonhalle, in a concert of the International Society for Contemporary Music.

Awaiting the great pleasure of receiving you and Madame Stravinsky here at Rychenberg, I ask you to believe me, dear friend, to be

your faithfully devoted   Werner Reinhart

---

[14] Stravinsky had written to Oeberg, August 21, 1924, indicating that he had never given Scherchen permission to perform the Octet.

Nice
                                                                  July 25, 1925

Dear friend,

You should have received a letter from the secretary of the Allgemeine Musikgesellschaft in Basel concerning me. Having received a proposition from this organization for next season, I answered that in principle I would like to come,
but that I am obliged to make my appearance there contingent on other engagements in Switzerland, the question we discussed last autumn with M. Andreae.

The point now is to know whether this short tour can take place. On the
same subject, I have just received a letter from a M. Hans von der—? the signature is illegible—telling me that he had heard from you indicating "the proba-
bility of an engagement by the Swiss Section of the International Society for
Contemporary Music." This is so vague and, in truth, so far from what I had
expected to obtain as engagements in Switzerland that I really do not know
what to answer, without vexation. Meanwhile, time presses, and I must organize my tours for next season now.

Permit me to tell you openly what I think, as I have always done with you.
Henceforth, to earn my livelihood, I see myself obliged to devote a part of the
year to concert tours, as I already started to do last year. Little by little this organizing of tours becomes a routine business, as in the case of other artists,
with their established fees, dates, and programs. Your country, which (as you
know) I love very much, is very limited in resources, for which reason, wanting
to come to you, I ask only half the fee that I receive everywhere else in Europe
(Germany, Holland, England, Warsaw, etc.). This lowering of my fee forces me
to increase the number of engagements to at least four. Tell me if this seems
possible, if you think you can arrange the matter this way, and if four engagements can be fixed for me not later than August 15, since I have many others to
settle.

Excuse me for this business letter, dear friend, when I want to talk to you
about very different things. Believe me to be

                              your faithfully devoted   I. Stravinsky

Winterthur
                                                                  July 29, 1925

Nice

My dear friend,

I have just received your letter of the 25th, and I thank you for having spoken so
frankly about the question of your Swiss tour. I perfectly understand all that
you say on the subject, and you can believe me when I say that I have done my
utmost to organize the tour for you beyond your concert at Winterthur. Meanwhile, I have been very disappointed that until now only Basel has responded.
Andreae, who had promised you a concert for next winter, told me again, recently, that he has had such great difficulties with his committee on the subject

of modern works that, for the moment, he has been forced to withdraw your concerto from the programs of the subscription concerts. And unfortunately, in Bern and in St. Gall, where I had high hopes, nothing at all has resulted.

I see now, from your letter, that you must count on at least four engagements under the special conditions fixed for Switzerland last year (which is to say 1,000 Swiss francs for a concert). At present I can propose to you only the following:

Zürich: November 10, concert by the Swiss Section of the International Society for Contemporary Music under the direction of Andreae, with rehearsal, I think, the night before (November 9, evening). Piano Concerto.

Basel: November 14, concert by the Allgemeine Musikgesellschaft, Dr. Suter. Rehearsal, I think, also the night before. Piano Concerto.

Between these two dates I see only one other possibility, which is for you to give a private concert at Winterthur, where you would perhaps be prepared to play your sonata and to accompany or conduct the song cycles (*Berceuses, Pribaoutki*). Since we have a subscription concert on November 11, with the program and soloist set, you would have to choose the 12th. If I fully understand your letter, you must have a sum of 4,000 Swiss francs for your Swiss tour. If a fourth concert cannot be arranged in the week of November 8 to 15, would you permit me to make up the difference? I would be much obliged to you for a word on this question and on whether we can count on the proposed dates. Would you also tell me what you will eventually propose as a program for Winterthur?

At this time I would like to speak of several matters that I have wanted to discuss with you for some time. First, Scherchen told me that, at the moment, you are busy with the composition of a symphony. You know with what interest I always look forward to each new work from your pen, and I wanted to ask you if there were any possibility of including this work on one of our programs next winter. It could be given in the concert of December 9 that Ansermet has agreed to conduct here. I wrote to him in Buenos Aires to ask him to perform one of your works on this occasion. It would be wonderful if we could have the premiere of your symphony. If this is possible, I will naturally leave it to you to name your terms for such an *"Erstaufführung."*

Second, the organizing committee of the Venice festival has requested that I approach you again to ask if you would consent to come to Venice to play your sonata on September 8. I do not have to tell you of the pleasure that we would all have in joining you there and hearing the work performed by you yourself, but we also understand that it is probably difficult for you to come to Venice only for that. For this reason I ask you to tell me, also very frankly, the terms that would make this possible. Perhaps you know that Schoenberg is also coming to Venice, to conduct his Serenade.

Third, one of my friends, the excellent violinist Alma Moodie, has heard that you have transcribed the *Pulcinella* Suite for violin and piano and that you have reserved it for Kochanski. Would you eventually agree to allow Mlle Moodie to perform it in certain countries? I can tell you that the work would be placed in the best of hands. This artist, perhaps not yet known to you, has had an exceptional success everywhere. Apart from being an accomplished virtuosa, she is a musician of the first order, and to give you an idea of her qualities, her playing has inspired such composers as Pfitzner, Krenek, and Hindemith to dedicate concertos to her. I will be very grateful if you can grant my request and thereby also render a great service to my friend. Here too, naturally, you must also indicate your terms completely openly.

You will soon receive visits from Scherchen and Krenek, and I only regret that I cannot accompany them. I have asked them to give you all of my best regards.

I often think of you and of all your family, and I hope that Madame Stravinsky, to whom I ask you to convey my respects, has completely recovered from her illness. Excuse me, dear friend, to have tired you with so many business questions, and believe me to be

your very cordially devoted   Werner Reinhart

STRAVINSKY TO REINHART   *Nice*
August 1, 1925

My dear friend,

I was very touched by your letter, and I thank you most sincerely. Permit me to reply point by point to all of the questions that concern us.

1. It is agreed for November 10 in Zürich, November 14 in Basel, and between these two dates a private recital in Winterthur as you proposed. As for the fourth concert, I would nevertheless like you to find it for me in order to save you this considerable expense. If this should prove to be impossible, I see myself obliged to partake again of your generosity, above all since I am bringing with me not only my wife but also my elder son—a pleasure that I cannot refuse him. Concerning the concert in Winterthur, I agree to play the Sonata, to conduct the *Pribaoutki* and the *Japanese Lyrics*—in preference to the *Berceuses* in that these require three clarinets; but this is for you to decide. I can also let you hear my *Ragtime* for eleven instruments, which has never been played in Switzerland; I will send you the full score one of these days.

2. Scherchen, whose visit I still await, was half correct concerning the Symphony: in effect, I have proposed to myself to compose one this year, and if I have the time I will do it for the spring, because at present I am working on something else [Serenade], which I hope to finish in October.

3. At the moment I am also working on the Suite for violin and piano taken from the music of Pergolesi. It seems to me that it would be difficult to let Mlle Alma Moodie play this without Kochanski's permission. Nevertheless, I will try to obtain some concessions from him to please you.

4. I think that it will be possible for me to come to Venice at the beginning of September, but, between you and me, I will do it only because you are the intermediary. My terms are the same as last spring in Rome: 5,000 French francs.

It is my turn to excuse this business letter, and, awaiting news of you, I send you, very dear friend, my affectionate regards and my greetings to your brothers.

Igor Stravinsky

STRAVINSKY TO REINHART   *Nice*
                                                    August 11, 1925
Very dear friend,

With these lines I will try to provoke a response from you to my letter of August 1, not yet having heard from you. I am forced to disturb you and to press you about Switzerland and Venice because at this very moment I am in the midst of establishing my tours, in order to organize my time. People are pressing me for replies from all sides.

Shall I also reply to Basel (for November 14), or will you do it?
In haste,

very sincerely yours,   Igor Stravinsky

STRAVINSKY TO REINHART   *Nice*
                                                    August 12, 1925
My dear friend,

Scarcely had I sent my letter yesterday when I received a very nice note from Kochanski assuring me that he will not be jealous if the suite is played by someone else. Legally speaking, I have the right to do with it as I see fit, and if I made you wait for this word from Kochanski, the reason is simply that I did not want to give the suite to another without informing him. It is agreed, therefore, for Mlle Alma Moodie. But when and where will I see her, and how will I get in touch with her, through you or directly?

Best regards from

your very sincerely devoted   Igor Stravinsky

REINHART TO STRAVINSKY   *Winterthur*
                                                    August 14, 1925
My dear friend,

I have just received your letter of the 11th, and I ask you to pardon me for not yet having replied to that of August 1. The reason is that I have been making inquiries in several directions to find the fourth concert for you, since this is more or less the stipulation for your tour in Switzerland.

Unfortunately, the results have been negative until now, and it is also very difficult to get answers, nearly everyone being in the country at the moment. Scherchen, to whom I wrote to ask if he could find something for you in Germany immediately after November 14, has just replied that, unfortunately, nothing can be arranged.

At present I can confirm only that the three already definite concerts are:

Zürich:	November 10 (with rehearsal probably on the evening of the 9th)
Winterthur:	November 12 (private recital)
Basel:	November 14

These are set, and I have already informed Zürich and Basel. Nevertheless, perhaps it would be good for you to deal directly with M. Hans von der Mühl, the secretary of the Allgemeine Musikgesellschaft, Basel, concerning the exact time of the rehearsal.

These concerts have been negotiated according to the terms you gave me, 1,000 Swiss francs per concert. If I cannot find the fourth concert for you, it is understood that the 1,000-franc difference will be made up by me.

As for the Winterthur concert, I am not yet ready to establish a final program. The committee, with which I have spoken, fears that to find a singer suitable for your works at the indicated date will probably be very difficult, quite apart from the question of cost. The occasion would be very beautiful if it were realized as you proposed it, but I ask you to give me the liberty of transforming this concert into a private reception at my home, where you will give me and some friends the privilege of hearing your sonata and possibly one other work for piano.

Scherchen has been asked to go to Milan and Turin with our instrumentalists at about the same time and to play your works (Octet, *Soldat*, [*Pulcinella*] Suite, etc.). Since this tour will probably be impossible for him, he asks me if you might like to do this with our musicians in his place. What do you say to this proposal, and do you want us to explore further possibilities through M. Luigi Ansbacher (via Armorari 8, Milan), who wanted to present these concerts?

I thank you very much for having so agreeably consented to come to Venice and play your sonata there. I passed this news along to Casella, who answered me—from Champoluc (Val d'Ayas), Piemonte, Hotel Breithorn—that he is delighted by your participation and accepts your terms. As you know, the date is September 8, and for all other information you can eventually address yourself to the secretary of the organization at the Liceo Benedetto Marcello, Venice. I thank you personally for having so kindly acceded to my request.

The mail has just brought me your other letter. Mlle Moodie is now at the Hotel Riederfurka, near Mörel (Valais, Switzerland), until about the 23rd, when she leaves for Germany, but she will be in Venice, and you will have an opportunity there to reach an agreement with her. Many thanks for your friendly words, which I will communicate to her, since I leave for Riederfurka tomorrow myself.

I look forward to seeing you soon in Venice (where my address from September 2 will be: Hotel Britannia) and, above all, to the pleasure of having you, Madame Stravinsky, and your son Theodore with us in November. Meanwhile, please convey my best regards to your entire family, and believe me, dear friend, to be

your cordially devoted   Werner Reinhart

REINHART TO STRAVINSKY

Winterthur
September 25, 1925

My dear friend,

Thank you very much for your letter from Genoa, and I hope that you are already back with your family.

On my return from Venice I immediately took the necessary steps for your visas, and Andreae personally took a letter to the department of the Zürich police in charge of aliens. Andreae telephoned me the day after his visit that all will be in order for you, for Madame Stravinsky, and for your son Theodore. I also sent the necessary precaution, since police business moves a little slowly here; I think that in a few days the Swiss Consulate in Nice will have the authorization for your visas. You might stop by there toward the end of next week, and if there is still a hitch, I ask you to send me word. For the period of your stay in Switzerland, I asked for the whole month of November, to give you some latitude in your arrangements.

Before leaving [Venice], I did not find an opportunity to settle with you the question of author's rights for the *Pulcinella* Suite. According to what you had said, you would agree to accept a lump sum and to forfeit your rights. But since it is a little difficult to foresee the number of performances of the piece that Mlle Moodie can give, I hesitate to name a figure that would satisfy you. Do you think that the sum of 1,000 Swiss francs would correspond to your ideas, and, with that, can you give Mlle Moodie exclusivity for the work for Europe for one or two years, which is to say until the work is published in this new form? I ask you to tell me, in friendship and perfectly frankly, what you think of this proposition.

Mlle Moodie, in Zürich at the moment, is very eager to receive the violin part that you promised her for the end of the month. She must depart soon on a tour, and she would like to have the music before leaving Zürich.

I greatly look forward to seeing you again, and Madame Stravinsky and your son, in November. I have not forgotten the hours spent in your charming company in Venice, and I send you and all your family my very friendly regards.

Werner Reinhart

Thank you again for the beautiful photograph. I will send a copy of it in turn to Mlle Moodie.

STRAVINSKY TO REINHART   *[Beginning of October 1925]*

Very dear friend,

I was very touched by your letter, and excuse me for not having answered immediately: I have so many things to do.

I thank you and Andreae for your efforts concerning our passports.

Turning to the question of Mlle Moodie's exclusivity for my suite, I am
fully satisfied with the sum that you propose, but, unhappily, I cannot extend
the period beyond June 1, 1926, because of obligations to Kochanski, who also
wants to play it (already having worked with me) after his return from America
at about that date. I hope that you will understand my embarrassment at not
being able to grant a longer exclusivity to Mlle Moodie, and I ask you to send me
a note on the subject. On the same matter, I am now negotiating with the Wolff
agency in Berlin for my chamber-music concert there on November 21, and I
have strongly requested that the thing be arranged.[15] Would you, on your part,
let me know if Mlle Moodie will be free to come to Holland at the end of February or beginning of March, since there, too, I want to put this suite on my program.[16]

The photograph came out very well. Would it be indiscreet to ask you to
send me another one of each, because I sent these to Madame Sudeikina, who
asks me to forward to you her friendly greetings.

At the same time as these lines, I send you the violin part of my suite for
Mlle Moodie.

Awaiting news of you, please believe, dear friend, in my very affectionate
thoughts.

REINHART TO STRAVINSKY   *Winterthur*
                                          October 5, 1925

My dear friend,

Thank you very much for your letter. I have noted and will communicate to
Mlle Moodie what you say on the subject of the arrangement of the *Pulcinella*
Suite. I am sure that she will understand perfectly the reasons that prevent you
from granting her exclusivity for the work after June 1, 1926. If I understand
you correctly, Mlle Moodie can continue to play the work after this date, and

---

[15] Stravinsky had written to Wolff & Sachs, September 29: "Concerning the new violin
and piano suite, I ask you to address Mlle Moodie through the intermediary of my
friend Werner Reinhart, who looks after the affairs of this young and very talented violinist. . . . Perhaps, through M. Reinhart, you can obtain a very good fee for her. I will
play the suite with her in one of my concerts in Frankfurt." The point of the second
sentence is that Stravinsky did not want Mlle Moodie's honorarium to be deducted
from his.

[16] On January 27, 1926, Stravinsky wrote to Mengelberg's secretary, S. Bottenheim:
"Tell me if Mengelberg still wants me to conduct *Le Sacre du printemps*, and what

Kochanski will not have exclusivity in Europe then as he has now in America. Would you send me a further note on this subject, if you please?

I have not yet received the violin part that you mentioned, but it is probably on the way, and I will send it to Mlle Moodie immediately. She is not in Germany. At this very moment the part has come. Many thanks. If you wish to communicate with her at this time, you need only write to her at her home address in Berlin: Viktoria Luise Platz 12, Berlin.

I am holding for your deposit the sum agreed upon and I await your instructions for an eventual deposit.

Concerning the concerts with Mlle Moodie, you can reach a solution on this question with the Wolff agency, with whom she has an exclusive contract for her concerts. This office has all of the information on her free dates.

All is in order for your passports, as was confirmed to me the day before yesterday by a communication from the Zürich police department in charge of aliens. I do not have to tell you that it will be a great pleasure for me to have you, Madame Stravinsky, and M. Theodore stay with me during the days when you are busy in Zürich, which is only thirty-five minutes from here by car, but if you find it more practical to be nearer to the Tonhalle and to Andreae during this time, I invite you and your family to stay at the Hôtel Baur-au-Lac in Zürich. I ask you to decide this question yourself and to tell me when you expect to arrive here so that I can make the necessary arrangements.

The parts for your concerto are here, and Andreae is going to prepare the work for his orchestra.

The Società del Quartetto of Milan wrote to us (Musikkollegium) apropos of the participation of our musicians for a Stravinsky concert (Octet, *Soldat* Suite, etc.). The dates, which are those immediately following your stay in Switzerland, are free. I mention this in case you can take part in the event. M. Luigi Ansbacher, via Armorari 8, Milan, will write to you directly about this.

Would you please tell Madame Stravinsky, before I thank her directly for her friendly letter, that I am sorry about the delay in receiving the glass from Venice, but since my own came only this morning, I trust that the package for Madame Stravinsky will also arrive in due course. The store in question was not very efficient with this transaction and also gave me some problems with customs, even though I had arranged in advance to avoid these expenses. I must excuse myself to Madame Stravinsky in the event that she, too, is obliged to pay something for the little present that I sent her.

I will ask Mlle Moodie to send you another set of the Venice photographs.

---

should be the approximate length of the symphonic program. As for the *Kammermusik,* I must know whether I will have a small chamber orchestra (about thirty musicians) at my disposal or only some soloists. In the latter case, I cannot offer a program of more than an hour and ten minutes, with, as the other performers, Alma Moodie and a clarinetist: Trio from *Histoire du soldat,* Sonata and Serenade, Suite for violin and piano, Three Pieces for Clarinet Solo.''

Awaiting the great pleasure of seeing you again soon, I ask you to convey my respects to Madame Stravinsky and to believe me, dear friend, to be

your cordially devoted   Werner Reinhart

REINHART TO STRAVINSKY   *Winterthur*
                                                          October 7, 1925

Dear friend,

I am sorry that, as a result of a mistake in my office, we probably sent you a letter intended for a police officer, while the letter you should have received went to another destination. Having been very busy these days, I could not personally supervise the mailing of my letters. My reply will therefore reach you a little late, for which I ask you to accept my apologies. Another question: have you instructed Pleyel to provide a good instrument for you in Zürich and Basel? You will recall that the one last year was muted and did not satisfy you. Since Casadesus will also play this winter in several Swiss cities, Pleyel would do well quickly to send one of their best instruments to their general representative in Switzerland. If you have not already done so, would you recommend this to them?

Friendly greetings.

Your   Werner Reinhart

STRAVINSKY TO REINHART   *Nice*
                                                          October 10, 1925

My dear friend,

Thank you for your letter of the 5th. In the meantime, you should have received my letter in which I tell you about the impossibility of granting absolute exclusivity to Mlle Moodie, though I am fully in accord with your request to permit her to perform this suite at the same time that Kochanski plays it. I only want to put more order in our little agreement, and to add the following: Everything that I have said pertains to the period ending June 1, 1927, but if this suite is published between June 1, 1926, and June 1, 1927, Mlle Moodie must return my manuscript to me. Then, in case she needs the music, she can obtain it from my publishers.

My wife and I are very grateful for your kind invitation, but it will be more convenient for us to reside near Andreae for the rehearsals.

My wife also thanks you for your kind words, and she asks me to tell you not to bother yourself with the question of customs, which is of no importance. What does annoy us is that the package must be lost, since we have not yet received it.

Awaiting news of you, I send you, my dear Reinhart, very affectionate greetings.

I. Stravinsky

REINHART TO STRAVINSKY

Very dear friend,

Just before leaving for Trieste on a business trip, I would like to thank you again for your two letters. I am sorry to hear what you say on the subject of the Pergolesi suite, and I wonder if a conclusion exists somewhere on the part of the Wolff agency in Berlin. I have received a letter from Mlle Moodie in which she expresses her joy in the violin part, which she is practicing. She tells me that everything is arranged for Frankfurt, Winterthur, etc. She has seen Wolff, who showed her your letter. Before you make an agreement with another soloist, I recommend that you put yourself in direct communication with Mlle Moodie at her permanent address in Berlin: Viktoria Luise Platz 12.

I regret that Madame Stravinsky has still not received the Venetian glass. I will make inquiries at the store.

Excuse these hasty lines, and believe, dear friend, in my best wishes.

Werner Reinhart

REINHART TO STRAVINSKY

My dear friend,

Back from Trieste, I find Madame Stravinsky's kind letter on the subject of the piano that you will play in Switzerland. I have made a note about the matter.

Since I must leave again on business on the 29th (Germany and Holland) and probably will not return until November 8 or 9, perhaps it will be best for you and your family to stay in Zürich first. Also, you will be closer to the Tonhalle. I assume that you are in direct communication with Volkmar Andreae (Hans Huberstrasse 4, Zürich) on the question of the rehearsals. He can also reserve your rooms at the Hôtel Baur-au-Lac, if you want to arrange that directly. I will see you on my return, November 10 at the latest, if not the evening before.

For Winterthur, I thought of inviting only a small group of friends for the recital of the Piano Sonata, the Pergolesi suite, and, as I hope, movements from the Serenade that you mentioned to me. I think that you will also find this program agreeable.

Excuse this hasty note. Please present my respects to Madame Stravinsky, and believe me, dear friend, to be

your cordially devoted   Werner Reinhart

STRAVINSKY TO REINHART   *Nice*
                                                  October 22, 1925

Dear friend,

Thank you for your letter of the 20th, just received.

In the end, it will be more convenient for me to stay at the Hôtel Baur in Zürich because of my rehearsals with Andreae. Therefore, would you kindly reserve two rooms for the three of us beginning the evening of November 8.

I am delighted that everything is now settled with Mlle Moodie for my violin and piano suite, and if I spoke to you of a certain restriction in the exclusivity that I gave her, this would take effect only in the event that she finds it impossible to perform with me and thus would deprive me of a very important piece in my own program. Tell me if you are in agreement with this. Answer me in Paris at the Maison Pleyel (24, rue Rochechouart), where I will be on Wednesday morning. See you soon, dear friend.

                        Your very devoted   Igor Stravinsky

REINHART TO STRAVINSKY   *Winterthur*
                                                  October 27, 1925

Paris

My dear friend,

A word in haste to tell you that I am in full agreement with your proposition concerning the Pergolesi suite: in cases where you cannot play the composition with Mlle Moodie, you are free to play it with another violinist. I have just received a card from her asking me to tell you that she can perform the suite with you here, in Frankfurt, and in Berlin.

Excuse me if I again take the liberty of sending you a copy of a letter from M. Luigi Ansbacher of Milan (via Armorari 8) on the subject of the proposed Milan concerts. You will see that this committee is divided over your terms. Perhaps M. Ansbacher's explanations will allow you to make concessions. Obviously, this is for you to decide.

I reserved your rooms for the evening of November 8 at the Hôtel Baur-au-Lac, Zürich, where I look forward to seeing you on the 9th, if possible.

In haste,

                        your cordially devoted   Werner Reinhart.

I believe that Mlle Moodie will also be in Zürich beginning the 8th. Her address is Susenbergstrasse 100, telephone 3763 Hottingen.

STRAVINSKY TO REINHART

Winterthur

Dear friend.

It has been a long time since I have heard from you. In the meantime, Bischoff, whom I saw not long ago, told me that you were back in Switzerland and that if I wished to correspond with you, I had only to write to Winterthur. This is what I am doing, in the hope that these lines will reach you soon.

I am spending this summer in the Savoie, on the Lake of Annecy, as I have done these past few years, and am working at the moment on my new piano concerto, which I intend to play here and there this season in Europe. I also wanted to come and play it with Andreae in Zürich and in Winterthur but have not yet written to him, wanting first to know from you if there is some way to arrange these two appearances, one right after the other. What do you think? Will you be there yourself? I would like to do it, if it is feasible, at the end of November.

Hoping to have a few lines from you, I send you, dear friend, my friendly regards of long standing.

Igor Stravinsky

REINHART TO STRAVINSKY

My dear friend,

I fear that my long silence may have surprised, if not worried, you. I cannot even say that my frequent trips and my busyness in general are sufficient excuses. After all, one ought to find the time to write to one's friends now and then.

When your letter written in August arrived here, I was still in North America. That is why, to my great regret, I could do nothing concerning your project of playing your new piano concerto here and in Zürich. I knew that by that time the programs were already set in our two cities. My friend Andreae, whom I saw upon my return, also regretted not being able to invite you this season, but both of us hope that this can be arranged for the beginning of next season (October 1930).

Meanwhile, you have had the sorrow of losing your great friend Diaghilev. I was truly grieved by this sad news, knowing what a big role this friend played in your life. I met him only once (in London) and was immediately struck by his towering personality. Everything he undertook bore the extraordinary imprint of this great choreographic creator. I do not think that people yet realize what art in general owes to him. Thus, though a bit tardily, I wanted to express my deepest sympathy to you, dear friend.

Last spring, I had the opportunity to hear your *Baiser de la fée* at La Scala in Milan with Ida Rubinstein and was deeply moved by your work, whose piano score you had so kindly given to me some time ago. I had to say to myself as well, alas, how far our present-day audiences are in general from grasping the meaning and all the beauty of music that is so simple and pure. One must, in my opinion, go all the way back to Haydn to find a language whose richness is in its simplicity.

Soon (December 4) we are going to hear this work here, in a concert conducted by Scherchen, and I am delighted in anticipation.

I often regret that we are unable to see each other as often as in the past, but I hope that you will return to Switzerland one day or that I can meet you in Paris or in Nice. I hope that you and yours are well and would be delighted to hear from you when the opportunity arises.

In the meantime, dear friend, please convey my respects to Madame Stravinsky.

Your cordially devoted   Werner Reinhart

REINHART TO STRAVINSKY

Winterthur
January 23, 1930
[Telegram]

Nice[17]

Would it be possible for you to come here and play your Capriccio with Ansermet on March 19? If so, please let me know your terms. Friendly greetings,   Werner Reinhart

Hotel Fürstenhof
Berlin
January 23, 1930
STRAVINSKY TO REINHART   *[Draft of a telegram]* [18]

I will play the Capriccio on March 19 with pleasure. Terms $500. Respond to Kaiserhof, Leipzig. Friendly greetings,   I. Stravinsky

REINHART TO STRAVINSKY

Winterthur
January 27, 1930
[Telegram]

Hotel Kaiserhof
Leipzig

Agreed to your terms. Am delighted to be seeing you again. Friendly greetings,   Reinhart

---

[17] Forwarded to Berlin.
[18] In the hand of Vera Sudeikina.

Winterthur
                                                    January 30, 1930

Leipzig

Dear friend,

I would have liked to write to you right away to tell you of my joy at receiving
your telegram accepting our proposal for March 19. I was very busy at the time,
however, and beg you to excuse the delay. This morning I received your nice
lines from Leipzig, and I am very touched that you have so kindly consented to
come and play your Capriccio, despite the inconvenience caused by the proposed date. I am overjoyed at the thought of seeing you again soon and of being
able to hear your new work, about which René Morax wrote to me with great
enthusiasm the day after the premiere in Paris, which, unhappily, I was unable
to attend myself.

Our board has agreed to your terms, namely, $500.

Ansermet has already sent us several proposals for the program, which we
are now considering. He will arrive here from Prague on March 14 to begin the
rehearsals, which will take place on the 14th, 17th, 18th, and 19th (open rehearsal at 1:30 in the afternoon).

If, after your current tour, you feel the need to come here and rest, I think
it unnecessary for me to tell you that you are always welcome at Rychenberg.
Will I also have the pleasure of seeing Madame Stravinsky again this time? I
hope so.

For the orchestra parts, I will address myself directly to M. Païchadze in
Paris.

Excuse, dear friend, these hasty lines.

                    Your cordially devoted   Werner Reinhart

Winterthur
                                                    February 28, 1930

My dear friend,

I hope that you received my letter of January 30 addressed to Leipzig and that
in the meantime you have returned safely to your family.

Your publisher in Paris has written to me saying that you possess the only
parts for the Capriccio and that he has asked you to send them to us upon the
conclusion of your tour. As we are in the habit of having our musicians study
their parts even before the rehearsals begin, I would be much obliged, unless
you have already done so, if you would send all the orchestra parts to my address here so that I may distribute them to the players immediately.

I would also like to relay to you the program we have decided upon with
Ansermet, namely:

1. Handel: Concerto Grosso in G minor, Op. 6, no. 6
2. Mozart: Symphony in D major, K. 504

3. Capriccio
4. *Le Chant du rossignol*

I have already ordered the parts for *Rossignol* from Paris and am delighted to be able to hear this work under the direction of our friend Ansermet. It has not yet been done here, and up until now I have not had the opportunity to hear it elsewhere.

I hope to hear from you soon. Please present my respects to Madame Stravinsky, my dear friend.

Your cordially devoted   Werner Reinhart

STRAVINSKY TO REINHART

March 6, 1930
[Draft of a telegram]

Nice

Please arrange for the concert a Steinway of the *heller Klang spielart leicht* type. Friendly greetings,   Stravinsky

STRAVINSKY TO REINHART

March 12, 1930

Winterthur

My dear friend,

Delighted to come and play for you and to see you again soon!

I arrive on Tuesday (leaving Geneva about 11:00) around 5:00 in Zürich, and I hope to get an immediate connection to Winterthur; I only hope that I do not miss my rehearsal.

Madame Ansermet will take the same train as I in Geneva, and you will find us together at the station if you come to fetch us.

Until then, dear friend. Cordially.

Your   Igor Stravinsky

STRAVINSKY TO REINHART

March 27, 1930

My very dear friend,

Thank you for the handsome Japanese salad bowl that I have just received, and thank you again for your great hospitality; I am very grateful for this remembrance of my stay with you at Rychenberg. There were so many things that gave me real pleasure. Some of them one does not mention, wanting to keep them to oneself. As for the others, one would like, on the contrary, to shout with joy. . . .

REINHART TO STRAVINSKY   *April 9, 1930*

My dear friend,

Thank you for your kind letter and for the wonderful photographs, which capture the unforgettable memory of your visits with us in such a lively way. I still think of the delightful hours spent in your company and of the magnificent concert, and I only regret that you could not stay a little longer.

If I have not been able to settle the question of the concert that we had discussed, the reason is that we have had to wait for Scherchen's dates. You know that this friend is always very busy and is able to come to Winterthur only at certain times. Now he informs us that his first concert will take place on October 8. I do not think that it would be a very good idea to schedule the second concert (under your direction) for October 15 (the date following Zürich). First, these dates are very close; second, you know that we must borrow a large number of our musicians for the *Sacre* from Andreae, which will be inconvenient for the simultaneous preparation of a concert at Winterthur. For this reason I would like to ask if you can give us some alternate dates, perhaps on the return from your German tour. For us, the day of the concert, as you know, must always be a Wednesday. Scherchen's dates, after the October 8 concert, are October 28, November 5, February 25, April 1.

Before discussing the question again with our committee, I would like to know what other possibilities you envision for next winter.

My sister and brother-in-law told me of the great pleasure they had in meeting you on the train to Geneva. I hope that everyone at home is well, and I ask you to present my respects to Madame Stravinsky and to believe me, my dear friend, to be

your very cordially devoted   Werner Reinhart

REINHART TO STRAVINSKY   *Winterthur*
                                                         April 17, 1930
Nice   *[Telegram]*

October 15 unfortunately impractical. Other dates still possible are November 19, December 17, January 21, February 4, March 18. Please telegraph Musikkollegium.

STRAVINSKY TO REINHART   *Nice*
                                                         April 17, 1930
Musikkollegium   *[Telegram]*
Winterthur

Agreed for January 21.   Stravinsky

REINHART TO STRAVINSKY   *Winterthur*
                                                          April 23, 1930

My dear friend,

Excuse me if, because of the Easter holidays, I have not yet confirmed our exchange of telegrams. I greatly regret that an arrangement with your Zürich concert (October 14) could not be worked out for the reasons that I explained to you in my first letter. We always depend on a certain number of musicians from Zürich for our concerts, and, reciprocally, this time Zürich will need (for the *Sacre*) a large number of supplementary players from Winterthur. Conflicts in rehearsal schedules between the two cities are therefore inevitable. We also regret that we must oblige you to make a special trip to come to us, and we thank you very much for having so kindly accepted the January 21 date for the concert. If you wish, we can now set the rehearsals for the 19th and 20th, as well as for January 17. If you have suggestions on the subject of the rehearsals, please give them to me.

For the program, you proposed *Apollon Musagète* and *Le Baiser de la fée* (complete), and this has been accepted by our committee. I assume that the fee, as in Zürich, is $500.

I greatly look forward to the prospect of seeing you here again next season, and I hope that on this occasion it will be possible for Madame Stravinsky to accompany you. Excuse this hurried business letter. With my respects to Madame Stravinsky, believe, dear friend, in my faithful friendship.

                                                    Werner Reinhart

P.S.   Between April 26 and May 16, I will be at Karlsbad (Czechoslavakia), "Haus Columbus."

STRAVINSKY TO REINHART   *April 27, 1930*

Karlsbad

Thank you, dear friend, for your letter of the 23rd. My terms will be the same as for last time.

I think that if all goes well with us here, I will be able to come with my wife and perhaps with my elder daughter.

For the rehearsals, I will tell you later, not being able today to calculate the time necessary.

In haste, I send you my friendly and faithful greetings, my dear!

                                                    Your   I. Stravinsky

REINHART TO STRAVINSKY

Karlovy-Vary
Karlsbad
May 10, 1930
[Postcard] [19]

Many thanks, dear friend, for your kind letter received here, where I am taking a very good cure. I will write to you upon my return on the subject of the rehearsals. I expect to be back by the 18th. Very friendly greetings,

your   Werner Reinhart

REINHART TO STRAVINSKY

Reykjavik
Iceland
August 11, 1930
[Postcard]

Charavines-les-Bains
Isère

My dear friend,

For the past two weeks, for a change, I have been exploring here with a friend. The desolation and the grandeur of the land are unparalleled. Now we are on the west coast, with its beautiful fjords. We will leave Reykjavik in a few days for Copenhagen. I thank you again for your kind letter and send you my best wishes.

Werner Reinhart

REINHART TO STRAVINSKY

Winterthur
September 24, 1930

My dear friend,

As the date of your Zürich concert draws near, I would like to ask if, this time, you and Madame Stravinsky would give me the great pleasure of staying here with me. I suppose that you prefer to stay in Zürich during the period of the rehearsals and the concert, but if you could come here a little earlier, with Madame Stravinsky and any of your children who may come with you on this trip, you could spend some days at Rychenberg. That would give me great pleasure.

I greatly look forward to seeing you soon, dear friend, and to hearing the Zürich concert. I hope that you spent a good summer, and I send you and yours my very cordial wishes.

Your very devoted   Werner Reinhart

REINHART TO STRAVINSKY

Winterthur
September 25, 1930

My dear friend,

Many thanks for your kind postcard. I am distraught not to be able to hear and applaud you in Basel, but a long time ago I promised Othmar Schoeck to attend

---

[19] Picture postcard of the Russian church in Karlsbad.

the premiere at Dresden of his new opera, *Vom Fischer und syner Fru* (the story by Grimm). Since this takes place on October 3, I am obliged to leave on Thursday afternoon. I would so much have liked to hear you in Basel, but I hope that you will excuse my absence. One of these days I will try to speak with you on the telephone to fix the details of your visit. If you wish, you could also try to telephone me before Thursday at 1:00. The office number is 27.61, the home number, 352. From the 3rd to the 5th I will be at the Hotel Bellevue, Dresden, then at Rychenberg on Monday, October 6, in the afternoon. I hope that all goes well in Basel.[20] I will be very happy to see you soon, and, in the meantime, my dear friend, I send you my very cordial wishes.

Werner Reinhart

STRAVINSKY TO REINHART   *October 9, 1930*

Very dear friend,

As I told Andreae, who came to see me the other day in Basel, I will arrive in Winterthur with Theodore this Saturday at 4:48 p.m.

I very much look forward to seeing you again, and I embrace you, my dear, in friendship.

Your

Winterthur

REINHART TO STRAVINSKY   *January 2, 1931*

The new year has begun before I have sent a note to you, but I hope that these lines will reach you in time for the Russian new year, and I send my best wishes to you and your family for that occasion. May this new year be a good and happy one for you. My pleasure in having you and your son Theodore at my house was so great that I am already anticipating the thought of seeing you again soon— you and, as I hope, Madame Stravinsky as well. The rehearsals do not begin until Monday the 19th and are scheduled as follows: January 19: 9:30 a.m., strings only; 2:00 p.m., winds; 7:00 p.m., full orchestra; January 20: 9:30, full orchestra; January 21: 1:15 p.m., dress rehearsal; 7:30, concert. I hope that you will come on Saturday. The orchestra is away on the 17th. I would like to invite some friends for dinner on Sunday, January 18, and you would be very kind to send me word about your arrival and that of Madame Stravinsky.

I hope that everything went smoothly for you in Germany in spite of the unfavorable weather. I think of you often and send you, dear friend, my sincerest wishes.

Your   Werner Reinhart

---

[20] From Munich, on October 2, Reinhart sent Stravinsky a "best wishes" telegram in care of the Music Casino in Basel.

[*Card enclosed in the same envelope*

My letter was already written when I received your kind lines. Many thanks, dear friend, for your good wishes. I will arrange the program according to your instructions. I look forward to seeing you again, you and Madame Stravinsky, on the 17th,[21] and I will await further word about the exact hour of your arrival.

Very cordially yours,   W.R.

REINHART TO STRAVINSKY *Winterthur*
January 28, 1931

My dear friend,

Many thanks again for your kind postcard from Geneva. I will write to you at greater length another time. Today I would like only to forward a letter from Mr. Siegfried Fritz Müller, the young pianist from St. Gall, at his request. I attach a copy typed in my office to make it easier for you to read (Mr. Müller's handwriting not being very legible).

I hope that you had a good tour, without any indispositions brought on by this season of colds, and that you will soon rejoin your family in good health. We continue to talk about the unforgettable days with you and yours. [?] left me on Sunday and returned to Lignières, where I forwarded your card to him. We will certainly not forget your kind invitation for April 18, and I hope to be able definitely to settle the end of February for you as soon as I see my way more clearly concerning other trips that I might have to undertake. In the meantime, my best regards to your family. I send you a friendly embrace.

Werner Reinhart

STRAVINSKY TO REINHART *Nice*
February 10, 1931

Very dear friend,

A word in great haste—have you heard from Andreae and from Basel (Weingartner)? I am being asked to accept certain dates for my engagements next season, and I cannot answer without knowing if our projects will be realized, and, if so, when (at approximately what period). I will be here in Nice until this Saturday, then go to Paris (Pleyel), then London (in care of Madame Courtauld, 20 Portman Square) until February 4, then again for a few days to Paris. Andreae promised to write, but up to now I have received nothing.

Thank you for your kind letter, and thanks also for having sent that of Mr. Siegfried Fritz Müller. I wrote him a short thank-you note.

---

[21] On January 19, Ansermet, in London, cabled Stravinsky at Rychenberg: "Everything arranged. I am at the Strand Palace Hotel."

Do not forget your promise to come and see us in April. We are counting on this very strongly. I embrace you very cordially.

REINHART TO STRAVINSKY   *November 26, 1931*

My dear friend,

Many thanks for your words. I am enormously happy to be able to come to Cologne to hear the Violin Concerto and to see you and to hear you on this occasion. I will also be in Mainz on Saturday, arriving on the *Rheingold,* and I will probably see you at the concert [in Mainz] at 5:00 as well as at the banquet afterward. My hotel in Mainz is the Holland Haus. Sunday I leave Mainz, also on the *Rheingold,* and in Cologne I will be staying at the Dom Hotel. Unfortunately, I must leave on Monday at midnight, after the open rehearsal. But I am happy to be able at least to have done my best and to have absented myself for two days. I will see Alma Moodie[22] on Sunday.

Until soon, dear friend, and very cordially,

your   Werner Reinhart.

My best wishes to Madame Sudeikina.

REINHART TO STRAVINSKY   *Winterthur*
                                                         December 31, 1931
Voreppe   *[Postcard]*[23]

My dear friend,

I thank you for your good wishes and send you and yours my best greetings and my friendliest thoughts for a good New Year.

Your   Werner Reinhart

STRAVINSKY TO REINHART   *Voreppe*
                                                         June 4, 1932
Winterthur

My dear friend,

I understand that someone from Winterthur has requested the parts of my *Symphony of Psalms.* Is it the board of the Musikkollegium or another organization that has made this request? If it is the Musikkollegium that intends to perform it, I would like to know if your board would be interested in having me

---

[22] Mlle Moodie had written to Stravinsky from Cologne, November 9, inviting him and Madame Sudeikina to spend the Saturday evening with Reinhart at her residence, and the Sunday evening as well.

[23] Picture postcard of the Ringacker Chapel at Loèche-la-Ville.

present this important work to your audiences myself, as we had already discussed when I last passed through Winterthur.

Dear friend, I am sure that you will forgive me the indiscretion of this question if you think of my longing (a bit jealous, I admit) to do it myself in your city (as I have done these last few years with all of my recent works) and if you think of the financial side of my conducting activities, which I could not neglect without dealing a mortal blow to this principal source of income.

I make no secret of it, dear friend, I counted a great deal on the concert next autumn, as I did on the one at the Zürich Tonhalle and on that of Basel with Weingartner, with whom you kindly intended to put in a good word in my behalf. Andreae, who sent me kind congratulations on my fiftieth birthday (he is my elder by one month—May 18 instead of June 18!), does not breathe a word of this projected concert, which he claimed (a year ago) to be forced to postpone to next season.

I had also planned to give some chamber-music concerts in Switzerland this autumn with Dushkin. The program would be the same that I performed with him in Italy two months ago with such success, nothing but the duos for violin and piano: (1) *Pulcinella* (20 minutes), (2) p [iano] / violin concerto (23 m [inutes]), (3) duo for violin and piano (in the process of being composed— about 12 min [utes]), and, to finish, the Berceuse from *Firebird* and the Danse russe from *Petrushka*.

What do you think of this project? Should I write to Walter Schulthess to find out what must be done at that end?

A word from you would give me great pleasure. I have not heard from you in a long time.

Your faithfully devoted

REINHART TO STRAVINSKY   *Winterthur*
                                          June 13, 1932
My dear friend,

Thank you very much for your kind letter. You have reason to be annoyed with me for leaving you so long without news, but I think you know the kind of life I lead here, which unfortunately forces me to neglect and to put off so many things, especially during the winter. On top of that, I was ill with tonsillitis from the beginning of January into February. So my sister and I went to take a rest at Cap d'Antibes; we sorely regretted that you no longer live in Nice, in which case we would surely have come to see you. Having already lost a great deal of time, I unfortunately also could not stop by en route in Voreppe, but I still hope to be able to avail myself of your very kind invitation to come and see you there. I hope that you had a good winter and that everyone is well. I took advantage of a trip to Basel this spring to see the administration of the Kunsthaus concerning your son Theodore. I was told then that, owing to numerous other questions, they had not yet been able to come to a decision, and that Theodore's photographs as well as his drawings were still with the committee. I am really annoyed at the way that this has dragged on. Do you know anything about it?

Answering your question concerning the *Symphony of Psalms,* I can assure you that your work will indeed be performed here on November 3 by the Gemischter Chor, an association not connected with the Musikkollegium and led by Walter Reinhart. The concert will take place in our Protestant church, with which you are familiar, and as part of a subscription series. Since Reinhart has not conducted here for several years, the board was inclined to accede to his request to conduct the entire program, which includes, moreover, music by Handel and Bach. You understand, then, I think, the reasons that prevented us from passing the baton on to you this time to conduct your piece yourself. I am certain that Reinhart and his chorus will give it an excellent performance. They have already been working enthusiastically on it for several weeks. On the other hand, and in principle, your project of coming here with Dushkin interests me very much, and I will submit it to our board with pleasure. With this object in view, could you, dear friend, tell me what your terms (lump sum) would be for such an evening? I have also spoken about it to Schulthess, who promised me that he would write to you directly. I am surprised that Andreae has not spoken to you about the performance of the *Symphony of Psalms* that he gave on March 15 in Zürich, which was excellent. As for Basel, you know that, unfortunately, my approaches to Weingartner have been unsuccessful up to now. Ansermet, who was here yesterday, has already told me about your new duo, and I am counting very much on being able to hear it here in the autumn. What are the dates (more or less) of your Swiss tour?

My letter will reach you a few days before your fiftieth birthday, which I have certainly not forgotten. Chance has even placed in my hands a little something with which I hope to be able to afford you a bit of pleasure and that I will send off in time for the 18th. It is only a small sign from me to let you know that I will be thinking especially of you and wishing you and yours the best on that day. I will also be recalling anew all that I owe already to your friendship, and I have but one wish, that it will continue for a very long time, and also that I will have the pleasure of seeing you again a bit more often in the future.

Please convey my best wishes to your family, my dear friend.

Faithfully, your very devoted   Werner Reinhart

STRAVINSKY TO REINHART   *Voreppe*
                                                   June 17, 1932

Winterthur

My dear friend,

I was very touched by your letter of June 13, and while awaiting the opportunity of writing to you at greater length (I am leaving for Frankfurt, where Rosbaud is performing *Mavra* with the Rundfunk on June 23), I will restrict myself to these lines answering your question concerning my project of a Swiss tour next autumn.

As a matter of fact, I received a letter from Schulthess and responded immediately, entrusting him with carrying out my chamber-evening project with Dushkin in Switzerland. Unfortunately, I have not received anything from him enabling me to tell you, even approximately, the dates of these projected concerts. The best and most practical thing would be for you to deal directly with him in joining my Winterthur concert, if this is to take place, with those that I hope to find through him.

As for my terms (to submit them to your committee), I would prefer that you set them yourself: your terms will be mine. I will share the fee that I am to be paid for this concert with Dushkin, according to the terms established between the two of us for similar evenings of chamber music. Thus you need not concern yourself with Dushkin's fee.

I hope to hear from you soon, and send you, my very dear friend, my faithful regards.

STRAVINSKY TO REINHART

Winterthur

Voreppe
July 16, 1932

My dear Reinhart,

I am in the process of corresponding with Schulthess concerning my chamber concerts (with Dushkin), about which I have already spoken to you. He makes no secret of the difficulty of finding these for me, since, as he says, few organizations exist (none, as it were) in Switzerland able to take part in such a venture, given the size of the fee that must be guaranteed. Still, he will try once more with Bern and St. Gall to see if someone could arrange something for me there.

In another connection, he would like to enter into negotiations with Dr. Andreae concerning my conducting the Tonhalle concert, at which Dushkin will play my Violin Concerto, on March 27/28, 1933. But Andreae is on vacation, and the decision on this engagement is also destined to be put off for some time. Could you not lend us a helping hand with Andreae in this business? It would be so kind of you!

Schulthess asks me when my chamber-music concert with Dushkin in Winterthur could take place. On this question, too, I was distressed not to be able to give an answer, as I have heard nothing concerning this since our last letters. Where does this matter stand? If your committee would like to agree to this concert, could I ask you to schedule it close to the Zürich dates (immediately before or after March 27/28)? I would be infinitely grateful if you would help me out in all these matters, for I am now making my arrangements and setting the dates for next season.

Thank you in advance, my dear friend, and do not bear me too much ill will for the bother that I am causing you with these questions.

Affectionately, your   I. Str.

REINHART TO STRAVINSKY   *Winterthur*
                                                   July 25, 1932

My dear friend,

Many thanks once again for your two letters. I was happy to see that Weber's little "Albumblatt" pleased you.[24]

I am finally able to give you the details of your chamber concert here with Dushkin. The committee was able to set it for March 29, 1933,[25] on the terms that you stated to Schulthess, namely, a lump sum of 2,000 Swiss francs. Unfortunately, I have not been able to do anything about Andreae, who is still away, but Schulthess told me that he will write to him again, insisting that the Tonhalle Gesellschaft invite you to conduct your Violin Concerto on March 27 and 28. As for Bern and St. Gall, the prospects of arranging something for you there do not appear to be very good, as things now stand, according to Schulthess, and unfortunately I cannot use my influence in these areas, with which I am not very familiar.

I went to see Gamper last Sunday, who told me that you enjoyed his poems. To me they recall so well the memory of our stay with you.

Beginning the 26th of this month, I am going to spend two weeks at my Château de Muzot, in Sierre.

I hope that you are having a good summer in Voreppe and ask you please to convey my best wishes to your family.

                    Your cordially devoted   Werner Reinhart

REINHART TO STRAVINSKY   *Winterthur*
                                                   August 26, 1932

My dear friend,

Before leaving (am taking off again for two weeks in England), I wanted to thank you very much for your nice parcel. This Pater Noster is a beautiful composition, and you gave me great pleasure in sending it. I am going to show it

---

[24] Doppel Canon a 4 by Carl Maria von Weber, the original manuscript, signed and dated by Weber: "Dresden, September 25, 1819." Reinhart inscribed the verso: "To the great friend and great musician Igor Stravinsky, as a token of an ardent affection and with heartfelt good wishes for June 18, 1932." Stravinsky affixed this fiftieth-birthday gift to the wall of his studio.

[25] On August 3, Stravinsky wrote to the administration of the Musikkollegium: "My friend Mr. Werner Reinhart has informed me that you have chosen the date of March 29, 1933, for my chamber-music evening with Mr. Dushkin. Unfortunately, it seems that Mr. Dushkin is engaged by the Amsterdam Concertgebouw for March 30 and is required at a rehearsal with Mengelberg on the morning of this day. Would you kindly advance the date of our chamber-music evening to a day before the Zürich Tonhalle concert, where Mr. Dushkin will appear as soloist on March 27/28, 1933? I am sorry to have to inconvenience you with this change of date."

to Hermann Dubs[26] as well, who is sure to be especially interested in such a composition.

I know—from your son Nini—that you too are traveling. Nevertheless, could you send us the exact program of your chamber concert, addressing it simply to the Musikkollegium, St. Georgenplatz, Winterthur? I would like to publish it in our general program, which should appear in mid-September.

My best wishes to your family and my friendly thoughts to you, my dear.

Your devoted   Werner Reinhart

STRAVINSKY TO REINHART   *Voreppe*
                                                August 31, 1933
Winterthur

A note, dear friend, to thank you for your kind letter answering that of my son (who wrote for me, since I was somewhat weak after three days of fasting because of an intestinal infection).

Very cordially yours,   I. Stravinsky

REINHART TO STRAVINSKY   *Winterthur*
                                               January 13, 1934
My dear friend,

I had intended to write to you for Christmas, but the end of the year always brings me such an overload of work that my correspondence with friends suffers in consequence. I remember, however, that I am still in time to send you my wishes for the Russian new year, which you must be celebrating now. Above all, I wish you and your family good health, especially your son Nini; I was upset to learn from him that because of illness, he had to cancel his recital in my home. I hope that the mountain [Sancellemoz] will restore his health.

It is a very long time since we exchanged news, and I hope that you have begun the winter well and in better health than when I saw you last spring. Between times we have successfully inaugurated our new concert hall, the Stadthaus. Scherchen gave us an excellent performance of your *Firebird,* and I think that you would have been pleased had you heard it. Is the date of the premiere of *Perséphone* already set?[27] Unhappily, I cannot promise to be there on that day, in spite of my great desire, since the winter generally does not permit me to be away from here very much. Nevertheless, I am interested to know when this work will be given at the Opéra.

---

[26] Choral conductor. The Stravinskys were fond of him, and he was one of the few people they visited during their stay in Zürich in October 1968.

[27] Scherchen wrote to Stravinsky on January 25, saying that he would like to see the score of *Perséphone,* which he has heard about from Werner Reinhart.

I am sending you today, or with a short delay, a little Christmas gift, the first volume of *The Mosaics of St. Sophia*. Perhaps you already have this volume, which has recently appeared, and in this case the copy will, I think, please your son Theodore.

Once again, with all my best thoughts for you and yours, I am, my dear friend,

very cordially yours,   Werner Reinhart

REINHART TO STRAVINSKY   *Winterthur*
                                          April 29, 1934

My dear friend,

I had counted on being able to come to Paris for the premiere of *Perséphone*. But to leave my work just now is really too difficult for me. I am very unhappy, because I would so much have liked to hear the piece from a place near you. Dear friend, the day will come when I will attend the premiere of one of your new works. Since the unforgettable time of the *Soldat,* I feel so extraordinarily attached to you and to your music that to have to miss a beautiful premiere is really painful. I hope, dear friend, that I do not have to tell you that my thoughts will be especially near to you tomorrow evening. I do not abandon the hope of being able to attend one of the other performances of your new ballet.[28] I will let you know about this. I ask you to remember me to your family and to believe me, my dear friend, to be

your very affectionately devoted   Werner Reinhart

REINHART TO STRAVINSKY   *Winterthur*
                                          October 22, 1936

My dear friend,

It seems an eternity since we exchanged news. I should have told you long ago how much I look forward to seeing you here again, and soon. With the date of your concert approaching, I would like to settle certain questions with you. I know that you have to be in Zürich on November 8 (in the morning with Ramuz[29]), 9, and 10, the date of the performance in the Tonhalle. As I think that in this case you will prefer to stay in Zürich first, my sister has asked me to tell you that she and her husband would be very pleased to have you and your son stay with them (address: Prof. Felix Nagel, Freie Strasse 30, Zürich). Of course you will tell me if this is convenient for you. As for Winterthur, we want to propose, for the rehearsal, Tuesday, November 10, from 10:00 a.m. to

---

[28] Stravinsky wrote on the upper corner of this letter: "He came to the last performance, May 9, 1934."

[29] On November 8, Ramuz read part of his *Souvenirs sur Igor Stravinsky* as the first part of the program.

noon, and for the dress rehearsal Wednesday, November 11, the day of the concert, beginning 2:00 p.m.

It goes without saying that Scherchen would be pleased to prepare the accompaniment of your concerto before your arrival, so that the Tuesday rehearsal and the open one will be sufficient for you. I would like to tell you again that we have changed the program of the Winterthur concert slightly, dropping the Mussorgsky (*Night on Bald Mountain*) in favor of the Tchaikovsky. The order of the program is as follows:

1. Tchaikovsky: Symphony No. 5, Op. 64
2. Stravinsky: Piano Concerto
3. Stravinsky: Concerto for Two Solo Pianos[30]

Please tell me once again the exact duration of the two concertos.

I hope that all is well with you. Please remember me to Madame Stravinsky, and believe me, dear friend, to be

your very cordially devoted   Werner Reinhart

STRAVINSKY TO REINHART   *Paris*
                                                 October 23, 1936
My dear friend,

Thank you for your friendly lines. I am very touched by the kind invitation from the Nagels, and I accept it with pleasure; I will write to thank them and to confirm my acceptance.

The Tuesday rehearsal, November 10 (10:00 to 12:00 in the morning), suits me if I do not have any rehearsals in Zürich. I think that with this rehearsal and the open one, in which I will need a good hour of work, I will have every possibility of preparing the performance of my concerto. I prefer to prepare it myself, so please do not ask M. Scherchen to polish this music before my arrival, as you suggested.[31]

Very happy to see you again soon, I send you, my dear friend, my very cordial greetings.

---

[30] Stravinsky and his son played the Concerto per due pianoforti soli again in Naples on November 29.

[31] Stravinsky had turned against Scherchen since October 1934. On the 24th of that month, Scherchen conducted a concert in Strasbourg with a program consisting of the *Firebird* Suite, the Piano Concerto, and the *Sacre*. Soulima Stravinsky was the piano soloist. He wrote to his father, October 20 and 24, severely criticizing Scherchen ("Scherchen is really terrible, and everything he is doing is a great mess"). Apparently suspecting this, Scherchen sent a long letter to Stravinsky detailing the amount of rehearsal time given to each piece and expressing admiration for Stravinsky's music and for his son's exactness in the Concerto. (Stravinsky himself had played his concerto, with Scherchen conducting, in two concerts in Milan in June

STRAVINSKY TO REINHART   *Paris*
                                                          January 3, 1938

Dear friend,

A few words to you on the subject of my new ballet, *Jeu de cartes*. I believe that the piece is listed in the programs of the symphonic season in Zürich and in Winterthur and that Ansermet is to conduct.

I have just learned that Ansermet made cuts in his [Orchestre de la] Suisse Romande performances recently, in spite of my categorical interdiction. (Two months ago we had a very painful exchange of letters on the matter.) I lack the necessary time now to explain to you the origins of the strange obsession from which he has suffered for some time. Today I want only to inform you of my wishes as the author. For this reason you will find enclosed the copy of a letter that I sent to the Tonhalle at the same time as this one.

I avail myself of this opportunity to wish you and yours a good and happy year.

                                              Your faithfully devoted

REINHART TO STRAVINSKY   *Winterthur*
                                                          January 5, 1938

Dear friend,

I thank you for your letter and good wishes, and I would like, in turn, though more than a little late, to send you and your family my best wishes for the year that has just begun. I hope that you are all well and that Madame Stravinsky's health will cause you less worry in the new year.

I read with interest what you told me on the subject of your ballet *Jeu de cartes*. I had enormous pleasure hearing the work conducted by Ansermet at the subscription concert in Zürich (November 16). At that time, not having had the pocket score in hand, I did not suspect that Ansermet had introduced cuts. Not until last month, when I saw Ansermet here, did he speak to me of the matter, about which he said you were very unhappy. I perfectly understand your point of view, as you have set it forth in your letter to the Tonhalle of

---

1926 and expressed no criticism.) On October 22, Stravinsky replied to his son's first letter in a telegram indicating his disbelief in the quality of the performances. On the same day, Stravinsky telegraphed to Charles Munch, director of the Strasbourg Conservatory, declining his invitation to attend the concert. Stravinsky filed all of the relevant documents of the occasion under the heading: "H. Scherchen, his hypocrisy, my answer, and the performance of my concerto by Nini under Scherchen's direction."

Scherchen conducted a Schoenberg memorial concert in Venice in September 1951, shortly after the third performance there of *The Rake's Progress*, but Stravinsky was already in Milan. The two former friends did not meet when they were together in Rome in April 1954. But in 1955, Stravinsky began to admire some of Scherchen's Bach recordings for Westminster, and in Berlin, in September 1956, after Stravinsky heard him conduct Henze's *König Hirsch*, cordial relations were resumed.

Zürich, and I feel that in a case where a conductor judges your work too long for a certain program, he should perform separate excerpts but not make cuts. At Winterthur, we have not yet scheduled the piece for one of our programs, having, as you know, counted on *Histoire du soldat* for this season. All of us have much regretted that this project fell through because of the insufficient number of engagements for the ensemble, but we hope that this will only be a postponement until next season and that we will finally have the pleasure of hearing your work in an authentic performance by its authors themselves.

The other day I met the new conductor of the Zürich Opera, Hans Swarowsky,[32] who told me that he will give your *Jeu de cartes* in ballet form at the theatre, together with Falla's *Tricorne* and a new ballet by a young Swiss composer, [Walter] Müller von Kulm. I take great pleasure in the anticipation of seeing this realization of your new work.

If you have the time to give me news of you, I will be very happy. I would like to know what you are doing and what your projects are. Will I perhaps have the pleasure of seeing you in Switzerland again this season? I reread with pleasure your *Chroniques* in the German edition, which seems to me well done from every point of view.

The day before yesterday I went to the funeral of Alice Bailly, the sad news of whose death you have undoubtedly heard. She had been overworking herself without rest for nearly two years, with the large job of decorating the foyer of the Théâtre de Lausanne. A good friend has disappeared, one who shared successes with you in Switzerland and in Paris, where I was also present. I return the copy of your letter addressed to Zürich, and I send you, dear friend, my very cordially devoted thoughts.

Werner Reinhart

---

[32] Hans Swarowsky (1899–1975), Hungarian conductor.

CORRESPONDENCE WITH

1917 ⚮ 1938

ANDRÉ GIDE

STRAVINSKY TO ANDRÉ GIDE

Fougères
Les Diablerets
Switzerland
August 2, 1917

Dear friend,

It was impossible for me to visit you tonight, simply because I do not feel well. Perhaps I have the beginnings of a cold, as a result of the change of altitude.[1] Rest well, and I will come to see you tomorrow morning.

Very sincerely, your   Igor Stravinsky

STRAVINSKY TO GIDE

Fougères
August 13, 1917
[Hand-delivered note]

Dear Gide,

Will you and your nephews join us for dinner at the Col de Jillous? One eats very well there, and besides, it is a lovely walk. Do you agree? When my son delivers this note, just tell him whether you will come to read the letter[2] to me, or whether you prefer that I come to you.

Cordially, your   Igor Stravinsky

GIDE TO STRAVINSKY

Cuverville
March 8, 1918

My dear Stravinsky,

More than once I have attempted to write to you, primarily to express, a little better than I was able to do over the telephone, how strongly I shared your grief.[3] . . . Oh, what sorrow still, and what horror! . . . Also, I want to tell you how much I liked your article in *Le Temps* and how touched we were when we read it.

Thank you for sending the little music workbooks [Eight Easy Pieces],

---

[1] Stravinsky had moved from Morges to Les Diablerets in mid-July.

[2] Probably from Ida Rubinstein, since Gide was in Switzerland to discuss with Stravinsky her project to stage Gide's French version of Shakespeare's *Antony and Cleopatra*.

[3] Gide had been in Les Diablerets when Stravinsky received the news of his brother Gury's death.

which I read with interest and played with a young student—but I fumed at the total absence of markings (A, B, or C—every eight measures, for example, as in some editions): you find your place just as you lose the child, or the child loses his place. . . . I also wanted to send you some photographs as a memento of our visit. . . . My nephews still speak of you in such lyrical fashion!

Finally, I wanted to tell you that my translation of *Cleopatra* is finished, and to ask how you feel about the work. I mean, can we expect you to write a score to illustrate the text? As you know, my deepest wish, now and always, is for you to do the music. I questioned Madame Rubinstein on this subject, but she claims . . . not to have heard from you in ages.[4] I was convinced that she, too, desires your collaboration, so I told her that I would write to you again and inquire about your intentions. The question cannot be put off any longer, and I thought that perhaps you could write more candidly to me than to her, if you have reservations or objections.

If you wish, I will send you a copy of my translation—now decidedly good—on which I have carefully indicated those points where music is required—in particular, at the moment of the battle of Actium (which takes place in the wings, or perhaps with the curtain lowered). A little later, at the time of the second battle, symphonic music is required, then a military symphony. I would be inconsolable if these pieces were not composed by you. Thus I await word from you. How reassuring it would be to know that you will do it.

Good-bye. Please present my respects to Madame Stravinsky, remember me to the children, and trust in my true affection for you.

André Gide

STRAVINSKY TO GIDE   *Morges*
                                                                    April 7, 1918
My dear Gide,

Thank you so much for your kind letter. Someday I will send an equally substantial communication to you, but at the moment, and with deep regret, I can only tell you that I have had to dismiss the idea of our proposed collaboration on *Antony and Cleopatra.* After quite a few letters and telegrams, and many financial concessions on my part, Madame Rubinstein, through Charles Péquin, her agent, has said that she will not go above her last offer, which was far from satisfactory for me. I was surprised, therefore, to learn from you that she still expects me to be in communication regarding the project, unless her agent does not keep her informed but acts on his own. But even if Rubinstein were to accept my terms, I could no longer do the work, having started another one [*Histoire du soldat*], which is fascinating and has me captivated.

---

[4] On November 10, 1917, Lyudmila Botkina had written to Stravinsky from Montpellier, where she was working in a military hospital: "I saw Bakst only on the fourth day of my visit to Paris, and at that time the borders were still closed. . . . He insists that he did not receive a telegram from you stating your terms, which he was to have submit-

I follow events in France and on the entire French front with growing anxiety. But who follows the fate of *my* unfortunate country?

Sincerely, your   Igor Stravinsky

Voreppe,
Isère
December 26, 1932
[Postcard]

STRAVINSKY TO GIDE

Many thanks, my dear Gide, for the beautiful gift. I never tire of looking at those wonderful pictures. What a beautiful collection! I am very touched.

Please tell Marc Allégret[5] that I am moved by the attention he has shown me. By the same mail, my dear friend, I am sending my latest photograph [by Lipnitzky] to you. All good wishes for the New Year.

Your admirer,   Igor Stravinsky

1 bis, rue Vaneau
Paris
January 20, 1933

GIDE TO STRAVINSKY

Ida Rubinstein has asked me to write to you. I am thrilled by the ballet proposal I just submitted to her. She says that if you are equally enthusiastic, you will [surely] agree to collaborate with me. The thought of connecting my name with yours, on a work that I have had in mind for some time, gives me the greatest pride and joy. If your response is positive, I will gladly go to Berlin* to discuss the project with you, and the sooner the better. I am dining at Ida's on Monday the 23rd with Sert,[6] who would do the set designs and is very excited by the idea.[7] Could you meet me on Wednesday? It does not matter where.** Please send a note or a telegram to Ida Rubinstein or me saying whether we could call you Monday night between nine and ten (remember the one-hour difference in Central Time), and, if so, at what number?

Sincerely and hopefully,   André Gide

* or elsewhere

---

ted to Ida Rubinstein, then wire you about the outcome. Just to be certain, he promised to write to me as well, so that I could also telegraph you; but he has not written. In any case, he promised to send the 5,000 advance that you requested. . . . Later, I received a letter from Bakst with only these words: 'Madame Rubinstein has telephoned to say that concerning the music for *Antony and Cleopatra,* she will consider Stravinsky's terms with her agent.' "

[5] Marc Allégret (1900–73), French film director and close friend of Gide.

[6] José-Maria Sert (1876–1945), the Spanish painter, with whom Stravinsky was on *tutoyer* terms.

[7] On January 24 Païchadze wrote to Stravinsky that Gide wanted to arrange a meeting

** I just had a telephone call from Madame Rubinstein informing me that you plan to be in the Midi soon, where I could easily meet with you. Also, will you perhaps be passing through Paris? That would spare me the trip to Berlin. . . .

GIDE TO STRAVINSKY   *February 8, 1933*

My dear friend,

First, I must tell you that our Wiesbaden reunion had a profound effect on me. I reported to Madame Rubinstein, without exaggerating, that the meeting was perfect. I think that she will be our biggest ally in fighting the intrusions of a set designer, whoever he may be. She seemed thrilled by our conception of the subject as the celebration of a myth. Consequently, [I have decided] to remove the episodic element—which I had originally been tempted to include—because it smacks of "entertainment." I am having a new edition of the *Odyssey* sent to you, a translation that contains the Homeric hymns. The last of the hymns (to Demeter) was my inspiration, and I am certain that you, too, will experience the extraordinary exaltation that I did when I first read them. I will concentrate my efforts on sustaining the nobility of this exaltation, inherent to the subject, which, as you will see, lies between the natural interpretation (the timing of the seasons, the seed that falls into the earth must die and be reborn through the apparent sleep of the winter) and the mystical one, for the myth is related both to the cult of ancient Egypt and to Christian doctrine.

I was very impressed by what you told me in Wiesbaden about your interest in emphasizing the cycle of the seasons. This cyclic form will be essential. Let the work begin with the autumn, despite the attraction of Proserpine's descent to Hades, though that would be to distort the Greek myth outrageously, as you will see when you read the hymn to Demeter. Persephone has nothing to do with autumn, however, and, by the way, the Greek year has only three seasons. Persephone is the personification of spring.

In two days I will send the first draft of the first scene, which has a recitative, some dances, and some songs. Madame Rubinstein tells me that it is impossible to have choristers dance or dancers sing. The chorus must therefore be placed in the orchestra pit, or on the side of the stage in the front. This has to be studied; what is important [for me] to know at this point is the timing of the first scene.

---

with him, and on January 30 and 31 the composer and writer conferred at the Hotel Rose in Wiesbaden.

Grand Hôtel
Le Lavandou
Var
February 24, 1933

This little note is to welcome you on your return to Voreppe, which was due to take place on the 25th. I am working relentlessly for you. You should already have received the sketch for the first scene,[8] but I consider this text to be definitive only to the degree that you find it so. The same is true of the second scene, which I plan to type today, and which you will receive very soon (in a day or two). The role of the narrator (Eumolpus, the founder, or the first officiating priest, of the mysteries of Eleusis) should be sung by a baritone (is that the correct spelling?), and the role of Pluto by a bass (the deepest possible). The choruses should be female only. As you will see, and at your suggestion, I have eliminated the anecdotal aspect, even the part of Eurydice. I fear that the scene of the encounter with Eurydice dragged, like all of the episodic passages, but it could be restored if the text is insufficient to cover the development of the music. Madame Rubinstein appears to be pleased, and I would like you to be also. I will listen to all of your criticisms, instructions, suggestions. Good work! I am full of hope and anticipation.

Very affectionately, your   André Gide

GIDE TO STRAVINSKY   *February 24, 1933*

Dear Igor,

Your special-delivery letter has just arrived. I sent the first scene to you in Milan, in care of Ida Rubinstein. Fortunately, I have a copy on hand, which I will enclose with this letter. I would suggest paying a visit to you in Voreppe, but I am afraid of becoming fatigued and catching cold, since I have not been well recently. What bothers me most is not working. I hope to be able to send the remainder of the text to you in a week or so (the provisional parts of it, that is, for they must be redone—so much the worse).

Very affectionately,   André Gide

STRAVINSKY TO GIDE   *Voreppe*
February 28, 1933

My dear Gide,

A word. Together with your own copy of the first scene, which I am returning to you, I have just received the one I thought was lost in the mail. Ida Rubinstein sent it to me from Paris, via Païchadze.

I will study the entire manuscript immediately and give you my opinion. Won't you come here for a few days (even two days)? Then we could travel

---

[8] Païchadze sent this to Stravinsky, who acknowledged its receipt on the 27th.

together to Paris, where I join Dushkin in March, for a tour, beginning in London. Say yes.

Yours very affectionately,   I. Stravinsky

I think there is a train direct from Le Lavandou to Grenoble, with sleeping cars. From there you must come to Voreppe by automobile. We will fetch you.

STRAVINSKY TO GIDE
Voreppe
March 5, 1933

Thank you for the end of the second scene, and particularly for the beautiful verses that fill your work. We need a little tranquility in which to examine the libretto together from the theatrical perspective. I must make you understand my conceptions and ideas about the role of music in theatre in general, and in your piece in particular. I love your work deeply, seriously, and I am seduced by your magnificent text, celebrating the mystery of the ancient Persephone. I will devote all of my energies to erecting a monument in sound to stand next to yours in words. Like yours, this monument will be a tribute to the mystery, but a monument that will also be an independent musical organism, serving neither to embellish the text (beautiful in itself), nor to color it, nor to guide the public (*Leitmusik*—Wagner) in the development of the plot. It hardly matters whether this concept of the music differs from I.R.'s and surprises her. In the final analysis, I am certain she will realize that I have not done her a disservice, and that the value of success with the subscription audience at the Opéra* is not indisputable, but, on the contrary, worth very little. In my last letter I proposed that you come to my house. Owing to the miserable weather these days, I am inclined to abandon this idea. I fear that you would be uncomfortable in the tiny, unheated room. So until Paris, my friend. . . . In a few days I will send my exact travel itinerary.

* Who like to leave the theatre whistling the tunes that they have heard (to provide them with these is felt to be one of the composer's responsibilities).

GIDE TO STRAVINSKY
March 7, 1933
[Telegram]

Impossible to leave Marseille.[9] Deep regrets. Very attentively yours,   André Gide

---

[9] On March 16, Stravinsky and Gide lunched at Madame Rubinstein's in Paris. Three days later, Count Harry Kessler wrote in his diary: "A visit from André Gide, who told me that he and Stravinsky are writing a ballet, *Perséphone*, for Ida Rubinstein. . . . Later we drove to a Stravinsky concert at the Salle Pleyel."

GIDE TO STRAVINSKY

You will have received the several verses of Eumolpus's introitus. Enclosed are the final verses of the first scene.[10]

STRAVINSKY TO GIDE   *Voreppe*
                                                       July 29, 1933

My dear Gide,

A small problem:

> *par-le nous du prin-temps, Per-sé-phone im-mor-tel-le*[11]

is good—but

> *par-le nous en-core, Per-sé-phone*[12]

---

[10] In this new version of the speech, Gide placed Persephone's final verse in the first scene *before* Eumolpus's aria. Stravinsky had indicated that the aria should be a march. Also, after the word *"fiancé,"* Gide wrote parenthetically "two syllables," but Stravinsky gave it three.

On April 8 the composer and the librettist worked together in Paris. On the 13th, Païchadze wrote to Stravinsky saying that Rubinstein had postponed a meeting about the contract. This was signed on April 22; two days later 25,000 francs was forwarded to Stravinsky. Meanwhile, he had started to compose, and on May 3 he was able to inform Païchadze that "Eumolpus has already begun to sing"—to which the publisher replied, May 4, expressing pleasure that "you have begun to sculpture *Perséphone.*"

On June 2, Stravinsky, Gide, and Rubinstein went to a service at St. Louis des Invalides to hear a children's chorus. On June 26, the composer asked Païchadze to obtain the second installment of the commission, and, when this was done (June 29), instructed him to send "3,200 francs to Vera Arturovna from the money you received from Ida Rubinstein." But as a letter from Païchadze, July 4, reveals, he had obtained the August installment as well. On July 7, the composer told Païchadze that the first scene was almost finished. Païchadze wrote from Aix-les-Bains (Koussevitzky's Villa St. Christophe), July 25: "Before leaving Paris, I saw Ida Lvovna, who told me that she has found a very good apartment for you. . . . Incidentally, we waved to you on the road, you on your way to Paris, I leaving the city with Prokofiev in his car." (Stravinsky had told a reporter in Copenhagen, November 30, 1925: "I have had a car for a number of years, and I can drive it, but I do not have a permit and will not have one until I pass the driver's test in Paris, which is where I learned to drive." On November 29, 1926, Prokofiev wrote to Stravinsky: "Please tell me the address of the establishment that taught you how to drive. As it happens, we are staying in that area, and I would like to take advantage of the opportunity to learn to drive myself.")

[11] Nos. **100–101**.

[12] Nos. **110–111**. Stravinsky changed the line to *"par-le nous, par-le nous, par-le nous, Per-sé-pho-ne."* Note that the melody starts in the minor mode and is a whole tone higher in the early version.

does not fit, because the number of feet (thirteen) is not the same. The *"encore"* disturbs me because of the silent *"e."* If you could insert a word with two syllables, accented on the last one, such as, for example, *"toujours,"* this would be perfect.

Be an angel and find it for me. Is it unacceptable for the second line to have twelve feet?

Perséphone gives me great pleasure, and I think of you often.[13]

Your   I. Stravinsky

GIDE TO STRAVINSKY   *1 bis, rue Vaneau*
                                                                    Paris
My dear Igor,   *August 8, 1933*

Excuse the delay. I found your letter yesterday evening on my return from a short trip to Belgium.

"Encore" is written (in poetry) either with or without the final *"e,"* depending on the requirements of the rhythm and the rhyme. I propose—*ad libitum*—for the second verse:

Parle encor, parle encor, princesse Perséphone,

which is better than my previous proposal.

Parle-nous, parle-nous encor, Perséphone

is perfectly possible with the silent *"e"* (and so would satisfy your request for two syllables), but the verse would have only eleven feet, because we do not count the final syllable as a foot if the *"e"* is silent.

According to the musical indication you gave me, *"Parle encor, Parle encor, princesse Perséphone"* seems to fit beautifully.

Happy to know you are working well. I shake your hand.

---

[13] Two days later, Stravinsky wrote to Willy Strecker: "I am consumed by my new romance with *Perséphone*, which gives me not a moment's respite, first making me savor the splendors of spring, then plunging me in Pluto's abysses, a somewhat fatiguing combination but full of delicious moments." Strecker wrote, November 23: "I told [Edward] Clark in London what an impact your *Perséphone* had on me and recommended that he include it in the radio festival there in May. He was receptive to the idea. . . . I urge you to facilitate this performance, since it may not be easy to secure engagements in England in the near future. I hope that I will be able to attend the premiere in Paris in February. . . . Based on what you played me that evening I could judge only the music, not the text." On January 12, 1934, Strecker wrote saying that he hoped "you have finished the orchestration of *Perséphone* and are now in the middle of proofreading and rehearsals." By February 9, Stravinsky had informed Strecker of the postponement of the premiere, and on April 20, Strecker wrote: "Sam [Dush-

STRAVINSKY TO GIDE   *May 26, 1934*

"Amicale communion[14]!" Why, my poor Gide, did you believe it incumbent to add the dedicatory formula, "André Gide to Igor Stravinsky"? This remedies nothing and fails to palliate the complete absence of rapport, which obviously originated in your attitude.

GIDE TO STRAVINSKY   *1 bis, rue Vaneau*
                                                              Paris
My dear Stravinsky,   *May 28, 1934*

I hope that because I did not attend the rehearsals of your, of our, *Perséphone,* you will not doubt my affection for you and my admiration for your work.[15] Or do you harbor some other grievance against me of which I am unaware? Since I have no grievance of any kind against you, I plan to continue in my ardent feeling of friendship for you.

                                                         André Gide

GIDE TO STRAVINSKY   *December 9, 1938*[16]

My dear Stravinsky,

Nadia Boulanger and Darius Milhaud have told me about the terrible bereavement you have suffered, which leaves you in anguish still. I, too, have just been

---

kin] told me that *Perséphone* is definitely scheduled for April 30, and I have arranged to attend."

[14] Thus Gide inscribed the copy of the *Perséphone* libretto that he sent to Stravinsky. As André Schaeffner wrote to the composer, Gide "has published the text of *Perséphone* as it was before your composition. What you have done in the area of dramatic structure is therefore evident, as are the essential discrepancies between your dramatic musical conceptions and his, not to mention the [absurdity] of his stage directions: the music does this, it expresses that. . . . Why not also have it pee when ordered to do so?"

[15] Gide wrote in his *Journal,* March 31, 1948: "The very night [of the premiere], throwing the whole thing up in disgust, I left for Syracuse in search of a classically antique setting of the sort I had wanted for [*Perséphone*]. I think Stravinsky has never quite forgiven me for not attending the first performance of his very beautiful score; but it was more than I could stand. The music, I think, was applauded. . . . If ever this 'ballet' is revived (and Stravinsky's score deserves to be heard again), I beg the producer to adhere strictly to the directions that I have given." (Stravinsky read Gide's *Journal, 1889–1939,* Pléiade edition, on the voyage to New York, September 1939.)

[16] Stravinsky never saw Gide or corresponded with him again, but the present writer was with Stravinsky on February 20, 1951, when he heard of Gide's death, and Stravinsky was deeply moved and silent for many hours.

cruelly tested, and this helps me to understand your sorrow.[17] Out of a profound feeling of friendship, I offer you my sympathy. I only wish that you could know how intense that sympathy is. Permit me to embrace you, very sadly.

André Gide

---

[17] Stravinsky's elder daughter, Lyudmila, had died of tuberculosis in November.

CORRESPONDENCE WITH

1938

PAUL CLAUDEL

PAUL CLAUDEL[1] TO STRAVINSKY

11 bis, rue Jean-Goujon
Paris 8
June 9, 1938[2]

Dear sir,

I did not dare to battle the suffocating throng that besieged you last night, but I want to tell you without further delay that your magnificent concert delighted me. What an Elysian language you make your music speak! What perfection! What sovereign elegance! The whole spirit focuses in the hearing, and the need for words, ideas, and even feelings vanishes, to give more attention to the concerted divine voices, which diverge only to be reconciled again. But how can a foreign element be introduced into this superior and self-sufficient realm? The principal impression that I retain from yesterday evening, one of the most beautiful of my artistic life, is intimidation.

I shake your hand affectionately.

P. Claudel

CLAUDEL TO STRAVINSKY

11 bis, rue Jean-Goujon
June 16, 1938

Dear sir,

I received your letter, and I fear that you attribute to me merits that I do not possess. What happened the other night on hearing your works was absolutely new for me and somewhat disturbing.

I do not have your address, which is not shown on your letter, or in the various directories; thus I do not know where to send this, or whether it will reach you. . . . Let us trust in Providence!

With the greatest uncertainty and diffidence, I have begun the work you requested. If you could come next Tuesday, I could give you the first pages. Lord knows what you will think of them!

---

[1] Stravinsky met Paul Claudel (1868–1955) in June 1910, at the time of the *Firebird* premiere, and disliked him intensely. A note from Claudel to Stravinsky, May 24, 1920, invites the composer to the poet's home for dinner.

[2] See Stravinsky's letter to Willy Strecker of B. Schotts Söhne of June 1, 1938, in the present volume.

If Madame R [ubinstein] were here, I would summon her as well. But God knows in which stratosphere she has managed to volatilize herself.

Have you read *Les Aventures de Sophie?*

With all my heart,   P. Claudel

STRAVINSKY TO CLAUDEL
June 20, 1938
[Draft of a pneumatique]

Dear sir,

I received your letter and will gladly come to see you tomorrow at five o'clock.

I am happy to learn that you have begun the work that we discussed. It is Prometheus, is it not? You know my point of view, and, after having reflected on this at length, I feel more and more convinced about not doing something for the theatre on a subject taken from the Scriptures, despite all the grandeur and beauty that the poet would bestow upon it.

Very cordially, your   I. Stravinsky

CLAUDEL TO STRAVINSKY
11 bis, rue Jean-Goujon
June 21, 1938

No, dear sir, the subject is not Prometheus, of which I never dreamed, even for a moment, but Tobit, the first part of which I am just completing. Nothing in the world would induce me to stick my nose into that ancient, pagan frippery, threadbare with use, and which only brings Offenbach to mind. So, a thousand regrets! and sorry to have bothered you this afternoon.

Be assured of my kindest regards.

P. Claudel

CLAUDEL TO STRAVINSKY
Château de Granges
Morestel, Granges
Isère
June 25, 1938

Dear M. Stravinsky,

A saintly, charming, and delightful invalid whom I often see wrote me the following lines about a work of yours: "Those coruscating clarinet solos [evoked] all of the liberty of the countryside of Attica, a biting poetry, a goat with his hoof on the extreme point of a rock, and rockets, and ruins, the rose, the nightingale, and the wind! All of this burst forth from that flat instrument (I do not agree with her here) with an incredibly lush greenness; I sensed the fragrance of the earth just after it has rained." That makes my mouth water! I would so much like to hear the piece in question.

The inspiration for Tobit has come, and I think that I will finally complete this work, on which I labor *con gusto e amore.*

I think that, in fact, we were not made to collaborate. You are too great a musician, and we would never have been able to enter into each other's minds.

I shake your hand very affectionately.

P. Claudel

STRAVINSKY TO CLAUDEL   *Paris*
                                                      June 27, 1938[3]
Dear M. Claudel,

Thank you for your note. Evidently it is impossible for me to give you any precise words whatsoever . . . after those vague instructions.

As for the fact that we were not made to collaborate, I am not sure of this, because the only obstacle that I saw was the choice of a Scriptural subject.

Be assured, dear M. Claudel, of my sincere regrets and my unalterable and always cordial friendship.

I. Stravinsky

---

[3] See Stravinsky's letter to Willy Strecker of B. Schotts Söhne of June 25, 1938, in the present volume.

A LETTER FROM

1 9 5 2

ALBERT CAMUS

29, *rue Madame*
Paris 6
[Summer 1952][1]

Dear friend,

Here is a letter that I hope will not take much of your time and that will leave my conscience free. Have you read René Char?[2] In my opinion he is our greatest living poet. He has made a ballet (for Cuevas) that I find marvelous. And he will not accept any of the composers who have been proposed to him: a hospital of anemics. I told him that you are the only one who can create the music (fire and ice) required for this strange ballet and that he must send it to you before anyone else. You will say no if you find it false. Everyone will understand, and, what concerns me, this will not compromise the gesture of my affectionate admiration. But, I do not want to miss, through negligence, the opportunity of a great conjunction between a poet and a musician whom I admire.

Having said this, I step aside, but not before sending my respectful remembrances to Madame Stravinsky and not before telling you of the free and very personal friendship that I found in our too-short moments together at the avenue Montaigne.[3]

Faithfully yours,   Albert Camus

---

[1] Stravinsky wrote to his son Theodore on August 1: "I have been very busy completing my Cantata. Very touched by what Camus told you about me. I, too, liked his article enormously, which I read in English in the *Partisan Review*. After all, he is the only one in France who can stand up to Sartre, who has a very powerful brain, but for whom, unfortunately, I have absolutely no sympathy."

[2] At this date Stravinsky had not yet read anything by Char, but in the years 1956–65 the two men were friends without ever having met, Char being either ill or too shy. He sent several of his books to Stravinsky with dedications.

[3] Stravinsky and Camus had shared the same loge in the Théâtre des Champs-Elysées during a performance of Berg's *Wozzeck* in May 1952 and then spent the evening together.

CORRESPONDENCE WITH

1917 ✒ 1962

FRANCIS POULENC

FRANCIS POULENC[1] TO STRAVINSKY
47, rue du Faubourg St.-Honoré
Paris 8
[No date]

Dear sir,

I am making an investigation among modern musicians to determine "what they think of Franck." D'Indy, Debussy, Dukas, Satie, and Saint-Saëns have already been so kind as to give me their views. Thanks to my friend Jean-Paul Boulard, who has often spoken to me about you, I learned that you are accessible to those of us who flounder about in uncertainty, so I dare to hope that my timid request will not remain unanswered. In the meantime, very dear sir, I beg of you to accept my thanks in anticipation, along with the homage of my immense admiration.

Francis Poulenc

POULENC TO STRAVINSKY

February 1917

Dear Igor Fyodorovich,

I am in the studio of Dmitri Simonovich Stelletsky, with whom I very often talk about you. I told him yesterday of my annoyance at not being able to obtain your trio [*sic*], which I would like to have performed. Dmitri Simonovich, saying that only you can help me, has advised me to write to you directly.

My good friends Satie and Viñes having encouraged me to hope that you might give me the honor of a favorable reply, I conclude, dear sir, by sending you the homage of my profound admiration.

Francis Poulenc

POULENC TO STRAVINSKY

47, rue du Faubourg St.-Honoré
Paris
March 5, 1917

Dear sir,

Dmitri Stelletsky showed me your letter yesterday.

I do not know what I had in mind when I wrote entreating you for a trio!!! I meant to request the Three Pieces for String Quartet: those three pieces, per-

---

[1] 1899–1963. An editor's footnote in Poulenc's *Correspondence, 1915–1963* states that the young composer first met Stravinsky and Apollinaire at the home of Valentine Gross on April 28, 1918, but Stravinsky was in Switzerland on that date. (See n. 2.)

formed for the first time at the Salle des Agriculteurs by Yvonne Astruc, Darius Milhaud, et al.

Excuse me, dear sir, for bothering you again, but be certain that I would not have dared to write to you again had Dmitri Stelletsky not given me strong encouragement.

Please accept, dear sir, my homage and immense admiration.

Francis Poulenc

POULENC TO STRAVINSKY

83, rue de Monceau
Paris

Morges

September 25, 1919

Dear sir and friend,

Having just received several copies of my Sonata for two clarinets from London, I hasten to send one to you, in the hope that you will be pleased to have this work.

I cannot express what a joy it was for me to make your acquaintance and to hear your "Rags";[2] they are truly marvelous, and I look forward to hearing them again soon in Paris.

Hoping as well for the pleasure of seeing you again soon, I beg you, dear sir, to be assured of my affectionate admiration.

Francis Poulenc

STRAVINSKY TO POULENC

October 1, [1919]
[Postcard]

Thank you, my dear M. Poulenc, for your kind note and for sending your . . . [Sonata for] Two Clarinets, which I like very much. I shall keep them always, in memory of the charming evening we spent at the Hugo's.

Sincerely yours,   I. Stravinsky

POULENC TO STRAVINSKY

4, rue de la Muette
Nogent-sur-Marne
Seine

My dear Stravinsky,

[July 10, 1922]

I finally succeeded in seeing Mr. Hammond, Jr., yesterday afternoon.[3] He is a charming boy, about twenty-five years old, and seems very informed and very

---

[2] Earlier that month, while in Paris to receive from Diaghilev the manuscripts of the music to be used in *Pulcinella*, Stravinsky had played his *Piano-Rag Music* at the home of Jean Hugo and his wife, Valentine Gross. In *Entretiens avec Claude Rostand* (1954), Poulenc stated that he had introduced himself to Stravinsky at his publisher's in Paris in 1916, which is probably true, but of this Stravinsky had no recollection.

[3] Richard Hammond (1896–1980), a pupil of Nadia Boulanger and one of the Stra-

Two cartoons of Georges Auric by Jean Cocteau, 1923, given by the artist to Vera Sudeikina.

rich. I spoke with him for a long time about *Mavra*, the Concertino, the Symphonies, and *Pulcinella*. He was very excited about everything. He took your address and will write to you, since he cannot possibly see you before his return to London (within the next few days). Moreover, I think that everything can be arranged by letter, according to your wishes, for he is a "businessman," and not a "dreamer" like your [Otto] Kling. Upon my arrival at home, I had a telephone call from Wiéner.[4]. . . I understand perfectly your astonishment at having heard nothing from us, but I was waiting to meet with Hammond so that I could inform you of the outcome.

I will see him again on Thursday and encourage him. That should not be too difficult, since he is intoxicated with the idea of publishing you.

Enclosed I send you the promised clippings. Perhaps by the time these arrive they will duplicate others that you will have received, but I could not obtain them any sooner, thanks to my clipping service, which twice confused the dates.

Auric and I often speak of the good times we spent with you this spring. Your stay in Paris was a great consolation for us both. The world of *La Revue*

vinskys' closest friends in the California years. Poulenc's reference is to a request from Stravinsky to encourage Hammond concerning a project to publish Stravinsky's music. See *S.S.C.* I, pp. 155–6.

[4] Jean Wiéner (1896–1982), pianist; founder in 1921 of the Wiéner concerts specializing in contemporary music; co-founder with Doucet of the club Le Boeuf sur le Toit.

Musicale is so ordinary and dull;[5] one must taste music oneself. Contact with you revives my taste for work. Thank you for that.

After consulting with Diaghilev and Marie Laurencin, I have a clear conception of my ballet [*Les Biches*], which will have no subject, simply dances and songs. I am thrilled by this decision and plan to begin work on it right away.

I plan to remain in Touraine until quite late and perhaps visit you at the end of November. I will discuss this again later.

I hope that you found your family well. Please present my respects to Madame Stravinsky, and keep for yourself, dear friend, the assurance of my profound affection.

Francis Poulenc

P.S. Write to me at Nogent. That is where I now live.

I hope that you received my Impromptus. I crave any indulgence you may wish to bestow upon them. These are some not terribly successful "attempts," which I sent to you under the cloak of friendship.

POULENC TO STRAVINSKY

83, rue de Monceau
Paris
[July 31, 1922]

My dear Stravinsky,

Thank you for the very nice letter, which deeply touched me; thank you as well for the errata of *The Nightingale*. I have taken so long in replying because I have been insanely busy this week. I spent many hours at the Bibliothèque Nationale looking for song texts for my ballet. I found some excellent ones. I will begin work on them in the latter half of August, when I return from Salzburg.

I am sending you the most recent issue of *Les Feuilles Libres*, containing my article about *Mavra*. I was given so little space that I had to do it in résumé style. Such as it is, may it testify to my admiration for *Mavra*. I will also send you Maurice Brillant's *Correspondant* article, which shows a certain goodwill. What do you think of Boris de Schloezer's article in *La Nouvelle Revue Française?* We'll have a good laugh about it five years from now. Have you had a reply from Hammond?

I will write from Austria to tell you everything that is going on.

In the meantime, please present my respects to Madame Stravinsky, and be assured of my profound affection.

Francis Poulenc

P.S. I would be grateful if you would tell me what sort of pen you use to com-

---

[5] Poulenc had been deeply impressed by Ansermet's article on Stravinsky in a 1921 *Revue Musicale*. Replying to Paul Collaer's observation that "you are suffering from an attack of Stravinskyitis," Poulenc wrote that in the Ansermet study, "One understands the craftsmanship of this man. CRAFTSMANSHIP, that is what is so admirable in Stravinsky. . . . For the last two days I have buried myself in *Renard*. The counterpoint is unforgettable."

pose. I have a dozen different kinds on my table, all of them ineffective . . . after one page. Is it impossible to find your stave-tracer for sale anywhere in Switzerland?

STRAVINSKY TO POULENC   *Paris*
                                                    September 9, 1922

My dear Poulenc,

Let me assure you that a day does not go by without my thinking that I owe you a long letter—which is what I am thinking at this very moment—but I find it impossible to concentrate. You will excuse me; I have many diverse preoccupations right now. But I will write when I am more relaxed.

Your article gave me *great* pleasure. M. Brillant's is like that of Madame Manuel.

The pens you want can be obtained in London; I have exhausted my stock, so I will try to procure a new box and send you half of it.

How is your work coming along? I worked quite well in Biarritz. I will be in Paris for a few days longer, then back in Biarritz again.

Keep in touch, as I am always pleased to have news from you.

Fondly, your   I. Stravinsky

STRAVINSKY TO POULENC   *January 1, 1923*

Happy New Year, my dear Poulenc.

I saw you only briefly at the concert; and your so sudden departure after the concert, and your somewhat dejected mood during the concert—to what is all this due? Am I being indiscreet?

Myself, I left the theatre in despair and utterly disgusted. Ansermet, too. The rehearsal promised *Mavra* a good performance. And you saw what the singers did to me. There are many things to be said, in addition, about the performance of my music and the places where it is performed, because these are designed for dressed-up music, whereas mine, what I have been doing for two years now, is naked but finds itself in the hands of couturiers, against whom the courageous Ansermet struggles desperately. I am in a very bad humor, and I have reason to be.

Your   Stravinsky

POULENC TO STRAVINSKY   *Le Grand Hôtel*
                                                        Brussels
                                                February 17, [1923]

My dear Stravinsky,

Yet another joy I owe to you! Two days ago I heard the instrumental rehearsals of the suite of the *Soldat;* I am mad about it. You cannot imagine the superb performance that it will be given here, where it has been rehearsed every morning for the past two weeks. You will judge the result yourself. What beautiful music, full of healthy rhythms and framework; my stay here has been thrilling. Finally I hear my music, interpreted well in a chamber-music hall and before an audience that is not there for a laugh. I swear that my last concert at Wiéner's left me thoroughly discouraged. You know that the *Sacre* will be given here in May. They are already working on it. What do you think of such conscientiousness? Each instrumentalist must learn his part at home before the first reading.

These people deserve some encouragement, and you would therefore be very kind (if you do not mind, of course) if you sent a little thank-you note to the conductor of the *Soldat,* M. Arthur Prévost (154, avenue d'Anderghem, Brussels), who would be wildly appreciative and who merits your gratitude.

I hope that you are well and that you, too, have already forgotten the stupidity of the contemporary Paris public.

I return to Paris in two days. Will I see you there soon? I hope so, with all my heart.

Give all of my respects to Madame Stravinsky . . . and be assured of my unalterable affection.

F. Poulenc

POULENC TO STRAVINSKY

Nazelles
[September 1923]

My dear Stravinsky,

I am ashamed to have deprived you of news for nearly two months now. Excuse me, and do not take crude measures—I am hard at work. I finished and submitted to Serge [Diaghilev] my recitatives for *La Colombe.*[6] I did that work meticulously, attempting to avoid a pastiche or a lesson in harmony *à la* Reger. I hope this will not seem too nasty to you. In ten days I go to Paris and take along the completed *Biches.*

And you, dear friend, what has become of you? I heard through Robert Lyon and later Auric about your trip to Weimar. Was it not dangerous in this time of political tension?

I suppose that you are now in Biarritz. Did the good, fat Georges [Auric] visit you? Perhaps you will see me at the "Rochers" in November, if the weather is good.

And your work? The Concerto for Piano and Orchestra?

You know that I often dream of the beauty of the Octet; it is so magnificent, so sure and solid.

Have you made arrangements with the Danes for that and for my beloved *Mavra?*

---

[6] Gounod's comic opera based on verses by La Fontaine, presented by Diaghilev in Monte Carlo on January 1, 1924.

It would be kind of you to reply to all of these questions in a good letter, which I await impatiently. Give my best to your wife and son, and be assured of my profound admiration.

Poulenc

POULENC TO STRAVINSKY

Nazelles
[September 1923]

Thank you, my dear Stravinsky, for your pretty letter. Your bather has nice enough breasts, but such contorted legs!

You ask me very nicely what else I have done this summer besides orchestrate *Les Biches*. Well, I completed it, the score is twice as long as it was; I am also working on a quintet for four strings and clarinet and some military marches for orchestra. This last is hard to do, at least from the viewpoint of construction. I think I may stick to a kind of "Harlequin" of brief marches sounding together, each of them giving the illusion of developing the other.

Auric wrote me an enthusiastic letter about his stay with you. I hope you would like me to visit one of these days. It would be a joy for me to visit that much-loved Biarritz again in your company.

Are you working hard? I heard of your Weimar triumph with joy. I hope that the *Soldat* will not dally in coming to France.

I will certainly go to Paris around October 20, if only to see you. Meanwhile, write to me if you have time, and give me news about the Concerto. That would make me very happy.

Present my fond respects to your wife, and keep for yourself, my dear friend, the assurance of my immutable friendship.

Poulenc

POULENC TO STRAVINSKY

Hôtel du Lion d'Or
Amboise
My dear Stravinsky,   *[October 5, 1923]*

I am overjoyed to see your Octet announced on the Opéra posters. I will go to Paris on the 18th without fail. I went there four days ago to play the complete *Biches* for Diaghilev, who was not yet familiar with it. He was pleased, as was Auric. I am eager to have your opinion, which I will cherish more than anyone else's. I am now orchestrating energetically. I am not unhappy. Would you be so kind as to send me, as quickly as possible, the address of the bookbinder who bound *Noces* for you? Mine requires three weeks to do *Les Biches*, and I cannot allow him to have my manuscript for that long while I am orchestrating.

I hope to see you often during the week I will be in Paris.

In the meantime, be assured of my lively affection.

Francis Poulenc

And the Concerto? How far has it progressed?

STRAVINSKY TO POULENC   *Biarritz*
October 6, 1923

Dear Poulenc,

The address of my bookbinder, if I am not mistaken, is 24 (?), rue Condorcet, and his name is neither more nor less than Adam. I think that his shop is between rue Turgot and rue Rodier.

Happy to know that you have finished *Les Biches.* If you need some advice, don't be ashamed to approach me—you will only meet with the same appreciation I have always had for your work and for *Les Biches* in particular, the remainder of which interests me enormously.

I will be in Paris around the end of the week and look forward to seeing you. Until then, my old friend.

Your   Igor Stravinsky

The Concerto is coming along very well, thank you.

POULENC TO STRAVINSKY   *Sunday [1923?]*

Dear friend,

It would be very kind of you to give me Diaghilev's address. I need to write to him. Haven't you already forwarded a letter to him that I sent to you? Since I leave on Thursday for eight days in Paris, he should send the requested information to 83, rue de Monceau.

I hope that my bottles of Chinon were delivered to you in good condition. If there was any damage, let me know and I will have them replaced.

In the meantime, I send my fondest wishes to you and Madame Stravinsky.

Poulenc

POULENC TO STRAVINSKY   *Amboise*
[October 1923]

Dear friend,

I arrive on Thursday to hear the Octet. I fear that I may not be able to obtain a seat in the afternoon for the same evening.

Please be so kind as to have Zederbaum[7] reserve a ticket for me and keep it at rue Rochechouart, where I will go to see you and pick it up. I always have one when I am in Paris, so this should not present any difficulty. It will be a joy to see and applaud you.

In the meantime, my dear Stravinsky, be assured of my profound affection.

Poulenc

---

[7] Koussevitzky's secretary.

STRAVINSKY TO POULENC   *Biarritz*
                                                February 3, 1924

My dear Poulenc,

. . . I have a great desire to see you again soon and to discuss with you in detail
the music of your *Biches*—the only aspect of the work that I have seen, though
Benois told me many good things about the production. Of one thing I am certain: *Biches* is a very beautiful score.

But when will I see you? From now until March I am here working on my
concerto,[8] then I go to Barcelona for two or three weeks to conduct three concerts of old things of mine. After that, back to Biarritz until mid-April.

Where are you and what are you doing? Keep writing to me and believe,
my dear Poulenc, that I remain your continually devoted   I. Stravinsky

POULENC TO STRAVINSKY   *[February 1924]*

Dear friend,

Many thanks for your deeply moving letter. You know that no encouragement
flatters me so much as yours. Yes, *Les Biches* went well. I cannot exaggerate
the beauty of Nijinska's work. She really is a creature of genius. A great compliment to Nemchinova, adorable in the leading role. Since our return, Auric and I
have felt a lot of jealousy and bad humor, quite naturally. M. Satie is particularly enraged. Having quarreled with Jean [Cocteau], Georges [Auric], and
myself, Satie is telling all Paris that our "tricks" are ignoble and, furthermore,
that we are skunks and that we deliberately organized the silence with which
his Gounod recitatives[9] were greeted. . . . He published an initial article to this
effect in the program of the *Indépendantes,* and a second will follow in *Paris-
Journal.* This is not very nice, is it? Very surprising from that otherwise admirable creature. After two weeks of errands and purchases, I will return to work.
The military marches will occupy all of my time. You cannot imagine how I am
dying to hear your concerto. You say you will stay in Biarritz until April 15. Perhaps I will visit you. . . . While awaiting the pleasure of seeing you again
this spring, dear friend, I send you many fond regards to be shared with your
wife.

                                         Your loyal   Poulenc

---

[8] Stravinsky inscribed a score of his Concertino: "For Francis Poulenc, this score,
which I promised him, but which he bought for 15 francs!!! His friend who likes his
music very much, I. Stravinsky, Café de la Paix, this February 16, 1924."

[9] For Diaghilev's production of *Le Médecin malgré lui* in Monte Carlo on January 5.

POULENC TO STRAVINSKY   *[October 1924]*

Montboron
Nice

Dear Igor,

In a letter from Jean [Cocteau], which pursued me from Touraine to Paris to
Fontainebleau and finally caught up with me, I learned that your children are
ill, particularly Theodore. You will wonder if this upset me. Thank God, I found
out immediately thereafter, from Vera, that the danger is now passed. I am annoyed not to have heard about this sooner, since you might even have thought
that I was indifferent. Be assured that, much to the contrary, everything which
affects you is close to my heart.

   Fortunately you are in a beautiful, sunny area, and I am certain that your
children will recover quickly. Pardon my silence—I have worked very hard this
summer. I completely reorchestrated *Les Biches,* finished my trio, and began
my Military Marches for piano and orchestra. I know that you completed a sonata, and I cannot wait to hear it. I am distressed still to be waiting for *Mavra*
and the Octet. The delay for the Concerto is more easily excused. I know that
you will soon be going on tour. Sad at the thought that I will not see you for a
long time, I nevertheless wish you an immense success . . . and embrace you
wholeheartedly.

                              Your devoted   Francis P.

Tell your wife that I think of her often. Special regards to my friend Theodore.

POULENC TO STRAVINSKY   *La Lézardière*
                                                  Nazelles
                                                  Indre-et-Loire
Dear friend,   *[Postcard]* [10]
                                                  [1924?]

I want you to be one of the first to receive this photograph of my house in
Touraine. May its appearance inspire you to visit one day. I send you many fond
regards.

                              Poulenc

POULENC TO STRAVINSKY   *Nazelles*
                                                  [September 1925] [11]
Dear Stravinsky,

I am ashamed to have taken so long to reply, but I have had an onslaught of
work to finish (some orchestration, a transcription of Mozart's *A Musical Joke,*

---

[10] Picture postcard of Poulenc's home, buried in ivy and aptly named La Lézardière.

[11] On March 21, in Paris, Stravinsky had autographed the title page of Poulenc's

proofs to correct), and also many friends passing through who have very nicely molested me.

The excellent copyist whom I used in Monte Carlo is named Iviglia, Bibliothèque de l'Opéra, Monte Carlo. You can trust him with anything; he is splendid. My recommendation would be superfluous; he will be more than proud to work for you.

I have done a lot of work this summer but with few results. I will not conceal from you the fact that I am in a certain state of anxiety these days. Here I am in the midst of the so fashionable *"alla* Scarlatti," *"alla* Haydn," etc. I find that musicians have misunderstood the lesson of the Octet and the Concerto. I would like to take better advantage of that lesson. The taste of perfection and science is what I owe to your last works, but this is difficult for those of us who do not have your giant's muscles.

I am doing a sonata for piano and violin, which is to say that I am taking the bull by the horns. Sonata in four parts, comprising a largo, an allegro, a romance, and a gigue. The first three tempi move along diversely, the final one in the [illegible]. I hope nonetheless to work more rapidly now.

How was your summer? I am dying to hear what you are working on, about which you keep silent. Is Theodore still painting a lot? How are the other children? I think often of all of you and regret being so far from Nice-Montboron.

I am certain that your advice will stimulate my courage.

I have no news from the gallant Serge, as usual. Do you know his plans?

Please write to me; your every word gives me joy for an entire week, and I am particularly in need at the moment.

Hoping to see you again soon, I beg you to be assured of my loyal and profound affection.

Poulenc

Many good wishes to your wife.

I listened to *Pribaoutki* again; how I love that piece!

POULENC TO STRAVINSKY   *Nazelles*
                                               [Autumn 1925]
Dear Stravinsky,

What has become of you? For a long time I have wanted to write to you but have set to work since my return from Vichy, for which reason, and as usual, I have neglected my correspondence a little.

---

pocket score of *Le Sacre*, incorporating his inscription into the printed name and title:

IGOR STRAVINSKY

who signs this book for Poulenc who loves it

LE SACRE DU PRINTEMPS

and him as well

I will be in Touraine for the entire autumn. On the piano I have the beautiful photograph that Vera took of you in front of a mirror and a lot of your music. This is to let you know that if I neglect to write, my thoughts are nonetheless with you.

I like your sonata so much. Would it be indiscreet of me to ask for news concerning your work? Is the Serenade coming along? I am so curious about it after what you told me in the spring. I am certain that you are doing well, but I would like details concerning your projects for the winter. Will you go abroad again or stay in Nice? If you find time, write to me; you know how happy it will make me. In any case, I hope to see you again soon, be it in Paris or in the Midi. I send many good wishes to your wife and Theodore. Be assured of my loyal and profound regards.

Poulenc

I hope that you have received my Ronsard, unimportant a thing as it may be.

POULENC TO STRAVINSKY

Moncontour
Vouvray
Indre-et-Loire
[December 30, 1925]

Villa des Roses
Nice

My dear Stravinsky,

From Touraine, where I am completing my recovery, I send you many wishes for happiness and health in 1926. I am very happy, because my hand gets better and better.

I will be in the Midi around January 20 and will hop over to Nice right away. In the meantime, I send you many fond regards to be shared with your whole family.

Your faithful   Poulenc

POULENC TO STRAVINSKY

Wednesday
[January or early February 1926]

167 blvd. Carnot
Nice

Dear Stravinsky,

I have been in bed for two days with flu and fever. What a dangerous place, where summer and winter alternate on an hourly basis. I do not think that I will be able to leave before the end of the week. Then I will come to see you, next Monday or Tuesday. Let me know which will suit you better.

I rejoice at seeing you before your tour in Holland.

Be assured that I am

your very faithful   Poulenc

POULENC TO STRAVINSKY   *[April] 8, 1926*
                                                        [Telegram]

167 blvd. Carnot
Nice

We will dine where you wish. Unless otherwise instructed, I will come by your
house Monday around 6:15. Fond regards.   Poulenc

POULENC TO STRAVINSKY   *Cannes*
                                                     [April 1926]
Nice

Dear Stravinsky,

Summoned back to Paris for my concert of May 2, I am leaving Cannes now.
Before my departure I want to thank you for the wonderful evening spent at
your house on Monday. How kind of you to have given me all of that good advice. I have modified the first tempo in the trio. It is completely different. Until
soon. Many, many fond regards to you, your wife, and your children.

                                                  Francis Poulenc

P.S. I love [your] Serenade.

POULENC TO STRAVINSKY   *Nazelles*
                                                    May 14, [1927]
24, rue Rochechouart   *[Telegram]*
Paris

Will be thinking of you tonight. Be assured of my affection and admiration.
Poulenc

POULENC TO STRAVINSKY   *[1922? 1929?]*

Dear friend,

M. Jean Demaraist, 50, rue de Clignancourt (18th *arrondissement*), is the one
who played *Renard*.[12] I also find in my address book M. Liminot, 5, rue Audran
(18th), and Doriguier, 9, rue Geoffroy-Marie (9th). I hope that with the three
addresses you will find your man.

     In haste, many fond regards.

                                                  Francis Poulenc

---

[12] Stravinsky inscribed Poulenc's piano score of *Renard:* "... in all friendship. Igor
Stravinsky, Paris, May 18, 1922, day of the premiere of *Renard* at the Opéra."

A 1939–40 New Year's greeting from Poulenc to Vera Sudeikina: "Dear Vera, What has become of you? I embrace you for the new year and wish you happiness in proportion to my affection, which is to say a great deal. I will be staying in Touraine through January. I hear that you will be following Igor to America. Fortunate woman. See you soon, in any case. Many fond regards, Francis."

POULENC TO STRAVINSKY

My dear Stravinsky,

Le Grand Coteau
Noizay
Indre-et-Loire
[April 3, 1931]
Holy Thursday

I am sending you a short article I wrote about the *Symphony* [*of Psalms*]. Accept it as I offer it, which is to say, as a small testimony of my admiration and affection.

I am working hard. On June 1 (Salle Chopin) I am giving a concert of new chamber-music pieces. If you attend, I beg a great deal of indulgence in advance.

Do not forget your promise to visit me here this spring. Lots of good wine and affection await you.

I hope that all of your family are well. I am with you often, thanks to your recordings.

I send you, my dear Stravinsky, my fondest regards.

Fr. Poulenc

POULENC TO STRAVINSKY

5, *rue de Médicis*
Paris
December 28, [*1945*]

[Hollywood]

Dear, very dear Stravinsky,

The beautiful package of music—which awaited me at my home upon my return from a long stay in England—thrilled, dazzled, and comforted me. Once again, it is your presence, your genius, your example.

I have missed you terribly for the past six years, and I hope, for myself and for us both, that you will return this year to your bruised Europe, where music is sometimes found. I have so much to tell you that I refuse to do so here.

At any rate, be assured that I am one of those for whom you carry the light. You must have heard talk of the polemics surrounding your recent works. Allow me to say that I find it beautiful to be as misunderstood at age sixty as at age thirty.

I will not discuss what I have composed since 1940. I have done what I could but often not what I wanted, for life has been so difficult, from all points of view, that I was obliged to give too many concerts, to write two films, some incidental music for the theatre, etc. . . .

I hope, when you hear my recent works, that you will find that a few good blades have grown in the crabgrass nevertheless. During the tragic times that we have just lived through, what sustenance I took from the memories of the past. It was a comfort to think that, twenty years before, we had the epoch of *Noces, Mavra, Pulcinella.*

When your new works are published, try to send them to me. (I already have the *Danses concertantes,* Sonata for Two Pianos, *Circus Polka,* and *Scènes de ballet,* which is especially ravishing.)

I embrace you affectionately, as well as Vera, and send you my best wishes for 1946.

Your devoted   Poulenc

STRAVINSKY TO POULENC

Hollywood
January 10, 1946

What joy, my very dear Poulenc, to have your kind letter. I received it just this moment, as I am about to leave for my concert tour, which explains the brevity of this note. Agreed, I will have some of my recently published works sent to you from New York, as well as the photostatic copies of some of my still-unpublished works.

My God, there is so much to discuss, but when and where? When will we see each other again? I have no idea, bogged down as I am, perpetually, in a pursuit that allows no *stoping* [*sic*].[13]

You will soon see Nadia B.; her departure from the U.S. (on January 4)

---

[13] In English in the original.

has left a void that will be difficult to fill. We saw a lot of each other in recent years.

Very dear Poulenc, send me some of your music, I beg of you; you know that I always had devoted and tender feelings for your entrancing Muse.

Very affectionately yours,   I. Stravinsky

New York, Boston, Baltimore, Havana, Dallas, San Francisco and ... *back home*[14] end of March.

POULENC TO STRAVINSKY

Hotel Ambassador
North State Street
Chicago
February 20, [1948]

Dear, very dear Stravinsky,

It is truly sad for me to miss you everywhere. I was overjoyed to find you again in America, [but] we are playing hide-and-seek, unless by some miracle you will be in New York from March 21 to 30.

I cry at the thought that I will not see *Orpheus,* whose every measure I love, and not hear the new *Firebird,* and not even glimpse the [score of the] opera. This is really too sad.

Since I do not have Soulima's address, Yvonne [Casafuerte] will deliver this letter, which brings you, Vera, and all of yours many tender thoughts and the assurance that you are, as when I was twenty, "my musician."

Francis Poulenc

POULENC TO STRAVINSKY

New York
November 23, 1948

1260 N. Wetherly Drive
West Hollywood
California

Dear Igor,

What joy at seeing you again soon! Alas, I will stay only two days in Los Angeles. I would like so much to go and see you on December 2 with my friend Bernac.[15] Upon my arrival at the Hotel Biltmore, on the morning of the 1st, I will call you to make the arrangements.

So many things to tell you.

I embrace you very affectionately, as well as dear Vera.

Poulenc

---

[14] In English in the original.

[15] On December 1, Stravinsky attended the recital of Poulenc and Pierre Bernac at the Wilshire-Ebell Theatre. The program contained groups of songs by Lully, Gounod, Schubert, Debussy, Ravel, and Poulenc.

POULENC TO STRAVINSKY

Noizay
Indre-et-Loire
September 7, 1956

Teatro alla Fenice
Venice

Dear Igor,

Needless to say, I will be listening on Thursday, sad to be far from you and from that *Canticum Sacrum* which I read, perhaps indiscreetly, at Nadia's house and found *sublime*. How I long for the time when we will see each other with some frequency! What is admirable is that you are always a model of youth, faith, and lucidity.

    I embrace you and Vera tenderly.

Francis Poulenc

POULENC TO STRAVINSKY

Noizay
Indre-et-Loire
August 5, 1962[16]

Fonda Hotel
Santa Fe, New Mexico

Very dear Igor,

Since no one gave me your present address in a precise form, I entrusted Boosey & Hawkes with the responsibility of relaying to you these birthday wishes, which are no less full of affection and admiration for being quite late. I spent all spring in the country listening, every evening, to all of your recordings. I always marvel at your music, *exactly* as I did when I was twenty years old; if possible, my awe has even increased.

    Very recently, at Aix, *Noces* plunged me back into one of the most wonderful periods of my life. Alas: I never see you anymore and suffer true sorrow as a result. In any case, you may be certain that you are always in my heart.

    If I no longer send you my music, this is because I simply do not think it would interest you.

    Embrace Vera as I embrace you, dear Igor, which is to say very tenderly, and know that I am forever

your   Francis Poulenc

How I like *A Sermon, A Narrative and A Prayer!* It is wonderful.

---

[16] At the bottom of the letter, Stravinsky noted that he answered with a postcard from Sante Fe on the 12th. Poulenc died in Paris on January 30, 1963.

III

1 9 2 8 ~~ *1 9 3 9*

to *B . S C H O T T S   S Ö H N E*

Stravinsky's letters to Willy Strecker of B. Schotts Söhne, Mainz, extend from 1924 to 1958, the year of the publisher's death (at age seventy-four), but the selection offered here is limited to the decade of the five major works that Strecker published: the Violin Concerto, the Concerto per due pianoforti soli, Jeu de cartes, the Concerto in E flat, and the Symphony in C.

The composer's connection with B. Schotts Söhne[1] *antedates his acquaintance with Strecker. As early as June 1909, Alexander Siloti, negotiating on Stravinsky's behalf, had secured the publisher's agreement to engrave* Fire-

---

[1] B. Schotts Söhne concluded contracts with Stravinsky as follows:

1909	*Fireworks*
3/5/1929	"Pastorale," voice and woodwind quartet
	Berceuse (*Firebird*), arrangement for violin and piano
	Prelude (*Firebird*), arrangement for violin and piano
1930–1/7/1931	Concerto for violin and orchestra
12/8/1931	Berceuse (*Firebird*), arrangement for violin and piano, with Dushkin
11/9/1932	Scherzo (*Firebird*), arrangement for violin and piano, with Dushkin
7/20/1933	*Pastorale, arrangement for violin and wind quartet, with Dushkin*
7/18/1933	*Firebird (1910) (purchased from Forberg)*
	Firebird Suite (1919) (purchased from Forberg)
1935	Concerto per due pianoforti soli
9/30/1936	*Jeu de cartes*
5/17/1938	Concerto in E flat (*Dumbarton Oaks*)
6/7/1939	Symphony in C
1942	Symphony in Three Movements (originally published by Associated Music Publishers, New York, the American representative of B. Schotts Söhne)
6/19/1942	*Danses concertantes*
6/19/1942	*Circus Polka*
11/10/1942	*Four Norwegian Moods*
10/19/1943	Ode
12/10/1945	Pas de deux (Blue Bird)
9/25/1950	*Babel*
5/19/1953	*Firebird Suite (1945) (acquired from Leeds)*
	Firebird Suite (1919) (contract with Chester, 1958)

works. *In the mid-1920s, B. Schotts Söhne became involved in a dispute over the proprietorship of* Firebird *in which Stravinsky's right to publish his revised (1919)* Firebird *Suite was contested.*[2]

In November 1930, Willy Strecker commissioned Stravinsky to compose a concerto for Samuel Dushkin, the Russian-born American violinist. Strecker had been introduced to Dushkin in 1913 by the American composer Blair Fairchild, Dushkin's adoptive father. Stravinsky had known Fairchild since the end of World War I, when, as director of the Franco-American Alliance, he contributed to the bursaries collected in America to assist Stravinsky, then deprived of his Russian income and, in many countries, of royalties. Dushkin met Stravinsky through Strecker in 1930.

Dushkin often insisted to the present writer that although Willy Strecker's older brother and business partner, Ludwig, was a Nazi party member, Willy was not and had never been a sympathizer. In a letter to Stravinsky, April 18, 1933, however, Willy makes a revealing statement with reference to the Nazis:

This movement has so much that is healthy and positive that no one can regard the artistic and other consequences quite calmly. The battle is directed primarily against the communists and Jews, whose influence is being checked to a considerable degree. A welcome cleaning-up has been undertaken . . . in an attempt to restore decency and order. No doubt there will be a reaction here against non-German art, but the really valuable will again be recognized as before. You must not worry about this, but our Dushkin, on the other hand, will find himself in an unfavorable position.

Strecker's communications to Stravinsky carefully avoid the word "Nazi," though a few letters to Strecker from Telefunken and other German companies, forwarded to Stravinsky, end with "Heil Hitler." Strecker displays masterful diplomacy in his efforts to keep the composer in good standing with the ruling powers in the German music world, powers that included Joseph Goebbels and the Nazi Reichsmusikkammer; the publisher was obliged to obtain permission for Stravinsky's concert engagements directly from Berlin. At the same time, Strecker took pains to shield Stravinsky from criticism abroad, to which, astonishingly, the German publisher seems to have been more sensitive than the most cosmopolitan of all the great composers.

The reader must wonder how Stravinsky could continue to visit and work in the Reich after Dushkin, a close friend and artistic collaborator, was forbidden to perform there; moreover, how could Stravinsky persist in attempting to secure concerts in the Germany of 1937–39? As the letters show, money was Stravinsky's motive, and he was the only composer for whom Strecker, or anyone else, succeeded in exporting sums of it from Hitler's state (arranging for payments to be made in Paris and London). Yet Stravinsky was not suffering

---

[2] See *S.S.C.* II for the history of this complicated affair, a consequence of the Russian Revolution.

any real deprivation, and he was not, as one wants to believe, politically naive. Friends kept him posted on developments in Germany, as in these insightful comments in letters from G. G. Païchadze:

Since no one has any money, life in Germany has come to a standstill. The shops are empty . . . the theatres, restaurants, movies, and even the bars are deserted. The activity in the streets is scarcely a third of what it was a year ago. . . . The coming months, no doubt, will be fraught with events. . . . The Germans themselves do not see a solution to the situation, and other countries refuse Germany any real aid. This, it seems to me, is the complete failure of Versailles. . . . The struggle between the political parties is further complicated because no combination of them can give the government a clear majority. The Nationalist movement is gaining strength now. . . . I pray that I am wrong, but I think that . . . we can expect an explosion in Germany by the end of the year. [August 24, 1931]

Hitler won a majority but not enough to wrest power from the socialist minority. . . . I do not believe that he can hold this position. The forces behind him will probably push him toward some illegal act, some *coup de force.* [April 25, 1932]

So far from being politically unaware, Stravinsky held deep convictions about forms of government. He was devoted to Mussolini,[3] *whom he knew personally and with whom he corresponded; Stravinsky gave Mussolini a score of Duo concertant and a gold medal to be melted down for the support of the Italian campaign in Ethiopia. Furthermore, Stravinsky had scheduled a concert in Italy for September 1939, even seeming to have found plausible his younger son's prediction—in a letter of August 28, 1939—that "there is a general desire to reach a peaceful agreement, especially on Hitler's part."*
    But Stravinsky's admiration for Fascist Italy and Spain—as late as 1938 he accepted honorary degrees from the rectors of the universities of Salamanca and Santander—is more comprehensible than his behavior toward Germany. That he esteemed German musical culture is natural; in 1932, he told an interviewer in Königsberg: "Nowhere is the art of music so consciously cultivated as in Germany, and that is a sign of a love for music. In the southern countries, the concept of music is less serious, while in America it is treated as a sport."[4] *(Ostpreussische Zeitung, November 4). But the Nazis contributed nothing to music. Apparently Stravinsky only once expressed sympathy for victims of the*

---

[3] Stravinsky preferred Mussolini's Fascism to British and French democracy, and when the *Manchester Guardian* described his music as "democratic" (February 22, 1934), he underscored the word and drew a large question mark next to it in the margin.

[4] After his 1935 and 1937 tours in the United States, Stravinsky changed his mind. Here is an excerpt from an interview in the Serbian-language Belgrade newspaper *Politika,* July 29, 1937: "I have become convinced that interest in . . . serious music, old

Nazis—in March 1939, in a letter to the Czechoslovakian Minister in Paris.
    After the war, Stravinsky and Willy Strecker continued to be good friends and saw each other both in Europe and in the composer's Hollywood home.[5] *On March 8, 1958, Stravinsky wrote to Nicolas Nabokov that he was "over-whelmed" to receive the news of his "dear" Willy Strecker's sudden death:*

Perhaps at our age it is natural to pass away like this; nevertheless, my reaction is one of pain. . . . We . . . do not know the details of Strecker's death: I hope to learn them from Strobel,[6] who is writing to Bob about this sudden and unexpected death.

STRAVINSKY TO WILLY STRECKER   *Nice*
                                                      December 24, 1928

Mainz[7]

I greatly appreciate your search for C. M. von Weber's symphonies, of which I am so fond, and I impatiently await your package containing the First Symphony (including the orchestra score, if possible), and the 4-hand reduction. Please look for the Second Symphony as well (orchestra score, piano 4-hands—or both). . . .
    . . . I just learned that the Königsberg Theatre presented *Noces* and hope that you are the one who arranged this, so that my [author's] rights will not be lost (i.e., pocketed by [J. & W.] Chester). . . .

                                                            Talloires
STRAVINSKY TO STRECKER   *August 10, 1929*

I hope your silence does not mean that you have forgotten me or that the proofs of the *Pastorale* and *Firebird* (for violin and piano)—which I sent a month

---

and new, is steadily increasing among Americans. And musical culture itself is developing there under much more favorable conditions than in Europe. The best orchestras in the world are now in America. . . . While squabbles between the conservative and the progressive artistic circles continue in the Old World, the New World has awakened to real musical art, and this fighting seems to them insignificant. . . . My eminently Slavic works—*Firebird, Petrushka, Le Sacre du printemps,* and *Noces*—seemed to please the Americans most at first, but this only led the way to their understanding my later works. The further development of musical culture in America has made the American public receptive to my works of other inspiration."

[5] On November 5, 1955, Stravinsky noted in his diary that Strecker had arrived in Hollywood.

[6] Heinrich Strobel (1899–1970), critic, author of *Stravinsky: Classic Humanist* (New York, 1955).

[7] Strecker's address, unless otherwise indicated, is that of B. Schotts Söhne, Mainz. Greetings and salutations and all of the formal apparatus of the letters have been omitted. With the exception of one communication in German, Stravinsky's letters are

ago—were never delivered. I am writing to you now not for acknowledgment of their receipt but to find out about the progress of your negotiations for concerts in Germany. The Wolff agency[8] and Ludwig Koch (Lindstrom) sent me discouraging letters on this subject. [Wolff] managed to secure only two engagements for me, with Klemperer in Berlin and at the Gewandhaus, which is not much of an accomplishment, since Klemperer himself had already proposed this to me some two months before Wolff. . . . The gentlemen who operate these agencies seem incapable of imagining alternative routes and inevitably approach the same, established philharmonic societies, which, of course, will never increase their standard fees. I doubt that I will ever succeed in making these people understand me. For this reason I am now directing my sights to the possibilities that we discussed in London long ago, and I would be grateful if you could give me a hint as to where the matter now stands. As you know, I ardently desire to introduce my works to your country myself, but nearly all of the German conductors find this objectionable. Will it be possible to realize this desire? I would also like to know if my new piano concerto could somehow be included in Scherchen's tours. . . .

STRAVINSKY TO STRECKER

Nice
December 27, 1929

Not long ago I was in Paris and played the premiere of my Capriccio for piano and orchestra, conducted by Ansermet. Virtually no other work of mine has ever been received so positively; the enthusiasm was unanimous, not only in the audience—which filled the Salle Pleyel, including standing room—but even in the press (with a few minor exceptions, of course). I hope that Berlin and Leipzig will greet the piece as warmly.

On January 20 I will be at the Hotel Fürstenhof. I play my Capriccio with Klemperer (at the Kroll) on the 23rd, conduct a concert at the Funkstunde on the 26th, repeat the Capriccio with Klemperer on the 30th at the Gewandhaus, then go to Düsseldorf to conduct a concert of my works, organized by the municipality, with the Wiesbach Orchestra. On February 7 I leave for Bucharest, where I will play my Capriccio with [Georges] Georgescu on the 12th and conduct a program of my works on the 16th. From Bucharest I proceed directly to Barcelona to conduct certain of my works (at the end of February and beginning of March). On March 7 I repeat my Capriccio, with Ansermet, in a Stravinsky festival in Paris. I give you this itinerary so that you will be able to reach me if necessary.

Your amiable intervention on my behalf with Madame Courtauld[9] was effective. She came to see me in Paris the other day, and we reached an

---

in French, but they are sprinkled with German phrases. All of Strecker's letters are in German. At the time of this letter, the two men had already been writing to each other for four years concerning the *Firebird* litigation.

[8] Wolff & Sachs, Stravinsky's German concert agents in Berlin.

[9] Elizabeth Courtauld, founder (1929) of the Courtauld-Sargent Concerts.

in-principle accord for two concerts, either at the end of October or in March–April 1931. In one concert I will play my Capriccio under [Malcolm] Sargent, and in the other I will conduct some of my works. . . .

I am infinitely grateful for your beautiful gift (that magnificent volume of *Neues vom Tage*). . . . Is it too much to ask you, in addition, for the piano score of the work?

Enclosed are my two photographs, which I have signed.

I am glad it occurred to me, the last time I was in London, to speak to you about my a cappella choruses,[10] which have been in the safe at the glorious J. & W. Chester Ltd. for ten solid years now. Had you not intervened, they would have spent another ten in that dirty flea bin before an English governor, brandishing fleabanes, would have come to revive my choruses in the name of that triumphant decade.

Will I see you in Berlin? That I would greatly enjoy. . . .

STRAVINSKY TO STRECKER

Nice
May 5, 1930

. . . Attached you will find the corrected proofs of the choruses.

I think the German text is very well done, in tone as well as in prosody. I am delighted. The translator's name is missing, but it should definitely be printed; please congratulate him for me.

Will you be coming to Paris? I go there tomorrow but leave again for Brussels and Amsterdam in ten days.

STRAVINSKY TO STRECKER

December 19, 1930
On the train between Amsterdam and Paris

. . . I concluded an agreement with the Concertgebouw of Amsterdam for the premiere of my Violin Concerto,[11] which I will conduct there in three concerts devoted to my works at the end of October or the beginning of November 1931. . . .

STRAVINSKY TO STRECKER

Nice
December 25, 1930

My heartfelt Christmas greetings and best wishes for the New Year, dear and esteemed friend.[12] Now I will switch to French, since you know very well that my German is not as good as it might be. This is a business letter, regarding the future of my Violin Concerto, and I address myself to you rather than to your brother (with whom I outlined the agreement) because I have misplaced the

---

[10] The Four Russian Peasant Choruses (*Podblyudnye*) for female voices were composed in 1914–17 but had not yet been published.

[11] Stravinsky's first sketch for the concerto is found on his bill for Brack's Doelen Hotel, Amsterdam, November 1930.

[12] This letter is to Ludwig Strecker.

number and name of his street in Wiesbaden. Thus these lines are intended as much for him as for you.

A week ago I sent a telegram from Amsterdam to inform you of my agreement with the Concertgebouw for the world premiere of my Violin Concerto. . . . Upon my arrival in Paris, however, I learned from your cable that you had simultaneously promised the premiere to the Berlin Radio. You can imagine the sticky situation in which I now find myself. The terms for conducting this concert are those I established with your brother Willy in Mainz, $750. But what am I to do now, since I managed to secure such a good honorarium for these three concerts precisely because it was to be the premiere? I immediately sent a telegram to Amsterdam, warning the Concertgebouw of your agreement with the Berlin Radio—which must have been executed at exactly the same time as my contract with [Amsterdam]—and requested to know their reaction to these new circumstances. Thus far I have received no reply.

I am also waiting for you to send the contract promised in your brother Willy's letter of December 2. . . .

In Paris I saw Païchadze, who told me that he had received Willy's letter (of December 9). . . . Païchadze was very favorably impressed and plans to ask two things in exchange: (1) that you place him, rather than Eschig, in charge of your representation in France; (2) if circumstances permit him to resume business in Russia, that you also let him represent you there. . . .

STRAVINSKY TO STRECKER

Nice
January 2, 1931

. . . Thank you for the contract. . . . Unfortunately, I have noticed several errors, which should be corrected before I sign. These concern the questions of: (1) mechanical rights, (2) the rights I reserve for myself in sound films, these stemming automatically from the rights for mechanical reproduction, which belong to me; (3) the manuscript of the work, which must remain in my possession. Here are my views on these questions:

A. I request not only the royalties that I automatically collect from mechanical reproduction (according to our agreement in Mainz) but also the rights that, in your contract, go to the publisher (see line 3 of this contract). In effect, if I leave this point as it now stands, I would have no recourse against the rental of my music for mechanical reproduction to interpreters whom I may find thoroughly undesirable. I would receive payment for author's rights from all mechanical reproduction but would have no voice in the matter.

B. Logically, the question of sound films falls under mechanical rights, which I reserve for myself, and I ask you simply to delete these words at the beginning of the contract: *und des Rechts zur Wiedergabe durch mechanischmusikalische Musikwerke oder Verrichtungen für Tonfilme.* . . . Points 4 and 5 should be modified accordingly and made into one point, as follows: Since the rights for mechanical reproduction and sound films remain the property of the author, the publisher would be indemnified by specific prices for the rental of the orchestra parts. In case of possible difficulties with organizations over the establishment of these prices, the organization would have to reach an accord with the publisher.

C. I generally keep my manuscripts for my family, and I therefore ask you to change the fourth line of page 2 so that the manuscript will remain my property. . . .

Do not neglect to inform me of the nature of your agreement with Païchadze. . . . I await your reply.

I enclose my signed copy of the contract, as well as the extra pages concerning Samuel Dushkin and my concerts. . . .

Nice

STRAVINSKY TO STRECKER   *January 10, 1931*

. . . . Thank you for the Strauss operas. Yesterday I received the other two you mentioned.

I will be in Berlin on the 14th at the latest. Write to me there at the Hotel Fürstenhof.

I ask you to help me in dealing with Chester about the little Valse [from the Suite No. 2 for Small Orchestra], which I will conduct at the BBC on February 1. . . . I am certain that, as usual, Chester will provide parts that are impossible to play.[13] Could you send them one of your copies of the little Valse, which is now correct and very easy to follow? As you may know . . . I will play these suites in Berlin on the 15th.

Nice

STRAVINSKY TO STRECKER   *February 7, 1931*

. . . Will I see you in London? I arrive the night of the 27th and will be staying at the home of Madame Courtauld, who is now a close friend.

I am here until the 14th, then to Paris (Pleyel) until the 27th. . . .

Nice

STRAVINSKY TO STRECKER   *March 26, 1931*

Amsterdam, deeply offended at being deprived of the premiere of the Violin Concerto, no longer intends to do a Stravinsky festival next season. Therefore, please tell [the] Walther [concert agency], that I am free at the end of October and beginning of November. Apart from concerts in London (November 16 and 17, with three or four days of rehearsal before the concerts) and probably in Paris (December 17 and 20, also with a few days of rehearsing), he can dispose of my time after the end of September as he wishes. . . .

Tell me, have you written to Païchadze about Columbia and the publicity that my recordings are supposed to receive?

---

[13] The repeats and da capo signs were confusing.

STRAVINSKY TO STRECKER

. . . I have finished the first part of the Violin Concerto, both the music and the instrumentation, but the latter is not yet in orchestra score form. Now I am working on the piano reduction. This first movement will comprise approximately nineteen pages in the piano score with a duration of five minutes, in tempo allegro ($\quarternote = 96$). That is all the information to which you are entitled at the moment!

STRAVINSKY TO STRECKER

. . . See if you can find a way for me to conduct something other than *Firebird* and *Petrushka,* which I do all the time everywhere. You would be an angel! . . .

On the 19th I go to Trieste to play the Capriccio and to conduct at the Teatro Verdi, on the 23rd or 24th. . . .

Thank you for [Weber's] *Turandot* [march] : the photocopy gave me immense pleasure!

STRAVINSKY TO STRECKER

Antwerp . . . has now requested that I advance the date to November 9, 1931 . . . owing to the jealousy of the displaced resident conductor, alas! . . .

Thank you for the letter of the 14th. Tomorrow I leave for a week in Trieste (Excelsior Palace Hotel).

STRAVINSKY TO STRECKER

. . . While reading the Russian papers in Paris, I discovered that *Firebird* is being staged in South America. In what city? By which theatre? Nothing is clear. I would be grateful if you could unravel this mystery for me. Forberg should know, since he alone has the complete parts of the ballet. I would be interested to learn how my author's rights were handled and who drew up the contract. . . .

I hope that you have already begun to engrave the first movement of the Violin Concerto.

As for the American copyright, the formula you deem the only acceptable one is very difficult for me to accept. Let me reflect on it a bit longer; I do not think that there is any rush.

I continue composing without interruption and will soon finish the second movement (Aria da capo). . . .

STRAVINSKY TO STRECKER   *June 7, 1931*

Along with this note I am sending the corrected proofs (violin and piano-violin) of the first movement. Please insert the corrections, including them in the second proofs that you send me. I would appreciate it if you would send two copies of the second proofs; I want to keep one for my library. . . .

Thank you for the nice telegram the other day acknowledging the receipt of the second movement and expressing the pleasure that this Aria da capo gave you (to judge by the flattering words you employ). The second Aria is shorter than the first and totally different in character; this I have just completed and will send to you in about eight days. . . .

                                                             Nice
STRAVINSKY TO STRECKER   *June 14, 1931*

. . . Tomorrow morning I will send the manuscript (piano and violin) of the third part (Aria II). I await the following from you: the second proofs of the first movement and the first proofs of the second movement. These will probably arrive tomorrow. . . .

I am tempted to settle for two rehearsals in Vienna, but this will depend on the orchestra. If it is the same orchestra with which I played my Capriccio,* then [two rehearsals] would suffice, since the musicians have already played many of my works. . . . If, on the contrary, it is another orchestra, I must know whether they have played my music before, and exactly which pieces, before I accept only two rehearsals. Will the Violin Concerto be done in Vienna?

. . . Berlin postponed the concert of October 9 until the 23rd; what a surprise! Does this mean that the Violin Concerto cannot be given before the 23rd? . . . What shall I do during October before the Berlin premiere?[14] And during the whole month of November? Do you really think that Leipzig and, eventually, Vienna represent enough work for two whole months? . . .

* Unable to recall the name of that orchestra, I enclose the program, from which Walther should be able to determine whether or not it is the same.

                                                             Nice
STRAVINSKY TO STRECKER   *June 22, 1931*

I have a liver infection, thanks to which I must follow a strict diet; if the condition does not worsen, I will take the train for Paris on Sunday, instead of driving by car with Dushkin, as planned. Write to me at Pleyel (252, rue du Faubourg St.-Honoré, Paris 8). When I return to Nice, on July 16 or 17, I think that I will go directly to the country (not far from Grenoble) and stay there until September 20.

Wish me a quick recovery, for it is imperative that I continue my work. . . .

---

[14] Arthur Lourié wrote to Stravinsky, October 14, 1931: "I would very much like to go

STRAVINSKY TO STRECKER

Voreppe
July 2, 1931

. . . I plan to send you the whole first movement of the orchestra score at the beginning of August. The other movements will follow automatically, and you need not give them another thought. . . .

Tell Strobel[15] that I would be delighted to see him any time after the beginning of August. Voreppe (Isère) is 14 kilometers from Grenoble, and I will send my automobile to fetch him at the Grenoble station. In the meantime . . . a book about me, by André Schaeffner, has appeared in Paris. You will receive a copy one of these days. Schaeffner's documentation is precise. . . .

That is all for now. I am curing my colitis by resting. I hope to recover, finish my work, and be in good, fresh shape for the coming season. . . .

STRAVINSKY TO STRECKER

September 12, 1931

. . . Herewith I am sending the last part of the piano score, by registered mail. Please alert the printers to the measures of violin music written in pencil on page 7, and on page 19, at one measure before **128**. I left these in pencil because I was waiting for Dushkin to decide upon the definitive version, but since I will not have it until Monday, I am mailing the package today, so as not to hold up everything for the sake of a few measures. This way you can begin work on Monday. Have the printers set the penciled insertions (very important for the spacing), because the triplets will not change; probably only the octaves will be modified, and this is easily done. . . .

On Monday I will send the manuscript of the orchestra score of the second Aria, as well as your engraving of the first movement of the orchestra score (corrected). Please ask your printers what purpose is served by the double numbers and figures (on pages 18 and 19). To save time, I have not bothered to copy into the orchestra score the repeated music from the beginning of the piece (**3** and **10**, inclusive), but I did indicate the corresponding numbers (**38** and **39**, etc., corresponding to **3** and **4**, etc.) to guide the placement of these numbers in the piano score. Perhaps in the parts the repeat is not written out, and the double [rehearsal] numbers were printed to assist the conductor. I still do not understand the double *page* numbers, though, and I therefore ask you to have the printers delete them according to my corrections in the proofs, and not to insert these double numbers in the parts. . . .

Starting today I will concentrate on the orchestra score of the last movement. . . .

---

to Berlin with Vera and hear the premiere of the Concerto, but I cannot even afford to dream about that now. Please write me your impressions of Germany. . . ."

[15] A note in Stravinsky's hand in one of his files reads: "August 1931. Visit to Voreppe of two reporters, Strobel and [Guido] Gatti, and the banal results—two articles, in the *Börsenkurier* and the *Ambrosiana*."

Here is the explanation of the telegram Dushkin just sent to you.

1. A measure of silence must be inserted between the last measure of **122** and the first of **123.** This idea occurred to me after I sent the manuscript of the last movement, piano score. I hope that the telegram arrives before the printers begin that page.

2. I also realized at this late date that each movement of the Concerto should have a title, so that the audience has an idea of the character, especially since the tempi are only metronomic indications. . . .

. . . Sincere thanks for the gift of the *Kneippbuch,* just received; I am very touched.

If you see any way to salvage the *Psalms* performance in Berlin, please do me this great service, for which I would be infinitely grateful. This was the only concert in Germany of the season that interested me. I really find it discouraging always to conduct the same things, while watching others conduct and "interpret" my [newer] works.

Since I am only a stone's throw from Geneva, where I must see some friends on Saturday night, why, great God, am I being sent to Oslo via Paris?

I hope that you have received the last pages of my manuscript, which Dushkin sent by airmail to Mainz last Saturday. . . .

I just received new proofs of the piano score of the Capriccio [the fourth movement of the Violin Concerto], along with the old corrected proofs, and new proofs of the second Aria with its old corrected proofs. I will attempt to correct these new proofs and send them off again today before the post office closes. Many thanks for the Hindemith, enclosed in your package. . . .

Along with this note, I am sending the corrected proofs of the following:

(1) piano score, fourth movement (second proofs);
(2) orchestra score, fourth movement (first and second proofs);
(3) orchestra score, third movement (first and second proofs);
(4) manuscript of the last pages of the fourth movement.

Please check the new insertion (on pages 54 and 57 of the orchestra score) to see that it is exactly as I indicated to you (by my scissoring and pasting system) in the first proofs. Check the orchestra score again, comparing it with the piano score, to be certain that all of the rehearsal numbers are in the right place. I do not have time to verify them here, or in the other movements, which you already have.

By now you must have received the final score of the solo violin, which Dushkin was to have sent you. Please coordinate that part with the corresponding music in the piano and orchestra scores. Of course, the fingerings and bowings should not be inserted in the orchestra score, but only in the piano score. I am referring here only to Dushkin's violin solo, not to the solo to be played by the concertmaster in the fourth movement.

After correcting what I send today, please forward the complete orchestra score to me at the Hotel Bristol in Oslo;[16] I will have a few free days there and would like to study it from the point of view of the conductor before I arrive in Berlin. . . .

P.S. Make certain that the arco is at **125** in the solo violin part, because, if I recall correctly, it is missing in the orchestra and piano parts.

STRAVINSKY TO STRECKER

Voreppe
December 29, 1931

. . . What is this you say about Markevitch's *Rebus,* which I heard him conduct on the day of my arrival in Paris?[17] In all honesty? Insofar as one can judge from a single hearing, there are excellent measures and ideas, which, unfortunately, never evolve into a cohesive work. Once again Prokofiev is the model—I really think that it is time to put an end to this habitual borrowing from Prokofiev, and [Markevitch's] technique is too accomplished for us to attribute the principal shortcoming of the work to that. The piece is just boring. I confess that I, more than anyone, did not want to walk away with this impression of a twenty-one-year-old composer, especially one who is considered by most to be extraordinar-

---

[16] Stravinsky conducted two concerts in Oslo in October 1931. George de Meck, a relative of Nadyezhda Filaretovna von Meck, Tchaikovsky's patroness, was living in Oslo, and he showed Stravinsky some Debussy manuscripts dating from the time that the French composer was employed by Madame von Meck. On returning to Germany, Stravinsky informed Strecker of this and arranged for their purchase by Schott. De Meck wrote to Stravinsky from 13 St. Olav's Gate, Oslo, December 20, 1931: "I have just concluded the affair of the Debussy manuscripts with Schott, and my first thought is to write to you to thank you with all my heart for what you did for me. . . . I received the 1,500 marks that Schott offered, and because of the devaluation of the Norwegian crown, this money is a small fortune for us. I know that it was realized through your kindness and your intervention. . . . The time that I spent with you had a profound effect on me—your music, but also your views on many questions of life, have made me think of you often."

[17] Tuesday, December 15, at the Salle Gaveau. The remainder of the program consisted of the two Bach chorale preludes in Schoenberg's orchestration, Satie's *Parade,* and *Le Sacre du printemps.*

ily gifted and by me to be very gifted. In my opinion, Markevitch is not a *Wunderkind* but an *Altklug,* which is perhaps even more dangerous to the future of his art than if he were a veritable *Wunderkind.* If I could follow the composition with a score in hand, my judgment would be much clearer, but I do not think that it would change substantially from the one I have just shared with you.

STRAVINSKY TO STRECKER

Voreppe
February 8, 1932[18]

Many thanks . . . for the attention you always give to my errands. I am ashamed to have pestered your wife—whom I was so happy to see again in Paris—with these. In effect, [I would like] the new photographic apparatus by Zeiss-Ikon, about which I should write to Weber[19] but have not yet found time. . . .

    I look forward to seeing you, since I will play my Capriccio with the Concerts Siohan (Théâtre Pigalle) on March 5 and you plan to be in Paris at that time. . . .

STRAVINSKY TO STRECKER

Voreppe
February 14, 1932

. . . Exactly when will you arrive in Paris? I will probably be there on March 2.

    Where is your brother-in-law, Ito Don Carlos?[20] It seems that I will be going to Buenos Aires (this is strictly confidential for the moment), and I would

---

[18] Strecker had written on February 6: "As for paying you, we must first secure permission from the Exchange Office (Devisen Zentrale), even if we just deposit the money in your German account (though then you could only be paid in marks). I could also arrange for you to be paid the equivalent amount in French francs through [Editions Max] Eschig in Paris; you may find this preferable, to avoid losing in the exchange. But for this, too, I must obtain permission from the German authorities. Unfortunately, other currencies, such as Swiss francs, are not available for purchase. Please let me know your preference, since the times are becoming increasingly complicated, and new and unexpected ordinances are passed down daily."

[19] Fyodor Vladimirovich Weber was the director of the Berlin branch of Koussevitzky's Russischer Musik Verlag.

[20] Strecker replied on February 18: "My brother-in-law, Carlos von Bernard, is leaving for Buenos Aires on the S.S. *Atlantic* on March 2 or 3. His address is: Once de Septiembre 1830. I will write to him today, since he will surely be glad to see you in Buenos Aires. For the next few days he can still be reached at the Hôtel Bristol, Beaulieu, but you could try to see him in Paris before his departure on March 2. . . . My mother-in-law, Frau von Bernard, will travel back on Monday on the *Cap Arcona,* so you will find friends in Buenos Aires. . . . Your *Scherzo fantastique* was enormously successful in Vienna under Clemens Krauss. The audience wanted it repeated, and the reviews were excellent. I believe this piece is definitely experiencing a revival and will be performed numerous times this winter."

like to know if I will see him during my thirty-four-day sojourn there. What is his current address? . . . I would like to ask him a few questions. . . .

P.S. If you think of it, please bring a package of the pills[21] to Paris with you.

STRAVINSKY TO STRECKER   *Voreppe*
                                                          February 20, 1932
Wiesbaden

Many thanks for your letter (of the 18th) and for carrying out my numerous errands. . . . I will be in Paris on March 11 and 15, just for a few hours, on the way to and from Antwerp, and then will be continuing on to Italy. . . .

I await a definite reply from Buenos Aires, via a telephone call from Mr. Susini (a friend of your brother-in-law, I believe), who leaves for Argentina on February 24.

He is the one negotiating with [the Teatro Colón] , . . . and if all goes well, I will leave for there on May 20, aboard the *Cap Arcona,* a beautiful German ship. . . . For this reason, I would like to ask you or your brother-in-law whether the administration of the ship can be expected to make a fuss about Madame Sudeikina's accompanying me. All this is *entre nous,* of course, for I would not like anyone to know that I have consulted you on the matter. . . .

STRAVINSKY TO STRECKER   *Voreppe*
                                                            March 9, 1932
Wiesbaden

. . . Would it be too much to ask you [another] favor? I need some spare batteries for my flashlights, and these can be purchased at the big store on the corner in Wiesbaden where all sorts of metal objects and kitchen hardware are sold. I enclose the dimensions of my two flashlights. . . .

                                                                  Voreppe
STRAVINSKY TO STRECKER   *April 6, 1932*

Returning to Voreppe, . . . I hasten to ask you to outline for Walther his part . . . in my three Italian concerts.

I agreed with the Moltrasio & Luzzato agency in Milan that I will pay 4 percent to Walther and 6 percent to Moltrasio & Luzzato from my honorarium. (Dushkin must arrange his accounts with Walther himself.)

I earned $500 in Venice, so I owe Walther $20; in Florence I earned $300, so from that I owe him $12; and in Milan I earned 5,000 lire, thus 200 lire. . . .

---

[21] A calmative for the stomach.

STRAVINSKY TO STRECKER   *Voreppe*
                                                       April 9, 1932
Wiesbaden

. . . Enclosed you will find a telegram and a letter from Furtwängler, and from this bit of correspondence you will be able to form a supplementary opinion as to the worth of this man (since you already have a general opinion). On the telegram you will find my response (in ink), with *"ausserordentlich gefreut"* [extraordinarily happy]. I would not mind if Luisa Wolf and others involved with the conductor's activities are made aware of this. I see, alas, that only my premieres are of interest to this kind of conductor.[22]

Do not worry about the little mechanism for my new camera, which you forgot to send the other day. . . .[23]

STRAVINSKY TO STRECKER   *Voreppe*
                                                      April 22, 1932
Wiesbaden

Wolff & Sachs have relayed the Commedia Tonfilme Gesellschaft's proposal that I conduct one of my works (twenty-some minutes long) for a film. I have accepted, but since they asked me to set an exact date between May and October, . . . I must ask you for some information.

First of all, I do not think, because of Susini's silence (no news since his departure at the end of January), that the South American [tour] will take place (at least not this year). Second, I would like to combine the Tonfilme engagement with the Homburg (vor der Höhe) performance of *Renard*, if that is to take place. I would be infinitely grateful if you would tell me immediately

---

[22] Furtwängler had written to Stravinsky on March 23: "Dear *Meister,* I was overjoyed that you agreed to appear in my concert series. . . . [But] for the time being, it is not possible for me to repeat a work; this would break the tradition of my concerts, because the pieces were performed in previous years. [Stravinsky wrote in the margin here: "What a reason!"] On the other hand, I would be very happy if I could perform one of your new works in Berlin. Of course, I have no idea what you are composing now, but . . . if you had a purely orchestral work, I would be happy to give it in Berlin. In that case we would have to postpone your solo participation for several years." On June 12, Arthur Lourié wrote to Stravinsky from Paris: "I have been seeing a lot of Vera lately, at the Horowitz recital and on Friday at a banquet that Furtwängler attended. At the banquet Vera pointed out the Countess Zubova, but I already know her well. I write to you about her because evidently she is Strecker's mistress; she spoke too persistently about him, leaving no room for doubt. And that you know her [in the same way] is really piquant." Stravinsky knew Count Sergei Zubov and his wife in Paris before World War I.

[23] Strecker had written on April 6: "I still have a little automatic release switch for your camera, and I will send it to you as soon as possible. Unfortunately, it was left behind in my suitcase."

whether our radio project with Rosbaud[24] is still on; if so, give me the approximate date, so that I can give Wolff & Sachs a date for the Tonfilme recording. Apparently this will be done in Berlin, either with the Philharmonic Orchestra or the Staatsoper (unless it is recorded with the Orchestre Symphonique in Paris, which is also a possibility). . . .

STRAVINSKY TO STRECKER   *Voreppe*
                                                         April 25, 1932
Wiesbaden

. . . The ballet master Boris Romanov[25] just received an offer to present the ballet season in Buenos Aires (Teatro Colón). He immediately accepted and thanked me for having recommended him, while I, on the other hand, still have not heard anything [from the Colón]! Incredible!

Spring is in full bloom here, too, but with a lot of rain, unfortunately. . . .

                                                              Paris
STRAVINSKY TO STRECKER   *May 16, 1932*

. . . I will be in Frankfurt on June 23. Everything has been settled with Rosbaud, who will do *Mavra* and *Oedipus Rex*, and I have asked Weber to arrange for me to conduct *Petrushka* at the Berlin Opera immediately after the 23rd. Please send the 309 [marks] 67 [pfennigs] to the Russischer Musik Verlag and have the sum credited to my account there.

                                                             Voreppe
STRAVINSKY TO STRECKER   *May 28, 1932*

. . . I am waiting for Wolff to schedule my recording for the end of June, as I requested.

Legislation concerning the author's rights in sound films is so confused and obscure that it presents quite a problem with a contract such as this one [Tonfilme]. I think it would be prudent to have you examine the contract before I sign, so I will send it to you as soon as I receive it. . . .

                                                             Voreppe
STRAVINSKY TO STRECKER   *July 16, 1932*

I was greatly amused to learn, from the *Allgemeine Musikzeitung*, of my participation as a pianist in Ravel's Concerto under his direction in Antwerp. You suppose that I will deny this fastidiously. On the contrary, it would be wonderful to encourage the *Allgemeine Musikzeitung*'s self-confidence (re-

---

[24] Hans Rosbaud (1895–1962), Austrian conductor.
[25] Romanov had staged the dances for Diaghilev's production of *The Nightingale* in 1914.

garding the information they furnish) to the point of reading, one fine day, that Furtwängler played the violin in my Concerto in D under the direction of Ernest Newman. My only fear is that Darius Milhaud will take advantage of this opportunity and submit a notice to the press to the effect that his new masterpiece, *The Emperor Maximilian,* triumphed under my direction at the Paris Opéra. . . .

STRAVINSKY TO STRECKER

Voreppe
September 14, 1932

Thank you for your postcard from the Mumms',[26] which awaited me on the table when I returned from my trip around France. I was away for three weeks, and I am now back at work, exercising my fingers for the chamber-music concerts with Dushkin. How ironic! I have only one concert—in Danzig! Walther has not breathed a word about Frankfurt, on which we were firmly counting. Rosbaud, too, is mysteriously silent. Perhaps you could give them a prod for me?[27] It really is absurd to give the premiere of my new Duo concertant in Danzig![28] Berlin still is undecided, after several talks between the Radio and Wolff & Sachs, who are trying to obtain the price we agreed on last year.

STRAVINSKY TO STRECKER

Voreppe
October 6, 1932

Wiesbaden

Precisely when will you arrive in Paris, when will you go to London, when will you return—and where, to Paris or directly home? A nice questionnaire, is it not? I must know, because I intend to ask a small favor of you in London, if you please. I ordered some knitted woolen shirts from Hilditch & Key in Paris, who

---

[26] The postcard reads: "We hope to listen to the Capriccio recording on the gramophone soon, alas, without you, dear *Meister.* We embrace you, Olga Mumm [Strecker's daughter], Willy Strecker, Paul Strecker [Willy's brother], Elena Orlova [Mumm], Maria Balasheva, [Peter] Balashev [Olga Mumm's nephew], Orlov." When Peter Balashev was nine years old (in January 1933), he sent a card to Vera Sudeikina because, as his "babushka" informed her, "*cette dame m'a tappé dans l'oeil.*"

[27] Rosbaud wrote to Stravinsky on October 25: "I went to Austria for a little vacation and met with Anton Webern in Bad-Fischau, from where I sent you that desperate letter. . . . When I received no answer from you, I became more and more miserable, supposing that the contents of my letter had left you angry not only with the situation in Germany . . . but with me." Stravinsky had last seen Webern, together with Alban Berg, at a reception in Vienna in 1926.

[28] Strecker replied on September 19: "Of course it is ironic that your Duo concertant will be performed in Danzig, but the premiere is less significant for this kind of piece than for an orchestral work, since each of your premieres makes a sensation here. I feel certain that you will have many opportunities to repeat this work and the other chamber-music pieces in the course of the next few years, as soon as things have set-

then passed the order to their London house, 48 Jermyn Street, SW1. I was advised to have someone returning to the Continent bring the package to me, to avoid paying the duty (of 150 francs for the three shirts). I will be in Paris for a few days before my Berlin concert, scheduled for October 28. . . .

STRAVINSKY TO STRECKER

Voreppe
January 15, 1933

Thank you . . . for the first proofs of the Scherzo for violin and piano from *Firebird,* received yesterday. . . .

I leave for a concert tour the day after tomorrow . . . going first to Hamburg (from January 20 at the Hotel Vier Jahreszeiten), where I play my Capriccio with Muck on the 22nd and 23rd. Next I play it in Ostrava, Czechoslovakia, on the 26th, proceeding then to Germany, where I give a concert with Dushkin in Munich on February 2. Then to Italy, where I have a series of engagements: Milan, February 11; Turin, the 17th, Rome, the 23rd (the last two are for Italian Radio, so you will be able to listen to them).

I could conceivably stop in Wiesbaden on my return to Germany for my Munich concert. I will have three or four free days, as you see. This idea is tempting; I will write you a note from Hamburg about it. . . .

STRAVINSKY TO STRECKER

Voreppe
April 14, 1933
Holy Saturday

Here are the genealogical details that I promised to furnish for my biography. I was born in Oranienbaum, near St. Petersburg, on June 5 [18 New Style], 1882. My mother and father were Orthodox (Greek-Catholic).

My father, Theodore de Stravinsky, Court Singer at the Imperial Opera of St. Petersburg, was a member of the hereditary Russian nobility. He studied at the Niezhen School (in southern Russia), an institution reserved for children

---

tled down. . . . [The premiere of Duo concertant took place in Berlin instead; Stravinsky and Vera Sudeikina stayed at the home of Gregor Piatigorsky and his wife, Lida.] These are very unfortunate times: because of the political situation, conductors and concert agents approach foreign artists very hesitantly. Rosbaud himself, because of his Austrian nationality, is having difficulties maintaining his position at the Radio. He told me that if he were to engage Dushkin or [Beveridge] Webster at this time, he would be dismissed immediately. Twice already he has been summoned to Berlin, where they have outlined for him the conditions under which he will be allowed to keep his job. I believe that this will be ironed out as soon as the political situation stabilizes, but for the moment he reflects the nervous tension that prevails in the whole of our artistic life." On February 19, 1933, Rosbaud wrote to Stravinsky from Frankfurt: "The situation will be even worse when Dr. Goebbels becomes the commissioner of all radio broadcasting. I cannot tell you how unhappy I am, most esteemed Herr Stravinsky, that soon we will not be permitted to play your music here." Nevertheless, in April 1933 Stravinsky received a personal invitation to attend an "international congress" in Bayreuth in August.

of the hereditary Russian nobility. My father's ancestors, the Counts Soulima-Stravinski, all landowners, were Polish and Catholic. More than one hundred years ago the line of the Counts Soulima-Stravinski became part of the Russian nobility, under the name "de Stravinsky," as stated in the sixth book of the Senate, a volume devoted solely to hereditary Russian nobility of foreign provenance (Balts, Poles, etc.).

My mother, daughter of Cyrille *de* Kholodovsky, a Privy Councillor and Minister of Agriculture under Nicholas I, was also a member of the hereditary Russian nobility and belonged to the landowner class, who, in that epoch, were given important functions in civil and military affairs of state.

Both of my grandmothers were Russian Orthodox and of the same class of Russian society as my grandfathers: one of them was the daughter of a minister under Alexander I and the other the daughter of a landowner.

As for myself, I have lived abroad for twenty-three years, settling first in Switzerland, in 1910, for the sake of my wife's health (my first cousin, born *de* Nossenko), and moving, after the war, to France, where I live today.

I have not returned to Russia. What would I do there? I loathe all communism, Marxism, the execrable Soviet monster, and also all liberalism, democratism, atheism, etc. I detest them to such a degree and so unreservedly that any connection with the country of the Soviets would be senseless.

I hope that this bit of biographical information, coming directly from me and thus authentic, will be of service in achieving the end that concerns you.[29]

I avail myself of this opportunity to wish you and yours a Happy Easter.

Your cordially devoted   I. Stravinsky

---

[29] Stravinsky made this declaration at Strecker's request. On March 29 Strecker had written: "Back in Mainz, I find that the mood in Germany is on the whole quite excited, although for the moment absolute calm and order prevail. A militant culture group (*Kultur Kampfbund*) was formed whose aim is to advance German art above all other art and to suppress everything Jewish and Bolshevik. Your name is on the list of the Jewish composers! I consider this insignificant, because such lists are hastily drawn up by inexperienced patriots and will certainly be examined by competent authorities. Hindemith, too, is implicated, but only as a musical Bolshevik [not as a Jew]. With the help of leading musicians and artists who are among the officials in charge, this propaganda will surely be curtailed. The case could arise, however, in which it would be helpful to have concrete evidence at my fingertips to counter the rumors, particularly that of your being a Jewish Bolshevik. I would therefore be grateful if you would send me a short declaration that seems appropriate to you. My general strategy is to ignore such assertions, but, in the future, it might be prudent for me to send authentic, reliable proof directly to the authorities. Hindemith, whom I saw in London, remains calm in appraising the situation. He feels certain that reason will very soon prevail, at least in matters of art. Anyway, the season is ending, and one hopes that by next season the atmosphere will have cleared." On April 18, Strecker acknowledged the receipt of Stravinsky's "declaration," adding: "I consider it beneath your dignity to publicize your deposition prior to an official attack, and besides, I do not think that it will be necessary to do so. Hindemith shares my view. I was happy to see that Monteux

STRAVINSKY TO STRECKER

I enjoyed your letter and congratulate you on your new acquisition. I hope that this third marriage of my daughter, *Firebird,* will satisfy her for the rest of her days and give her the happiness of a normal life, which she has sought now for more than twenty years. I also hope that her passing flirtations with the English gigolo will be completely erased from her memory and that her father will be free of such annoyances for good.[31]

Attached you will find two signed copies of the *Pastorale* contract, on which I have taken the liberty of adding my name before the title ("Igor Stravinsky's"), and the indication *"für Violine und Blasquartett"* after the word "Pastorale," both omitted by your typist. The new, enlarged version of the piano and violin reduction is not yet finished, whereas the ensemble score (with oboe, English horn, clarinet, and bassoon accompanying the violin) has already been recorded by Columbia (with Dushkin and myself). The recordings and the

---

conducted a work of yours in Berlin not long ago, along with some other French works, and that the concert was ostentatiously attended by government people, which is a sign that the higher-ups have quite reasonable views."

[30] On July 20, Strecker had written: "Here in Germany the situation is beginning to clear. I have had some rather harsh correspondence and negotiations about your 'degenerate Bolshevik art.' I think that the danger has now passed and that the guidelines set down by the new music commission will prove to be quite rational. Your music should come into its own again. I had some interesting deliberations [about your music], and [I conclude that] the people in the leading circles have great insight and understand the need to present the *good* things that other countries may have to offer." At the beginning of August, Strecker wrote again: "German theatres, expecting new guidelines from the government, have avoided presentations of practically all foreign works in the past six months. This explains the unusually small royalties in the last statement." In pencil at the end of this letter he wrote: "Warm greetings from Paul Hindemith, who happens to be here." On August 7, Strecker informed Stravinsky that the *Firebird* ballet would definitely be performed in Zürich the next winter, "but otherwise I have nothing to report, since political conditions are difficult, and programs have not yet been assembled." By January 30, 1934, Strecker felt that "in the course of the next few months the [official] evaluation [of music] will become less dogmatic, and performances [of your music] will again take place by the fall. . . . We look forward to your daughter's visit." (In May 1934, Lyudmila Stravinsky went to Mainz and stayed with the Streckers, intending to carry her father's royalties home with her, but she was stopped at the border.) On November 28, 1934, Richard Strauss's comment that Stravinsky *"begeistert zu den Ideen Adolf Hitlers"* [is enthusiastic about the ideas of Adolf Hitler] was published in the *Frankischer Kurier.* Two days later, Strecker wrote: "I enclose the newspaper article, which is currently being printed everywhere. Stupid though it may be, the effect is certainly excellent. This is partly a result of the information you put at my disposal a year ago. One must remain quiet now and let the thing run its course."

[31] The metaphor refers to Schott's acquisition from Forberg, on July 19, 1933, of the original *Firebird* ballet and the 1919 suite. The "English gigolo" is J. & W. Chester.

manuscript of this work are at my house, and I await Sam's arrival from America to submit the fair copy for printing and to review, correct, and copy the score. When will I find time to do all of this? Furthermore, I am searching for a furnished apartment in Paris, where I have decided to live during the winter months (October to June), since my children can no longer stay in Voreppe year-round. It is a busy time for me! . . .

STRAVINSKY TO STRECKER

Paris[32]
November 17, 1935

. . . I am still considering your invitation to spend a little time with you in Wiesbaden and arrange some interesting [concerts] for the near future. I decided to cancel my trip to America; I received a cable from Sam [Dushkin] in New York informing me that my manager will be in a sanitarium for several weeks, but his secretary is doing all she can in an attempt to save the tour. All this is not very reassuring. Hence we must think about fixing engagements elsewhere. Don't you think that we could arrange something in Frankfurt again this season, including several appearances with my son in my new Concerto [per due pianoforti soli] ? . . .

Did you receive the photographs of me from a young photographer in Wiesbaden, and have you chosen one from which to make postcards? I think the most successful one is that in which my body is visible down to the knees. Another, against a vague background of a library, is not bad, either (head and hands), but the right side would have to be tailored a bit: my elbow did not come out well. . . .

Païchadze says he is terribly busy but has not forgotten the project you discussed recently. If I understood him correctly, he feels that another conversation would be superfluous. . . . In respect to [Païchadze's] "gloomy" silence, I must say in his behalf that he has had an excess of work lately because his firm has just assumed representation of the Editions Belayev. . . .

STRAVINSKY TO STRECKER

January 18, 1936

A second letter has arrived from Baden-Baden, this time inviting me to play my double concerto with my son in their festival.[33] . . .

I could, of course, put aside the [other] proposals if I were well remu-

---

[32] Unless otherwise specified, all of Stravinsky's letters from this date forward were sent from 25, rue du Faubourg St.-Honoré, Paris.

[33] Strecker wrote to Stravinsky two days later advising him that "the Baden-Baden performances, together with Furtwängler's presentation of the *Firebird* Suite during the tour of the Berlin Philharmonic, should break the spell and clear the way for further performances of your works in Germany." Strecker wrote again on January 25: "Enclosed is the copy of the reply from Baden-Baden. Again, I strongly suggest that you accept this offer, because it will mark a brilliant new departure for your art in Germany."

nerated for the Baden-Baden concert. But since these gentlemen do not even mention the honorarium, I cannot very well broach the subject by suggesting that they make up the 700 francs that I will lose. Could you make this proposal for me? If they are willing, I will break off my other negotiations and prepare to go there with my son to do my concerto. . . .

STRAVINSKY TO STRECKER   *January 27, 1936*

. . . I am very moved by the interest you have taken in my reappearance in Germany, this Germany that was always so attentive to my music. For this reason I gladly accept the proposal from Baden-Baden, where they have gone out of their way to make my appearance possible.[34] . . . In scheduling the concerts, keep in mind that the S.S. *Cap Arcona* leaves Boulogne on April 9 and that I have business to attend to in Paris on the 7th. Since Baden-Baden suggested April 3, 4, and 5 (as the dates of their festival), come to an understanding between Baden-Baden and Rosbaud[35] concerning when I am to be there. . . .

As for the parts, since only a double concerto without orchestra is concerned, assure Baden-Baden that they will not have to pay anything.

Speaking of the Concerto, I would like you to publish it.[36] What do you think?

---

[34] On February 14, Strecker wrote: "I have just heard from Rosbaud that we finally obtained permission for your Rundfunk concert. You will see from the enclosed letter how difficult that was; [Rosbaud] went himself to the committee and thus was granted oral permission; the written confirmation is supposed to follow. . . . If we finally succeed in breaking this resistance, it will be crucial to the future of your art in Germany." Eight days later, the publisher wrote again: "I went to Frankfurt yesterday to find out about the status of your proposed concert. Rosbaud told me that, unfortunately, some intrigues have flared up again against your appearance with the Frankfurt Rundfunk, though he has already obtained permission from the top Rundfunk administration, as well as from the Reichsmusikkammer. . . . It is extremely important for your total artistic significance in Germany that this Rundfunk concert take place, and I hope that we will succeed in this. . . . I suggest that for now we settle for the Baden-Baden and the Rundfunk concerts, which would signify a new beginning for you in Germany. Let us hope that the autumn and winter will bring opportunities for large orchestral concerts."

[35] On September 21, 1936, Stravinsky wrote a letter of recommendation for Rosbaud: "May these few lines have the desired effect on those who are attentive to genuine manifestations of musical art, who remain unimpressed by the futile glitter and passing glories of amateurs and opportunists, so numerous in an epoch of decline. I know Hans Rosbaud, a pure-blooded musician, an aristocrat among conductors. I know his fine talent, his exemplary humility, his perseverance, his tenacity, the exactitude of his baton, his artistic conscience and integrity. A serious and significant organization such as the Frankfurt Rundfunk should be pleased and proud to have such a conductor."

[36] Strecker wrote on February 3 expressing his desire to see the manuscript, and adding that the work "made an extraordinary impression on me that time in Paris." Ac-

I request that the two organizations, Baden-Baden and the Rundfunk, obtain permission for me to take the money out of Germany at the appointed time so that I will not run into trouble at the border. . . .

STRAVINSKY TO STRECKER   *February 1, 1936*

. . . The concert that you are planning with Wetzelberger—in which I am to play my Capriccio—is worrying me a lot. I have not played the Capriccio in a long time, and many hours will be consumed before my fingers can memorize it again, hours that I do not have. . . .[37]

I would be delighted, as I told you, if [Schott] were to publish my double concerto. I am happy that you, too, view this project with "great joy." The sum you mention is close to what I was going to ask—2,000 marks, or 12,000 francs—and I hope that this tiny 2,000-franc discrepancy will not create a conflict between us, the more so since neither of us really wants to make it into a commercial enterprise. We will certainly reach an agreement, as we always do, on the particulars (percentages, performance rights, etc.). One urgent question: could the engraving be done immediately? I will send you a copy at a moment's notice. . . .

STRAVINSKY TO STRECKER   *February 8, 1936*

My agent in charge of the trip to Argentina writes that he has spoken with Mr. [Athos] Palma, director of the Teatro Colón in Buenos Aires, about using the fees I earn in Germany to pay for my travel expenses on the *Cap Arcona*.[38] Unfortunately, Mr. Palma plans to pay for the trip himself, and in foreign currency. . . . I must therefore have Baden-Baden and Frankfurt obtain authorization for me to remove the money from Germany.[39] . . .

Undoubtedly my score of the double concerto is in the process of being

---

cording to a letter from Catherine, August 6, 1935, Stravinsky had first offered the Concerto to the Edition Russe de Musique.

[37] Strecker replied two days later: "Perhaps you will agree to conduct a piece yourself, then, and have Wetzelberger present you, too. He is your admirer and friend and has done a great deal in your behalf. The important thing is for you to be present at the concert and to participate in some way."

[38] On February 27, Strecker wrote to the Hamburg-America Line, having arranged for Stravinsky to travel on its ship the S.S. *Cap Arcona* to Buenos Aires at the beginning of April: "It is important to me personally, as the composer's publisher—as it may also be to your company, considering Stravinsky's reputation—for him to be satisfied." Strecker also mentions that his wife's family are the von Bernards from Buenos Aires, and he closes the letter: "I remain, with the German salute, very sincerely yours."

[39] Permission was finally obtained by Strecker on March 25. He wrote to Stravinsky the next day: "You will receive the 700 marks in French francs at the official German exchange rate, along with the permit allowing you to take the money out of the coun-

engraved as you read these lines, since you would not waste time, and I mailed it on February 3, immediately after I received your last letter. I hope that this score is correct, but I am not certain that the transitions, which always give me some difficulty, will be entirely smooth.

When do you expect to obtain permission for my fees? I still have not heard from Eschig. I refer to the payment for *Firebird* at the National Opera of Sofia, along with a note to the effect that the 158 marks, 80 pfennigs would be transmitted through Max Eschig in Paris. . . .

STRAVINSKY TO STRECKER   *February 10, 1936*

I hope that you can send me a copy of my concerto in the next few days, because my son and I leave on the evening of the 18th for Milan, where we will play [the Concerto] the next day. I will need it a few days in advance, to review the piece a little, since I have not touched it in over a month. . . .

STRAVINSKY TO STRECKER   *February 16, 1936*

In great haste, a note to thank you for the marvelous edition of my concerto, which I received in two packets, yesterday and this morning. I have been correcting it but do not know if I will manage to finish before my departure for Milan (Hotel Continental). I go there this Tuesday, and my son and I play the Concerto on Wednesday; the same night we leave for Paris, where we will stay for a week (beginning that Thursday morning). After that, we return to Italy on the 28th (Rome and Genoa), going from there to Barcelona, Madrid, and finally England, via Paris. We have an engagement in Bournemouth (near Southampton) on the 27th and will be back in Paris on the 28th, only to depart immediately for Germany! . . .

Enclosed you will find the lecture I delivered at the Université des Annales:[40] I discuss my new concerto and give a brief analysis of the four movements, and this is exactly what you need for the German performances as well as for your edition. Translate it into German, and I could perhaps show it to the Rundfunk.[41]

---

try. . . . It might be wise for you to write a letter to Generalmusikdirektor Albert, telling him that all is in order, thanks to his efforts. . . . I have written to my brother-in-law Carlos von Bernard in Lausanne, who will certainly contact you if he goes through Paris."

[40] Stravinsky is referring to his lecture on the Concerto per due pianoforti soli, which he also delivered on other occasions.

[41] Stravinsky had also suggested that the title page of the Concerto edition have an artistic design, to which Strecker replied on the 18th: "Personally, I would be happy with a . . . black-on-white pen-and-ink drawing, but I hesitate to recommend this. We in Germany reject anything too modern, anything showing Picasso's influence."

STRAVINSKY TO STRECKER   *February 25, 1936*

. . . I have decided to do the concerts in Baden-Baden and at the [Frankfurt]
Rundfunk, which will take up only three days and five nights, including travel
time. . . . I am overjoyed to have a chance to see you on March 24, as you promise. I leave for [Bournemouth] the following day. . . .

STRAVINSKY TO STRECKER   *February 28, 1936*

. . . I just saw *El Pájaro de fuego,* which is to say the film of *L'Oiseau de feu,*
entitled here *Firebird,* as you see in the attached program. Not only was the
title of my piece taken without my permission, but also fragments of my music,
which were played as an accompaniment to the film, with impunity, in France
(where I am supposedly protected), as well as in South America! I summoned
an agent from Edipho to see and hear the film and to verify the piracy. He
came yesterday with a process-server in tow. Today one of the directors of
Edipho will visit me to discuss how to recover our rights. I plan to give him
the little dossier on Argentina that you brought me last autumn (the poster and
the clippings from the Buenos Aires newpapers). I will discuss this with you
again on March 24.

    I leave for Rome (Hotel Excelsior) tonight and will be back on the morn-
ing of the 5th. On March 8 I leave for Barcelona (the Ritz), returning on the
17th. . . .

STRAVINSKY TO STRECKER   *March 5, 1936*

I hope that you received my letter of February 28. It must have crossed in the
mail with your letter to Madame Bouchonnet regarding the score of the *Firebird* Suite for Barcelona (in which you claim not to have had any news from me
on the matter). I assure you, dear friend, that everything is in order. . . . Just let
me know that the letter of the 28th did indeed arrive; I also acknowledge
therein receipt of the second proofs of the Concerto. Edipho is now investigat-
ing the film *Firebird.* . . .

STRAVINSKY TO STRECKER   *March 7, 1936*

I just received . . . a curious letter from Baden-Baden, which I enclose. . . .
How do you explain the sentences that I have underlined in blue? With you as
intermediary, I agreed to a totally distinct arrangement with these gentlemen.
Their *initial invitation* (object of the present letter) became, after an exchange of letters, propositions, and counterpropositions, a *definite engagement,*
and I was now expecting an official confirmation from them detailing the conditions, which you were so kind as to transmit to them and which they

Russia, 1901.
Stravinsky is second from the right; Catherine, his future wife,
is third from the left.

Clarens, 1912

Top: With Ramuz and the Murets, Lens, spring 1918.
Bottom: G. G. Beliankin, Stravinsky, Serge Poliakov, and Vasily Kibalchich, Switzerland, 1919.

Rouen, January 19, 1923.

With Hermann Scherchen,
Weimar, August 18, 1923.
Photo by Vera Sudeikina.

With Boris Kochno, Paris, January 1923.

With Ramuz, Paris, May 17, 1924.

Venice,
September 6, 1925.

Monte Carlo,
summer 1925.

Practicing
in Steinway Hall,
New York,
January 1925.

Le Lavandou, summer 1925.
Photo by Vera Sudeikina.

Vera Sudeikina,
Ostende to Dover,
November 13, 1931.

Villènes-sur-Seine, July 2, 1926.

With Ramuz, Lausanne, 1928.

Nice, 1929.

Lausanne, 1930

Nice, 1930

Holland, 1931.

Nymphenburg, 1930.

With Werner Reinhart,
Winterthur, 1932.

Plombière-les-Bains, 1932.

With Vera Sudeikina, Berlin, October 1931.

Dover, October 1931.

Opposite, top: The marriage of Arthur Rubinstein
to the former Mrs. Amelia Muntz, Paris, July 1932.
Opposite, bottom: With Vera Sudeikina, Biarritz, September 1932.

Milan, 1933. The Teatro alla Scala is in the background.

Vera Sudeikina, c. 1930. Photo by Igor Stravinsky.

Reinhart, Alice Bailly,
Stravinsky, and Dushkin,
Winterthur, 1933.

With Ramuz and his family, 1932.

With Cingria
and Ramuz, 1936.

Monthoux, summer 1937.

At the Escorial,
Madrid, March 1955.

Above: With Prince Max Egon von Fürstenberg, Donaueschingen, October 1958.
Opposite: Hollywood, 1953. Photo by Tom Kelley.

Top: At a recording session with Aldous Huxley, Hollywood, October 17, 1955.
Bottom: With Gerald Heard and Robert Craft, Hollywood, 1960.

With Ingmar Bergman,
September 16, 1961.

At the Taronga Park Zoo,
Sydney, November 22, 1961.

Paris, May 1952.

New York, January 1957.

Hollywood, 1947.

Above and below: Copenhagen, May 1959.

At an exhibition of Stravinskyana, Leningrad, October 6, 1962.

Listening to a rehearsal of *The Flood*, Hamburg, May 1963.

At home in Hollywood, December 1966.
Photo by Arnold Newman.

Hollywood, March 1966. Photo by Claudio Spies.

Venice, April 15, 1971.
The funeral.

Mrs. Stravinsky at home,
New York, 1977.
Photo by Inge Morath.

accepted. Instead, I receive this letter! Their offices must be in a chaotic state.[42]

I await a note from you about this at the Hotel Ritz in Barcelona. . . .

STRAVINSKY TO STRECKER   *August 1, 1936*

. . . I just learned from . . . Madame Bouchonnet (the secretary of de Basil's Ballet Russe) that this company will dance *Firebird* and *Petrushka* in Berlin around October 1.[43] M. de Basil has invited me to conduct one or two of the performances beginning this series, so if I can make an agreement with him, I may have the pleasure of seeing you this autumn in Berlin. M. Païchadze tells me that Weber [of the Russischer Musik Verlag] is drawing up a contract for *Le Baiser de la fée* at the Staatsoper, as mentioned in your letter of July 21, which will be a joyous event. You understand my apprehension concerning the *Histoire du soldat* performances you mention, for we are in danger of losing all of the ground that we have gained. For this reason I am in no hurry to arrange the reductions that [the Jewish Kulturbund] requested. Furthermore, that was the advice you gave me (see your letter of July 6), and I

---

[42] The Baden-Baden concert finally was arranged, and on July 6, 1936, Strecker wrote to the composer: "The Baden-Baden performance has undoubtedly had great import for your music in Germany, and people are now less fearful [of presenting your works]. The boycott has been broken and new possibilities unearthed; the influential people change their attitudes from day to day, though, and contracts that one has just drawn up are superseded a few weeks later. . . . The Jewish Kulturbund in Germany has asked to perform *Histoire du soldat* in Berlin and elsewhere. I did not consider it wise to tell this organization pointblank that we do not want the work presented, so instead I demanded 100 marks per performance—a price I was certain they could not pay—maintaining that this was the minimum price agreed upon by our contract. I said that you were in South America, and I gave your address as the Teatro Colón. They will write to you there, and I fervently urge you not to make any concessions. Best of all, should the letter ever reach you, do not answer it, or simply send it on to me. You have often been attacked here in Germany precisely for *Histoire du soldat;* if you permit the Jewish Kulturbund to perform it, your enemies will gleefully term you, as well as your art, 'Jewish,' spoiling everything we have managed to nurture. In any case, these people cannot pay a decent price, so it is not worth the risk." But on July 21 Strecker wrote again: "Regarding the Jewish Kulturgemeinde performance of *Histoire du soldat,* I have fixed the condition that permission must be obtained from the German Reichstheaterkammer. Should authorization be granted, we could agree to the performances, which would take place in the Jewish quarter, exclusively for that audience, and, I made sure, would not be mentioned in any newspapers. I also heard that the Berlin Staatsoper wishes to present your *Baiser de la fée.* If this works out, it would indeed be good news, a widely recognizable sign that the government has no objections to your works."

[43] Antal Dorati conducted these performances, danced by Danilova and Massine, at La Scala, Berlin.

am unaware of any subsequent developments that may have changed your attitude. . . .[44]

August 22, 1936
STRAVINSKY TO STRECKER   *[Telegram]*

. . . I am very happy that you are so enthusiastic about my new ballet [*Jeu de cartes*]. I have noted what you said concerning an eventual edition, and we will discuss this again when we see each other, I hope on September 15.[45]

Eschig just sent me the accounting for the most recent [royalty] statement. . . . Thank you. . . .

STRAVINSKY TO STRECKER   *September 17, 1936*

I send you this note in great haste to tell you not to copy the last two pages (81 and 82) of the manuscript: some notes are missing (flute, oboe, English horn) in the penultimate measure; and on page 81 the indication of the change to B-flat instruments is missing in the clarinets. I will make those insertions in the copy when you come to see me at the beginning of October. I hope that this tiny inadvertency on my part will not interrupt your work too much; please excuse me. Païchadze just telephoned to tell me that he fixed the rental fees for *Petrushka* with M. de Basil: up to fifteen performances, $65 each; beyond fifteen, $45 each. . . .

STRAVINSKY TO STRECKER   *September 21, 1936*

. . . Attached you will find the penultimate measure of page 82 (the ending of the music I have already sent), including the parts for the three missing instruments. Please insert these two notes in pencil in each of the instruments, along with the instruction "Clarinet in A = B-flat" on the preceding page, just after the end of the clarinet music. . . .

---

[44] Evidently Stravinsky had not yet received Strecker's letter of July 28, in which he stated: "The [Reichs] theaterkammer has authorized the Jewish Kulturbund concert; when the official authorization arrives, I will ask you to write me a letter to the effect that you have decided to 'make an exception under these circumstances' and to 'allow a small reduction of the contractual 100 marks.' " On August 3, Strecker explained his new decision to the composer: "I have changed my mind because the German authorities gave written permission. If we refused now, our refusal would be interpreted as an explicit act of unfriendliness toward Jews. Abroad, this could have unfavorable repercussions for you. In America, for example, it would surely be known that you refused the German Jews a performance even after the German authorities agreed. . . . Having ascertained that the performance definitely will not be publicized, I have no further reservations."

[45] Strecker had written on August 20: "The more I think about [your new ballet], the

STRAVINSKY TO STRECKER   *October 16, 1936*

I am sending my score to Mainz today with sixty-one new pages to be photo-copied. I hope that you have alerted [the printers] to the urgency of this task and that my manuscript and the new copy will be returned in a week.

I still have not received anything from London (a small check from Schott that was supposed to be sent to Morgan & Greenfeld) or from Germany (via Eschig). . . .

STRAVINSKY TO STRECKER   *October 22, 1936*

London

. . . It is sad to make such a statement, but Harry Kling had to die in order for justice to triumph.

I impatiently await the return of my score (with the new photocopies) from Mainz. Fortunately, I will not have to stay long in Switzerland, since *Soldat* was postponed until next year. This is better for me, in light of the work and innumerable details to which I must attend for my new ballet. I will be gone only a week, from November 6 to 12. . . .

STRAVINSKY TO STRECKER   *November 3, 1936*

. . . I am sending you the manuscript of the piano score—eighteen pages—by registered mail for the printer. Notice the titles of the "deals": for example, the new Second Deal should begin on a new page; in the manuscript I sent, it begins on the bottom of page 2, just as a continuation. As we decided, these "deals" are to replace the existing titles of "First Tableau," etc. With this manuscript I include the first eighty-two photocopied pages of my manuscript of the orchestra score, showing my corrections in red for the proofreaders and printers. On this subject, I have appended a sheet in German as well, explaining that the reprise is developed in such a way that it no longer fits on pages 96, 97, 98, and 99 of my manuscript.

Friday I leave for Zürich, where I will stay with friends (Professor Felix Nagel, Freie Strasse 30), rather than at the Hôtel Baur-au-Lac as I had told you.

The day after tomorrow or Friday I hope to send you my manuscript of pages 27–28 with the new instrumentation. . . .

---

more I like this extraordinarily original idea, and I am honored that you will entrust it to my publishing house. You know that I will do everything in my power to promote it. . . . Unfortunately, we cannot struggle against world developments; but much can be done, nevertheless, and we in Germany, especially, will be able to squeeze out more opportunities for an increasingly visible success than America or England, let alone unhappy France. . . . I am eager to know how you will read your cards. I see several

STRAVINSKY TO STRECKER   *November 4, 1936*

I am sending you . . . my manuscript with thirty new pages of orchestration. Please alert the printers to yesterday's letter (about the reprise of **79**)—the changes of the numbers there—and to the double numbers on pages 145–8, which will now follow correctly in the printing thanks to my development of the reprise. . . .

I look forward to having the manuscript with the thirty new pages of photocopies upon my return from Switzerland (on the 13th) so that I may continue my instrumentation. Perhaps the pages of the piano score will also be ready? . . .

STRAVINSKY TO STRECKER   *November 15, 1936*

Received your letter of November 6 in Zürich, along with the engraved pages of the first seventy [rehearsal] numbers. The orchestra score with the new photocopies was also delivered to me. The thirty-five engraved pages are being corrected by a student of Nadia Boulanger ([Léo] Preger), but I am going to glance at it myself when he brings it (next Friday). Thank you very much for all of your deliveries and your admirable precision.

I have begun working again after a week of rehearsals and concerts: I have eight new pages of orchestra score, but the composition is still not complete. I work all day, practically without pause. I sleep well, eat well, and suffer atrociously ([being] hypersensitive) from the bad weather.

I would be happy if something could be arranged with Courtauld for next autumn. I could propose to present a program of mixed music, such as I will direct with the New York Philharmonic: an overture by C. M. von Weber, a Tchaikovsky symphony (first or third), *Jeu de cartes,* and *Firebird,* all conducted by me. What do you think? The late Madame Courtauld paid me 300 guineas for the pair of concerts. . . .

STRAVINSKY TO STRECKER   *November 24, 1936*

Along with this note I send you thirty-one new pages of orchestra score. It is not yet finished: about fifteen more pages will follow. . . . I go to Naples on Friday and will be back on the 30th. Upon my return I hope to have received photocopies of these thirty-one pages. . . .

Tomorrow or Thursday I will send you the proofs of the first pages of the piano score and of the orchestra parts.[46] Today I enclose the new pages

solutions, but I am convinced that you will have found your own way by the time we see each other.''

[46]On November 26, Strecker wrote reminding the composer to "include the final text for the inside title page—'scenic arrangement in collaboration with N. Malayev,'

(19–31) of the piano score; please return these to me by the end of next week with the new proofs. . . .

STRAVINSKY TO STRECKER   *November 27, 1936*

I am sending (by registered mail) these lines and the engraved proofs of the orchestra score (pages 1–35), meticulously corrected. . . .

Please have the printers carefully review the numbers after **79** (i.e., after the place I already mentioned). On checking the manuscript of the piano score that I sent you the other day, I noticed that I made a mistake (my letter of November 4). In this manuscript I have corrected the mistake in pencil (there is a note for the printers about the development of the reprise), and I ask you to correct all of the numbers in the orchestra score following this correction in the piano score, renumbering them in order through to the end of the work. This is hard to explain by letter but easy to understand when you have the pages in front of you.

I am going to Naples and will be back next Tuesday. . . .

Upon my return I will attend to the synopsis and scenario, which are finished but need a little revision . . . As agreed, I will pay 1,500 francs to the musician who is preparing the piano score,[47] so we must simply add 750 francs to the last payment of 25 [pounds]. When will you do this? Will I see you before my departure for New York on December 18?

STRAVINSKY TO STRECKER   *December 1, 1936*

I returned this morning and found your two packages: (1) orchestra score manuscript; (2) pages 36–60 of the engraved orchestra score. . . . Kahn is coming at five o'clock with the continuation of the piano score. Just this minute I received the photocopies of pages 170–201 of my orchestra score, which I will hand over to Kahn this evening. I agree with you about deleting the wrong numbers (after **79**) once and for all, but I ask you to be sure to position these four numbers in the following manner: **79** is in place but consists of five measures instead of, as now, four; **80** includes eleven measures (music of horns, English horn, and oboe); after this, the music with three flats will be shared between **81,** which takes the first five measures, and **82,** the last four measures (**82** is in the right place). Please correct this in the piano score and parts, dear friend. . . .

---

etc.—as well as your synopsis of the action, so that I may translate it. Also, I must present the synopsis to the Reichstheaterkammer to obtain permission for our company to publish it." See *S.S.C.* II, p. 313.

[47] Erich Itor Kahn (1905–56), composer and pianist. He did not receive any credit for his work on *Jeu de cartes*.

STRAVINSKY TO STRECKER   *December 7, 1936*

On Wednesday I will send you the end of my orchestra manuscript, the continuation of Kahn's piano score, and the end of this piano reduction, which I am in
the process of doing myself to save time. After this work I will begin correcting
the proofs of the orchestra and piano scores that you sent me, along with the
proofs you promised to send in your last letter.

STRAVINSKY TO STRECKER   *December 10, 1936*

Thank you for acknowledging receipt of the end of the manuscript of the orchestra score. . . . Yesterday I sent you the end of the piano score manuscript,
done in part by Kahn and in part (the end) by me. In that package I also included proofs of pages 17–27 of the piano score. This morning I sent the second
proofs of the piano score (pages 1–16), which, after scrutinizing my remarks
and changes, you may print. . . .

   As you know, I leave in a week (the 18th) on the S.S. *Normandie.* Please
send two copies of the piano score on white paper of a size that is easy to handle,
and by Thursday morning at the latest, so that I can deliver them to Warburg[48]
in New York. Apart from these, you should send me the usual green proofs of
the last pages, which I will correct either during the crossing (if it is smooth) or
in New York. I will return these to you along with the second proofs of the piano
score (pages 17 to end), which I certainly will not manage to correct before
New York. Also send me the title and first pages showing M. Malayev's name so
that I can reassure him. . . .

   I just received the attached letter from the secretary of the Courtauld-
Sargent Concerts. I want your advice before I reply. Send this back to me by return mail; also tell me whether you have informed them of my terms. . . . The
obstacle to my conducting the whole program is unquestionably Sargent's jealousy, as you see. Hence the whole concert or a single work of mine conducted
by me in two concerts will cost them the same amount, i.e., what the late Madame Courtauld always paid me, 100 guineas per appearance, or 200 for a double concert. Also, they are wrong in saying "like the one time you conducted
Symphony of Psalms," because I also conducted *Firebird* and played the Capriccio in another pair of concerts during a different season. If they do not want
to accept these conditions, we will be obliged to turn to the BBC.

   In the next few days I will correct the proofs of the orchestra score, and I
will send them off to you before my departure. Will you send me the second
proofs in New York, as well as the parts, so that I may hand them over to Warburg and also examine them myself in my spare time?

---

[48] Edward M. M. Warburg, the banker and Harvard classmate of Lincoln Kirstein who
commissioned *Jeu de cartes* for their American Ballet.

STRAVINSKY TO STRECKER   *December 11, 1936*

. . . Since my boat leaves from Le Havre at noon on Friday, you should make
certain that the last package of proofs . . . arrives in Paris on time; I will be leaving the house very early in the morning, and it is imperative that I take the two
copies of the piano score with me. . . . As you wrote, if you can send them to me
by airmail on Wednesday, after submitting them to the routine checking I will
certainly have them by Thursday. Please assure me that I will have at least
these two copies and the last pages of the green batch . . . to carry under my
arm to New York.

The last pages of the engraved orchestra score could perhaps be sent by
airmail directly to the S.S. *Normandie*, Le Havre, to save time. What do you
think?

I keep forgetting to tell you that some time ago a musical antiquarian here,
a certain M. Legoni, informed me that he has a lot of music that belonged to
Diaghilev. The official liquidator [of Diaghilev's estate] gave it to Legoni to ap-
praise, in preparation for the public sale at [the Hôtel] Drouot. Among other
things, he has the complete parts of *Firebird* and of my two orchestrations of
Chopin for *Les Sylphides*. All of the copies are, of course, messy and in dreadful
condition, as Legoni told Païchadze, who will probably attend the sale. I suspect
that Eschig will go too, and he should be given instructions, since it would be
imprudent to let these parts, which you do not sell but rent, fall into private
hands.

Though it may be very dirty, the set could always be of service to us, as it
was to Diaghilev. . . .[49]

STRAVINSKY TO STRECKER   *December 15, 1936*

I am sending you by airmail the last pages (35–45) of the piano score, which I
just received and corrected. The last pages of the engraved orchestra score
(91–101, green proofs) arrived as well. I have twenty-five more pages of the orchestra score to correct. Yesterday your letter of December 9 arrived, and I hasten to reply. Let me say first that I was astonished not to have had any response
to my letters of December 10 and 11. The former contained a letter from the
Courtauld Concerts, which I asked you to read and return. Did you receive it? I
am very anxious; also, I had wanted to allow time to reply to London, which I
did not want to do without your advice, and especially not without their letters.
I am impatient to receive two copies of the complete piano score (white proofs)

---

[49] On March 5 [1937?], Strecker wrote to the composer: "The Diaghilev materials will
be auctioned on Monday. I have instructed Eschig to purchase the *Firebird* score if the
price is within reason. I had a letter sent to the auctioneer stating that ownership of
the score does not imply performance rights. Païchadze should make this clear to the
auctioneer as well, if only by telephone. I fear that Massine or some American troupe
will purchase the parts, since no protection exists in America." In fact, the *Firebird*
parts were sold at this auction to Hutchinson, London.

for Warburg as well. Will you have time to correct and send me two copies? I repeat, I am leaving Friday at 9:00 a.m. [for the S. S. *Normandie*]. Since I am not absolutely certain that this package will arrive in time, I cannot send you the end of the piano manuscript, as you requested, with the green proofs (which I am sending by airmail right now). . . .

Now something else. The beautiful engraving of the orchestra score unfortunately contains many more mistakes than expected, evidently because the engravers worked from the photocopies of the manuscript. I imagine that this is what happened: one engraver had before him the even-numbered pages, in which I marked the instruments, while the other was looking at the odd-numbered pages. Instead of figuring out which instrument follows on the line from the preceding page—as marked on the photocopy—the engraver determined which lines seemed to correspond according to his own judgment. Thus you find the tuba playing the trumpet's music and the trumpet placed in the lines for the horns. To extract the parts from this will involve an immense clean-up job. The parts will have to be checked against my corrections in the orchestra score before they are sent to me in New York. Convey all of this to your printers, dear friend, and also tell them that I acknowledge the effort they have made and regret that we have to face this fatiguing and thankless task. . . . Hugo[50] is having lunch at our house tomorrow. . . .

STRAVINSKY TO STRECKER   *May 20, 1937*[51]

. . . Do come on June 4; I will still be in Paris. I have a million things to tell you. I will not send you the corrected parts for the ballet because it requires verbal explanation, without which I would not dare to let you make the final edition.

---

[50] Strecker's son.

[51] While in America from January to April 1937, Stravinsky did not keep copies of his correspondence. The following are excerpts from Strecker's replies: "I am enormously happy about your intention to write a symphony; the world has awaited this from you for a long time. I am honored that you offer [Schott] its publication and gladly accept. . . . Enclosed I send you a letter from the Westdeutsche Konzertdirektion about our engagement in Frankfurt. I would be glad if this could be realized, since the Frankfurt Museum-Gesellschaft is, after all, one of the oldest and largest concert organizations, and through this you would be in our vicinity and would also have the prospect of other concerts in Germany as a result. . . . They are slowly beginning to play your works here, thanks to your appearance in Baden-Baden. The concert in Frankfurt would, from this point of view, be worth a sacrifice. . . . Klemperer sent a telegram requesting the concert premiere of the ballet. I asked for a fee of $500 for an American premiere, since I know that equivalent prices are paid for other works of similar caliber. Today Klemperer sent another telegram saying that you will probably want to do the premiere in concert form yourself. If that is the case, please have Associated Music Publishers ask at least as high a sum [$500] from the particular organization—which will certainly be paid, as Klemperer would have paid it. . . . I heard from the West-

STRAVINSKY TO STRECKER   *June 18, 1937*

Please give me your advice. Madame Bouchonnet has asked me, on behalf of
the management of La Scala of Berlin, to conduct one or two performances
of *Petrushka* and *Firebird* with de Basil's ballet there at the beginning of September.

Do you think it worthwhile, if their terms are favorable (I have the impression they will be), to give this serious consideration? The Berlin Philharmonic
would be invited to do the concerts, and I could have as many rehearsals as I
wish. I am perplexed, especially because of the dates: in effect, what audience
exists in Berlin in September, when everyone is still in the country?

Have you had a reply from the Biennale in Italy? It is very important that I
know as soon as possible, because the [Biennale] concert should immediately
follow the one in Berlin. . . .

STRAVINSKY TO STRECKER   *June 23, 1937*

. . . The new duty on author's rights (which is no longer a duty on income but
on capital). . . . surprised me, since our contract contained no provision for it. . . .

Time is running out, particularly in respect to Germany, where proposals
have been made for the beginning of September. . . . Hurry, straighten this out
with these idiots, who, in their dazed carelessness, remain silent!

As for the original score of the first Russian edition of *Firebird*, I have conducted from it many times in my life, as have other conductors (to judge by the
polychromatic pencil marks). I am perfectly willing to lend it to you, but to mail
it frightens me a little because the copy is so rare and is bound in a parchment
box;[52] I would prefer to give it to you in person, when I come to Germany, for
example. Are you in a rush? . . .

STRAVINSKY TO STRECKER   *June 29, 1937*

Yesterday my friend Lord Berners, the English composer, visited me; his ballet
A Wedding Bouquet just had a very big success at the Sadler's Wells Theatre in

---

deutsche Konzertdirektion regarding the Frankfurt Museum Concert: 'In regard to
the pecuniary question, I can only tell you that this is not so simple . . . but with such a
figure as Stravinsky, the German State will do everything to settle this matter quickly,
just as the German State did for . . . Mengelberg.' With a bit of patience we should be
able to obtain the transfer of these amounts." Stravinsky's eagerness to perform in
Germany seems not to have been checked by his wife's report, in a letter of January 3,
1937, that "Father Vassily is very depressed by the fact that everything is so tightly
tied to politics in Germany. . . . The Germans either want to or already have imprisoned
a former Russian priest (from Wiesbaden) in a concentration camp, just for some
careless word."
[52] The score, now in the possession of the present writer, contains many changes made
by Stravinsky himself.

London. . . . I have always been devotedly sympathetic to his music, which, until now, has been handled by J. & W. Chester, as you know. On that subject, [Berners] informed me that Chester is on its last legs and that Hawkes is endeavoring to balance the accounts. If this is so, you had better take urgent measures. . . .

STRAVINSKY TO STRECKER   *July 22, 1937*

. . . Delighted to have the German premiere in Dresden.[53] . . . . I will conduct it [this autumn?] probably in Zürich and [illegible] .

                                                              Château de Monthoux
STRAVINSKY TO STRECKER   *August 2, 1937*

. . . What are the possibilities of my conducting a certain number of concerts this winter in Germany, including *Jeu de cartes,* with Frankfurt as the base?[54]

STRAVINSKY TO STRECKER   *August 8, 1937*

Thank you . . . for sending me the Hindemith sonatas. . . . Many good wishes to the Hindemith couple. . . .

STRAVINSKY TO STRECKER   *September 4, 1937*

I just received a letter from my old friend Edwin Evans, the music critic, saying that he will write the program notes for the Courtauld Concerts. Thus he asks me to send him a pocket score and a piano score of *Jeu de cartes,* as well as the

---

[53] Strecker had written on June 19: "The German ballet premiere has finally been set for November in Dresden. This is good, and the ballet mistress, Frau Kratina, enjoys complete support from all the officials—which is very important these days. Thus her work will be presented under politically as well as artistically propitious circumstances." On July 6 Strecker wrote: "I have arranged a number of concert performances of *Jeu de cartes,* with the first staging in Dresden in November . . . Furtwängler in Berlin, and concert performances in Hamburg, Stuttgart, Wiesbaden, Münster, with five or six performances after the holidays." (Valeria Kratina [b. 1892] was a German dancer and choreographer who studied with Dalcroze, Laban, and Wigman.)
[54] Two days later, Strecker wrote: "What happened to the engagement you had in Berlin in August? Let me know if it is to take place, because . . . Frau Kratina wanted very much to meet with you in Berlin to discuss . . . the Dresden performance. Too bad that nothing will come of your Swiss concerts. I do not think that Scherchen is the one opposing you; perhaps it is the almighty old [Volkmar] Andreae, who has a decided influence on the question of all foreign artists who wish to perform in Switzerland. Unfortunately it is a bit late to arrange winter concerts in Germany now."

most favorable excerpts from the American reviews, which, undoubtedly and as always, will be mediocre and ignorant. . . .

I will be in Venice on Monday night for rehearsals. . . .[55]

STRAVINSKY TO STRECKER

Sancellemoz
September 29, 1937

. . . Ernest Ansermet conducted *Jeu de cartes* in Vevey; have you heard anything about this? Only in Paris has *Jeu de cartes* never been requested: not, of course, by the theatres, nor by a single concert organization. . . .[56]

STRAVINSKY TO STRECKER

Paris
November 5, 1937

. . . *Jeu de cartes* was an immense success not only in London and in Amsterdam . . . but in Switzerland as well. Were you able to listen to the broadcast?

Could you possibly reduce the rental fee for Naples? They have asked me to intervene in their behalf: their budget is apparently very tight. . . .

I expect you on Sunday as planned. Telephone as soon as you arrive (Anjou 61-45). . . .

STRAVINSKY TO STRECKER

Sancellemoz
November 17, 1937

London

I arrived in Sancellemoz yesterday and have begun to work. I am continuing the composition of my new concerto, for which you have the full score. I just added six measures at the end of the first movement, for which reason I ask you to send me the last page right away so that I may complete the instrumentation of this movement. I promise to send it back to you without delay. Do not send the whole thing; just detach that page. . . .

STRAVINSKY TO STRECKER

Sancellemoz
November 18, 1937

London

In yesterday's letter I completely forgot to tell you the "big news": M. Rouché, with whom I spoke by telephone two hours before leaving for Naples, asked me which ballets I would like to have the [Paris] Opéra present. I said it would be

---

[55] One week later, Strecker wrote: *"Le Baiser de la fée* was quite successful in Berlin, even though it was preceded by a small attack against you in the papers. What I fear most is the anxiety that [such articles] may produce in your friends. For the moment, I consider any kind of a sensation undesirable."

[56] Five days later, Strecker wrote: "The Reichsmusikkammer has arranged a show entitled 'Modern Music' in Frankfurt. Your picture will be exhibited among others, as

logical to proceed in chronological order beginning with *Firebird,* and he answered, "It is understood." We plan to see each other in early December. . . .

The French Radio cabled acceptance of my terms for the December 6 concert (*Oedipus, Jeu de cartes, Firebird* Suite). . . .

I hope that this good news will please you, unless, of course, it is not such good news (i.e., if it will not be as well done as the last time, by Diaghilev). . . .

P.S. I just received a proposal from the Westdeutsche Konzertdirektion to conduct at Bad Nauheim on July 10 for 1,300 marks. They hope to link this to several other engagements as well. . . . What do you think?[57]

Sancellemoz
November 25, 1937

STRAVINSKY TO STRECKER

I agree to the printing of my score according to our discussion. The Hindemith score seems very clear, and there should be no problems in conducting from it. Thank you also for the manuscript page, which I received in time. . . . I will attempt to return this page, with a few final measures, either from here or from Paris within the next few days.

On December 1 I have a rehearsal for my radio concert (on the 6th), and then my son and I go to Riga and Tallin (Revel), where I will conduct Tchaikovsky's Third Symphony, and Nini will play my Capriccio. Then on the 17th we have the Riga concert, then home. . . .

Sancellemoz
November 27, 1937

STRAVINSKY TO STRECKER

A note in great haste to implore you to give Max Eschig's head a good beating. Here is why. About a month ago, the above-mentioned representative of your firm announced to Pierre Monteux that the only available orchestra score of *Jeu de cartes* is now in New York. Monteux had wanted to conduct *Jeu de cartes* in Paris; fortunately, he was not able to, owing to my own performance with the French Radio (that's why I say "fortunately"). [Eschig] also gave out this same absurd bit of information to the Radio, with whom, as you know, I begin rehearsals this Wednesday, the first of the month, for the December 6 concert. The management of the radio station reported: "We requested the orchestra parts of *Jeu de cartes* from Max Eschig, Schott's representative, who replied that there are only two scores, one in New York, and the other in Stresa (*sic!!!*), where it has just been played."

---

well as a manuscript (the piano part of the Violin Concerto, which you gave me as a present)."

[57] On November 27, Strecker wrote urging Stravinsky to accept this engagement: "We will have to fight strong antagonisms and animosities here. Not many people dare to engage you, since they expect to produce too great a sensation and thereby opposition. But one must start somewhere, and every opportunity must be seized. Nauheim, an

Please send the complete orchestral parts by airmail to the Service de la Radiodiffusion, Orchestre National, 18, rue François Ier, Paris. Also, tell Eschig that his stupid and unpardonable negligence has caused me great difficulties. . . .

STRAVINSKY TO STRECKER
Paris
December 1, 1937

. . . These few lines are to ask your advice about Telefunkenplatte, from whom I just received a letter. Is this a serious, quality firm, and, if so, what terms should I set?

. . . I just rehearsed *Jeu de cartes* with the Orchestre National from a score that probably has never been corrected, since very old mistakes were discovered. . . .

STRAVINSKY TO STRECKER
Paris
December 7, 1937

Thank you for your letter. I responded immediately by asking these gentlemen [Telefunkenplatte] to meet me at the railway station (Schlesischer Bahnhof) in Berlin tomorrow morning to discuss the matter. I hope that they will come; I have a 20–25-minute stop there (North Express). I intend to ask 15,000 francs (including travel expenses). We shall see. When we agree on the basics, I will leave the contract to you.

Did you hear my concert yesterday? It was a great success, and I was overjoyed. . . .

P.S. Send urgent communications by airmail to me in Riga, Hotel Rome (until the 17th).

STRAVINSKY TO STRECKER
Paris
December 18, 1937

The enclosed letter from Telefunkenplatte awaited me upon my return from Revel and Riga. When I met with these gentlemen on December 8 in the Schlesischer Bahnhof, we agreed upon 10 percent, with an advance of 1,000 marks. . . .

. . . In my contract with Columbia, my percentage is reduced by two-thirds if I record one of my works already done by Columbia with another company, while [Telefunkenplatte] wants, in the same case, to eliminate my percentage altogether. . . .

The orchestras in Revel and Riga had never played my music before and had no symphonic routine whatsoever; thus the concerts were arduous. At

---

international spa, is convenient for this reason, and we will perhaps secure another concert engagement directly thereafter. If not, [Nauheim] will still pave the way for the more extensive concert touring next season. Conditions here are unusual, and many currents exist whose meaning and influence are difficult to assess."

many spots I was obliged to dissect the music for them measure by measure. . . .

The reduction for two pianos of the first movement of my [new] concerto is finished, as are the four measures at the end of the orchestra score. . . .

STRAVINSKY TO STRECKER   *January 3, 1938*

. . . Please return to me the scores of *Jeu de cartes* that were used in those performances that were deliberately maimed by Ansermet.[58] Please warn him, when he next tries to obtain my works from you, that no rearrangement or cuts in those of my works edited by your house will be tolerated. . . . You, my publisher, are the only one who can defend me and prove that this is not merely the whim of an obstinate author. Please hold on to . . . this paper explaining my reasons for defending my works against the shamelessness of my impudent "interpreters." . . .

Chamber concerto: the composition of the second movement, an allegretto, entitled "Intermezzo," is finished. But I would like one movement to follow the other, which is why I did not draw thick bar lines to separate the three movements that make up the piece.

I hope that it is not too late to request two copies of the proofs. The second copy is for Nadia Boulanger, who goes to America on January 19 and will conduct the premiere of the Concerto in a gala evening at the Washington home of Mrs. Bliss[59] in May: *Soldat*, Duo concertant with Sam [Dushkin] and Beveridge [Webster], and the Concerto. Since Mrs. Bliss is the one who commissioned this concerto [and its first performance], leaving me at liberty for all other performances of it, she should, of course, be sent a score beforehand and without charge. As for me, I am giving her my manuscript, to be preserved in the library of her Washington estate, which, along with all its treasures, she will bequeath to the government. I think I already discussed this with you.

Perséphone: I greatly appreciate your having placed this on the program of the music festival in Baden-Baden in the spring. I would certainly be even more pleased if I could conduct it myself, but after what you told me, I realize that financial difficulties would surely prevent such a possibility.

---

[58] Ansermet had made cuts in his Geneva Radio performance of October 27, 1937. See the correspondence with Ansermet in *S.S.C.* I and with Werner Reinhart in the present volume.

[59] Mildred Bliss, the wife of the American diplomat Robert Woods Bliss. The premiere of the Concerto at Dumbarton Oaks, her estate, was in celebration of their thirtieth wedding anniversary, May 8, 1938. Stravinsky wrote to Mrs. Bliss, October 25, 1937, promising to have the Concerto ready for performance in May (he had previously agreed to finish it only by July) and requesting that Nadia Boulanger conduct the piece.

STRAVINSKY TO STRECKER   *January 20, 1938*

. . . I received two checks, one from Berlin and the other from Polydor here;[60] the total sum is close to what we had estimated. Enclosed is the receipt for the Berlin check, and I thank you in advance for forwarding this receipt to them.

Please do not forget to let me know the number of the last page of the orchestra score, and the rehearsal number. I completely forgot to note the page number, and this is not conducive to the continuation of my work. . . .

STRAVINSKY TO STRECKER   *January 28, 1938*

What about the 4-hand transcription of my concerto? I would like so much to have a copy of the first two parts, which are with you. Pleyel has recently furnished me with a new piano, and we plan to put it in the room where my son works (to prepare ourselves for the Columbia recording of my double concerto on February 14 or 16). I would like to play that transcription with him before fixing its final form for the edition. . . .

I am scrupulously correcting the proofs of the first part of my [chamber] concerto. In the absence of Sam [Dushkin], I have Jeanne Gautier assisting me in checking the violin and viola parts for bowings and articulation, so that the instrumentation will be impeccable. That is what is delaying my return of the proofs.

I conduct *Jeu de cartes* here again with the Orchestre National on February 28 in a concert devoted to the music of Debussy and myself, and marking this organization's five hundredth performance. I also will conduct *Symphony of Psalms*. . . .

STRAVINSKY TO STRECKER   *February 1, 1938*

Unfortunately, it is absolutely impossible for me to come to Mainz for *Firebird* on February 24, because I have a rehearsal here on the 25th for my concert on the 28th. I am truly disappointed, for I would very much have liked to attend and to be with you on that day. . . .[61]

---

[60] Strecker had written to Stravinsky on January 14: "The Berlin performance . . . was very successful and the reviews unanimously favorable, yet I have the impression that the conductor, [Eugen] Jochum, treated the work too romantically. I am glad that the recordings will avail the public of your interpretation, and, in Germany at least, this will be studied and followed as the authentic one. I am collecting the reviews and will send you some excerpts. From all I have seen and heard, the prejudice against you in official circles is waning . . . but one must still proceed cautiously."

[61] Stravinsky's reply is to Strecker's letter of January 28: "The [opening] performance of *Firebird* in Mainz was excellent and represented a real triumph. The director thought he might be able to arrange another performance on February 24, so that you

Could you send me several copies of my Concerto for Two Pianos? I do not have even one copy, and I will need at least three for the recording. . . .

Thank you for the letter from Telefunkenplatte. Must I now ask them to draw up the contract, or will we do that when I go to Berlin? . . .

STRAVINSKY TO STRECKER   *Paris*
                                                      February 27, 1938

My dear friend (and grandfather),[62]

. . . Everything went very well in Berlin at the Singakademie. I was very happy to record my *Jeu de cartes* with that magnificent orchestra, and I hope that these will be quality recordings.

I will probably return [to Berlin][63] at Easter to conduct *Petrushka* at La Scala with [Herr] Duisberg, who has engaged the de Basil ballet for two weeks.[64] I have stipulated that the Berlin Philharmonic do this perform-ance. . . . He is now trying to arrange this, and I await his reply. If so, perhaps Telefunkenplatte would like to take advantage of this occasion and make new recordings of *Petrushka,* with the latest technological improvements. My Co-lumbia recordings are already ten years old.

The third movement of my concerto is coming along. It is still difficult for me to say on exactly which day I will finish (probably in three weeks). My work is constantly interrupted by concert tours. Happily, the month of March be-longs to me; I have only the radio concert on March 4 (*Jeu de cartes* and *Sym-phony of Psalms* at the Salle Gaveau), after which I will devote myself entirely to finishing the third movement and correcting the proofs. . . .

Which pieces should I propose to do in Bad Nauheim, this village of baths? Can a complicated program be presented to the international set that has come to take the waters? I would like to do four ballet suites, or, rather, two suites and

could stop here and see it . . . on your way back from Berlin. . . . Your presence at such an otherwise harmless occasion might be politic, since it would be noticed in all of southern Germany, and the people of Mainz would be further strengthened in their brave and commendable stand in your behalf. There would certainly not be any dem-onstration against you, because it would already be the fifth performance. . . ."

[62] Strecker's daughter, Gerda, had just given birth to a son.

[63] Strecker wrote on March 4: "I am glad that you were satisfied by your reception in Berlin and that you will soon return." In the same letter, the publisher promised to "send your correction about your nationality to Baden-Baden. It cannot have been in-tentional; just a mistake, which will be corrected in future publicity." (In the first printing of the programs for the Baden-Baden concert of April 24, Stravinsky was identified as "Russian," and his comments survive on his copy: "Russian? Not since 1934. Russian music? Also not. In what sense 'Russian'?")

[64] The leaders of the Third Reich were among the enthusiastic audience for the Berlin season of the de Basil Ballet Russe. Fokine caused a stir by refusing to visit Goering's box following the first performance of the choreographer's new production of *Le Coq d'or.*

two [complete] ballets: *Apollo* and *Jeu de cartes* (together totaling 50 minutes), and Divertimento [from *Le Baiser de la fée*] and *Firebird* Suite (40 minutes altogether). What do you think?[65] Apart from that, I would like them to send me the contract, which should specify that the money will be paid to me in France. . . . M. Henri Jourdan, the cultural attaché to the French Institute in Berlin, gave me this advice, in the presence of Grenzbach. It should also be made explicit that the enterprise that engages me must rent the parts from my publisher. Is this the only concert, or will others follow, as the Westdeutsche Konzertdirektion assumed?

Thank you for the commissions in London. The Phonographic Company never replied. . . . Thank you also for the manuscript of the second movement of my concerto, which was delivered to me the other day. When will I receive the second proofs of the first movement, which I sent while you were [in England]?

STRAVINSKY TO STRECKER

Paris
March 20, 1938

. . . Tomorrow I will send you by registered mail twenty-seven pages of the full score of the third movement of my concerto; this is about four-fifths of the whole. You should have received the proofs of the second movement, as well as the second proofs of the first movement, which I also sent by registered mail a few days ago. . . .

Could you begin to extract the parts of the Concerto? I think that with what you already have, you could do so without waiting for the end, which, God willing, will not be long now.

Concerto in E flat: I have received the proofs, but I have not yet corrected them, since I am busy finishing the instrumentation of the second movement (for which the two-piano reduction has just been completed). I will send both together in five or six days.[66] You can leave the double bar at the end of the first movement as it is, in large characters, because we will begin the second movement separately, on another line, like a new piece (with new indications for the participating instruments). . . .

STRAVINSKY TO STRECKER

[*Early April* 1938]

I finally received the proofs of the last section of my concerto (pages 27–37 inclusive), with pages 66–92 (inclusive) of the manuscript. Unfortunately, only one copy was delivered, rather than the usual two, and I must send this copy to

---

[65] In his March 4 letter, Strecker also said that he had "written to Bad Nauheim and sent them your program proposals, which I found appropriate."

[66] Strecker had written on March 16: "I am beginning to worry about finishing the engraving of your concerto. . . . The printing of the instrumental parts requires a certain amount of time if it is to be done carefully, and I cannot begin until I have the final proofs, at least of movements I and II. . . . If no time remains for printing and correct-

Nadia Boulanger via the S.S. *Europa*. She ... just sent me this cable: "Bliss premiere in May definite. Send urgently needed manuscript. Will copy it here. Fond regards, Nadia Boulanger, 63 Garden Street, Cambridge, Massachusetts."

Since I, too, need my manuscript, to verify pages 27–37, I request a second copy of the proofs, to be returned to you as soon as they are corrected. I am sending [Nadia] the first copy of these pages in print rather than in manuscript form. I will correct them right away with my violinist Mlle Jeanne Gautier (who will play the first violin part in my concert at La Sérénade[67] on June 16[68]), and put them in the mail this afternoon so that they will leave on the S.S. *Europa* tomorrow.

Thus, given the [lack of time], Nadia and Mrs. Bliss will have to copy what they already have there (the first two movements of the Concerto and pages 27–37 of the last movement), and we must send the rest as soon as it is printed. ... Consequently, you may extract the parts at your leisure and send them here; we will verify and correct them during the rehearsals for the June 16 concert, so you can then print the edition from a score that has been used. ... Another performance is scheduled for the beginning of July with the Orchestre National here in Paris. They want to perform the new concerto in a radio broadcast, along with Satie's *Socrate* and my Capriccio (with my son at the piano). ...

P.S. I heard that Ansermet performed *Jeu de cartes* in Warsaw, and I wonder if the copy of the parts he received contained the notice, which I sent you,[69] forbidding cuts.

STRAVINSKY TO STRECKER

Paris
April 20, 1938

I just learned that the S.S. *Europa* departs from Bremen early on the 25th, i.e., Monday morning. To be certain, address yourself to the Mainz branch of the

---

ing, the conclusion of the piece might have to be performed from your manuscript; we could send Nadia Boulanger a photocopy of the third movement." Strecker wrote again on the 23rd: "The manuscript of the third movement arrived yesterday. ... While movements I and II are relatively classical and conservative, in the third movement your personality stands out in a surprising way, lending the whole work that absolutely original character which is uniquely yours. I look forward to hearing it, and I am sure that the ... little march in the third movement will enchant the audience."
[67] A chamber concert organization in Paris founded by the Marquise de Casafuerte.
[68] Misia Sert was in the audience of the Paris premiere of the *Dumbarton Oaks* Concerto. The next day she sent a letter to Stravinsky: "Dear Igor, I did not dare to disturb you by telephone and could not bear to speak to you last night, after your wonderful music, when you were surrounded by all of those people. ... Thank you, a second time, for the great joy you gave me in playing that music, which touched me to the heart. I embrace you affectionately. Your Misia."
[69] Strecker replied on April 8: "We sent [*Jeu de cartes*] to Warsaw with your instruc-

Norddeutscher Lloyd, and have them send the material to their Bremen office on Saturday morning. . . . This is the only way to guarantee that the music will leave on the *Europa*. My agent here says that the ship may even be leaving on Sunday evening (or night)—so you will have just enough time. Do not forget to send it express, so that Nadia will receive it in Cambridge, Massachusetts (63 Garden Street), as soon as possible after its arrival in New York on May 1. . . .

I cannot understand Nadia's negligence or absent-mindedness, since she received my letters of April 6 and 11. I wrote saying that I would send the orchestra score of the last movement, as she requested in her telegram, adding that she could extract the parts for the whole work.

STRAVINSKY TO STRECKER

Paris
April 27, 1938

. . . Several days ago I sent a cable to [Richard] Copley in New York authorizing him to conclude a series of contracts for February–March 1939. . . . Next winter, therefore, I will conduct my new concerto in America. In this case, the question of Nadia's exclusivity [in conducting the piece] does not work. . . . I have the impression that [the Americans] do a much better job of extricating themselves from difficulties of this kind than we do.

With your help I would also like to resolve the question of the 60 percent (for me) and 40 percent (for you), according to the [agreement with] Forberg. I signed with him before I was a member of Edipho (now BIAR). As a member, I am obliged to cede 20 percent of what I receive from all mechanical reproductions of my music to them. Thus . . . I am confronted with the following figures: 60 percent minus 10 percent (commission) = 50 percent; 50 percent minus 10 percent (Edipho) = 40 percent. . . .

I am very happy about the success of *Perséphone* in Baden-Baden, and I thank you for having told me about it (in your postcard).[70] . . .

P.S   If you are certain that the parts of the Concerto arrived before the departure of the S.S. *Europa* and are now on their way to New York, then everything is all right. If you are not sure of this . . . perhaps we should cable Nadia so as not to leave her in such a state of uncertainty one week before the concert! . . .

---

tions that the work must be played without cuts (as we now indicate upon each rental). . . . Unfortunately, we did not realize that Ansermet would be conducting it [in Warsaw]; otherwise I would have attached a special letter as well."

[70] Strecker had written to Stravinsky on April 20: "If the Baden-Baden performance [of *Perséphone*] is good . . . I think it would be diplomatic to send the conductor, musicians, singers, dancers, and spa administrators a brief note expressing your appreciation. In this letter you should acknowledge the idealistic strivings and the international significance of Baden-Baden's achievements, particularly since they worked so energetically and selflessly. A note of this sort would be publicized and thus would be helpful to us in the future." Strecker wrote again on the 26th: "I have just returned from Baden-Baden, where *Perséphone* had a great success. We sent you a postcard after the

STRAVINSKY TO STRECKER

. . . I forgot to insert two things in the proofs: (1) the tempo in the first move-
ment, which should be "Tempo giusto," ♪ = 152; (2) the dedication to Mrs.
Bliss, which could be done in facsimile if there is enough space, as with the
Violin Concerto. . . . If you think that there is enough room on the first page, be-
neath the title, then please insert: *"A Madame R. W. Bliss,"* or "To Mrs. R. W.
Bliss."[71]

Thank you for sending me that magnificent recording.

I was certain that the Bad Nauheim affair would end in a refusal.[72]

STRAVINSKY TO STRECKER

I write to you from bed, where an abominable head cold has held me captive for
two days now.

From yesterday's cable you learned that I am considering the questions
raised in your letter. In effect, must the prices be fixed by your New York representative? Here (in France and Germany) such people are incompetent with
respect to these matters. So please reach an agreement for me with your New
York representative (since I am still in bed with a little fever).

Also, I have decided that it is not necessary to grant exclusivity for the
Concerto to anyone. In the cities where I plan to conduct the Concerto, it would
be desirable if no other conductor had done it before me, though. . . . Your reasoning about exclusivity seems to me entirely correct. . . .[73]

---

performance. Werner Reinhart was present; we were all very moved by the performance, which was infinitely superior to the Paris premiere. The first accounts in the
press have been entirely positive, and so far no opposition from any quarter has been
expressed. I am extraordinarily pleased . . . since such a performance was risky, after
all. . . . Even so, it is better that you were not present, because demonstrations might,
in that case, have ensued, and these would be ammunition for your enemies."

[71] Strecker replied on May 3: "Send me a facsimile of your dedication of the Concerto,
since all of your other works have a facsimile. I think that a handwritten dedication set
on a separate page preceding the music would be best. And if I know Americans, the
French dedication is preferable."

[72] Strecker had written on April 20: "I have bad news. The authorities did not approve
your Bad-Nauheim concert. I sent someone to the Reichsmusikkammer to inquire as
to why permission was not granted. He was advised not to force the issue. . . . The individual in charge of the district of Nauheim happens to be an avowed enemy of your
music, as well as an influential person. If we were to request that this refusal be lifted,
the case would be made into a precedent for an overall injunction against your works."

[73] Strecker had written on April 30: "I have just received a letter from Nadia. . . . To
give her exclusivity [for the Concerto] in America would preclude performances by
Klemperer, Koussevitzky, Stokowski, etc., etc. Nadia would probably ask a $25 fee for

STRAVINSKY TO STRECKER

... Yesterday I saw Koussevitzky, for whom I will conduct five concerts in Boston next winter. He asked me to let him do the premiere of the Concerto in mid-October in a Stravinsky festival there; he would also conduct the *Sacre* (on the twenty-fifth anniversary of its premiere in Paris) and *Le Chant du rossignol.* [Koussevitzky] claims that the committee will not allow him to pay more than $100 [for the Concerto premiere], but, on the other hand, he will play it three times and proposes $200 as the price for these three performances. Given the duration of the piece (10–11 minutes), I find his proposals reasonable, and I promised to speak to you about it immediately in support of his demand. Thus I ask you to accept, as a personal favor. You are familiar with his capricious and distrustful character: he could easily suspect an intrigue on my part if these prices are not accepted, thinking that I concocted the whole thing in order to conduct the performances myself. . . . I will conduct the Concerto in other cities, and, moreover, I find the system of exclusivity . . . totally senseless.

I have received cables from Mrs. Bliss and from Sam about the Washington performance. The piece was a real success (Sam took part in it), but Nadia apparently did not conduct, for reasons that the cables did not give me. Illness? Or maybe at the last minute she feared that she did not know the work well enough? . . .

Now something else: Walt Disney's proposition inspired me with the idea of composing something original for him, i.e., for animated cartoons.[74] I am going to mention this to my agent in New York, Mr. Maurice Speiser, who is prominent in America in the field of film contracts, etc. Soon he will be moving to Hollywood, and . . . he intends to give special attention to me. Thus his move there is very timely. . . . Also, negotiations about *Firebird* should be put in his hands, because I think he could obtain the best terms. Please write him a letter on this subject. . . .

I leave tomorrow morning for Brussels (Grand Hôtel), where I conduct Thursday night. . . .

---

each of her six to eight performances, while at the same time all other conductors would be disgruntled. Such exclusivity would guarantee good engagements for Nadia, which I wholeheartedly wish for her. However, . . . she probably is not even going to America until January or February 1939, which means that the Concerto would lie fallow for the first half of the winter . . . and you would not be able to conduct the work yourself, either."

[74] Strecker replied on May 17: "To make an original film with Disney is an excellent idea, but I do not know what he will think of that. You will have to discuss it with him. . . . It is difficult for me to judge whether he is enough of an artist to create a truly original work in collaboration with you. . . . Incidentally, I was amazed to learn that, to date, Disney has just broken even with his films because his production costs are so high: only *Snow White* was a real financial success."

STRAVINSKY TO STRECKER

Paris
May 22, 1938

After all of those painful rehearsals, I returned from Brussels and went straight to bed again. I hope that this will not last long. I received your letter of May 17 and . . . accept the terms you propose for the Concerto (with Koussevitzky in Boston). At the same time, I received Mrs. Bliss's letter (of May 4, i.e., four days before the performance in Washington). . . . She mentions Nadia casually, saying that they are working together. In conclusion, she says that "the big day of Dumbarton Oaks is approaching." I was astonished to read this same name in huge type on the letterhead and [thought it must be] the name of the conductor! Mrs. Bliss's telegram began: "Concerto performance Dumbarton Oaks worthy of the work." . . . This I dismissed as a simple error, and I looked in vain for Nadia's name [on the program]. . . . [When] Sam and his family arrive, I imagine we will have a laugh about that.[75]

. . . Old Ida Rubinstein has just asked me to compose something for her. I will meet with her as soon as I am well enough. . . . I would like to arrange the collaboration through you, as I did through Païchadze for *Le Baiser de la fée* and *Perséphone*. This is impossible to do by letter; your presence would be indispensable. I will have to meet with her next week. . . .[76]

STRAVINSKY TO STRECKER

Paris
May 26, 1938

. . . First, the piece must be called "Dumbarton Oaks Concerto in E flat," as it was listed in Mrs. Bliss's program at its baptism on May 8. She has informed me, through Dushkin, that the work need not be dedicated to her, but that she would like very much for the work to bear the name of her property—an estate with a park, houses, library, which costs her enormous amounts of money to maintain. Also, she will continue to give concerts there . . . and Sam thinks that I could go on tranquilly composing Dumbarton Oaks Concertos as Bach did his Brandenburg Concerti.[77] But, for the moment, let us not consider the many

---

[75] Strecker replied on May 24: "This riddle about the conductor is surprising and amusing. I do not understand, since Nadia's own name was good enough. But she is clever and knows what she is doing, so there must be some reason behind this. Sam, to whom I ask you to relay my best regards, will be able to explain it." Boulanger did conduct the Concerto but did not have her name included on the program.

[76] By this time, Strecker had an option on Stravinsky's new works, and, in any case, the Edition Russe de Musique was scarcely functioning. Strecker wrote in his May 24 letter: "Ida Rubinstein's new proposal is interesting. I will gladly serve as a middleman, but I cannot come to Paris before the second week in June. I hope that you will be able to postpone negotiations until then."

[77] Strecker replied on May 31: "Frankly, I do not like the title 'Dumbarton Oaks Concerto.' Bach did not call his concertos 'Brandenburg Concertos': this title was attached to them gradually, over the years. No one outside of America will understand the designation or be able to pronounce it, and stupid remarks may even be made about the name, since it resembles duck or frog sounds in French and German pronunciation. A

possibilities that may emerge with this new Frederick the Great, but turn our attention instead to correcting the large number of mistakes in the parts. . . . I hope that you will still be able to make the necessary corrections, as you indicated to me in your letter of May 13. Nadia just sent me the parts and the printed orchestra score—from which the work was performed in Washington. Thus I have both a virgin score (the one you sent to Madame Casafuerte) and Nadia's. The latter is the one I will use here, after putting it in order; the former I am meticulously correcting with the help of a proofreader from Païchadze's firm, and I will return it to you (either directly or through Eschig) for the final printing. . . .

I am going to add the words "Dumbarton Oaks" to the title of the work in our contract, as well as "in E flat," which is missing.

How soon will you be able to send the remainder of my money for the Concerto to my London bank?

Too bad that you will not be here for the [European] premiere. . . . I will wait for you at the end of June, as you promised, when I hope to be able to settle all questions of an "artistic" order with Ida Rubinstein (who is generally dilatory). I will keep you up to date. . . .

STRAVINSKY TO STRECKER   *May 27, 1938*

Zürich

. . . Some friends who just came from Germany have informed me of an exhibition in Düsseldorf entitled "Entartete Musik" in which my name, along with that of Hindemith, heads the list [of "degenerate" composers].[78] And this after the great success of *Jeu de cartes* and *Perséphone* (repeated the day before yesterday in Braunschweig), while *Firebird* is played . . . all over Germany!

---

solution might be to set 'Dumbarton Oaks' and the date of the premiere above the title. Otherwise, Concerto in E flat is sufficient. 'Dumbarton Oaks' could be added to the title on the programs in America, or whenever desired." Strecker's criticism was shrewd: at the time of the June 16 concert at La Sérénade, a French newspaper spelled the title "d'Umbarton Oak."

[78] The *New York Herald Tribune* published a description of this exhibition in June 1938: "The Nazi leaders have issued a declaration of war against atonality and 'modernism' in general in music and are proceeding with their customary thoroughness to stamp out in the Third Reich this phase of 'Jewish cultural Bolshevism.' At the current exhibition at Düsseldorf of 'degenerate music' they have hit on the novel means of making the German public safe for pure 'Nordic melody.'. . . ." The official program of the Entartete Musik exhibition (written by Dr. Hans Severus Ziegler) states that: ". . . The exhibition . . . [is] a veritable witches' sabbath, portraying the most frivolous intellectual and artistic aspects of Cultural Bolshevism and the triumph of . . . arrogant Jewish impudence. . . . At the same time, I must point out that . . . the after-effects can still be found in today's musical life, though they are gradually . . . disappearing." (In a neighboring column of the *Tribune* is an article about the theft of Mussolini's "Alice

Listen to the *Sacre* on the radio Monday night, if you can. I have just come from the rehearsal of the Orchestre National, excellently conducted by the young Rosenthal.[79]

I shake your hand cordially and wish you and Hindemith a great success with *Mathis*.[80] . . .

P.S. Please save all information (and programs) about the Zürich production of *Jeu de cartes* for me.

STRAVINSKY TO STRECKER   *Paris*
                                                              May 30, 1938
Zürich

Attached you will find a copy of the letter I just sent to I. Philipp[81] after our conversation with him (and following your letter of the 28th). Philipp knows

---

blue pink" automobile from "the curb of the fashionable café Boulevard Vittoria Veneto. . . . The luckless thief . . . confessed in prison tonight that he was ignorant of its ownership.")

[79] Manuel Rosenthal (b. 1904), French conductor.

[80] Strecker had written to Stravinsky on March 14, 1934, after the first performance of the orchestral suite from *Mathis der Maler* in Berlin: "I am just back from an extraordinarily successful performance of Hindemith's new work. . . . The opera is not yet finished, but to judge from these pieces, we may expect a very unusual work, about the fate of the painter Grünewald. The performance was important for the recognition of modern music [in Germany], since in the past year Hindemith has been subject to strong enmity from reactionary segments. Had this concert failed, his adversaries would have howled triumphantly, and modern music would have been defeated for years to come. . . . This decisive success with the audience and the press also fortifies Furtwängler, . . . who risked his own [reputation] to conduct the concert. . . . For the time being, he is the only one whose position is sufficiently strong to influence general opinion and trends." On May 24, 1938, Strecker mentioned to Stravinsky that he was leaving for Zürich to attend the premiere of the complete opera on the 28th, and on the 31st the publisher reported: "The performance of *Mathis* was enormously successful, and it is really a beautiful work. Hindemith was very happy to receive your good wishes and regards."

[81] Stravinsky's letter to Isidor Philipp asks him for his "assistance in protesting the disagreeable surprise of reading in the German papers . . . that my musical activity and even my person are presented to the public in an absolutely inadmissible fashion. . . . I consider this [exposition] to be the work of . . . certain German musical circles who are trying to create an effective weapon against the expansion of my music in Germany, as well as in those countries where the German press is influential. Since these are not the first acts of hostility and seem to me to be part of a calculated campaign, I hope that our ambassador will find the occasion to defend my rights as a French citizen and musician—which have been severely violated—before the German authorities."

our ambassador to Berlin [André François-Poncet] [82] and is happy to help me in this affair. Furthermore, I met with (again on Philipp's advice) an important functionary,[83] who asked me to prepare a brief memorandum of material justifying my protest. Unfortunately, I have very little documentary material of this sort (only two articles, which [F. V.] Weber is sending to Païchadze today). I hope nonetheless to gather as much as possible, and I ask you to furnish some more information to substantiate [these] purely objective facts.

Philipp is sending a registered letter (including my letter to him, the copy of which is now before you) to François-Poncet today. . . .

STRAVINSKY TO STRECKER

Paris
June 1, 1938

. . . The negotiations with Ida Rubinstein began yesterday, and it is very likely that I will be collaborating with Claudel. This could be a large work with chorus and speakers (narration as well as stage action). Keep that to yourself for the time being. I expect you on June 14. I hope that our negotiations will by then be advanced enough for you to intervene and assume the business aspect. . . .[84]

STRAVINSKY TO STRECKER

Paris
June 25, 1938

. . . The collaboration with Ida Rubinstein is over: I simply said no. She informed me *through her secretary* that the poet P[aul] C[laudel] was so carried away with excitement over my music that I absolutely must work with him, rather than P[aul] V[aléry], with whom she envisages no collaboration at this time. She would not come to the telephone herself, so it was impossible for me to convince her [to use] a Greek subject. I saw that there was no hope of making her see my point of view, so I broke off relations with her, expressing my regret at having wasted a month for nothing when she knew from the begin-

---

[82] In June 1958, Bernard François-Poncet, French Minister of Foreign Affairs and son of François-Poncet, married Marian Sachs, daughter of Arthur Sachs, Stravinsky's friend since 1924 and a close friend in Santa Barbara during the war.

[83] On May 31, Stravinsky wrote to M. Marx of the Ministry of Foreign Affairs, mentioning, among other things, that the caption under his portrait (by Jacques-Emile Blanche) at the exhibition read: *"Wer hat das Märchen erfunden, dass Strawinsky aus russischen Adelsgeschlecht stamme?"* The composer states: "My adversaries even go so far as to make fallacious insinuations . . . implying that I am a Jew, [ignoring] that my ancestors were members of the Polish nobility, in an attempt to place my origins in doubt. This has nothing to do with music; and such an assertion would not ordinarily provoke any protest from me. But, knowing the unfortunate significance of this question in Germany, . . . I cannot remain indifferent to it." Marx replied, June 14, informing the composer that a formal complaint had been registered at the Bureau of Foreign Affairs of the Reich in Berlin.

[84] See the correspondence with Paul Claudel in the present volume.

ning of our talks that I did not want to and could not do a theatrical piece of the kind [she proposes].[85]

I just received a reply from M. Jourdan.[86] He told me all his thoughts on this sad affair and expressed his sympathy and that of his superior, promising to follow the matter attentively. He thinks that I may expect a letter of apology within the next two weeks, and, if not, one will be demanded. . . .[87]

The day after tomorrow (Monday) I will send you the corrected proofs of the two-piano reduction of my Concerto in E flat (do not forget the flat in the contract, please!). . . .

I was so happy to see you again. . . .

STRAVINSKY TO STRECKER

Paris
July 4, 1938

. . . I just had a visit from M. Jourdan, who is hopeful about the efficacy of the steps they have taken. He returns to Berlin around July 15 and hopes that by then there will have been a positive reaction of some sort. If not, he will institute new measures, which should have a decisive effect.

Please tell your proofreader that I have just found two more errors in the orchestra score and parts. I hope that these [corrections] will not arrive too late. . . .

STRAVINSKY TO STRECKER

Paris
July 12, 1938

. . . I await M. Jourdan's answer impatiently (he should be back in Berlin any day now). His impression was clearly favorable, because he states that these gentlemen are ashamed, not having expected the matter to take on such a formal aspect. [Jourdan] was not yet able to tell me what form the apology will take, but he is certain that the official circles will arrive at an honorable solution one way or another. . . .

Thank you for the insistent attitude you showed Telefunken; a week ago they wrote to say that everything is now in order. Nevertheless, I still have not

---

[85] Strecker replied on June 27: "I hope that your newly won freedom will allow a new masterpiece to come forth naturally, from your heart, free from the dictates of this woman [Ida Rubinstein]. . . . Although the business aspect of my visit to Paris was therefore in vain, . . . I was still enormously glad to have seen you and hope that the new treatment [for your wife and daughter] will relieve your worries about your family."

[86] Head of the French Cultural Institute in Berlin.

[87] In Jourdan's reply of June 23 he warns Stravinsky that "in general the Reich does not volunteer public apologies. . . . I am sending you several photographs, which speak for themselves." Strecker wrote to the composer on June 27: "I was happy about Jourdan's answer. By the way, he will be in Paris in the next few days and will probably look for you. Let me know . . . as soon as you hear anything. A great deal depends upon the response that he promises."

received anything, not even your payment (directly to Paris, according to your letter of July 2). It is July 12. What happened? . . .

STRAVINSKY TO STRECKER

Paris
July 29, 1938

How can I ever thank you, my dear friend, for your very kind attentions! Tchaikovsky's First Symphony is impossible to find, and you have given me immense pleasure by obtaining it for me. But why not give me the satisfaction of sharing

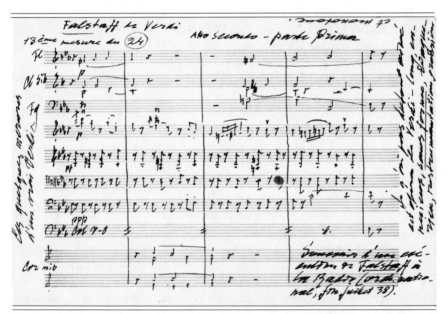

Stravinsky heard a radio broadcast of Falstaff on July 26, 1938, and, as his marginal comments indicate, disliked the opera intensely—with the exception of these four measures, which he calls "d'un vrai Verdi."

the costs of the photocopies of the orchestra score? . . .

I am very happy about your reaction to my concerto.[88] The radio performance[89] the other day, which I attended, in my opinion left something to be desired, and would have been more precise with a greater number of rehearsals. . . .

I just wrote to Jourdan to ask if anything has happened. This two-month silence is already somewhat alarming. . . .

[88] Strecker had reported on July 27: "Recently I heard a very good broadcast of your [*Dumbarton Oaks*] Concerto, which made an extraordinary impression on me. In its economy [*Sparsamkeit*] it is one of the most intricate scores I know."
[89] Conducted by Manuel Rosenthal.

Finally, an evasive and embarrassed response,[90] but a response nonetheless, which, it seems to me, inspires hope that [I] will not suffer humiliation in the future. This is something. This response (not the original text, which I must obtain) I received from two sides, one communicated to me here and via Jourdan. Here are some excerpts from his letter: "According to the purport of this text, it is necessary to establish a distinction between a technical orientation, of which you would be the perhaps involuntary precursor, and your work itself, as a whole. This work, like yourself, is virtually untouchable, and the German reply stresses the fact that your works continue to be played in the territory of the Reich. Regrettably, the note fails to mention the painful exhibition of your portrait. But all in all, taking into consideration the embarrassed tone of this note, which clearly implies that your work is beyond reproach, you and your publisher may count on a benevolent neutrality."

And this is what was communicated to me [from the Quai d'Orsay]: "First, it was indicated at the beginning of the exhibition that certain artists would not therein be treated as individuals but only as representatives of certain orientations of musical art. Thus your involvement came about only because you were named as the precursor of a determined musical orientation. Second, the fact that one of your works was presented for quite a long time at the beginning of 1938 can only confirm that the exhibition intended to denounce neither your person nor your work."

If we can count on a "benevolent neutrality" (which has already been contradicted, since *Petrushka* and *Firebird*, my most popular works, are not allowed to be presented in theatres in Berlin and Düsseldorf), we must now determine how to make the most of this with other interested enterprises (theatres and other concert organizations).... .[91]

Would you please communicate the content of this official response to F. V. Weber? Thank you. I will try to obtain the original of this reply.

---

[90] Jourdan had written on August 4: "By now you have undoubtedly received the response finally communicated to us at the Embassy on July 26. The exact text will be transmitted to you through the Quai d'Orsay [office]." Stravinsky answered Jourdan on August 6, thanking him and adding: "If the reply to our ambassador is not all that we had hoped for, it is nonetheless a dissembled avowal of their gaffe, which, I hope, they will be careful not to repeat." Stravinsky also asks Jourdan to try to obtain the exact text for him. Strecker wrote to Stravinsky on August 9: "Do try to obtain the official letter and request permission to cite it, should the need ever arise. All that the declaration should say is that neither your person nor your work has been denounced and you may count on a benevolent neutrality. All other questions can be dismissed." Not until September 21 did Jourdan write to assure Stravinsky that the authorized German response had been sent.

[91] Strecker wrote on November 21: "The [Düsseldorf] exhibit seems already to have been forgotten in Germany. Two days ago, *Jeu de cartes* was played on the Leipzig

STRAVINSKY TO STRECKER   *February 1, 1939*[92]

. . . Unfortunately I have no good news to give you about my family, for my wife
is not at all well. Since our terrible sorrow her lungs have weakened considerably and lost all resistance, and the cavity has become much larger. Despite the
doctors' assurances that the cavity is in the process of stabilizing, she stays in
bed all the time and is very feeble, owing to a cough that leaves her exhausted.
For three weeks now she has not been able to shake a debilitating flu. We
should take her to Pau, for its salutary air, which calms the nerves and the irritated bronchi. But in her present state she cannot be moved. What am I to do? I
have no idea. I wait, I hope, I am full of anguish. . . . I have to cancel my American tour, of course. Copley has asked me to cable him as to whether or not I will
come next year. How am I to reply, in view of the present situation? Each hour,
each day holds immense discouragement for me. I wait, I wait, I wait. . . .

. . . Thank you for the pleasing news that I will soon receive the 700 marks,
a payment that now, in my cruel inactivity, is especially desirable. . . .

                                                                Sancellemoz
STRAVINSKY TO STRECKER   *April 1, 1939*[93]

. . . Given the conditions under which I have had to work recently, it is difficult
for me to say when [the Symphony in C] will be finished, as you will understand.[94]

Now there is another question, which, as you will see, is somewhat complicated. Some friends in America, knowing of the pecuniary difficulties in
which I find myself this year, conceived the idea of raising a sum of money for
me, in exchange for which I would bequeath my manuscript to the National

---

Radio. This work will also be broadcast from Munich, and the orchestral suite will be
presented in Karlsbad. *Firebird* will be presented in a radio broadcast from Berlin and
in a concert in Wiesbaden. Rosbaud is conducting the Concerto in Mainz and
Münster, and Furtwängler will do *Baiser de la fée* in Berlin. . . . Everyone knows about
your negotiations [with Jourdan] by word of mouth, so you have achieved the desired
effect, even if the written German response was not all that it might have been."

[92] A six-month gap exists in Stravinsky's side of the correspondence, during which period he apparently kept no copies, but Strecker's letters survive. On October 10, 1938,
for example, the publisher wrote to say that his trip to Paris would be postponed for
two or three days, "since I have to see Hindemith in Switzerland first. I probably will
not be in Paris before the 22nd, but I will call you as soon as I arrive." Strecker wrote
again on November 29, from London: "The letter from Jourdan was brought to Mainz
by an acquaintance. I will save it and forward it to you as soon as possible. I think about
you a great deal and am with you in your troubles." Stravinsky had conducted in Rome
on the 29th, and the next day, while he was on the train for Turin, his daughter Mika
died.

[93] Strecker had written on March 13: "I hope that we will see each other at the Maggio
Musicale in Florence. If at all possible, I will come. Hindemith will be there as well!"

[94] Catherine Stravinsky had died on March 2.

Library of the White House [*sic;* Library of Congress] . Furthermore, the world premiere of my symphony would be given in Chicago under my direction. Details are supposed to arrive by the next mail, and I will immediately relay these to you. As you see, it is better, under these conditions, to wait before scheduling my BBC program. . . .

STRAVINSKY TO STRECKER

Sancellemoz
July 9, 1939

. . . My new bereavement[95] has interrupted our correspondence. Permit me to tell you on this sad occasion how much I appreciated your sharing in my grief.

Thank you as well for taking care of Chester, Telefunken,[96] and the BBC in London.

As for the world premiere of my symphony at the BBC, I must still see what has happened in America on that subject. N. Boulanger, who just arrived there, surely will not delay in sending information about this.

Attached I send the contract for my new symphony with my signature; the copy you signed I will keep. . . .

STRAVINSKY TO STRECKER

July 29, 1939

. . . . I will stay here until August 31, when I go to Venice. I will conduct my opera *Mavra* in the first concert and the *Dumbarton Oaks* Concerto on September 4, at the Biennale. On September 6 I must be in Paris, where you can write to me in care of Madame Sudeikina (31, rue de l'Assomption, Paris 16). I leave for New York on September 27 on the S.S. *Ile de France.* Will I see you in Paris before my departure? . . .

---

[95] The death of Stravinsky's mother on June 7.

[96] Strecker had written to Stravinsky on January 28: "In mid-November, Telefunken asked for information by express mail, and they were sent an outline based partly on the genealogical letter you wrote me years ago [see Stravinsky's letter of April 14, 1933] . . . . Incidentally, the world knows enough of you and about you that this small mistake will cause no harm [Telefunken had identified Stravinsky as "the conductor of the Diaghilev Ballet"] . . . . I can happily inform you that your standing in Germany is apparently entirely restored. They play you again, and without any objections. This will develop fully only next winter, since most concert programs are already set in the spring, and last spring was a critical time for you here. Even now you are not officially promoted, but if no objections are raised against your works, then the more timid souls will slowly begin to perform you, too. . . . The *Dumbarton Oaks* Concerto was also played here several times; of course, it will take a while for this piece to become established. It would be good to agree to a recording with Telefunken. When you write to Grenzbach, wouldn't you like to offer this to him as a kind of reparation? . . ."

Excerpts from *STRAVINSKY'S LETTERS*

1940 ✦ *1947*

to *ASSOCIATED MUSIC PUBLISHERS*

STRAVINSKY TO ERNEST VOIGT

124 South Swall Drive
Beverly Hills, Calif.
July 14, 1940

25 West 45th Street
New York, N.Y.[1]

. . . A note in reply to your nice letter of the 5th. The last movement of my symphony is quite far along but not yet finished. I would have sent it to you at the end of July, had my work not been interrupted by a trip to Mexico. I go there at the end of this week for a two-week guest-conducting stint in Mexico City, returning around August 10. I will resume the composition then and hope to send you the finished orchestra score by the end of August. Thus you will have two whole months to extract and verify the parts, which should be sufficient for the task.

For your information, let me add that the orchestra score of the last movement will be about fifty pages long, with four to five measures per page. If you think that . . . two months will not suffice, could you perhaps begin extracting the parts from the first three movements now?

Within the next few days I will send you (through a friend who is returning to New York) the photostats of the first two movements of my symphony (those that W. Strecker made), in order for you to enter certain corrections (ties, bowings, etc.), marked in pencil and noted in the margins, in the new photostats (those that you made yourselves), as well as in the extracted parts. Return these old photostats to me later (at the end of September).

The terrible events in France and the anguish in which I have been living recently have slowed my work, which would otherwise have been completed a long time ago.

Until July 20 I will be here, and thereafter you can write to me at the Orquésta Sinfónica de Méjico, Isabel la Católica 30, Mexico City. AIRMAIL, please! . . .

---

[1] All the letters are addressed to the office of Associated Music Publishers in New York. As the American representative of B. Schotts Söhne, A.M.P. became the publisher of most of Stravinsky's music composed during the war years. His one close friend in the company, Hugo Winter, had been Webern's friend in Vienna. A.M.P. was eventually purchased by G. Schirmer.

French is the original language of Stravinsky's letters unless otherwise noted. Random English words and phrases in the French letters are indicated by italics.

124 South Swall Drive
Beverly Hills, Calif.
August 23, 1940

STRAVINSKY TO VOIGT

. . . Finally I have finished my symphony and sent it [to A.M.P.] today, airmail special delivery.

Please be so kind as to acknowledge receipt and, as soon as you have photocopied this manuscript (of the fourth and last part), send me a copy, as you did with the other three movements. After making the photocopies, send the manuscript . . . to Washington, D.C., Librarian of Congress, Division of Accessions, asking them, in turn, to send me an acknowledgment of the receipt of the *entire* Symphony in C (the manuscripts of the first three movements were already delivered in June), along with a check for $1,000. This follows the stipulation of their letter of July 8, 1939, to Mrs. Robert Woods Bliss (3101 R Street, N.W., Washington, D.C.), signed by Mr. Herbert Putnam, Librarian of Congress, and by the Chief, Division of Accessions. Thank you in advance.

Did you read the card from Willy Strecker, which [A.M.P.] forwarded to me? Read it and return it to me, please, and tell me what you think. Could we send him the photostats of the last two movements of my symphony by clipper? . . .

124 South Swall Drive
Beverly Hills, Calif.
September 3, 1940

STRAVINSKY TO VOIGT

. . . I am replying immediately to your question concerning my arrangement with the Chicago Orchestra, since it is important that you be up-to-date on the details of this issue before you begin negotiating the rental fee.

This piece is dedicated to the Chicago Symphony, as you know, in honor of its fiftieth anniversary. This organization expressed a desire to have me conduct the world premiere . . . myself, at the beginning of the symphonic season, and concluded an agreement with my manager, Mr. Paul H. Stoes (119 West 57th Street, New York, N.Y.), for a week of guest-conducting . . . starting November 7. My manager has the contract, signed by him and by Mr. Voegeli. Further information regarding the rental fee, should you need any, can be obtained from Mr. Stoes. Personally, I made no special agreement with the Chicago Orchestra. I simply informed Dr. Frederick Stock,[2] at the time of my last Chicago concerts, that the question of rental fees does not concern me and is to be resolved directly between the Chicago Symphony and your publishing company. I suggested the sum of $250 for the world premiere, which was Willy Strecker's idea, at the time of our last meeting in France, one year ago, just ten days before the war broke out. . . .

Apart from that, I have based all of my guest-conducting engagements for this season on the novelty of my new symphony, and naturally I should be the one to conduct it and to establish the tradition for its interpretation. I will con-

---

[2] Frederick A. Stock (1872–1942) had become conductor of the Chicago Symphony Orchestra in 1905.

duct it with the Boston Symphony as well as the New York Philharmonic (with whom Mr. Stoes is negotiating). . . . Please do not give my symphony to any other conductors, at least for this 1940–41 season. I will probably see you in December, at which time we could discuss the possibilities for the 1941–42 season. . . .

From September 6 to 13 I will be taking a little pleasure trip, by automobile, to San Francisco (c/o Mrs. Charles N. Felton, 3311 Pacific Avenue, San Francisco).

STRAVINSKY TO VOIGT

Beverly Hills
September 4, 1940

. . . I am writing to you today about a proposal I received from a certain Moses Smith of Columbia Recording Corporation (799 Seventh Avenue, New York), worded as follows in his letter of August 22: ". . . I should very much like to know what would be your desire so far as both payment for conducting and payment for rights to use the music on records are concerned [regarding the new symphony]. I do hope that, in formulating your demands, you will take into account the fact that we have a royalty contract with the Chicago Symphony Orchestra. I am most eager to have the work recorded, but must naturally be guided by certain iron business considerations with which we are both familiar. I hope I have not been presumptuous in writing to you rather than to your manager about this matter. I look forward to an answer from you on the subject."

I replied on the 26th: ". . . on the question of my terms, I still prefer that proposals be made directly to me . . . about my conducting and author's rights (I also own all rights to mechanical reproduction). The arrangement should be established between your company and me directly, since neither my agent nor anyone else has anything to do with this. The payment should be based on a fixed sum for my conducting and a percentage of the record sales (to be calculated from the retail rather than the wholesale price). This payment *'for the right to use the music or records'* was defended by the Bureau International de l'Edition Musico-Mécanique just prior to the war, and by Edipho in Paris before that. Given the present situation in Europe, I am obliged to protect my rights to musico-mechanical editions myself, until the situation returns to normal." To this letter I received the enclosed reply from Mr. Moses Smith, which I ask you please to return to me after examining it.

. . . What do you advise? Should I accept 2 cents per side (the duration of my symphony is about 23 minutes, thus seven sides can be expected)? In my opinion, this is far from equitable remuneration for serious music that will never sell the way that light music does. Of course, I would not give them exclusivity for very long (perhaps only one year). The rental of the orchestra parts will have to be arranged between you and Columbia. As for my conducting fee, I will have to reach an agreement with Mr. Voegeli, as I did with Mr. Zirato when I recorded the *Sacre du printemps* and *Petrushka* last April with the New York Philharmonic. . . .

I would be happy to find your reply as well as the last photostats of the Symphony upon my return from San Francisco. . . .

Beverly Hills
September 17, 1940

. . . Last April I received $1,500 for conducting the recording session with the New York Philharmonic (the author's rights were handled separately), by contract with Mr. Zirato. It seems logical to me that I should receive the same amount from the same Columbia by contract with Mr. Voegeli—what do you think? . . .

Beverly Hills
September 30, 1940

Thank you for your letter of the 20th and for the photostats of my symphony (fourth movemment, and for the first two showing my corrections), which just arrived.

I have written to Mr. Voegeli and Mr. Smith about recording my symphony and await their replies. . . .

The victim of a *misunderstanding,* my manager Paul Stoes neglected to include any indication about the rental of the parts and the rental fee for the world premiere in the contract with the Chicago Symphony. I had discussed this question personally with Dr. Stock last winter. . . .

An important musical group has formed here, made up of studio musicians. They meet twice a month, placing themselves at the service of composers and conductors who wish to do readings of their scores. The other day, I was informed that the group would like to play one of my works under my direction, if possible the Violin Concerto (published by B. Schotts Söhne). I promised to write to you on this subject. . . . Would you please be so kind as to send me a copy of this concerto, if you have a *set* available (normal strings), free of charge—since these are not public concerts, but two-hour rehearsals, twice a month, to examine the score in shirt-sleeves. . . ? Reply immediately, please; I must give them an answer, for this reading is supposed to take place in two weeks. . . .

October 2, 1940

Confirming our verbal [*sic*] understanding, I herewith authorize you to represent me during the period of one month, from October 3, 1940 to November 3, 1940, for the purpose of carrying on negotiations with BMI in securing for me an engagement as conductor of my own compositions.

In addition to this and should the necessity arise of using my larger orchestral works such as *Petrushka, Firebird, Le Sacre du printemps, Pulcinella,* and *The Five Fingers,* you may with my consent make your own arrangements of the above mentioned works for any combination of instruments and in any form.

If at any time your arrangements of my compositions are accepted for publication, I am to receive 50% of all royalties due you. For this I grant you permission to use the following inscription on the title page of all your published arrangements of my works: EDITED BY IGOR STRAVINSKY. . . .

[*Original in English*]

STRAVINSKY TO VOIGT   *October 16, 1940*

I just received the orchestra parts of my Violin Concerto, along with your letter of October 11, and I thank you. Attached you will find a little accompanying note indicating in red the 8–7–6–5–4 of the strings that I found instead of the 9–8–7–6–5. The reading-rehearsal will take place on October 27. I will either return the score by the same means by which it came or bring it to you personally in New York in December.

Attached you will also find two corrections on a scrap of paper, to be introduced in the score of my Symphony in C as well as in the oboe parts and the first bassoon, third measure, of **98**, second movement. I just discovered these errors in the photostat of my manuscript.

Mr. Moses Smith claims that 2 cents per side for the recording of my new symphony . . . is the maximum that Columbia can offer. I guess that in this case I have no choice but to accept. But how, then, do I arrange this payment with you? By my contract with Schott, I am the sole proprietor of all my mechanical rights, and I should therefore receive the whole 2 cents in question. How, then, to reconcile this with your arrangement with Schott, which you explained to me in your letter of September 20 [1939]? I think that the easiest way, for the moment, would be for you to deal directly with Columbia, through Moses Smith, and then we will discuss it again when I come to New York.

As for *Jeu de cartes,* I received no advance from Schott for performance rights, which belong to me. Before the war, Schott collected these rights for me and took a certain commission for this task. . . .

Write to me, dear Mr. Voigt; I will be here until November 3; then I go to Chicago and Cincinnati. . . .

STRAVINSKY TO VOIGT   *Beverly Hills*
                                                              October 19, 1940

My letter of the 16th must scarcely have been delivered to you when I learned, from reading the New York newspapers, that my ballet *Jeu de cartes* is being presented by the Ballet Russe [de Monte Carlo] company under a different title: *A Poker Game.* Yet this ballet was duly registered and copyrighted in Washington under the English title *A Card Game.* By what right is my title changed without my authorization? Did you give permission? If not, please take all necessary steps to reinstate the authentic title.

This change in the title is all the more bizarre and incomprehensible because Balanchine mounted this ballet under my direction three years ago at the Metropolitan Opera House using the correct title.

Please keep me informed on this subject, which astounds me because of the flippancy of these gentlemen. They have probably forgotten that I am the author of the piece, which is to say that I composed the libretto and scenario of the ballet and christened it. . . .

Beverly Hills
October 24, 1940

STRAVINSKY TO VOIGT

. . . As for the title *A Poker Game,* I understand your argument very well, and I myself would not have had any objection, had I been asked to approve that title. But the Ballet Russe did not show the elementary decency of consulting the author of the work about changing its title. The same company also did not consult me about making cuts in my other ballet, *Le Baiser de la fée.* This time I therefore had no choice but to remonstrate with them. In the future they will be more prudent. For this reason I would be much obliged if you would point out to them the illegality of their action, adding that it is entirely up to me whether to accept or reject their explanation. . . .

1260 N. Wetherly Drive
West Hollywood, Calif.
November 2, 1941

STRAVINSKY TO VOIGT

The orchestra score for my Symphony in C (the one from which I conducted in Mexico last July), along with all of my corrections, is now in the hands of Mlle Boulanger. I saw Mlle Boulanger on numerous occasions, and I asked her to contact you about the parts of the Symphony. In effect, the *set* from which I conducted my symphony last winter and this summer, in Mexico, must be completely redone: too much time is wasted in rehearsals with that hastily and negligently compiled material. Mlle Boulanger (c/o Mrs. Edward W. Forbes, Gerry's Landing, Cambridge, Massachusetts) . . . will indicate everything that needs to be done. Get in touch with her as soon as possible. But do not forget that before you begin to make a new, legible, and correct score, you must send the old one . . . to San Francisco, where I will conduct my symphony in January (9–10), and perhaps St. Louis, where I will conduct *Jeu de cartes,* among other pieces, on December 19 and 20. . . .

Attached you will find the questionnaire I signed before the notary public; please deliver it to Mr. Hugo Winter. . . .

Exactly what parts of my symphony did you send to Hugo Strecker in London? Were they at least corrected according to my score? Because if I myself had trouble with the performance using those parts, I can imagine what will happen in London with a conductor who is not at all familiar with the music. Frankly, I would not like to be in his shoes. . . .

STRAVINSKY TO VOIGT   *February 20, 1942*

. . . As I told you last year, when we made our arrangements, I unfortunately had no contract with Schott—everything remained in Europe. I only remember that I was paid 15 percent of the sale and 85 percent of the performance and rental fees. I do not think that my memory is far off in these figures. You would do me a great service to pay me my share; I am not an *enemy alien,* after all. . . .

What should I do about my new compositions, given the present situation? . . . I need a publisher who will protect my music. The war has dictated that I live in the United States, where I happened to be when it broke out. I decided to stay here, bought a house in Hollywood, and, almost two years ago, took out my *first papers.* Events have transferred my musical activity here, and I have no reason to believe that a normal life will resume in Europe after this gigantic conflict is over. . . .

I must inform you that after June 22, 1942, I will no longer be a member of SACEM.[3] Mr. Gene Buck of ASCAP has been alerted to this. He sent me a very nice letter expressing the hope that I will join their organization. . . .

STRAVINSKY TO VOIGT   *March 7, 1942*

. . . As for the question of my membership in ASCAP, I thank you for having so kindly taken my interests to heart. I think that . . . ASCAP is perfectly well informed about control of my performances and editions. I am convinced that Gene Buck will not be deterred by the copyright issue, since he has a singular desire to see me join ASCAP. . . .

Tell me sincerely what kind of a contract you could offer me. I am rather embarrassed to make such a proposal myself, given my special case: I have my position vis-à-vis Willy Strecker in mind. Thus I await news from you, and I am already certain that we will have no difficulty in reaching an understanding adequate to our reciprocal interests.

STRAVINSKY TO VOIGT   *March 19, 1942*

. . . The question of your conversation with Mr. Libidins brings us indeed to the general question of our eventual collaboration. The prospect of this ballet is still somewhat problematic, as the mailing of the musical material (fragments of Donizetti's operas) they promised me is much delayed and I am not sure to be able to compose this work for their autumn season as they wanted it.[4] But at the same time they were interested in producing my last work—*Danses concer-*

---

[3] Société des Auteurs, Compositeurs, et Editeurs de Musique, the French copyright collecting organization.

[4] On March 10, Stravinsky had written to Vittorio Rieti: "A month ago [Serge] Denham and Massine invited me to compose a Donizetti ballet. I advised them to address themselves to you, since you would be the one to do it; but I did not realize that you

tantes. This work I have conducted on its world premiere about a month ago at the Werner Janssen Symphony concerts. It is about the same duration as *Jeu de cartes,* scored for a small orchestra, and is foreseen as well for symphony performance as for ballet exploitation. I have already copyrighted it and I am in possession of the photostatic score and the complete set of orchestra parts. I also

Stravinsky's copies of excerpts from Linda di Chamounix *for use in a "Donizetti ballet" (1943).*

recently composed a small work entitled *Circus Polka.* This composition was suggested by George Balanchine who actually is composing the choreography for "a young elephant" (*sic*), and the first performance will be given in

were in the middle of working on Bellini [*Night Shadow*]. They were insistent, demanded my conditions, and came to my house, with their pianist in tow, to play fragments of Donizetti's operas. They asked my opinion of their selection of fragments, which I found suitable. Upon their departure from Los Angeles, they requested that I begin working as soon as I received the material. . . . 'First of all, [send] the contract,' I added, 'according to our oral agreement.' Well, I have received neither the Donizetti material nor Denham's contract, and I wonder if they have decided to postpone this project until the 1943–44 season. I will wait another week, then inform them that I cannot prepare this work for next autumn. All of this is to explain that there is little chance of our Bellini/Donizetti ballets coinciding. And even if they did, why should anyone complain? I do not find it improper."

New York in April at Barnum and Bailey. The work exists actually for piano (two hands) and military band (as used by the circus) and I intend to make a normal symphony orchestration for it as well. The duration is about 3½–4 minutes. I think it would be a good idea to have this polka published for the New York performances. . . .

I think you will be interested to know that I have been proposed to compose music for an important film production. . . . Though we are actually only in the preliminary phase of conversation I accepted in principle the collaboration . . . and you certainly will hear soon about this prospect from Mr. Abe Meyer to whom I just gave the representation of my interests for this particular case. . . .

[*Original in English*]

STRAVINSKY TO VOIGT   *April 13, 1942*

. . . As you see I took in consideration the actual international musical situation. Though the proposed amounts are far from my usual arrangements, I actually do not want to discuss them, leaving this question to the moment when it will be again possible to settle the definite amounts with Willy Strecker himself. It is why I wired you that I accept the amounts you proposed me, as an account on my eventual future transaction on these works with Schott. . . .

. . . I gave to the Circus the rights of performance for one year. . . . As for the symphonic scoring I shall send it to you as soon as I will finish it.

As up to date I heard very little about the production of the *Polka* I should appreciate immensely if you could let me have the clippings you mention. . . .

[*Original in English*]

STRAVINSKY TO VOIGT   *April 25, 1942*

. . . As for the payments—$500 for the *Danses concertantes*, $250 for the *Polka* and $125 reimbursement of material expenses (mentioned in my last letter, April 13) would you be kind enough to deposit them on my bank account at the Public National Bank and Trust Company, 37 Broad Street, New York City.

I take the opportunity to tell you that Mr. Ingolf Dahl, an excellent musician and pianist [plans] to make under my supervision an arrangement for piano of the *Danses concertantes*. He will write to you on this account and I would appreciate immensely your welcome meeting of his letter. . . .

[*Original in English*]

STRAVINSKY TO VOIGT   *May 2, 1942*

In reply to your letter of April 29 I am sending you an extract of my letter to Mr. Milton Bender (personal manager of Mr. Balanchine) of January 31, 1942 with the conditions regulating my arrangement with the Barnum & Bailey Circus. . . .

As for Mr. G. Balanchine, we have just spoken with him lately by telephone and he was interested to be acquainted with the music and he should be happy to produce the *Danses concertantes* on the first opportunity. It certainly belongs to you as the publisher of the work to arrange the eventual financial agreement with him or his ballet in due time. . . .

[*Original in English*]

STRAVINSKY TO VOIGT   *June 28, 1942*

I am very glad to know (from your letter of June 25, 1942) that you arranged with [Victor] Babin for the 2 pianos version [of *Circus Polka*], which can be published in the same time and right away as my original version for 2 hands. I had to delay somewhat its symphonic version. I am actually taken by a very urgent work. . . .

I wrote you that there is already a violin transcription by Mr. Sol Babitz made under my personal supervision and which can be used perfectly for publishing and performances. Notwithstanding my personal friendship to Sam Dushkin there is no reason to wait for his eventual transcription of my *Polka* as we have Babitz's at hand. . . .

As for the Dougherty private [piano] transcription still of the same *Polka* . . . I do not see any utility of it as we have the excellent Babin's transcription verified and corrected by myself. . . .

. . . I am wondering if Mr. Dahl who recently was in New York got in touch with you. He was the person most suited to transcribe my *Danses concertantes* for 2 pianos as he had the opportunity to hear this work several times at my rehearsals and performance. . . .

[*Original in English*]

STRAVINSKY TO VOIGT   *July 25, 1942*

Of course what I wrote you about private transcriptions of my works was a general statement. . . . I want you only to understand the point that I am in the impossibility to control all the transcriptions of my works as it would take me much time. And without controlling them there is no sense to give my approval. . . .

As for the violin arrangement I just finished to revise and correct Mr. Babitz's transcription which he is going to send you within the next few days. . . .

I recently composed a little suite on Norwegian folk tunes. . . . The duration is about 7 minutes and it is scored for rather restricted orchestra (woods by 2, 4 horns, 2 tromp., 2 trb., tuba, timp. and strings). . . .

[*Original in English*]

STRAVINSKY TO VOIGT   *September 4, 1942*

Before sending you the set of my *Norwegian Moods* I shall rehearse it here with the musicians of the studios. They are getting together every week to facilitate composers to hear their works. I shall profit of the opportunity to let them hear also my Symphony in C. So I ask you send me *immediately* (after reception of this letter) its material (orch[estra] parts and the score) which I used in all my performances until now. That will be a private rehearsal as two years ago when you sent me the material of my violin concerto. Do you remember? I accepted to work with them the 14th of September and also a second time one week later. . . .

[*Original in English*]

STRAVINSKY TO VOIGT   *October 9, 1942*

. . . I already terminated the symphonic orchestra score of the *Circus Polka*. . . .

[And], as I wrote you on September 4th, I already corrected the parts of my *Norwegian Moods* and I am sending you the photostatic score and the orch[estra] material under separate cover. . . .

[*Original in English*]

STRAVINSKY TO VOIGT   *October 17, 1942*

. . . I haste[n] to write you to prevent the definite printing of my *Danses concertantes* orch[estra] score before you will receive from me a small list of errata I discovered in my manuscript recently. . . .

[For] your knowledge I inform you that I never requested . . . Mr. Ormandy nor any other conductor. I simply gave him the information. He asked me by mutual friends to let him know a recent composition of mine available for a performance for his concert season. As you see there is no question about a *request* from my part but a simple *indication*.

I hope you [sent] to London the material of my symphony in a *corrected* copy because the material of this work was the most abundant in mistakes of any . . . I ever met in my musical career. Please, set my mind at rest. . . .

[*Original in English*]

STRAVINSKY TO VOIGT   *October 24, 1942*

Answering your question (your wire of October 23). Of course you can spell my name with a V instead of a W. I personally use the W as an old habit gotten in Europe (because of the German pronunciation). . . .

As to the piano score of this *Polka* which I received from Mr. A. Mendel some days ago (in green proofs) I shall correct it in few days and send him back in the beginning of the next week. . . .

[*Original in English*]

STRAVINSKY TO VOIGT   *November 1, 1942*

. . . I do hope that . . . Miss Marcelle Manziarly, my friend, who just has arrived from here in New York, has remitted to you the piano proofs of my *Circus Polka* and the promised errata sheet of my *Danses concertantes*. By the way, Miss Manziarly's address is 302 East 66th Street, New York City. Please keep me posted if all is in order.

Concerning my new symphonic orchestration of the *Circus Polka:* In about ten days I will rehearse it with an orchestra of studio musicians who gather weekly to read new scores. This material which I have prepared for you I will then verify and send to you, the complete set, in the best condition. . . .

[*Original in English*]

STRAVINSKY TO VOIGT   *November 18, 1942*

Answering your wire: the *Polka* sketch with the elephants was returned to you by mail two days ago. I do not find it necessary to have an *illustrated* title page but prefer a standard lettered cover especially established for all my works published by you. Therefore I shall appreciate to receive from you such a layout in gray and black for my approval.

. . . A slight flu had laid me up for a few days preventing me [from] rehearsing my new orchestration of the *Circus Polka,* which explains the delay in sending it to you. . . .

. . . Now, dear Mr. Voigt, you will understand my surprise at seeing my name *linked* to Mr. Dougherty's for my *Polka* on this program. Do not misunderstand me, but I must candidly state that it disappointed me. I do not doubt that he has made an excellent arrangement . . . (which I have never seen) for two pianos for which, upon your request only, I gave my authorization—but certainly I did not extend it to the printing of my name in the way Mr. Dougherty did it. For the future I earnestly ask you to see to it that on programs and other printed matters this indiscretion will not be repeated. In general an arrangement of a piece is not necessarily a collaboration and in this case by no means, [was it] one. . . .

[*Original in English*]

STRAVINSKY TO VOIGT   *December 7, 1942*

. . . I am sending you the title page of the *Circus Polka* with some alterations, and a design by Eugene Berman, the renowned painter, my friend. This design I wish to be as a trademark on the cover of all my works published by you. Naturally it must be printed directly on the sheet reduced to the size as cut out on the enclosed proof. The price index as indicated on same. Color of the paper can vary between light gray as you have chosen, ivory, beige or white. Please send me a proof before final printing. Mr. Berman has generously dedicated and presented to me the design for the use of the trademark. Please return to me this valuable sketch signed by his initials. . . .

[*Original in English*]

STRAVINSKY TO VOIGT   *December 12, 1942*

. . . The orchestra rehearsal I hoped [for and] wrote you about did not take place. The gasoline ration makes it more and more difficult for the musicians to gather for such rehearsals. Consequently I am compelled to correct the parts myself note by note which takes an awful amount of my time. I was most anxious to do it myself as I could not entrust anyone with this arduous task. Besides I have promised to you to deliver it in perfect shape. So now you can go ahead in confidence. . . .

[*Original in English*]

STRAVINSKY TO VOIGT   *February 15, 1943*

. . . Mr. Stokowski called on me and I indicated all the necessary directions of performance of my Symphony in C.[5] At the same time I gave him my own and only copy of the orchestra score as your copy was mailed to you together with the complete orchestra set the day before. Kindly take my copy (black binding) after performance and mail it to me, duly insured.

Please let me know by return mail, better still wire me, the exact time of performance of the broadcast and do not forget to mention the corresponding time here on the coast. . . .

[*Original in English*]

STRAVINSKY TO VOIGT   *August 30, 1943*

. . . *Circus Polka:* I am in complete agreement with your proposal to publish the orchestra score in facsimile. I do not understand, however, why you ask me to send my manuscript, when you have plenty of copies. . . . [It is true that] my calligraphic manuscripts resemble those of no other author. Thus I await your reply on this question.

Danses concertantes: I am still waiting for my author's copies of the orchestra score, which was finally printed. As for the two-piano reduction, Mr. Dahl (whom I telephoned this morning) has not yet received the proofs. Have they been lost?

That is all for today. But . . . not quite. Since you now have the complete catalogue of my works, would it be too much to ask you to reply on my belief to the attached ASCAP survey? You would do me a great service; I do not have the list at hand, and, moreover, I am a little tired (heat and work), so starting tomorrow I plan to take a one-week vacation. Perhaps Mr. Mendel would attend to this. . . .

STRAVINSKY TO HUGO WINTER   *September 5, 1943*

. . . *Circus Polka:* You will find enclosed herewith my original manuscript of its symphonical orchestra score in pencil. Please send me it back as soon as you will finish with photographing it, duly insured.

Danses concertantes: Ingolf Dahl is already working on the proofs of the two-piano arrangement. The published orchestral scores did not yet reach me. . . .

---

[5] Stravinsky wrote to Vittorio Rieti on March 10: "I just heard a new Leopold Stokowski arrangement on the radio. First Bach, now it is Mussorgsky's turn: *A Night on Bald Mountain* and *Pictures at an Exhibition* were not enough for him (or for Rimsky and Ravel); this time it's *Boris Godunov! Boris Godunov*, Symphonic Synthesis by Leopold Stokowski. 'Symphonic Synthesis'! What a clever idea to give a vulgar potpourri such a title. At least the title sounds good. Poor Mussorgsky has no luck; what a

I will conduct the Ode at Boston Symphony the 13, 14, and 15 of January 1944. . . . [At] the end of the month I will start my tour beginning with New York and conducting [*Petrushka*] in the Metropolitan Opera House the 4th and the 6th of November. . . .

[*Original in English*]

STRAVINSKY TO WINTER   *September 8, 1943*

Just a note to ask you to grant Nicolas Nabokov's request to borrow the orchestra scores of my most recent compositions (Symphony, *Norwegian Moods, Polka,* Ode) for a week or two. He is in the process of writing an important article about these compositions for *Harper's,* and you would do our common cause a great service by placing this music at his disposal. . . . I just received the proofs of *Danses concertantes* (two-piano) from Mr. Mendel, and I still await my author's proofs of the orchestra score. Mr. I. Dahl, to whom I gave these proofs, is going to correct them and send them directly to Mr. Mendel.

STRAVINSKY TO WINTER   *September 23, 1943*

Just this moment I received a telegram from the Boston Symphony that Koussevitzky is going to give the premiere of the Ode on October 8, which is in two weeks.

I hope that you will have time to extract the parts from the transparencies (master copy), which I just sent off to you one minute before receiving the telegram. . . . If you send [the material] by special delivery, Boston will receive it on the morning of the 4th. Please do not forget to enclose this set of my photostatic orchestra score (with my corrections in red pencil), which you will find in the envelope containing the transparencies.

Did you receive a request for the Ode from the Boston Symphony? The telegram I just received came as a complete surprise to me, since I was planning to give the premiere myself in my guest-conducting engagements in January. I advised Koussevitzky of this in my letter of a few days ago and gave him my program for these concerts.

STRAVINSKY TO WINTER   *September 24, 1943*

Attached you will find the transparencies of the Ode, which I have checked. Thus you can go right to work and print the desired number of negatives. I did

---

decided irony that this is the music that arrangers have concluded sounds bad. The honorable speaker of the South[ern] California Gas Company–sponsored Evening Concerts candidly explains that Stokowski composed this Synthesis from Mussorgsky's original text. But so did Rimsky! This piece, with its Soviet brio, destined to excite American listeners, will surely be a big success with Shostakovich."

not have this done here, because I did not know how many string and wind parts you intend to print. The transparencies cost me $36.80, which I would like you to add to the $500 that will be coming to me by contract. . . .

Along with the transparencies you will also find a copy of the photostatic positive of the Ode, like the one I had sent to you but including corrections (in red). Please ask Mr. Mendel to insert all of my corrections into your score and then to return my copy to me.

I hope that you received my manuscript of the *Circus Polka,* which I sent on September 16. . . .

STRAVINSKY TO ARTHUR MENDEL   *October 12, 1943*

Before replying to your questions (of October 4), I would like to call your attention to a serious confusion in the string parts at the end of the Ode (page 23), which I discovered the other day while listening to Koussevitzky's broadcast of October 3 (Boston). . . .

Page 23 contains three lines of music, six measures a line. In following the broadcast with my score, I heard the orchestra play the second line (the music of the oboes, clarinet, and horn) together with the third line (music of strings syncopated by the timpani), resulting in total cacophony. Here is the cause: in my orchestra score, the bars of these measures were, unfortunately, placed too regularly, one beneath the other, and the copyist must have thought that these two lines were one. I did not notice this when I corrected the masters!!!! Unpardonable! Thus, attached you will find a new photostat of page 23, with 44 at three measures later, giving seven measures to 43 and seven to 44. . . .

Circus Polka: Since my plans have changed and I will not be coming to New York, please send me my manuscript. I will return it to you with corrections, which should not take me long, especially since I intend to play the *Polka* in my concerts in Boston (January 13, 14, 15, 1944); it is in our best interests for the orchestra score to appear before the New Year.

Danses concertantes: I am in complete agreement about calling it a "Concert Arrangement," because if we call it a "Reduction for Two Pianos" I fear that the piano-duettists will not use it. That would be a pity, for the transcription is very well done and has every right to occupy a comfortable position in the repertory of these duetti.

As for the details of the proofs of this piece, about which you corresponded with Mr. Dahl, I leave these decisions entirely up to you. . . .

STRAVINSKY TO WINTER   *October 24, 1943*

. . . The paragraph three (f) you found "vague" was motivated by reasons explained in our correspondence with [the] late Ernest Voigt concerning my European publishing conditions which, he realised, were indeed superior to the present ones. He found this "vague" formula in order to avoid embarrassing precisions. You will, I am sure, get a clear picture of this question in glancing through our exchange of letters of that period. . . .

[Original in English]

STRAVINSKY TO WINTER   *October 16, 1943*

. . . Have you heard anything about Koussevitzky's Ode performances in Boston and Cambridge? I just received a telegram from him thanking me for mine (I sent him a telegram after hearing the [radio] *broadcast* last Saturday) and saying that he played it again last Thursday in Cambridge *"with repeated success and profound impression. . . ."* So much the better. . . .

STRAVINSKY TO ARTHUR MENDEL   *October 27, 1943*

. . . *Danses concertantes:* Unfortunately, there are two important mistakes to be corrected, in ink, if possible; otherwise a small errata sheet will have to be attached to the score. . . .

Page 1 and page 105: The slurs are missing in the second measure of the violas. . . .

Page 64: In the last measure of the bassoon, the penultimate note is a B flat, not a B.

Page 110: The first two measures of the bassoon should be in the C clef.

STRAVINSKY TO WINTER   *December 3, 1943*

. . . I am going to Santa Barbara for five days and will be back at the end of next week. By then I hope to have received the manuscript of my *Circus Polka,* whose receipt I will acknowledge without delay. . . .

I am also playing the *Norwegian Moods* in the Boston concerts, just before the *Circus Polka.* You can listen to this performance on the radio on January 15 at 8:00 or 8:30 p.m.—this will make up the first part of the broadcast program. You will also hear the *Pulcinella* Suite and *Jeu de cartes* conducted by me.

I plan to come to New York on January 17 for only two days, since I must be in Chicago on the 19th to give a lecture at the university on the 20th. I will probably stay at the Ritz Towers, as I did last time. . . .

I hope that you received the Alien Property Custodian's approval for my check for mechanical rights, as mentioned in your letter of October 21. . . .

STRAVINSKY TO MENDEL   *December 10, 1943*

This note is to alert you to another mistake in the orchestra score (and probably in the parts) of the Ode: second clarinet, no. 10, page 6: the sharp signs at C and at F are missing, since the second clarinet should be playing the same notes as the first, only staccato. The first quarter-note (before this passage) is missing as well. . . .

As for the trumpet at **39** (in answer to your letter of November 1), the most practical solution would be to put the instruction "Tr. B-flat *muta* in Tr. C" at **38** on the preceding page.

I intend to come to New York the night of January 16, after my Boston concerts, and leave for Chicago on the 19th. . . .

STRAVINSKY TO GRETL URBAN   *January 30, 1944*

. . . Attached is the manuscript of my *Circus Polka,* which has made plenty of *round trips* (Los Angeles–New York) this year, unfortunately with no appreciable result, so far as I can tell. . . . What are these remaining technical difficulties you mention? Mr. Winter told me that you had to abandon the facsimile method used on Hindemith's scores because the photographic results were less than satisfactory.

Have you changed your mind again? Just take care in returning the manuscript to me, since the edges were already damaged on one of those *trips.*

I will send you the correspondence with ASCAP (the photocopy of my contract as well as a letter from D [eems] Taylor) . . . in a week or ten days. . . .

Attached you will find a letter from Mr. Rudolf Nissim of ASCAP, along with innumerable forms to be filled in about the catalogue of my works. May I ask you to facilitate this chore for me, since you have the catalogue in question and can telephone Mr. Nissim? . . .

Thank you for sending my *Firebird* Berceuse for violin and piano. This reprinting took me by surprise.

When must I send you the orchestra score and parts of my new version of the Danse sacrale (*Sacre*)? Or must you send me the contract beforehand?

Please tell Mr. Winter that I would very much like to have a copy of Hindemith's *Ludus Tonalis,* which has just appeared.

In the meantime, let me express how much I enjoyed the exquisite afternoon spent in your company. . . .

STRAVINSKY TO WINTER   *February 11, 1944*

. . . I did not know that Koussevitzky intended to repeat my whole program the other day in Boston, as you informed me. From our last telephone conversation in Boston, when he spoke with so much enthusiasm about my symphony (which he had heard for the first time) and of his plan to record my *Polka,* I thought that he was going to present my symphony once more this season but record the [*Polka*] only. So much the better if he wants to go all out. In the meantime, it would be a good idea for you to send him your *records* (Symphony, *Norwegian Moods,* and *Circus Polka*), so that he will have the document of my performance at hand, leaving no room for conjecture. Why did you prefer to send him my score of the Symphony, which should have been copied and photostated as soon as you received it, rather than one of the new copies? I am eager to have my manuscript back, as you see. I spoke to you about Alexis Haieff, who made that copy so quickly and so well; have you abandoned the idea of making pocket scores from his copy?

I just signed a contract with the New York Philharmonic to do a week of guest-conducting at the beginning of February 1945. I intend to conduct the Boston program and my *Danses concertantes* for the Sunday *broadcast*. . . .

STRAVINSKY TO WINTER   *February 15, 1944*

Just a note to accompany the orchestra score (band score) of *Circus Polka* . . . which I am sending today . . . following a request from Sergeant Robert Weatherly, U.S. Air Force Band, Bolling Field, Washington, D.C.:

> I would like to know if there is any possibility for our band to obtain by renting, borrowing, or buying the band arrangement of your famous *Circus Polka*. In as much as our U.S. Air Force Band gives regular concerts in Washington as well as weekly NBC coast-to-coast broadcasts we would like to play your music. [*Original in English*]

I have just replied, referring him to you and telling him that I am sending you the *band orchestration* by the same mail. . . .

STRAVINSKY TO KARL BAUER   *February 24, 1944*

You have sent me 6 records. . . . [In the] *Norwegian Moods* [the] first two movements, Entrada and Song, are missing; [the *Circus*] *Polka*—missing too. . . . Please, send me a new side VII with the *Circus Polka* on its reverse side, and one new record of *Norwegian Moods* with Entrada on one side and Song on the other.

I just tried to play automatically my symphony and to my utter dismay the records did not fit. It is impossible to use those records on my Stromberg-Carlson because of their slightly larger diameter (I mean your records) than the usual records of this size. I am afraid that you will have to make for me this entire set anew.

P.S. I recommend a more substantial wrapping in view of the delicate material.

[*Original in English*]

STRAVINSKY TO WINTER   *March 5, 1944*

You will be receiving a letter from Mr. Nat Shilkret concerning his proposal that I compose a piece of music (4½ minutes long) for an album of records on the text of the Bible. He wishes to reserve all ownership rights, in exchange for a payment of $1,000. Although I am not bound exclusively to your company by contract, I thought it natural, given our excellent relations, to advise him to contact you about his request. . . . I think that he would give me full freedom regarding public performances of the piece. . . .

I forgot to thank you for Hindemith's *Ludus Tonalis*, which I received, unfortunately maimed by the relentless post. If you have time, it would be very kind of you to send me another copy, securely wrapped between two pieces of cardboard. . . .

STRAVINSKY TO WINTER   *March 27, 1944*

[*Circus Polka*]:

1. I do not like the gigantic figures of the meters, and I ask you please to return these figures to their normal size. . . .

2. Remember to show the names of the instruments on every page.

3. Remember to put in the rehearsal numbers—there are thirty in this score—because, at the moment, they are missing altogether. I think that you insert these last.

4. When you have done all of this, please send me a copy to examine before the final printing. . . .

STRAVINSKY TO WINTER   *April 3, 1944*

Today I wish to discuss my new version of the Danse sacrale of the *Sacre du printemps.*

In discussing my guest-conducting concerts next year, Artur Rodzinski[6] gave me complete freedom in choosing the program, except that the *Sacre* must be excluded, since he intends to conduct it himself next season. I promised not to do the *Sacre* but took advantage of this opportunity to mention my new version of the Danse sacrale, employing deliberately vague terms. Attached is an excerpt from my letter, and his reply.

Since I was not certain of his reaction, I thought I should remain vague. Now that he has shown an interest, I will be more precise and refer him to you.

Now I will break the news that this version does not involve, as he supposes, a few changes—"*which can be put in* [*his*] *score,*" but a new arrangement, with respect to the transcription and measures (without any change in the music itself).

I will also tell him that I have put you, not Galaxy[7] (with whom I broke off relations two years ago), in charge of the exploitation of this new version.

---

[6] Rodzinski had been appointed permanent conductor of the New York Philharmonic in 1943.

[7] Galaxy Music Corporation, the New York branch of the Edition Russe de Musique.

Also, would it not be easier to send you the complete *set* of the Danse sacrale before we make any definite arrangements? Keep in mind (for our accounts) that the parts I am sending (the strings must be extracted) cost me about $100. . . .

Along with the Danse sacrale parts, I will also send a score of the Sonata for two pianos that I mentioned to you in New York and have just finished. . . .

Thank you for your letter of March 14 about Mr. Shilkret's request. I have seen him since and spoke to him in the tone you suggested. He seems to be in agreement. . . .

STRAVINSKY TO WINTER   *April 17, 1944*

Your airmail special delivery [letter] of April 11 arrived on the 15th! I awaited it impatiently, in order to give you a substantial reply, since I was only able to give you an in-principle *OK* in my last telegram.

Unfortunately, the problem of an eventual edition (*printed music*) of the piece in question is not entirely clear to me. In effect, is P[aul] Whiteman with you, A.M.P., or with another publisher? Otherwise, what relation does P. Whiteman's overture to me have to the money that an eventual publisher would pay me? . . . This point is even more obscure and incomprehensible to me than the three paragraphs that, according to your letter, constitute the conditions of the commission, but in which no mention is made of the question of a printed edition of the piece.

. . . These conditions I would find perfectly acceptable and clear, for the issues of the *advance* on the author's rights . . . and the sale of the music, for which the publisher will pay me. [If these issues were resolved] the matter could be settled immediately, even though you do not think that the Blue Network's [WOR] offer is exceedingly generous. Obviously, if you can obtain something better, I would not object, but the Blue Network's offer (down payment of $1,000 with no advance conditions) interests me more than that of Nat Shilkret, which you deem a handsome fee. . . .[8]

STRAVINSKY TO WINTER   *April 23, 1944*

I just received your letter of April 20 and hasten to reply, by letter rather than telegram, for clarity.

In rereading your two letters about the Blue Network's proposal, I see the thing exactly as I did when I wrote to you on April 17. This is to say that if you can obtain more favorable conditions (such as you mentioned) from P. Whiteman, so much the better. If he will not compromise, I have decided to accept the $1,000 he offered *as advance payment of my record royalties with the right for him in the course of a year of the first broadcast and public performance.* The sum of $1,000 comprises: (a) the $500 advance on my record royalties, to

---

[8] See *S.P.D.*, pp. 373-4.

be reimbursed as soon as the gramophone company pays me; (b) the $500 for the right to the public premiere and radio *broadcast*. In addition, I agree, following your suggestion of April 11, to give them two years to record ... the 4½ minutes of music I will compose for them. I hope that this time everything is clear. . . .

Would it be too much to ask you to tell Mr. Mendel that I need to excerpt several items from the biography that A[ndré] Schaeffner did of me, which [Mendel] has. I would be infinitely grateful if he would let me have it for a while. . . .

STRAVINSKY TO WINTER   *May 16, 1944*

The enclosed letter from P. Whiteman just received speaks for itself. I presume that you were in touch with them after our long distance telephone conversation in Santa Barbara on May 7th. Please do attend to this matter at once. . . . As to the biographical data—give them necessary items to be found in any encyclopedia which, alas, they will anyway distort. . . . I will appreciate your doing it for me as I am just in the middle of working on the *Scherzo à la russe.*

[*Original in English*]

STRAVINSKY TO WINTER   *June 4, 1944*

I finally received your letter of May 25, in which you acknowledge receipt of my letter of May 16 (*your typewriter put* "May 7"). . . .

Sonata for two pianos: Apart from the general difficulties of reserving a piano premiere, the present case is complicated by the fact that I distributed many copies of the Sonata to various musicians at the same time as to you, two months ago. Since then I have received quite a few enthusiastic letters on this subject, and thus it will be very difficult, if not impossible, for me to guarantee the virginity of this piece for the premiere, given the many months separating us from next season. It is a pity that you did not foresee this, or bring it up back at the beginning of April, when you received the work. What do you plan to do with the Sonata now? Will you make a certain number of copies directly from my manuscript to distribute to musicians, or do you intend to publish it immediately to sell? Bear in mind that I have not yet applied to Washington for the copyright. . . .

P. Whiteman: The instrumentation of *Scherzo à la russe* is nearly finished, and the contract has not yet arrived. I do not find this situation entirely normal. Also, you never told me whether he has been informed of the title, *Scherzo à la russe.* . . . Thank you for having sent him the biographical notes and photographs. By the way, which photographs were they? If they are the same ones you sent me (Mr. Bauer's), I must confess that I do not like them: they do not resemble me, and the retouching is overdone. Instead of signing the five you asked me to return, I am sending you some much better ones, five signed and three for your files. . . .

Danses concertantes: I saw Denham and Balanchine the other day. The latter told me that the dancers in the company that Rieti discussed with you (the Marquis de Cuevas's new company) are inferior to those in Denham's. Consequently, [Balanchine] is reluctant to accept the proposal to mount *Danses concertantes* on them. Moreover, he told me that in terms of business, this would not make any difference for you (us), since he (Balanchine) has persuaded Denham not to request exclusive stage rights for the composition. All the better for us, since practice has shown me that exclusivity is advantageous only for the enterprise that secures it. Furthermore, my impression is that Denham has no objection to your terms, since he would otherwise have asked me to intervene in his behalf. Thus I saw no reason to meddle in it any further. . . .

Here is the text of the telegram I just received from New York:

> Will appreciate by fastest return mail brief description *Danses concertantes* including whether programmatic or if intended for ballet. Desire your own explanation for my broadcast commentary. Thanks.

I sent [radio announcer Ben Hyams] the following reply:

> *Danses concertantes* is a suite of instrumental pieces composed in the form of a Sonata, or better still, in the form of a Concerto Grosso.
>
> The two parts entitled "Pas de Deux" and "Pas d'Action" borrowed from the choreographic terminology are none but the two principal movements of a Sonata, its allegro and its andante, constituting the kernel of a Symphony, a Concerto, a Quartet, etc.
>
> In applying choreographic titles to pieces composing my *Danses concertantes,* I emphasized the close relationship of the structural principle on which both arts are based, namely the architectural, inherent to music as well as to choreography.
>
> In spite of the fact that this work was composed without any idea of a dramatic action, be it ballet, or pantomime, this music nevertheless, by its dance and structural character, lends itself naturally to a classical choreography stage presentation. [*Original in English*]

STRAVINSKY TO MENDEL   *June 15, 1944*

I just received the proofs of the orchestra score of *Norwegian Moods.* The photostat of my manuscript—which I left with you last January after my performance in Boston—was not enclosed. I need it, for I inserted several changes that I now do not remember by heart. Please be so kind as to send me that photostat with my corrections by the next mail. Be especially careful not to confuse this photostat with the first one, which I sent to Mr. Winter when A.M.P. bought the work, and which does not contain my later corrections.

STRAVINSKY TO WINTER   *June 27, 1944*

Just a few lines to tell you in all haste that I still await the Blue Network's contract (and check) for *Scherzo à la russe*. In your letter of June 20, you explicitly
promised to send me this, as well as Billy Rose's contract.

　　With respect to the latter, I would like to warn you that Anton Dolin will be
arriving in New York and will contact you to discuss his scenario (the ballet libretto) and the title *in connection with the publishing of my music*. The title
and scenario apparently belong to him, since he is the author of the idea and its
choreographic realization. But I would not like for his rights to hinder us in any
way when we publish the music alone. The libretto involved is not complicated
or developed in the literary sense of the word; in effect, it consists of several
choreographic numbers linked together by a general literary and psychological
idea. This ensemble of numbers will form a whole, a ballet of romantic character, that will have a title and belong to Dolin. This is the point to which I wish to
call your attention. We should secure the right to use the title *in connection
with my music* without this title's becoming an obstacle in other than strictly
choreographic executions of my music, i.e., without our having to make ridiculous pecuniary sacrifices to Dolin.[9]

　　I hope that this note reaches you before [Dolin's] visit, since he left for
New York today. . . .

　　If it is not too late, please inform the printers that the beginning of *Danses
concertantes* lacks a metronome for the quarter, which should be inserted.

STRAVINSKY TO WINTER   *July 3, 1944*

Yesterday I received Billy Rose's letter-contract (a single copy), signed by him.
Today I received your letter of June 30 with three copies of that contract.

　　I have signed and hereby return these three copies to you. I signed them
despite the many lacunae I noticed, in the firm belief that these will be rectified
in the additional letter that [Rose] will send either to you or directly to me.
These lacunae are:

　　1. The term: In effect, B. Rose says at the beginning of his letter-contract:
"The score, together with all parts extracted by me, is your absolute property
and is to be delivered to you at the termination of this license." Nowhere in the
contract does he mention the duration of our agreement. Is it for one year, two
years, or forever?

　　2. The advances: There is no indication as to the date when the payment
of $2,000 and the *"additional"* $3,000 must be effected. I hope that you will
obtain the first sum right now; the second must be sent to me upon his receipt
of the orchestra score, September 20.

　　3. A confirmation that we have absolute freedom to exploit the work in the
symphonic domain would be desirable as well.

---

[9] See *S.P.D.*, pp. 374–6.

No mention is made of the piano reduction of this ballet, which is indispensable for the ballet master's choreographic rehearsals. Thus I request your authorization for me to broach the subject with Ingolf Dahl, because I will not have time to make the piano score myself, given the few weeks left before September 20 (during which time I must finish the composition and instrumentation of the work). . . .

Received a nice letter from [the duo pianists] Dougherty and Ruzicka—kindly tell them that I am very touched but have absolutely no time to write to them. . . .

STRAVINSKY TO URBAN   *July 15, 1944*

Thank you for your kind letter of the 13th and for sending the Blue Network contract. . . .

Thus I await the return of one of the copies with their signature (how bizarre that they neglected to sign), along with the check, after which you may send them the orchestra score of *Scherzo à la russe.*

I also find it strange that they did not think to mention the title of the piece, which they have known for more than a month already, in the contract.

Thank you for the news about the performance of my *Norwegians* and my *Polka* at the [Lewisohn] Stadium in the presence of General de Gaulle. Did they receive a warm welcome under Mr. [Efrem] Kurtz's baton? . . .

STRAVINSKY TO URBAN   *July 27, 1944*

. . . I am somewhat confused about the way you consider the publishing of my works.

You realize perfectly that simple multiplication of a facsimile made in a given number of copies of orchestra works (orchestra scores) resolves only the practical side of eventual performances but does not represent a real publication and a launching of works as usually done by miniature scores, piano reductions, etc., available for sale to everybody. In other words, the publisher's activity consists not solely to be an agent between the composer and the conductor, but particularly between the composer and the average buyer. For instance, I hardly could imagine to have a work like my Sonata for two pianos to be presented as a temporary photostatic publication. The same applies to the piano reductions of my ballets, as for the one I am composing. . . .

In spite of my rather long telephone conversation of yesterday (for which, incidentally, I have to apologize), I was unable to see what your intentions are in this matter of publication and how you conceive this in principle. . . .

[*Original in English*]

STRAVINSKY TO URBAN   *August 22, 1944*

Just a few words in answer to your wire. . . .

Sorry not to be able to tell you an amusing story concerning my *Scherzo à la russe* for there is no story to it. Besides if a music by itself does not take hold of the listener then an amusing story will be of no profit. Thus all I can tell you about my *Scherzo à la russe* is, as the title shows it, that it is composed in the spirit of Russian folk music, although without use of a special folk tune.

You asked me, what was my inspiration in composing it. I answer: the object of my inspiration lies, as always, in music itself and never in things exterior to the music.

[*Original in English*]

STRAVINSKY TO URBAN   *August 31, 1944*

. . . I must insist to have your propositions (project of the contracts) by return mail this time. This is particularly urgent as I completed already the composition of my ballet for Billy Rose and Mr. Ingolf Dahl completed his piano arrangement. By the way . . . I do not know the condition you consider for my [ceding the rights] of this ballet. This also seems to me rather embarrassing.

I really cannot accept to have these matters delayed any longer and I hope you will act this time consequently.

The title of my new ballet also must be decided right now in connection with the conversation Mr. Winter had with Anton Dolin who is the author of the ballet libretto. Mr. Winter promised to write me about it (his letter of June 30) but he never did it.

[*Original in English*]

STRAVINSKY TO WINTER   *September 16, 1944*

Yesterday I sent you (airmail special delivery) a complete copy of my new ballet, entitled *Scènes de ballet*, including the orchestra score and piano reduction (by Ingolf Dahl), which I ask you to deliver to Billy Rose, in exchange for his check. As you know, the remainder of the sum he owes me is $3,000.

At the same time, I am sending a copy of the orchestra score to the Library of Congress for my copyright.

I now await your contract for the ballet, which should be established under the same conditions as the *Danses concertantes*.

I also await the contract for the Danse sacrale.

I finally received the two-piano transcription of *Danses concertantes*, which spent two entire weeks in the mail!

I am sending you a packet of my photographs, to distribute to those people who constantly request autographed photographs. Not having time to reply myself, I ask you please to do me the favor of mailing out these photographs on my behalf. The recipients will have only to pay the cost of the photograph, or 25 cents each.

So the performance of *Scherzo à la russe* was not good? Who conducted it, in the end? David Diamond[10] wrote to say that he was enchanted by the piece, so I concluded that it must not have been too terribly disfigured in this performance.

Happy to hear of the great success of *Danses concertantes,* despite the ignorance and provincialism of the New York press. . . .

STRAVINSKY TO MENDEL   *September 21, 1944*

Did you receive my note concerning the Sonata for two pianos in time? I sent it on August 31. Please be so kind as to acknowledge receipt, and assure me that the corrections I pointed out were inserted.

Here is the text of that note:

. . . In the proofs of my Sonata for two pianos there are two little omissions, unless they are already corrected (I do not remember if I corrected them)— I quote:

1. Sign of repeat (of the period finishing on page 6) on the start of the Sonata.

2. Indication—"Tempo Primo"—missing on page 30 (on the 2d line).

[*Original in English*]

STRAVINSKY TO WINTER   *October 8, 1944*

In reply to your letter of October 4:

Scènes de ballet—As you know, I sent Miss Urban two orchestra scores on October 6, following her telegram of the same date. These are intended for Mr. Abravanel, who I suppose is Billy Rose's conductor, though neither you nor [Rose] has ever informed me as to who will conduct my ballet, and I am not otherwise familiar with the name Abravanel.[11] Your letter also mentions this Abravanel, who *"needs three more copies of the* Scènes de ballet *piano score."* Not very clear! First, as a conductor, why would he need all of these *piano scores,* and second, why did Miss Urban not breathe a word about *piano scores,* saying only that he needs *two conductor's scores?* In order not to waste more time, and having absolute confidence *"that I can rely on your protecting my interests fully, on this or any other work, even before the contract is signed"* (I quote you), I enclose the *master sheets of the piano score* of *Scènes de ballet.*

Contract for the Sonata for two pianos and *Scherzo à la russe*—I know that

---

[10] David Diamond (b. 1915), American composer.

[11] In fact, Stravinsky had heard Maurice Abravanel conduct two operas by Kurt Weill in Paris in 1933.

your company always takes ages to complete contracts, but in this case the time loss could really be avoided. All of the time-consuming changes are not owing so much to me as to the fact that you do not adhere to the structure of our previous arrangements, which you explained to Mr. Sapiro[12] so clearly. Let us hope that in the future things will take their normal course.

Messrs Dougherty and Ruzicka—I beg you to advise these artists that my sonata was, as you know, already played last summer in Bloomington, Indiana, by R. S. Tangeman and Nadia Boulanger. Thus their performance on October 29, 1944, at the Library of Congress . . . cannot be considered a world premiere.

When you send me the contract for *Scènes de ballet,* remember to add another $150, the amount I paid Ingolf Dahl for you (see my letter of September 16), to the $500, as well as another $100 for the material of the Danse sacrale (see my letter of April 3), which you neglected to include in your down payment for this composition. . . .

STRAVINSKY TO URBAN   *November 4, 1944*

. . . Yes, *at last,* I received your long-awaited check for $100.

The justification for this delay . . . is not, to my mind, a well-founded one. . . . In all seriousness, what logical relation exists between the $100 your company owed me and the so unexpected authorization you awaited from me to publish the orchestra score of my Danse sacrale? No relation whatsoever, in my estimation. First, it is more than evident that you never need to receive written permission from me, since you already have these rights by virtue of our contract for the score. Second, it is really too naive to think that an author exists anywhere in the world who would object to a publisher's establishing . . . a better-quality orchestra score than the one furnished by the author. Thus such an authorization from me would be of no value whatsoever to you.

This is similar to asking me for permission to do whatever is necessary to avoid the needless loss of time in the establishment of our contracts, . . . the delay in payment of amounts due, i.e., to accelerate the publication of my works. Although it is not up to me to give you such an authorization, I confess that, despite its absurdity, I would at this point be tempted to do so. . . .

[*Handwritten at the bottom*] On the advice of my agent, A. Sapiro, I did not send this letter.

STRAVINSKY TO MENDEL   *December 13, 1944*

This note is to point out a troublesome error that I have just discovered in my Sonata for two pianos. In the last measure of Piano II, before Variation IV (conclusion), on page 32, the right hand should change clef. . . .

---

[12] Aaron Sapiro was Stravinsky's Los Angeles lawyer until 1959.

A metronomic change must be introduced at Variation II, page 22: ♪ = 125 and not ♪ = 108.

Thank you in advance. Please assure me that this will be taken care of.

A.M.P. is preparing an orchestra score of my new ballet, *Scènes de ballet,* for my performances in Philadelphia and New York on February 3 and 4. For this score to pass before your perspicacious eye before my rehearsals would be highly desirable, if not indispensable. Say yes. Thank you.

STRAVINSKY TO URBAN *January 11, 1945*

In reply to your kind letter of January 8, I hasten to inform you that my wife and I will arrive on January 27 and will be staying at the Drake Hotel (Park Avenue and 56th Street).

The program I will conduct with the New York Philharmonic has been fixed as follows:

Program of February 1 and 2

> Overture to *Ruslan and Lyudmila*—M. Glinka
> Second Symphony—Tchaikovsky
>
> Ode—Igor Stravinsky
> Piano Concerto—Stravinsky
> *Norwegian Moods* and *Circus Polka*—Stravinsky

Program of February 3 and 4

> The first part is identical
>
> *Scènes de ballet*—Stravinsky
> *Norwegian Moods* and *Circus Polka*—Stravinsky

I also plan to conduct *Norwegian Moods* and *Circus Polka* in my concert of March 1, in Rochester. . . .

STRAVINSKY TO WINTER *May 3, 1945*

Too bad that only now I am writing you and even now hastily. Miss Urban undoubtedly told you about how busy I am at present.

Concerning my *Babel* Cantata I must say that this is absolute news to me. I have not heard a thing about Werner Janssen for a very long time. As to the rights of the Cantata all I can tell you now is that Mr. Shilkret has all the rights and probably has made the musical material [parts] of it. Nevertheless, the contract stipulates the possibility of an outside publisher to be approved by both parties on certain percentage conditions.

Now about Leeds Musical Corporation. Indeed, I was approached by some of their people and I believe that out of it may come something profitable for you too. As it stands now it is still in a very vague state. As soon as I know more of it I shall in due time write you.

[*Original in English*]

STRAVINSKY TO WINTER   *May 31, 1945*

. . . Concerning Dr. Walter's plans for Toronto on my behalf, as you know, all such arrangements are made through Columbia Concerts (Mr. Bruno Zirato in charge), consequently such plans must be submitted to them. I believe that they probably will be in contact with the Canadian agent, Mr. N. Koudriavtzev of Montreal; besides, you or Miss Gretl Urban have previously been in contact with that Russian gentleman.

In a few days I shall mail you the photostats of my symphonic version (orchestra score) of the *Scherzo à la russe* which I have just finished. Together with that copy I shall send you two additional ones at your expense—about four dollars which you will owe me. . . .

[*Original in English*]

STRAVINSKY TO WINTER   *July 5, 1945*

Thank you for sending me the different scores of my music which I asked for, in the letter of May 26 in which I asked you also another matter concerning my orchestration of Tchaikovsky's Blue Bird which you never answered. So I conclude that this question is dropped.

I have at hand a letter from Zirato telling me that you have never contacted him about Dr. Walter's proposition for Toronto. Yet in my letter of May 25 I have asked you to get in touch with Zirato on that matter. It appears that Zirato is waiting to hear from you and you are waiting a word from him. Something must be done to change that state of things which causes only one thing—loss of precious time. Please do not wait longer but attend to it, we have already lost a month.

P.S. You have not acknowledged the receipt of the photostatic copies of *Scherzo à la russe* of which the few additional ones cost me exactly $5.00 according to the bill. Do not forget to mail me this big amount.

[*Original in English*]

[*Stravinsky's handwritten outline of what he intended to say to Gretl Urban over the telephone*].

August 20, 1945

1. Denham (a) See no reason to change the condition for the past year. He should pay according to signed agreement.

        (b) For a new year we could request $25 per performance (maybe guarantee too?).

2. Symphony (a) I have finished it and will [send it] to you now.

        (b) Please send me the contract and check for $1,000, according to our contract: first installment of $500 was paid, and thus . . . $1,000 remains to be paid to me.

3. *Scènes de ballet* (a) Received the Columbia Records statement (*as artist-conductor*); have you received same for the author's royalties? My 3 percent has brought me, in the first three months (25,000 records sold), a little over $600. The 2 percent author's royalties that you should have received would amount to $400. It is a success! [Goddard] Lieberson happy?

4. Ode (a) A while ago Winter told me that as soon as the work on Danse sacrale was finished they would send Ode to the printer. Well?

        (b) Please ask Lieberson of Columbia Recording Co. when the recordings of this work will be released for sale. . . .

STRAVINSKY TO URBAN   *August 24, 1945*

. . . As for Mr. Denham, I was convinced that he would never let go of [*Danses concertantes*]; he was simply trying to intimidate you. The best strategy now would be: before allowing him to continue the performances, make him pay what he owes you for the past season or year; only then accept his new advance of $250 for ten performances and continue with the performances, paying $25 for each additional one. . . .

    Yesterday I reached an agreement with Miss Lucia Chase of Ballet Theatre, giving me exclusive rights to my orchestration of Tchaikovsky's Blue Bird.

STRAVINSKY TO URBAN   *August 30, 1945*

Enclosed is the photostatic orchestra score of my Symphony in Three Movements, whose receipt I ask you to acknowledge.

    You will surely need at least two more copies for the copyright and the copyists (extraction of the orchestra parts). Here a copy of that size costs $20 (the 107 pages of this score); in New York it would probably be more expensive. Let me know exactly how many copies you will need, and I will order them for you. . . .

STRAVINSKY TO URBAN   *September 6, 1945*

. . . Tomorrow I will send you the two other *photostatic copies* of my symphony. The title Symphony in Three Movements is preferable, and I must have been distracted when I put the word *parts* in the contract. The third movement of this symphony begins with page 68. In the two copies I am sending I have added this in ink (in Roman numerals), along with the word "attacca" at the end of page 67 in order to avoid an interruption between the last two movements.

Finally, how many performances of *Danses concertantes* have been given in the past year, and, consequently, how much did the upstanding Denham pay you, beyond the guaranteed sum of $1,200 for thirty performances?

It seems really extraordinary that a man of state as busy as General de Gaulle would think of taking my recent scores back with him to France. That could only cause pleasure.[13]

By the way, I just received a note from Darius Milhaud saying that Francis Poulenc implores me to send him all of my works that you have published during the last few years. Poulenc asks that the music be sent to him via the Foreign Affairs Office: M. Jacques Rouché, Service de la Valise, Quai d'Orsay, Paris; or via the French Embassy in Washington, addressing the package to M. J. Rouché. . . .

A week ago I sent Miss Lucia Chase (Ballet Theatre) a letter-contract to confirm our oral agreement (she visited me here during her stay in Los Angeles) concerning my reorchestration of Tchaikovsky's Blue Bird. According to this agreement, Ballet Theatre would give me exclusivity on this reorchestration. Since we discussed this at the beginning of the year, I felt I should let you know about it, and I ask you please to tell them that the photostatic orchestra score and parts may be delivered . . . directly to you and not to me, to avoid unnecessary trips. I now await their signature by return mail. . . .

I have the manuscript here.

STRAVINSKY TO URBAN   *November 10, 1945*

. . . Roger Desormière, who conducted my *Danses concertantes* so brilliantly last year in Paris, is a superb conductor and musician, and an old friend of mine and my music. So if he has requested to give the Paris premiere of my new Symphony in Three Movements (after my world premiere in New York at the end of January 1946), I see no reason to refuse. I therefore accept with joy and ask you to send him the parts as soon as possible, perhaps, once again, via the French Embassy in Washington (as with the music for Poulenc).

Why is it that the Blue Bird cannot make up its mind to fly into your arms, especially since it is so near to you, in the same house? Do you frighten it?

---

[13] De Gaulle had called A.M.P. when he was in New York and requested copies of the two-piano scores of *Circus Polka* and *Danses concertantes* and the miniature score of *Four Norwegian Moods*.

STRAVINSKY TO WINTER   *April 8, 1946*

Just this word in answer to your very kind letter of April 5. Indeed, the pianists Gold and Fizdale wrote me on the same subject some days ago but did not mention the *Scherzo à la russe;* they spoke only about the Sonata (and also about Five Easy Pieces, J. & W. Chester, London), but, never mind, I answered them I am glad they recorded the Sonata (and now also the *Scherzo à la russe* of course, why not, after all!). Otherwise, I don't see obstacles whatsoever. . . .

[*Original in English*]

STRAVINSKY TO URBAN   *June 4, 1946*

This note is to tell you that I will give two concerts (same program) with the Orquésta Sinfónica de Méjico in Mexico City at the end of July.

Among the compositions making up this program (which I sent [to Mexico] today) are my Symphony in Three Movements, *Scènes de ballet, Scherzo à la russe,* and *Circus Polka,* all published by A.M.P. Please be so kind as to contact the manager of the Orquésta Sinfónica de Méjico, Mr. José Rojas Garciduenas (Isabel la Católica 30, Mexico D.F.), giving him the details about rental of the scores and sending him, without waiting for the rest of the parts, the piano part of the Symphony, so that their pianist will have sufficient time to learn this difficult part before the rehearsals.

I leave for Mexico on July 15, returning on August 4. . . .

STRAVINSKY TO URBAN   *June 27, 1946*

I just received the orchestra score of my Symphony in Three Movements . . . and I thank you.

Nevertheless, I must admit that the provisional photostat came as something of a surprise, since I was expecting to receive a number of little pocket scores. When will you publish them? I know that there is a great demand among musicians, especially since the recordings will be released around the end of November or beginning of December.

When may I expect the final publication, in normal format? . . . Because, I repeat, the score I have just received is nothing more than a provisional edition, . . . in its general appearance, its awkward layout (too big for the conductor's stand), and the thickness of the pages (which makes them difficult to turn while conducting). . . .

Tell Mr. Mendel that I received the proofs of the Ode (finally). . . .

May I ask you to send my pocket scores and an old copy of the Symphony in Three Movements to Mr. Nicolas Nabokov, ODIC/OMGUS APO 742, c/o Postmaster, New York, New York . . . who is a colonel with the official American mission and has been in Berlin for many months? He has implored me to send him my music, of which he has been deprived for so long. Apart from the favor to him, this could perhaps be useful propaganda over there for my recent works. If possible, also include the Sonata and the Elegy.

STRAVINSKY TO URBAN   •   *September 1, 1946*

. . . The Denham question (*Danses concertantes*): I do not see the reason why you make it look as if the fulfillment of the contract . . . has to be referred to me. I do not think it is in your interests. It also creates the situation where I might have strained relations with him . . . because I certainly would refuse to give him any new concessions. To tell you the truth, the so-called friendly relations with Denham serve only for his benefit, as he mainly uses them for bargaining. . . .

[*Original in English*]

STRAVINSKY TO URBAN   *November 6, 1946*

Attached is a letter from the conductor Mr. Victor Desarzans [of Radio Lausanne], which I just received this instant. Please read and return it to me. I ask you to reach an understanding once and for all with the Chappell Company so that the orchestra parts of *Scènes de ballet* may be delivered to Mr. Desarzans without delay.

    You must admit that the facts of which Mr. Desarzans informed me were unacceptable, as was the total absence of any report, which Chappell is obliged to give me by virtue of our tripartite contract. I think that there may have been a breach of contract. If I do not receive satisfactory answers this time, I will be forced to put this matter into the hands of my lawyer and have him break the contract. . . .

STRAVINSKY TO URBAN   *November 27, 1946*

You say that the "accounting of $551.76 is solely for U.S. rights due on *Scènes de ballet,* as per statement attached to the check," which is not entirely the case, because Elegy (with 3-cent royalties—somewhat comical in itself) is also mentioned, thus contradicting your statement. Moreover, this statement offers no details as to the kind of mechanical rights, sums collected, commission retained, etc.; in short, this is not a detailed statement such as I would need to . . . exercise control. Further, there are other compositions (aside from *Scènes de ballet*), such as the Sonata for two pianos and the *Scherzo à la russe* (not to mention the Elegy), whose performance Chappell is managing abroad, in Europe and elsewhere. . . .

STRAVINSKY TO URBAN   *February 6, 1947*

This morning I received a letter from Mr. Victor Desarzans, asking me to support his request for the parts of my Symphony in Three Movements, which he has placed on the program in Winterthur (Switzerland) for March 26, 1947. Thus I ask you please to make certain that this material is delivered to him on time. Thank you in advance. His performance of *Scènes de ballet* enjoyed great success in Geneva. As you recall, it was thanks to your intervention that the material arrived on time for that performance, and I hope that your intervention will have the same decisive effect on this occasion.

The recordings of *Perséphone* (my broadcast of January 15 on "Your Invitation to Music") arrived from A.M.P. this morning. Is Mr. Fassett[14] the one who asked you to send them to me—he promised I would have them upon my return—or is A.M.P. responsible?

Have you done whatever is necessary with regard to your Paris representatives (Eschig?) so that the orchestra parts of all of my music . . . will be waiting for me? My first concert in Paris is scheduled for May 18—I will play my Symphony in Three Movements. . . .

STRAVINSKY TO URBAN   *February 15, 1947*

. . . Mr. Ralph Hawkes has written to me from London asking whom he must address for the rights for choreographic performance of my *Scènes de ballet* . . . in Covent Garden.[15] Must this be done through Schott, or must such arrangements be concluded directly through Chappell and Co. in London? I would be much obliged if you would reply by return mail, because Mr. Hawkes asked me to answer immediately. . . .

STRAVINSKY TO URBAN   *August 17, 1947*

. . . Is it Hugo Strecker who does such a terrible job of attending to my recently acquired works, or are the old bureaucrats of Schott & Co. in London to blame? Little does it matter who is at fault, as long as this is settled as soon as possible. Could you send the parts [of the Symphony in Three Movements] to Venice, since you have quite a few sets? Be kind and help them, because this performance is of some importance, and the conductor (Roger Desormière) is very good.

Did you receive the statement [about the Symphony in Three Move-

---

[14] James Fassett produced the CBS late-night "Your Invitation to Music" broadcast.
[15] Choreography by Frederick Ashton, decor by André Beaurepaire, first presented on February 11, 1948, by the Sadler's Wells Ballet with Margot Fonteyn and Michael Somes. Ashton attempted in this ballet to create floor patterns that would be equally effective when viewed from any angle.

ments] from the Columbia Recording Co., showing that a substantial number of records has been sold?[16]

Your two letters have been received, and I thank you sincerely. Only through these did I learn of the change at A.M.P. I was not notified by A.M.P., which would, it seems to me, have been natural after many years of close professional relations. Well and good that you are again at the helm of A.M.P., with whom I continue to deal, although the bulk of my compositions published by them was purchased last year by Schott of London.

I appreciate your readiness to cooperate with me. I shall take advantage of it when needed.

Thank you also for your energetic measures in sending my symphony to M. Desormière in Venice. Undoubtedly it is by now in his possession. I know that he will present it as brilliantly as he did at the European premiere in Paris about a year ago. . . .

---

[16] Apropos of the Symphony, Stravinsky wrote to Vittorio Rieti on September 23: "Frankly, I am not enthusiastic about the plan you describe [to use the Symphony in Three Movements for a ballet]. I would not like for [Todd] Bolender and [Corrado] Cagli to interpret this as a sign that I lack confidence in them. On the contrary. I like their work, and I like both of them personally. My apprehensions are of a distinct order: the problem is the music, i.e., the execution of this music in ballet performances, which, alas, have ceased to be of an acceptable caliber. Thus I would not like to see my music, written for concert performance (in which, from time to time, we still have decent renderings), *to be played in the pit and backed* by a spectacle (good as it might be), for which my music was not intended."

Stravinsky's letters to his publisher Boosey & Hawkes, Ltd., for the years 1946–68, constitute the largest segment of his business correspondence. The principal value of these communications is in the composer's revelations about the development of his works in progress; his intentions concerning the performance of his music, new and old; and his projects and plans, whether or not fulfilled. The letters also offer a glimpse of Stravinsky's daily life, musical and otherwise. Most important of all, they illustrate some of his essential qualities: meticulousness and immense vitality, not to mention the incredible creativity.

Partly for reasons of space, only excerpts are offered here, and these from less than a quarter of Stravinsky's letters. Another reason for the abridgement is that an ample portion of most communications is devoted to details regarding contracts; commissions; royalties; concert, radio, and television fees; the minutiae of correcting proofs—none of them matters of general interest. Yet these snippets amount to a surprisingly comprehensive biography of the composer's everyday world in his American years.

Addresses are given only when relevant. The majority of the letters were sent to members of the London branch of the firm—the location of the editorial and central business offices—but a great many were sent to New York, and a few directly to Paris and Bonn.

English is the original language of the letters except where otherwise indicated. (In the 1960s Stravinsky resorted to Russian to discuss his banking affairs, as if this would conceal them from the United States tax authorities.) He corrected proofs in French or German, according to whether the engraving was being done in Würzburg or Paris. A few "silent" orthographic corrections have been made. I have not identified the obtrusion, in 1951–54, of the alien voice of Andre Marion, Stravinsky's son-in-law and time-to-time secretary, since his mixture of jargon, cliché, and off-target metaphor clearly distinguishes his communications from the composer's ("Thank you for the 'low-down' on the . . . 1951 income." "Mr. Stravinsky . . . has no time to let himself be bothered by the Smithes and Joneses of music").

Serge Koussevitzky telegraphed to Stravinsky, December 3, 1945, that Ralph Hawkes would be in Los Angeles beginning on December 15 and asked the composer to meet with the publisher, who had just purchased Koussevitzky's Edition Russe de Musique. Hawkes met the Stravinskys in Los Angeles on Decem-

ber 28, *the day that they became American citizens. Having acquired the pro-*
prietorship of most of Stravinsky's music of 1912–34, Hawkes also wanted to
publish the new and future works. He offered the composer a yearly retainer of
$25,000, as well as a bonus for earnings above that sum. An agreement was
reached, but not immediately, and until 1947 Stravinsky was free to publish
new works wherever he chose.

In April 1946, G. G. Païchadze, director of the Edition Russe in Paris,
came to the United States to assist Koussevitzky in preparing an inventory of
the Galaxy Music Corporation, the New York branch of the firm, and to try to
obtain an accounting for the war years. Here are passages from three of
Païchadze's "American" letters to Stravinsky, April–June 1946 (originals in
Russian):

I have been in America for more than a week now. . . . Since the French have
made it so arduous to get a visa, it was very difficult for me to come here. . . . I
had to negotiate for half a year before finally obtaining permission for the
trip. . . . I am sure you will be interested to learn that just before leaving Europe, I placed *The Nightingale* on next season's agenda of the Royal Opera in
Copenhagen. . . .

You probably know that our firm was badly battered in Germany during
the war, and that now we are faced with the task of rebuilding all that we lost in
the bombings. . . .

When I return to Paris, I will attend to your London account. A sum of
money accumulated for you there during the war (actually quite a bit, I think).
But until now it has been practically impossible to transfer significant amounts
out of England. . . .

Europe should hold no [pecuniary] interest for you. We were forbidden to
arrange any performances during the occupation or during the war. Since the
liberation, performances have increased, but the income from these will all go
to the account for 1946. Incidentally, when Svetik [Soulima] was having difficulties, I paid 10,000 francs to him out of your European accounts. . . .

Musical life in Europe, particularly in Paris, is returning to normal, but
very slowly so far. Many requests for music are addressed to us, but as yet we
have no way to cope with them adequately. I am not just referring to the sale of
scores, which is hampered by a lack of paper and the loss of the old warehouses
during the war, but also to concerts. The public attends enthusiastically, but
what they hear is not terribly interesting. . . . Requests for Russian music,
especially Soviet music, are very numerous indeed. [April 4, 1946]

I was away in New York and have only recently returned. I made all the arrangements for transferring the $2,000 to you, which I hope you received
promptly.

Thank you for sending the copy of the Alien Property Custodian's letter: I
will write to my lawyer in New York and enclose the copy, but its contents will
not be news to him. He has already been notified that Galaxy paid the Custo-

dian only for the Mussorgsky-Ravel *Exhibition,* since that work is copyrighted and is subject to the copyright laws.

The situation with Galaxy is complex. I will try to explain it to you briefly. When America entered the war, a law was passed here amounting to a freeze on all alien properties, which then came under the jurisdiction of an Alien Property Custodian. Without permission from the custodian, nothing could be touched or returned. Thus Galaxy began to regard itself not as *our* agent but as the Custodian's. For the time being, it is impossible for us to demand not only our money but also our orchestra scores. I already informed Galaxy that we no longer consider them our representative, instructing them to transfer their representation to our new agents, Boosey & Hawkes. Galaxy is ignoring these instructions, still claiming to be responsible only to the Custodian. . . .

This state of affairs will continue until another bill is passed and implemented, removing the freeze on alien properties. According to my lawyer, one such bill has gone to Congress but will not even be drafted in proper form for another month. Only then will our lawyer be able to demand the release of our property from Galaxy. . . .

To your second question, I can answer that I did not bring any contracts to America with me, because I had not expected to do accounts here. Our practice was to do them in Berlin, but now they will be done in Paris, as soon as I receive the information. . . .

As I said in my earlier letter, nothing of any significance for you has happened in Paris during these last six years, since almost all performances of Russian music were forbidden during the occupation, and any pittance earned for the new performances that *were* permitted had to be sent directly to Berlin.

I cannot give you any information right now about Disney's payment for the *Sacre;* I do not have Galaxy's account of it with me, and I cannot remember much about it offhand. When I return to Paris, I will look into it and let you know. . . .

I am extremely pleased that your musical work is "beyond reality," as you wrote. That is how it should be. Reality can change ten times, but what you create must remain. You are so right: "What has any of this got to do with music?" (April 21, 1946)

I have managed to settle business matters with Galaxy, negotiating all controversial questions and obtaining from them all accounts for recent years. We will have to wait a little while for the money they owe us, since that issue depends on the Alien Property Custodian. Because our firm was German based, the money cannot be paid to us without the Alien Custodian's authorization. Our lawyer will argue for the release of the money on the grounds that although we published in Berlin, our sole owner is an American citizen, Sergei Alexandrovich [Koussevitzky], and so the firm must be considered American property. . . . The $1,000 advance you received from Galaxy, coupled with the $2,000 that I sent you, constitutes almost the entirety of your bonus, but I will give you an exact accounting from Paris. . . .

We have parted company with Galaxy, and beginning next season we will be represented in America by Boosey & Hawkes, 668 Fifth Avenue, New York 19.

Sergei Alexandrovich, Olga Alexandrovna,[1] and Henrietta Leopoldovna[2] have asked me to give you and Vera Arturovna their very best regards. [June 20, 1946]

After reaching an agreement with Stravinsky to republish his Edition Russe repertory as well as to publish all new works, Ralph Hawkes installed Betty Bean in the New York office. He had introduced her to Stravinsky in 1946, before she was associated with the company. In 1950 Hawkes died suddenly, which left his inexperienced young friend in the difficult position of supervising the publication of a large number of Stravinsky's works in his newly revised editions, as well as preparing the scores and parts for the String Concerto, Orpheus, the Mass, *and* The Rake's Progress.

When Bean left the company in 1952, Stravinsky's main correspondents were Erwin Stein, the senior editor, and Ernst Roth, neither of whom had even met Stravinsky. In 1958 Stein, Schoenberg's pupil, died, and Leopold Spinner, Webern's pupil, became Stravinsky's principal editor. Among the other members of Boosey & Hawkes to whom Stravinsky's letters are addressed are David Adams, Hans Heinsheimer, Sylvia Goldstein, Rufina Ampenoff, Edgar Bielefeldt, Mario Bois, Hans Swarsensky, Robert Holton, and Stuart Pope.

Stravinsky's marginal comments on many of the letters from *Boosey & Hawkes cannot be reproduced, if only because they are too unflattering ("senseless," "what a people"). Still another important omission is that of the memos he kept on his meetings with members of the company's staff, ranging from a simple reminder about a discussion of a Mr. Arthur Ehrlich's proposal to film* Oedipus Rex *(New York, April 25, 1952), to a receipt for delivery of a copy of the Epitaphium manuscript to David Adams (Hollywood, June 17, 1959).*

STRAVINSKY TO RALPH HAWKES   *August 15, 1946*

I would like to add that I just finished my Concerto for string orchestra written for the Basler Kammerorchester (Paul Sacher), the work I told you about the last time I saw you. The parts will be ready by the end of the month and I shall mail the whole thing to you to be shipped to Switzerland immediately.

---

[1] Koussevitzky's last wife.

[2] Henrietta Hirschman, sister of Paul Léon, who was James Joyce's secretary in the late 1930s and a close friend of Vera Arturovna Stravinsky in France and later in America. Madame Hirschman had known Stravinsky since 1905, and her letters to him are of considerable interest.

STRAVINSKY TO HAWKES   *August 27, 1946*

I just received a letter from Massine, in addition to our cable exchange. Unfortunately he repeats again his senseless and very naive appeal for my permission to perform *Petrushka* ... by a reduced orchestra. Of course he is unable to specify how, correctly, the reduction will be made, ... the only thing I ought to know; instead of which he continues to name the number of players in the pit, which in itself does not illuminate anything. He argues, quite awkwardly, saying that *Petrushka* had a great many performances with reduced orchestras, mentioning, as an example, the pitiful Hurok performances, as if I ever approved of those. To tempt me, he points out, on behalf of Dr. Braunschweig [*sic*] (who is this gentleman?),[3] that this show will bring me £3000 a year. Cautiously he does not say anything about the question of taxes ... gross or net, nor the planned run of the show. Also he never mentions whether they use the whole of *Petrushka* or just one part, as you inform me. I believe that ... they will not leave me in peace, so I decided, in order to have no responsibility in their machinations with my score, to grant the permission under the following condition: they will have to print in the program of the show this notice: "In view of the limited seating capacity in the orchestra pit the present reduced orchestration of *Petrushka* is made with the permission of the composer but without his knowledge and without his actual participation in this arrangement." Besides, I am including a copy of my reply to Massine in this letter.[4]

STRAVINSKY TO HANS HEINSHEIMER   *February 7, 1947*

Just yesterday I shipped you three copies of my Basler String Concerto together with the full orchestra score (157 black negative pages) of the new *Petrushka* orchestra version which Mr. Hawkes also requested. ...

   Returning home from my concert tour I find a cable from Paul Sacher sent after the premiere of this concerto with the Basler Kammerorchester (January 21). ...

   I will perform it myself in Paris, on June 19, in my Paris-Radio concerts.

STRAVINSKY TO HEINSHEIMER   *February 19, 1947*

I met in San Antonio Fritz Reiner and I spoke with him about my Basler String Concerto. He was very anxious to have the American premiere of it and I prom-

---

[3] Julian Braunsweg, manager of de Basil's Original Ballet Russe.

[4] Stravinsky and Massine had misunderstood each other; the choreographer wished to use Stravinsky's 1946 version but had been wrongly informed that this required forty-five, instead of sixty-eight, players. Stravinsky's letter to Massine begins: "In answer to your Russian letter of August 21, I am typing in English because I address this letter not only to you but also to your associates. ... I wish people to understand that the

ised to write you about it. Indeed I would be glad if the thing could be arranged with him. He is a wonderful musician and such a fine technician.

STRAVINSKY TO HEINSHEIMER

February 24, 1947
[Telegram]

Object staging these suites therefore declining theater offer.[5]

STRAVINSKY TO HEINSHEIMER   *March 14, 1947*

This is to tell you that I am not going to Europe this year. Although I have no worry about my health, I have to be careful . . . for my present work (*Orpheus*); being entirely absorbed by it [does] not allow me to undertake this year such an important thing as my European concert tour. So I postponed this tour to the next year leaving only my Washington (Dumbarton Oaks, April 25) engagement unchanged. I therefore shall be in New York for my rehearsals April 23d. . . .

Other thing. Don't you think your negotiations with Mitropoulos (premiere of my Basler String Concerto) could easily set Fritz Reiner against us because he was so anxious to get this premiere himself. . . . [Also,] he told me about his intention to have me the next season in Pittsburgh as guest conductor.

STRAVINSKY TO HEINSHEIMER   *March 29, 1947*

I will be in New York on April 23 rehearsing for my Washington concerts (April 25 and 26), and back in N.Y. April 27 for recording (*Dumbarton Oaks* Concerto). Staying probably at the Ambassador Hotel. . . . May I ask you to . . . fix for Mrs. Stravinsky and myself a double bedroom for April 23 and 24 (going to Washington April 25th in the morning), as well as for the last four days of April.

STRAVINSKY TO HAWKES   *April 18, 1947*

No European trip this year. . . . I feel relieved of great anxieties—the relief is quite indispensable for my work now and I am already nearing two thirds, to be exact, of *Orpheus*. . . . I do hope we shall continue on "speaking terms." . . .

Heinsheimer wrote me that you are returning to the States in May. I would ask you a little favor of getting me a dozen of those toetips (label en-

---

number of players does not mean anything; it is not the number but the way the instrumentation is made, which is the really important thing."

[5] Jerome Robbins had wanted to choreograph the Two Little Suites (the orchestrated versions of the Eight Easy Pieces) for Ballet Theatre. Stravinsky's objection seems to have been that the music was in the public domain.

closed) unknown here. Such a comfort not to tear the socks. Obtainable, as I remember, at Austin's on Regent Street. Will you also oblige me in bringing with you the English Columbia Records of my *Histoire du soldat,* also not to be found here.

STRAVINSKY TO HAWKES   *May 11, 1947*

Your reaction to Frederick Ashton's desire to lengthen *Scènes de ballet* is absolutely right because [no] . . . such thing can be done with any of my works.

The new English Opera Group is indeed very welcome. I am also looking forward to Britten's *The Rape of Lucretia* here in California and will be glad to be with you on its production this summer. Do come. . . .

May I ask you to inquire concerning Columbia Records statement which I did not have since 1939.

STRAVINSKY TO HEINSHEIMER   *June 2, 1947*

As to *Orpheus,* . . . 6 1st violins, 6 2nd violins, 5 violas, 4 v-cellos, 3 c-basses. This string section is in its number a MINIMUM. It could be augmented if there is a place in the pit.

STRAVINSKY TO HAWKES   *June 23, 1947*

What a shock, the leaving of Hans Heinsheimer. . . .

I must tell you that there are some small but important revisions and some changes in *Apollo.* Fortunately I have a photostatic copy of its orch. score and could send it to you corrected with annotations in red ink easy to compare with the old score. . . .

As to Chicago Opera Theater project I have already a wire from them, their manager, Harry Zelzer, telling me about projected staging of *Mavra, Histoire du soldat, Pulcinella,* asking me to conduct early October. I wired that I could conduct at that time asking for all details of the presentations. . . .

Last week I attended the Westcoast premiere of *Lucretia.* Strictly *entre nous* the presentation was *very* amateurish. Hope that the Chicago one was to the contrary.

As to composing a new operatic work, you are right—impossible for some time to come. As soon as I finish *Orpheus* I have to complete my Mass. . . .

I will be in New York in April and probably sail to Europe in May (beginning) for 3 or 4 months. . . .

P.S. Has Ingolf Dahl seen you before his sailing for Sweden?

STRAVINSKY TO HAWKES   *July 4, 1947*

The Ballet Theatre (Lucia Chase) . . . has in its possession my personal complete set of parts & score of *Apollo* and Lucia Chase continues to perform this ballet. I made with her an arrangement some years ago (ignoring Galaxy, a delightful feeling!) according to which a guarantee of $200 for a minimum of ten performances a year was paid out. . . . But the . . . agreement expired in May 1947. . . .

Pulcinella. . . . The orchestra set (parts & score) of this Suite is indeed in the possession of the Monte Carlo Ballet and Mr. Denham who got it from Galaxy is using fragments of it in his performances of a ballet entitled *Commedia Balletica* (what a ridiculous title!). Mr. Denham told me that he has never paid any royalties (performing or rental fee) to Galaxy for it (how did he manage it with Mr. Kramer I would like to know—it looks like an authentic miracle) thus owing you* a lot of money, I presume, because there were a lot of performances of this *Commedia Balletica* the last two years and Mr. Denham continues to play it everywhere. As to my personal set of parts (with transparent masters of strings & ordinary copy of the rest) which I ordered to my copyist the last year for my concert tour (ignoring Galaxy, a delightful feeling!) I have paid for it $255.97. If you wish to profit of it for your library, I would be glad to sell it to you just as the material of *Apollo*. . . . You also ought to know that the *Klavierauszug* of the complete ballet of *Pulcinella* is the property of J. & W. Chester Ltd., London. Strange situation, one would say, but it is just so. When in 1919 I composed *Pulcinella* and made a contract with the late O. M. Kling for a series of works I composed during the years of the first world war, he, O. M. Kling, was also interested in purchasing *Pulcinella's Klavierauszug,* the orchestra score did not interest him at all—*de mortuis aut nihil aut bene*—so I included this *Klavierauszug* in my contract with him (Chester) and some years later sold the orchestra score to Koussevitzky.

Baiser de la fée. Speaking about Denham, I would tell you that he also is in possession of the complete orchestra material of this ballet (orchestra parts and a written copy).** . . .

Divertimento. That is the title of the Suite of *Baiser de la fée.* There is a printed score (orchestra) and I got it recently from my library in Paris together with the full orch. score of *Pulcinella,* its suite and the full orch. score of my opera-buffa *Mavra.* Within two months, in September I have to record this Divertimento here for RCA-Victor with whom I just signed a three years exclusive contract. . . .

* He, Denham.

** The orch. score was never published by Païchadze (*sic!*). . . . Can you procure it? It is imperative to publish it and to reprint its *Klavierauszug* as soon as possible.

STRAVINSKY TO HAWKES   *August 4, 1947*

Before your Bermuda trip I sent you as required the corrected (in red) *Apollo* photostatic score and the whole *Pulcinella* orchestra score which was duly acknowledged by Harold Winkler (July 22d). You also received my letter of the 4th of July with detailed notes about *Apollo, Pulcinella, Baiser de la fée* and Divertimento and you promised me a letter concerning this subject. So I am expecting it now.

STRAVINSKY TO HAROLD WINKLER   *August 5, 1947*

The orchestra material, the only one existing in U.S.A., of my Divertimento, has been sent by you to Mexico City for a performance on August 30th. I am exceedingly worried for the following reason.

   I am going to record this work . . . for RCA-Victor on September 16th and 18th, and know by sad experience that in most cases of mailing important orchestra material, the delay of delivery from Mexico to Los Angeles is unbelievably retarded, causing tragic situations for its performances at a definite date. . . . Bear in mind that the 31st of August falls on a Sunday, preventing shipping of material, [apart from] custom procedure on both sides. I beg of you to entrust this precious material to be shipped to a most reliable and responsible person. Will you also let me know who exactly is performing my work, Orquesta Sinfónica de Mexico (Carlos Chavez) or any other organization?

STRAVINSKY TO HAWKES   *September 15, 1947*

I am at the last pages of *Orpheus* and will mail you the copy of its full orchestra score, as well as a copy of its summary sketches (for the choreographer's use in rehearsals at the piano) before you leave for London. I want you to start immediately with its orchestra parts in order to let Lincoln Kirstein have them in good time and also to give time to your copyist for careful revision and correction before delivering the material to the Ballet Society. As soon [as] I shall finish the score you will receive a wire from me.

STRAVINSKY TO HAWKES   *September 26, 1947*

Glad to tell you that I have completed the music of *Orpheus* and will see to it that it reaches you in time before you leave for London. . . .

   I shall resume work on my Mass, which I hope to finish early next spring. Be advised that this Mass is for children and male chorus, accompanied with the following instrumentation: 2 oboes, 1 Eng. horn, 2 bassoons, 2 trmp., 3 trmb.

   After that is done I plan to begin the composition of an opera which we discussed vaguely at our last meeting. The theme will be based on William Hogarth's famous masterpiece *The Rake's Progress*. As librettist, . . . advised by my good friend Aldous Huxley whom I see frequently here, I suggest that you contact . . . W. H. Auden, whose address according to Huxley is: c/o Haverford College, Pennsylvania, where [Auden] is apparently a professor of English. Am anxious [for] you [to] do it before leaving for Europe, or we [will] have to postpone until you return. . . .

P.S. My concerts here in California are: in San Francisco on February 12th, 13th, and 14th; and in Los Angeles on March 18th and 19th. In these concerts I am planning to conduct my Basler String Concerto.

STRAVINSKY TO HAWKES   *October 7, 1947*

If you speak in your letter of a transcription of the Mass for organ, you can have it done, but naturally you did not think of adding an organ part to my instrumentation to facilitate its performance, God forbid, or it will simply turn out *à la* "Bach-Stokowski." Neither do I favor the idea of the female chorus instead of the children's voices. . . . I am afraid that once started with female chorus, never will there be a chance of having the children's voices, so infinitely precious, especially for this particular spiritual purpose. . . .

How fortunate that Mr. Auden walked into your office just at the right time. I have already written him as per enclosed copy which speaks for itself. . . .

Concerning my Symphonies of Wind Instruments, which is not a part of your Koussevitzky catalogue, . . . I have no knowledge whether Païchadze ever published it before France's debacle. Anyhow, I have firmly decided after a thorough examination to rewrite it, . . . make it easier for performers as well as for audiences, and that without sacrificing any of my intentions. I think I can have it ready by about the first of December.

STRAVINSKY TO HAWKES   *October 11, 1947*

Petrushka—You speak about the publication of the new version and the suppression of the old one. . . . I don't see really any reason to rent the old one. . . . As to the recording of this *new version by me* next April with the San Francisco Symphony, I think you are mistaken. It is P. Monteux, and not I, who should record the *old version* with RCA-Victor and with the San Francisco Orchestra next April. Unfortunately for me and for my new version, indeed. I spoke about it with Mr. [Richard] Gilbert, and I still hope he will be able to convince Monteux to let me do it myself. I think your interference in this matter could greatly help to change things in my favor. . . .

For the re-issue of *Petrushka*'s piano score, I presume you are speaking about the 4-hand score, the only one I know. . . .

Oedipus Rex—I airmailed you today my vocal score with many red-ink corrections and alterations quite sufficient to obtain a new copyright. As you probably know, the orchestra score of this important work was *never* published by Koussevitzky during the 20 years of its existence! It is imperative you publish it (as well as *Perséphone*) in, at least, a pocket score.

STRAVINSKY TO HAWKES   *October 13, 1947*

Glad *Orpheus* arrived on time. My contract or rather agreement with Lincoln Kirstein concerns only his exclusivity of its stage premiere. . . .

Don't forget to mail me the *Symphony of Psalms* for corrections and some alterations needed for a new copyright.

STRAVINSKY TO HAWKES   *November 4, 1947*

As to the argument of *Orpheus,* all the action sequences are clearly indicated in French throughout the score. It is quite easy to compile them into an explicit argument and then translate it into any language desired. Please have it done by someone at hand because I really have absolutely no time to do it myself. The reason—I am working . . . to finish my Wind Instruments Symphony for the new copyright as you know, and as soon as I finish that I will proceed with the new markings of the Psalm Symphony score, just received from your office.

As to the storm raging in the newspapers about my . . . *Firebird* theme [used in] a slow foxtrot titled "Summer Moon," I have absolutely *no* part in it. All that is put on by the loud Broadway merchants (L. Lewy & Co of the Leeds Corporation) greedy for sensation. . . . I am refuting this assertion in the press, requested by A.P. I will send you a clipping of it. However if they manage to make big profits, you will be the first to take notice of it, as Leeds has to go through you. . . .

A piece of good news to please you. I have invited Mr. W. H. Auden to be my guest in my home and am paying his flight here. I am looking forward to work with him in person, as it would have been too complicated and unsatisfactory to do it by correspondence. Will keep you posted on our *progress* [*Rake's Progress*]. Apropos this I wish you could bring me from London that remarkable publication of Byrd's work, I saw in 1937 there, [and] maybe there is a similar [edition] of Purcell. Try to find them, as I may need it as a sample of music in Hogarth's time.

STRAVINSKY TO HAWKES   *November 9, 1947*

Enclosed a formal denial concerning my . . . participation in juke boxes business. Enclosed also a copy of my letter . . . to let you know exactly all about the brazen manners of the Leeds Music Corporation, and, if necessary, to deny it on my behalf.

I mailed yesterday back to your office in N.Y. . . . the orchestra score of my Psalm Symphony with red ink notes I made there for a new copyright. . . . Mr.

Auden is coming tomorrow to spend with me a few days to discuss our fascinating project.

STRAVINSKY TO HAWKES   *November 25, 1947*

To add to my "errands," . . . I need . . . the complete record albums of the Glyndebourne Festival Co. conducted by Fritz Busch: *Così fan tutte, Don Giovanni* and *Nozze di Figaro*. Besides those I also need Handel's scores of *Messiah* and *Israel in Egypt,* if possible the orch. scores too. Also, please, try to get me the Mozart opera scores. All that is impossible to find here. . . .

I not only have completed the new version of the Wind Instruments Symphonies, but already ordered its parts. . . .

Wystan Auden spent 7 days with me in my home. . . . The text and verses, he said, would be ready by March, before his departure for Europe on 7th April.

I have to be in Washington beginning of April for my concert there on the 4th. On my return after that to New York I shall see you and Auden too.

STRAVINSKY TO BETTY BEAN   *December 10, 1947*

I have just finished a revision of an . . . arrangement I made in 1929 of Parasha's Song from my opera *Mavra*. It was already published in 1929 by Mr. Païchadze with a copyright mention, but I doubt the value of such. This new revision ought to be copyrighted at once. The reason for the haste is that a young singer, Mrs. Vera Bryner (former Pavlovsky) is engaged to make a record of my songs (J. & W. Chester Publications). One side will be open and I suggested the above mentioned Parasha's Song. Maybe you know that some years ago I . . . arranged this music for violin & piano, which I recorded previously with Dushkin and recently with Szigeti for Columbia Records. The title of it is "Maiden's Song" or "Chanson Russe." I wish to retain this same title for this present vocal piece without mentioning the opera *Mavra,* from which it is extracted—in view of the dubious copyright issued for *Mavra* itself, the note "Edited by A. Spalding" hardly [being] helpful.

STRAVINSKY TO HAWKES   *December 10, 1947*

Can you bring with you Palestrina's Masses, unobtainable here?

Wind Instruments Symphony. . . . You say that Ansermet projects to conduct it early in January. Where? In Europe or in New York, where he is expected, as I heard. If in Europe, naturally I'll be delighted if he conducts this newly revised symphony. But if you mean in New York, here is the problem. I have promised the newly organized young Chamber Arts Society (one of its programs enclosed) with Robert Craft conductor, to conduct this symphony on the program of my works in April, when in N.Y.

STRAVINSKY TO BEAN   *December 20, 1947*

Symphony for Wind Instruments. . . . It took me exactly two months to rewrite anew this intricate score. . . . Ansermet can play it in his NBC concerts (the new version . . . because the old one is to be destroyed). . . .

I was photographed together with W. Auden for *Vogue* during his stay here, at my home, by George Platt Lynes, but as yet I did not receive these photographs. Please, contact him directly, his address is: 8706 Sunset Plaza Place, Hollywood 46, Calif.

STRAVINSKY TO ERWIN STEIN   *January 2, 1948*

I think you are right in accelerating the production of *Orpheus* and to help you I would be glad to dispense with seeing the proofs because I rely on you and your house corrector. I ask you only the following: in engraving my composition, please do repeat the accidentals when they are actual [ly] notes tied between measures, as I use to mark my scores. I remind you about it because of my last experience with my String Concerto in D when your engraver intentionally omitted the repeating of the accidentals. . . .

As to your [query] concerning the missing cello and double bass notes [in *Orpheus*], you are absolutely right, but you made a mistake in figure **126**. It is not in the figure (4 measures after) **126** but in **124** where these notes are missing. So please rectify it in accordance with the bassoons, as you suggest, and it will be correct.

STRAVINSKY TO BEAN   *January 12, 1948*

I have to be back in New York a few days before going to Washington and coming back (N.Y.) where I shall be till my European trip, my departure depending upon the available ship in the first half of May. . . . [The score of] *The Beggar's Opera* just received. Thank you.

STRAVINSKY TO STEIN   *January 20, 1948*

F-sharp on the 3rd fourth of the 3rd bar after **180** [*Orpheus*] is intentionally omitted and trumpet's E (sounding D) in the next bar is also correct. As to the missing "arco" in **249**, you are right—it is to be corrected.

STRAVINSKY TO BEAN   *January 26, 1948*

String Concerto in D. Why didn't you inform me of its American premiere in Pittsburgh under Fritz Reiner Jan. 15/16? How did it come off, and what reaction in general? . . .

Oedipus Rex. When I conducted it last time in 1939/40 with the Boston

Symphony, Galaxy, at that time Koussevitzky Editions representatives, furnished the entire orchestra material and undoubtedly also its text for the narrator in English, Paul Leysac at that time. Will you inquire or look up your files of that defunct Galaxy inheritance.

   Petrushka. . . . Correct timing, *of course,* is 42–43 minutes. . . . Koussevitzky's timing is undoubtedly that of the Suite and not of the entire ballet, and the correct timing is 20 minutes and not the 17 of his performance. As to Mr. Bernstein's 33⁶ minutes duration of the entire ballet, this is his own irresponsible and unaccountable musical treatment, which I prefer rather to deplore than to explain. . . .

   Now, your last question: "will *Petrushka* Suite differ from the full ballet in duration." What a puzzle! Indeed, how can a part be as long as its whole?

STRAVINSKY TO HAWKES   *February 28, 1948*

These few words in answer to yours of 25th last. 1—For my European dates ask Mme N. D. Bouchonnet, 45, rue de la Boétie, Paris, who is my agent (Office Artistique International) and is aware about my available time (probably in July). 2—My acceptance of conducting concerts depends mainly on the number of rehearsals the organizations are able to put at my disposal for each program. The more new compositions in the program, the more rehearsing time required, as you realize. 3—The amount of money I would be able to withdraw after deductions of taxes and 15% commission to Mme Bouchonnet is also to be taken in consideration, before acceptance.

   I'm here [Mexico] till 2d March, afterwards in Los Angeles until the end of the month. . . .

P.S. Yesterday—a brilliant success of my Basler Concerto which I repeat tomorrow morning.

STRAVINSKY TO BOOSEY & HAWKES

March 22, 1948
[Telegram]

Will be Washington morning March 31 Hotel Raleigh. Completely free this day and next afternoons till 4th April. If Auden coming there already 31st am almost sure alterations could be made . . . in few days.

STRAVINSKY TO BEAN   *May 9, 1948*

Did Robert Craft already start with the corrections of the *Orpheus* printed material (score & parts)?

   Was Roger Desormière finally given permission to play 10 June *Orpheus* in Paris Radio (Nadia Boulanger's cable)?

---

⁶ Bernstein's timing is correct, not Stravinsky's.

STRAVINSKY TO HAWKES   *June 28, 1948*

Enclosed, as promised, a reproduction in negative and positive of an old drawing (XVII century) for the cover of my Mass. I came across it in one of the cata-
logues of rare books and prints sent to me from time to time. Can't remember
its origin, hope it will not arouse objections in regard to copyright.

Its negative is still more interesting for our cover and I will be glad [if] you
[agree]. Please answer before leaving.

STRAVINSKY TO BEAN   *July 7, 1948*

Answering yours of 30th June.

The Mass—I will try to see Dr. Finlay Williamson of the Westminster
Choir School. But my idea was to *conduct myself* this Mass, at least its world
premiere, and I wonder if his interest in preparing this work for someone else
(even for me, its author) would not weaken his enthusiasm in this promotion.
Besides, this (my conducting the world premiere) was precisely what we
planned with Ralph last April. Sorry you did not mention it in your parley with
Dr. Williamson, as this would have helped me in my eventual discussion with
him. As to the League of Composers sponsoring the promotion of the Mass, I
frankly cannot see any interest in this project because this would mean publicity for them rather than for me and, besides, they never had any money worth
. . . speaking of.

Orpheus—Dear Betty, do you really believe in the importance of such pla-
tonic rewards as that of the Music Critics Circle, who did not even advise me
directly. . . . When you are a little older you will get rid of all this juvenile enthusiasm.

STRAVINSKY TO HAWKES   *August 2, 1948*

Your letter from Engadine (25th July) just received. I wired you through B. &
H. London in order to let you know immediately that I don't want the Mass to
be performed by anyone until I myself establish the tradition by a definitive first
performance. I wish to arrange a performance of it as explained in my cable,
during the last week of February while I am still in New York. . . . Merely to
perform the Mass is in itself not as important as to perform it as only I know
how.

                                                                      August 2, 1948
STRAVINSKY TO BOOSEY & HAWKES   *[Telegram]*

Tell Ralph must conduct Mass myself before any performance whatsoever.
Have time New York last week February. Insist he stops all plans until see him.

STRAVINSKY TO HAWKES   *August 4, 1948*

Your cable just received, and, I must confess it confuses me very much. First, I do not understand at all what you mean by this phrase of your cable: "RE MASS DO NOT SEE DIFFICULTIES NEW YORK PREMIERE"—neither do I, as you can see from my telegram, where I explain in this phrase, "HAVE TIME NEW YORK LAST WEEK FEBRUARY." Perhaps you have other *difficulties* in mind and, in this case, please advise. Are you referring to *difficulties* of *my* tentative New York performance or of *difficulties* of *any* New York performance including that of Ansermet? . . .

As you see from my letter of 2nd August, it is not a question of my maintaining reservations about particular conductors, Ansermet and/or Milano, it is not such differences that make me anxious but the realization that the *only true performances can stem from myself.*

STRAVINSKY TO BEAN   *September 25, 1948*

Enclosed my wire of today to Eugene Ormandy in answer to his letter and a very odd wire from John Finlay Williamson, who even does not know that my Mass, as all my works now, are published by Boosey & Hawkes. Besides is Bob Craft not in touch with him and his Westminster Chorus? Isn't it strange?

STRAVINSKY TO HAWKES   *November 6, 1948*

Sacre. . . . I must know what you mean by "The new scores do not correspond to the old parts. . . ." Are *new scores* already printed? If so . . . after which one of the two existing editions (or versions). There is the old one with many mistakes, misprints, etc. which was replaced by Païchadze by a new one, unfortunately not completely corrected by me, in the 20s. I have here a big full score of the old edition with many substantial corrections and handwritten pages. This served Païchadze for the second edition. But since then I made new changes in it, and I feel very upset that I was never asked either by you or by London to help you (with this valuable old copy) in order to establish a new and correct edition for a new copyright. Too bad. I also intended to convince you to make an arrangement with the Associated Music Publishers for the new version of the Danse sacrale. . . . Although for the same large orchestra, this music, entirely re-written, is much easier to read and to play and of a definite better balance and sonority. I think it is you who must have this version and not A.M.P. . . . As for the parts, I am afraid I have nothing here. So Dorati (of the Dallas Symphony) will be obliged to postpone his performance there.

STRAVINSKY TO STEIN   *November 10, 1048*

Enclosed—my red, blue and black answers to your questions concerning my Piano Concerto.

As to *Baiser de la fée,* I wonder if you alone will be in a position to master this intricate problem.

The full orchestra score of this ballet was never published by the late Edition Russe de Musique. One of the few badly written copies now in your possession will be the only score after which you have to deal in engraving this work.

Don't think Paris can be of any help to you in giving you useful information about "corrections to be inserted" in the score which is in your library, as you say. In Paris they know exactly nothing. I am the only one who can help you, but, to do so I must have an orchestra score of the work. . . . My original manuscript is in Switzerland, and it would be rather complicated (and not safe at all) to let the volume be sent over here. . . .

As I know, one copy is at the Paris Opéra (the work is in their repertoire), another in your hands and a third one probably in Boosey & Hawkes library in New York (I myself conducted it after a badly copied score two years ago with the Monte Carlo Ballet in N.Y.).

Please, check up and tell me what do you think about it.

Will be glad to know if my Mass which you heard the other day broadcast from Milan (many thanks for your kind lines about it) was sung *by children.* I have the suspicion it was not.

STRAVINSKY TO HAWKES   *December 10, 1948*

I became an ASCAP member 25 November 1942.

Petrushka. Mr. Sapiro told me that when he had lunch with you in San Francisco, you had not yet come to any kind of an agreement with Monteux regarding his using my new version. The same evening, when you kindly phoned me from the airport here, you gave me the good news that you had managed to convince Monteux to play and record my new version. Please, tell me exactly where we stand? If Monteux is still opposed to the new score, then I will try to make arrangements with Victor to record the new *Petrushka* in full myself.

STRAVINSKY TO HAWKES   *December 17, 1948*

Baiser de la fée, Perséphone (full score). What do you mean by saying that you are "without further news"? Logically it is up to you to get this news. 1—it is up to you to have Ormandy send me the full score of *Baiser de la fée;* 2—it is up to you to have the full score of *Perséphone* sent over here from London.

And after all I do not believe it is [in] your interest that these engravings stand by waiting for my corrections. . . .

Petrushka—Monteux. I am not surprised, because knowing old Monteux, I am used not to take such "good news" at face value. Concerning the recording I am entirely opposed to have anybody use the old material, notwithstanding the matter of cost.

STRAVINSKY TO STEIN   *December 26, 1948*

Thinking again about *Baiser de la fée* I come to the conclusion that we actually don't even know if your score and the one I have just in hand are 100 per cent identical. Even [though] they [were] copied [from] the same original I cannot know what happened to them while changing hands from one ballet company to another.

If it appears to you that the best way out of all this is for me to clean up the whole score itself, the only thing to do is for you to send me your score because *I cannot send the one in my possession outside of the U.S.A.*

As I shall be in New York in February, the best thing to do is to send the score to your New York office where I will be able to go through it.

STRAVINSKY TO BEAN   *January 8, 1949*

Thanks for yours of 3 January.

O.K. for 19 February: probably between 6 and 8 will be the most convenient for me after the concert.

Enclosed a list of friends and associates you asked me to send you. . . .

Mr. Wystan Auden, 7 Cornelia Street, N.Y. Cy
Miss Mercedes de Acosta, 471 Park Avenue, N.Y. Cy
Mr. Stark Young, 320 East 57th Street, N.Y. Cy
Mr. Luc Bouchage, 32 East 62nd Street, N.Y. Cy
Mr. & Mrs. George Balanchine, 41 East 75th Street, N.Y. Cy
Miss Dagmar Godowsky, 502 Park Avenue, N.Y. Cy
Mrs. P. Kochanska, 141 East 56th Street, N.Y. Cy
Mr. Léon Kochnitzky, 925 Fifth Avenue, N.Y. Cy
Princesse Al. Krapotkin, 122 East 76th Street, N.Y. Cy
Mr. Lincoln Kirstein, 225 East 74th Street, N.Y. Cy
Mr. George Platt Lynes, 145 East 52nd Street, N.Y. Cy
Mr. & Mrs. Nicolas Nabokoff, 1350 Madison Avenue, N.Y. Cy
Mr. & Mrs. G. Pittaluga, 740 Madison Avenue, N.Y. Cy
Mr. & Mrs. V. Rieti, 312 East 66th Street, N.Y. Cy
Mr. Vladimir Sokoloff, Barbizon Plaza Hotel, N.Y. Cy
Mr. Carlton Smith, 850 Seventh Avenue, N.Y. Cy
Mr. & Mrs. Saul Steinberg, 410 East 50th Street, N.Y. Cy
Mr. Alexander Schneider, 31 Beekman Place, N.Y. Cy
Mr. Paul Tchelitcheff, 360 East 55th Street, N.Y. Cy
Mr. Virgil Thomson, 222 West 23rd Street, N.Y. Cy
Miss Kiriena Ziloti, 170 West 73rd Street, N.Y. Cy
Mr. Alexander Iolas, 25 East 56th Street, N.Y. Cy
Mr. & Mrs. Harold Shapero, 56 Clinton Place, Newton Center (Mass.)
Mr. & Mrs. R. Gilbert, 44 East 80th Street, N.Y. Cy
Mrs. Nell Tangeman, 177 East 71st Street, N.Y. Cy

STRAVINSKY TO BEAN

Received yours of January seventh. No question renounce 26 February Mass premiere for projected May concert. Craft in touch with Tietjen taking care of all problems.

STRAVINSKY TO STEIN   *March 15, 1949*

Delayed by my concert tour, this is my answer to yours of 26th January concerning *Apollo.*

First violins on the 6th bar after rehearsal number **7** in the full score are wrong (the piano score is right). Sorry, I forgot to notify you about it when I sent you my revised version. So please correct it. . . . Please correct also violin solo II, viola sola and cello solo in the 5th, 6th, and 7th bars after number **59:** only the second sixteens of each group of two slurred notes . . . must be dotted. In my score you will see that both notes under slurs are dotted and this is wrong. Same in the 3d and 4th bars after number **60** for the whole violin section (solo and altri).

STRAVINSKY TO BEAN   *March 21, 1949*

Basler Concerto. Enclosed find my own corrected orchestra score inside which I have put the pages newly engraved in London. The revisions made by Stein are OK but I have added some corrections and new improvements so I am sending the whole thing to you. . . .

Tzigane from *Baiser de la fée.* . . . Please don't call it "Tzigane Song"; call it Ballad for Violin and Piano (from the ballet *Baiser de la fée*). Give me some more time so I can put the piano part in final shape; the violin is already correct.

Suite from *Petrushka.* The numbers I take from the ballet *Petrushka* for a concert performance as a suite are the following (take in mind that the rehearsal numbers below are those of the new version, of course): One can start the suite by playing the whole First Tableau which ends with the fifth measure after **90,** mentioned "For ending." But usually one starts with number **58** till the same ending mentioned above. After this, one usually plays the Second Part of *Petrushka* from **95** till **119** (excluded). And the Third Part of the suite is the Fourth Part of the ballet which starts with number **161** until the last measure of page 164, switching there to page 172 entitled "Ending for Concert Performances."

STRAVINSKY TO HAWKES   *March 29, 1949*

Just received the proofs of *Perséphone* from Paris (A. Rabenek).[7] There was no handwritten score after which the full score was printed. . . . Tell me, also, have I to write my notes in the margins in French or in English?

STRAVINSKY TO HAWKES   *April 17, 1949*

I have received lately a pamphlet from [Ballet Theatre] where I read that they will perform my *Apollo* on 27 April and *Petrushka* 3 times on 30 April, 5 and 7 May in New York I presume. You probably already know it and are ready to watch for the use of the material of *Apollo*. As to *Petrushka* I am interested to know whether they will use our new version or perform and mutilate the old one without paying you a penny?

STRAVINSKY TO HAWKES   *April 22, 1949*

The enclosed card will show you what my surprise was when I received your catalogue without a single correction from the ones I had made. . . . The only exception is in regard to the name of your firm which is not even printed but simply stamped.

What a shame!

From now on I see I'll have to check up every detail myself before anything goes to press.

STRAVINSKY TO STEIN   *June 6, 1949*

Thank you for your letter of 31st May. Touched by what you say about the *Rake.* . . .

Mass—First, I prefer the priest's intonation before the Credo as it is in my score. Ansermet, as it appears, prefers another version. Mine is one of several official versions available.

---

[7] Arthur Lvovich Rabenek, of the Edition Russe, wrote to Stravinsky, March 10, 1949: "Dear Igor Fyodorovich, In accordance with instructions we have received from London, from the Boosey & Hawkes firm, we are sending you a registered packet containing the proofs of the *Perséfone* [sic] score. This was engraved in France, but London did the proofing of it, and, as you will see, all of your latest corrections have already been entered on the covers. Thus the score is ready to be printed. But we, of course, will hold off on the publication until we receive instructions from you, in order to give you a chance to study this proof. . . . It was a great pleasure for all of us to hear your new works, Mass and *Orpheus.*"

STRAVINSKY TO BEAN

June 19, 1949
[Collect telegram]

Answering your 16th June wire. As my birthday now over a birthday article seems rather inappropriate. As I hope to finish my opera in about 18 months can't give performance information now.

STRAVINSKY TO SYLVIA GOLDSTEIN

September 16, 1949

As to the date at which I may finish Act II (as you ask me re copyright purposes), I can only tell you that I hope to finish this Second Act (which includes 3 Scenes) about January or February 1950.

STRAVINSKY TO STEIN

October 17, 1949

I would like to know (if possible by return air mail) whether *Perséphone* is printed and will be available soon. I am especially anxious to see this score out without further delay in view of an important performance of it in Carnegie Hall in New York by Robert Craft, within about one month. [At] present he is having the utmost difficulties with the handwritten and dirty copy which is the only one we have here.[8]

STRAVINSKY TO HAWKES

October 17, 1949

You know well enough that I (as well as yourself) shall never consider the Met as a possibility for the kind of Chamber Opera that the *Rake* is going to be. You were yourself feeling very much the same way regarding this purely chamber work. . . . You ought to know (as we have discussed this point already so many times), that the *Rake* will not be finished until 1951; this would mean that we could present it in the late spring or early summer of 1951. . . .

It is of course preferable to speak than to write about it and I shall be glad to learn that you are coming as planned in November on the occasion of Britten's Los Angeles appearance.

STRAVINSKY TO HAWKES

November 20, 1949

As to the world premiere in Edinburgh in August 1951, a lot of work should be done by the other conductor preparatory to my arrival. He would have to prepare the singers, choruses and orchestra so that I would need only some rehearsals myself to check up all details and create the tradition of the *Rake*'s performance. That conductor would have to conduct all following performances in England and the Continent (except my premieres).

---

[8] Stravinsky wrote at the bottom of this letter: "Receiving no answer air mailed him a copy 31 Oct."

STRAVINSKY TO STEIN   *December 10, 1949*

Re yours of 7 November: I have no time right now to go through the mistakes of the *Sacre* (the score of which I received indeed); but Robert Craft being due here in a few days will help me in clearing this problem, and I hope I will be able to send it to you before the end of the month.

STRAVINSKY TO BEAN   *December 28, 1949*

Have no time to answer these stupid questions. . . . I take advantage of this to answer yours of December 16 concerning my Urbana concert. In that concert Octet for Wind Instruments is the only piece from Boosey & Hawkes and Dr. Kuypers has already been coaching and rehearsing it since last September; it seems that your worries are coming rather late. . . . Don't bother, dear Betty.

STRAVINSKY TO HAWKES   *January 3, 1950*

I shall be in New York from 20 February to conduct *Orpheus* and the *Firebird* at the City Center [New York City] Ballet.[9]

By that time I hope you will at last be able to gather all the European accounts which I never received, as you know; you call them "complications" (your letter of 6 December) but this does not explain anything. To me it means only the impossibility to settle any accounts as long as we cannot have a complete and full picture.

Switching now to Miss Goldstein's note concerning a special copy of the summary sketches of *Rake*'s Act I: OK, I am going to mail you C.O.D. that copy by regular mail; you probably need it for your translations.

STRAVINSKY TO HAWKES   *January 14, 1950*

I sent you today by regular mail the full score of *Sacre du printemps* with all the remarks and queries by Erwin Stein of London. Those queries were answered a few days ago in a separate note.

I hope you gave full attention to Robert Craft's letter to you of 27 December, re Symphonies of Wind Instruments, because I just received today from London a *"calque"* of the old version they got from Paris. How, on earth, did it happen, and how is it possible that Erwin Stein never got a copy of the new version that I performed myself as well as Ansermet 2 years ago in New York? Please straighten this at once.

Just received your note of 10 January, re Mass performed liturgically in

---

[9] On January 18, Stravinsky wrote to his younger son, who lived on West 72nd Street, New York: "We expect to leave for New York on the 6th or 7th of February in a new Dodge that Vera is just acquiring in exchange for our old one. . . ."

Essen on 8 December. I was very glad to read about it. It happened that on the same Church festivity, on 8 December, my Mass was performed during the liturgy in St. Joseph's Church in Los Angeles by the excellent UCLA–Roger Wagner Chorus.

STRAVINSKY TO HAWKES   *January 23, 1950*

From the intentional or merely natural confusion of point "3" in your letter of 18th January, am I to read an apology for the inconceivable negligence in not notifying your London office of the existence of my new version [Symphonies of Wind Instruments], as it happened to be the first work I did with you?

STRAVINSKY TO HAWKES   *May 20, 1950*

Despite my lack of enthusiasm to have my chamber *Rake* played in large theaters like the Met, Covent Garden, Grand Opéra Paris, and above all La Scala, unfortunately we have to solve this dilemma in the only way offered us.

Of course it has always to be kept in mind that the world premiere in the U.S.A. will, under all circumstances, take place before Europe.

STRAVINSKY TO HAWKES   *May 22, 1950*

As you know, when Bob Craft was recording *Mavra* just two weeks ago, you were debating with the recording company the question of the duration of *Mavra*. You had in mind that *Mavra* should take much longer than the timing figured out by the company and Bob Craft. Their figures were right as *Mavra* lasts in fact around 23 minutes only; you probably got your own figures mixed up by the Boosey & Hawkes catalogue which, unfortunately, has been put out all full of mistakes including the timing of my works. This catalogue has been printed and edited without any proof having been sent to me. And you probably remember that upon discovering what a terrible confusion the whole thing was I had sent Bob Craft (who was working for you at that time) to Betty Bean with all corrections in red pencil on one of the copies.

One of the most surprising omissions in that catalogue, which did not affect me personally, was the total absence of the name of your firm, and when I received some time afterwards the supposedly corrected catalogue, I found the correction work had been limited only to the name of your firm. Under such circumstances it is no surprise indeed, if or when you happen to be wrongly informed by your own uncorrected catalogue.

Going through my files and your statements I noticed that you had made a debit towards me of $4.58 for a collect telephone call. . . . It should have been easy to understand that the reason for the call was a strictly business one motivated by the carelessness of some of your staff. Maybe they misinformed you; nevertheless, you charged the call to me and this in itself should prevent you from giving me cautious advice through Vera and also anyone else from telling unkind stories about my discharging my social duties at your expense.

STRAVINSKY TO HAWKES   *May 23, 1950*[10]

Friends of mine who attended a performance of *Apollo* in Mexico City by Ballet Alicia Alonso of Cuba, have given me the enclosed program. I send it to you so you can take all necessary steps towards controlling their performances in order to find out where they got the material from, because the copyright limitations are applied only to the U.S.A. while all other countries of Central or South America are under the regime of the Bern Convention which means under your authority. . . .

STRAVINSKY TO HAWKES   *June 19, 1950*

Yours of 15 June on hand.

You are 100% right this time in pointing to me the C.O.D. shipping of *Baiser de la fée*. It was only a small amount and in such instances my intention has always been to suffer the expense myself alone.

The whole thing, indeed, was a mistake from my secretary [Andre Marion] who had two other more important C.O.D.s to send that day and who mailed everything the same way at the same time.

In order to straighten the whole thing, I am enclosing my check for this small amount of $1.29. . . .

STRAVINSKY TO HAWKES   *June 28, 1950*

You shouldn't have made that payment without my formal requirement. I had asked you in New York if you would be able and willing eventually to pay certain amounts of money to the Stravinsky bank account no. 10937, Crédit Commercial de France, Agence Malesherbes, Paris. You answered me you could and then I told you to wait until I could find out and let you know whether I needed such payment in France to be made or not.

The tentative financial plans (Berman, Edel or others[11]) that I had in mind then did not materialize for various reasons, and it is why I just put the whole idea in dead storage.

---

[10] Stravinsky had returned to California in the middle of May, as he wrote to his younger son on May 25: "We returned with Bob on the 17th in the evening, after a beautiful ten-day trip in the car, via Pittsburgh, Chicago, Yellowstone, San Francisco."

[11] Stravinsky had wanted to exchange his francs for the dollars of friends who were going to France.

STRAVINSKY TO HAWKES   *July 24, 1950*

I am on the eve of my motor trip to Aspen where I give 2 concerts (2 and 8 August). I expect to be back around 15 August. . . .

Perséphone—I am willing to approve your suggestion concerning the percentage proposed for Gui.[12] But does it really concern me? Gide is the author, I am the composer, and the translation is made from Gide not from me. Maybe you should secure Gide's agreement and let him divide his share with Gui. Of course Gui cannot expect [many] performances in Italian (i.e. in Italy or Switzerland . . . a rather limited field). . . .

STRAVINSKY TO HAWKES   *August 12, 1950*

Just back from Aspen. . . .[13]

Petrushka—I give you my agreement to let Babin and Vronsky get two and one-half per cent (2½%) of the sheet music royalty from their two-piano version of the new arrangement of *Petrushka*.

Rake's Progress—The second act, vocal score, has been duly received with the list of queries. I will try and take care of them as soon as I get rid of my backlog of correspondence, and I clear all matters which have been piling up during the last two weeks.

STRAVINSKY TO HAWKES   *August 30, 1950*

Here are my observations concerning each contract in particular:

—Ballet Works—*Baiser de la fée*—The title appearing on page I should read: "The Fairy's Kiss" ("LE BAISER DE LA FÉE") Ballet in 4 scenes

Sacre du printemps—The title appearing on page I should read: "Rite of Spring" ("LE SACRE DU PRINTEMPS") Ballet for Orchestra. But what "revised version" is the contract covering? I have never made any "revised" version and the one you have reprinted after "Edition Russe de Musique" is not at all revised, nor even completely corrected, as I see. Moreover, you have just reprinted the previous "Edition Russe de Musique" score without mentioning the "new version"; then what do you plan to do about it?

Apollon Musagète—The title appearing on page I should read: (here we should

---

[12] The conductor Vittorio Gui had made an Italian translation of *Perséphone*.

[13] Stravinsky wrote to his elder son, August 22: "My trip to Aspen went well. We made a circuit of 8,000 kilometers in seventeen days by car. . . . The Busoni Prize was conferred on me in Rome, but I sense that it is conditional and doubt that I can dispose of these 2 million lire in Italy unless I agree to conduct a series of concerts there. I wrote to the Accademia Nazionale di Santa Cecilia and am waiting for what will probably be an evasive reply."

keep the French title because we cannot translate properly "musagète"): "APOLLON MUSAGÈTE" Ballet in 2 Scenes for String Orchestra. . . .

OCTET—The title appearing on page I should read: "Octet" for Wind Instruments. Here let us drop the French "Octuor." "Octet" is an international word and it needs no French translation.

Symphonie de psaumes—The title appearing on page I should read: "SYMPHONY OF PSALMS" ("SYMPHONIE DE PSAUMES") for Chorus and Orchestra

Symphonies for Wind Instruments—The title appearing on page I should read: "SYMPHONIES OF WIND INSTRUMENTS" ("SYMPHONIES D'INSTRUMENTS À VENT")

—Chorus a Cappella—
Pater Noster, Ave Maria—It would be OK except for a rather funny note given by the mention "composer-arranger-author of text." Please scratch out "author of text"; we do not want to be ridiculous, neither you nor I, as everyone knows that the Pater Noster's author is Jesus Christ Himself and the Ave Maria's author is the Archangel Gabriel. The title appearing on page I should read: "PATER NOSTER," "AVE MARIA" with Latin Text. Revised Version.

—Violin and Cello Arrangements—
Ballad—The mention "arranged for violin and piano by Jeanne Gautier" is not right. On page I it should read: "BALLAD," for Violin and Piano, from the Ballet "THE FAIRY'S KISS." The Violin part has been established by the Author in collaboration with Jeanne Gautier. This is exactly what you can read on the copy I sent to you.

Russian Maiden's Song—For this contract I shall not raise the same point I did about Jeanne Gautier as I did not take part in the arrangement of the cello part. The piano part is still that of my piano-violin version, for which I did with Dushkin the same as I did with Jeanne Gautier for the Ballad. The title appearing on page I should read: "RUSSIAN MAIDEN'S SONG" for Cello and Piano, Cello part arranged by Dmitry Markevitch.

STRAVINSKY TO HAWKES   *August 31, 1950*

After going through all the contracts for revised versions . . . and checking them against the catalogue, I let you know the following works (in their new versions) prove to be still missing to this date; I am listing them below with the exact titles they should bear; here they are: —1—"PERSÉPHONE" Melodrama in 3 parts for Tenor, Speaking Voice, Mixed Chorus and Orchestra — 2—"SONATA FOR PIANO SOLO" —3—"SERENADE IN A" for Piano Solo —4—"CONCERTO" for Piano and Orchestra of Wind Instruments. I am giving the titles in English and not in French, as the new versions will be copyrighted by you, an English publisher, and I cannot see any reason to stick to French titles.

STRAVINSKY TO BEAN   *September 13, 1950*

It has been quite a shock both to my wife and to myself when we . . . learned the terrible news [of Ralph Hawkes's death] on our return from a week's trip North last night.

Thanks for your telegrams which I read yesterday only.

We have cabled at once to Mrs. Hawkes and I beg you to bring her once more the expression of our deepest sympathy. It must have been a sad blow to everybody in your office.

STRAVINSKY TO ERNST ROTH   *September 20, 1950*

I shall appreciate your help in the matter of the Pathé-Marconi-Columbia matrices. I hope the Columbia people, who are known to be extremely slow, will not make you beg again and again for some kind of an answer.

Your letter came to me shortly after my return from a week's absence and it was a great shock to me when I learned upon my arrival back home that Ralph Hawkes had died suddenly in New York 5 days before.

STRAVINSKY TO BEAN   *September 26, 1950*

Yesterday's mail brought me Ralph Hawkes's obituary. . . . Knowing how much he appreciated your collaboration and the high esteem in which he kept you I was particularly pleased to see that you [are] going to pursue his work yourself in cooperation with his brother.

STRAVINSKY TO LESLIE BOOSEY   *September 27, 1950*

Even before the shocking and tragic death of Mr. Ralph Hawkes, who was such an outstanding personality in your world wide firm, I have always wished to meet you, but circumstances have never favored it so far; nevertheless, I do hope as much as you do that we shall meet in the very near future. . . .

I shall be in Los Angeles except from 11 December until 18 December when I will be guest conducting at the San Francisco Symphony. My private Los Angeles telephone is: CRestview 1 4858.

STRAVINSKY TO BEAN   *October 13, 1950*

In the case of the *Rake* my work comes to reach a scope with no precedent in all my experience. By putting myself through a terrific strain I have managed to give you one completely composed act every season (orchestra plus summary sketches score). The third and last act is made of 3 scenes (as the other acts) plus a short epilogue. It is by far not only the longest but also the most dense of the three. I am well able to visualize the end of the fully completed *Rake* this current season if I am given the means and the incentives for devoting all my energy and time to my opera without taking my usual series of seasonal commitments. . . .

Translations: This is a subject on which my point of view is of necessity always incompatible with that of any publisher. As a composer of music for a definite text with definite words and syllables, I know that it is impossible to make a translation of the original text without losing most of the musical links between the words or syllables and notes.

To avoid this it would be necessary to re-write the music according to each translated text. . . . From the experience I have had with my previous vocal music I can only assure you that whenever the singer's part in the vocal score is made of a piling up of translations (see *Mavra* score) it becomes so hard to read for the singers in all the other lines in excess of two that practically nothing useful can come out of it. In other words, if you plan to make translations in German, Italian and French, I think it would be a fair compromise to publish the full vocal score with the original English text adding to it only the German translation (as it will be the closest to the English text).

As to the Italian or French texts, if you are planning to have them made, I think their markets will always be rather limited, mostly the French one. Why won't you publish them both (Italian and French) in a special edition without piano accompaniment but keeping the vocal lines in a small libretto-size booklet, as it has been done sometimes with famous Italian works. . . .

That's enough writing for today. I'd better go back to my *Rake*.

STRAVINSKY TO STEIN   *October 16, 1950*

At last I am through with your vocal score of Act 2 of my *Rake's Progress*. This time it has been a huge task indeed.

In many instances the reduction for piano of my orchestra score was satisfactory. In other—quite a few—[cases] I had to go through an extensive overhauling of whole sections of your piano reduction. My idea in doing this has been not only to give the piano reduction a better "pianistic" cut but also (and mainly) to bring it acoustically closer to my original orchestra score. . . .

Please also remove the signs "–" or "÷" [wherever] they appear in your vocal score. I use these signs to get a sharp though light start of instruments (especially strings) in the orchestra score; but in the vocal score it looks rather odd and I am afraid nobody would understand it.

Something else: What happened with the full scores of *Perséphone* and *Baiser de la fée*? I have never seen any of them so far though you have had the proofs for a long time already.

You will have the visits of Nadia Boulanger and Igor Markevitch. They will ask you to let them have a look at the *Rake*. Please be kind enough to do so.

I think that's all at this time.

STRAVINSKY TO BEAN   *October 18, 1950*

Concerning *Rite of Spring*[:] I have sent a long time ago a long list of answers
to the numerous queries then written by Mr. Erwin Stein in London. If you are
contemplating to make a "revised version," you should only enter into it all the
corrections I listed for Mr. Stein. . . .

Concerto for Piano and Orchestra of Wind Instruments: In order to avoid
any confusion please consider this above title as the only correct one.

On other points of the same list: OK.

I believe this time we are really on the eve of straightening all this out. . . .

P.S. Do you know what happened with *Perséphone* and *Baiser de la fée* as well
as Divertimento? It has been more than a year since London received my corrected proofs.

STRAVINSKY TO BEAN   *October 23, 1950*[14]

Thanks for sending me a copy of your letter of 13 October to Judd concerning
Le Sacre du printemps.

From my letter of 18 October you know by now what is the general situation concerning the state of corrections in the score. I suppose the parts have
been checked against the corrected score.

Whenever you give Munch, or someone else, the material for performance
or recording, please make sure that you are giving the corrected one.

I heard Mr. Erwin Stein is in New York for a while; if that is so, it will give
you a chance to review the matter of *Le Sacre* and the corrections with him once
and for all. . . .

P.S. You must have in your files a copy of the list of errors in the score of *Le
Sacre.* This list was sent [to] Mr. Stein a year ago. You could probably locate
your copy in Long Island.

STRAVINSKY TO BEAN   *October 27, 1950*

Petrushka is not in the public domain outside of the U.S.A. and, except in the
U.S.A., I do not see how [the Grand Ballet du Marquis de Cuevas] could use
any material without paying a fee to Boosey & Hawkes. . . .

P.S. . . . I believe you will be able to force the Cuevas gang not only to pay for
the material, but actually to play it. I am not interested in the earnings only but
also in not having my music mutilated publicly by shameless arrangers.

---

[14] On October 24 Stravinsky wrote to his daughter-in-law in Geneva in reply to her description of "a beautiful performance of the *Sacre* by Ansermet" in that city.

STRAVINSKY TO BEAN   *October 31, 1950*

Last evening I had the visit of Mr. Edward Dryhurst.* He was supposed to see
you in New York this morning as he was traveling by plane overnight. This producer is going to make a movie under the title "Bullet in the Ballet." It is an old
project originating back in 1939 and stopped by the war. Then Païchadze had
been carrying negotiations with them and it could have been very important . . .
financially. I hope this time the [negotiations] will go through as it could be
very profitable both for Boosey & Hawkes and myself. But [don't] tie us up too
much as far as the exclusive rights to *Petrushka* are concerned. In any case I
will appreciate hearing from you about the outcome. . . .

* Edward Dryhurst, Hallmark Productions Ltd., 35 Portland Place, London W1
(England)

STRAVINSKY TO BEAN   *November 6, 1950*

Marquis de Cuevas Ballet: I have just received your letter of 3 November with
copy of your letter to Emerson Buckley.

    Thanks for taking this very firm stand. I believe you will win as far as
money is concerned, but, unfortunately, I am not so optimistic about the use of
my new version by them as they are looking much more for cutting down their
expenses than for gratifying the composer's requirements. . . .

    I have been approached by both Dr. Carl Ebert and Dr. Raymond Kendall,
head of the Department of Music at USC. They wanted to undertake the
[*Rake*] premiere for the fall of 1952 but I told them at once it would be too late
and they would have to give the world premiere before 1 November 1951. I had
in mind your own position which I want to make as easy as possible in view of
the various decisions you may feel obliged to take as publishers even before my
composition is completed; . . . at the same time, [since] Dr. Kendall seemed to
be very anxious to commission this opera, I thought he could offer both of us
the most satisfactory solution as it would give me the incentive for completing
my work on the *Rake* score this season and it would enable you not to miss the
opportunities you might have at hand. . . .

    I have agreed to accept $10,000 commission; this figure would have been
raised to at least $15,000 should I have accepted to conduct the premiere. But
on the other hand, as Otto Klemperer—whom I met here a week ago—is so enthusiastic about the whole thing, I prefer to leave to him the conducting even
for the premiere and to give all my energy to the supervision of rehearsals and
preparations which will take place here on the spot. This will permit an exhaus-
tive schedule of rehearsals which nobody else could afford and it will help in establishing the best possible genuine tradition for my opera.

STRAVINSKY TO STEIN   *November 7, 1950*

I am glad you have already made the corrections in *Rake*'s vocal score first act (which you called by mistake the "2nd act"; you could not possibly correct the 2nd act as you were waiting to receive it). . . .

When Ralph Hawkes made a stop over here on his way back from Australia in August 1949, I gave him some photostats of the cover of the Mass. He intended to reprint the cover anew as he was as much dissatisfied with it as I was myself. Could you find out whom I should get in touch with in order to know what happened since then?

STRAVINSKY TO BEAN   *November 22, 1950*

De Cuevas: Unfortunately we have more or less to leave our fate in the hands of the gods. . . .

RCA-Victor recording, *Le Sacre du printemps:* . . . [I] certainly . . . prefer [Munch] not to try his hand on my music at all. . . .

I am guest-conducting in San Francisco on 14, 15, 16 December, plus a Standard Oil broadcast on 17 December.

The management of the San Francisco Symphony Orchestra is due to put the order to you in a matter of days for the material of: *Petrushka* (fragments), *Orpheus* (fragments), Divertimento.

I have not made a final decision concerning Divertimento which I plan to play on the Standard Oil hour broadcast only (the whole or fragments of it); it all depends on the exact time allowed me. In case I need it, the material *must* be on hand already now.

It always takes about a week for parcels to travel from coast to coast, so please tell your library to act at once as soon as the order comes in from San Francisco. I must start rehearsing 12 December in the morning.

Concerning *Orpheus,* I plan to play only a few fragments of it (about 7 minutes in all); nevertheless, you will have to send the whole ballet material as there is no special orchestra material for fragments. If possible I would like you to send the set I used for my recording with RCA-Victor in 1949.

As to *Petrushka* I will play excerpts from it for a total of about 24 minutes. You will have to send the complete material, of course, but please *make sure* that your library will include with the material a very important page, "Ending for Concert Performances," which is page 172 of the full score. This has to be put in every part for each instrument. Of course, I am speaking of the "New Version." . . .

I shall go to Havana for the first twelve days of March to conduct two concerts there (probably *Petrushka*, Divertimento and fragments from *Apollo;* I will tell you more about it soon).

STRAVINSKY TO BEAN   *December 1, 1950*

Yesterday I received your telegram concerning the Boston Symphony–RCA-Victor offer for *Le Sacre du printemps.* You certainly have read my answer by now and I scarcely have anything more to say. Of course they are not too generous but on the other hand they probably have reason [not] to be: we are in no bargaining position ourselves. . . .

STRAVINSKY TO BEAN   *December 4, 1950*

RCA-Victor recording, *Le Sacre du printemps:* My letter of 1 December has probably made my point of view quite clear to you by now. While *Le Sacre* is on the order of the day I am wondering how the same problem [was] solved the last time when the same Monteux* made the same recording for the same RCA-Victor with the San Francisco Symphony Orchestra. . . .

* I still suppose Monteux will conduct the recording; did you get confirmation of it? Please let me know.

STRAVINSKY TO STEIN   *December 6, 1950*

I sincerely appreciate your words about the music of *Rake's.* Your assistance throughout this exceptionally large score of mine is most precious to me during all these months of preparatory work.

STRAVINSKY TO BEAN   *December 22, 1950*

. . . I am back from San Francisco[15] and I have still nothing new to tell you about the Kendall-USC project. . . .[16]

    Please send me a single word to relieve my soul.

---

[15] Stravinsky had returned from San Francisco on December 18 after conducting a week of concerts there. He wrote to his children afterward: "We ate in some good French restaurants and returned happy and tired, Vera having gained 5 pounds." On the 22nd he wrote to Soulima: "My opera is going well; I am in the process of finishing the eighth scene and hope to complete the whole thing before going to Havana in March. Unfortunately . . . the local negotiations with USC, begun eighteen months ago when Hawkes was here, have come to nothing. Nevertheless, this project pleases me the most, both because I would not have to travel and because Dr. Carl Ebert would have young and competent people."

[16] Following the University of Southern California's proposal to give the premiere of *The Rake's Progress,* Ingolf Dahl played parts of the music at the piano for Dr. Kendall, Stravinsky, and the present writer at the beginning of December 1950.

STRAVINSKY TO BEAN   *December 23, 1950*

My Havana trip is already too long in itself and it has forced me to refuse another profitable engagement in Mexico with Chavez in order not to jeopardize my work on the *Rake.*

RCA-Victor—*Sacre du printemps* recording: OK on the figures you mention. Monteux, in San Francisco, had already told me he would do it. So much the better. . . .

Commission—piano concerto: I am sorry to disappoint you but I do not want to be commissioned for any piano concerto. . . .

Rake's Progress—Juilliard: If, as I understand, they want only a New York premiere, I think it is worth considering and taking. But the $5,000 should be in payment only of the guarantee to be given them that they would have the New York premiere, but nothing else. I cannot tie myself up with them now for 1952 on a program of side activities such as lectures, etc. . . . (these do not pay because they take too much of my time, as I experienced at Harvard, despite a fee of $10,000).

On the other hand, if they want to have me as conductor of my own works I will accept with pleasure for a special fee (to be fixed in due time).

But as far as their ballet projects are concerned, I shall be rather puzzled until I will be given a chance to know whom they intend to cooperate with. If it is Kirstein-Balanchine, OK. . . . But with most others I shall refrain.

STRAVINSKY TO ROTH   *January 13, 1951*

Thank you very much for your note concerning the release (at last) of my old Pathé-Marconi recordings. It is good news indeed.

I had lately a letter from Mr. Stein and another one from Betty Bean in connection with their tracing the full score of *Perséphone* which I was supposed to have received for some time but which never reached me. Will you be kind enough to find out what has happened. I have been waiting patiently now for over a year and I would appreciate your helping me.

STRAVINSKY TO BEAN   *January 19, 1951*

Just two words to tell you I have just shipped 1st class mail registered 2 sets of my summary sketches (which we call "vocal score") of *Rake* Act 3, Scenes 1 and 2. . . .

I expect to send you the orchestra score of the same two scenes of Act 3 about the end of this month.

STRAVINSKY TO STEIN   *January 31, 1951*

Please find enclosed a list of corrections to be entered into the orchestra score of *Rake* Act III, Scenes 2 and 3. . . . I am adding to the typewritten list a tiny handwritten list to be included both in the orchestra score and the summary sketches.

STRAVINSKY TO BEAN   *February 10, 1951*[17]

I am going to leave for my Cuba concerts on 21 February, motoring between here and Miami. This means I will not be able to be reached except during my stay in Havana proper (where I will be from 28 February until 7 March at the Hotel El Presidente).

STRAVINSKY TO BEAN   *March 16, 1951*

In reference to your letter concerning the National Institute of Arts and Letters' request for an address from me on the occasion of their annual ceremonial, I am . . . not interested at all in receiving this Gold Medal for the reason that all such monkeying has nothing to do with creative art which is my . . . concern.

    I am not going to write any address. Please do not feel embarrassed about my attitude. I am writing them today stating more mildly than I am doing here my reasons for being uncooperative. . . .

    I have heard from Lincoln Kirstein that he is contemplating to produce the *Rake* in New York sometime in November 1951. . . .

    Another project originates from Carlos Chavez in Mexico. I am supposed to talk things over at length with him when I go and conduct my concerts there at the end of July. . . .

STRAVINSKY TO BEAN   *March 17, 1951*

Dario Soria of Cetra-Soria Records . . . wrote me the other day in Cuba and right now he must be awaiting an answer from his Italian counterpart, who is himself in contact with La Biennale. . . .

    . . . I think that owing to the first-rate connections Cetra-Soria has with the Biennale (via Labroca of Radio Rome) no other outfit would be able to use all the facilities available; and, on the other hand, I do believe too that no other

---

[17] On February 17 Stravinsky wrote to his son Soulima: "I have just finished the third act. What a relief. . . . We will leave Tuesday afternoon or Wednesday morning in our new Buick, take the airplane from Miami to Havana on the 28th, staying [in Cuba] until March 6, then flying back to Miami on the 7th, and reaching here around the 13th." Two days before, Stravinsky had written to his daughter-in-law in Geneva: "The premiere [of the *Rake*] is supposed to take place in Venice on September 12 under my direction. Keep this a strict secret. . . . You can imagine the joy with which I look forward to seeing you, since I am sure that you will find the means to come to Venice. We will go directly from New York to Naples."

recording of the *Rake* in full could ever possibly be made in this country owing to the costs involved. . . .[18]

Of course, please present the idea as yours and not mine, and whenever you talk to Dario Soria do not mention my writing you about this. . . .

STRAVINSKY TO STEIN   *March 19, 1951*

On my return from Cuba I have read your three letters of 22 February, 5 and 9 March 1951.

I found also the two packages containing your vocal score of the first two scenes of Act 3.

I am already working on those, but at the same time I am carrying on with my orchestrating of Scene 3 as I believe it is the most urgent job to be completed. Anyhow, I am doing everything I can to reduce delays . . . and I shall send you back everything air mail as soon as it will be ready.

. . . I can tell you this new transcription of yours for piano is much easier to use than the others and I believe I will have less to do myself in the way of alterations.

STRAVINSKY TO STEIN   *March 26, 1951*

I am sending you by air parcel the last scene (Scene 3) of Act 3 of the *Rake*'s orchestra score. . . .

I hope by now you have received the same scene (Act 3 Scene 3) in summary sketches.

STRAVINSKY TO BOOSEY   *March 28, 1951*

I strongly wish you will not hesitate to come over here as it is too bad that I have never met you and Dr. Roth before and—mainly at the present stage, and with all the Italian developments—there are too many things which need nothing more than reviewing and discussing straightforwardly.

STRAVINSKY TO ROTH   *April 2, 1951*

I have the greatest regard for the City Center activities mainly in the ballet field where Kirstein and Balanchine have enough weight to impose both an excellent tradition and taste and despite their limited budget they always manage in the end to give enough rehearsals.

---

[18] In a March 27 letter to his son Theodore, Stravinsky reveals that the rehearsals were to have taken place in Rome, "from the middle to the end of August, and after that the final work will be done in Venice. . . . I am working on the Epilogue."

Unfortunately the situation is quite different in the City Center operatic field. Halász is a very capable opera conductor but he is never given the means to do a real fine and thorough job because the management does not have the money to pay for a decent preparation (rehearsals). This question of rehearsals is the real bottleneck in the production of the *Rake* and it will never be overcome except with the backing of a modern "Mécène." It is why, if Kirstein can find such a "Mécène," I will [vote] for him as he may give us a better chance.

STRAVINSKY TO ROTH   *April 14, 1951*

I have told Ballo I would like—sentimentally—to see Auden take part; but it is not within my authority. . . .

I have just finished the Epilogue. . . .

I have received directly from Sturtz, Würzburg, the green proofs.

STRAVINSKY TO STEIN   *April 20, 1951*

I have just received your letter of 18 April 1951.

Your telegram of yesterday read: "Please cable when we can expect manuscript vocal score first scene third act."

While you were away I wrote Dr. Roth on 15 April advising him, as I did in my telegraphic answer to you yesterday, that . . . Scenes 1 and 2 . . . were sent back to London airmail-registered with my corrections on 14 April. . . .

Will you tell Dr. Roth that I have just been informed [by] Wystan Auden himself [that he] has arrived in Italy from India. He is supposed to stay there now; he has probably taken his former address: via Santa Lucia 22, Forio d'Ischia, Prov. di Napoli. If you have decided to send one of the librettists the proofs (*another set of course* than the one bearing my corrections; see my letter to Dr. Roth of 15 April 1951), I think it will be much safer and better to send them to Auden in Italy.

STRAVINSKY TO BEAN   *April 26, 1951*

While you were away, Chandler Cowles came here and we spoke of a tentative New York production of the *Rake*. Cowles is budgeting the thing for the millionaire Farrell who owns the Mark Hellinger theatre and is planning to back the production. Kirstein would likely bring his talent too. . . .

Rake—Mexico: I . . . suspect the Opera Nacional is the group in competition with Chavez. On the other hand I do not know what Chavez's [position] is now. He seems to have more or less faded away lately, supposedly for undergoing an operation, but I won't be suprised if it were a political one. Who knows in Mexico??? Maybe you could find out what has been going on there. . . .

Mavra: As to the English text, important alterations (most necessary and a good many) were made in pencil by Bob Craft during his concert performance and recordings. Such alterations were entered directly into the singers' vocal scores. . . .[19]

I am giving Bob Craft my score at once and he is going to start re-writing a complete English translation. I will follow his work here so that everything will match with my original music. My part in this is my own responsibility but I have told Bob Craft I will pay him $40 for his work. This of course I will charge to you.

STRAVINSKY TO STEIN   *May 3, 1951*

I am sending you enclosed . . . the orchestra score (photocopy—1 set) of the Epilogue pages 402 to 417 incl. . . . the orchestra score (photocopy—1 set) of the Prelude to the whole work . . . the *Klavierauszug* (two pages on transparent paper) of the same Prelude, which I arranged myself in order to spare your time. . . . Will you please give instructions to your engravers in Würzburg to use the same wide layout I have used, in order to fill two pages. The reason for this is that with one page only we should not be able to put the Roman figure "I" and so the Prelude won't be numbered; while with two pages there won't be any number page I but page II (Roman) will be numbered and the whole Prelude will so appear like the Preface to a book, usually numbered in Roman before the beginning of the Arabic [numerals].

STRAVINSKY TO BEAN   *May 7, 1951*

Rake, Chicago Symphony: Actually some time ago I received a letter from Mr. Kuypers to whom my secretary answered that my opera had to have a stage premiere and not a concert performance. . . .

I do not see any possibility for using the music of *Rake* in concerts; the numbers are too short to be placed in a concert program and I do not plan to make any suite of separate numbers which could take place in a concert program as does a suite from a ballet.

The Strauss music may offer such possibilities but my music simply does not, neither in length nor in style.

---

[19] On March 29, Stravinsky had written to his son Soulima: "As for the English text, Bob tells me that he did not make any changes, except where they were absolutely imperative." In another letter, May 4, Stravinsky wrote: "The English text in the printed scores is very bad. Bob corrected and improved it for his performances. . . . I will send the LP that he made, since you will find the complete text on the jacket. If you play the recording, you will see that it is not excellent. I don't like the Parasha very much [Phyllis Curtin]; the technical side is bad and the instruments cover the voices, and the music even changes pitch (something unhappily common now with LPs); also, there are some wrong tempi. At **93** the indication in the score was wrong; it should be a dotted quarter = 44, not a quarter."

STRAVINSKY TO BEAN   *May 14, 1951*

The Rake's Progress is completed . . . and by now you actually are in possession
of the whole music both in summary sketches and orchestra score.

STRAVINSKY TO STEIN   *May 16, 1951*

Not a single word of the original libretto should be changed unless I could be
given another chance to re-write my music on the alterations in the text (this
means about 3 more weeks' delay in mailing the proofs back and forth another
time from you to me).

STRAVINSKY TO BEAN   *May 21, 1951*

Rake: concert performances: Whether the Chicago Symphony or any other
concert organization may be involved, I positively disapprove of making or even
discussing any such plans until the stage premiere has taken place, in order to
give me a chance to hear the work myself and thus decide how and if it can be
performed in a concert program. No menace of any deadline should make us
alter our course.

STRAVINSKY TO ANTHONY GISHFORD   *May 25, 1951*

You are asking me an article, after all!!! and I am afraid and sorry that I am absolutely unable to help you. . . . I am not much of a writer in any language and I
cannot undertake such a major project (for me) at this moment. You may well
realize how busy I am, 3 months before the premiere of the *Rake.* Let me give
you a suggestion. Why not commission an article to Robert Craft who has been
living near me here since the beginning of my work on the *Rake.* He knows
about all you want to know and he is very capable both in music and literature. . . . His address is: Robert Craft, 8624 Holloway Drive, Hollywood 46, California and whatever he will write before sending you he will certainly have me
check it. This is the most I can do, but I shall do it with pleasure both for you
and for Robert Craft.

STRAVINSKY TO STEIN   *June 5, 1951*

You will find enclosed on transparent paper . . . a correction in order to have the
music fit . . . Kallman's new writing (which, I must say, I plainly approve). . . .
I do not see why he wants to remove those stage directions, but as a composer it
does not concern me much and if it can only please them it is all right with
me. . . . I must tell you that the version you read in my score was actually composed by Auden himself a year ago. . . . If you can make these corrections in the
printed score it will be better for everybody. Otherwise in any case you will have

to do it in the orchestra score already now and the same will apply to any other corrections still to be suggested by Kallman and accepted by me before he is through with his reading.

STRAVINSKY TO ROTH   *June 9, 1951*

It has been a very long time indeed since we last wrote each other about the Italian premiere and the *"pasticcio"* ahead of it.[20]

Actually I had been left without any information from either the Biennale or the Scala for weeks, I should even say months, until I finally received a letter from Ballo mentioning that they had come to terms with Dr. Ghiringhelli under the auspices of an official representative from the Italian government. Under the agreement the Scala is supposed to produce the opera at the Venice Festival.

STRAVINSKY TO ROTH   *June 11, 1951*

I am writing you today in reference to my Symphonies of Wind Instruments. There is, as you know, a new version of it which is covered by a copyright with your New York office.

In December 1949 and January 1950 there was an exchange of correspondence between myself and Ralph Hawkes as I was more than surprised that this new version of mine had not yet been dealt with by any one of your offices. Mr. Stein certainly remembers this now. . . . The situation was all the more odd

---

[20] Stravinsky had written to his son Theodore on April 19: "I have a contract with the Biennale, but B & H seems to be in hot water, having promised the premiere left and right without telling me. Finally, B & H has more or less concluded an agreement with La Scala, which is naturally jealous of the Biennale and wants the premiere for itself. in fact, La Scala threatens to sue B & H. . . . While we wait for this Machiavellian struggle between the Biennale and La Scala to be settled, we lose time for the choice of artists." Stravinsky wrote again May 17: "I find myself caught between my publisher (who is the proprietor of my work and its performances, including the world premiere), who is demanding that I do it at La Scala, and my own agreement to conduct the premiere at the Biennale. . . . Berman, who was a candidate to create the decor from the very inception of the work with Auden (November 1947), is a victim in the battle of the cliques and has probably lost his standing. Suddenly Balthus is being proposed, on the pretext that Berman would be too expensive." On June 8, Stravinsky informed Theodore that "La Scala has taken charge of the entire production of the opera for the Festival of Venice in September." The composer informed his younger son on June 15 that the Italian Consul in Los Angeles had confirmed this agreement with La Scala, and asked, "Will we still have time enough to find English-language singers?" In a final letter to Theodore, July 16, Stravinsky tells his son: "I am hoping that we will all meet in Venice, but I leave it up to you to make hotel reservations. . . . Bring my manuscripts . . . with you to Italy, and I will take them with me to America."

as this was the first work I had completed and handed to your firm under our five-year contract. Actually it had been performed by Ansermet with the NBC orchestra in New York on 31 January 1948, and by myself some months later in Town Hall in New York.

It seems that after you received the score some 18 months ago the whole matter sank again into oblivion.

STRAVINSKY TO BEAN   *June 14, 1951*

Thank you for your letter of 1 June (which incidentally was misdated "1 July") 1951. I was too busy to write you until today. . . .

Your "tip" on Columbia [Records] is very interesting though I would like to have some more details whenever possible. . . .

Will you check if your accounting department has not overlooked my June payment which is not covered by the ASCAP check you sent me on 7 March (Miss Goldstein's letter of 7 March 1951).

STRAVINSKY TO STEIN   *June 14, 1951*

You will find enclosed the corrected proofs of *Rake* Act 3, pages 139 to 159 incl., which came directly from Würzburg 2 days ago.

I went through it all carefully but nevertheless I wish you will check it again yourself with your experienced eyes, and especially the German text for which my competence does not equal yours.

STRAVINSKY TO STEIN   *June 27, 1951*

I hasten to answer your question about the cembalo problem in *The Rake's Progress.*

Originally I had in mind the sound of a harpsichord which would have had to play chords accompanying the recitative parts. But . . . in Act 3, Scene 2 (Churchyard scene) [if] a harpsichord [is] used for the cembalo part in the duet, the harpsichord would likely be inaudible. For that reason I have decided to use a piano forte instead of harpsichord. . . .

Please leave the word "cembalo" throughout the score as it is probably already engraved, but in the index of the instrumentation, characters, etc. . . . preceding the score, you will have to add "piano forte" as follows: cembalo (piano forte).

The above explanation will also make it clear to you that the conductor will not be the player of the cembalo and therefore it is compulsory for the cembalo (piano forte) player to be given a separate part.

STRAVINSKY TO STEIN   *June 29, 1951*

I wish you would make sure that your people in Würzburg will not drag before sending me the balance of the green proofs. I mean the last two scenes plus Epilogue. I must have them in time to be able to make my corrections *before I leave here on July 30.*

STRAVINSKY TO ROTH   *June 30, 1951*

Strange as it may be, I am still without any direct and detailed news from Dr. Ghiringhelli. On 13 June he cabled me that a solution with Venice was imminent, that he was delighted, and that he wanted me to conduct 2 concerts after my opera (not mentioning where, when and fee . . .). On 14 June, I cabled him: "Accept in principle conducting 2 concerts following my conducting opera Fenice but can answer definitely only after knowing exact date premiere. Please also wire schedule rehearsals."

Well, nothing has come since that date and you may well realize that even with the most cooperative and lenient disposition, I cannot feel very happy about the way the Dictator of the Scala is treating me. Nevertheless I do not want to complicate still more the already very complicated atmosphere.

STRAVINSKY TO ROTH   *July 3, 1951*

While going through my scores and archives I came upon my instrumentation of "Chanson de Mephistopheles" by Moussorgsky, published (around 1912/13 probably) by Bessel and by Breitkopf & Härtel.

This was made by me at the request of A. Siloti for the centennial of Goethe's *Faust.* At the same time I also made an instrumentation of Beethoven's song of the same "Chanson de Mephistopheles."

This I cannot find in my library but as I see that Edition Russe de Musique (Concert Catalogue) had published in Russian in 1913 Beethoven's original song ("Mephistopheles' Lied vom Floh") for voice and piano, I wonder if, at the same time, they had published my instrumentation of it. I would be very glad if you could check and find out.

STRAVINSKY TO STEIN   *July 10, 1951*

You will notice on page 203 that I added 2 measures I had overlooked in my summary sketches as well as in my orchestra score. Thus I am enclosing page 358 of the orchestra score which I had had photocopied especially for you and your engravers in Würzburg with the 2 missing measures restored. Please make sure that your engravers in Würzburg will not overlook entering this very important correction in the layout of page 358. . . .

In the 250 provisional copies for the singers, etc. . . . you will have to enter these 2 measures some way or other.

STRAVINSKY TO STEIN   *July 13, 1951*

Two days ago I received from Würzburg Scene 3 in full from page 209 to 230 incl. This I will airmail to you Monday July 16. . . .

As you know I am leaving here on 30 July and I will not be available afterwards. Maybe you should clear the matter by telegram.

STRAVINSKY TO ROTH   *July 14, 1951*

Thank you for your letter from Paris of 10 July 1951. . . .

I am leaving here 30 July. I will stay in New York (Hotel Lombardy, 111 East 56th Street, New York 22, N.Y.) from 2 August, until the day of my sailing (7 August) with the S.S. *Constitution* (American Export Lines). I will land in Naples 15 August. I have not heard yet what the schedule of rehearsals will be but I presume I will go directly to Milan and later move to Venice. You can therefore write c/o Scala after 15 August.

Dr. Ghiringhelli has cabled me that my concerts in Milan are scheduled for 27 and 28 September. I have concluded with Cologne for 8 October, Baden-Baden between 10 and 16 October; I will probably go to Munich (Musica Viva—Karl Amadeus Hartmann) after 18 October. I will go back to Italy afterwards and I have made my reservations for the sailing of the S.S. *Constitution* on 29 October.

I have no agent as I prefer to handle these limited European concerts directly. I do not think I will be able to undertake any other engagements outside of the ones I have already mentioned.

As to *Baiser de la fée* I am glad to hear it is being readied. The stage directions mentioned in the piano score must indeed be inserted also in the orchestra score. I only want to draw your attention upon a small mistake which is repeated 7 times (pages 20, 29, 30, 31, 33, 35, 39) in the stage directions of the piano score: the character "Jeune Homme" has been printed with a small "h" (Jeune homme); it should be with a capital "H" (Jeune Homme).

STRAVINSKY TO STEIN   *July 16, 1951*

Two days ago I have received the stitched book (temporary edition) of the first 2 acts of *Rake*'s *Klavierauszug*. There was an accompanying slip asking to return it after inspection. This inspection I am doing now and you will find my corrections throughout the book in red pencil. I hope to mail it back to you in a few days.

                                                               July 18, 1951
STRAVINSKY TO BOOSEY & HAWKES   *[Telegram]*

Desperately waiting missing green proofs also provisional edition third act. Mailing you back provisionally printed *Klavierauszug* first two acts unfortunately full of mistakes.

STRAVINSKY TO STEIN   *July 18, 1951*

I am still without the green proofs of *Rake*'s Act 3 beginning of Scene 2 from page 185 to 194 incl. and it seems to be a rather tragic situation unless you have already wired Würzburg about it.

In the meantime I have inspected and checked the provisional edition of the first 2 acts. I have found quite a few mistakes, a list of which you will find enclosed.

I am afraid you will have to rework all those plates and in the meantime it will be imperative to have the corrections hand made or to give at least errata.

STRAVINSKY TO BEAN   *July 21, 1951*

I am working under terrible pressure as I have only one more week to spend here before I will start on my trip to Italy. I will be in New York from 2 August until 7 August. . . . Therefore it will be more convenient to discuss all pending matters . . . in New York. . . .

Thank you for your phone call. I am awaiting particulars about the German visas. Robert Craft's passport number is 387873. Looking forward to the pleasure of seeing you in New York.

STRAVINSKY TO STEIN   *July 21, 1951*

Please do as the librettists want. I have reached agreement with Auden on this.

But do not forget to have the German translation match exactly whatever alterations are made to the English text.

                                                               Venice
STRAVINSKY TO ROTH   *September 22, 1951*

A note to inform you that I have just received a telegram from Geneva accepting the date of November 4 as definite. So much the better. The two rehearsals that Schenker of Radio Geneva mentions are as you telegraphed to me, November 2 and 3. . . .

Keep me informed; I will be in Milan tomorrow evening, at the Hotel Duomo. [*Original in French*]

                                                              Baden-Baden
                                                          October 10, 1951
STRAVINSKY TO BOOSEY & HAWKES   *[Telegram]*

Met [ropolitan Opera] obviously preferable but impossible to weigh such complicated and voluminous matters while traveling. Please have Weissberger contact Bing.

STRAVINSKY TO BOOSEY & HAWKES

Baden-Baden
October 15, 1951
[Telegram]

Thanks for yours 5 Oct. Flying 21 Nov from Rome to New York. Could conduct one ballet in Stravinsky night 25 Nov for fee mentioned.

STRAVINSKY TO BOOSEY & HAWKES

Hotel Schweizerhof
Bern
October 23, 1951
[Telegram]

Answering yours 19 October. Will conduct *Apollo* provided two rehearsals with required instrumentation. All other matters till seeing you. Craft sending required *Apollo* instrumentation.

STRAVINSKY TO BEAN

Hôtel des Bergues
Geneva
November 1, 1951

Of course I will conduct *Baiser de la fée* Sunday night 25 Nov. [in New York]. Since this will be its first performance I will need two rehearsals.

We arrive on Pan American in the morning of 22 November (Thanksgiving). This flight leaves Rome the previous day. Would you kindly arrange hotel accommodations. We would like a suite with kitchenette at the Lombardy Hotel. Please call Mr. King, head manager of the Lombardy, and ask him to make the best possible price he can. Kindly notify us at the Hassler Hotel, Rome, of the results of the negotiation. We will be in New York at least 16 days.

There is of course no change in my original statement about a production of the *Rake* at the Metropolitan. I definitely prefer it there to any other place in America. All other questions will have to wait until my arrival 22 November.

STRAVINSKY TO BOOSEY & HAWKES

Rome
November 14, 1951
[Telegram]

Sorry cannot accept Met broadcast interview. Arriving 22 November Pan American ten a.m. Hope you arranged Lombardy Hotel.

STRAVINSKY TO ROTH

Hollywood
January 3, 1952

There is a little project which I have discussed already with Robert Craft and Andre Marion who are working on a translation in English of my son Theodore Stravinsky's book *Le Message d'Igor Strawinsky*.[21] This translation should be completed before long and I believe plans could be made already now for its quickest release.

---

[21] Stravinsky wrote to Theodore on January 11: "Bob and Andre are working continually on the translation. . . . Bob intends to write a short preface to bring the book up-

STRAVINSKY TO BEAN   *January 8, 1952*

The Rake's Progress, vocal score: I have sent word immediately to Auden telling him to get in touch at once with you and Dr. Roth and give you the corrections (concerning defective scansion in a few places) to be entered before it is too late. If you do not hear from our "poet" shortly it might be a good idea for you to call and awake him to the urgency of the matter.

Cuvelier: I will be glad to see him when he comes here. I cannot answer anything off hand concerning Belgium. I first have to know . . . my schedule and commitments in Paris because Nabokov & Co. are trying to have me conduct the premiere of the *Rake* in Paris in May, and we are negotiating. . . .

New composition: You already know from our recent conversations what my feelings and wishes are on this subject. I had time before leaving New York to fix with Auden the main lines of a short new opera in one act[22] calling for a small chamber ensemble. . . . [But] I would like to have the work fully commissioned before starting my composition.

My commission should be $10,000, not including my conducting the premiere (of course) which should be made compulsory and the object of a separate contract and fee. Naturally another contract will have to be drawn and concluded with Auden and Kallman for their libretto.

STRAVINSKY TO BEAN   *January 9, 1952*

Sam Dushkin has written, . . . forwarding . . . a tentative proposal for a composition to be delivered by the end of 1954 at the latest to a symphony society which wants to stay anonymous for the moment and will be celebrating its 25th anniversary in 1955. Enclosed is a copy of my answer to Dushkin. If you are in a position to know more about it, please keep me posted.

Moreover, the morning mail has also brought me a letter from Simon Harcourt-Smith concerning the old film project of *Odyssey.* He writes that they are getting ready to shoot around August 1952 and he is planning to come and confer with me in this country if I am still interested.

STRAVINSKY TO ROTH   *January 11, 1952*

Paris—Nabokov—Rake: I have written Nabokov telling him I will accept conducting one or all acts of *Rake* at the Paris premiere for a special fee of $5,000. . . .

Montevideo: Buenos Aires being out of question on account of both "atmo-

---

to-date, which is to say that the English edition will mention my most recent compositions." Stravinsky wrote again on January 22 saying that Boosey & Hawkes had agreed to publish the book in English.

[22] Kallman did not return from Europe until January 1952, and the libretto of *Delia* was sent to Stravinsky several weeks later.

sphere" and exchange situations, Montevideo could be the only South American alternative worth my considering. But I have not an extraordinary appetite for it unless they are willing to pay a high fee.

American Premiere: You are probably aware by now of the situation with the Met . . . for February 1953.

STRAVINSKY TO ROTH

This word to ask you to . . . let me have some copies of the booklet (a kind of introductory guide) which was issued and sold in accompaniment to the *Rake's Progress* program in Zürich. I had one copy of it (which I think you had given me) and it has disappeared during my trip. It is a very good booklet, well made. No doubt you will have it translated into English.

STRAVINSKY TO BEAN

Auden—Royalty on *Rake*'s libretto: Here is what happened: Auden, *on his own initiative (not mine)*, told me in [April] 1948 in New York that he felt I had to have a share in his royalties from the sale of the libretto because, he said, the sale will be influenced, indeed, by the added prestige of my name. Though I answered I did not want [this], Auden insisted that I should have a share of 2½ percent. For this reason the clause you mention [was] introduced in my contract dated 29 April 1948.

Now [you] ask me to give up something which I never claimed but was given to me as a gift. Of course precisely because it was a gift and Auden made it to me from his own inspiration and good heart I won't stage any fight for it. If Auden has changed his mind today for some reason unknown to me let him take the negative initiative just as he took the positive one.

STRAVINSKY TO BEAN

This is the continuation to my writing of yesterday in answer to your three letters of 28 January.

Mexico: I will fly with Andre (Mrs. Stravinsky will stay here) to Mexico on 1 March and back here 10 March. . . . We will stay at the Del Prado Hotel. My concerts are scheduled for 7 March (night) and 9 March (morning). . . .

Baiser de la fée: The other day I received the proofs from your office. I have already made corrections and I am giving a last look to the score. . . . As you have already noticed, the titles of the four scenes are in English in this full score. . . . I am afraid that, owing to the snail-like speed of your French engravers, we will never see the end of it and for this reason only I am inclined to give up the stage directions in the full score, inasmuch as stage directors or choreographers work always with the piano reduction and not with the full score. . . .

Orpheus: . . . I want to go through it and I will make all corrections for a new edition which is badly needed (please don't drag it).

Dali: I have not heard a thing from [him]. I guess the matter must have been dropped. . . .

Rake's—vocal score: Auden must have given you the latest correction concerning the word "initiated" (page 49/50).

Rake's—Metropolitan: Good news as to the contract and congratulations to you.

Concerning the singers . . . I knew [Mack] Harrell 12 years ago (Creon and Tiresias in *Oedipus* with the Boston Symphony under my direction); but, after all, I do not know if he is the same now. I prefer to leave all this to Reiner and Auden-Kallman. . . .

Columbia: Lieberson was here for lunch with me Saturday, 26 January. It was all very friendly.

Yesterday a letter from Gilbert was telling me quite frankly that *Perséphone* at Philadelphia is off for the next season, but he mentions "another possibility" and maybe you will know exactly what it is before I do.

STRAVINSKY TO BEAN   *February 2, 1952*

Here is the print of the photograph of Vera and myself which I hope you will like. . . .

This week Sanford H. Roth, who is an extraordinarily gifted photographer . . . has made a series of portraits of me. Yesterday he brought two of them here and they are really wonderful. He will have more of the other poses ready next week. You should write him directly.

STRAVINSKY TO ROTH   *February 8, 1952*

I have just received a letter from Nadia Boulanger whom I had asked to give me her opinion about the French translation of the *Rake*.

Her answer is not too cheerful.

I understand that the French translation of this Mr. de Badet (by the way, I have never understood who commissioned him: you or the Grand Opéra?) in many instances is completely off, and, still worse, has led to some musical changes which completely erase the original rhythmical sense. . . .

Please contact Miss Boulanger and ask her to handle herself the problem of straightening out the mistakes. I cannot do it from here; time is running short and moreover Miss Boulanger is at hand and perfectly aware. Till Monday 18 February, she will be lecturing on the *Rake* at Le Palais de Monaco, Principauté de Monaco. Thereafter she will go back to her regular address, 36, rue Ballu, Paris 9.

STRAVINSKY TO ROTH   *February 15, 1952*

As to things in Paris, they are far from settled. What is certain is that I will be there in May at the Théâtre des Champs-Elysées to conduct *Oedipus Rex,* a symphony and a ballet. But the schedule is somewhat vague, and, in order to let my first reappearance in France in 13 years not be wasted through poor management and programming, I have written Nabokov a few days ago telling him that I suggest one performance with *Oedipus Rex* only, one full symphonic program with Symphony in C, Capriccio or Piano Concerto, and Symphony in Three Movements, and a third appearance to conduct only one ballet (*Orpheus*), the rest of the program being left to another conductor. I do not know if Nabokov will endorse this plan.

Concerning *Rake's* at the Opéra I know nothing of what they have planned or decided. I wrote [Emmanuel de] Bondeville insisting that they should take Cocteau to stage my opera, whether I participate or not.

STRAVINSKY TO BEAN   *February 22, 1952*

This morning I received the following telegram: "New Friends of Music planned a concert devoted to your chamber work next season. Would be honored have your suggestions for such program with your participating concert on a Sunday afternoon during series from mid November to March. Please wire reaction and time preference—Herbert Barrett mgr 250 West 57 St New York City."

I answered: "Accepting [in] principle conducting program my chamber works Sundays December twenty first or twenty eighth of January. Going now to Mexico will write you details and program suggestions around middle March—Igor Stravinsky."

. . . While waiting for some commission to . . . materialize, I have been and am still working on some pieces taken from old English poetry. For these songs I am writing music for small chamber ensemble. For the time being I cannot foresee how many such songs I may [compose. As] to the Friends of Music, . . . I would like to give a program similar to the one I conducted here last month, i.e. Octet, *Dumbarton Oaks* Concerto, *Danses concertantes,* but instead of *Histoire du soldat* I would give them the premiere of my new songs. . . .

Furthermore, in this chamber music program Columbia could record Octet and, of course, the new songs (this will even be *the main thing to record*). . . .

Please answer me as soon as you can; if too busy to do it before my leaving for Mexico 1 March, write me air mail between 1 and 10 March: Hotel Del Prado, Mexico D.F.

STRAVINSKY TO ROTH   *February 22, 1952*

I have heard from Nabokov that the Grand Opéra will definitely not give the
Rake in May but in October. I hope your stay in Paris has enabled you to
straighten out the unpleasant details connected with the French translation of
the *Rake*. I entirely agree that errors in translations are unavoidable, but I think
it is a good thing to use all goodwill and competence to discover and mend
them.

STRAVINSKY TO ROTH   *February 29, 1952*

I am awaiting the final schedule of my rehearsals and appearances in Paris from
Nabokov. . . .

 Rake—Paris: What I read in your letter is quite new to me. The last time
Nabokov wrote me concerning the *Rake* was on 13 February. . . .

 I believe that behind all this there is an intricate political *"pasticcio."* Nevertheless your information seems fresher. As to Desormière, I . . . suggested
him because he has always well presented and played my music. I do not pre-
tend to impose him . . . moreover I have no conditions to put because I won't
even conduct the *Rake* myself. My conducting would have been the result of a
collaboration between Nabokov and the Grand Opéra, and now, from your letter, I suspect that Lehmann-Bondeville do not want to be tied in any way with
all this American business.

 When you will know my dates at the Festival you may engage my presence
to the *Rake* in a box provided it does not mean an extension of my stay and what
I will see and hear at the rehearsals will meet with my approval.

 You know and they may know at their convenience what my intentions are
concerning the *Rake* and therefore if they want to stick to them they can do it.
But I won't endorse with my own presence anything which will be "fancy interpretation."

 By the way, if Desormière is not engaged, do you know who will be? Would
they take Morel? And for the staging, Cocteau being *"tabu"* whom do they consider? . . .

 Mexico: I have just canceled my trip to Mexico tomorrow because I am in
bed with a strong flu. . . .

 I strongly advise you against putting the stage directions in the full score
of *Baiser de la fée:* 1. You would have to translate them in English as all titles
are already in English. 2. You would have to make a second proof-reading which
would delay things still more. 3. All this would be useless anyway because the
conductors do not need it and the stage directors or choreographers use the
vocal, not the full score.

STRAVINSKY TO ROTH   *March 10, 1952*

I want to let you know that I am working on some transcriptions of previous
works such as: Two Poems of Verlaine, former Jurgenson Edition, for baritone
and orchestra, and Concertino for string quartet, Hansen Copenhagen Edition,
which I am putting into a chamber music version for 12 instruments. I had the
idea of doing it because I have sometimes demands for conducting chamber
music programs which I am always at a loss to put together because I am rather
poor in chamber works.[23]

STRAVINSKY TO ROTH   *March 10, 1952*

Don't you think it would be better to forget about any European concert outside
of Paris this year? This may sound like a change of mood on my part but I had
not realized till now how involving the Paris Festival will be for me and my energies have to be kept fresh for the coming fall and winter season (Cleveland
concert and recording of the whole *Pulcinella* and Symphony in C plus the Met
Rake's premiere and recording).

[As for the] *Rake* in Paris, indeed I believe the matter is safe in your
hands. There is so much political intrigue always in France that I am unable
and unwilling to analyse the situation clearly from here. Even the fact that
Lehmann has written me a few days ago that he had taken Desormière means
nothing to me. . . .

When Schwarzkopf sang her aria in Geneva, who conducted? Ansermet or
someone else? . . .

Mexico: I will be there (Hotel Del Prado, Mexico D.F.) from 22 March till
30 March.

STRAVINSKY TO ROTH   *March 15, 1952*

I am enclosing a copy of the letter I have just received from Mr. de Rohozinski.
Will you please see if this is of any interest and advise me of the fee you feel I
should receive. Of course it must be substantially more than for regular conducting, and they should pay me *here*. I am writing Mr. Rohozinski myself telling him to negotiate with you both for my participation and your publisher's
rights. . . .

My son Theodore has wired me yesterday asking me if I would accept to
conduct the *Rake's* premiere in Geneva on 2 May. I have cabled him I would
exceptionally (on account of Theodore's participation) advance my flying to
Europe to do it if they are willing to pay me not less than 10,000 Swiss francs
but possibly more, up to $5,000. I am awaiting their answer.

---

[23] Stravinsky chose the ten wind instruments because they were already engaged for a
program that included the Octet and the Mass.

STRAVINSKY TO ROTH   *April 1, 1952*

I have just received your telegram in answer to my cables of 28 March (from Mexico) and 31 March (from here) concerning the Brussels concert on 29 May.

I hope it is not an afternoon affair because I am not going to take any afternoon dress along with me on the plane, having no space in my baggage.

Will you please get in touch with the Belgian management and let them know my program, which is: Symphony in 3 Movements, either Capriccio (with Monique Haas) or Violin Concerto (with Jeanne Gautier), intermission, Symphony in C. The program will be about one and one half hours. If they choose Capriccio it will be identical with my Paris concert of 22 May. . . .

Moreover, I shall not stay in Brussels after the concert because I want to go to Holland to rest for a few days and I will fly direct from Amsterdam back to New York not later than 10 June.

STRAVINSKY TO GOLDSTEIN   *April 3, 1952*

Upon my returning here from Mexico I have read Miss Bean's letter of 27 March 1952, concerning the use of *Firebird* in the film *Tonight We Sing*. This matter is so confused owing to the former Jurgenson Edition rights which are now in the hands of Schott, that . . . I am unable to answer you in any pertinent manner. Therefore, I suggest that you or your film agents should get in touch with Schott.

STRAVINSKY TO ROTH   *April 4, 1952*

When I wrote you on 1 April concerning the Brussels concert, I had no idea that Brussels, like Paris, wanted to have *Oedipus Rex* with Cocteau. I do prefer it also myself. In that case the program I drafted in my preceding letter is void.

In Paris I will give *Scènes de ballet* (16/17 minutes) as a prelude to the *Oedipus Rex* stage performance. If Brussels is satisfied with a program of *Oedipus* only (as I did in the past in Germany) it is all right with me. If so, we will have an intermission between the 2 acts of *Oedipus*. . . .

If Brussels can manage to have Peter Pears I shall be delighted. Otherwise, do they intend to have the Paris cast?

STRAVINSKY TO ROTH   *April 5, 1952*

I have just received your letter of 2 April, concerning BIEM,[24] SACEM, the Belgian Radio, and the boycott. Unfortunately I must admit that I have been dragged into this by BIEM which asked me to sign a protest in 1948. At that

---

[24] Bureau International de l'Edition Mécanique, the French copyright collecting organization.

moment it looked sound to me, probably because I had no other source of information.

Of course, [if] the cooperation between Boosey & Hawkes and myself
[had] been as close then as it has been lately, I can now regretfully say that I
certainly [would not] have signed anything of this kind without first taking
your experienced advice. . . .

I am enclosing the whole file I have on this stupid matter. You will see that
back in 1950 I got from the Brussels Tribunal the copy of the decision rendered
against Honegger and myself. I never did anything more after that because I
was not really interested and it seemed to be hopeless.

I did not pay anything either because, after all, it was BIEM's business.

Now I realize that I do not know what they have done. Have they paid the
court charges or not? And am I going to find some *huissier* waiting for me at the
door of my green room at the Palais des Beaux Arts in Brussels before or after
my concert on 29 May?

STRAVINSKY TO ROTH   *April 21, 1952*

I am leaving by plane for New York the day after tomorrow.

Trip to Europe: I am flying TWA flight 922, leaving New York Monday 28
April at 5 p.m., calling at Paris-Orly for an unknown number of minutes, Tuesday 29 April around 1:30 p.m., and arrive Tuesday 29 April at 4:10 p.m. I will
assist [i.e., be present] at the dress rehearsal, the premiere and the second performance of the *Rake* in French, and I will fly back to Paris on 6 May.

In Geneva I will stay at Hôtel des Bergues. In Paris: Hôtel Plaza-Athénée.

Television *Oedipus Rex:* A letter from Rohozinski has just come in from
Paris (his address there: 40, rue Lauriston, Paris 16ème). He seems to be worrying about the delay. . . .

Royal Philharmonic Society: I have not heard anything from them
directly. . . . Let me confess frankly that I hate all of these things, medals,
scrolls, etc., . . . whether with or without social fuss. But I will do my utmost to
be nice and to act in view of what may be helpful to you, provided they do not
require my going specially to London . . . because this would really be asking
the impossible.

STRAVINSKY TO ROTH   *July 4, 1952*

I have found rather important misprints in the vocal score of *Rake* (in the full
score these notes are correct). I am stapling herewith the correction.

. . . From the tape recordings he let me hear, I guess [Paul] Collaer followed in the steps of someone (Leitner???)[25] who inaugurated some wrong
tempi.

---

[25] Ferdinand Leitner conducted the second and third performances of the opera in
Venice, following Stravinsky's premiere.

STRAVINSKY TO DAVID ADAMS   *July 11, 1952*

As you know, I am going to perform *Pulcinella* in Cleveland and record it also. This will be the first time that it will be performed here in the full original ballet version (so far, the Concert Suite has always been played).[26] I assume that your office does not have the orchestra material of the full ballet; therefore you will have to get it from Europe.

STRAVINSKY TO STEIN   *July 18, 1952*

When I was in Brussels, Paul Collaer played for me the tape recording of his broadcast and then I noticed most of the tempi were wrong. On this, Collaer told me he had merely followed the tempi as they were given in a list of corrections he found in the orchestral material. . . .

I would like to have a look at this list in order to check it. Moreover, I am curious to know who established it.

Now something more to be taken care of in the printed vocal score:

1. page 202 at **197**; the first note of the right hand of the piano must not be a C but a third higher, an E.

2. page 203: at the third eighth (F), a sharp is missing. In the same measure, in the last chord of the right hand, a flat is missing at E: it should be a C minor and not a C major chord.

Of course there should be some more corrections, but, first of all, I would like to see the list Paul Collaer had referred to.

STRAVINSKY TO ROTH   *July 21, 1952*

You will find enclosed one copy (photocopy) of my Concertino in its newly orchestrated version for twelve instruments. You are fully aware of the situation with Hansen and I wonder if you foresee now the possibility of making some arrangement with them. . . .

I am also enclosing one copy of Two Poems of Verlaine (which, I believe, I mentioned to you in Europe). This is a recently made orchestration (small orchestra) of the Two Poems of Verlaine for piano and bass voice, composed in 1910 for my late brother who was a bass baritone of the St. Petersburg Imperial Opera. I have just completed it and I am handing it over to you for publication. . . .

This brings up the matter of the former Jurgenson Edition, to which the Two Poems of Verlaine originally belonged. What kind of arrangement can you conclude in Europe (of course here it is free) with Jurgenson/Forberg? This is an interesting point because some other works of mine in the Jurgenson cata-

---

[26] Stravinsky is mistaken here: the first performance had taken place in November 1949 at Carnegie Hall, the present writer conducting. See *S.S.C.* I, p. 368.

logue might be considered by you for re-publication. Among them I would like to mention: *Deux poésies de Serge Gorodetzki: Novice et sainte rosée,* and Quatre études pour piano.

My new Cantata is in its final stage; actually my composition is complete.

STRAVINSKY TO ROTH   *July 23, 1952*

I believe I spoke to you in Paris or Brussels of the awkward experience I had with the orchestra material of *Oedipus Rex.* . . .

I found out that the Paris orchestra had been provided with parts that did not follow the new version while the score given Rosbaud and myself was the engraved score of the new version.

Moreover, the singers had the old vocal score which did not follow the two "reprises" that I put in the new version (aria of Jocaste and duetto of Jocaste and Oedipe in Act II).

Please make sure that from now on the material will be . . . in accordance with the newly printed orchestra score, whether the old parts are adapted and corrected, or new parts are made.

STRAVINSKY TO ROTH   *July 28, 1952*

I have just received a small brochure-program from the Bayerischer Rundfunk in which there is the following announcement: 7 Oktober 1952, Igor Strawinsky zum 70 Geburtstag, *Orpheus, Apollon musagète,* Leitung: Igor Strawinsky.

Knowing that I won't be in Europe at the moment I draw the conclusion that they are going to play my recordings of *Orpheus* and *Apollo.*

I wonder if you have any control over this and if they are going to pay us anything.

STRAVINSKY TO ROTH   *July 28, 1952*

When the piano score of my Piano Concerto (Concerto pour piano et orchestre d'harmonie) was published in 1949 no mention was printed that it was actually a "revised version." As a matter of fact, we even signed a new copyright contract for it. . . .

Speaking of "revised versions" I do not find [those] of my Piano Sonata and Serenade in A. I do remember I revised them even with the fingering details, and you must have those corrected copies somewhere in your files. . . .

I have here the printed vocal score of "Introduction, Chant du Pecheur et Air du Rossignol" from Act I of *Le Rossignol.* Do you have this fragment [in full score] separately published for concert performances? I think Païchadze did it.

I also have "Chanson de Paracha" pour Chant et Piano, from *Mavra,* in the printed edition (1929). I remember I had made a special orchestration of it and I thought this had been printed. Do you have it?

STRAVINSKY TO STEIN   *July 28, 1952*

Are you going to put all these [*Rake*] corrections on an "errata" list or do you
plan to make a new corrected edition? Of course the latter alternative is a much
better one. . . . The provisional edition (in 3 volumes) of the full score, given
me in Venice, is on such inadequate paper that the "recto" side shows through
the "verso." . . . Another great inconvenience to the conductor comes from the
engraving itself, which is so dense that it makes the eights, especially in recitatives, look exactly like sixteens, . . . but I think that better paper would at least
partly overcome this.

STRAVINSKY TO ROTH   *July 30, 1952*

I have just sent you via air mail–registered: one copy of the Cantata full score
with most of the piano reduction written by myself in red pencil and ink. In
some instances you will find the piano reduction on photocopied sheets which I
stapled to the score. In other instances, I have written the piano reduction on
the score in red pencil.

    In both cases I have done it so that there won't be any doubt left in Mr.
Spinner's mind. But there are some [places] where I have not made the piano
reduction. Those are the ones where no doubt should take place.

    In other words, now it is just a matter of material work. Therefore when
you will publish the *Klavierauszug* you should mention the vocal score has
been made by myself.

STRAVINSKY TO ADAMS   *July 31, 1952*

The *New York Times* of Sunday July 27, 1952, has printed the following:

> Music from Igor Stravinsky's newest opera, *The Rake's Progress*, will have
> its American premiere on "Your Invitation to Music" on CBS Radio, Sun-
> day, August 31, from 1:00 to 2:30 p.m. The excerpts to be heard were re-
> corded by James Fassett during a recent trip to Holland and were played by
> the Residentie Orchestra of The Hague, conducted by Igor Markevitch
> with Elisabeth Schwarzkopf, soprano, as soloist. They include the two
> principal arias of the opera, from the first and third acts.

I wonder if you are aware of this and if you . . . have given permission . . . to
broadcast excerpts . . . before the premiere at the Met.

    Outside of the fact that I personally do not think it is wise to do it at this
moment, I am very much afraid that the thing will not at all make Mr. Bing
happy.

STRAVINSKY TO ADAMS   *July 31, 1952*

Did you hear anything from Dr. Rosenwald (New Friends of Music)? Please do
not show him the score of my Cantata before he signs his contract with me.

STRAVINSKY TO ROTH   *August 2, 1952*

I have just received the green proofs of Capriccio sent by your office. As they
seem to have been engraved in Germany I will endeavor not to write my corrections in French as I did with the scores engraved in France. I am starting to
work on that right away but I will not progress too fast because during the coming two weeks I have to get ready for my local concert at the Hollywood Bowl
where, in fact, I am going to give this Capriccio with my son Soulima.[27] It may
even help me find some more details to straighten out. . . .

   Please send me some pocket scores of Four Etudes for Orchestra. By the
way, do you plan to make a new edition of the full score in normal size, because
the Païchadze edition, which I have here, is full of mistakes. I have made the
corrections in my copy and whenever you would like to have it I would be glad
to send it to you.

   When do you plan to make a new edition of my Mass? You must have in
your files some excellent and unaltered photostat prints of the cover of the vocal
score. I had them made at the request of Ralph Hawkes to whom I handed
them. The first published vocal score had this cover, but it had been tampered
with and Ralph Hawkes agreed it was rather bad and he promised to change it
and use the unaltered drawings for the new edition.

   What about Octet? About a year ago Betty Bean requested me to correct a
copy of the full score to make a revised version for a new copyright. I did the
work and sent it to your New York office. Since then I had no news whatsoever.
Is the new printing under way?

STRAVINSKY TO ADAMS   *August 9, 1952*

In reference with the CBS Radio broadcast of excerpts of *The Rake's Progress*, I
am glad to hear that you have already been in touch with the Met on this matter, [and] I am quite satisfied . . . with the fact that the broadcast will be limited to two arias.

STRAVINSKY TO STEIN   *August 15, 1952*

Cantata: After reading your comments on the spelling I have made a careful
check in the Oxford Book of English Verse (1900 edition) with my friend

---

[27] Stravinsky had written to Soulima on July 25: "Both of us must be dressed the same,
and, personally, if it is warm I will wear a white *smoking*. But one never knows what
the temperature will be here, and if it is cold I will wear full dress. Also, do not forget to
bring the manuscripts that you did not sell."

Aldous Huxley. Nothing has to be changed in the score I sent you except an actual slip-of-the-pen. In the "Lyke-Wake Dirge," first interlude, it should definitely read: "The whinnes shall prick thee to the bare bane." . . .

As to my using "shall" instead of "sall" it is perfectly all right linguistically and it is by far much better in view of the singers who might make too often a mistake in pronouncing the "sall." So, let us keep "shall."

The title "The Maidens Came" is all right also.

STRAVINSKY TO STEIN   *August 16, 1952*

Rake's Progress: I am enclosing the errata list (6 pages plus addenda) and also 4 additional slips. I hope this can be considered final as far as the full score is concerned. I do not speak about the vocal score which is still full of mistakes of its own. . . .

Capriccio: While conducting here a few days ago, I made a slight change in the orchestra score (it does not concern the piano score). I wish you will also make this slurring in the green proofs I mailed back to you the other day when you receive them. Please refer to the enclosed slip.

STRAVINSKY TO ADAMS   *August 18, 1952*

When I saw Mr. Lester, President of the Los Angeles Chamber Symphony, the other day, he asked me whom he had to deal with for the material of the Cantata and Concertino. . . .

There is no question of charging a special "premiere" fee because . . . I have been commissioned for the premiering of these two works by the Los Angeles Chamber Symphony. . . .

But since Mr. Lester has come forward I believe he may be expecting to have to pay something. This is why I told him to get in touch with you, and I think if you charge him a moderate rental fee, he will not cry too much.

STRAVINSKY TO ADAMS   *August 20, 1952*

I am writing you now in reference to the film proposal.

In principle, I have nothing against it, provided it pays what a film should pay. But in order to enable me to state my material and artistic requirements, I need to know more details:

1. What is the subject or rather the story? . . . I cannot endorse a proposal in the blank.

2. What quantity of music (in minutes) do they need for this one hour feature?

3. If I undertake this commission, at the time of my composing I will have to be given a precise schedule of the music requirements by the producers or directors.

They will have to decide themselves what sections have to be with music and the exact timing of the music for each section, [however] short it may be.

STRAVINSKY TO STEIN   *August 25, 1952*

Enclosed, you will find the corrected first proofs of the vocal score of my Cantata. . . . If the work keeps progressing at the same fast pace and you airmail the second proofs here, I think there will not be much delay incurred and everything will be ready to let the soloist singers have the vocal score at least a month before they start rehearsing.

STRAVINSKY TO ADAMS   *August 28, 1952*

The CBC-Toronto project is quite acceptable to me in principle, but under the following condition: a program of one hour and a half should be given at least 4 rehearsals. My practice shows that for the average concert of 75 minutes of music the orchestra needs from 4 to 5 rehearsals, which I am careful to use with the greatest efficiency. I am not the one who needs the rehearsals, the orchestra needs them. . . .

I will never again accept to do what I did at Hollywood Bowl where we had only two rehearsals for only 45 minutes of my own music,[28] and the result was disgusting. Fortunately it was not broadcast.

STRAVINSKY TO STEIN   *August 29, 1952*

Thank you very much for your very kind letter of August 25, from Harewood House. . . . I am glad you like my Cantata and I also wish you will have a chance to hear it soon in London. . . .

As to the full score, . . . I am in full agreement with your suggestion . . . not to publish it until after my premiere in order to allow for any possible corrections. . . .

This cover is now satisfactory. My only objection concerns the color and kind of paper used. It must get spoiled very quickly. A paper not so coarse, even white, would keep better.

STRAVINSKY TO BOOSEY   *August 30, 1952*

I have to go to Vancouver, B.C., on the last days of September, for the rehearsals preceding my concert there on October 5. I will fly back on October 6, arriving here probably late that day.

---

[28] Stravinsky had filled out the program with Tchaikovsky's Second Symphony.

STRAVINSKY TO ADAMS   *September 8, 1952*

Pulcinella ballet material: You mention that you are going to receive 2, 2, 2, 2, 2. I will need 3, 3, 3, 2, 2. I will ask you to send this material to me here, because I want to check it myself well in advance, owing to the fact that it has not been used for so many years (the Suite only has been played in concert performances . . . a different material). Moreover, if I find it possible, I may use two numbers from the tenor and soprano parts of the ballet, in addition to the Suite, when I . . . perform it here on November 11. Have you any idea when this material may arrive?

STRAVINSKY TO STEIN   *September 9, 1952*

If the full score second proofs have not yet been sent to me when these lines reach you, please do be so kind to enclose also the first proofs of the full score bearing my corrections. . . . After checking and re-checking, I decided to settle for "Cancrizans," which is the English spelling. I have already written it that way (with "z") in the full score, and I am doing the same now in the vocal score.

STRAVINSKY TO ADAMS   *September 11, 1952*

Cantata chorus: My original intention is to manage with 8 girls (4 sopranos and 4 altos). If the first practice here shows that [this] is too [few] I may decide to do it with 6 and 6 in New York. In this case we will be able to use also the parts already used here.

It is good news to hear that London is working so fast. Anyhow, if the engraved parts have not arrived for the Los Angeles and New York performances, it will not matter, because we have . . . the masters and the prints for two complete sets.

STRAVINSKY TO ROTH   *September 12, 1952*

I have been in constant touch with Mr. Stein concerning the proofs and the editing of my Cantata. I am delighted to see how fast you have actually been acting and I want to congratulate you on the fine work of engraving done.

I thought that a standard cover won't be up to par with the rest of the edition and I asked my daughter (Milene Marion) to compose an appropriate cover in the style I wanted. She did an excellent job, which, I am sure, you will also approve.

STRAVINSKY TO STEIN   *September 19, 1952*

My reason for writing you today is in connection with the "v" or "w" in my name. I fully endorse your point of view as far as the German speaking people are concerned, but another pronunciation trap exists in English with the "w." Whatever spelling is used, it should not make much difference in my case, as my name is now known well enough.

Anyhow, if you believe the "w" is more likely to make more people happy, please use it.

STRAVINSKY TO ROTH   *September 22, 1952*

The original [Concertino] manuscript happens to be now at the Library of Congress after being presented there by a member of the Quatuor Flonzaley. You could tell your New York office to get a microphotography of it if necessary, and compare it with the so-called Burt version, the copyright of which would then appear so shaky indeed that Hansen would very likely prefer not to raise the question officially. (This Burt business is like the Spalding and Schneider protection of my works for Edition Russe. Kalmus, Marks, and other smart people knew that they could just overlook it.)[29]

STRAVINSKY TO ADAMS   *September 23, 1952*

Thank you for your letter of September 19, 1952, which accompanied the script for the film project. . . .

If they consider getting Balanchine I certainly would prefer him to anybody else, because I am so used to work with him and, besides, we are personal friends. . . .

I will fly to Vancouver Wednesday October 1st and back here Monday October 6 (my address there: Vancouver Hotel, Vancouver, B.C.).

STRAVINSKY TO STEIN   *September 23, 1952*

In reference [to] new editions of my Piano Sonata and Serenade in A, I have here only my own single scores of both works (with the old Edition Russe cover) in which there are many corrections and fingering marks of mine.

---

[29] Koussevitzky's secretary, Vladimir Zederbaum, had written to Stravinsky on April 2, 1924: "A few days ago I saw the violinist Spalding, who told me that in the U.S. a society is being organized, along completely new lines, to protect authors' and publishers' interests (regardless of nationality or citizenship), and Spalding has taken an active part in organizing this society. . . . He will be in Paris at the end of April and will explain everything at that time. I don't know if you know him. . . . He and Sergei Alexandrovich are great friends."

STRAVINSKY TO ROTH   *September 26, 1952*

Today, after completing the corrections in the proofs of the new version of the
Octet (which I airmailed at once to Mr. Stein), I started to go over this *Pulcinella* material, and I found it in a *disastrous condition.*

Every conductor who used it made his own various and numerous cuts,
marks, etc. . . . , in the score, and the musicians did the same in their parts. It is
a complete mess. Moreover, the paper, being in very bad condition, does not
allow for easy erasing.

I cannot spend hours and hours of my own time here trying to clean all
this and to patch up the pages. And in Cleveland rehearsal time will be too precious to be wasted on this stupid business.

I am asking you to take emergency measures in this instance. Can you
send me *at once* a completely new (untouched) set of the *Pulcinella* ballet material? I will then make my corrections into it, because, indeed, there are misprints, and corrections are needed.

If no new material is available, I will have to get authority from you to give
all this job here to a copyist and pay him to do all this dirty work.

STRAVINSKY TO ADAMS   *September 26, 1952*

I just read the script you sent me. . . . [Its] qualities, though attractive, are not
quite enough to let me commit myself to the project. . . .

Do you know whether Balanchine has been contacted and could you find
out directly from him what his reaction actually is? Has he also examined the
script?

STRAVINSKY TO STEIN   *September 26, 1952*

I am sending back to you herewith the corrected first proofs of the Octet which
I received a few days ago. . . . I would like to see this new revised version come
through in time for my being able to use it when I will record the Octet with
Columbia in New York next December. . . .

Thus we will avoid being deprived from a financial return as we would necessarily be should I be compelled to use the old version, the protection of which
by Albert Spalding is very shaky.

STRAVINSKY TO ROTH   *September 29, 1952*

I just learned from Mr. Stein that Paul Sacher is going to conduct *The Rake's
Progress* at the BBC early next year. . . . Please do everything you can to bring
Sacher to follow closely my tempo indications which I have checked again recently and for which Mr. Stein has a corrected list of errata (which concerns
also the notes). How do you feel about this broadcast? Aren't you afraid it may
hurt the Edinburgh and Covent Garden projects if it is not done properly?

STRAVINSKY TO ADAMS   *October 8, 1952*

After returning from Vancouver, I received . . . an answer to my letter with reference to the terrible condition of the *Pulcinella* material. . . .

The orchestra strings are going to be completely made anew on transparent masters. The other parts (solo strings and winds) will be cleaned.

Everything will be ready in the middle of November and I will send the whole material directly to Cleveland then. . . .

I have seen Mr. Leslie Boosey yesterday and we are having lunch together today. It is nice meeting him again, indeed.

STRAVINSKY TO ROTH   *October 8, 1952*

Upon returning from my Vancouver concert, I found a letter from Hansen, a copy of which I am enclosing, as well as a copy of my answer to him . . . *"pour la forme."*

I must confess . . . that there is an unknown element of difficulty resulting from the fact that I have lost (with part of my files which I had left in France during the last war) my copy of my contract with Hansen.

I would rather not tell them that, [and] acknowledge the fact by asking them for a duplicate.

Therefore, if it is true that they have bought from me the Concertino in its arrangement for string quartet as well as *all other arrangements,* I believe that, legally, they would have a valid title to my new instrumentation of it, unless this new instrumentation would not be copyrighted under my name (inasmuch as anybody can copyright an arrangement from the original).

This, I cannot tell them, but you can. Moreover, you can also scare them by saying that, if they persist in trying to have everything for themselves, I might, as a last resort and to stop all this nonsense, simply withdraw my new instrumentation and keep it for myself in my files.

Therefore, it sounds more sensible for every party concerned to share something than to have nothing.

STRAVINSKY TO ROTH   *October 13, 1952*

Serenade and Sonata: the scores have just arrived. I hope you do not have too many of them in stock because I am willing to revise these two works in view of securing a new copyright.

Forberg: very pleased to learn you have made a deal with him. . . .

I was very pleased to see Mr. Leslie Boosey here last week.

STRAVINSKY TO ADAMS   *October 17, 1952*

The chorus master does not seem very much aware of the music and instru-mentation of my Cantata: otherwise he would know that 24 is a figure which would throw everything off balance. . . .

My . . . plan calls for eight singers (that I will have here). If Dr. Rosen-wald's[30] chorus master wants to go as far as twelve, this [is the] *maximum* ac-ceptable to me.

STRAVINSKY TO ADAMS   *October 22, 1952*

Thank you also for the information in your letter of October 13, concerning the film proposal. The best thing to do at this point seems to be to wait till my arrival in New York in December.

As to the New Friends of Music, I was aware of Dr. Rosenwald's resigna-tion.

STRAVINSKY TO ROTH   *October 23, 1952*

Ansermet—*Rake:* Of course, Ansermet is a serious craftsman and I believe he will do quite a good job, though he never heard me do the *Rake.*

Rake—Brussels: Glad Collaer does it in Flemish at the Beaux-Arts, pro-vided, of course, that this time he follows strictly my tempos (you have the complete errata list now).

Rake—score: I heard from Mr. Stein that you planned to publish the full orchestra score in 3 volumes. Don't you think that this is less practical than one single volume, even big?

As to the pocket score, Mr. Stein wrote me that you did not intend to pub-lish it. If so, please think it over again, because in my opinion it would be a great mistake to deprive musicians of the possibility of getting acquainted with the work in its original orchestral form.

Baiser de la fée: For the pocket score it is my wish and hope, indeed, that you will publish it because Divertimento is only one third of the whole score.

STRAVINSKY TO STEIN   *November 1, 1952*

As for the proofs of my instrumentation of Verlaine's songs, it is very fortunate, indeed, that you noticed what I did not notice, i.e., that I had jumped over six bars, probably in the rush to copy from my pencil sketches in order to let you have the score without delay.

I should have checked more carefully myself and I am sorry that this is going to cause you some trouble now.

---

[30] Formerly of the New Friends of Music, New York. Stravinsky conducted the Can-tata for this organization in December.

STRAVINSKY TO ROTH   *November 3, 1952*

Rake—Brussels: I am not worried about the singers, still less if they are the ones from Holland. They were so wonderful in *Oedipus* last June. But let us hope that Collaer will straighten out his tempos, because what I heard of his Flemish performance recording was far from exciting. . . .

Odyssey film: (confidential)

Since I have seen him, I am not interested at all in any project in which Harcourt-Smith[31] is involved. On the other hand you may remember that I am rather interested in the Michael Powell idea of having Dylan Thomas (or some outstanding poet like him) compose a libretto in view of my composing the music.

STRAVINSKY TO STEIN   *November 4, 1952*

Here are the pages with the six bars missing from the orchestra score photocopy of my Verlaine poems. . . . You will also note that in these six bars I made some changes, especially in the voice part of the original vocal score.

In connection with this, I believe some day I will have to think of making a complete new vocal score. Anyhow, I have no time for that now.

STRAVINSKY TO ROTH   *November 5, 1952*

Enclosed is a copy of my letter to Hansen in reply to their recent mail. As you may see, my answer is rather strongly worded and I wish it will help make them either more lenient or at least less stubborn.

STRAVINSKY TO ROTH   *November 12, 1952*

Cantata: The premiere last night was a great success. Soloists, chorus, musicians, all were excellent. As you know, Hugues Cuénod sang the tenor part. He will do it again in New York with me next month. This part is very strenuous owing to its length without any kind of respite; and Cuénod did it very well.

I think you should write down the duration as being "about 30 minutes."

The only change or correction that I wish to make in the score is in the Westron Wind duet, 2 bars before **10.** There, I have removed the fermata.

That is all and you can go ahead with the printing. Please inform Mr. Stein on my behalf about this.

---

[31] Stravinsky had met Simon Harcourt-Smith in Paris in May 1952.

STRAVINSKY TO ADAMS   *November 24, 1952*

Three days ago I sent to Cleveland the complete material (either cleaned or made anew) for the *Pulcinella* ballet. . . .

The old string parts . . . are . . . so full of mistakes of all kinds that *they have to be completely withdrawn from circulation.* My advice to you altogether is to destroy them as soon as you can. . . .

Did you hear anything from the New Friends since Dr. Rosenwald's resignation? . . . I do not even know how many rehearsals are scheduled and when they are scheduled. Could you get some information and forward it to me? . . .

I am flying from here to Cleveland on Saturday December 6[32] and I will stay in Cleveland till December 14. Address in Cleveland: Wade Park Manor Hotel, Cleveland 6, Ohio. I will leave Cleveland by air for New York either in the evening of December 14 or the morning of December 15, depending on when the recording session will end on Sunday the 14th. In New York, I shall stay at the Gladstone Hotel, as usual.

STRAVINSKY TO STEIN   *December 1, 1952*

The two songs must have a common title indeed, and it should be: Two Songs (Poetry of Paul Verlaine), Orchestral Version 1951.

. . . From December 15 I will be in New York (Hotel Gladstone, 114 East 52nd Street, N.Y. 22) till after the premiere of the *Rake* at the Met sometime in February.

STRAVINSKY TO ROTH   *January 16, 1953*

I have just received your letter of Jan 12th, together with that of Michael Powell. . . . I ask you to enter into negotiation with him for me. For the moment I shall confine myself to my own demands (leaving the details of meeting with Dylan Thomas and Michael Powell, etc. until I have his reaction to this first letter).

1. Suppose we decide upon the Nausicaa scene—which I think is an excellent idea—and the scene lasts 20 minutes, then in this case I could compose circa 12 minutes of music, to be divided into the following numbers: Prelude or Interlude; Dance, or Song or Chorus-song, 2nd Dance; Hymn (chorus).

2. The orchestra would be a small chamber-music ensemble.

3. For this I will ask twelve thousand dollars. If later film or television will be in question you will determine what arrangements to make at the time.

4. As Michael Powell is asking this for next January 1954, I have to have an answer immediately. I have other propositions which I will be able to stall off

---

[32] Stravinsky went to Cleveland and New York accompanied by his son-in-law, since Mrs. Stravinsky was recovering from a thyroid operation.

for only a short time. If D. Thomas can finish a libretto by June it would give me enough time.

5. Please tell Michael Powell that D. Thomas is expected in the U.S.A. very soon, and that it would save a lot of time and money for me to discuss the libretto with him while he is here. Also tell Mr. Powell that I will be in Hollywood only from March 10th to April 1st and that until then I will be here in New York, and after that time I will be on tour in Cuba and Venezuela. I may go to Boston to conduct *The Rake's Progress* at Boston University. At any case I should be in June in Hollywood.

STRAVINSKY TO BOOSEY   *July 21, 1953*

For a long time I have [been] planning to write . . . but, as you may know, I was away in Cuba and Venezuela in April, then in May I conducted two performances of *The Rake's Progress* at Boston with the Opera Workshop of the Boston University. The first one was very good, the second one (with another cast) was not so good unfortunately. Staging[33] and decors excellent.

But it was a very tiring experience indeed,[34] and I was glad to come back home in June. . . .

May I ask you to send me Benjamin Britten's *Gloriana* in which I am greatly interested?

STRAVINSKY TO ROTH   *July 21, 1953*

I do not know whether you were in Paris for the premiere of *"Le Libertin."* The press which I got quite in full proved to be stupid, incompetent and nasty. What are your comments?

My *Rake* recordings with Columbia are excellent and will be released early in the fall.

STRAVINSKY TO BOOSEY & HAWKES   *July 21, 1953*

You must have received by now both the instrumental score and my two-piano transcription of my new Septet 1953 through your New York office. If so, I suppose you are already working on the engraving. When do you expect to send me the proofs?

The negotiations I was carrying on with the Dumbarton Oaks Foundation

---

[33] By Sarah Caldwell.

[34] Stravinsky had elaborated on the ill effects of this experience in a letter to his son Theodore on June 8: "I am happy to be at home finally. This terrible crisis of spasms of the colon was aggravated as a result of the enormous task, very trying for my nerves, with the Boston students. This work added to the already debilitating effects of the four attacks of influenza I have suffered between February and May. But already I have regained my strength, and now I will put on the 3 kilos that I lost."

for the premiere of Septet 1953 finally came to a conclusion. Therefore I will conduct 2 consecutive performances at Dumbarton Oaks at the end of January 1954 and immediately after I will record it with the same players for Columbia in New York. . . .

When I saw Mr. Adams here last month I advised him of the new instrumentation I had just completed of my Tango, originally published as a piano score by Mercury Music Corporation, New York, in 1941. This new instrumentation is rather unusual, with 4 clarinets, 1 clarinet bass, 4 trumpets, 3 trombones, guitar, and a small string section (3 violins, 1 viola, 1 cello, 1 double bass). The instrumental parts are already extracted on masters and photocopied. The premiere will take place here in an all-Stravinsky program of one of the Evenings on the Roof concerts during the fall or winter, under the direction of Robert Craft. . . .

I have selected two (the first and the last) of the Four Russian Songs, the two ones which could fit the instrumentation I chose (flute, harp, and guitar). The titles are "The Duck" and "A Russian Spiritual." The original Four Russian Songs for voice and piano published by Chester in 1918–19 were in Russian with a French translation by C. F. Ramuz. Ramuz's translation, though very beautiful in itself, is, like all translations, necessarily different from the original phonetics on which my music is based. For this reason, I did not attempt to write an English translation in the score under the notes. I only gave the translated meaning in a short foreword. In this foreword I also give a "key" for the pronunciation of the Russian sounds by English speaking people and I have written in the score under the notes of the singer the phonetic combinations in English sounds. . . .

I am enclosing a copy of a letter I wrote to La Guilde du Livre, Lausanne, about Ramuz's share in the recordings of *Histoire du soldat*. Thus you will be aware of the matter in case they contact you.

STRAVINSKY TO BOOSEY & HAWKES   *July 21, 1953*

After much delay since the whole idea first took shape some 6 months ago, I have just signed contracts with both Nabokov (International Conference, Rome 1954) and the RAI. These two contracts cover my stay in Rome for 8 days for the labors of the International Conference "Situation de la Musique au XXe Siècle" with the award of prizes, and in connection with this, but in plus, also two concerts in Rome and one in Turin with and for the RAI.

Altogether this should amount to spending roughly the month of April busying myself with this Italian schedule, as the Conference is supposed to take place beginning April 5, 1954. . . .

As Mr. Boosey knows, I have already been asked by the Royal Philharmonic Society to conduct a concert there on May 27, 1954. . . . Moreover, I have accepted the Royal Philharmonic Society's invitation and fee assuming that Mr. Boosey will manage to have the English money converted for me into dollars after payment of the British taxes. But I want to point out to you that I am accepting this engagement more as a friendly gesture than as business, because, as you may well understand, there is no money to be made in England with the outrageous tax situation. Therefore, I shall not stay in London any longer than strictly necessary for the rehearsals and my concert because, though I love London, it is too much of a non-profitable proposition.

STRAVINSKY TO BOOSEY   *August 5, 1953*

With reference to my Royal Philharmonic concert of May 27, I understand from your letter that the matter of the broadcast is being dropped for the benefit of a special studio concert to be broadcast by the BBC. This is all right.

Now, my fee for this BBC appearance should be of course not less than the £500 which the Royal Philharmonic is paying me. I do not know if you can get me more than £500. I want to point out that £500 is less than $1,500, which is my minimum fee anywhere, notwithstanding the travelling expenses for which I always get a special allowance whenever I take an engagement outside of a combined tour.

STRAVINSKY TO JEANETTE WIÉNER   *August 5, 1953*

Upon my return home from the hospital I read your letter of July 23, with reference to *Histoire du soldat* and the New Orleans Opera House.

Will you kindly advise them that I cannot possibly take any additional commitment as my schedule is already too heavy and would not allow me to be in New Orleans in the beginning of December.

STRAVINSKY TO ROTH   *August 11, 1953*

This morning a letter came from Vienna to which I am answering as per copy enclosed.

I want to add that, between you and me, I will never go to either Vienna or Berlin for reasons you may guess. Western Germany is the most Eastern place I am willing to go. . . .

I have been in the hospital for 10 days for a prostate operation.[35] Home since a week ago I am now quite well and back to my work.

STRAVINSKY TO BOOSEY   *September 10, 1953*

Many thanks also for the beautiful edition of *Gloriana* which arrived safely. Now, I wish to have a chance to hear it because I find the music very interesting.

---

[35] Stravinsky wrote to his son Theodore on August 22: "I continue to convalesce, and

STRAVINSKY TO ADAMS   *September 10, 1953*

Please read the enclosed copies of my correspondence with Mercury.

Let me point out that *they* took the initiative, probably because they had got hold of one of the Evenings on the Roof programs (personally I never told them nor wrote them anything).

Also Milton Feist is, I believe, the brother of the one you plan to contact about Tango.

STRAVINSKY TO ROTH   *September 15, 1953*

I am in perfect health now and back to my work here until the start of my conducting season which will begin with a group of Los Angeles Philharmonic performances at the end of November. Just before Christmas I will leave for my tour including a series of concerts in Philadelphia, Washington, Baltimore, New York, Chicago, New Orleans, Portland, Seattle.

With reference to my European tour I have received a letter from Erich Winkler (Deutsche Welle, Köln Funkhaus) suggesting that he might arrange a schedule of engagements for me in Germany. I am now in a position to answer Winkler and I will tell him to go ahead.

I will be in Rome from April 5 till April 18 or 19, my concerts with the RAI there being on April 15 and 17. After that I will go to Turin for another RAI concert on April 23. Therefore Germany should take place after April 23 and before May 22, because I suppose I will have to be in London by May 24 to rehearse my Royal Philharmonic program of May 27. As I wrote Mr. Boosey last week the date of May 27 is the extreme limit for my stay in England and I have to depend on my leaving London the next day.

STRAVINSKY TO ADAMS   *September 25, 1953*

Lincoln Kirstein is going to . . . advise you of a new project which is about to be . . . launched. They are willing to commission [from] me a ballet for $10,000. I asked for $5,000 down now and as soon as they will make this payment our arrangement will go into force.

I plan to . . . compose a kind of symphony to be danced. . . .

I will play *Petrushka* (usual excerpts) with the Philadelphia Symphony at the end of December.

STRAVINSKY TO ADAMS   *October 1, 1953*

Just a few words to tell you that when you will ship the *Symphony of Psalms* material to the Los Angeles Philharmonic Orchestra it will be necessary to dou-

---

my doctors guarantee that the post-operative side effects will disappear in one or two weeks. It is slow and requires patience, but I feel well in spite of a certain feebleness."

ble the harp and therefore there should be 2 harp parts. Please do not forget! . . .

Thank you very much for having mailed me the Symphonies of Wind Instruments score which I will receive probably in a few days.

Re: Septet, you have my OK for this tentative New York performance. I only wish Galimir would hear me conduct either the rehearsals in New York or the Washington premiere with the ensemble of Sasha Schneider. By the way, David Oppenheim will play the clarinet, and I am delighted.

Incidentally when I saw David Oppenheim here two weeks ago he told me that Columbia will record Septet and Octet (he will play in both) in New York right after the Washington performance during the three days I have before flying to New Orleans for my guest conducting there.

STRAVINSKY TO ROTH   *October 23, 1953*

I have just completed three songs for mezzo-soprano accompanied by a trio (flute, clarinet, viola).

They are three pieces from Shakespeare's poetry: one sonnet and two songs from his plays. . . .

I dedicated these songs to Evenings on the Roof, a Los Angeles organization which I greatly admire. It is made of the best musicians to be found anywhere, who are willing to accept nominal and ridiculous fees for the sake of music itself.

The founding and acting brain of the whole thing is Peter Yates who is really worthy of every praise.

I wanted to give them some proof of my sympathetic understanding and I decided to dedicate this work to this remarkable organization (16 years old now) and to let them have the premiere of it.

STRAVINSKY TO STEIN   *October 23, 1953*

I am very pleased to know that you enjoyed Septet 1953 (this is the correct and complete title). . . .

I am very glad to know that my Cantata will be performed with Peter Pears and the excellent Greek soprano whom I heard and enjoyed very much last year.

STRAVINSKY TO ADAMS   *October 29, 1953*

The English translation of *Mavra* by [Thomas] Scherman which you sent: *very confidentially*, . . . I do not like it at all. The whole meaning of the original play has been completely altered, especially [in] what *he* calls the Coda. . . .

You should ask Bob Craft to make such a libretto by overhauling com-

pletely the old English translation of the vocal score. . . . The job will be done
here and under my supervision (provided it is commissioned right away because as you know I am leaving in the middle of December).

Of course you will have to pay a fee to Robert Craft but not a fortune. I
think $75 will do it.

STRAVINSKY TO ROTH   *November 2, 1953*

Both full and piano scores of my new Three Songs from Shakespeare left here
via surface mail ten days ago. Therefore you should have them in about two
weeks. This will enable you to have the material ready in time. . . .

Will you kindly tell Mr. Stein that the duration of Septet is about 12
minutes.

STRAVINSKY TO STEIN   *November 20, 1953*

The discrepancies in the spelling result from the fact that I used Auden's
American edition, which, unfortunately, appears to be not always correct. But I
will make the necessary corrections according to the Nonesuch Press text
which is quite official.

As to the two verses missing in the last song ("When daisies pied . . .") it
is indeed a double oversight which I cannot explain myself.

STRAVINSKY TO STEIN   *November 27, 1953*

This will be a good surprise: enclosed you will find a fully corrected copy of both
full and vocal scores of my Three Songs from Shakespeare. . . .

(All my corrections, etc. . . . have been made according to the text of the
Nonesuch Press, as I wrote you on November 20. This is why the last piece is
now entitled "Spring.")

I have just received your letter of November 23. Thank you for writing me
about my Cantata performance.

I agree entirely with you. I understand very well Peter Pears' feelings and I
also believe that too much rigidity and an excessive overcaution not to go astray
create a general uneasiness and dullness which is as detrimental as too much
liberty or "interpretation." It is entirely a matter of tact (as Cocteau once said:
"le tact c'est de savoir jusqu'à où on peut aller trop loin").

STRAVINSKY TO STEIN   *February 19, 1954*

Re: Piano reduction of my Verlaine Songs, please do go ahead and do it yourself.

I am leaving here March 13 and will arrive in Rome April 2. I will stay, in
Rome, at the Hotel Hassler, until April 19.

STRAVINSKY TO ROTH   *June 16, 1954*

I am back home since last Friday evening after an excellent and very fast flight from Lisbon; we left Lisbon Thursday at 6 p.m. and landed here Friday at 7 p.m. My stay in Lisbon was very pleasant, the weather good (at last) and the temperature very nice. The concerts had a very big success. . . .

I found that to be safe I had to steer a cautious course with the orchestra. Therefore I gave up Basler Concerto. I also abandoned *Pulcinella* Suite because of somewhat different difficulties.

STRAVINSKY TO STEIN   *June 29, 1954*

Enclosed please find the first proofs corrected of the full score. (I know it will cost a little more, but in the future I would appreciate if you could send me the proofs printed only on one side of the page. You know that I like to be able to cut, clip, paste, etc., and I cannot do it if the page is printed recto-verso). . . .

Enclosed also you will find 3 additional pages (11, 12, 13, by my manuscript numbers) to *In Memoriam* [*Dylan Thomas*]. As you will see they are to follow the Song (which ends with "attacca subito"). I am using the same music as in the Dirge-Canons, but inverted. I mean that in this "postlude" 2 augmented canons of the string sections of the beginning (A and C) are played 3 times one octave lower by 4 trombones, while the canon of B (page 2) and that of the beginning are played by strings one octave higher.

STRAVINSKY TO ROTH   *July 7, 1954*

I have just completed an instrumentation of the Two Poems of K. Balmont which were already in your catalogue. This instrumentation is identical with that of *Lyrique japonaise* (soprano, 2 flutes, 2 clarinets, piano and string quartet) which is also in your catalogue. I have done this in view of a chamber music concert (of the former Evenings on the Roof now renamed "Evening Concerts") scheduled under the direction of Robert Craft for the opening of the regular season in October 1954.

The plan is to perform this new instrumental version of Two Poems (I dropped the "of K. Balmont" because he is known only to Russians), the *Lyrique Japonaise,* and the Three Songs (From the Recollections of Childhood) in the instrumental version of 1930.

These Three Songs and *Lyrique Japonaise* already exist in English, but not Two Poems. Therefore an English text is needed for it. Robert Craft is going to do this English text under my supervision. This way is of course the most convenient to me because I can watch the job while it is in progress.

STRAVINSKY TO ROTH   *July 20, 1954*

I was very interested and very glad to read your own comments on *The Rake's Progress* performance at Glyndebourne. Moreover I know that if you found it good, it *was* good.[36] I have immediately sent a word of congratulations and thanks to Dr. Ebert and also to Paul Sacher. I hope this will help sustain their enthusiasm. Thank you also for sending me the Glyndebourne program,[37] which I received this morning with the proofs of the last pages—or "postlude"—of *In Memoriam.*

STRAVINSKY TO STEIN   *July 21, 1954*

I am returning to you, enclosed, the second proofs—corrected—of *In Memoriam,* and the first proofs of the "postlude." You will note that I have made some corrections in both. To save you time and trouble, you [need] not send me any second proofs of the "postlude." Will you kindly check them yourself?

STRAVINSKY TO ROTH   *July 26, 1954*

I am enclosing the Two Poems (formerly 2 Poesies de K. Balmont) which I referred to in my letter to you of July 7, 1954.

The title—in English this time—will be: Two Poems, for soprano, 2 flutes, 2 clarinets, piano and string quartet. The poems are entitled: I—"The Flower"; II—"The Dove."

Robert Craft succeeded in making a very nice translation in verses of the Russian text with rhymes from time to time. It will be very easy to sing. . . .

As to the full score of *Lyrique Japonaise* it is evidently out of print (the copy you sent me is a photostat of the original Koussevitzky edition). Considering that the new instrumentation of these Two Poems is identical with that of *Lyrique Japonaise* I would suggest that you publish both together. There is already an English text for *Lyrique Japonaise;* it is in the vocal score but was not in the full score, but you could use it as is.

For Two Poems as well as for *Lyrique Japonaise* it will be entirely up to you to keep the Russian text or to do away with it. But if another text is to be printed in addition to the English it should be the original one (i.e. Russian).

---

[36] Nicolas Nabokov had written to Stravinsky from Paris, November 29, 1952: "I heard a massacre of the *Rake* by the Hamburg Opera, a performance recommended to me by Dr. Roth (*sic!*) as one of the finest."

[37] Someone at Boosey & Hawkes sent Stravinsky a review from the *Sussex Daily News* containing the statement: "There is a kind of continuo given by the bassoon running through the whole work." Stravinsky put four question marks in blue pencil over the sentence.

STRAVINSKY TO GISHFORD   *July 26, 1954*

I was very touched by your kind letter after the Glyndebourne performance of
The Rake's Progress.

Your comments are most interesting indeed. It is too bad that Shadow was
a weaker element because it is an important part.

Your London office sent me a program and I am very glad to have it.
Among the cast only Richard Lewis is known to me.

I am still enjoying the pleasant memories of my short London visit.

STRAVINSKY TO EDGAR BIELEFELDT   *August 4, 1954*

Will you kindly find out *urgently* from Musikantiquariat Hans Schneider,
Tutzing-Über-München, . . . if the following items listed in their catalogue No.
34 just received here, are still available:

       No. 73—Guillaume de Machaut   200 marks
       No. 75—Luis Milan—Saemtliche Werke   80 marks
       No. 77—Schütz—Saemtliche Werke   1,450 marks

If any or all of these items are available, please get them for me at once and
have them shipped to me.

STRAVINSKY TO RUFINA AMPENOFF   *August 11, 1954*

I am enclosing the copy of a letter I am sending to Baden-Baden. Dr. Strobel,
before going on his vacation, had written me that he would like to have the European premiere of my new work *In Memoriam—Dylan Thomas* for the festival
of Donaueschingen.

There seems to have been some misunderstanding as to the date of the
world premiere here. This premiere will take place on September 20, 1954, and
will be given by the Monday Evening Concerts (formerly Evenings on the
Roof) at Los Angeles, under the direction of Robert Craft. . . .

As to Mr. Craft's fee for the translation of Two Poems I think it could be
settled satisfactorily with $50.

STRAVINSKY TO ADAMS   *August 25, 1954*

Mr. Fanning wrote me some 3 weeks ago, but very shortly, about his idea, and I
referred him to you. But, of course, the piano performance had not been mentioned then. . . .

I am absolutely against a performance with piano only, at least during the
first years, and until the work is known enough. . . . To give a performance with
the piano vocal score . . . could only greatly mislead the audience on a work like
In Memoriam—Dylan Thomas. I consider the vocal score only as a guide for rehearsing.

STRAVINSKY TO ADAMS   *September 7, 1954*

Indeed the *In Memoriam* material has been duly received by myself and Mr. [Lawrence] Morton. Please do thank also Miss [Gertrude] Smith for having airmailed me so promptly the material for the Three Songs from Shakespeare. I am doing the recording next Monday and having the material enabled me to start rehearsing Friday of last week.

STRAVINSKY TO GISHFORD   *September 14, 1954*

Thank you so very much for your lines of August 26th and also for the delicate attention you had in sending me this very interesting Diaghilev catalogue. . . .[38]

I was not here myself when Mr. [Franz] Waxman performed *Oedipus Rex* this last spring but I have heard from reliable professional sources that he had not selected a proper cast and that—though he could have used my Columbia recording as a reference—his tempos were somewhat unorthodox. Therefore I can only give you a word of extreme caution.

STRAVINSKY TO ROTH   *September 14, 1954*

With reference to Two Poems & *Three Japanese Lyrics* I am delighted at your intention to do the German text yourself. . . .

The Russian has to be printed; . . . the Balmont poems as well as the Russian *Lyrique* both are good poetry. . . . This brings us to [the question of] 3 [languages] and I am not in favor of having more than 2 printed under one stave because it puts the third text too far from the music. . . .

The cover should bear only the compound title: Two Poems & Three Japanese Lyrics. But the first pages of the Two Poems and the first page of the Three Japanese Lyrics should bear the respective title in 4 languages with the names of all the translators.

STRAVINSKY TO ROTH   *September 21, 1954*

The premiere of *In Memoriam Dylan Thomas* took place here last night. I hasten to tell you that it was a truly fine performance and an immense success.

STRAVINSKY TO ADAMS   *September 21, 1954*

I am enclosing . . . the program and a copy of some informative notes I wrote for the Donaueschingen Festival in Germany where this work [*In Memoriam Dylan Thomas*] will be performed next month.

---

[38] Of Richard Buckle's exhibition at the Edinburgh Festival.

STRAVINSKY TO ROTH   *September 22, 1954*

Giving the matter some thought later in the day I figure that this material [of *In Memoriam Dylan Thomas*] having been unusually and thoroughly checked by myself for the recording performance with Columbia here last week, all the red pencil markings I made in my own hand should be kept as reference and this full score and these parts should be used as "masters."

    If it is still possible, your engravers should make corrections accordingly in the full score.

STRAVINSKY TO ADAMS   *October 18, 1954*

I am in full agreement with your point of view and I am absolutely opposed to let Mr. Dorati create one more version of *Petrushka*. If he does not want to do the new version as is, then let him not do any and let him drop the whole thing. It is not only a matter of copyright, but the new version sounds much better than the old one.

STRAVINSKY TO ADAMS   *October 30, 1954*

I have just returned from Chicago where I conducted *Petrushka* twice last Monday and Tuesday with the London Festival Ballet for Hurok.

    I had previously made sure that they would bring with them the new version, which they did. But, unfortunately, the material which they have been given (by London I assume) is in a terrible condition. It is altogether falling apart and full of all sorts of wrong and contradictory markings. . . .

    I am going to conduct *Petrushka* again with the same company on December 7 at San Francisco and December 25 at Los Angeles. I have told the ballet people to write you and ask for a replacement set of the *Petrushka* material in order to enable me to do my job without having to repair both the material and musical damage, thus wasting all my rehearsal time which is already . . . too short.

STRAVINSKY TO BIELEFELDT   *November 1, 1954*

With reference to the Glazounov booklet, I was never asked anything by Mr. Gunther. But it is just as well because I wouldn't have accepted to do it.

STRAVINSKY TO BIELEFELDT   *November 6, 1954*

Since I wrote . . . a few days ago I have found myself in need of the following item: Alban Berg, Violin Concerto, full score (Partitur), Universal Edition 10758. Will you be so kind to get it for me and send it to me here at your earliest convenience.

STRAVINSKY TO ROTH   *November 15, 1954*

I have already been contacted by telegram for the 1955 Edinburgh Festival but I had to answer that I could not possibly commit myself to be there due to my schedule of work here. In fact I have to fly back from Europe to California in the very first days of May.

My European tour will be quite short and somewhat limited. It will include: Madrid (March 25), Rome (April 6), Baden-Baden (between April 20–22), Lugano (April 28), Stuttgart (May 3).

STRAVINSKY TO ROTH   *November 23, 1954*

It is good news indeed to learn that Glyndebourne will do *The Rake's Progress* again in the coming season and that the BBC will televise it.

Do you know if it is still going to be performed in Germany, Brussels and Paris? The last [Société] Dramatique statements do not mention *Le Libertin* any more.

STRAVINSKY TO ADAMS   *November 29, 1954*

As to the programs of my concerts in the U.S.A., here is some more detailed information.

Portland:	Ode, *Orpheus, Pulcinella, Firebird*
Birmingham:	[I conduct the] second part of the program only, First Symphony in E flat, *Firebird*
Atlanta:	Mozart Serenata Notturna, Tchaikovsky Serenade, *Scènes de ballet, Petrushka*
Pittsburgh:	Same program as Atlanta

Will you kindly make sure that the new version of *Petrushka* will be supplied (besides you know well my wishes concerning this).

STRAVINSKY TO ROTH   *December 20, 1954*

I am writing you today with reference to my Quatre études pour orchestre which I will be conducting at my Baden-Baden concert on April 22, 1955.

I have here my own copy of the full score (large size) in which I made corrections and even partial changes when I performed the work with the New York Philharmonic. . . .

Something has to be done so that you may provide me at Baden-Baden . . . with material which agrees with what I have corrected and changed in 1952. Therefore will you kindly send me as soon as possible a brand new copy of the large score. I will correct and adjust it and send it back to you.

STRAVINSKY TO ROTH   *January 4, 1955*

I am returning to you enclosed the first proofs corrected of Two Poems and *Three Japanese Lyrics* which I received from your New York office yesterday.

I am very glad that I had a chance to see them and correct them just before leaving for my U.S. tour to Portland, Birmingham, Atlanta all this month of January. . . .

Will you also be so kind to send me a printed copy *as soon as possible* because I am scheduled to record Two Poems and *Three Japanese Lyrics* in full here for Columbia on February 14 & 15.

STRAVINSKY TO ADAMS   *February 5, 1955*

Re: *Le Roi des étoiles*

With reference to your letter of February 3rd, I wish to suggest that you order a photostat copy of the score directly from the New York Public Library where you will get it cheaper than here, faster also, and, anyhow, you will save the shipping expenses from Los Angeles to New York.

If you run into any difficulty in New York, then—useless to say—I shall act here in order that Mr. Bielefeldt may get the photostat he needs.

STRAVINSKY TO ROTH   *February 5, 1955*

Le Roi des étoiles: Do you intend to print it?[39] I suppose you do. Then I would like to suggest that before publishing it we should ask Robert Craft to do an English translation (he gave the American premiere in New York some years ago) and I would like to ask you to do the German one. I do not think the French will be necessary.

To facilitate performances I would reduce the 8 horns to 4 without any harm.

If we have the material I could play it at Cleveland next December (I will play *Perséphone* then) and record it with Columbia.

STRAVINSKY TO ROTH   *February 15 [?], 1955*

If you are interested to publish *[Le Roi des étoiles]*, I think you have to make an arrangement or a purchase with Robert Forberg. If Hansen was intractable for

---

[39] Apparently the Edition Russe had intended to publish the piece (*Zvezdoliki*) in 1938. At any rate, Stravinsky answered an inquiry from Vladimir Zederbaum, Koussevitzky's secretary, on July 21 of that year: "The only printed copy of my cantata, *Le Roi des étoiles,* is here with me, and I do not want to send it out anywhere. But if you would like us to copy it *here,* let me know, and by what date you will be needing it. . . . Koussevitzky has another copy in America." J. & W. Chester also had a copy, as well as the vocal score inscribed by Stravinsky to Debussy. (In the spring of 1961, the daughter of

Concertino it doesn't mean that Forberg will be intractable for *Roi des étoiles*. Incidentally, it was not I who proposed a new publication of it but Mr. Bielefeldt.

STRAVINSKY TO STEIN   *February 19, 1955*

As to [your projected] book, *Form and Performance,* I think it is a most fascinating and useful project. I hope you will complete it soon and I shall be looking forward eagerly to read it. The points that you outline in your letter are already giving proof that your knowledge and experience will not be left idle and that they will keep bearing fruit even after you have decided to lead a less strenuous life.

STRAVINSKY TO ROTH   *February 19, 1955*

I do not know at all what the position is regarding *Le Roi des étoiles*. I assume it is still the property of Jurgenson, i.e. Forberg.

I wish to remove a slight misunderstanding. . . . I did not know if Mr. Bielefeldt asked a score of this work for re-publishing, but I thought that was the idea after my conversation with Mr. Adams in New York. . . .

At this point I would like to ask you directly if you will eventually seek to conclude an agreement with Jurgenson not only . . . for *Le Roi des étoiles* but [also] for my [other] works in their catalogue. I think you had mentioned your intention to do so previously.

As far as I am concerned, I would be very favorable to such a project, and I would be glad to see my former Jurgenson works added to the Boosey & Hawkes catalogue. Maybe it is feasible . . . after all Forberg may prove to be softer than Hansen.

STRAVINSKY TO ADAMS   *February 23, 1955*

When I returned from Atlanta I found on my desk a letter from Charles Munch asking me to compose something for the 80th birthday of Pierre Monteux.[40]

I first answered that I had to put this on a waiting list, and last week when I began to see my way more clearly, I wrote Munch that I was going to compose a *Greeting Prelude* which I would send to Boosey & Hawkes when completed.

This *Greeting Prelude* I am now enclosing, and I will ask you to prepare the

Konstantin Balmont sent to Stravinsky the eighth volume of her father's poems, the one containing the text of the cantata.)

[40] Munch had asked Stravinsky to compose "a very brief *touche,*" and Stravinsky had answered on February 9 that this "requires a certain time that I do not have." On the 19th, Stravinsky wrote to Munch that the *Greeting Prelude* would be finished "in the first days of next week." In June 1951 Samuel Barber had written to Stravinsky asking him to harmonize "Happy Birthday to You" as a present for Mary Curtis Bok (Mrs.

necessary parts so that the Boston Symphony can rehearse it before April 4, on which date the performance will take place at a concert planned to celebrate the occasion of Monteux's birthday.

Will you kindly let Munch know that you have this *Greeting Prelude* at hand and that you are preparing the material. As to fees, I leave entirely up to you to decide if you want to charge the Boston Symphony something or not.

STRAVINSKY TO ADAMS   *March 4, 1955*

Enclosed 3 copies of the full score of my *Greeting Prelude* as per yours of March 1st.

I will be in New York (at Gladstone) for a few hours in the morning of Monday, March 14, at 2 p.m. going to Lisbon. Maybe I'll call you then to say goodbye.

STRAVINSKY TO ADAMS   *May 14, 1955*

It has been announced in a press release that Stokowski is going to perform my Mass in Santa Barbara in June, or July, I think. Please do stop this at any price. It is going to be strictly an exhibition of showmanship, which will have nothing to do with music in itself and still less with my music in particular. Therefore, it could be most detrimental to the Mass. . . . It is said that it will be done with a chorus of 150 voices. . . . You can imagine. . . .

STRAVINSKY TO ROTH   *May 14, 1955*

State Opera Vienna: I am enclosing in a few sentences a condensed statement, as you suggested. I wrote it in English in my own hand in order to enable them to reproduce it in facsimile. I also enclose a German translation of it, typewritten, to prevent being misunderstood. They can print it with the facsimile. . . .

Agon (this is the title of my new ballet with Balanchine): I had to stop or rather postpone its composition because of the Biennale commission. Therefore it is better not to speak too much about *Agon* for the moment.

Biennale commission: . . . For the moment we can safely say that the work will be a sacred concerto for soloists, chorus, and limited instrumental ensemble, based on the Gospel of St. Mark and fragments of the Old Testament

---

Efrem Zimbalist) on her forthcoming seventy-fifth birthday. (Barber's letter reminds Stravinsky that they had met at the Tintoretto show in Venice in 1937.) Stravinsky promptly sent the following, marking it "better in $\frac{6}{4}$":

(Psalms), to be premiered in Venice (probably at St. Mark's) in September 1956.

STRAVINSKY TO ADAMS   *May 25, 1955*

Re: my Mass and Stokowski, it is out of [the] question to quote my letter of May 14. Nevertheless I would like you to tell them, or him, frankly that I composed this Mass for a chamber chorus of about 16 singers accompanied with only 10 solo instruments and that I am totally opposed to any change in the "ratio" for acoustical and esthetical reasons.

STRAVINSKY TO EDWINA JACKSON   *June 4, 1955*

With reference to my *Greeting Prelude:* in my opinion the demand of Keith Prowse & Co., Ltd. to have us print a sub-title reading, more or less, "A Canon on the Melody of 'Happy Birthday to You' " is out of proportion with the thing itself.

Nevertheless, if they are not willing to be satisfied with something shorter or in the form of a footnote, then I still prefer to accept their ultimatum than to prevent the publishing of my *Greeting Prelude.*

STRAVINSKY TO JOHN ANDREWES   *July 3, 1955*

A few words in answer to yours of June 28th re "house cleaning" in *Mavra.* Mr. Craft fully agrees with your suggestion of "clean-ning house."

As everything is settled now the new English text will be published without delay, I hope.

STRAVINSKY TO ROTH   *July 9, 1955*

With reference to Danse sacrale and the rights of A.M.P. and Schott I am inclined to share your opinion. Nevertheless this is only my "feeling" and it may require . . . authoritative legal advice before being used to any further extent.

I believe the following excerpt from my contract with A.M.P., dated September 1944, will be of interest to you or your counsel:

> Stravinsky hereby waives all right and interest in and to the said new arrangement which he produced as a work for hire under the engagement of his services in and to the manuscript thereof, and for himself, his heirs, executors, administrators, successors, assigns and statutory copyright successors, hereby conveys, transfers and assigns to Associated, its successors, and assigns forever, all right, title, and interest in and to the said work, the manuscript thereof and title thereto, and the copyright therein for the United States of America and for such other countries of the world

in which copyright may be secured together with the right to secure copyright and statutory protection in the name of Associated, and on his behalf and on behalf of his statutory copyright successors to apply for and secure in its name all renewals and extensions now or hereafter conferred by law, including but not limited to, all ownership in and to the rights of publication, execution, representation, performance, transcription, arrangement, version and reproduction in all forms and methods of whatever kind, and all other rights whatsoever, now or hereafter conferred or created.

STRAVINSKY TO BIELEFELDT   *July 16, 1955*

I am sorry to give you a negative answer but, indeed, I do not want to let the correspondence I had with Dylan Thomas be published during my lifetime.

I have already been asked to release some Dylan Thomas letters and I have always refused.

STRAVINSKY TO ROTH   *July 16, 1955*

I would like to say frankly that, even outside of any question of copyright, I do prefer to have this Danse sacrale performed with the *Sacre* instead of the old version. It is better in my opinion and it is also easier to perform and more economical. Therefore if you have a chance to take it over and to help promote it, I shall only be delighted.

STRAVINSKY TO ROTH   *July 27, 1955*

I have finally got the right title: *Canticum Sacrum, Ad Honorem, Sancti Marci, Nominis* in five movements (with a Dedicatio as a short prelude) for two solo voices (tenor and baritone), mixed chorus and different groups of instruments. The text is in Latin. I composed it after the Vulgate; phrases of the first and last movements are those of St. Marcus gospel's last verses, the parting words of Christ to the Apostles. The text for the other movements is taken from the Old Testament, fragments of Canticum Canticorum, Deuteronomy and Psalms. . . .

P.S. I was glad to receive the following wire. "Happy to report that *Rake's Progress* again scores greatest success in third successive season Glyndebourne Festival. Sincerely, Carl Ebert, Paul Sacher, and Cast."

STRAVINSKY TO BIELEFELDT   *August 9, 1955*

I would be very grateful to you if you would buy and send to me these two books. . . .

1. Rimsky-Korsakov, *Traité d'instrumentation*
2. Herbert Eimert, *Lehrbuch der 12-ton Technik*

[*Original in German*]

STRAVINSKY TO ROTH   *August 14, 1955*

Do you know if Hans Keller's article on *In Memoriam Dylan Thomas* appeared in *Tempo*? Mr. Gishford sent me its proofs in February and wanted to release it in his spring issue. Since then—complete silence. Did this article ever appear?

Enough for today: so many letters still to write, no secretary because Andre Marion is working now in a travel agency and I see him once a week and only for bookkeeping.

STRAVINSKY TO GISHFORD   *August 29, 1955*

Please tell Mr. Roberto Barry that from the end of June to the end of December 1956 I have to be in Europe conducting. . . . So Buenos Aires and Montevideo—out.

As to my *Canticum Sacrum,* I make no secret about composing it. What I ask . . . is only to let nobody have a look at it before the work is complete. . . . I found it suitable to give my friend Robert Craft some details concerning the text, music and construction of this cantata to enable him to write about it in an article (Mr. Lindlar asked him for Bonn's *Musik der Zeit*) dedicated to my last works after the *Rake.*

Also I think it would be an excellent idea to ask him [to write] an article for your *Tempo,* when I will complete the composition, for nobody will know better this music than he who is a first class professional musician and writer.

STRAVINSKY TO ADAMS   *September 5, 1955*

Nothing special to report except our daily complaint of the ferocious heat and almost unbearable smog violently attacking our eyes and lungs.

STRAVINSKY TO BIELEFELDT   *September 29, 1955*

I received the other day the two Giselher Klebe violin sonatas and I thank you very much.

May I ask you today to send me Anton Webern's Variationen für Orchester, Op. 30. I cannot find [it] in my library; I probably lent it to somebody [which] means that I have to consider it as lost.

STRAVINSKY TO BIELEFELDT   *October 4, 1955*

I am glad to hear you are able to get me the complete 18 volumes of [the] Spitta-Schering Schütz (for DM 1500) and I ask you to ship me it by separate packages as you did it the last time with the Schütz 7 volumes. Do not worry about the latter. I am almost sure to be able to sell them here or to make an exchange with my *Musikhändlers* here.

STRAVINSKY TO ROTH   *October 6, 1955*

When will I receive the proofs of my *Greeting Prelude*? Are you already preparing the parts of my *Canticum* and what did you decide for the engraving of it? Will you do it now or after the performance? I think the latter is safer, for the full score, naturally; the vocal score could be printed right now.

STRAVINSKY TO BIELEFELDT   *October 12, 1955*

Many thanks for the score of Webern's Orchestra Variations, which I received today. Attached is an announcement for the Moser *Musiklexikon*. The note says that this price is good only until October 31, 1955 (which cannot apply to me, since I am very far from Hamburg and received the notice only today, October 12). If you can obtain the two volumes for the advance price of DM 39.50, please do so and send them to me.

[*Original in German*]

STRAVINSKY TO ROTH   *October 18, 1955*

I must tell you that I had the project to go to London but only after Germany, i.e. in December, to give there a concert with BBC this time, before going back home for Christmas on a good liner sailing from Southampton.

 William Glock had already asked Robert Craft to do the *Canticum* at the end of November or beginning of December in one of the London churches, St. Bartholomew's. I believe such a church would be a better site for the work than a concert hall. Also the *Canticum* should not be played in an orchestra concert, but only under the best—most intimate—conditions of chamber music. It will last probably not more than 15 minutes and would best be heard twice on the same program. As I plan to conduct it somewhere in Germany (and maybe in Switzerland too) during my Oct.–Nov. concerts, there won't be much "premiere" value left by December for the BBC.

STRAVINSKY TO ADAMS   *October 26, 1955*

Answering yours of October 24th.

 Robert Craft is quite willing to make the English translation of my opera

Le Rossignol. Right now he is rather busy with his recordings and rehearsals for his next Monday Evening Concerts program. But later in November and in December he can do it, and deliver it to you the first week of January. He will ask you for it the modest sum of $200.00. I personally will be glad to have him do it for both literary and musical reasons.

STRAVINSKY TO BIELEFELDT   *October 27, 1955*

One more favor: Can you find and send to me Anton Webern's edition of the second volume of Heinrich Isaak's *Choralis Constantinus* in the Denkmäler der Tonkunst in Österreich (1909) publication?

[*Original in German*]

STRAVINSKY TO STEIN   *November 6 [?], 1955*

I will send B. & H. tomorrow some six new pages (in full and vocal scores) which is the IVth part—Brevis Motus Cantilenae—of my work in order to help the engravers to have as much as possible of the manuscript. [Do not] wait for the ending (the next Vth part which will be short).

I will be here till the 1st day of December, going to Cleveland for my concerts there and afterwards to New York for one month (Gladstone Hotel, 114 East 52 St.) from Dec. 12th.

STRAVINSKY TO ROTH   *November 7, 1955*

[This is] only to tell you that I will have tomorrow from my photocopier the copies of the IVth part of my *Canticum,* called Brevis Motus Cantilenae (baritone, chorus, instruments): some 6 pages of full score music (about the same for the vocal one), and I will ship it to you by surface mail in 4 copies (both full & vocal scores, as before).

STRAVINSKY TO ROTH   *November 10, 1955*

BBC program for December 5th, 1956: 1—Symphony in C (about 30'), 2—*Symphony of Psalms* (23'), 3—*Pulcinella* complete (about 36'). That is the program which seems to me ideal since I definitely want Bob Craft to do the London premiere of my *Canticum Sacrum* at St. Bartholomew's even with less satisfactory acoustics than that of the beautiful Festival Hall and a lesser "event.". . . So, kindly tell Mr. Howgill that I prefer the BBC concert of December 5/56 to have the program shown above. And concerning my fee, I leave it to you to decide. But do not forget to ask the BBC for the necessary rehearsals and good singers for *Pulcinella.* For example—Richard Lewis, Margaret Ritchie and a good basso.

The most difficult thing in this program is the Symphony in C, especially the 3rd movement. Therefore I insist that some important preliminary rehearsing should be done before my arrival, because I probably will not be able to be in London before 1st Dec. I'll tell you when.

Some days ago the representative of Dr. Seefehlner, Mr. Martin Taubman, came to see me and invited me (quite officially) to conduct a concert in Vienna the next year in the fall. I accepted in principle provided it is combined with a group of my German concerts in Nov./56, i.e. before London. We went even so far as to discuss the program of this concert—*Canticum* (twice), Cantata, Jocasta's Aria from *Oedipus* and the 3rd scene of the 1st act of *The Rake's Progress* with Magda Laszlo. . . . As to Piovesan's letter—he must be informed that there is no other religious work of mine that I can play with the *Canticum*: the Mass cannot be "performed" in a Catholic church, the Cantata is not a religious work, and the *Symphony of Psalms* would be harmful in juxtaposition to the *Canticum*. However I want to do the following program which will very effectively situate the *Canticum*:

1—Ricercar for 4 trombones	Andrea Gabrieli
2—Psalm for 5 voices	Heinrich Schütz
Motet No. 14 ⎫ for 7 voices	Carlo Gesualdo
Lauda Jerusalem ⎭	Claudio Monteverdi
3—*Canticum Sacrum*	Igor Stravinsky

* * *

4—*Canticum Sacrum*	
5—Choral Variations (instr. ensemble)	J. S. Bach
("*Vom Himmel hoch, da komm' ich her*")	

You will notice that I propose to make an instrumentation of the "*Vom Himmel hoch . . .*" variations of Bach (duration about 25′), but I will write you about this later.

STRAVINSKY TO STEIN   *November 14, 1955*

Canticum Sacrum: The enclosed page of the vocal score, as you will see, is the repeat of the last section of Caritas (bars 116 to 129 incl.).

As I decided to enlarge this section by repeating it, because of the new text (1st Epistle of St. John) I had to write it entirely out. . . .

I had no time to write out these 14 measures for the full score. There will be no difficulty for the engravers because the instrumental music (trumpets), counterpointing the chorus, remains the same.

STRAVINSKY TO ANDREWES   *November 21, 1955*

To answer yours of Nov. 18th re: *Mavra* vocal score.

    1. The tempo of the Overture is [quarter note] = 104. Kindly mark it in the full score of your stocks.

    2. The C you are speaking of is a sharp, as in the full score (cl. picc. E flat), but the next note, a B, must be a natural, as in the full score (same cl.).

STRAVINSKY TO ROTH   *November 25, 1955*

I am sending you today or tomorrow, under separate cover, via air mail, the fifth and final part (vocal and full scores) of my *Canticum.* . . .

    Please do not let anyone—outside of Boosey & Hawkes—know that I have delivered the work to you in full. . . .

    Because Piovesan & Co. are still worrying about the shortness of *Canticum,* I want to avoid any discussion as to the amount of work I have put into it. By working day and night and refusing a lot of engagements I have been able to complete my task in a few months less than originally scheduled, but this is my own affair.

    I will ask you to notify Piovesan on March 31, 1956, that you have received the completed work. In the meantime it will remain our secret.

STRAVINSKY TO BIELEFELDT   *December 1, 1955*

Is it possible to find a small and rare book by Ferdinand Keiner, *Die Madrigale Gesualdos von Venosa* (57 pages with music examples)? This doctoral dissertation for the degree of philosophy at the University of Leipzig was published in 1914 and printed in Leipzig by Oscar Brandstetter.

    You can write to me in Cleveland (Hotel Park Manor), where I will be until December 12, or at the Hotel Gladstone, 114 East 52nd Street, New York 22, N.Y., where I will be until January 12, and after that, home.

[*Original in German*]

STRAVINSKY TO ADAMS   *January 18, 1956*

This is to answer yours of Jan. 16/56.

    If you like the De Grab photos and want to use some of them for publicity purposes, that's all right with me, but I prefer the Columbia ones [that] Deborah Ishlon gave you. Unfortunately I cannot supply you with the De Grab originals because my wife gave you the only copy we had. Besides, I don't like them at all.

STRAVINSKY TO ROTH   *February 6, 1956*

In answer to your letter of February 2nd I can only tell you that Robert Craft
has received no letter from Piovesan since the 7th of November/55 at which
time Piovesan inquired whether I would accept a Hammond in case the San
Marco organ was out of tune. . . .

  As to the Bach Variations, the instruments I am using are those included
in the instrumentation of my *Canticum;* no other instruments are required. . . .

  I have many other engagements in Europe which are dependent on the
Venice date (which I still do not know). I am here only through May: singers
have to be engaged, materials have to be prepared and corrected. Please . . . find
out . . . what is the situation and what are . . . the intentions.

                                                       February 14, 1956
STRAVINSKY TO BOOSEY & HAWKES   *[Telegram]*

Please airmail me here complete new version *Petrushka* material according
Robert Craft's letter. Thanks in advance.

STRAVINSKY TO ROTH   *March 3, 1956*

Answering yours of Feb. 13th and 28th. Good that Dr. Seefehlner finally agreed
to my fee of $2000. As to the date and the program of my concert there
(Vienna) kindly get in touch with Erich Winkler (Deutsche Welle, Köln Funkhaus) who organises the dates of my concert tour after Venice: Switzerland,
Germany and Vienna.

  Glad the matter with Piovesan is now cleared up and I am hopeful he will
finally arrange a concert with Robert Craft.

STRAVINSKY TO ADAMS   *March 9, 1956*

I am enclosing here the original [*Fantasia* contract] (dated "January 4th,
1939") for that is the only one in my files. What is the license Jan. 4/49 you are
speaking of?

  It will be good, of course, if you get some additional fee for their fresh use
of the *Rite of Spring.*

  By the way, you forgot to enclose the correspondence between Walt Disney Productions and the Harry Fox Office you mention in the beginning of your
letter.

STRAVINSKY TO GISHFORD   *March 11, 1956*

Erwin Stein is not only a highly professional musician but in the present case
the one who knows better than anybody this composition [*Canticum Sacrum*],
working on its proofreading very efficiently all these last months.

STRAVINSKY TO ROTH   *March 21, 1956*

The only information I can give Dr. Strobel re *Agon* is that I have not yet finished its composition. . . .

Please, let me have some copies of the *Greeting Prelude.* I received some
time ago only one or two.

STRAVINSKY TO ROTH   *March 29, 1956*

I can only say that I have nothing to add to the score on the subject of the commission. Also the 1st performance's date is not yet known *(sic)*. As to the duration of the work it must read: "about 17 minutes" and not "ca. 15 minutes." It
is however important that the Latin text be printed on a fly-leaf at the beginning
with the corresponding English text from the King James Bible. . . .

Today I airmailed you two copies of my Bach arrangement.

STRAVINSKY TO ROTH   *April 9, 1956*

My arrangement [of the Bach Choral Variations] must be sung everywhere in
German.

STRAVINSKY TO ANDREWES   *April 15, 1956*

Now I am answering yours of April 9th. (1) Caritas—"Diliges Dominum
Deum . . ." taken from Deuteronomy you will find in King James Bible, chapter VI–5, and ". . . diligamus nos invicem . . ." in his 1st Epist. Joannis,
Chapter IV–7. (2) Spes-Chorus words—"Sustinuit anima . . ." etc. taken
from Psalm CXXIV–4, 5, 6 in the Vulgate and Ps., CXXX–5, 6 in the King
James Bible. (3) Of course it should be "Domino cooperante" in the last
movement.

STRAVINSKY TO ROTH   *April 17, 1956*

Correcting the 2nd proofs of *Canticum*'s full score I wanted to tell you the following:

In printing the chorus parts, it is very important to give pitch leads. That
is, each chorus part should make clear what instrument, or solo voice in some
cases, has its pitch. . . .

We leave here early in June motoring to New York where we will stay in
Gladstone Hotel for 4 or 5 days before sailing on the *Vulcania* June 27. Then we
will be at the Hôtel Grande Bretagne in Athens through most of July, arriving
there the 10th. From the 6th till the 15th of August we will be at the Hilton
Hotel in Istanbul and in Venice in the last days of August. Incidentally, I still
have not the date of Venice, nor any answer to my letter of 6 weeks ago, and in 6

weeks we leave! This when every detail of every other festival has been announced months ago. How to wrench from them an answer?

One thing more. Can you get from the BBC people my Labor Permit before I leave for Europe in order to avoid the complications at the pass control I had the last time in London? Thank you.

I am conducting in Berlin (Oct. 2) and in Munich (Oct. 10) my Bach arrangement in a program of my works. I wanted to do the same in Zürich (Oct. 16) but, I am afraid, it will be hardly possible because of the chorus.

STRAVINSKY TO GISHFORD   *April 17, 1956*

Please send me the article (*Canticum Sacrum*) of Dr. Stein before it appears in *Tempo.*

Please also bear in mind that we leave here for Europe early in June and our address through July will be Hôtel Grande Bretagne in Athens, Greece.

STRAVINSKY TO ANDREWES   *April 26, 1956*

Your note of April 20th and the last page of the 2nd proofs (full score of *Canticum*) received and I corrected everything and air-mailed it to you today under a separate cover. Now I want to see the final corrections made, therefore kindly let me have a clean copy of the full score (before printing it) together with the second proofs. In sending it to me, please, check it with your office for correct post rating because each time I receive from you such packages I have to pay a special post duty (not custom!) of 15 cents. Something must be wrong. Thank you. Certainly I will be glad to check the letterpress material (Latin and English text on the same pages) which is to be printed in both vocal and full scores. Also I would like to see the title page and other pages preceding the first page of music. . . . Check with my own arrangement of titles, size of letters and disposition of words.

STRAVINSKY TO ROTH   *May 1, 1956*

The size of Boosey & Hawkes letters should not be the same size as those of my name. Not because I find myself more important than Boosey & Hawkes but because precisely the equilibrium would suffer. . . .

Biennale:

a. Only thanks to you I finally get the important information about the 20th of September which is the limit of my stay in Venice because of my concert in Montreux on Sept. 25th, rehearsals starting the 22nd. My many letters on this subject were never answered.

b. I suggested to them that R. Craft conduct the old Venetian music before I conduct the *Canticum.*

Piovesan probably does not understand my reasons which are: Craft has a great deal of experience conducting and recording this music, whereas I have none; the *Canticum* is by far the most difficult work of mine to sing and for the whole ensemble. I anticipate such conducting problems for myself that I do not want to take on the additional worry of conducting baroque music, even though it is short in time. Now Piovesan will probably re-propose that I conduct a program all of my own music. But I know the *Canticum* will suffer if first performed together with any of my earlier compositions. And, I know better than they do what kind of piece the *Canticum* is.

It is annoying at this late date of May 1st, and especially after I made a big sacrifice in my price, to have this pettiness.

STRAVINSKY TO ADAMS   *May 2, 1956*

Just answering yours of April 30.

Venice—between 10th and 20th of September.
Montreux (Switzerland)—Sept. 25th.
Berlin—October 2nd.
Munich—October 10th.
Zürich—October 17th.
Winterthur—October 24th.
Vienna—November 4th.
London—BBC—December 5th and 7th.
New York—January, 1957—10th, 11th and 13th.

STRAVINSKY TO GISHFORD   *May 15, 1956*
                                          [Telegram]

Impossible [to conduct *Canticum* in York Minster]. Send me *Life of Mozart* of Franz Niemetschek.

STRAVINSKY TO ROTH   *May 16, 1956*

A cable from Piovesan of May 11 in answer to mine of May 5, a copy of which I airmailed to you the other day: "Situation paragraph two clarified in my letter of May 7. I confirm acceptance of payment terms and am searching for a solution for Craft. Cordially,   Piovesan." [*Original of cable in French*]

I waited till today for his announced letter and having not received it I wired him: "Your letter May seventh not received. Accept conducting entire program but in Fenice only as follows: *Canticum*, Mass, *Canticum*, Bach Variations. You must engage Craft for full rehearsals before my final ones. Chorus, soloists must be prepared before our arrival. Awaiting cable acknowledgement."

The naive malice of Piovesan's answer is self-explanatory. Naively too I am still trying to make an order in this chaos. But in one month I'm going to take my train to New York to sail to Athens and even this absurd correspondence will be impossible.

STRAVINSKY TO ADAMS   *May 16, 1956*

This is to answer yours of May 14th. Let Mr. Walter Koch (Bonn) ask Mr. Erich Winkler about all details of my European concerts: he is the one who organizes my German and Swiss concerts. His address is: Deutsche Welle, Köln Funkhaus, Köln am/R, Germany.

STRAVINSKY TO ADAMS   *May 17, 1956*
                                        [Telegram]

First performance of my arrangement of Bach's Choral und Variationen taking place May 27 in Ojai Festival under Robert Craft direction. You can give CBS the necessary clearance for broadcasting it. The chorus will be that of Pomona College Glee Clubs.

STRAVINSKY TO ROTH   *May 23, 1956*

I just received the following cable from Piovesan: "Every detail will be arranged for perfect organization your concert. Letter follows re contract, performances. Maestro Craft situation solved. Await president to confirm Fenice performance. Piovesan, Biennale"

This is the answer to my last cable of May 16th. . . . He did not even apologize for his letter of May 7th which he probably never sent me.

STRAVINSKY TO STEIN   *May 30, 1956*

Just these lines to thank you for your very interesting *Canticum Sacrum* article analysis.

Although in a hurry before my leaving to Europe, I wanted only to tell you that in your article the titles III & IV do not need parentheses for the words *Hortationes* and *Cantilenae*. It must read (just as is in the score) as follows: III, Ad Tres Virtutes Hortationes, and IV, Brevis Motus Cantilenae. We are leaving Hollywood for Europe in two weeks by train and boat. Will I see you in Venice?

STRAVINSKY TO ROTH   *July 13, 1956*

At the moment it seems that we shall be here at Athens for the next two weeks and you can write me (or wire) here until the 26th.

STRAVINSKY TO BOOSEY & HAWKES   *July 31, 1956*
                                                 [Telegram]

London

Am installed here at Bauer Grünwald. . . . Cancelling my November trip to Egypt, can now arrange for Hamburg concert second half November.

STRAVINSKY TO ROTH   *August 9, 1956*

The schedule, the number and the duration of rehearsals proposed by BBC is not acceptable; it must be changed. I am asking 4 rehearsals of 2½ hours each and I don't want to rehearse the day of the concert. Also the interval of one hour between the rehearsals is too short for me. I hope you will succeed in changing this schedule.

STRAVINSKY TO ADAMS   *August 9, 1956*

The *Canticum* does not belong on orchestral programs. It will suffer in company with orchestra repertory.[41] It should be encouraged by chamber music societies and by the universities.

    We are enjoying a stay of six weeks here in Venice, up to the premiere on the 13th of next month, that is.

STRAVINSKY TO ANDREWES   *August 13, 1956*

There is a misprint in the [*Canticum*] full score on page 11, bar 73 in the flute part: the third and fifth sixteenths *should be C flats* instead of A flats. Please, let it be corrected.

STRAVINSKY TO ROTH   *August 28, 1956*

I agree for the recordings of my *Canticum* and the *"Vom Himmel hoch"* Variations by Robert Craft with Vega Company in connection with his Paris concert (November 10th/56) in Pierre Boulez's programs.

    We start here the *Canticum* instrumental rehearsals in two days, and I hope I will receive from London a second copy of *Canticum*'s full score (playing proofs) because the one I have here is not enough.

---

[41] After the *Canticum Sacrum* had been performed in Tanglewood in July 1957, Stravinsky received a telegram signed "violinists and cellists of Boston Symphony Orchestra" that read: "Congratulations on your superb orchestration *Canticum Sacrum*." Stravinsky snapped back with a telegram: "Too bad clarinets, tuba, horns and percussion didn't share your enthusiasm for my *Canticum* superb instrumentation. Best wishes."

STRAVINSKY TO KOCH   *November 12, 1956*

I will be leaving the hospital on Saturday, November 17, and I will be needing some money. Thank you in advance. My address is: Krankenanstalt Rote Kreuz, Nymphenburger Strasse 163, Munich. Fortunately, I am much better and will go immediately to Rome to conduct the *Canticum* and my Bach Variations.

[*Original in German*]

STRAVINSKY TO ROTH   *November 19, 1956*

Since yesterday I am here [out of the Munich hospital] and we are going to Rome next Thursday. We will leave Rome for London probably the 30th by train and I will confirm . . . by wire from Rome for Savoy Hotel reservations as soon as I will have the tickets in my pocket.

STRAVINSKY TO ROTH   *January 19, 1957*

I certainly accept your suggestion of exchanging letters concerning the uninterrupted continuation of our contract until December 31, 1961, in case there will be no devaluation of European currencies. . . . Please send me [this] letter in two copies (both signed by you). I will send one of them back to you with my signature. I will join this [rider] to the two copies of our contract signed by me. We are leaving N.Y. Wednesday, Jan. 23rd for Hollywood by train.

STRAVINSKY TO ADAMS   *February 15, 1957*

Enclosed the continuation of *Agon* in full score, pages 63–72 incl., and the piano reduction, pages 54–60 incl. . . .

    May I ask you to inquire at Columbia Records why the unions still withhold the money they owe me for my 6 hours conducting the records of *Perséphone* on January 14, 1957.

                                                            April 11, 1957
STRAVINSKY TO BOOSEY & HAWKES   *[Telegram]*

Tell Roth have agreement conduct *Agon* European premiere Sudwestfunk Orchestra Paris October 12. Please arrange dates my German concerts accordingly. Please phone Glock private house in Dartington or nearby not as guests most convenient solution.

STRAVINSKY TO ROTH   *April 12, 1957*

You see from my wire of yesterday I accepted Boulez's proposal for the European premiere of *Agon* in Paris on October 12th. The German premiere could be reserved to München (Hartmann) the world premiere being as you know here on June 17th (in Waxman concerts). Waxman told Bob he can have the parts of *Agon* extracted in a few days by his studio copyist without mistakes. Boasting, of course, but that is a good idea to have it done here under my control. I have a month and a half still to work.

STRAVINSKY TO ADAMS   *April 16, 1957*

Will you be kind enough to tell me what shall I do to force the unions to pay me the money they owe me for my recording of *Perséphone* . . . with N.Y. Philharmonic Orchestra. I asked Columbia (through Deborah Ishlon), the unions promised to pay immediately, Columbia asked Zirato to intervene, the unions promised to pay immediately. Result: I never was paid. Shall I ask Petrillo to help me?

STRAVINSKY TO ADAMS   *April 24, 1957*

Enclosed the four copies of the *Apollo* Variation contract (J. Szigeti)[42] signed by me which I am sending you back as you asked me to do so in yours of April 15th.

STRAVINSKY TO ADAMS   *May 3, 1957*

I mailed you a copy of what was left of *Agon*'s full score: (1) new reduction of the first eight pages and (2) the last pages of the ballet—pages 73–98 incl.

 The other day I noticed in my own copy that the photostat printer repeated twice page 83 and left page 84 missing. I wonder if your copy (which I had no time to verify) is correct. Please verify these pages and see whether the sequence is correct throughout.

STRAVINSKY TO ROTH   *May 8, 1957*

You will receive from N.Y. the last pages of *Agon*'s full score. . . . Today I discovered two mistakes in them and I enclose the corrections. Please let it be immediately introduced in the pages of the full score you will receive before you engrave them.

 You also will receive (with these pages) a new reduction of the first 8 pages of *Agon*. Please destroy the old ones and engrave the new version. Bob is telling me you already started the engraving; I am very sorry to disturb your engravers with these new 8 pages but I decided to introduce the mandoline part and this might cause trouble for the engravers. Let us hope that this trouble will not be too serious.

---

[42] Joseph Szigeti had made an arrangement of the violin solo (following the introduction).

STRAVINSKY TO ROTH   *May 10, 1957*

I mailed you today by air under separate cover Illumina Nos, a seven-part motet by Gesualdo, Bob Craft wrote you about. If you need more photocopies of it let me know. . . .

You will be kind to tell the engraver of *Agon* that there is a big mistake in the bar [numbers]: the number 519 is missing—after 518 comes 520 on page 84. In the piano score which I finished now and the end of which I will send next week . . . I could not correct it, it was too complicated. So I prefer your engraver takes care of it.

STRAVINSKY TO ROTH   *May 18, 1957*

Many thanks for yours of May 14th as well as for that [which] you wrote to Bob concerning my concerts.

Rome: the date of October 21st, i.e. 9 days after my Paris concert seems to me the most convenient of the three dates they propose. So let us take it. Hope they will accept $2000 instead of the former fee of $1500. To whom must I write as to the program?

Do not worry about the facsimile of the first four bars of *Agon* which will be after all the same music but less complete in its instrumentation. The people might take it for a sketch—that's all. Too bad David Adams did not send you the eight first pages by air. I asked him to do it immediately and he did it but by surface mail: too bad indeed.

Hope you are in possession of a photocopy of Illuminia Nos with my piano reduction to photocopy underneath the choral score. Please, do the same in printing. A propos: you are right—let *The Score* have the first page of it but not the entire sacred song which is a long affair of 15 pages. Craft will send you a foreword of 200–300 words for the fly-leaf of Illumina Nos which I hope will illumine us—explanation about the Gesualdo Sacred Songs. I think he will be glad to have $50 for it, and I hope you will accept it.

STRAVINSKY TO ROTH   *May 20, 1957*

Many thanks for your two letters of May 15th & 16th.

May 15th letter: glad you did not lose time in engraving my Gesualdo *Sacra Cantione* and I do hope you did not forget to give your engravers orders to leave the place beneath the vocal score for the piano reduction. I . . . airmailed you a new photoprint with my piano reduction on May 15th. By now you probably have it. Please reassure me about it.

You will be an angel to answer for me Mr. Jaenike's letter. I certainly have no time (and between us no particular interest) to do a requiem for Pergolesi for the next spring (and probably for little money). So, please, tell him I have no time to undertake it. On the contrary I am negotiating with Paul Sacher to whom I promised last year a composition more or less important in size (from

12 to 15 min. of music). This unfortunately I will be obliged to postpone because of my European trip on one side and on the other side this terrible loss of time in my birthday period—television, concert, trip to Boston. The 10th or the 12th of July going already to Santa Fe for the *Rake*'s performance (Bob Craft conducting) and from there [at] the end of the month to New York to sail on *Liberté* to Plymouth. So you see what is going on!

STRAVINSKY TO ADAMS   *May 22, 1957*

This morning I received your word of May 20th and this afternoon a new page of the beginning of *Agon* in transparent manuscript flew to London. . . . That was the fastest way to do it: to bring to my reproduction service, to wait a few hours, to miss the post service I preferred to make in 45 minutes a new page (four bars) for the periodical *The Score,* and to airmail it immediately.

STRAVINSKY TO ADAMS   *May 24, 1957*

In answer to yours of May 22 I mailed to you today (parcel-surface) two copies of the two-piano reduction of *Agon.* . . .

If you are going to [give] one of these copies to Balanchine . . . ask him not to show for the moment the music to curious people before it will appear . . . sometime in the summer.

STRAVINSKY TO ANDREWES   *May 24, 1957*

Agon:

1. OK for the trumpets above horns throughout.

2. Your engravers are right following my score for the mandoline and the castanets and the harp in Bransle Gay (pages 61 & 62).

3. Page 81, as before and later I prefer you follow my manuscript as per my cable to you in answer to yours of May 20th. The order [of] the instruments in my score is much more convincing for the readers and the young generation of conductors than the order of instruments in a standard orchestra score.

STRAVINSKY TO ROTH   *May 29, 1957*

In answer to your cable I wired you my acceptance of the Rome dates and my program provided they give me 3 rehearsals in these three days of October 21/22/23 (day of the concert if the other two prove impossible). . . .

Yesterday I sent you a cable full of hope that you will receive in 4 airmail days my two envelopes: (1) Bob's foreword to Gesualdo, two photostats for the cover, and his letter to you with explanation, and . . . (2) proofs of Gesualdo's Sacra Cantione received in the morning and corrected in the afternoon.

STRAVINSKY TO ROTH   *June 3, 1957*

This word—about Basler String Concerto in D which I am conducting in Munich and Rome, as you know. . . . I am asking you in advance to let Bonn and Milano be sure to furnish me the right material, i.e. the one with the enlarged . . . 3rd movement. Unfortunately there are still some sets (and full scores, too) in circulation of the primary version.

STRAVINSKY TO ROTH   *June 7, 1957*

I am answering yours of June 3rd, just received. If Rome insists on *Agon*, please cancel the concert because meanwhile Strobel has proposed me to conduct *Agon* in Donaueschingen October 21–22, and this is much easier for me.*

However, Hartmann has the rights for the first German performance, has he not?

If Rome refuses to do the concert without *Agon* (which, between us, is too difficult to do there and does not go at all with the *Firebird* Suite), please cancel Rome, and telephone Strobel to arrange Donaueschingen for me even if it is only $1500.

* At that time I will already have conducted it with the same orchestra (of Baden-Baden) in Paris, and it is just one piece of the program.

STRAVINSKY TO ROTH   *June 9, 1957*

Terrible two weeks with TV, concert, two days of recording *Canticum* and *Agon* on June 18 & 19.

                                                           June 9, 1957
STRAVINSKY TO ADAMS   *[Telegram]*

Imperative you stop performance *Canticum* Munch Stokowski. Too serious danger misinterpretation by wrong people and also because I plan conduct it myself New York this fall. Please help me.

STRAVINSKY TO ADAMS   *June 21, 1957*

I enclose here a letter from Westminster which embarrasses me very much: first—I am a Columbia artist and as such cannot give to another firm for advertisement purposes a photo of mine or permission to reproduce it without hurting Columbia . . . which I don't want at all. Second—I don't want [Westminster] to release my *Canticum* before my own Columbia recording.[43]

---

[43] Westminster wrote to Boulez on June 26, and he sent the letter to Stravinsky, explaining that Westminster represented Vega in the United States, and that the record,

STRAVINSKY TO ROTH   *June 22, 1957*

Bob is already in Boston for my three concerts he is conducting there [with] Soulima at the piano for Capriccio, Boston Arts Festival in my honor. Afterwards we are going to Santa Fe where Bob is conducting three performances of the *Rake* in the new Bowl-theater, July 17, 18 & 20. The 22nd of July by train to New York to take *Liberté* sailing to Plymouth the 29th. . . .

David Adams was here for my concert and my recordings. *Agon* and *Canticum* are now recorded and I will edit them when in New York (end of July). Now, before going away in 2 weeks I must check the proofs of the full score of *Agon* from which Bob conducted its premiere here. It was a very successful performance and the audience greeted my new work with real enthusiasm. Of course I could not expect the first proofs free of mistakes and misprints. The main corrections were already done by Bob during the rehearsals.

STRAVINSKY TO ROTH   *June 27, 1957*

I received a French catalogue of manuscripts the cover of which is as follows: *Lettres autographes et manuscrits de musiciens—Marc Loliée, Expert près du Tribunal Civil de Versailles, 40, rue des Saints-Pères, Paris 7, Téléph.: Littré 40–19, Numéro 90. At . . .* page 30 of this catalogue, under Nos 155–156, are two letters of mine; one—for Fr. 10,000 and another for Fr. 11,000. May I ask you to acquire these two letters for me and to bring them with you at Dartington in August. Many thanks.

Only today can I start to work on your full score proofs of *Agon*. It was again a very busy week. In ten days we are going to Santa Fe for Vera's show there and my *Rake's Progress*.

STRAVINSKY TO ROTH   *July 4, 1957*

In a few days I am leaving Hollywood. So write me, please, c/o Miss Mirandi, Thunderbird Shop, Santa Fe, New Mexico, U.S.A. I will be there till July 21st attending the performances of my *Rake* (Bob conducting) July 17th, 18th and 20th. Afterwards going for a week to New York, taking S.S. *Liberté* (still on strike!) on August 1st for Plymouth.

. . . All these last weeks it was a hell of life! It was such a mess in our house: the NBC television people flooding three days our house, 27 people three days without interruption (making a film of me [and] an interview with R. Craft for TV later in the fall). No sooner were we through it [than] we had to start rehearsing the concert, afterwards my concert and the Columbia

---

with the *Canticum* conducted by the present writer on one side and the Webern cantatas conducted by Boulez on the other, was scheduled for release in America. Stravinsky sent the Westminster letter to A. Gishford, who visited Stravinsky in Dartington on August 14, at which time Stravinsky gave permission to release the record.

recording of *Agon* and *Canticum*. And only after all these very tiring days could I take care of the *Agon* proofs.

STRAVINSKY TO ROTH   *July 6, 1957*

I notice that in my last letters to you I did the same mistake: I wrote you having wrongly in mind your staying in England until the end of August. Today re-reading your letter of June 18th, I noticed in your P.S., to my utmost disappoint-ment, that you are leaving the 28 of July and not of August. How very stupid I am to make such a mistake! . . . Now, dismiss my letter of June 27th, unless your people in Paris can take care of it and hand me over the purchased letters when I will be in Paris for my concert there (Oct. 12th). . . .

The Donaueschingen concert (my performance of *Agon*) is settled with Dr. Strobel for Oct. 19th, flying from Zürich the 20th to Rome.

STRAVINSKY TO BOOSEY & HAWKES   *July 27, 1957*

Paris

Could I ask you to send on my behalf to M. Alexei Remizov,[44] 7, rue Boileau, Paris 16, the sum (in French francs) equivalent to $25 (twenty-five dollars), debiting my account with Boosey & Hawkes also of the expenses of this remit-tance.

[*Original in French*]

STRAVINSKY TO ROTH   *September 21, 1957*

Enclosed a letter . . . which I ask you . . . to answer for me; . . . I just made such a film for NBC and my contract . . . does not permit me to make another film. . . .

I corrected and airmailed yesterday the piano score *Agon* proofs. While correcting them I found a dozen . . . mistakes and misprints in the orchestra score. This must be corrected in a new edition I dream to have as soon as possi-ble to replace the ugly present one. . . .

---

[44] Stravinsky wrote to Suvchinsky on November 20 from Hollywood: "On my table I find, completely unexpectedly, Alexei Remizov's book, which has appeared here in a totally mysterious way, his *Tristan and Isolde* autographed and inscribed to me in the calligraphic scrawl of the poor, blind man. It is a miracle. Apart from my name, what is written is very difficult to decipher. A pity. In all likelihood this is an answer to my salu-tation to him on his jubilee. I am writing to you also to ask you to buy for me the twelve books of his that have appeared in the Opleshnik and that are listed on the last page of this book." Stravinsky wrote again on December 30: "I found out about Remizov's death from his own books, which were sent to me, eight of them with an inscription or

STRAVINSKY TO ROTH   *November 17, 1957*

To answer you about your London and Switzerland suggestions I must let you
know first that I am conducting a concert in Hamburg on 13th October 1958.
And in the very beginning of November I have to be in Paris for two pairs of
concerts to conduct at the Domaine Musical (Pierre Boulez), November 7th &
8th and Nov. 14 & 15 (French premiere of *Threni*). Thus the only time for
your proposal could be between October 14th and 31st. As I cannot accept both
(London and Switzerland) I take the less fatiguing—Switzerland, with Winterthur, Zürich and Basel; same program for the three concerts and the rehearsals
in Winterthur with their orchestra. The concerts have to be spaced in order to
let me have a little rest between. The program you asked me could be the same
as it was planned for Winterthur the last year: *Danses concertantes,* Violin
Concerto (with Peter Rybar, soloist), *Dumbarton Oaks* Concerto and Suite of
Pulcinella.

The concert I am conducting in Hamburg will be the third I contracted
with Hamburg Radio (Rolf Liebermann) in succession of the two Biennale
concerts (in the second half of September/58) in Venice where I will conduct
the world premiere of *Threni* (or Lamentationes Jeremiae Profetae). The first
concert will be—*Sacre* and *Oedipus.* The second one—Wind Instruments
Symphony, *Dylan Thomas "In Memoriam,"* *Threni, Threni* (repetition) and
Mass. . . .

The combination of *Agon* with *Perséphone* and *Petrushka* in La Scala is
certainly not a very good one because the difficult young *Agon* cannot yet compete with the success of such well known compositions as *Petrushka* and
Perséphone.

STRAVINSKY TO HANS SWARSENSKY   *November 20, 1957*

Kindly pay Mr. Pierre Suvchinsky [for the] purchasing and shipping of a dozen
books I need. It will be probably around $30–35.

STRAVINSKY TO BOOSEY & HAWKES   *December 6, 1957*
                                                              [Telegram]
London

Cancel concerts as have just accepted four Swiss concerts conducting only
Threni with Hamburg Orchestra. Much easier for me.

---

a dedication on the first page by a hand I do not recognize. Some of the inscriptions
were dictated by Remizov and one is in his own hand. Then another informs me of his
death, peaceful and painless, in a half-sleep, on November 26. In one of the books I am
told about the interest and excitement with which he awaited accounts of my concert
of October 11 at the Salle Pleyel, and in another, about how my regards were given to
him on the day before he died. God rest his soul." In a letter to Natalya Victorovna
Reznikova, April 26, 1964, answering one from her thanking him for his comments on

STRAVINSKY TO SWARSENSKY   *December 11, 1957*

Did you ever receive my note of November 20 asking you to send Madame Olga Sallard,[45] Tauzin, Illats, Gironde, the equivalent of $25? Probably not, since I have received a letter from Madame Sallard saying that she never received this sum.

Would you therefore please send her this money at your earliest convenience.

STRAVINSKY TO KOCH   *December 14, 1957*

May I ask you to secure me a Düsseldorf Städtische Bühnen Program booklet 1955–56 (Heft 9)—that of Mozart Festivals. . . .

STRAVINSKY TO ROTH   *December 28, 1957*

I have no contract and even no verbal [*sic*] agreement with Balanchine and Kirstein [for *Agon*]. The only understanding . . . was that they were to have first performance rights. And, as you know, even that was modified as they allowed us to give the music here and in Paris before the ballet. . . .

I understand Balanchine's wishes in that City Center has paid a good sum of money for a work which will now be given to anyone—that he has no exclusivity. Perhaps also he plans to perform *Agon* in Europe with his ballet (though that I doubt because of his wife's condition;[46] and he did not mention any European plans to me). He does not think Scala capable of doing the piece well (nor do I) but I don't see how Europe can be prevented from doing it and in that case how La Scala can be discriminated against.

I think Balanchine (or rather City Center [New York City] Ballet) has a moral right to enjoy at least some stage exclusivity for, say, one year. Personally I find it fair to recognize the City Center's exclusivity and not only for U.S.A. We must not forget that it was the City Center who paid me for the composition of *Agon* and generously agreed to our concert world premiere in Los Angeles at my birthday festival (George Balanchine present) before their stage world premiere on November 27th. Knowing in detail the difficulties, musical intricacies and subtleties of the score and having arranged with Balanchine a well established choreographic construction for this plotless ballet, you can easily imagine my complete lack of interest for a staging of *Agon* by strangers of . . . La Scala in a total ignorance of my ideas and of how we realized it with Balanchine. . . .

Flying Jan. 2nd to Houston (Texas) for my concerts there and coming back the 9th. Please answer me what will be your decision about the whole

---

her translations of Rozanov, Stravinsky says that he has "treasured the works of Remizov since the years of my own youth."

[45] A close friend of Vera Stravinsky.

[46] Tanaquil LeClercq had been stricken with polio in October 1956.

thing. I hope by now you have my reply to your letter of Dec. 13 airmailed to you the 18th with the proof of *Agon's* sketch for the cover which I am awaiting now back for the *bon à tirer.*

STRAVINSKY TO ADAMS   *January 1, 1958*

Enclosed two photocopies of the first 24 pages of *Threni,* I spoke about by phone the other day: one copy for your office and the other one to be shipped immediately to London.

STRAVINSKY TO ADAMS   *January 28, 1958*

I guess by now you received the second portion of my new work, pages 25–50 (incl.), I surface-mailed you the other day. Now, I ask you to show *nobody* my score before I give you special permission for it.

STRAVINSKY TO ROTH   *February 2, 1958*

The proposition of BBC . . . to finish my program with *Scherzo à la russe* seems to me a little bit unpractical because after its last number, i.e. *Apollo,* 30 minutes duration and in a special string orchestra sitting, the full orchestra must be gathered together for a normal sitting which will take some time, with the time of my bowing after *Apollo*—and all this to conduct 3½ minutes of music. Don't you think that the effect "to finish up with a flourish for the whole orchestra" (to use your phrase) will be spoiled because of this change of the orchestra for a very short piece of music! . . .

As *Threni* is mainly a vocal composition for soloists and chorus I think that a *Klavierauszug* would be rather difficult to establish. But if you find that it must be done in any case I will ask you to entrust it to Leopold Spinner (if he is still with you) because I doubt I will have the time necessary and the patience to do it myself.

STRAVINSKY TO ADAMS   *February 5, 1958*

Enclosed two photocopies of the full score of *Threni*—pages 51–66 inclusive. One copy for your office, the other one for London.

STRAVINSKY TO ROTH   *February 11, 1958*

Answering in order your 6 questions . . . of February 5th.

1. Yes, the parts have to be written out in the conventional way.

2. To facilitate the reading of the full score I am now writing for the clarinets *the real notes,* leaving it to the copyist the writing out [of] the parts as

Stravinsky's marginalia on a letter of agreement for a concert in Rome in November 1958.

usual, i.e. in B flat or in A according to the lowest note of the section. In this *Threni* score I left only the four horns in F as transposing parts.

3. I know, the deep C of the bass clar. is always an undesirable note but recently (in America at any rate) the players have managed to produce it by a special key. As to the Germans—surely they have it.

4. The bugle contralto in my score is a saxhorn (in German *Flügelhorn* in B). . . . I write it in C, i.e. it sounds as written. The tuba which is playing with it is actually the bass saxhorn (E flat or C) of the family.

The questions 5 & 6 are answered by the leaflets (with many corrections) I am enclosing here. . . .

P.S. As you will notice I replaced the contrafagotto by the sarrusophone. Please notice that in this score the contrabassi and the sarrusophone sound *an octave lower,* [like] the tenor with his treble clef. The English horn, of course, sounds a fifth lower.

STRAVINSKY TO ADAMS   *February 26, 1958*

Enclosed find pages 67–82 for the full score photocopy of *Threni* in two copies: one for your office, the other for London as usual.

STRAVINSKY TO ADAMS   *March 6, 1958*

Reading today your acknowledge[ment] of receipt (March 4th) of the last shipment of *Threni* I was surprised not to find your reaction on my St. Thomas Church concert of March 2nd conducted by Robert Craft, attended by about 2000 persons, sponsored by Mrs. J. D. Rockefeller and the Ballet Society. . . . But even so, it should not escape your attention especially since the entire program was composed of Boosey & Hawkes works and the material could not be rented otherwise than through your office.

STRAVINSKY TO SWARSENSKY   *March 16, 1958*

You would be most kind to send Madame Olga Sallard the equivalent of $50, to the same address as the last time (Tauzin, Illats, Gironde), debiting my account with Boosey & Hawkes of this sum.

[*Original in French*]

STRAVINSKY TO SWARSENSKY   *March 21, 1958*

Once again I am writing to you, asking you this time to send the equivalent of $25 to Mlle Zika Kamenetzky, 20, rue de Seine, Paris 6ème.

[*Original in French*]

STRAVINSKY TO ROTH   *March 26, 1958*

My score of *Threni* is finished and I am sending today the last eight pages. . . .

I have an awkward contract. Hamburg does not pay me my commission on the completion of the score but only when they have all of the materials in hand. Naturally I am anxious to have the money. I therefore would like to hear from you immediately how soon you think it is possible to complete the preparation of the material.

STRAVINSKY TO ADAMS   *March 26, 1958*

Enclosed the last pages of my *Threni* (83–90 incl.) in two photocopies; as usual—one for your office, the other one for London. You will also find two photocopies of pages 51–2. Please let the old ones be destroyed and replaced by these new ones which are now correct. . . .

Please send me the piano reduction of my *Orpheus* which I need and which is strangely missing in my library. May I ask you to get me from Schirmer's Arnold Schoenberg's Piano Concerto (in full score and piano reduction if such exists). I prefer to do it through you rather [than] directly. Thank you.

I was so pleased to spend a very nice evening after the last "Monday Evening" concert with Anthony Gishford. To Leslie Boosey—my best regards.

STRAVINSKY TO ROTH   *April 3, 1958*

Glad you energetically push the work on *Threni* material ahead and I am enclosing here my corrections which you already had plus new ones. . . . When will you send me the first proofs of the full score and the vocal score? Am pleased to know the latter is already finished.

STRAVINSKY TO ADAMS   *April 8, 1958*

This is just to tell you that I will be in San Francisco for my concerts from this Saturday April 12th till Sunday 20 April in the Clift Hotel.

STRAVINSKY TO ADAMS   *April 20, 1958*

Thank you for the scores of Schoenberg and *Orpheus*. Enclosed please find a check for these Schoenberg scores. I do not pay, of course, for my *Orpheus* piano score because I never pay my publishers for copies of my own compositions when I am in need of them. It was billed probably by some newcomer in your office. Enclosed also some mistakes in the full score of my *Threni* on pages 27, 37–38 and 55, just discovered. Please, let it be corrected in your score immediately.

STRAVINSKY TO ROTH   .   *June 12, 1958*

We are leaving July 20th Hollywood by train to New York and taking *Cristoforo Colombo* July 29th. Arriving the 7th of August in Genova (Savoy Hotel) and going by car (with the whole baggage) to Venice the 9th.

Are you going to Sirmione as usual, and when exactly?

When are you going to send to Hamburg the remaining *Threni* material? I am [asking not out of] curiosity but by necessity . . . because . . . [the] final payment to me [is] after the delivery of the material.

STRAVINSKY TO ROTH   *June 17, 1958*

In my last letter of June 12th I wanted to ask you about the new orchestra score of *Agon* and I completely forgot it. Since our last correspondence in November/ 57 and in Jan./58 I never heard about this new full score of *Agon* which is to replace the absurd size of the first one. Was . . . something done about it?

STRAVINSKY TO ROTH   *July 4, 1958*

I would like to add something about *Agon*.
     Will you be kind to notice that in the new edition (in a correct size) the useless and funny German and French translations of "Ballet for Twelve Dancers" and "Full Score" which appear on the page following the cover ought to be completely eliminated. Also on the back side of this page, below the "Instrumentation," the duration of 20 minutes must be replaced by 23 *minutes.* . . .
     That's all for today's American 4th of July.

STRAVINSKY TO ROTH   *July 25, 1958*

I received your letter of July 22nd with the news of Erwin Stein's death, which made me very sad. I sent a cable to Boosey & Hawkes in London asking to convey [to] his family my feelings [of] deep sorrow. How unexpected! Was it a heart attack?

STRAVINSKY TO ROTH   *July 26, 1958*

I am performing in Venice the *Sacre* with the new Danse sacrale. I certainly agree with you that this Danse sacrale should come under the terms of our general contract. I am very glad that you finally managed to arrange the thing with B. Schott. . . .
     . . . May I ask you to write to Carisch (Milan) for a small muted pianino (a spinet or an upright small piano) to be put in my room at the Bauer Grünwald during my stay there (10 August–24 Sept.). It must be . . . felted (muted) in order not to disturb the neighborhood and not to be heard myself. I hope he can find something in Venice without sending it from Milan.

STRAVINSKY TO ROTH   *August 11, 1958*

Many thanks . . . for writing to Carisch about the muted cembalo I am expecting this afternoon and about the money, the news of which is not yet received. If the control of the government makes the payments so difficult, better to give it up. After all, I am not in a critical position; I wanted only to profit, in order not to spend my dollars, if there was some money on my account at Carisch's.

STRAVINSKY TO ANDREWES   *August 18, 1958*

Please find enclosed the four letter-press pages of *Threni* I partly corrected; I changed the second page into English and I added on the 4th page to the De Elegia Quinta—"Oratio Jeremiae Prophetae" (with below the English translation) which was omitted, a title I let be sung by two basses.

You speak . . . about three typographical errors which you already corrected. Strangely enough I see only two of them, because the second one (bar 346)—"*cogitationes*" is correctly engraved with dashes belonging to the same word. So what is the trouble?

It is absolutely necessary to make some small changes as to the first and second clarinets because the firsts don't like to change their embouchure to play in a low register. It must therefore be the second clarinet who takes the alto clarinet after bar 134 and not the first one. It is why we have not to put on pages 52, 54 and 55—"Cl. I" instead of "Cl. II."

Not having at this moment under hand the last full score of *Threni* you sent me, I wonder if there are still mistakes in some places I enumerate: (1) bar 33—tempo missing? (2) bar 188—is there a "p" missing in "sem*p*re" (stesso tempo), (3) bar 115 "arco" at VC missing? (4) bar 231 "arco" missing at CB?

STRAVINSKY TO ANDREWES   *September 1, 1958*

I hope a correct full score and vocal parts (chorus and soloists) as well as the piano transcription of *Threni* was shipped to Pierre Boulez who was anxiously awaiting it to start the rehearsal in Paris. Please reassure me on this, because he is preparing . . . the rehearsals of *Threni* and I am directly interested in the preparation of the singers in good time conducting *Threni* in Paris in the first half of November.

STRAVINSKY TO ROTH   *September 6, 1958*

Robert Craft just phoned me from Hamburg where he is preparing . . . *Threni,* that Brussels still has no music of *Threni* which Craft has to conduct there in one month! On the other hand P. Boulez writes him the same for his Paris group of musicians which he is anxious to start preparing for my concert of November 14th!

STRAVINSKY TO ROTH   *September 14, 1958*

I am writing today to ask you to help me in hotel reservations for our stay in London in December (two single rooms each with bath, communicating, for me and Vera, and one single with bath for Bob). We will leave Rome the 6th of December and will be the 7th in London. So, please, get in touch with the Claridge Hotel where we want to stay this time till December 17th, the day of our sailing to New York on the *Liberté.*

May I also ask you to remind the BBC people about the labor permit. As I plan to ask Bob Craft to help me in conducting some of my rehearsals (because two rehearsals a day is too strenuous for me) I wonder if he also has to secure a labor permit for it. . . .

Sorry but the timing of *Threni* must be marked not 35 min. but circa 30 min. This is what I hear from Bob after his Hamburg rehearsals.

STRAVINSKY TO ROTH   *October 5, 1958*

We are going Tuesday the 7th of October by car to Hamburg stopping for two nights at Munich and Frankfurt.

STRAVINSKY TO ROTH   *October 10, 1958*

Enclosed two copies of the assignment for Danse sacrale signed and initialled by me, the third one being kept for my files. That is the answer to yours of the 2nd Oct. which I received just a day before I met you in Munich.

STRAVINSKY TO ROTH   *November 2, 1958*

Would it be possible for you to tell the Claridge Hotel that we will arrive only the 2nd of December. We cannot leave Rome before the 30th of November because of the show of my wife. So we will be the 1st in Paris and the 2nd in London. . . .

We are leaving Vienna Saturday the 8th of Nov. for Paris, Hôtel Berkeley, 6, avenue Matignon.

STRAVINSKY TO ROTH   *November 13, 1958*

I am thinking now about my rehearsing schedule and my program in BBC and I am starting a little bit to worry about it.

1—two rehearsals the same day which is extremely fatiguing, 2—two very difficult works never played by BBC orchestra which takes much time to rehearse (Hans Rosbaud . . . last year prepared . . . *Agon* in 6 rehearsals!)— *Agon* and the Symphony, 3—*Apollo* requiring only strings means a rehearsal apart from these 4 rehearsals, a thing which never was mentioned in my contract with BBC.

Unfortunately I cannot count on Robert Craft's help this time because he was not well all this last time (he had to cancel his Hamburg engagement after rehearsing there the whole week) and continues to be under a menace of an appendix operation! And we have to go the 20th to Rome (our concert there is scheduled for the 27th) before London.

STRAVINSKY TO AMPENOFF   *December 22, 1958*

So much thanks for your letter of Dec. 18th with all these enclosures and your answers to all the useless people writing me useless letters. Thank you very much, indeed.

Today only these lines to acknowledge this and also to tell you that till now—no notice from my bank in Basel about my two Italian checks sent to this bank by the gentlemen of Liechtenstein.

STRAVINSKY TO AMPENOFF   *January 10, 1959*

Since your letter of December 30 to me, I heard nothing from you concerning Liechtenstein and the money to deposit in my Swiss bank. Did you investigate . . . it? Tomorrow we are going home where we count to be in the afternoon of the 14th of January.

STRAVINSKY TO AMPENOFF   *January 15, 1959*

As to the Liechtenstein payment, I received from the Swiss bank an information (or rather a confirmation) [that they received] this money (paid as Liechtenstein said on Dec. 29th) only Jan. 8th!! This incomprehensible delay of 10 days was the reason I bothered you.

STRAVINSKY TO AMPENOFF   *January 17, 1959*

Enclosed a letter from an unknown person (in a very poor Russian) which I received here in August when I was already in Europe.

Please, read this letter and my remarks . . . because we have to stop this Herr Hinnonthal from printing my *Pulcinella* Tarantella. I do not want him to know the source of the Pergolesi fragments I used in composing this ballet.

STRAVINSKY TO ROTH   *January 26, 1959*

I received a letter from a poor priest whom I knew in Paris years ago and who is in want. I am willing to help him and ask you to do it through your Bonn office. Please let them send him $25 charging my account in Bonn for it. Thank you very much in advance. His address is: Subdeacon Mr. Alexander Koutroff, 3 Odos Rangavi, Neon Faliron, Athens, Greece.

STRAVINSKY TO BOOSEY   *January 31, 1959*

Thank you for your note of January 29th. The best evening for us to have you for a comfortable dinner will be Wednesday February 11th. I hope this date will be convenient.

STRAVINSKY TO AMPENOFF   *February 7, 1959*

Enclosed two strange letters, one from Mr. G. H. Trent and another a credit note with a mention of a "Russian Easter Carol" I never composed. On the other hand in the bunch of statements I received for 1958 (Mechanicals, Sheet music, Rentals Hire, Performances, etc.) the important list of an ensemble of all this (usually there to alleviate the verification) was missing this time.

STRAVINSKY TO ROTH   *February 19, 1959*

I do not understand what exactly Leslie Boosey had in mind telling you that I find "the B. & H. editions leaving something to be desired." When I spoke with him about the printing, engraving and editing problems, I just said that the latter sometimes [left] something to be desired, having in mind things which were already discussed with you, improved and corrected since; as, for example, the disproportionate size of the title of *Agon*'s first full score, and the advertisement on the cover's back-pages and their cheap look. But all of this you know, and I have absolutely nothing else or new in mind. Please believe me, that, if I had to say something, being not satisfied with something, I would certainly first of all tell you about it.

STRAVINSKY TO ADAMS   *March 20, 1959*

We are flying to Japan via Honolulu (2 days), Manila (2 days), Hong Kong (4 days) and Tokyo, Imperial Hotel, where we shall be the 6th of April. My concerts will be—one in Osaka (the 1st of May) and two in Tokyo (between the 3d and the 6th of May). The 7th, flying back (via Honolulu). Till the 20th of May in Hollywood, afterwards flying SAS to Copenhagen, conducting there the 25th (Royal Danish Ballet and Music Festival) and flying back the 26th same SAS. Here at Franz Waxman's festivals in middle June conducting in concert performance my opera *The Nightingale* and in July in Santa Fe's Cathedral my *Threni* in connection with the Santa Fe Opera Association performance this summer.

Now I have to pack. I want you to wish me *"bon voyage."*

STRAVINSKY TO ROTH   *June 5, 1959*

1. Everything was in order with the [orchestra parts] in my Japan concerts. The whole trip interesting but the flight a little bit fatiguing.

2. Movements for Piano and Orchestra—not yet finished (two thirds of the piece is composed, full score and two-piano reduction already photostated and one copy with Margrit Weber).

3. Rolf Liebermann came specially to Copenhagen to see me and to discuss with me the first two performances of Movements which he proposes to

me conducting his NDR Hamburg orchestra in Köln June 17th 1960 and Hamburg one week [or] 10 days later.

4. Pierre Boulez came to see me there also. He wants to have the first French performance of Movements in his "Domaine Musical" concert in June 1960 under his direction in a program dedicated to my chamber music. As he told me he must do it before June 28th, he has to place this concert between my two German concerts of 17 and 25 (or 27) of June. On the other hand he must do it with Mme Weber who has the exclusive rights for one year from the day of its first performance. . . . So she took note about our decision with R. Liebermann. . . .

6. Yes, I wrote a very short piece (one page) in the memory of late Prinz Max Egon zu Fürstenberg to be played in Donaueschingen in the fall of 1959 in the first concert before a program dedicated to Anton Webern, as I was asked to do so by H. Strobel. . . . This piece is composed for three instruments: one flute, one clarinet and one harp.

STRAVINSKY TO ROTH   *June 12, 1959*

I answered William Glock accepting his proposal to conduct at BBC November 7th & 9th. As program he was already decided to do my Symphony in C and *Oedipus Rex* on November 7th in the Festival Hall and only *Oedipus Rex* in the studio on November 9th. Of course I ok'ed this suggestion. But nevertheless I will be glad [if] you get in touch with him to be quite sure that everything is all right. . . .

How was *Threni* received in William Steinberg's direction? Why do you think the Festival Hall is a wrong place [to] play it?

I must stop—rehearsals of *The Nightingale,* I am conducting the 15th!

STRAVINSKY TO ROTH   *June 27, 1959*

Enclosed the corrected proof of my Epitaphium to which I added, as you can see, the second name of the Prinz. . . .

In order not to lose time, please write me at Santa Fe Opera, P.O. Box 1654, Santa Fe, New Mexico where I will be from June 29 until July 13th. Afterwards here until the end of August. I am conducting *Threni*[47] in the Cathedral of Santa Fe July 12th, Bob Craft conducting Bach and other religious music in the 1st half of the program.

---

[47] Stravinsky was particularly pleased when his daughter-in-law, Françoise, wrote to him later in the year after the release of the *Threni* recording: "It's a marvelous work. *Threni* has the grandeur and the intensity of conviction of the *Symphony of Psalms,* but with something more and more profound."

STRAVINSKY TO BOOSEY & HAWKES   *July 18, 1959*

Bonn

I received today the June 1959 catalogue of the firm H. Tiedemann, Rare Books
and Art Books, Berlin-Lichterfelde-West, Gardeschützenweg 110.
     I very much want to have the following items from this catalogue:

		DM
No. 105—Banchieri	. . . .	60
203—Berg	. . . .	5
500—Galilei	. . . .	24
525—Genua-Giazotto	. . . .	48
808—Borren. Orlando de Lassus	. . . .	14
920—Mersenne	. . . .	105
1007—Nenna (Madrigali)	. . . .	64
1012—Neumes	. . . .	45
1071—Piacenza-Bussi	. . . .	7
1094—Purcell	. . . .	18
1098—Westrop (Purcell)	. . . .	11
1117—Reaney	. . . .	52
1518—Willaert	. . . .	480

[*Original in German*]

STRAVINSKY TO ROTH   *July 23, 1959*

When do you plan to publish my little Epitaphium? Please, send me a proof of
the cover with my drawing.
     In Santa Fe Bob Craft broke his arm. The poor fellow conducted in the
Cathedral before my *Threni* the Bach *Trauer Ode* with his left arm. The surgeon here took off the cast the other day. It will take some weeks before he can
use it in a normal way. Poor Bob slipped on a concrete floor after a rehearsal and
he fell on his right arm.

STRAVINSKY TO BOOSEY & HAWKES   *August 5, 1959*

Bonn

Today I received from you a beautiful parchment with old liturgical script, and I
am wondering what the connection is between this gift and my letter, and
whom I should thank.

[*Original in German*]

STRAVINSKY TO AMPENOFF   *August 11, 1959*

As to October—we arrive in London (from Paris) the 28th and Bob Craft a little bit later, the 31st of October. . . .

I will bring copies of my new score Movements for Piano and Orchestra (in full—and piano scores).

Venice
STRAVINSKY TO ROTH   *September 25, 1959*

The matter with Liebermann (Cologne and Hamburg) is definitely settled: I canceled the contract because I did not want to go to Europe again in the spring. I gave Liebermann the right for the European premiere in Cologne and our exchange of letters and telegrams was very friendly. . . .

Margrit Weber was here for a few days (she played here the Martinu piano concerto) and studied with me every day my Movements.

Please, let me have the labor permit for BBC as soon as possible—I am leaving [Venice] (for Naples) October 12. It will be difficult to find me afterwards: Naples, Bologna, Paris and London! . . .

We will stay in the Ritz Hotel this time (Claridge's too expensive). Sir Isaiah Berlin arranged it.

STRAVINSKY TO ROTH   *September 29, 1959*

I still hope to receive the first proofs of Movements here before . . . leaving for Naples (on Oct. 12)—reassure me, please, on this.

I have just completed the bass parts of two of Gesualdo's 6-part sacred cantiones. I am mailing you today photostats of them for engraving and printing them afterwards together with "Illumina Nos." As they will be performed in my New York concerts in January I hope I can have proof copies by then.

I am coming with Vera to London (Ritz Hotel, as I wrote you) at 9 a.m. on October 27th; Bob is coming later from Hamburg.

STRAVINSKY TO ROTH   *October 2, 1959*

As to the recording of Movements by Columbia, I, of course, discussed the matter with the Webers, but I have not yet her definite answer concerning her release from the Deutsche Gramophon Gesellschaft; she hoped to have it very soon.

I spoke with the Webers about Nussio (Lugano) and Schulthess (Zürich) and about my intention to make a small Swiss tour with Movements. I will see what they will answer me about it. So, if you write to Nussio, tell him, please, to get in touch with the Webers and Schulthess and tell him also that I want to have these Swiss concerts with suitable rehearsals in the period between Oct. 20 and Nov. 10, 1960.

STRAVINSKY TO BOOSEY & HAWKES

October 4, 1959
[Telegram]

Please airmail Illumina Nos. Craft preparing new foreword covering all three Gesualdos which I hope to publish together. Can you pay hundred dollars for foreword to be sent this week?

STRAVINSKY TO ROTH

October 10, 1959

Just this word to tell you that I received the proofs of Movements (full & piano scores) only today. I won't be able to correct them tomorrow, which means that I will do it only in London. The *airmail* package *took 4 days* to arrive in Venice!

STRAVINSKY TO ROTH

New York
December 3, 1959

Thanks for yours of 30 Nov.

1. Please tell Ugrino Verlag that my edition of Gesualdo's 3 pieces belongs to you and if they want to print it in their complete edition of Gesualdo's sacred works, they must arrange this with you.

2. Bob Craft will air mail you tomorrow his preface to these 3 pieces.

STRAVINSKY TO ROTH

March 28, 1960

I write you today to tell you that I just finished to recompose three Gesualdo madrigals for instruments and that I will send you a copy of it in a few days. I call it Monumentum pro Gesualdo di Venosa, CD Annum. I will perform it in Venice (Biennale, September 26).

Will I see you in Europe this year? We are busy now with our affairs for a big South American concert tour from the beginning of August till Sept. 20th, where we are conducting half and half the programs with Robert Craft: Mexico City, Bogota, Lima, Santiago, Buenos Aires, Rio, Caracas. . . .

P.S. I still have not received the three Gesualdo [motets] published together with R. Craft's preface.

STRAVINSKY TO BOOSEY & HAWKES

May 12, 1960
[Telegram]

Recording *Monumentum* June eight. Please send parts and advise. Awaiting Movements and Gesualdo [motets] with Craft's preface.

STRAVINSKY TO MARIO BOIS

May 17, 1960

Please send my niece, Mlle Ira Belline, the equivalent of one hundred dollars, debiting my account with you. Her address is: "Art Africain," 54, boulevard Pasteur, Tangiers, Morocco.

[*Original in French*]

STRAVINSKY TO AMPENOFF   *May 20, 1960*

Thanks for yours of May 16th which I anxiously awaited because we needed here to be reassured that the parts of Monumentum must be here for rehearsals in the very beginning of June. . . .

Awaiting also Movements (why so belated?) and the Gesualdo motets with Craft's preface. As to the latter please remind Dr. Roth to transfer to Bob Craft (c/o my address) the $100 he promised for this preface. . . .

P.S. I am conducting here the 7th of June my Mass and *Les Noces* and the next day recording the Mass and *Monumentum.* July 3rd going to Santa Fe to conduct *Oedipus* (open stage performances) twice, the *Symphony of Psalms* in the Cathedral of Santa Fe afterwards, attend the performance of *The Rake's Progress* by Bob the 24 of July, returning home for a few days to pack and probably the first of August flying to Mexico City to start our South American concert tour. So you have our approximate timetable.

P.P.S. Enclosed a photostat of an arrangement I made of my Lullaby from *The Rake's Progress* for two recorders. Let it be printed and please send me the proofs.

STRAVINSKY TO AMPENOFF   *June 12, 1960*

I recorded yesterday *Monumentum* (and Mass).

1. Enclosed new errors found in the score and parts. Please let them be corrected.

2. *Monumentum* material (parts) Columbia sending you back air mail today. This material should be that [which] I use in my Venice concert where I premiered this piece.

3. The first proofs of the full score of *Monumentum* not yet received. I will answer you if I wish to have (to see) the second proofs only after seeing the first ones. It must certainly be printed, both conductor's score (full score) and a pocket one.

4. Under separate cover I am returning to you the corrected proofs of the Lullaby (*Rake's*) for two recorders.

STRAVINSKY TO ROTH   *June 17, 1960*

A few days ago I received the first proofs of *Monumentum* which I corrected but which I should keep here a week longer for the editing of my records of it at the end of next week. Enclosed my sketch of the cover (rather front page) of Monumentum—my tracing of the other Gesualdo cover; let us duplicate this attractive format and print it on the same white paper as the other Gesualdo cover. Please keep the proportion of the letters in the size and color indicated. The word "Monumentum" shouldn't be so different from the rest of the title—

Gesualdo di Venosa—and it shouldn't be in such large characters as on your enclosed original plate. Also do not put any more a W in my name: the W is good only for Germans, because they pronounce it like our V, and our V like an F. This W was introduced first by Russischer Musik Verlag which was a German edition and we are Boosey & Hawkes Ltd which is an English house.

STRAVINSKY TO ROTH   *June 24, 1960*

Glad you heard in Cologne my Movements and you like it. Curious to know how Schmidt-Isserstedt conducted the piece. I heard his tempi were very slow.

STRAVINSKY TO BOIS   *June 29, 1960*

I have just received a letter from M. Robert Kanters of the Editions Denöel, a copy of which is enclosed.

Would you be so kind as to follow up on this matter, you being there and I about to leave on a long tour. Then again, you can always reach me by addressing your letters to this address.

It will be advisable to draw up a new contract with the Editions Denöel for this re-edition, which is not covered by the terms of the original contract, from this moment null and void.

[Original in French]

STRAVINSKY TO ROTH   *June 30, 1960*

We are leaving Hollywood for Santa Fe the 5th of July and we will be back the 26th. Starting our South American tour the 1st of August. Around the 20th of September (probably the 22nd) we will be at Bauer Grünwald in Venice. My Biennale concert will be at San Rocco the 27th with *Monumentum* and *Orpheus*.

STRAVINSKY TO ROTH   *July 1, 1960*

Before leaving Hollywood I am airmailing . . . a photostatic copy of the first 22 full score pages of a new piece I am composing for Paul Sacher. This is about the fourth part of the whole piece which we have to deliver [to] him in the fall of 1961. Maybe—to spare the time—you can already start the engraving? I composed quite a bit more than that but it is not yet instrumentated. I intend to finish the 2nd movement and its instrumentation in Venice, when I will be settled there.

STRAVINSKY TO TO ROTH

Puzzled your irate letters since my Sextant[48] contract is for a commission only and since Adams has been in charge of questions of rental and performance rights for the past two months.

STRAVINSKY TO ROTH

October 8, 1960

Venice

Many thanks . . . for the 3 miniature scores of my Piano Concerto which I received two days ago. The other 5 you are referring to, I prefer you send them to Hollywood.

STRAVINSKY TO ROTH

October 22, 1960

Venice

In spite of your sending my check to Liechtenstein on Oct. 12th (yours of Oct. 18th) nothing was received from my Basel bank. Why should it be so long? Are there some difficulties?

Glad you acquired my Op. 6 songs from the dead Forberg edition. No, there isn't a revised version of them, but, coming home in Jan. or Feb., I will see what can be done with [these] old songs and I will let you know.

STRAVINSKY TO ROTH

October 29, 1960

Enclosed find new 15 pages (23–37) orch. score of my new work. You just continue the engraving. It will be a kind of postlude following this music which will make a good ending of this II part. Unfortunately no more time to think about it now; I have to wait until I will be at home again (in January 1961).

Thank you for the information re Liechtenstein (yours of Oct. 26).

The weather continues to be awful and I continue to feel badly. Maybe with the change of climate I will feel better. We plan to make our tour (Venice–Genova–Roma–Sicily–Roma) in a very comfortable Cadillac and a good chauffeur we know well.

Know only that we will be in Genova at the Colombia Hotel until Nov. 14th. Afterwards at the Hassler Hotel in Roma until the 24th (day of my concert).

---

[48] Robert Graff's television production company. Graff had made a filmed interview with Stravinsky for NBC in 1957.

STRAVINSKY TO ROTH *November 2, 1960*

Enclosed the last two pages (I was speaking [to] you about in my last letter) which I succeeded to finish before leaving Venice. I am very glad. So the second movement of my new work is completed.

There may be some changes in our program, because I am trying to get rid of my Palermo engagement and come to New York earlier. That we will know before leaving (this Saturday).

Stravinsky and Robert Craft rehearsing The Nightingale, *Washington, D.C., December 27, 1960. Drawing by Prentiss Taylor.*

STRAVINSKY TO ADAMS *November 3, 1960*

We plan to come back earlier: our liner *Rotterdam* arriving in New York Tuesday December 6th.

My addresses now will be: from Nov. 5th–14th Hotel Colombia, Genova, and from Novémber 14th–25th Hotel Hassler, Roma. . . .

STRAVINSKY TO ROTH *November 6 [?], 1960*

Genoa

I received your word from November 1st but nothing concerning . . . the postlude to the second part of my new work.

We are going to Rome the 14th (Hotel Hassler) and leaving Rome Nov. 25th for Paris (Elysée Park Hôtel, 2 rue Jean-Mermoz, VIII) staying there until Nov. 30th, when going to Le Havre to take the liner *Rotterdam* for New York. So Sicily canceled.

STRAVINSKY TO ROTH   *January [?], 1961*

Your letter of January 10th received. . . . Why should Liebermann worry about a work which I expect to start to compose only in one year for Sextant???? I clearly told the press in Washington about it exactly this way and if they presented it to the public differently (as a completed work) what can we do? The lie of the press is our chronic social disease.

STRAVINSKY TO BOIS   *January 17, 1961*

A note to ask you to send me the exact amount of the two expenditures that you made on my behalf last November: (1) the three tickets with the reservations for Le Havre and (2) the bill from the Elysée Park Hôtel. I need these amounts for my American taxes.

[*Original in French*]

STRAVINSKY TO ROTH   *February 6, 1961*

I am sending . . . by air mail (Business Papers) under separate cover the third and last piece of my new work, the Prayer, pages 40–50 incl. . . . May I ask you also not to show or send to Paul Sacher this last part of my work. I will tell you later when I want you to do it.

STRAVINSKY TO BOIS   *February 16, 1961*

Today I ask you to be so kind as to send to M. and Madame Constantin and Olga Sallard in Tauzin, Illats, Gironde, five hundred new francs, debiting my account with you.

[*Original in French*]

STRAVINSKY TO ROTH   *February 27, 1961*

Sacher's program . . . is the result of my letter to him (of Jan. 26th). I am surprised he did not inform me he settled it.

As soon as I . . . write him telling him I finished the composition, I will ask you to mail him the last part of it (the Prayer).

I just received from L. Spinner the 1st proof of this Prayer with a letter in which he asked me to answer . . . some of his queries concerning the first and second part of the work. . . . I cannot do it because I sent him back all the proofs. Let him send me as soon as possible (by air) these prints.

As to Liebermann, we really have to stop him doing this senseless announcement concerning *Noah*. . . . This *Noah* which will be called *The Flood* will last no more than 25 minutes: it never was planned for the full evening.

STRAVINSKY TO ADAMS   *March 27, 1961*

Flying in two days to Mexico City to conduct *Sacre* (April 7 & 9)—back April 10th.

STRAVINSKY TO ROTH   *April 11, 1961*

I have just received yours of March 29th having returned only yesterday from my concerts in Mexico City.

I would be delighted to do a concert for the Swedish Radio, if they can meet my conditions: $2500 (start with this, and come down if necessary, but no lower than $2000); Robert Craft conducts first half of concert, because I cannot go there by myself and [conduct] all rehearsals myself. . . .

I have . . . received a prospectus from the Hamburg Opera announcing the performance of a *"Noah"* by me there in June 1962. I am considerably annoyed at this aggressive and tactless action on Liebermann's part. *The Flood* was commissioned by Robert Graff. It is far from finished and no performance date can yet be foreseen. Also it is *not an opera, not a ballet,* perhaps not a theater piece at all. . . .

I received the last proofs of the Prayer and its vocal-score proofs in L. Spinner's reduction.

STRAVINSKY TO BOIS   *April 11, 1961*

I have just returned from Mexico, where I had some concerts, and I am reading your letter of March 28, as well as a letter from France telling me the sad news of the death of Madame Olga Sallard in an automobile accident. Her last letter, dated March 20, told my wife that she had not yet received this sum. Did she receive it before her death? That is the question. She died on March 30.

[*Original in French*]

STRAVINSKY TO AMPENOFF   *April 20 [sic], 1961*

Good you told the Swedish Radio that Bob Craft is not included in my fees so they will write directly to him concerning his remuneration. Perfect.

Unfortunately—nothing doing with the Holland Festival—in June I will have here a concert to conduct and recording to do with Isaac Stern, and in July going to Santa Fe to conduct *Oedipus* and *Perséphone*.

STRAVINSKY TO AMPENOFF   *April 20, 1961*

This letter amends, corrects, supplements mine of yesterday wrongly dated April 20 (it should be April 19th).

The first half of the Stockholm concert should have the following program:

Symphonies of Wind Instruments
Quatre études
Symphony in C

Now, as we are sailing on the *Kungsholm* and will be in Sweden September 10th, I wonder if you could contact the Finnish Radio and see if something could be done about repeating the Stockholm program in Helsinki sometime between September 10th and 20th or, if the same program is not advisable, then the following:

Divertimento	R. Craft conducting
Jeu de cartes	
Orpheus	myself conducting

STRAVINSKY TO AMPENOFF   *April 20, 1961*

I just received a letter (with the contract) from the Swedish Radio dated April 17th and signed by Gereon Brodin.

In your letter of Apr. 17th I read the following phrase: "It is understood that Robert Craft conducts the first half of the concert and helps you with the rehearsals." Unfortunately this very important thing is totally missing in the contract. The mention of Robert Craft as my assistant conductor in . . . #14 does not mean . . . that he is conducting the first half of the program and myself the *Sacre* which makes the second half. Therefore I send this contract (with its copy) to you and ask you to explain . . . the omission. Mr. Gereon Brodin didn't even mention this . .   . in his letter to R. Craft or to me. In his letter to R. Craft he is speaking only about rehearsing and asking him his fee for this job; but not a word about conducting the first half of the program.

By the way, we slightly changed the program, which was short, replacing *Monumentum* (6–7 minutes) by my Symphony in C (about 28 min.). The second half of the program which remains unchanged is the *Sacre* conducted by myself. Please remind them that the last number of the score, La Danse sacrale, will be performed in my new 1943 version and its orch. material must be added to the Boosey & Hawkes material of the work. I had it this way just now in Mexico and two years ago in Venice when I conducted it in the Biennale with the Hamburg Radio Orchestra.

STRAVINSKY TO ADAMS   *April 22, 1961*

The work commissioned by Robert Graff and which I just started to compose is called *The Flood* and not *Noah.* . . .

    If Mr. Graff told you that the taping may take place during my visit to New York in September, I can only tell you that I started the composition not very long ago and have not the slightest idea when I will finish it and when the taping will take place.

    Bob Craft will be next week in New York for his concert in Town Hall (May 1st). . . . Bob will explain . . . the situation about the texts arranged . . . from the King James Bible and the York and Chester miracle plays.

STRAVINSKY TO ROTH   *May 2, 1961*

I will answer your letter . . . in a few days after consulting Robert Craft who is coming from New York where he gave a very interesting concert of Edgar Varèse's works yesterday.

    Please do not forget that we will need a special page for my new piece (*Sermon, Narrative & Prayer*) preceding the title page with indication of the instruments, some special remarks about them, duration, etc. . . .

    I received the Stockholm contract with the correction, . . . Robert Craft also.

STRAVINSKY TO ROTH   *May 20, 1961*

The Aldous Huxley house which burned to the ground was not his old house which was not far away from us but the new one, very distant from us, [which] he bought some years ago. It is a terrible disaster, and no insurance can compensate what was lost in this fire. . . .

    I will send . . . as much of the orchestra score of *The Flood* as I now have ready, as soon as you have completed negotiations with Robert Graff. I cannot say when I expect to finish the work.

STRAVINSKY TO ROTH   *May 22, 1961*

I never could welcome honors . . . in connection with anniversaries [and] jubilees when it concerned myself. So I ask you frankly—please drop your ideas and forget about it. Thank you. . . .

    Could you ask Dr. Tomek in Köln to send me a tape of the Köln Radio Chorus's performance of Schoenberg's *De Profundis.*

STRAVINSKY TO AMPENOFF   *May 27, 1961*

The complete history of the affair is this: Robert Wangermée, director of the [Brussels] Radio, wrote R. Craft in Venice last October, and André Souris (a friend of Wangermée) came to see me in Venice to propose a Brussels concert. I agreed, but they never concluded negotiations. I am no longer interested to go there for $1500 and conduct an entire concert. I have had no answer to my letter of five weeks ago to them, and Craft, who wrote them for me too from New York over a month ago, has not heard either. I will still keep the engagement however (for Oct. 10) and at the same fee but they will have to allow me to use Bob Craft conducting the first part of the program [which] I gave them the 22 of April (Symph. of Wind Inst.—Mass—*Orpheus*).

I would still like to arrange something for the period Oct. 10–Oct. 20, however, and as Vera might go to visit my niece in Tangiers then, perhaps Spain is a possibility. I have refused several offers to go there for $1500, though, and I cannot accept less than $2000 since I cannot conduct a whole program and do all the rehearsals myself. Madrid had a good orchestra when I was there last (spring 1955).* So has Santander, I am told; will you try these places and, if they do not work, Lucerne?

Would you ask Glock to send me a tape of Schoenberg's Suite for Strings in G—performed recently on the BBC. William Glock visited me here but we did not speak about my BBC fee because it was always understood that it is the same as usual. So kindly let them send me the contract for signature. . . .

* Miss Felicitas Keller of Madrid Agency Victoria (Alcala 30-5) was then a representative of the agency Quesada. She was working very well and since then she wrote me often proposing especially Barcelona which always asks for very long programs and I'm sure will not accept to [share] the program between me and Craft and pay us the Scandinavian fee.

STRAVINSKY TO ROTH   *June 2, 1961*

To explain my cable of yesterday reading as follows: "Airmailing photocopy for cover my new cantata. Awaiting proofs page with instrumentation, also Prayer's first page proof for some addition in title." I hope that this cable was clear enough and you understand it.

I composed a nice cover with a reproduction of a splendid XIII century stained glass from . . . Westminster Abbey (*English Stained Glass* by Herbert Read) representing the stoning of St. Stephen (the Narrative—the second movement of my cantata). I hope my sketch here enclosed with all my remarks will be clear to your printers.

I need the proof page 30 (the Prayer) to add under the title, rather than the words "(from Thomas Dekker)," a short dedication to the memory of a dear friend of mine who gave me this text and who died [at] the time I composed its music—Reverend James McLane. . . .

Too bad that Radio Brussels is sending . . . their contract—I hoped so much to avoid this disadvantageous concert, besides I don't see in [your] letter that they agreed to share the program with R. Craft. If they don't agree, I will not sign the contract.

Zürich—*Rossignol:* if they accept to pay me $2500—I am ready to go there, otherwise it will be too costly (the travel and a week expenses with R. Craft whom I will ask to accompany me and to help me in the rehearsals as he did it in December in Washington).

Paris? Never again! After the obvious hostility of the public and the press (my performance, fall 1958) I decided never to appear again in Paris.

This Sunday June 4th I am recording (Columbia) in stereo my *Symphony of Psalms* which I perform publicly with the Violin Concerto (Eudice Shapiro) on the 5th.

And in two weeks I will record this Violin Concerto with Isaac Stern who is [still] in Australia.

STRAVINSKY TO LEOPOLD SPINNER   *June 3, 1961*

I just received your letter of May 31st concerning the proofs of your vocal score of my new cantata, and I am somewhat puzzled. . . . Have you received . . . the last 2nd proofs of the whole cantata or only of the Prayer? . . . Please answer me as soon as possible—I will be busy the next weeks until my departure for Santa Fe where I will be the whole of July.

                                                            Santa Fe
STRAVINSKY TO AMPENOFF   *July 21, 1961*

I agreed with Glock to conduct *Ode* and *Perséphone;* and on the 29th October, the Royal Festival Hall public concert, we decided with him to perform only *Perséphone* from 5:00 to 6:00 p.m., *Perséphone* lasting about 50 minutes. Unfortunately they did not pay attention . . . and put in both contracts "*Perséphone* and other works," which is wrong and absurd because *Ode* cannot be called "other works." . . . Tell Zürich Opera that I will not change my mind and will conduct *Histoire du soldat* as agreed with them and not the *Rossignol* for which they sent me the contract. . . . I am here till the 4th of August.

                                                            Santa Fe
STRAVINSKY TO ROTH   *July 24, 1961*

I do not see any special urgency in engraving this vocal score [*Flood*] right away, and Mr. Graff's hope that the videotaping of the work can be done by the 1st of January 1962 is more than naive: (a) he, as it seems, does not realize the kind of music I compose and its density which takes much more time than . . . simpler music, and (b) he obviously doesn't want to pay attention to another activity of my life—my concert travels—which yearly takes 5–6 months from my composing. . . .

We are leaving Santa Fe for Hollywood Aug. 5.

STRAVINSKY TO ROTH

Sante Fe
July 28, 1961

Thank you for yours of 24th July assuring me that the Danse sacrale orch. material will be with the rest of the *Sacre* material in time for the rehearsals in Stockholm.

I am also pleased to know that everything concerning the new print of *Rossignol* (orch. & vocal score) is taken care of. Although I have no doubt that you are right telling me that "there are sufficient" corrected orch. materials (where, in Europe?) of *Rossignol,* the orchestra scores belonging to those materials which I saw in different places are in a perfect state of decay, and the sooner new scores and new material will be available the better.

And what about *The Rake's Progress?* I remember the never realized promise to publish a *corrected* pocket score (large size).

If the value of this score does not seem to justify the expense, perhaps the event of my 80th birthday might do so. But is it not regrettable to have to find such a pretext? The musicians interested in this score have already waited a decade, whereas the opera orch. scores of the younger composers (Henze) are made immediately available in pocket scores by their publishers.

STRAVINSKY TO ROTH

Santa Fe
July [?], 1961

As for the Zürich Opera, too bad that they change their mind so often. As for me—I do not want to change it and will conduct *Histoire du soldat* as they asked me to do . . . insead of *Le Rossignol. Le Rossignol* is a very fatiguing piece. My last performance in Washington one half year ago proved it, especially with a mediocre orchestra, and Zürich's opera orchestra, as I was told, is not a very good one (without permanent conductors and a lot of guest conductors). So tell them, please, to send me their contract for . . . *Histoire.* The *Rossignol* was never played there so they probably prefer me to make the dirty job [of rehearsing it].

STRAVINSKY TO AMPENOFF

August 19, 1961

Yesterday I airmailed Boosey & Hawkes, attention L. Spinner the last four pages (44–47 incl.) of *The Flood* photocopy of the (full) orch. score and a few days ago Spinner's vocal score of the first 43 pages of my full score. Please acknowledge . . . their receipt to my New York address (Hotel Pierre). . . .

I will be only till the 1st of September in New York. . . .

STRAVINSKY TO ROTH

December 31, 1961

I am so burdened with work in these few days before I go East (Benvenuto Hotel, Toronto 7–13 Jan.; Jefferson Hotel, Washington, 13–23 Jan.; Pierre Hotel, New York, 23 Jan.–3 Feb.) that I must ask you to help me with some of my organizational problems for 1962.

1. Hamburg: Liebermann, when I saw him in London, had proposed a festival of considerable artistic interest. He is unable to realize these plans now, and he has instead simply invited George Balanchine to import his dancers and choreography to perform my three "Greek ballets." I do not mean that these three productions are not of interest to me but only that they are not novelties and that therefore the whole point of Liebermann's invitation is to exploit my personal presence there on my birthday. I accepted Liebermann's proposal but conditionally some weeks ago, and I have not heard from him since. In the meantime I have had so many other invitations, including one from the White House, that I have decided not to appear at all on my birthday, but to take a holiday. . . . As a U.S. citizen, I cannot refuse the White House and the Stravinsky Festival in my home city (I have already refused both) and then go to Hamburg, even though Hamburg has done much more of my music than my so-called home city. I would be greatly obliged to you if you would telephone Liebermann and explain this to him.

2. The one invitation that I wish to accept is the Israeli. This is for the first two weeks in September, which is a good time for me. Moreover, the conditions are excellent. I want to stay in Europe for the last two weeks in September and I will see if it will be possible to go to Russia then to pay them a visit without giving concerts there.

3. Finally, I am just composing music for some verses of T. S. Eliot. This was at the suggestion of the Cambridge Hymnal who will have to arrange with you, if they wish to publish it, of course, though the music is so unlike other hymns, they might not want to. Meanwhile, I hope to include a photocopy of the music in a forthcoming book of ours to be published by Faber—if it is not too late—and as Faber is Eliot's publisher this will be easy for you to arrange an agreement later.

STRAVINSKY TO ROTH   *January 3, 1962*

For the Cocteau affair (King Oedipus), I have no idea who the composer is but I doubt his *Oedipus* could hurt ours. Theirs will be French, ours Latin, and I don't know what the legal point about that would be. Cocteau has probably rewritten it.

After our chamber music concert here (Jan. 6th) we are flying to Toronto—Canadian Radio engagement (Canadian Broadcasting Corporation) which takes place Jan. 12th. Jan. 13th in Washington, Jefferson Hotel till the 23rd (3 times *Oedipus Rex*) and afterwards in New York Hotel Pierre from Jan. 23 to Feb. 3.

STRAVINSKY TO AMPENOFF   *February 8, 1962*

Before going [on] my concert tour, i.e. Toronto, Washington, New York, the 7th of Jan., I sent . . . a photostatic copy of a new small chorus of mine called

Anthem and dedicated to T. S. Eliot, the manuscript of which I sent to Faber & Faber; they received it. And you?

Enclosed my answers to L. Spinner re *Rossignol.* . . . Some of the questions I cannot answer because my orchestra score is not here—it is at Boosey & Hawkes Ltd in London and Spinner is working on it for the new edition. . . .

Please send me from Faber & Faber our last book with Robert Craft *Memories and Commentaries.*

STRAVINSKY TO BOOSEY & HAWKES   *March 4, 1962*
                                                  [Telegram]

London

Zürich impossible. Answering your letters next week. Ten more full score pages will be en route.

STRAVINSKY TO ROTH   *March 8, 1962*

Still too busy to write . . . promised letter but yours of February 28 forced me to send you a letter I received from Massine Jan. 20 and answered sending him back two copies of the Bulletin de Déclaration to help him (and maybe also . . . myself) with my signature. And what about *Pulcinella*? Are the royalties frozen too? Please send me back this precious letter and advise.

Hope you received safely my last 15 pages of *The Flood* full score I sent you March 5th. . . . In one week I hope to send you more—I am working very hard—it is why no time for letters!

But you—write me please and I will answer what is possible. Sometimes Bob is helping but he is also so busy!

STRAVINSKY TO ROTH   *March 15, 1962*

Do not worry about Massine's intentions. My contract with the Société Dramatique was never "beyond" the Société Dramatique and always mentioned the choreographic rights of Fokine, Nijinsky, Massine, Balanchine in a given percentage (one sixth, as I remember) of my own rights.

I signed two Bulletins de Déclaration (replacing the old bulletins) in which Massine will receive . . . Nijinsky['s share] for the choreography. . . . The phrase, "adaptation by Léonide Massine" concerns only the choreographer and by no means the authorship [of the libretto] which belongs to me with N. Roerich (now replaced by his son Sviatoslav) [or] the composer rights [which belong] only to me.

As to *Pulcinella* . . . the best thing to do is: when I will be in Paris (May 15 & 16) I will see the people of the Dramatique and will let you know the situation. To write now to Massine about it is not safe. . . .

Am so happy to have finished *The Flood*. This weekend will start the recording business. I have Balanchine here these days discussing the staging of *The Flood.*

STRAVINSKY TO ROTH   *March 16, 1962*

George Balanchine came from N.Y. to work with me and Robert Craft on *The Flood.*

We established the scenario on the full score—the right place of different entrances (appearances) of the characters (before and during the music)—things so important in the scores (full and vocal).

So, please wait my sending you a full score [with] all this; your engravers must know how to print it (*la mise en place*). This also must be done by Spinner [in] the vocal score (still full of mistakes—mainly in orthography).

STRAVINSKY TO ADAMS   *March 20, 1962*

I received a letter from an important young Russian musician, Igor Blazhkov, a teacher or professor in the conservatory of Kiev. His address is: Tchkalov Street 79, Apartment 16, Kiev, U.S.S.R. Please send him the following music of mine:

1. Piano Sonata (1924)
2. Piano Serenade in A
3. Piano Concerto (with wind instruments)
4. Octet
5. Symph. of Wind Instr.
   All this in pocket score

6. The Japanese songs in full score
7. 3 *Histoires pour enfants* in voice and piano and if you have it in my instrumentation (small ensemble)....

The *Flood* orch. parts and chorus parts [were] copied here—we have *no time* to wait . . . because the recording of the whole thing will take place here *in one week,* Wednesday the 28 of March. . . .

STRAVINSKY TO AMPENOFF   *March 24, 1962*

Would you please contact Oslo again and see if they can arrange a concert around Oct. 6—i.e., to give us plenty of time coming out of Russia where we go ca. Sept. 15th and conduct in Moscow, Leningrad and Kiev. Try to get in Oslo the same conditions as in Helsinki or Stockholm for me and Bob. For the program

      String Concerto in D
      Firebird Suite   Robert Craft

> *Vom Himmel hoch* Variations
> *Monumentum*   myself
> *Norwegian Moods*
> *Pulcinella* Suite

STRAVINSKY TO ROTH   *April 8, 1962*

First let me have here before my leaving to Seattle (Apr. 18th) your annual statement and the money waiting for me. I repeat you this request. . . .

I will write again in a few days. Today—in a great hurry.

STRAVINSKY TO ROTH   *April 11, 1962*

I renounced Paris and Brussels. . . . Only Italy, in any case, would have free dates at such short notice as this. My plan is to do one concert before Rome (Filarmonia with Panni) and after Russia, then . . . fly to New York from Rome October 15th.

STRAVINSKY TO ROTH   *April 13, 1962*

I hope . . . your terms with Rolf Liebermann do not prevent Santa Fe . . . to stage *The Flood;* this Santa Fe . . . already staged *The Rake's Progress, Oedipus, Perséphone* and this year *The Nightingale.* I have the feeling that John Crosby's zeal really deserves a special reward and special treatment. What did the Metropolitan Opera do for me? Just the same as the Los Angeles Philharmonic—i.e. nothing!!! . . .

I made an important change in the score of *The Flood:* after . . . bar 489 (page 74 of my full score manuscript) I repeat the beginning of the work with its tremolos of the first six bars (or the first three pages of the work without the last fag., c-fag. and corni bar, to be quite clear) and . . . continue with Satan singing at 490 his music on page 74, which I interrupted by this insert. . . . Another thing: this insert, as you see, starts with an eighth upbeat; please, let them precede this note by a dotted quarter rest to make a two-four bar before the tremolo music continues in four/four.

STRAVINSKY TO AMPENOFF   *April 14, 1962*

Let me have *immediately* at Seattle, State of Washington, Hotel Olympic (we are there till the 21st of April) by air express two or three copies of my little new Anthem—conducting it in Toronto and have never received any copy nor proofs!!! . . .

Just received a cable from [Mario] Labroca [in Venice] telling me about the success of the whole concert dedicated to me and especially of my new cantata [*A Sermon, A Narrative and A Prayer*]. If it is not just to be agreeable to me but true I will know from your letter. . . .

STRAVINSKY TO ADAMS   *July 27, 1962*

Please send me a word to La Fonda Hotel, Sante Fe. . . . Did I [leave] with you the transparent masters of my orchestra score [Miniatures]? . . . [I] cannot remember what I did with the manuscript.

Taking the night train (Superchief) for Santa Fe at 9 p.m. this evening. Yesterday's concert [Hollywood Bowl] as well as the Ravinia one big success.

                                                    New York
                                              November 19, 1962
STRAVINSKY TO BOOSEY & HAWKES   *[Telegram]*

May 31 Festival Hall OK but when studio concert as usual? Bob must receive not less than 500 dollars for his studio concert because of his travel, hotel expenses.

STRAVINSKY TO ROTH   *February 7, 1963*

Glad the Irish Radio asked about the hotel reservations for our staying in Dublin (from 1st to 19th of June, the concert being the 9th). We will need with Vera two connecting rooms with a bathroom and one separate room also with a bathroom for Robert Craft. Please, let them know it.

STRAVINSKY TO ADAMS   *February 15, 1963*

Please send me the miniature scores of Britten's *War Requiem* and *Midsummer Night's Dream*.

And I urgently need a *Flood* orchestra score and orchestra parts (no chorus, no tenor, no dialogues, no vocal scores) because we perform the two [orchestral] pieces in our concert in Oberlin, Ohio on the 21st of March. We leave here March 15th and would need it 2 days or so before. We will be in New York March 22–April 8.

I also want at this time strongly to recommend that you publish the new Piano Trio of Ingolf Dahl (Music Department of USC Los Angeles where he is a professor). . . . Hope you will do it.

STRAVINSKY TO ADAMS   *February 27, 1963*

(1) Thanks for Britten. (2) I am told that Oberlin is already rehearsing the two pieces from *The Flood*. (3) Conducting there March 21, will be in N.Y. (Pierre Hotel) the 22nd.

STRAVINSKY TO ROTH   *March 10, 1963*

I finished one week ago the composition of *Abraham and Isaac*[49] and am sending you under separate airmail two copies of its photostatic copy (orchestra
score). Please do not show it to anybody and let L. Spinner . . . do the vocal
score (without showing it to anybody). I hope the work with the *Flood*[50] is finished by now and I feel it will be good to start the engraving of my new score
just now. As you will see, the music is composed on the Hebrew Bible text written phonetically with English letters. On a fly leaf the Hebrew text must be
printed parallel to the King James English. But before the text is printed I
would like to have it checked by one or two Hebrew scholars.

　　Please airmail me two orchestra scores of *The Flood* to Pierre Hotel in New
York where I will be on March 22nd.

STRAVINSKY TO ROTH   *March 11, 1963*

I forgot to tell you that the Hebrew text which I wrote phonetically in English
beneath the music must be printed in Hebrew and not in Latin letters, and the
Latin beneath the Hebrew. It is the Latin transliteration that has to be checked.
The work should have a key to pronunciation, probably prepared officially by
someone in Israel and printed as a foreword. . . .

P.S. Try to get A. Schoenberg's *De Profundis,* published by Israeli Music Publications U.S.A.: Leeds Music Corporation, New York. You will see how the Hebrew text and the Latin transliteration beneath the music has been resolved.

STRAVINSKY TO SPINNER   *July 4, 1963*

Sending you back your vocal score of *Abraham and Isaac* with the answered
queries as usual by airmail–Business Papers. There will be a few more corrections to be made after consulting Hebrew scholars in the first engraving when I
will receive it from you. I am going to Chicago (Ravinia) in one week and will
fly from there July 14th to Santa Fe, La Posada [Inn].

　　I was so glad to see you in Dublin.

---

[49] Stravinsky wrote to his son Theodore that same day: "I finished *Abraham and Isaac*
for baritone and chamber orchestra. . . . I am very relieved that I managed to do this
before our long trip. If I am alive and well, I will visit Israel again and conduct it."

[50] Stravinsky wrote to Theodore's wife on March 11: "We fly on the 17th to Cleveland
to conduct a concert on the 21st at Oberlin College. The 22nd we fly to New York
(Hotel Pierre), staying there until April 8. Then we embark on the *Bremen* for Hamburg, where Bob will conduct *The Flood,* staged like an opera by Rennert on April 30.
We will determine whether Liebermann's idea [to make an opera of a film] is justified
and will work. Since this is for a television show on June 1, I must already record the
music, to which Balanchine is going to set abstract dances for the whole composition
(25 minutes). The parts are being hurriedly copied now, and the choristers and so-

STRAVINSKY TO AMPENOFF

Received yesterday *Le Rossignol* full score. . . .

The concert in Ravinia (near Chicago) was a very good one, in spite of heavy rain which prevented many thousands [from] hear[ing] it. But the 3 thousand sitting under cover were extremely enthusiastic and at my third bow [the orchestra] played . . . a flourish of brasses. I was very touched by this most beautiful Chicago orchestra, especially after the Hamburg orchestra in Milano.

Here—very hot. We have a separate house here (5 rooms and a kitchen!!) and Bob a separate 3 room house.

STRAVINSKY TO AMPENOFF

Absolutely nothing is clear except what concerns those pieces that Lalandi[51] and I have already agreed upon. In the first place, does she agree to Bob's participation? Her letter does not contain a word about that. In the second place, the program must be changed: Bob will conduct the *Trauer Ode* by Bach, which lasts 35 minutes. After the intermission I will conduct the *Vom Himmel hoch* Variations, ending the concert with the *Symphony of Psalms*.

P.S. The Octet is a most ridiculous suggestion from a completely idiotic person. How could anyone suggest a chamber piece for a concert that will feature a full orchestra, chorus and soloists? I will not give any more concerts either in Oxford or in London.

[*Original in Russian*]

STRAVINSKY TO AMPENOFF

We are leaving here early Monday morning, the 19th, and will spend the night in Williams [Arizona]. From there we will drive to the Grand Canyon (500 miles, a whole day's trip), and then, on the next day, with God's help, another 500 miles home.[52] We will be in Hollywood for only a few days, since I must be

loists are learning the comparatively simple music." On January 19 Stravinsky had informed Suvchinsky that "at the beginning of April we will be sailing to Hamburg, where Bob will be conducting *The Flood*. . . . This will also be done in Zagreb and Milan with the Hamburg Opera. The production is by Rennert. Let us hope that Liebermann did not make a mistake in presenting *The Flood* as an opera. It is not my idea."

[51] Lina Lalandi, director of the English Bach Festival.

[52] Stravinsky had written to Andre Marion on July 30: "The Archbishop of Santa Fe, who was to present me with the Order of Saint Sylvester after my performance of my Mass in the cathedral here on August 18, died a few days ago, following an operation. Tomorrow is the burial, and someone else will make the presentation, but it is a sad event; he was always so kind and attentive to me." (The Archbishop had provided Stravinsky with a studio on the church property.)

in Rio de Janeiro on the 28th (the concert is on September 3). Perhaps, if the terms are suitable (and we will only be able to decide that there), we may give another concert in São Paulo. Then I will come home, and only in mid-November will I go to Rome.

[*Original in Russian*]

Santa Fe
August 17, 1963

STRAVINSKY TO AMPENOFF

This is in reply to your letter of 13 August '63, concerning a so-called small orchestra [version] of *Petrushka* now in possession of the London Festival Ballet. I never authorized any version of *Petrushka* for reduced orchestra except that made by myself in 1946 and published by you . . . and I do not permit any tampering with the music of *Petrushka* in the interest of further orchestral economy.

August 24, 1963
[Telegram]

STRAVINSKY TO BOOSEY & HAWKES

Accepting Oxford around July first if Bob is invited sharing indicated fee and program.

STRAVINSKY TO BOOSEY & HAWKES   *October 11, 1963*

Enclosed signed by me the contract of Jean Sibelius' Canzonetta,[53] arranged by me for a chamber music ensemble. Please see that the DM 1,500 are deposited in the Schweizerischer Bankverein in Basel, Switzerland for account no. 43656–111.

The Stravinsky automobile was in Santa Fe, driven there from Los Angeles by Mrs. Stravinsky and the Stravinskys' friend Bill Brown. Stravinsky and the present writer conducted a concert in Santa Fe on the afternoon of August 18 and drove to Albuquerque that night. On the afternoon of the next day, Mrs. Stravinsky dozed off while driving, whereupon the present writer seized the steering wheel and managed to avert an accident. A different route was taken to Los Angeles from the one Stravinsky described.

[53] Stravinsky orchestrated the Canzonetta as a gesture of gratitude for receiving the Sibelius prize. After receiving it, he sent gifts of money to each member of his family. He wrote to his daughter-in-law, Françoise, on October 23, explaining this and including an itinerary: "We fly to New York on November 5, stay a few days there, and continue to Rome (concerts in churches in Palermo, Catania, and Rome of my religious music), returning to New York on the 26th. We will spend two months in New York, where Vera has an exhibition at the beginning of December; I have five concerts with the Philadelphia Orchestra in January." (The concerts in Palermo and Catania took place in theatres, the one in Rome at Santa Maria Sopra Minerva.) Stravinsky wrote to his son Theodore on October 31, saying that the Sibelius money would come to them

STRAVINSKY TO AMPENOFF

New York
December 19, 1963

Please answer him [the vice-chancellor of Cambridge] that, in the first place, I never accept any of the numerous propositions that I get for the degree of Doctor of Music, and, anyway, in February I will be very far away, in California.

[*Original in Russian*]

STRAVINSKY TO BOOSEY & HAWKES

January 16, 1964
[Telegram]

Craft conducting *Abraham/Isaac* Tel Aviv sometime third week August. Of course *Himmel hoch* can be sung Hebrew. We are leaving New York for Hollywood Feb. 5. Do not want *Sacre* sketches published in my lifetime. Ask Adams send over here the new pocket score of *Peter Grimes*.

STRAVINSKY TO AMPENOFF

January 27, 1964

New York

At last I received the long-awaited orchestra score (first proof) of *Abraham and Isaac,* forwarded from Hollywood, but there is no sign of the letter you mention from L. Spinner. . . . I enclose two letters: (1) From that absurd Lalandi, who requests that we tell her what must be prepared before our arrival in Oxford. A few days before the rehearsals, the choruses of the *Symphony of Psalms* and *Vom Himmel hoch* should be ready. At this point, half a year before the performance, it is impossible to give any reply to her questions regarding rehearsals. Bob and I never rehearsed the choruses separately, only with the orchestra. She can arrange for a single piano rehearsal before the general rehearsals if she wishes. (2) A Russian letter that Boosey & Hawkes (i.e., you) will have to answer, for it concerns questions of copyright, money, number of rehearsals, etc., . . . questions that I cannot and do not want to answer. . . . We are leaving for home on the 5th, by train via Chicago. I will be glad to have a positive answer from Liechtenstein. . . .

[*Original in Russian*]

STRAVINSKY TO ROTH

February 16, 1964

Obviously *Abraham and Isaac* can only be sung in Hebrew; that is the whole point of the work. Just as *Oedipus* can only be done in Latin!

---

directly from Boosey & Hawkes, and adding: "The concerts of my religious music I will conduct with Bob in churches with good acoustics (if such can be found). . . . In January with the Philadelphia Orchestra I will conduct *Perséphone* and Bob my Symphonies of Wind Instruments and *Von Himmel hoch,* my instrumentation of which so stunned Radio Geneva that they have never pardoned that sacrilege."

STRAVINSKY TO AMPENOFF   *February 17, 1964*

We have planned to come to London in June to record *The Rake's Progress* as well as to go to Oxford. The recording is now cancelled, however, and the Oxford concert is not enough money even to pay the expenses (after British taxes) and not enough to justify the trips for my American taxes. Can you find one or two other concerts, but for no less than $3000 (tax free)? Germany, Switzerland, Italy, Belgium won't pay even that little, but perhaps you can get it from Warsaw . . . (as we did from Budapest last year). The time: 20–26 June and 30 June–10 July.

STRAVINSKY TO AMPENOFF   *February 25, 1964*

The enclosed letter by a certain Lewis will explain why I am sending the program notes of my Septet. He is free to use them, but please return his letter to me along with this sole remaining copy of the 1954 program that I conducted in Dumbarton Oaks and Washington, D.C. . . . .

　　　Tomorrow I will send you (i.e., Spinner) . . . a reply to his questions concerning *Sacre* and *Baiser de la fée.*

[*Original in Russian*]

STRAVINSKY TO AMPENOFF   *February 26, 1964*

You will find in this envelope my reply to Spinner (*Baiser de la fée* and *Sacre*); a letter from Hungarian Television, to which I shall ask you to reply (the only question concerns money, and that is the publisher's concern—I could not be against the performance, since it is *mine*); and, finally, the *Pulcinella* libretto in two languages, English and Russian. I do not know whether you have this there, but I do know that you *should* have it, because each time, the libretto has to be sent along with the orchestra scores that theatres require for a performance. In this instance I am thinking about Leningrad, which wants to produce *Pulcinella,* and if you decide to rent the orchestra score, then the theatre should know on what the subject was based when Diaghilev, Massine, and Picasso put it together; so copy the English and Russian texts for the firm and send them back to me.[54]

[*Original in Russian*]

---

[54] Stravinsky sent the original libretto of *Pulcinella,* in Massine's hand, and the present writer's translation.

STRAVINSKY TO AMPENOFF   *February 27, 1964*

(1) Please send £5 to Chatto and Windus Ltd Publishers, 40–42 William IV Street, London W.C.2. This is for a recording sent to me by Sir Julian Huxley. (2) Dates in England—we plan to arrive 16th June. Rooms should be taken at Oxford for the 29th only. The rehearsals are in London, and we will drive to Oxford in the morning of the 29th. Of course we could return to London after the concert, but it may be too tiring. (3) I suggested . . . Warsaw because Hurok said he can get $3000 there for me without difficulty. Also, there is so much more cordiality and appreciation in the East. Also I would be surprised if the Germans, who are organized up to about 1990, could make room for me in June. . . . (4) . . . Paris—I won't do a *public* concert, but if Barraud can pay for a broadcast or television $3000 (tax free)—O.K. Incidentally that should be in the first week of July and should have the Capriccio on the program as Columbia Records wants me to record it there at that time with Entremont, i.e. Paris 30 June–6 July.

Rushing, rushing!

STRAVINSKY TO SPINNER   *March 1, 1964*

Abraham and Isaac: . . . If adding the verse numbers in the vocal score will not complicate the reading of it, you can do it, but not in the full score, which deals mainly with the music and not with the sense of the text (concern of the singer).

Enclosed my answers to your queries concerning *Petrushka*.

STRAVINSKY TO ADAMS   *March 3, 1964*

I think *you* have my agreement with the Modern Art Museum for my pictures I lent them for my show "Stravinsky and the Dance." We are flying to Cleveland (Hotel—Wade Park Manor) next Sunday, 8th March. The 15th—to Cincinnati where Vera has her show. Just a word, s.v.p.

STRAVINSKY TO AMPENOFF   *March 23, 1964*

I received a touching letter from Bakhnitskaya in Warsaw. Please send her more assistance, the same amount as last time.

[*Original in Russian*]

STRAVINSKY TO AMPENOFF   *March 31, 1964*

I agree to conduct *Sacre du printemps* with the usual edition (i.e., *not* with the
new Danse sacrale) that was supposed to be used, since Dr. Roth cabled that
this orchestra performs *Sacre* from the usual edition.

[*Original in Russian*]

STRAVINSKY TO BOOSEY & HAWKES   *April 2, 1964*
                                                    [Telegram]

German projects no longer advisable as *Rake* recording now fixed. Working
every day London 15–27 June followed by Oxford. Cannot go Germany. Prefer
rest England few days before returning New York.

STRAVINSKY TO STUART POPE   *April 10, 1964*

Regarding the new edition of the 4 Etudes, I am sending you my old (Edition
Russe de Musique) full score under separate cover. It contains almost all of the
corrections as well as the revised instrumentation of the 3rd movement, on
which you will be able to secure a new copyright. I wish that your music editor
would take the new metronome marks from my new recording. This is not yet
available at Columbia Records and not even edited, I think, but will be before
the full score is finally engraved. All of the metronomes, but especially the 3rd
movement, are now very much faster.

    However another work of mine is in far greater need of printing and, as I
am conducting this work in two weeks, I take this opportunity to discuss it.
Mavra, which I will record with Columbia Recordings in Toronto, has never
been engraved, orchestra scores of any kind are unavailable, and the parts are
in bad condition. Of course the music is not and will never be a success and
there may be no demand or justification for printing it; and if I say that worse
music than *Mavra* is performed you may say that better music is also not performed. Still, I would like to see the work in print.

STRAVINSKY TO AMPENOFF   *April 13, 1964*

How irritating this first-performance business is!, and how can anyone know he
wants to perform music he has not heard, not seen? In any case, the *Elegy for
J.F.K.,* a tiny piece of chamber music, two minutes long and [using] only three
instruments and voice, cannot be performed in an orchestra concert.

    The Variations (I titled them "Some Variations") will be finished not ear-
lier than in one year. . . . Also as to the *Tempo* article I have no objection to
loaning out the score now, but I prefer that the critic hear the work before he
writes about it instead of just reviewing serial orders. As you know from my
cable we will be very busy in England. Therefore you can get us a big suite on
the Thames side of the hotel [Savoy] , so we can at least have some comfort . . .
for Vera.

While you are answering Glock please, ask him for the tape of Schoen-berg's Suite for Strings in G.

STRAVINSKY TO AMPENOFF   *April 19, 1964*

Elegy for J.F.K. . . . . The baritone version was already sung the 6th of April in the Monday Evening Concerts without being announced in the programs (the copies were ready when the program was already printed). . . . The mezzo-soprano version will be sung in a concert we will organize with Bob at the end of November in Town Hall in New York, a chamber music concert. B. & H. have to write as soon as possible to Wystan H. Auden, 77 St. Mark's Place, New York 3, N.Y. to settle with him the copyright matter for the *Elegy;* he is still in New York. Here is our schedule: Ann Arbor, Michigan, Philad. Orch., 29 Apr.–3 May;[55] Toronto (*Mavra* recording), 4–7 May; New York (different recordings), 8–20 May (Pierre Hotel); home; . . . Denver concert, 8–12 June; London 15 June–5 July (*Rake's* recording & Oxford); N.Y. (few days) and Chicago (Ravinia concert) July, then Bob to Santa Fe conducting *Lulu,* ourselves—home; 15 August to Israel; 22 August to Paris (few days) and Berlin (Festiv.). In a big hurry.

STRAVINSKY TO AMPENOFF   *April 22, 1964*

John McClure of Columbia Records has appealed to me for help to save the *Rake* recording project, saying that the rental fee is too high, in fact eight times what it was in 1953! Can you please cooperate, in my interest . . . because on a sale of only 5000 copies of the old recording in eleven years there is no justification whatever to do a new recording. It is only Mr. McClure's efforts at Columbia (against everyone else there) that have made a recording possible. And because my staying in London in June depends on this *Rake* recording. I do hope you have been able to reserve the Savoy suite for us, since those driveway rooms in the open-window season will not do at all.

The mezzo-soprano version (which must be engraved separately) of my *Elegy for J.F.K.* was airmailed yesterday to you.

We are flying to Michigan (Ann Arbor) just in one week and I hope to receive a reassuring answer to these lines from you.

---

[55] Stravinsky conducted *Perséphone* at a matinee in Ann Arbor, with the present writer conducting the Symphony in C and Schoenberg's Five Pieces for Orchestra in the first half of the program. Stravinsky's son Soulima and his wife attended the concert, and on May 13 she wrote to her father-in-law mentioning "*ces ravissants morceaux de Schoenberg.*"

STRAVINSKY TO AMPENOFF   *June 2, 1964*

Please tell this pest that an encore to the *Symphony of Psalms* is the stupidest suggestion and that is saying a great deal. NO. We are flying only the 11th, the 13th is our concert, the 14th flying to New York and the 15th—to London.

STRAVINSKY TO ROBERT HOLTON   *June 6, 1964*

1. The music of my Fanfare is not yet sent by me to Boosey & Hawkes; I will bring it to London where I shall be in 9 days.

2. My arrangement of "The Star Spangled Banner" was recorded by myself with Columbia one week or 10 days ago.

3. My opera *Le Rossignol* was recorded by myself with Columbia some years ago.

I will spend the night in New York probably Sunday (14th June) coming from Denver—I am conducting in Red Rocks the 13th (if it doesn't rain) or the 14th. The 16th I have already a recording in London at 6 p.m.!!!!

                                                           [June 1964]
STRAVINSKY TO BOOSEY & HAWKES   *[Telegram]*

Please meet flight 100 Panamerican Monday 21:35 London time with labor permits for Oxford and CBS Records.

STRAVINSKY TO AMPENOFF   *August 5, 1964*

I can imagine how busy you must be, since Bob has been waiting for the results of his participation in the Oxford concert for more than a month now, and Andre [Marion] for the same thing for the accounting. In your letter of July 31, you write that *next week* (i.e., *this week*) you will inform me of the (financial) results, but in the telegram just received you say that you will be seeing the tax people *next week*. Do not . . . take this as a reproach, but, rather, as an explanation of my situation, since I will be going to Israel on August 14 (in nine days), spending two days in New York at the Pierre Hotel to rest from the flight (on the doctor's advice), then flying to Paris on the 17th, where I will spend another two days at the Hôtel Berkeley, again to rest. On the 20th we are flying from Paris to Israel, where we have three concerts, on August 23, 25, and 26, in the Israel Festival. On the 27th we will be flying back, with stopovers in Rome and New York. If you cannot manage a reply about the financial results to me here (your last airmail letter took five days to reach me), then write to New York or to Paris during the dates that I just gave you.

We are incredibly busy here, what with arrangements for the new house[56] and then the moving, which will take place following our return from Israel. . . .

---

[56] Stravinsky had written to his son Theodore on March 23: "We have bought the house of the Baroness d'Erlanger, who died two years ago. It is on our street and very

I will be in Europe only four days—two days in Paris and two in Rome. In Rome I have been offered a film (which I may turn down).[57]

[*Original in Russian*]

STRAVINSKY TO AMPENOFF   *August 8, 1964*

Please let Mario Bois know immediately that we will be arriving in Paris (Orly) on August 17 at 10:00 p.m. Paris time, on flight 010 (Air France from New York). . . . Nabokov will be coming from somewhere else to see me, but it is doubtful that I will have time for other friends. Bois must come with a limousine, for there will be three of us (with Bob) and luggage. . . . Yesterday I turned down the film, because it would have meant more troubles, more nuisances, and more musical grief than I am prepared to assume. So from Israel (Jerusalem, King David Hotel), after a day of rest, we will be flying on the 28th to Paris, and spending two days resting there before returning to New York. . . . We will not be going to Rome.

[*Original in Russian*]

STRAVINSKY TO SPINNER   *September 9, 1964*

No time to write . . . because we are moving to a recently bought house—same street only the numbers slightly different, 1218. . . .

We are flying to Berlin already next Sunday the 13th, staying in New York two days and in Paris two days by doctor's advice.

As to *Pulcinella* I cannot understand why did you send me the full score of your rental library and not my own score. All the queries (or almost) refer to pencil marks made by different conductors and even cuts IN RED INK which shouldn't be allowed by the publisher. . . . I will send you back this mutilated score and ask you to send me my own in order to give you correct answers of your list of queries. I advise you to burn this crippled horror as soon as possible. I cannot forget what Arnold Schoenberg said once about his music: "The truth is not that my music is modern but that it is badly played."

---

near to us. A large two-story building, its 'Black Forest'–style exterior would be difficult to change, but the interior is comfortable." He wrote again on April 6: "Vera spends nearly the entire day in the new house with the contractors, estimating costs." In fact, the Baroness had died in Paris nearly five years before, on December 14, 1959. Stravinsky had known her since the 1920s, when she was a patroness of the Ballets Russes, but it is as a neighbor and close friend for eighteen years in Hollywood that she has a more than minor role in the composer's biography. Catherine de Rochegude was wealthy even before marrying the Baron d'Erlanger—in 1895, at which time she was a lady in waiting to Queen Victoria—and the obituaries mention that she once tried to buy Stonehenge. She owned the Villa Malcontenta, as well as a palace in Venice.

[57] Dino de Laurentiis wanted to use music by Stravinsky in his film *The Bible*.

STRAVINSKY TO ROTH   *September 23, 1964*

We are now already a week at home struggling with colds. As soon as I feel better I will correct the vocal score (first proof of *Abraham and Isaac*) received from Spinner.

This vocal score should be sent to Israel and the adding of the Hebrew letters and the correcting of the English phonetics should be done according to the State rules or uses in the University there. Every "Hebrew authority" I have encountered in the U.S. and England has a different opinion. This could be a great nuisance later. . . .

Also, as Bob informed Rufina [Ampenoff] some time ago, I had planned to perform the piece with the Philadelphia Orchestra in January, but this project has now fallen through because the recording (my real purpose) was not possible.

As for the recommendation of the Hebrew scholar in Israel, please ask the advice of Sir Isaiah Berlin, Headington House, Oxford.

STRAVINSKY TO AMPENOFF   *October 7, 1964*

This is the second day that we have managed without any help in the new house: chaos reigns here, the building of the swimming pool causes an unending racket, and our possessions are still being moved in. . . . I do not know how long it will be before order is re-established and I am able to work.

On August 28 you wrote: "Our bank will immediately transfer 947.209 to 'B' [Basel]." Imagine, so far "B" has not sent (through Fedya, as usual) any confirmation of the Swiss bank. Please write them and ask them to tell Fedya about this. . . .

I decided to send Kitty[58] 500 Swiss francs instead of the former 450. I hope that this is not any trouble for you.

[Original in Russian]

                                                      November 17, 1964
STRAVINSKY TO BOOSEY & HAWKES   *[Telegram]*

Until De Laurentiis sends contract to me refuse all negotiation. Variations premiere Chicago next year. Will write later about European premiere.

                                                      New York
STRAVINSKY TO AMPENOFF   *December 12, 1964*

We have finished our concerts, and they were very successful with the public. The critics were bad (as always), and in New York they were abusive; all they

---

[58] Catherine Mandelstamm Stravinsky, the composer's granddaughter (b. 1937), who was adopted by Theodore Stravinsky and his wife.

could find to say about *Abraham* was "monotonous and minor." And I really tried! Well, what can you do, not everybody can have Benjamin Britten's success with the critics.

We will be here until Christmas and will probably fly back on the 27th.

It was terrible of Stuart Pope to refuse to include an advertisement in our program, i.e., a list of Boosey & Hawkes compositions, an ad such as Columbia did, with my portrait and a full page listing the records I made with them. Stuart Pope came neither to our rehearsals (everyone else was there) nor to the concert. . . .

I would be very grateful if you could send to Cathy Berberian (she is the wife of the composer Luciano Berio), via Moscati 7, Milan, $100. She turned down some concerts that would have been quite profitable in order to participate in ours.

[Original in Russian]

STRAVINSKY TO BOOSEY & HAWKES

New York
December 13, 1964

Please hold up *Abraham* printing for few final corrections. Last proof score arriving by airmail.

STRAVINSKY TO SPINNER   *January 15, 1965*

Back home (after two weeks of flu in New York) I re-read your letters of 2 and 21 Dec. and 4 and 6 Jan. (wrongly marked in ink by you as December).

Thank you for sending me back my full score of *Pulcinella*. I am sending you by separate airmail as usual my answers on the list of your queries and also the 1st proofs of my Russian Credo (don't put "Orthodox" as you did under the Credo) which you can correct and print.

Hope Boosey & Hawkes received my last telegram from New York, 10 Jan. [saying] that I will continue the composition of the Variations.

STRAVINSKY TO SPINNER   *February 26, 1965*

I just airmailed the corrected 2nd proofs of Variations with an important alteration (pages 4, 5, 6, 7 of the previous proof included) concerning the 1st and the 12th violins to be interchanged. Unfortunately I forgot to ask you to do the same with the eleven measures (pages 9, 10, 11, 12) of the 1st and the 4th violins.

STRAVINSKY TO AMPENOFF   *February 26, 1965*

Send . . . the surplus to Basel.

I am sending the corrected proof of the Variations and a photocopy (two copies) of the choral "Zaupokoynyi," in memory of the unforgettable Eliot, with the instrumental accompaniment that is to be engraved. I will send the latter item in the next couple of days.

[*Original in Russian*]

STRAVINSKY TO AMPENOFF   *March 3, 1965*

Please send 20 copies of *Introitus* choral parts (or the vocal score if it will be soon ready and engraved) to Sylas Edman, Chicago Symphony, Symph. Hall, Chicago, Ill.

Please make sure that Spinner writes the tenor part in the treble clef (they cannot read the tenor clef!).

STRAVINSKY TO AMPENOFF   *March 8, 1965*

Premieres of Variations & *Introitus* will take place in Chicago in one month and I do hope to see your engraving very soon (the vocal score is less urgent)—the music is very simple and very short; it will take four pages [in all]. The choral parts are the most urgent for the choral master. If you need more photostats of the full score wire me immediately, I will airmail them to you also immediately. The timpani notes (there are much more than 8, so let Spinner take the "8" out) will be performed by two players (I consulted here with a specialist) and each player must have the two lines of the timpani before him—they will arrange themselves how to distribute the notes between them.

We have with Bob two important television projects, one with CBS (David Oppenheim, he will be with us on our trip to Bucharest and Warsaw where we give concerts in May), another with Liebermann, Hamburg, only for Germany. He is coming here in a few days to organize the undertaking starting in our new house.

STRAVINSKY TO AMPENOFF   *March 14, 1965*

Robert Owen Lehman has been asking me for a long time to allow him to reproduce my sketches of *Sacre*. He has done an outstanding job with Debussy, Chopin, and Mozart. Did you ever receive the letter of his that I sent? I insist on the cooperation of Boosey & Hawkes because it is not going to cost *anything*, and because he does not sell these splendid editions, but rather *gives* them away to conservatories and universities as documents. Please answer me right away why you have not replied to his requests.

[*Original in Russian*]

STRAVINSKY TO POPE   *March 22, 1965*

May I ask you to find out the address of Mrs. Aladar Racz and let her know that this (her, I am sure) statement is absolutely wrong and that she must take out the sentence I framed in red.[59] Yesterday I wrote a few words to Peter Bartók directly on his letter to me (in a big hurry), a letter which had the address of his organization. Too bad, I threw the envelope away, and I cannot write him to get in touch with Mrs. Aladar Racz. So I am forced to annoy you with this stupid affair. Please excuse me and help me.

STRAVINSKY TO SPINNER   *July 24, 1965*

There are, unfortunately, some important corrections in the Variations:

　1. The figure **40** should read:[60]

　2. The two septolets, violin-solo in figure **14** page 3 and bass clarinet in figure **62** page 13 should be 16ths and not 32nds.

　3. Page 10's note should read: "If ten violas are not available, the combination of four violins and six violas may be used."

Add to list of performances: first Canadian performance—Vancouver, 12 July 1965, and first English performance, 14 September 1965 (London).

　4. As I am recording the Variations in Los Angeles on 22 August, please try to airmail a few copies of the published score (you may publish it now) and correct the parts.

　5. Put fermatas between the variations in parentheses.

---

[59] "He even planned to include four cimbaloms in *Les Noces,* but at the persuasion of Ernest Ansermet substituted four pianos instead. The reason: he would never find four cimbalon players together in the same town who could read music, especially that by Stravinsky." In the margin, Stravinsky has written: "This is *absolutely wrong*—I never consulted anybody for my instrumentation of *Les Noces.*"

[60] The musical example in the letter is wrong (the sixteenths should not be equal), but Stravinsky corrected the mistake in a draft of the passage made at a rehearsal of the Variations in Vancouver in mid-July.

STRAVINSKY TO BOIS   *October 24, 1965*

I have received Michel Phillipot's book. I do not know his address, so please thank him for me, not only for the book but for his "subtly" French dedication as well. Since returning from my tour a few days ago, my wife and I have been swamped with housework in our big, beautiful new home. There are no servants to be found in the United States, where this is thought to be a humiliating job. What is not humiliating, in contrast, is to extirpate tips whenever possible, and even when impossible.

[*Original in French*]

STRAVINSKY TO AMPENOFF   *November 8, 1965*

Just this word to tell you I am sending you under separate cover and by special delivery, airmail, three copies of the canon I speak about in my letter to Madame Monteux, a copy of which I enclose here. [*Original in Russian*]

Please have the parts printed immediately as I should hear from her again very soon. The canon is after a popular Russian melody, thus I would like to ask you to take out a copyright on it.

STRAVINSKY TO AMPENOFF   *November 8, 1965*

I have just written to my son Fedya that today I will be writing you to have Boosey & Hawkes stop sending him those 5,000 Swiss francs every two months, and to send only 1,000 Swiss francs *every month*. Please write to me to confirm receipt of this letter, and also please tell me *when B. & H. made the last payment* of 5,000 to him. . . .[61]

Unfortunately I cannot write more, because I have been confined to bed for two days now with an injured knee. I hope to be able to get up tomorrow. Exactly one year ago I had the same problem with the same knee—a slight inflammation of the muscles resulting from my having to kneel in the bath! . . .

You are free to publish in a new Boosey & Hawkes edition, and to exploit, the last Hymn of the *Firebird* (which I sent today, three copies), since it comes from a new volume of Russian Folk songs, which is in the public domain. Schott has absolutely no rights to this edition.[62]

[*Original in Russian*]

---

[61] Stravinsky reduced his elder son's allowance as an act of reprisal for his and his wife's alleged harsh treatment of the composer's granddaughter Catherine.

[62] Stravinsky had composed an orchestral canon in memory of Pierre Monteux on the same melody used in the last movement of *Firebird*. The composer is explaining that the publishers of *Firebird* have no claim on the new piece, since he took the melody from a different source.

January 4, 1966
[Telegram]
STRAVINSKY TO BOOSEY & HAWKES

Tell Karajan am occupied American engagements until June but willing give televised talk for modest sum. Camera crew can come *chez moi* mid February. CBS televised me conducting *Sacre* snippets Warsaw last May but probably not usable. Performing *Sacre* last week February from which rehearsal film could be made except American unions costly. Appreciate Karajan's courtesy consulting me. Suggest he confer Liebermann for cameramen.

STRAVINSKY TO SPINNER   *March 21, 1966*

Finally at home I am sending you my *Mavra* orchestra score with many corrections, red ink marks, etc. . . . In this new score I want you to use only my original Russian text printed *under* the singing parts, and the English text of Robert Craft printed *over* it. I am here at home for about two months and don't hesitate to ask me if you have some doubts or decision to take. The German and the very mediocre French translations are in the vocal score and could be used by the singers in rehearsals and concert performances: they do not need [to be in] the orch. score. I wanted to have the latter as clean and readable as possible and four languages under one single singing line of music, arbitrarily changed every second because of different accents, is the most primitive technic used by old publishers.

Have you engraved the two pages of my canon? I am not sure if I wrote the repeat sign of the first four bars correctly because the repetition must be done *only before the last bar* of the piece, after finishing the Canon and not in the beginning.

June 1, 1966
[Telegram]
STRAVINSKY TO BOOSEY & HAWKES

Made some changes in Canon therefore want to hold it up and performances as yet not possible.

STRAVINSKY TO SPINNER   *July 29, 1966*

We must print a new vocal score [of *Mavra*] : one with the original Russian text and its English translation by Bob Craft (a C and not a K, as it is printed— B. & H. should know it) . . . . The discrepancies between the orch. and the vocal score are so numerous that I don't see any other means to present to the public my poor *Mavra*.

STRAVINSKY TO AMPENOFF   *August 16, 1966*

I am sending . . . four photocopies of my new work—*Requiem Canticles* (in eight succinct sections, of a duration of about 15 minutes). This is a commission of Princeton University (New Jersey), . . . composed to the memory of Helen Buchanan Seeger, the late generous donor who gave much money to this university, and whose son wanted to honor her memory by a musical work for a chorus and orchestra of a requiem character.

I would like Boosey & Hawkes to start the print immediately because I hope that the first performance may be done at Princeton in December.

STRAVINSKY TO BOOSEY & HAWKES   *August 29, 1966*

The first performance [of *Requiem Canticles*] will be at Princeton in the beginning of October. Hold up the European performance until you hear from me; we will do it ourselves in the spring.

1. Please try to send a proof copy of the orchestra score by the end of September. (We are in the Brown Hotel, Louisville, Kentucky 14–17 Sept., then in the Pierre Hotel, New York, until the performance.) Of course it would be better to have proof for the orch. parts, too, but if there is not enough time they could be copied here, or in New York.

2. . . . I will send you corrected score tomorrow; the one I sent you is full of errors.

STRAVINSKY TO AMPENOFF   *December 10, 1966*

1. I am surprised at [Peter] Diamond's "hope" that I will be able to conduct in Edinburgh on September 9. He must have been told that I would not be coming.

2. The question about the *Requiem* is simple: I will not allow it to be played until it has been published. I was at all of Bob's rehearsals and can see that this delicate music can be performed properly only if the orchestra and choral scores are presented in a *complete and orderly form*. To achieve this, proofs and more proofs. . . . I have to help Spinner; I haven't the time right now.

3. Lalandi is preparing concerts in Athens and in Oxford, as she does every year, and nothing is *new* in any of that. The performers, however, are different in each place, as was the case last year, and that is one of the reasons for my refusing to go to London. The orchestras are more or less the same, but while the chorus and soloists in Athens are good, the ones in London turned out otherwise, necessitating some special rehearsals.

4. I do not know whether we will be going to Europe this winter. It depends on my health and on Vera's, for lately she has begun to complain about pains in her heart, and her latest cardiogram shows the aorta to have widened somewhat since the last time, which worries me. For my part, I have begun to depend on the x-ray cure. And in January I will probably have to have another x-ray treatment.

5. I was saddened by [Mario] Bois's retirement, for I liked him and had

grown accustomed to him these last few years. . . . It is a pity that Boosey & Hawkes did not want him, or was not able to pay him the same as Salabert.

6. We will be here another two weeks, then we are off to Chicago, and then New York—to the Hotel Pierre, as always—and finally home again, unless something turns up in terms of concerts.

[*Original in Russian*]

STRAVINSKY TO ROTH   *January 17, 1967*

I enclose the corrected letter press, second proof of the *Requiem Canticles* which please be good enough to give to Mr. Spinner. . . . Please send the Appendix B back to Bob. I was under the impression that there were to be no prefaces by Boulez or Lesure,[63] and I still do not see what the relationship of these people is to *Le Sacre du printemps. Le Sacre* doesn't need "blurbs" by anyone. It is by no means French. Not one note of it was composed in France, and the French public hissed it, as you know, when it was first played there, now using it as a stick to beat me with for all my later music. I definitely do not want any prefaces by anybody. . . . We are still planning the Morocco trip in March, without any concerts at all.

Toronto
May 17, 1967
STRAVINSKY TO BOOSEY & HAWKES   *[Telegram]*

Wanted you to know that I promised *Requiem Canticles* Paris premiere to Domaine Musical conducted by Gilbert Amy in December. Please make for him necessary reservations of orchestra and chorus material of this work. Thanks.

STRAVINSKY TO POPE   *March 11, 1968*

I would like to recommend the music of Mr. Niccolo Castiglioni for publication by Boosey and Hawkes. I know of no worthier composer of the younger generation to have appeared in Italy in the last decade, and I think his name would enhance the Boosey and Hawkes catalogue. His music should be much more widely known and performed than it is at present.

STRAVINSKY TO ADAMS   *July 13, 1968*

I agree to the publication of Mr. [Erich] Kunzel's four-hand reduction of *The King of the Stars*, but with certain amendments. I do not like the word "edited" and would like it to be changed to "arranged for four-hands." Further, on page I . . . Mr. Kunzel describes the work as "for four-part chorus of men's voices." What about "and orchestra"? [And] he has omitted the four-chord a cappella

---

[63] François Lesure, director of the music department at the Bibliothèque Nationale.

motto at the beginning, which must be sung.[64] Then too, I don't know who decided on the Russian pronunciation but the title should be *Zvezdoliki,* it is pronounced *zvez,* not *zves.* The score should be printed with the Russian text in Cyrillic *and* in phonetic Russian but absolutely not in English. The (uncredited) English translation is dreadful and does not suit the music anywhere. (My God, "high noon": one expects Gary Cooper. . . .) What is the purpose of the phonetic Russian except to help choruses who do not know Russian? . . .

Is it possible that you could publish the full score? . . . The piece is in demand now. I am sending the manuscript to Mr. Pope today.

STRAVINSKY TO AMPENOFF   *September 3, 1968*

I enclose the scores of my instrumentations of the Wolf songs. They should be printed in the order, *"Herr, was trägt der Boden hier,"* first, *"Wunden trägst du, mein Geliebter,"* second. The cover should read *Two Sacred Songs from the Spanisches Liederbuch,* Hugo Wolf—instrumentation Igor Stravinsky. Please tell Mr. Spinner to check the score very carefully with the Peters edition of Wolf's originals. There are no added harmonies, and even the dynamics should follow Wolf's. Also, the tempo directions for the second song should be taken from Wolf and not from my score.

Answering your two letters of August 29, I would . . . be happy to have a television film of the *Sacre* made [at] Covent Garden [but] the Belgian . . . project is a very different story. . . . I did not see Béjart's choreography, but reliable opinion says that it is very bad. I will certainly not answer any direct inquiries from the Belgian television. . . . (They have been requesting an interview with me for a Debussy memorial program.) In any case, if you make a commercial transaction with them I do not want the phrase *"collaboration artistique"* used in connection with my name, no matter what they pay.

[Original in Russian]

---

[64] This contradicts earlier statements by the composer.

APPENDIXES

HISTOIRE DU SOLDAT: *The Musical Revisions,*
the Sketches, and the Evolution of the Libretto

THE MUSICAL REVISIONS

The *Histoire du soldat* that had its premiere at the Théâtre Municipal in Lausanne on September 28, 1918, was a very different work from the one with which we are familiar today. Stravinsky began revising the score soon after this unique performance, until only the Scene by the Brook and the Tango remained unchanged. The Royal March and the Triumphant March of the Devil underwent especially extensive revision; the latter, which Stravinsky expanded from 71 to 114 measures,[1] must have had a considerably less powerful effect at the premiere than it does today. Furthermore, the volume of the music was smaller in 1918, when the trumpet and trombone were muted, or coperto, almost throughout.

That Stravinsky began to revise *Histoire du soldat* soon after its first performance is verified by the manuscript of the trio version of the Little Concert, completed on December 1, 1918; this includes the music between **26** and **28** that he added to the full score after the premiere. The Lausanne stage premiere and the July 20, 1920, London concert performance were conducted by Ansermet from a copy of the manuscript made by the composer's wife, whose Russian script is found at the head of the second number. That this score was used on both occasions is shown by the cues it contains for Elie Gagnebin, the Narrator, and Closset, the violinist (participants in the premiere who never appeared in another performance together), and also by some revisions entered in a rather crude hand just before the London concert.

---

[1] Most of the revisions were made in late June and early July 1920, in preparation for the London performance. But on September 1, 1923, Stravinsky wrote to Otto Kling: "I have just returned from Weimar, where I introduced a very important change into the copy of the Triumphant March, which is now in Scherchen's hands. Since he is conducting the work throughout Germany, we will have to wait to get the score back from him before engraving it." In another letter to Kling, October 25, Stravinsky wrote: "I have just completed the new instrumentation of the Triumphant March, which I will conduct when I perform *Histoire* on November 7 in Paris." On November 20, he wrote asking for "the score used by Scherchen and myself. Since this score was employed at a great number of rehearsals and performances, it has many more corrections than the one you sent me." But the one Stravinsky wanted was in Leipzig for three performances there.

Some of the most substantial changes made in 1923 were in the Music to Scene II, where in the original score (unlike the published one) a pause is expressly forbidden before **2**; the curtain cue occurs at the beginning of the cornet solo; a complete break (silent measure with fermata) coincides with the entrance of the Devil at **4**; and the music does not resume until after the exit of the Devil.

The most important changes, completed by mid-July 1920, are as follows.

The Soldier's March (Part One)

The violin and bassoon parts between **11** and **13** were entirely rewritten, conforming to the published score.

The Soldier's March (Part Two)

In the first measure of the full score, in Stravinsky's hand, the trombone part at **5** is marked "cornet *or* trombone." The measure includes a score for the Narrator, the upper staff marked *"libre,"* the lower one *"rhythmée."*

But the publisher was confused by Stravinsky's abbreviated directions at **5,** and Kling wrote to him on October 28, 1923: "We believe that a passage is missing in the full score, in 'Part Two, Introduction.' The music stops after **4** in the full score, but in the piano reduction you have added several measures. Should we delete these measures in the parts, or should they be added everywhere?" On January 17, Kling sent the measures from the piano score and asked Stravinsky to orchestrate them. On January 19, the composer wrote that "these measures are exactly the same as in the first march of the Soldier." But not until a month later did he notice that "in continuing to correct the proofs, I have discovered that the reprise of The Soldier's March is missing—the fragment concerning which we exchanged letters in January—although it is included in the manuscript full score. To my great surprise, this music was not engraved in the proofs that I now have. As I explained to you, it is exactly the same music found in the first march beginning at **10**. . . . To guide you, I enclose the manuscript pages taken from the copy of the full score. Also, the pagination must be changed, since this fragment begins on page 16." (February 19, 1924)

Royal March

At **5,** the clarinet part in the original is given to the trombone, the violin part in the original to the clarinet. (In writing the trombone part in 1920, Stravinsky, Ansermet, and the proofreaders overlooked the key signature, and as a result the E's and the B lack natural signs to this day—in the only score in print.)

At 1 measure before **7,** Stravinsky changed the seven-note turn in the original bassoon part to a trill.

The clarinet part in the second measure of **8** was the trumpet part in the original score, and at 3 measures before **9,** the trombone part was the trumpet part (an octave higher).

The trumpet part at **11–12** was originally played by the clarinet, and in the original, the alternating and interlocking of the clarinet and violin parts in this passage were different.

Little Concert

In 1920, Stravinsky changed the barring before **16,** rewrote the bassoon part at **21,** reassigned the trumpet part to the trombone at 1 measure before **21,** and added the part for trombone from 2 measures before **26** (though in one of the sketches this "added" music is scored for bassoon).

In Paris on November 21, 1923, Stravinsky inscribed a handwritten part containing these added measures: "This conforms to the ensemble." On the same day he wrote on a similar manuscript of the percussion part between **4** and **8** in The Devil's Dance: "The family of one of the players made this copy for him, writing it in a different manner from that of the score, but the result is in conformity with the ensemble." Stravinsky wrote to Kling on November 30: "In the score of the *Soldat* that I sent to you via A. Bosc, you will find two manuscript pages, for the trombone and the percussion, on which I reply to your question about the noncorrespondence of the fragments with the score. . . . Obviously the parts should follow the score, but the musicians of each ensemble in every country have left their own markings, which are not in the score. To establish the correspondence between parts and score is an immense task for which I do not have a free moment until June (and far beyond that)."

The Soldier and the Princess

The only change in the Tango is that the first part of the piece was originally titled "Prelude." The Waltz, in the original, began with a bass-drum downbeat, and in the original Ragtime, the bassoon was alone in the last measure; the trombone was added in 1920 (but not yet the bass).

The Devil's Dance

Stravinsky added the cornet part at **2** in 1920.

Triumphant March of the Devil

The lowest eighth-notes in the bassoon part at the beginning were added in 1920; in the original this part had the same pattern as that of the trumpet and clarinet. In 1920, Stravinsky switched the bassoon and trombone parts in measures **2** and **3.** (The trombone did *not* play the ascending eighths and the repeated D quarter-notes in the original.) The "fade-out" music in the clarinet, bassoon, and cornet between **16** and **17** was added in Weimar, though a suggestion of it is found in an early sketch.

In 1920, Stravinsky added the trombone to the bassoon at 1 measure before **13;** hence the change to cornet must have been introduced at a later date. He also inserted off-beats to the bass music at **13.** Most important of all, however, is the addition of 41 measures from **3** to **9.** In the first sketch, the music at **9** is *"l'apel [sic] à l'enfer,"* and underneath the percussion part, Stravinsky introduces what may be a dance notation, with the sign "π" for the emphasized notes and "λ" for the unaccented ones.

The original score and earliest sketches require three side-drums without snare and a bass drum, and their parts are notated on four lines, as in the following sketch (large side-drum on the top line, middle on the second line, small on the third, bass drum on the bottom). Stravinsky added a verbal note (in

French) at the head of the sketch: "The notes with stems above are to be played with the right hand, the notes with stems below with the left hand. The bass drum should be placed to the left of the player, the large side-drum to his right, while the two other drums are in front of him, the smaller drum closer, the larger farther away, with their heads facing him. Timpani sticks made of hard felt are to be used."

Unfortunately, this arrangement is not followed consistently throughout *Histoire.* In the published score, moreover, Stravinsky changed one of the side-drums to a tambour and switched the positions on the staff of the large and middle side-drums. He later acknowledged that the percussion part should not have been written on a stave that might imply relative, high and low, pitches, and he wrote to Kling, April 14, 1925: "I draw your attention to the engraved parts of the *Soldat,* which in many places do not conform to the engraved score. Above all, this affects the percussion part, where there is a great confusion in the order of the different instruments. In addition to these faults, the last piece has the additional inconvenience of being unplayable for the musicians, who must turn the page while executing the solo part with both hands occupied. Your engravers and proofreaders might easily have avoided that. Also, instead of printing the part of each percussion instrument on a staff of five lines (something perfectly absurd, since these instruments do not have definite pitches), your engraver could have saved space and avoided page-turns entirely. At my last performance, in Barcelona, and in the one last autumn in Berlin, I had to omit the final number."

The percussion part in the last movement contains many errors, and it lacks important markings found in the sketches—where, for example, the composer describes the sound of the drum solo at the fourth measure of **13** (Triumphant March) as "the heels of a dancer."

THE SKETCHES

Some of the thematic materials of *Histoire du soldat* come from sources in popular music. For one example, the melody at **11** in the Music to Scene I is the well-known song

> I am pretty, I am pretty
> But I am poorly dressed
> And for that no one
> Will take a girl for his bride.

Stravinsky wrote these lines in Russian in the margin of his first sketch, and it is worth noting that throughout the sketches, more of the annotations are in Russian than in French. In one draft, beginning at the third measure of **5** in The Devil's Dance, he even refers to the Princess as the "Tsarevna." (At this point, incidentally, at 1 measure before **6,** a still earlier sketch contains the parenthetical indication "Valse.")

Stravinsky evidently diverted to his new work music that he had intended to use in Ida Rubinstein's production of André Gide's *Antony and Cleopatra*. Still other music was taken from sketches written long before, dating from 1915–17. In late 1915 or early 1916, the composer was apparently planning a piece, "Etudes and Cadenzas," among the sketches for which appears a motif (bassoon, 3 and 2 measures before **6,** continued in the violin, second and third measures of **9,** Music to Scene I) that was to become important in *Histoire du soldat*.

In 1916, Stravinsky drafted most of the motifs that were later to form Music to Scene II. The following two measures occur in the sketchbooks no fewer than five times, in different registers and with minor differences in harmony and figuration.

The evolution of the music between rehearsal numbers **3** and **4** can be traced on two pages of a small sketchbook for *Renard* and on one detached sheet. In the first entry, the tonality is the same as that of the final score.

The final four measures of this last example were worked out in smaller notes.

Stravinsky added a question mark at the end of the upper line, then an "ossia" between the two upper staves, with the words "Apparently so!" after it. He then crossed out both of these versions and wrote beneath the lower (third) staff: "So,"—and, after the music, "Correct!" The reader is left wondering about the piece for which this music was intended.

The sketches that Stravinsky composed for *Antony and Cleopatra* date from only shortly before he began work on *Histoire du soldat*. On December 16, 1917, he sent a telegram to Ida Rubinstein's agent, Charles Péquin: "Please communicate to Madame Rubinstein that I will write the music for the Shakespeare drama only if she agrees to a payment of 15,000 Swiss francs, half payable upon delivery of the manuscript. Will work without percentage." This message indicates how desperately Stravinsky needed money at the time, the October Revolution having deprived him of all income from Russia. The question of the commission had been dragging since June 26, 1917, when Péquin wrote to the composer proposing that he work on a percentage basis. Stravinsky rejected this offer, but he continued to negotiate. On November 15 he received a letter from Péquin offering 7,500 francs, with a 5,000-franc advance. No money was forthcoming, however, nor any answer to the composer's telegram to Léon Bakst (who had involved Stravinsky in the affair[2]) informing him that he was *already composing* and wished to know whether or not to continue. On December 6 Stravinsky telegraphed Péquin, requesting 10 percent of the box office and a minimum of 15,000 Swiss francs, 10,000 of which would be due upon delivery of the manuscript. Still no agreement came, and on December 19 Péquin conveyed Madame Rubinstein's regrets at not being able to alter her conditions.

The music in the following examples dates from November and December 1917, before the project was shelved. Proof of this is that some of it is found on the same page as a draft of the Berceuse, completed on December 10, that Stravinsky wrote for his elder daughter, and that from the inception of the *Soldat*, in February 1918, Stravinsky understood that only a single instrument, a violin, would be used; he soon added a bass, a clarinet, a bassoon, a cornet, a trom-

---

[2] See *S.S.C.* II, pp. 89–97.

bone, and, on about May 1, percussion instruments, but the *Antony and Cleopatra* ensemble would have been much larger.

Stravinsky's verbal notes for the *Antony and Cleopatra* music (red notebook, 1917–18, Paul Sacher Foundation) reveal that he intended to compose fanfares, marches, and dances. One of the first fanfares is a simple triadic bugle call scored for "baryton." Another, for small and large side-drums,

became the cornet tune in *Soldat:*

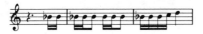

From a third fanfare

Stravinsky used the 7-note figure in reverse order in the harp part in the following sketch:

The harp motif is developed in a subsequent sketch that in some ways anticipates the Symphonies of Wind Instruments:

The relationship between this and the violin figure in the *Soldat* is evident:

The most interesting of the derivations of the *Soldat* from *Antony and Cleopatra* is that of the following melody:

The rhythm comes from a piccolo, flute, and side-drum, while most of the intervals are derived from the fanfare for two trumpets shown above. The following "oriental" dance for three trumpets and side- and bass drum in *Antony and Cleopatra* later became one of the principal motifs in the *Soldat:*

The chronology of the composition (and of the instrumentation) can be traced in a 16-page pocket-size *"croquis"* (Sacher Foundation), of which the Waltz fills about a third; the cornet enters in the final measures. Some sketches for the Ragtime follow, then notations for The Devil's Dance (between **4** and **5,** and **1** measure before **8**), for the Little Concert (from **9** to the second measure of **11,** a version of the violin figure at **13,** and the bass figure and chromatic violin figure at **7**), for the Chorale (complete, but scored without the strings), and for the beginning of the cornet part at **1** in the Royal March, albeit with the first note of the second measure a step lower than in the final score. Some of the percussion part for the Tango appears on the penultimate page, and the coda is dated March 16. The Little Concert (dated August 10) is found on the detached sketch pages, as are the Triumphant March of the Devil (August 26), The Devil's Couplets (composed in September), and the Little Chorale (completed last of all).

When did it occur to Stravinsky to identify the repeated quarter-note figure from the *Antony and Cleopatra* dance with the Devil in the *Soldat*? The sketches record considerable trial and error at the beginning of work on the Triumphant March. The first draft, below, marked "for the ending," reveals the composer's sense of the need for an irregular rhythm.

Perhaps after writing this Stravinsky remembered the passage at **15** in the Royal March. In any case, the next draft shows his grasp of the theme, pitches, and some of the accompaniment pattern.[3]

THE EVOLUTION OF THE LIBRETTO

In Ramuz's first draft of the libretto, sixty-nine bound, typewritten pages, Part One is divided into three scenes, as in the published edition, while Part Two, with four scenes, is much longer than in its final form, which consists of only two scenes.

---

[3] This example is found on a page of sketches for the Music to Scene I, the first page to include the passages **10–12,** from the third measure of **7** in that piece, and in the section **9–10,** where the theme of two pitches, related to the bassoon music at **1** and **6** in the Music to Scene II, first appears.

The second draft is handwritten and only eleven pages long; this is not complete, of course, but seems to be a kind of outline. Certain penciled changes in the first draft are incorporated here, but the second draft more closely resembles the third, which is typewritten and fifty-eight pages in length.

The fourth version is the one published by the Editions des Cahiers Vaudois in 1920, and the fifth and final version was issued by J. & W. Chester in 1924. The two published editions are structurally identical. Most lines remain the same, but there are scattered changes;[4] in line 9, for example, the word *"villain"* is replaced by *"fichu."* [5]

Part One

The narration in the first draft is much longer than in any of the later ones (approximately 52 lines, as opposed to 21 in the 1924 edition). Ramuz describes in some depth the place where Joseph, the Soldier, is seated beside the brook, and his sack of possessions. Ramuz also devotes about 15 lines to an explanation of his own intentions ("this is not a play, it is a story," etc.). The Narrator begins, "It is on the road from Denges to Chevilly. . . ," but this is crossed out, and the final version of the line appears in pencil: "Between Denges and Denezy. . . ." The most important discrepancy, though, is that the original *Histoire du soldat* opened not with music but with text: The Soldier's March begins seven lines from the end of the narration and continues while the curtain is rising.

Scene I consists of approximately 70 lines of uninterrupted dialogue, as compared with the 48 lines (with interjections from the Narrator) in the 1924 libretto. The dialogue follows the same course as in the later versions, concluding with the Soldier agreeing to accompany the Devil. (Already in this draft he tempts the Soldier with "Havana cigars.") The scene ends with the Devil playing the violin.

A 98-line narration (cut to 75 lines in the 1924 version) follows Scene I, describing the Soldier's trip home in the Devil's magic carriage. As in the later versions, the Soldier is at ease during the trip but upon arrival in his home town

---

[4] Henry Kling wrote to Stravinsky, February 8, 1924: "Please note that a small change has been entered in the stage direction before the dance in the sixth scene. Ramuz deleted this instruction in his new version; also, the Princess awakens and dances alone in the palace hall and not before the curtain." On May 12, a representative of Chester wrote: "We particularly call your attention to the note on page 33, at the beginning of the sixth scene, where M. Ramuz has eliminated the two ballerinas, if we understand correctly."

[5] On August 31, 1924, Mermod published an edition of 2,000 copies of the final version. In 1946, Elie Gagnebin sent this text to Stravinsky with some 190 added lines, inked-in on inserted pages, and with the identification: "First version, proposed to Ramuz by Elie Gagnebin and Alfred Roulet for the performances of 1946, read and approved by Ramuz." But the text is not identical to the first one, and, though improved in many ways and marked by Stravinsky on the cover "With Ramuz's last changes," it is not by Ramuz.

slowly realizes that he has been deceived, that in fact three years have passed and everyone believes him dead. Although almost all of these lines have been changed in later versions, the design remains the same. About six lines from the end, the narration is interrupted by the music, which continues while the curtain opens on Scene II.

Scene II, which is 60 lines long in this draft (cut to 34 in the 1920 edition), opens with the Soldier cursing the Devil, who then elaborates upon the opportunities the young man would have if they were to become partners in the beef business. (This exchange does not appear in the first published version.) Scene II of the first draft concludes with their partnership and the Devil's declaration that they are now like "a pair of legs." When the Soldier asks whether people would accept his money if its source were known, the Devil's repartee is that money does not speak or feel; he adds that the Soldier's mother finally may recognize him when he becomes a benefactor. This ending was carried over into the third draft but is deleted there and does not appear again.

The next narration, describing the Soldier's good fortune, contains approximately 105 lines in this draft but is cut to 91 lines in the third draft and 70 lines in the first published edition.

Scene III runs for 62 lines in the first and third drafts, but many of these are penciled out in the latter. In the 1920 and final versions, the dialogue has been cut to 40 and 37 lines, respectively.

This last scene of Part One opens, in the first draft, with the Soldier on the telephone, making business deals and then writing at his desk. The Narrator interrupts the dialogue to describe the business letter that the worldly Soldier is composing; it concerns his representative in Pondicherry, the wardrobe of that man's wife (who is twenty years his junior), and a warning about the character of the Dutch. This narration appears in the third draft in a somewhat diminished form, but with an X through it. The scene continues as the Devil enters with quick little steps, dressed as an old woman peddler in a deep red-violet, feathered hood and a secondhand silk coat, and carrying a milliner's satchel. The Devil launches into a speech about how beautiful and rich "she" once was, and says that "for a long time I have cherished the illusion of having you on my list of clients; I am like you: I buy and I sell." The Devil offers Joseph a variety of objects, none of which is of interest to him, for he has no material needs. The scene ends here almost as it does in the final version: the Devil saves the little violin for last, and when "she" produces it from the satchel, the Soldier jumps up, seizes the instrument, and begins to play—but he can produce only screeching sounds, at which the Devil laughs out loud. The Soldier throws the fiddle, aiming at the head of the Devil, who ducks and disappears. The Devil's violin music is heard from the wings, continuing through the end of the scene, while the Soldier tears up the Devil's magical book of the future. In the third draft, this scene ends in the same manner, but the old woman–Devil hints at their past connection (and his own identity) before revealing the violin by calling the Soldier "you, the old violinist." In the published version, of course, the violin remains mute when the Soldier endeavors to play. Since the Devil has already disappeared at this point, the violin is simply thrown into the wings.

Part Two

The opening narration of Part Two, with a musical introduction followed by a repetition of line 1, extends for about 58 lines. This is one section that was actually lengthened with each subsequent revision, totaling 70 or more lines in the 1924 version. Surprisingly, the main body of the narration is only slightly transformed in the final edition. Many lines, such as those describing the Soldier's experience at the inn, the encounter with the other soldier, and his message about the King's daughter, remain exactly as they were in this first draft. This narration ends when the Soldier is on his way into the King's gardens, whereas the final versions continue the narration through the Soldier's discussion with the King. The Royal March begins at the end of the narration and persists into the following scene.

Here the King addresses his cabinet in regard to the ailing Princess (approximately 67 lines), until the Soldier-doctor arrives. The King mentions that since her illness, he can no longer bring himself to read Horace, and that he has arranged for a violin concert in the evening to amuse his daughter. After this statement, the Royal March ends abruptly. The Soldier arouses the Princess's curiosity, and it is agreed that he will attempt to cure her the next day. The Royal March resumes.

This scene has been omitted in the third draft and a different one inserted, that of the Devil alone, in front of the curtain. He says that he arrived at the palace in the afternoon, whereas the Soldier arrived in the evening, already too late. The Devil claims responsibility for the illness of the Princess and plans, in his vanity, to cure her by playing the violin and thus stealing her hand from the Soldier by means of his own instrument. Neither of these variations of the scene appears in the published versions.

The first draft then moves into a 78-line narration, opening with a description of the Soldier's contentment as he ponders his return to cure the Princess the next day. He does not know what he will do or say but feels certain that his stars are lucky. Hearing a violin in the distance, the Soldier remembers the concert that the King mentioned and realizes at once that the violinist is the Devil. The Soldier listens, remarking to himself that the Devil plays well—too well, for his music seems too beautiful to be true. The Soldier has been drinking. He begins to draw cards from his deck, one by one: all are hearts. Fortified by this and no longer afraid, he implores Satan to come to him.

The Devil appears in the next scene, feigning surprise at encountering the Soldier after so many years and commenting that Joseph again has the appearance of a simple soldier. To the Devil's inquiries about his book of the future, Joseph replies that he has discarded it. The Soldier puts on the table all of the money he has left, and they begin playing cards and making bets. The Devil is losing. The Soldier wagers everything and draws the Queen of Hearts. Finally, as the Devil falls into a drunken stupor, Joseph takes up the violin and begins to play the music of Part One softly. The curtain comes down, and the violin arias are heard.

In the third draft, the second scene of Part Two begins with Joseph contemplating the chances of the next day. He hears a violin in the distance and knows instantly that Satan is playing it. "Ah, Satan, you have followed me again, always you! Violin thief, I see that this time you are after the girl." He begs Satan to come to him. The Devil enters in a tuxedo, masked, with a waxed mustache, carrying the violin. He brags about the concert, then hands the violin to the Soldier, saying, "One mustn't forget that it is not talent alone, but also the instrument, and for that all thanks are due to you. . . ." They end up playing cards, and the rest of this scene is repeated from the first draft with only minor revisions.

A narrative of about 45 lines follows in the first draft, a description of the preparations that the Soldier must make for the next morning: precisely how he will dress, how everything will be, and so on. For the first and only time, Joseph is referred to as "M. Wertheim." In the third draft, this narrative is only 10 lines long and is addressed to the Princess; the Narrator assures her that she will be cured.

In the next scene in the original version, the Princess is much better, and the King is happily reading Horace again. He remarks that she is nearly cured. But when the Soldier arrives, the Princess withdraws once again, turning to face the wall. When the King calls the Soldier just another "ass," the Soldier warns that if the Princess is to recover, the King must leave them alone. Then Joseph takes the violin from his jacket and begins to play the Prelude (Tango) and short arias. The Princess glances at him. By the third or fourth measure she turns toward him, sits up, then laughs; and when he plays the dance aria she stands, lets her robe fall to the floor, revealing a ballet costume, and dances: approaching him, backing off, reapproaching. When he finishes, she falls into his arms and kisses him. A terrible noise is heard from the wings, and the Devil enters, now exposing his true self. He is a howling black beast, on all fours, with horns and a tail. He begs to hold the violin for only a moment, but Joseph will not surrender it. The Devil prepares to pounce on the Princess, but the Soldier touches the strings of the violin, and the Devil freezes. The Soldier plays, and the Devil is obliged to obey the music. When it stops abruptly, the Devil collapses to the ground.[6] The Princess and the Soldier drag him off into the wings. From there he is heard repeating the lines that he says in the last scene of the 1924 version. The music begins, and the curtain falls.

This scene has a different beginning in the third version. It takes place in the Princess's bedroom, at night. The Soldier sneaks in, too impatient to wait until the next day. He plays the violin, and, as in the first draft, she is restored. The Devil interrupts them. The rest of the scene is the same as in the original.

---

[6] It is clear from Stravinsky's sketches that in his first conception he intended the Soldier and the Princess to dance together (in the music before **6**). Also, he writes the Russian for "convulsions of the Devil" to describe the end of this scene.

The next narration and the final scene are almost identical in the first and third drafts. The Narrator tells us that the Princess and the Soldier are married. The Soldier elaborates about his past and becomes nostalgic. The narrative is interspersed with music. He yearns to visit his mother and to find the things left behind in his sack. Finally, he persuades the Princess to accompany him to his village, despite her protests that the King will not be pleased. Reaching the boundaries of the kingdom, the Princess waits there, and the soldier proceeds for a way. Later he goes back for her, but she is nowhere to be found. The curtain opens on the final scene. The Soldier calls "Emmeline!"[7] The Devil's violin is heard, and the Soldier stops. The Devil appears, wearing a red Spanish bull-fighter's cape and billowing satin trousers. He approaches the Soldier, mimicking him, playing the violin. The Soldier follows him, slowly but without hestitation, and the Devil glances over his shoulder to be certain. From the distance, the Princess calls Joseph's name. He stops. The Devil plays furiously on the violin. They continue, walking off stage in single file.

---

[7] Only here is the Princess called "Emmeline." This was probably a joke, and Ramuz may have borrowed the name from his cook, Emmeline Morzhskaya.

PERSÉPHONE: *The Evolution of the Libretto*

Perséphone, André Gide's poem based on the fourth of the so-called Homeric Hymns[1] celebrating the Eleusinian mysteries of the cult of Demeter, must immediately have appealed to Stravinsky as an archetypal resurrection myth.[2] Certainly, as the first audiences recognized, Stravinsky conceived the work as a religious drama, though many were puzzled by its denomination. In an impassioned letter to Stravinsky after the premiere, Francis Poulenc wrote: "Since you have composed with the heart of a Christian ascetic, how do you expect me to accept [Gide's] Calvinist confection?" And Gide, after the premiere, wrote (in a still-unpublished manuscript offered for sale in 1967 in a Librairie Gallimard catalogue):

> *Perséphone* can no longer be defended and rescued except by the great beauty of the music. The piece is now a symphony with choruses, and the words are of no more consequence than their rhythm as syllables—according to a perfectly defensible theory of Stravinsky's. . . . Moreover, the Greek myth becomes a Christian mystery which will confirm my reputation, though already solidly established, as an *emmerdeur.*

Stravinsky grafts Christian sentiment and allegory onto Gide's humanist poem by, among other means, allusions to church music—the suggestion of plain-chant and organum (*"Si tu contemplais le calice"*), the use of antiphonal effects, the color of the all-male choir in Scene Three, the deliberate archaicisms (the parallel movement at *"Cependant sur la colline"*). Above all, the chorus *"Nous t'apportons nos offrandes"* is an Easter hymn that evokes the Russian Church, something that Stravinsky had refused to do in spectacle form for Diaghilev.[3]

On another level, the libretto specifies that the part of Pluto is to be sung by a deep bass voice, Gide having thought of it as an operatic role. But for Stravinsky, the King of the Underworld was the Devil in pagan guise, a terrifying presence, and to have had Pluto sing would have stripped him of his awesomeness and diabolism. At Pluto's entrance, Stravinsky wrote in the libretto, "SI-LENCE (long pause)." The composer planned to give Pluto's lines to the cho-

---

[1] Gide apparently used the Budoy translation.

[2] For at least a year and a half before receiving the *Perséphone,* commission from Ida Rubinstein, Stravinsky had been thinking about composing a large work. In September 1931, he wrote to Païchadze: "Can you guarantee me a fee of $3,000–$5,000 during 1932 for the purchase of a large-scale composition that I propose to work on after finishing the Violin Concerto?"

[3] Stravinsky acknowledged the Russian character of the music here and even jokingly referred to the whole work as "Persefona Ivanovna."

rus but finally transferred them to Eumolpus, son of Poseidon, the Eleusinian hierophant who is the narrator-historian of Gide's drama. In Stravinsky's creative world the dance, not the word, is the proper medium for the servitors of Pluto. Hence the formalization of their music in a saraband, part of whose power lies in the simple contrast between metrical regularity and inequality of phrase.

The most important discrepancy between the philosophies of the collaborators is in Persephone's resurrection, which is ephemeral, or part-time, in the libretto: her abiding emotion is pity for suffering humanity (*"la détresse humaine"*), while her return to the shades of the underworld to bring light and love is voluntary. At the time of the premiere (April 30, 1934), some critics attributed this sentiment, and such lines as *"Qu'un peuple insatisfait souffre et vit dans l'attente,"* to Gide's newfound communist sympathies, *Le Petit Parisien* even going so far as to refer to "the generous heart of M. Gide, neocommunist" (May 2, 1934). Such concern for the human condition is anachronistic, however, and virtually unknown in the ancient world. If the writer intended his *Perséphone* to be a legitimate version of the classical myth, his humanism is misplaced. Moreover, the feeling is Gide's but hardly Stravinsky's, for whom humanism does not exist, unless derived from divine revelation. His world is one of order, form, rule, and the acceptance of impositions from above; observed rituals are as inflexible for the composer as the cycle of nature. Thus Gide provided him with some, but far from all, of his prerequisites for a new theatrical masterpiece.

Gide's original opus was a poem, not a dramatic work, and even in his much-revised stage adaptation, the action is more described than portrayed. Instead of a dramatis personae, he employs three narrators: Persephone, whose part is spoken; Eumolpus, who sings formal arias as well as brief interjections; and the chorus, whose music is frequently homophonic to facilitate comprehension of the words. Eumolpus and the chorus stand immobile, in the tradition of the composer's *Oedipus Rex*. This profusion of narrative elements in *Perséphone* has often been a focus of criticism.

For Stravinsky, sacrifice is the basis of all religions: *Svesna Sviaschenaya*, or *Holy Spring*, is the true title of the *Sacre*, not the paganized *Rite of Spring*. Yet *Perséphone*, though typologically Christian, is a successor to the *Sacre* in presenting the rebirth of spring and fertility obtained at the cost of rape. The composer would have preferred to adhere strictly to one of the ancient forms of the myth, stressing the inexorable and including at least a symbolic rape of the goddess, rather than a mere seduction by a method automatically associated with the world capital of perfumes. Compelled by the usual "fatal" curiosity— do not look back, taste the forbidden fruit, open the box—Gide's Persephone cannot resist the dangerous scent of the narcissus. She thereby commits a sin that may be sufficiently strong to effect her "fall," but hardly her damnation.

The first of the three scenes, "Perséphone Ravie," centering on the flower seduction, is the weakest but also the shortest. At times both text and music, sung by female choruses and danced by Persephone's nymphs, are pretty to the point of insipidity. Hence, the agitato, when Eumolpus and the chorus warn the goddess not to approach the narcissus, fails to convey a vivid sense of peril. And while Gide's Eumolpus speaks directly to Persephone, *"Si tu te penches . . . si tu respires,"* Stravinsky strengthens the score by opting for the impersonal *"Celui qui se penche";* the composer's sacerdote remains aloof throughout, standing apart on a pedestal, commenting on the drama but never directly participating in it by word or deed.

Gide specified that Eumolpus was to deliver his introitus before the closed curtain, as well as to sing there during the two changes of scene. Stravinsky instead composed substantial orchestral intermezzi for the transpositions to Hades and back, and did not begin Eumolpus's music in the second and third scenes until after these symphonic pieces. At the very beginning, for contrast, Eumolpus sings after only two orchestral "tuning" notes, which recall *Les Noces* in pitch and the elimination of preambles. Though the chronology of the libretto is examined in detail later in this essay, it may be mentioned here that Gide did not send his final version of this first aria to Stravinsky until long after the composer had received the original poem and the "book" of Scene One.

On March 28, 1933, Gide dispatched the final two speeches of Scene One, Persephone's *"Nymphes, mes soeurs"* and Eumolpus's *"Perséphone, un peuple t'attend . . . ,"* together with a note suggesting that Eumolpus's music should precede Persephone's *"tirade."* The composer followed this change of order but ignored Gide's suggestion that Persephone declaim her lines during what Stravinsky had decided would be a slow march. Finally, Stravinsky transferred the couplet *"O peuple douloureux des ombres, tu m'attires! / Vers toi j'irai."* to the recitation in Scene Two, in Hades, thus establishing a continuity between the two realms through Persephone herself.

The libretto contains no indications for tempo except in stage directions ("Persephone rises slowly"), yet the verbal substance determines the pace of the work. And *Perséphone* is a journey, its three scenes, like those of the *Commedia,* providing the frame for a quest. The characteristic movement is slow, and the most beautiful examples of it are in the string-quartet music accompanying the goddess's speech after the chorus intones *"L'hiver,"* in the evocation of the frozen world of winter at the beginning of Scene Two, in Persephone's last speech and in the final chorus. Stravinsky sets these and other majestic pieces in relief through rapid music associated with Mercury, and one of the most remarkable achievements in the score is in the effectiveness of its allegros in the few places where the text allows them. The predominant mood, however, is one of gentleness, while the sonorities, in the main, are more voluptuous than those of any other Stravinsky piece. Well aware of the danger of monotony in the text, Stravinsky relies on juxtapositions in orchestral colors— for example, the percussive, "dissonant," and irregularly accented wind-and-piano chords at the beginning of Scene Two, after the sweet, feminine music of Scene One. Scene Three contains the most extended section of pure triadic harmony and diatonic melody in all of Stravinsky's work.

The composer's treatment of the poet's alexandrines provides the principal textual-musical interest in *Perséphone*. From the first line, with the caesura at the end of the sixth syllable, it is clear that Stravinsky intended to follow the classical meter. Yet the verse structure of the melologues is not complicated by musical notation, and the reviewer who complained "Is it really necessary to listen to one hour of implacable alexandrines?" is far off in his time estimate. Another reporter described Gide's versification as "falling between Paul Claudel and *La Belle Hélène*" (*Candide,* May 10), while still another remarked that such phrases as *"un peu d'amour," "retour du printemps," "grenade mordue,"* and *"mon terrestre époux"* sounded like titles of music-hall numbers for Lucienne Boyer (though, in truth, some of the language is fin de siècle); but these barbs were aimed at the vocabulary rather than at the rhythmic structure. As for the statement in *Paris-Midi* that the audience could hear only a few of Madame Rubinstein's apostrophes, the target is more general:

> Where am I? / What have I done?
> What am I doing here? [*sic*] . . .

Gide seems not to have allowed for a single melisma—though he did attach a note to an early draft of the libretto giving Stravinsky liberty to follow the requirements of the rhythm of his music and to repeat or transform the words where necessary, while warning that, above all, the words must be comprehensible to the audience. And the composer does bend the text according to his musical dictates, though he seems nevertheless to have become increasingly annoyed with Gide's directives: when he spells out that *"s'épanouit"* has four syllables, that this verse and all of the others have seven feet and, a little later, that "the following verse has eight feet and consequently is in a different rhythm," Stravinsky wrote in the margin: "MERCI."

Of all composers, Stravinsky—the supreme inventor of rhythmic structures, of changing meters, of asymmetrical phrase lengths, and, at another extreme, of rhythmic repetition (the ostinato)—was the one most fascinated by the exploitation of verse rhythms in music. What puzzles the listener in *Perséphone* is, on the one hand, the composer's acceptance of a text written in rigidly fixed quantities, which he frequently follows, and, on the other, his no less frequent disregard of the *spoken* verbal requirements of accentuation or stress. Stravinsky's argument was that to duplicate verbal rhythms in music would be dull; but the conflict that sometimes arises in his treatment of syllables as independent sounds, rather than as components of words, continues to disconcert part of his audience. Prose might have suited him better, except that *"En vérité, il n'y a pas de prose. . . . Toutes les fois qu'il y a effort au style, il y a versification"* (Mallarmé).

On April 23, 1934, Stravinsky wrote an *avant-propos* to his new work and published the statement in the *Excelsior* of April 29. A paragraph was omitted, however, whereupon Stravinsky obliged the editors to reprint the article complete, which they did on May 1:

I have been asked to write about the music of *Perséphone,* but since I hardly have time to do this, I would like simply to call the attention of the public to a word that contains all of the main points: "syllable," and the verb "syllabify." This word is my principal preoccupation.

Music is regulated time and tone, as compared with the confusion of sound that exists in nature. In [vocal] music, the syllable is a constant. Between the actual music and the style that bathes the work stands the word, which channels the otherwise dispersed thought and complements the discursive sense. But the word, rather than serving the musician, constitutes a cumbersome intermediary.

In *Perséphone* I wanted only syllables, beautiful, strong syllables, and only after that an action. With respect to that desire, I congratulate myself on having chosen Gide, whose text, highly poetic and free of jolts, provided me with an excellent syllabic structure.

Music is not thought. One says "crescendo," or "diminuendo," but true music neither inflates nor diminishes itself according to the temperatures of the action. I do not externalize. I understand the role of music in a completely different manner from that in which it is generally understood. Music is given to us specifically to make order of things, to move from an anarchic, individualistic state to a regulated, perfectly conscious one, which alone insures vitality and durability.

In this regulated state my own conscious emotion cannot be reflected to others, or even to me. From the instant one becomes conscious of emotion, it is already cold; like lava, it becomes a substance from which one makes brooches to peddle at the foot of Vesuvius.

Orchestral effects used for embellishment horrify me, and I must caution the public that it will not be dazzled by seductive sonorities in *Perséphone.* Long ago I abandoned "brio" as futile. The idea of wooing the public I find loathsome, even humiliating, though composers and conductors strive toward that end to the point of nausea. The crowd demands that the artist emerge and exhibit his entrails, which is taken for the noblest expression of art and termed personality, individuality or temperament.

I have used a normal orchestra, mixed choirs, and a children's choir. The only soloist is Eumolpus, the master of ceremonies of Demeter's cult in Eleusis; he reveals the action and directs the drama. Persephone's role is mimed, spoken, and danced. The delicate *parakataloghè* complements the ensemble remarkably well.

This score, as it was written and as it must remain in the musical annals of the era, forms an indissoluble whole. Many tendencies, affirmed in my preceding compositions—*Oedipus Rex, Symphony of Psalms,* Capriccio, the Violin Concerto, Duo concertant—are renewed here. In short, *Perséphone* belongs to and represents the present link in a continuum of works whose autonomy has in no way been diminished by my abstention from the spectacular . . .

Everything that is felt and true tends to yield enormous projections, which are not mere caprices of my nature. I am on a perfectly sure road. That point is not open for discussion or criticism. One does not criticize someone or something that is functioning. A nose is not manufactured—a nose just is. Thus, too, my art.

On May 2, Paul Valéry wrote to the composer:

I was unable to catch you Monday evening [after the premiere] to tell you that the music of *Perséphone* made an extraordinary impression on me. I am only a layman, but the divine *detachment* of your work touched me. It seems to me that what I have sometimes sought by means of poetic language you pursue and synthesize in your art. It is a matter of attaining purity through will. You stated it marvelously in yesterday's article [in *Excelsior*], which I enjoyed immensely. Long live your Nose!

Stravinsky conducted the first performances of *Perséphone* at the Paris Opéra, April 30, May 4 and 9, 1934, with "Les Ballets de Madame Ida Rubinstein." Kurt Jooss was the choreographer,[4] André Barsacq the designer, and Jacques Copeau the stage director.[5] Rubinstein declaimed and mimed the part of Perse-

---

[4] Rubinstein had proposed Fokine, but Stravinsky telegraphed to her, September 1, 1933: "To collaborate with him would be extremely painful to me. I am against all choreography for *Perséphone* except by Massine or Balanchine."

[5] Copeau, whom Stravinsky had known since January 1914, and who had been the Narrator in the first performance of *Oedipus Rex,* had been Stravinsky's choice to stage *Perséphone.* Copeau accepted in October 1933. He wrote to Stravinsky, asking for detailed information about the choruses, with a view to stage direction, and wrote again on October 22: "I cannot express my full joy in working with you, for you, to place myself at your service. I have wished for this for many years, particularly since *Noces.* As soon as you have something to show me, let me know and I will come." Stravinsky replied two days later: "Your note touched me. . . . For me, our triple collaboration (that of Rubinstein, you, and me) is a guarantee of success and will provide an atmosphere of work that is necessary for me. Until now, only Rubinstein has testified to an unreserved enthusiasm."

Later, when Stravinsky proposed to entrust the decor to his son Theodore, Copeau wrote to the composer, January 6, 1934: "It would be very unfortunate if a misunderstanding were to arise between us. Regarding your desire to have your son Theodore do the designs, I find myself in a difficult situation. I have already given the job to André Barsacq . . . because I did not want the realization of *Perséphone* to be hindered or its style altered by 'ideas' and pictorial fantasies. I also did it because I like Barsacq and have absolute confidence in him, having worked with him before, to my complete satisfaction. Furthermore, he is poor and little known, and this exposure, in connection with an important work, would be significant for him. . . . I cannot turn around now and demand that Madame Rubinstein have Barsacq withdraw his work, to which he has devoted so much energy."

Stravinsky answered on the same day: "It is really a pity that you did not inform me until today . . . of what was 'understood for a long time' but was actually hidden

phone, and René Maison sang the part of Eumolpus.[6] The role of Mercury was danced by Anatole Vilzak, those of Demeter, Triptolemus, and "La Génie de l'Amour" were anonymously mimed, acted, and danced. The Nymphs and the Hours were represented by female dancers, the Adolescents and Servitors of Pluto by male dancers, and the slaves of the underworld by the corps de ballet. The chorus of the Opéra was supplemented by the boys' choir of Zanglust, Amsterdam.

None of the reviews sheds much light on the piece, as Stravinsky wrote to André Schaeffner on May 3:

> I found your kind words in the mail along with all the new proofs of the stupidity and incompetence of the press in all that concerns my art. Your words were a precious gift after the premiere of *Perséphone,* which Gide eloquently . . . marked by his absence. I thank you with all my heart.

Comoedia noted the contrast between the simplicity of the poem and the complexity of form and means, both aural and visual, in the profusion of elements (dance, chorus, solo singer, spoken narration, and orchestra). And Domenico de' Paoli referred to "the influence of the golden age of Italian music, especially that of Cavalli and Scarlatti"[7] (*Il Lavoro*), though the same critic had already cited the influence of Gluck in the arioso in Scene Three, and of Pasquini's organ pastorales in Persephone's last monologue.[8]

---

from me, for reasons that escape me, and told to me only today, after so many months. To judge from this development, my role as the composer of *Perséphone* is considered to be a secondary one, since it did not even occur to you to consult me about the set and costume designer. Why, my dear friend, did you not mention this at my house the other day, letting me know that in your eyes the modest part that I wanted to reserve for my son was more a question of sympathy than anything else? In my opinion, an atmosphere of confidence and trust is more than indispensable to our work, but these circumstances do not confirm such as atmosphere."

[6] Stravinsky's first choice to sing Eumolpus had been Pierre Suvchinsky, but in a letter to the composer, November 11, 1933, the tenor canceled on the grounds that he believed Ida Rubinstein considered him too great a risk. Stravinsky answered this note the next day, promising Suvchinsky that if he did not sing the part in the spring, he would do it in the fall. In the draft of a letter to his London concert agent, Stravinsky says that "Madame Rubinstein will perform the role of Persephone; that of the sacerdote Eumolpus will be taken by one of the most beautiful tenors of today, Monsieur P. Suvchinsky." The letter also mentions that the orchestration includes two pianos.

[7] On August 30, 1933, de' Paoli wrote to Stravinsky: "I hope that the volume of Italian clavicembalists has been received, as well as the recordings." On November 16, Catherine Stravinsky, in Sancellemoz, wrote to her husband in Barcelona: "De' Paoli was here. . . . Very enthusiastic about *Perséphone.*" (Four days later, she wrote again to say that Rubinstein had telephoned to inquire how the Barcelona concert had gone.) According to another letter from de' Paoli in Paris, February 22, 1934, to Stravinsky in London, the composer had entrusted the Italian critic with the correction of the orchestra parts of *Perséphone.*

[8] At the time of the composition of *Perséphone,* Stravinsky was profoundly affected by

The *Feuilleton du Temps* review mentions a few details of the production not found in other publications:

> In the background, behind the arch of a nave, is a small temple with Ionian columns, consecrated to Persephone, where the tree of dreams extends its metallic foliage. . . . Persephone is led to the cave of the Nymphs by her mother, the goddess Demeter. Instead of embroidering divine figures on Demeter's blue veil, as in the myth, Persephone dances. . . . In the second scene . . . Pluto asks Persephone to share his throne and offers the crown, the scepter, and the cup of forgetfulness to the chaste goddess. She refuses these gifts: "Take back your treasures. For me the delicate meadow flower is a preferable ornament." Mercury, accompanied by the Hours, presents a pomegranate to the goddess, who tastes it and regains the meaning of life.
>
> In the third scene, Persephone has been called back to the light by Triptolemus. The Nymphs and the celebrants of Eleusis have combined their supplications with those of Demeter and Triptolemus to resurrect Persephone, and, to the great joy of Demeter, Persephone reappears among the living. She takes Triptolemus's hand. Impassioned with pity for the suffering Shades, she penetrates the abyss to bring a little love to those in misery beyond the shores of the Styx: "Et je vais pas à pas descendre les degrés / Qui conduisent au fond de la détresse humaine."

Scene One

Three drafts exist for Scene One with, in certain sections, substantial differences from one another. All are typewritten, but only one is bound, with a sturdy paper. Both the bound version, which is the second draft, and the first draft contain a note by Gide:

> The proposed text cannot be considered final unless I.S. finds it satisfactory. I give him full liberty, according to the rhythmic requirements of the music, to employ [or transform] the proposed chorus verses as he wishes. I fear that the last speeches of the chorus of Shadows will not be clearly understood by the audience, and, given their importance, perhaps it would be prudent to have the chorus sing only "Come!" and call "Persephone!" musically, letting Eumolpus sing the *"Quitte les jeux charmants . . ."* verse alone. The ending of Scene One will not assume a definite form until it has been examined in depth by I.S. and I.R.

Nadia Boulanger's Monteverdi transcriptions. It might also be mentioned that on May 10, 1933, Stravinsky attended the Paris concert of the Zagreb Madrigalists, whose program included Carissimi. As early as 1917, Henry Prunières had attempted to introduce Stravinsky to the music of Lully, during Stravinsky's stay in Rome (letter from Prunières, April 15).

The first draft reveals revisions and additions in Gide's hand but none in Stravinsky's, and the second draft, which was apparently submitted to Rubinstein, contains only one mark, on page 3, where the chorus of Nymphs sings "Do not approach the narcissus." This has been circled and canceled, possibly by Stravinsky, since the deletion is in pencil, which he used throughout. This verse does appear in the third draft, which is heavily marked by the composer and bears his signature on the front page. Very likely, the third draft is the only one (of these three) that Stravinsky saw.

Both the first and second drafts make note at the beginning that to elaborate upon the sets at this point would be useless. Gide goes on to say that they are very simple: the backdrop portrays a meadow bordering a seashore; on the right is a grassy embankment covered with flowers, most conspicuously a large narcissus in full bloom; on the left is the rocky gorge leading to Hades, where Persephone will venture. Attached to the first page of draft three is Eumolpus's introitus, which appears there exactly as in the published edition of the libretto (Boosey & Hawkes, 1949). In draft one, Gide has written the first stage direction by hand; draft two is identical in this; and in the third draft only the wording has been changed. The first speech of the Nymphs is the same in all three drafts and in the published libretto, but in draft three Gide has typed, in parentheses, that some lines will be added, ending with "Song of the first morning of the world." (Example 1) In the final libretto, "stay with us" is repeated several times, and the line "stay with us in happiness. . ." is added. Persephone's opening lines are identical in all versions, and her next speech is as follows in the three drafts: "I listen to you with all my heart, song of the first morning of the world."

The next speech of the chorus of Nymphs is sung, and no changes have been made from draft to draft. In the third draft, Stravinsky has circled the verse and written "second chorus piece," naming it "Dance of the First Morning of the World." (Example 2) (Stravinsky calls the next speech of the Nymphs the second, though it is technically the third; he must have considered the first two inserted verses as one musical verse, since they are interrupted only by a two-line interjection from Persephone.) The composer has also indicated that the dance is to halt during Persephone's next verse. Gide has added a new concluding line to this verse (in the third draft), to be employed ad libitum with the two preceding lines: [That the most timid soul] "Already abandons itself / Would abandon itself / Can abandon itself" [to love]. (Example 3)

The next verse of the chorus (beginning "Verbena, columbine") concludes, in the first draft, with "Of all the flowers of spring / The narcissus is the prettiest," but Gide wrote in here that these last two lines are to be given to Eumolpus. They appear this way in the second draft, and in the third the Nymphs are given a new ending line, "And all the flowers of spring." Also in the third draft, Stravinsky has indicated that the dance is to resume with these verses, and he has suggested the insertion of other flowers to the list following hyacinth: lily, iris, buttercup, anemone. (Example 3)

Eumolpus's next speech in the first draft begins "He who inclines toward its calyx / He who inhales its scent"; these lines have been crossed out here but are repeated in his next speech. In the second draft, Eumolpus sings the first two lines of the verse ("Of all the flowers of spring / The narcissus is the prettiest"), then speaks the others, ending "Will see." Here the chorus, in the first two drafts, breaks in, saying "Do not approach the narcissus," but in draft two this is penciled out. In draft three, this section is more concise, with fewer interruptions back and forth between the chorus and Eumolpus. His verse ends "He who inhales its scent / Sees the unknown world of Hades." Then the chorus gives Persephone its warning (seven lines long), after which Eumolpus repeats the three concluding lines of his last verse. In pencil Stravinsky has indicated that these lines could be given to the chorus rather than to Eumolpus. In draft three, this section is less choppy (Example 4)—in drafts one and two, the chorus sings two lines ("Be on your guard / don't take risks"), after which Eumolpus says "You will see," and Persephone dances toward the flower and gazes into its calyx. The chorus asks her what she sees, and she replies, "I see upon the meadow sown with asphodels / Shadows wandering about slowly," and the chorus asks "What are they doing?" In the first draft, Persephone's next verse is typed as follows: "I do not know, they roam plaintive and pitiful. I see a whole people wandering without hope, / Sad, anxious, resigned." Gide has made changes here indicating that the second line is to read "I see a world without hope," but this is changed back to the original in the second draft; in the third draft, Persephone continues uninterrupted, starting with "I see upon the" through "resigned." (Example 5)

Apparently mystified by the next stage direction in draft three, Stravinsky has put exclamation points and a question mark in the margin next to "An unknown disquiet has crept into the orchestra, which until then had expressed pure joy." Stravinsky also made a note, alongside the following verse of the chorus, "Do not pick that flower," that there is to be a reprise of the music for the "Be on your guard" verse from the previous page. Gide indicated that this verse is to be ad libitum, either completely or in part.

In draft one, page 5, the chorus of Nymphs sings, "Come with us / Do not pick that flower, Persephone," and she interrupts with

> Nymphs, my sisters, my charming companions,
> How could I ever again laugh with you?
> Now that I know
> That a doleful people is tormented?

Gide has added another line in pen:

> Toward them I shall go . . .

Then the chorus of Shadows sings from the wings:

> Persephone, a people awaits you,
> Come, you will reign over the Shadows . . .

> Wife of Pluto, Queen of Hades
> Come, we await you, Persephone

But Gide has crossed out all except the last line. This section is identical in draft two, and the canceled lines of the Shadows have been reinstated.

Draft one ends with Persephone, narcissus in hand, saying:

> Oh, doleful people of darkness, you draw me toward you!

Gide had changed this to

> Mysterious people of the Shadows, you draw me toward you.

and added a verse to be sung by Pluto:

> Already you belong to me, Persephone.
> Come to me. Be mine.
> Come! You will reign over the Shadows,
> Wife of Pluto, Empress of Hades.

This last verse does not appear in later versions.

In draft three, Stravinsky has changed the order of the concluding verses. (Example 6) The one beginning "Persephone, a people awaits you" (which belongs to Eumolpus rather than to the chorus in Stravinsky's draft) is inserted before Persephone's speech ("Nymphs, my sisters"). He also indicates that a prelude to the march is to begin with the last two lines of Persephone's verse ("O doleful people of darkness, you draw me toward you / I shall go to you ..."). Then the composer indicates that the march is to be played as Persephone descends into Hades, and he deletes her closing lines, which were a repetition of the last two lines of her preceding speech.

Persephone's final speech in Scene One is also found on a slip of notebook paper in Gide's hand and is identical to the published version, except that the verse still shows the last two lines from draft three. Stravinsky eventually persuaded Gide to drop these.

Two typed inserts to draft three, which do not appear in the earlier drafts, are contained on separate slips of paper. The first is to be inserted on page 1 at the "Song of the First Morning of the World":

> Among the birds and the flowers,
> The kisses of the streams,
> The caresses of the breeze;
> See the sun that smiles upon the waves!
> Stay with us in happiness.
> It is the first morning of the world.

The second insert follows the next verse of the chorus of Nymphs:

> The breeze has caressed the flowers,
> It is the first morning of the world.
> All is joyous like our hearts;

All smiles upon the earth and upon the waves.
Come! play with us, Persephone.
The breeze has caressed the flowers.

Scene Two

Two typewritten drafts exist for Scene Two. The earlier one is on paper of a greenish hue and contains myriad comments in Stravinsky's hand. At the top of page 1, he writes:

> The beginning must be established by the musical form so that the music is not enslaved by the dialogue. It is impossible for me to create a succession of musical pieces (forming a musical ensemble that will be logical and useful, and have a reason for existence on its own) while accepting the dialogue form.

Next to the first indication for the chorus of Nymphs, Stravinsky has written:

> Why Nymphs? What if a male chorus were to sing this part? Nevertheless, it is not mandatory that these verses be done by a character (or two) on the stage. [Example 7]

On page 2, Stravinsky has suggested a different ending for the first verse of the chorus of Shadows—"That which slips away and vanishes"—and he has crossed out all but the last line of Persephone's verse:

> Nymphs, my sisters, loyal companions,
> Oh, why have you followed me . . .
> What am I doing here? . . . [Example 8]

In draft two, page 3, a new stage direction appears, which Stravinsky has circled. (Example 20) In the green copy, after Persephone tells the Shadows to rest, the Danaides say "Never. Never."; while in the later copy they repeat the "Nothing is completed" verse. In their next verse, Stravinsky has changed "We" to "The Shadows" and "They," and suggested these alternatives for the third and fourth lines:

> They have no other destiny
> Than to begin again endlessly

He has also substituted, in the fifth line, "insane" (*"insensé"*) for "unfinished" (*"inachevé"*). (Example 9) Gide did not accept these last changes outright when he typed the next draft, but they do appear there next to the old lines as alternatives. (Example 20)

In the green copy, Eumolpus has the next line:

> Tell them about spring, immortal Persephone

which is given to the Nymphs in draft two, where Stravinsky has changed "them" to "us."

Persephone's next verse is the same in both copies, and the change Gide made in the green copy (replacing the word "immense" with "unique") is incorporated into draft two.

In the green copy Stravinsky has written that this verse is to be followed by the chorus and/or Eumolpus saying:

Tell us more, immortal Persephone.

In draft two, this is typed in as "Tell us, tell us more, Persephone," and Stravinsky has circled *"encore"* and written *"parle-nous"* again above it, indicating that three syllables are necessary.[9]

Stage directions follow, stating that Persephone is to approach the Danaides and touch their faces. Stravinsky has underlined in red crayon the indications for music in the green copy and reminded himself that this music must be followed by silence. He had crossed out Pluto's first line ("Persephone") and written "SILENCE" next to it. (Example 10) Gide did not incorporate this change into draft two, where Stravinsky has once again insisted that there be silence (and a "long pause") after this music. (Example 21).

In the green copy, the Nymphs say, "Do not let yourself be tempted, Persephone"; but Stravinsky felt that this line must go to a male chorus. Since the same indication appears unchanged in draft two (for the Nymphs), Stravinsky has deleted the line altogether.

The stage directions show that the music is to halt for an instant to allow Persephone to speak, then starts up again "as a scherzo after the call from Pluto." (Example 11) Stravinsky has not disputed this in the green copy, but he put a large question mark over this direction in the second draft. (Example 22)

Again, at the next indication for the Nymphs, Stravinsky has written, in the green copy, that this should be a male chorus; in draft two, where the indication appears precisely as it was ("Accept nothing from Pluto, Persephone"), the composer has deleted it altogether.

After Eumolpus's long verse, the Nymphs say, "What have you done? Why, Persephone, did you not defend yourself better?" (Example 12) This does not appear in the later draft. And Persephone's next speech (in the green copy) is "I have rediscovered the taste of the lost earth." Gide has struck this out and written (in hand) the "Where am I?" verse, which is incorporated into draft two. Stravinsky has written here "like a heartfelt cry" and "great nostalgia," alongside the next verse of the chorus, and then "By suggestion they persuade Persephone to look at the narcissus over there where she is not." (Example 24)

At Persephone's next verse, in the second copy, Stravinsky has written "on the proscenium." Here she is surrounded by the chorus of Shadows, as opposed to the chorus of Nymphs in the green copy; but Stravinsky has canceled the Nymphs throughout the second draft.

Then the chorus says, "Tell us, what do you see?" In the second copy Stravinsky has changed this to "Recount to us, [what do you see?]" or "Queen [tell us what do you see?]" and written "better" next to "Recount."

---

[9] See Stravinsky's and Gide's letters of July 29 and August 8, 1933.

In Persephone's next verse, Stravinsky has underlined *"Redemander partout"* in the green copy and indicated in the margin that this is to be repeated by the chorus. After the next chorus line ("no; Demeter will no longer hear your voice, Persephone"), Stravinsky has drawn a line in both copies, and in the second he wrote that this signals the end of the despair, and that from this point on Persephone goes into a trance. (Example 25)

Eumolpus's next lines were changed by Stravinsky in the second draft from "Do not despair, / Nymphs" to "Poor desperate Shadows"; and "Even the winter *cannot be* eternal" was chosen by the composer in preference to *"is not."* He also deleted the next lines of the chorus. (Example 26)

Gide changed the chorus's line after that, from "Thus in our enraptured soul / Hope is reborn" to "Thus hope is reborn in our enraptured soul."

Persephone's next verse is missing a section in the green copy, Gide having written in parentheses that this text is to be revised, but he has inserted part of it by hand. (Example 16) An empty space appears at this point in the second copy.

In draft two, Stravinsky had indicated that Eumolpus's next lines could be sung by the chorus or be repeated by them.

In draft two, Persephone's next speech contains a new line: "I will be Queen?"; and after Eumolpus's confirmation that she will be Queen of the terrestrial spring and no longer of the Underworld, Stravinsky had inserted a question mark and written, "Reprise of the chorus as before." (Example 27)

In the second draft of Persephone's last speech of Scene Two, Stravinsky has changed "Come, my sisters" to "Come, come." He has also indicated in this copy that the singers must go toward the back of the stage "as fast as possible" while the lights go down in the front. (Example 28)

Scene Three

Only one incomplete draft of Scene Three survives in Stravinsky's papers, typed in blue ink, three pages in length, and on the same greenish paper as the first draft of Scene Two. The pagination makes clear that this Scene Three follows that draft of Scene Two.

Eumolpus delivers the first speech, identical to that in the published libretto, during the scene change. According to the stage directions in this rough draft, the scene is a sunny landscape, blue and golden. In back, a hill dominated by a Doric temple. In front at the left is a tumulus with holm oaks rising above it. Alongside it, and seen at an oblique angle by the audience, is the entrance to a tomb, which is closed with heavy stone panels, in the Etruscan manner. In front of this stands the spirit of Death, an extinguished torch in his hand. Gide added parenthetically that from this point on, the text cannot be definitely established until the music and stage directions have been completed.

After the curtain goes up, Eumolpus continues his verse, which is the same as in the final version. Stravinsky changed "A happy people *invading* [the temple]" to *"hastening to."* He also drew an arrow away from the stage direction "a chorus of adolescents enters to join the chorus of Nymphs," crossing out the phrase "probably preceded by Eumolpus," and writing in its place that this section is to occur instead during Eumolpus's song. (Example 29)

In the introductory line of the first verse, sung by two choirs together, Gide suggested replacing *"We bring our* offerings" with *"You bring your,"* but the one finally employed is "We bring you our offerings." In line 4 of this verse, Stravinsky underlined the *"es"* in *"renoncules"* (buttercups), noting in the margin that it is to be a syllable—as, indeed, it is shown to be in the final score. (Example 30)

The first discrepancy between this rough version and the 1949 libretto is in the following verse of the chorus of Nymphs. In line 3, " [Persephone] leaves the sinister courtyard" becomes the command "Leave the . . ." in the final version. Line 4 in the rough draft reads: "Staggering and as if drunk / with night," which becomes in the final version "You make your way and as if . . ." and inserted three lines later ("Shadow still surrounds you / Staggering Persephone"). (Example 31) After this verse, Stravinsky indicated in the margin: "She advances toward Triptolemus: pure music finishes the dance." Some verses were inserted in the final libretto at this point, since in the rough draft the line following "and yet you live" is that of the children's chorus: "Speak, Persephone, tell us what the winters conceal." The added verses are found on a loose sheet of paper in the composer's *Perséphone* notes (Example 32)

In the margin of the page containing the first four inserted verses, Gide indicated that all of the lines are to be of seven feet. (For example, he writes *"s'épanou-it."*) Beginning with the lines "Speak, Persephone, tell us what the winters conceal," however, he notes in the margin that the lines will have eight feet, and consequently will have a different rhythm.

After this, Persephone's long speech, given when she rejoins the chorus and Demeter and Triptolemus, is not included in the rough draft but appears in Stravinsky's sketches on separate pieces of paper, identical to the final version except for one word in line 21: "I have seen what is hidden . . ." (the final version reads "I have seen what happens").

Some of Gide's earlier revisions are also revealed on these pages: in line 2, "that desolated [the winter]" was changed to "that darkened"; in line 13, " [strong] enough" was changed to "as [strong]."

Eumolpus's final speech also appears on these sketch pages almost exactly as in the published libretto. (Example 33) Stravinsky has underlined the last line or so of each of Eumolpus's last three verses and indicated that either the entire verse or only the underlined parts may be reprised by the chorus.

The rough version of Scene Three breaks off with the two choruses together singing, "Tell us, what did you see in Hades?" Gide wrote at the bottom of this page: "I await Stravinsky's opinion on the first two scenes before going any further. New address: Hôtel Splendide, Marseille." (Example 31)

Ier TABLEAU.
———————

        Avant le lever du rideau,EUMOLPE sur le devant de la scè-
ne doit annoncer par quatre ou six vers(à composer)la représentation des Mystères
d'ELEUSIS.
        Le rideau se lève sur une prairie au bord de la mer;à droi-
te,un talus gazonné et fleuri où s'épanouit la grande fleur du narcisse;sur la gauche,le défilé rocheux(qui conduit aux Enfers)où s'aventurera Proserpine.

———————

                        Demêter,avertie par Mercure qui
                        l'emmène,dit adieu à Perséphone,
                        et à la recommande aux Nymphes.

LE CHOEUR DES NYMPHES :
        (chanté)
                                    (bis ou ter,)
"Reste avec nous,Princesse Perséphone;"
                                    (ad libitum.)
"Ta mère Demêter,reine du beauté,"

"T'a confiée à nous;
    (quelques vers seront ajoutés,dont le dernier:)
    ("Chant du premier matin du monde")
    (voir lequel n° 1)

                        Perséphone,encore assise sans dou-
                        te,et comme à demi-endormie:

PERSEPHONE :
        (parlé)

        "La brise vagabonde"

Example 1

Example 2

- 2 -

"A caressé les fleurs."

                        Le choeur des Nymphes s'empresse
                        autour de Perséphone qui se lève
                        lentement.

LE CHOEUR DES NYMPHES :
        (chanté)
"Viens!Joue avec nous,Perséphone..."-(bis ou ter,ad libitum;sera peut-être augmenté.)
    (voir lequel n° 2)

            PERSEPHONE :
                (parlé)

        "Je t'écoute de tout mon coeur"

        "Chant du premier matin du monde."

                        Elle se mêle au choeur des Nymphes
                        et commence à danser avec elles.

LE CHOEUR DES NYMPHES :
        (chanté)
"Ivresse matinale"

 "Rayon naissant,pétales"

"Ruisselants de liqueur."

"Cède sans plus attendre;"

 "Au conseil le plus tendre"

 "Et laisse l'avenir"

 "Doucement t'envahir."

DANSE

- 3 -

PERSÉPHONE :
(parlé)

"Voici que se fait si furtive"

"La tiède caresse du jour"

"Que l'âme la plus craintive"
"Déjà s'abandonne,
(ad libitum.) "S'abandonnerait à l'amour."
"Peut s'abandonne"

Danses des Nymphes qui cueillent
les fleurs et tressent des guirlandes dont elles ornent Perséphone.

LE CHOEUR DES NYMPHES :
(chanté)

"Verveine, ancolie,"

"Jacynthe, safran,"

"Adonide, goutte de sang,"

"Et toutes les fleurs du printemps."

EUMOLPE :
(chanté)

"De toutes les fleurs du printemps,"

"Le narcisse est la plus jolie."

"Celui qui se penche sur son calice,"

"Celui qui respire son odeur"

"Voit le monde inconnu des Enfers.."

Example 3

Example 4

- 4 -

Le choeur évolue en dansant de
manière à empêcher Perséphone
d'approcher de la fleur. Perséphone, rompant le cercle des Nymphes,
s'est approchée de la fleur et
s'est penchée sur son calice

LE CHOEUR DES NYMPHES :
(chanté)

"Tiens-toi sur tes gardes,"
"Défends-toi toujours,"   }-(bis ou ter, ad libitum.)

"De suivre, hagarde,"
"Ce que tu regardes"
"Avec trop d'amour."   }-(bis ou ter, ad libitum.)

"Ne t'approche pas du Narcisse;"
"Non, ne cueille pas cette fleur"

EUMOLPE :
(chanté)

"Celui qui se penche sur son calice,"

"Celui qui respire son odeur"--(ad libitum.

"Voit le monde inconnu des Enfers

Danse mimée de Perséphone penchée
sur la fleur.

- 5 -

PERSÉPHONE :
(parlé)

"Je vois sur des prés semés d'asphodèles"

"Des ombres errer lentement."

"Elles vont.Elles vont,plaintives et fidèles."

"Je vois errer"

"Tout un peuple sans èspérance,"

"Triste,inquiet,décoloré."

> Le choeur entoure attentivement
> Perséphone,et se penche anxieuse-
> ment vers elle.Une inquiétude
> inconnue s'est glissée dans l'or-
> chestre qui jusqu'alors exprimait
> une pure joie.
>   Le choeur,essayant,malgré
> l'inquiétude nouvelle de retrouver
> sa joie et d'y entrainer Perséphone.

LE CHOEUR DES NYMPHES :
(chanté)

"Ne cueille pas cette fleur,Perséphone,"

"Défends-toi toujours"

"Ce suivre,hagarde,"

"Ce que tu regardes

"Avec trop d'amour."

"Viens!Joue avec nous,Perséphone.."

Example 5

Example 6

- 6 -
EUMOLPE

PERSÉPHONE :
(parlé)

"Nymphes,mes soeurs,mes compagnes charmantes,"

"Comment rirais-je avec vous,désormais..?"

"A présent que je sais"

"Qu'un peuple dolent se tourmente?.."

"O peuple douloureux des ombres,tu m'attires,"

"J'irai vers toi..."

> Une grande plainte envahit l'or-
> chestre.Perséphone a cueilli la
> fleur.Sa danse exprime l'inquié-
> tude et la désolation.Elle descend
> lentement du tertre gazonné où
> s'épanouissait la fleur du narci-
> sse et se rapproche des rochers
> sur la gauche.

EUMOLPE :
(parlé)
chanté

"Perséphone,un peuple t'attend;"

"Tu régneras sur les ombres.."

"Epouse de Pluton,reine des Enfers..."
(à allonger.)

> Les Nymphes veulent retenir Persé-
> phone,qui s'avance toujours comme
> hagarde,les yeux fixés sur la
> fleur de narcisse qu'elle tient à
> la main.

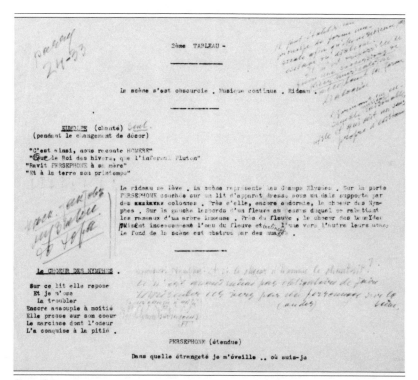

Example 7

Example 8

-3-

Cette eau vaine
Des fontaines
Qui s'enfuit toujours

PERSEPHONE

Reposez vous ombres douloureuses .

Le choeur des Danaïdes -

Jamais . Jamais .

PERSEPHONE -

Que puis-je pour vôtre bonheur ?

Le choeur des Danaïdes -

Sans maitre et sans amour, sans peine et sans envie
Que de recommencer sans fin
La geste inachevé de la vie

EUMOLPE -

Parle leur du printemps, PERSEPHONE immortelle .

PERSEPHONE -

Ma mère DEMETER, que la terre était belle
Quand l'amoureux éclat de nos rires mêlait
Aux épis d'or, des fleurs,et des parfums au
Loin de toi, DEMETER, moi, ta fille égarée
J'admire au cours sans fin de l'immense journée
Maitre de pâles fleurs, où mon regard se pose
Les bords gris du Léthé s'orne de blanches roses

Example 9

Example 10

-4-

Et, dans l'ombre du soir, les ombres s'enchantes
Du reflet incertain d'un souterrain été

PERSEPHONE s'est approche des Danaïdes et, compatissante, touche le front à
chaque d'elles (musique à chercher) . Le musique peu à peu , se fait plus tendre,
moins plaintive, et comme doucement rassérénée .
Cependant PLUTON est entré, comme une grande ombre, dont je ne pense pas qu'il
faille voir le visage . Il est en scène, derrière le lit de repos que PERSEPHONE à
quitte . Et soudain on entend sa voix très grave :

PLUTON -

PERSEPHONE ..

PERSEPHONE (s'arrêtant interdite)

Qui m'appelle ?

PLUTON (plus grave encore)
(un temps)
Tu viens ici pour dominer
Non pour t'apitoyer, PERSEPHONE .
N'espère pas pouvoir te montrer secourable .
Nul, et serait-il Dieu, ne peut échapper au destin
Ta destinée est d'être reine, Accepte ;
Et pour oublier ta pitié ,
Bois cette coupe de Lethé
Que t'offre les Enfers avec tous les trésors de la terre .

Des ombres, drapées de noir (Les Danaïdes sont vêtues d'un vert cendré) sortent
du palais de PLUTON, chargées de joyaux, de parures; l'une d'elles tient une coupe qu'elle tend à la dernière des Danaïdes . Celle-ci l'emplit d'eau du Lethé
Puis l'ombre s'approche de PERSEPHONE .

(musique pompeuse et morne)

Le choeur des nymphes -

Le chœur des Nymphes

-5-

Ne te laisse pas ~~xxxxx~~ tenter, PERSEPHONE.   *Chœur d'hommes*

PERSEPHONE (qui a pris ces bijoux et les
a regardés tristement les repousse)

Non, reprenez ces pierreries
la plus fragile fleur des prairies
M'est une préférable parure .

instant
La musique s'est tue un ~~temps-deux~~ (?) pour laisser parler PERSEPHONE , puis
reprend en scherzo après attaque sur l'appel de PLUTON .

PLUTON (en appel)

Viens Mercure ! .
Venez, heures du jour et de la nuit   *Orgue* *Musette* ff

nuages
Les ~~vignes~~ au fond de la scène , surélevée, s'entrouvrent, pour laisser bondir
~~bondit~~ Mercure suivi du cortège des heures (MERCURE rôle *muet*)   Chacune des
heures ~~voilées~~ , de tons graduées, couleur d'aube, d'aurore, de jour etc.. porte
un présent pour PERSEPHONE .

Le chœur des nymphes -

N'accepte rien de PLUTON, PERSEPHONE .   *Chœur d'hommes, pp sur la musique*
(musique prolongée)
mimique

EUMOLPE - *Orchestre Seul*

PERSEPHONE confuse
Se refuse
A tout ce qui la séduit
Cependant Mercure espère
Qu'en souvenir de sa mère
Saura le tenter un fruit
Un fruit qu'il voit pendre à la branche
Qui se penche
Au dessus de la soif fatale .
De Tantale

Example 11

Example 12

-6-

De Tantale
Il cueille une grenade mure
Et s'assure
Qu'un reste de soleil y luit,
Il la tend à PERSEPHONE
Qui s'émerveille et s'étonne
De retrouver dans sa nuit
Un rappel de la lumière
De la terre
Les belles couleurs du plaisir
La voici plus confiante
Et riante
Qui s'abandonne au ~~plaisir désir~~
Saisit la grenade ~~mûre~~
Y mord .... Aussitôt MERCURE
S'envole et PLUTON sourit .

Le rythme accéléré de la musique , ironique et stridente au moment où MERCURE
selon le Chant d'EUMOLPE , bondit pour s'emparer de la grenade . Il la tend
à PERSEPHONE , qui veut s'en emparer . Le chœur des nymphes s'interpose
jusqu'au moment où MERCURE rompt le cercle qu'elles ont formé . PERSEPHONE
a pris la grenade et y mord . Eclat de rire dans l'orchestre .Sur les dernies
mots d'EUMOLPE le cortège des heures , MERCURE et PLUTON se sont retirés .
L'on ne voit plus que PERSEPHONE et le cœur des nymphes .

LE CHOEUR DES NYMPHES -
Pourquoi
Qu'as-tu fait ? Qu'as-tu fait, PERSEPHONE .
Ne t'as-tu pas mieux défendue ?

PERSEPHONE -

~~J'ai retrouvé le gout de la terre perdue .~~
Où suis-je ?... Qu'ai-je fait ?.. Quel trouble m'a saisi ?
Soutenez-moi, mes sœurs . La grenade mordue
M'a redonné le goût de la terre perdue

Le chœur des Nymphes
Si tu consultais le calice
Du narcisse
Peut-être reverrais-tu
des près de laisser et la mere

Comme il advint que, sur la terre
Le mystère
Du monde infernal t'apparut...

```
  De Tantale
Il cueille une grenade mure
  Rts'assure
Qu'un reste de soleil y luit
Il la tend à Perséphone
Qui s'émerveille et s'étonne
De retrouver dans sa nuit
Un rappel de la lumière de la terre
De la terre
Les belles couleurs du plaisir
La voici plus confiante
  Et riante
Qui s'abandonne au plaisir désir
  Saisit la grenade mure
Y mord.... Aussitôt Mercure
S'envole et Pluton sourit .
```

> Le rythme accéléré de la musique, insolque et stridente au moment où Mercure selon le chant d'Eumolpe , bondit pour s'emparer de la grenade Il la tend à Perséphone, qui veut s'en emparer. Le choeur des nymphes s(interpose jusqu'au moment ou Mercure rompt le cercle qu'elles ont formé . Perséphone a pris la grenade et y mord . Eclat de rire dans l'orchestre . Sur les derniers mots d'Eumolpe, le cortège des heures, Mercure et Pluton se sont retirés. L'on ne voit plus que Perséphone et le choeur des nymphes .

```
LE CHOEUR DES NYMPHES -

Qu'as-tu fait? Pourquoi, Perséphone
Ne t'es-tu pas mieux défendue ?
```

```
              PERSEPHONE -

          Où suis-je?.. qu'ai-je fait?... Quel trouble me saisit?...
          Soutenez-moi, mes soeurs. La grenade mordue
          M'a redonné le gout de la terre perdue .
```

```
  EUMOLPE -    Dans le phare d'Euuuu
  Si tu contemplais le calice
```

Example 13

Example 14

```
                          -7-
  Du narcisse
Peut-être reverrais-tu
Les près délaissés et ta mère
Comme il advint quand sur la terre
  Le mystère
Du monde infernal t'apparut .
```

```
              PERSEPHONE -

          Entourez-moi, protégez-moi, nymphes fidèles .
          Cette fleur des prés, la plus belle,
          Seul reste du printemps que j'emporte aux enfers,
          Si, pour l'interroger, je me penche sur elle,
          Que saura-t-elle me montrer?...
```

```
    EUMOLPE -
    L'hiver .
```

> Perséphone, entourée du choeur des nymphes, sur le devant de la scène, a pris la fleur de narcisse qu'elle gardait a la ceinture et la contemple .

```
              PERSEPHONE -

          Où donc avez-vous fui, parfums, chansons, escortes
          De l'amour?... Je ne vois rien que des feuilles mortes.
          Les prés vides de fleurs et les champs sans moissons
          Racontent le regret des riantes saisons .
          Plus, au penchant des monts, les flûtes bacoliques
          N'occupent les bosquets de leurs claires musiques.
          De tout semble couler un lent gémissement
          Car tout espère en vain le retour du printemps.
```

```
  LE CHOEUR DES NYMPHES -

  Le printemps c'est toi, Perséphone .
```

```
              PERSEPHONE -
```

-2-

Alternons les accents de nos voix affligées
Nymphes .

LE CHOEUR DES NYMPHES -

Dis, que vois-tu ?

PERSEPHONE -

.... Des rivières figées;
Cesser la fuite en pleurs des ruisseaux et leur voix
S'étouffer sous legel . Dans les nocturnes bois
Je vois ma mère errante et de haillons vêtue
Redemander partout Persephone perdue .
A travers les halliers, sans guide, sans chemin,
Elle marche; elle porte une torche à la main.
Ronces, cailloux aigus, vents, ramureanoueuses,
Pourquoi déchirez-vous sa course douloureuse?
Mère, ne cherche plus. Ta fille qui te voit
Habite les enfers et n'est plus rien pour toi .
Hélas.. ah.. si du moins ma parole égarée
Pouvait ....

LE CHOEUR DES NYMPHES -

Non; Demeter n'entendra plus ta voix
Perséphone ....

EUMOLPE -

.... Ne soyez pas désespérées,
Nymphes. L'hiver non plus n'est pas éternel.
ne peut être éternel.

(C'est à partir d'ici que la musique commence le lent
crescendo, ou éclaircissement - enfin la montée qui doit
se poursuivre jusqu'à la fin de ce tableau et amener à la
solennité joyeuse du tableau suivant.)

Example 15

Example 16

LE CHOEUR DES NYMPHES -   -9-

Jusqu'à quand serons-nous captives
   Sur la rive
Du fleuve Léthé ?

EUMOLPE -

Au palais d'Eleusis où Demeter arrive
Le roi Séleacus lui confie
la garde d'un enfant dernier né,
   Démophoon qui doit devenir Triptolème .

PERSEPHONE -

Au dessus d'un berceau de tisons ardents et de flammes,
Je vois ... Je vois vers lui Démeter se pencher.

EUMOLPE -

Au destin des humains penses-tu l'arracher,
   Déesse? D'un mortel tu voudrais faire un dieu.
Tu le nourris et tu l'abreuves
Non point de lait
Mais de nectar et d'ambroidée.
Ainsi l'enfant prospère et sourit à la vie .

LE CHOEUR DES NYMPHES -

Ainsi dans nôtre âme ravie
   L'espoir renait .

PERSEPHONE -

Sur la plage, et des flots imitant la cadance
Ma mère,dans ces bras, en marchant le balance .
....
....
.... humectant sa marine

(texte à revoir)

-10-

Elle l'expose nu dans la brise marine.
Qu'il est beau, rayonnant de hâle et de santé
Il s'élance; il se rue à l'immortalité .
Salut Démophoon en qui mon âme espère .
Par toi vais-je revoir se refleurir la terre?
Tu sauras aux humains enseigner le labour
Que d'abord t'enseigna ta mère .

EUMOLPE -

Et, grâce à ton travail, rendue à son amour
Perséphone revit et reparaît au jour .

PERSEPHONE -

Eh quoi . J'échapperais à l'offre souterraine?
Mon sourier emplirait de nouveau les prés .....

EUMOLPE -

        Reine
Du terrestre printemps et non plus des enfers .

PERSEPHONE -

Déméter tu m'attends et tes bras sont ouverts
Pour accueillir enfin ta fille renaissante
Au plein soleil qui fait les ombres ravissantes
Venez, mes soeurs. Forçons les portes du trépas.
Non, le sombre Pluton ne nous retiendra pas
Nous reverrons bientôt , agités par le vent
Les branchages aux délicats balancement.
O mon terrestre époux, radieux Triptolème
Qui m'appelle, j'accours. Je t'appartiens, je t'aime.

        Perséphone accompagnée du choeur des nymphes s'est dirigée
        vers les fond de la scène qui s'illumine , tandis que le de-
        vant de la scène s'obscurcit.

RIDEAU -

Example 17

Example 18

            DEUXIEME TABLEAU

    La scène s'est obscurcie. Musique continue. Rideau.

        EUMOLPE (chanté)
    (pendant le changement de décor)

    "C'est ainsi, nous raconte HOMERE"
    "Que le Roi des hivers, que l'infernal Pluton"
    "Ravit Perséphone à sa mère"
    "Et à la terre son printemps".

        Le rideau se lève. La scène représente les
        Champs-Elysées. Sur la porte PERSEPHONE cou-
        chée sur un lit d'apparat dressé sous un dais
        supporté par des colonnes. Près d'elle enco-
        re endormie, le choeur des Nymphes. Sur la
        gauche les bords d'un fleuve au-dessus duquel
        se rabattent les rameaux d'un arbre immense.
        Près du fleuve, le choeur des Danaïdes puis-
        ent incessamment l'eau du fleuve et incli-
        nent l'une vers l'autre leurs urnes. Le fond
        de la scène est obstrué par des nuages.

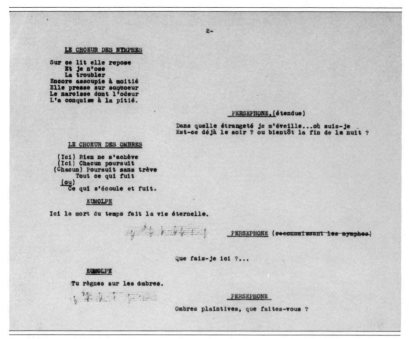

Example 19

Example 20

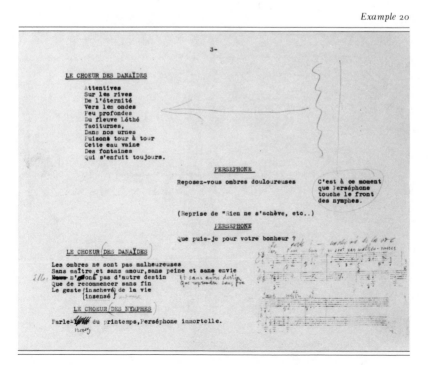

4-

PERSÉPHONE

Ma mère DÉMÉTER, que la terre était belle
Quand l'amoureux éclat de nos rires mêlait
Aux épis d'or, des fleurs, et des parfums au lait
Loin de toi, DÉMÉTER, moi, ta fille égarée
J'admire au cours sans fin de l'unique journée
Maître de pâles fleurs, où mon regard se pose
Les bords gris du Léthé s'orner de blanches roses
Et, dans l'ombre du soir, les ombres s'enchanter
Du reflet incertain d'un souterrain été.

CHŒUR

Parle-nous, parle-nous encore Perséphone.

PERSÉPHONE s'est approchée des Danaïdes et, compatissante touche le
front à chacune d'elles (mimique à chercher). La musique peu à peu se
fait plus tendre, moins plaintive, et comme doucement rassérénée.
Cependant Pluton est entré, comme une grande ombre, dont je ne pense
pas qu'il faille voir le visage. Il domine la scène, derrière le lit
de repos que PERSÉPHONE a quitté. et soudain, on entend sa voix très
grave.

PLUTON
Perséphone !

PERSÉPHONE, s'arrêtant interdite

qui m'appelle ?

Pluton !
Tu viens ici pour dominer
Non pour t'apitoyer, PERSÉPHONE.
N'espère pas pouvoir te montrer secourable.
Nul, et serait-il Dieu, ne peut échapper au Destin
Ta destinée est d'être reine. Accepte;

Example 21

Example 22

5-

Et pour oublier ta pitié
Bois cette coupe de Léthé
Que t'offrent les Enfers avec tous les trésors de la terre.

Des ombres drapées de noir (Les Danaïdes sont vêtues d'un vert
cendreux) sortent du palais de Pluton, chargées de joyaux, de
parures; l'une d'elles tient une coupe qu'elle tend à la dernière des Danaïdes. Celle-ci l'emplit d'eau du Léthé. - Puis
l'ombre s'approche de PERSÉPHONE.

(Musique pompeuse et morne.)

LE CHŒUR DES NYMPHES
Ne te laisse pas tenter, PERSÉPHONE.

PERSÉPHONE (qui a pris ces bijoux et les
a regardés tristement les repousse)

Non, reprenez ces pierreries
La plus fragile fleur des prairies
M'est une préférable parure.

La musique s'est tue un instant (?) pour laisser parler
PERSÉPHONE, puis reprend en scherzo après attaque sur
l'appel de PLUTON.

PLUTON (appelant)
Viens, Mercure !
Venez, heures du jour et de la nuit.

Les nuages au fond de la scène, surélevée, s'entr'ouvrent
pour laisser bondir Mercure suivi du cortège des heures.
(MERCURE, rôle muet) Chacune des heures vêtues de tons
gradués, couleur d'aube, d'aurore, de jour, etc ... porte
un présent pour PERSÉPHONE.

6-

LE CHOEUR DES NYMPHES

N'accepte rien de PLUTON, PERSÉPHONE.

(Mimique prolongée)

EUMOLPE

PERSÉPHONE confuse
Se refuse
A tout ce qui la séduit
Cependant Mercure espère
Qu'en souvenir de sa mère
Saura la tenter un fruit
Un fruit qu'il voit pendre à la branche
Qui se penche
Au-dessus de la soif fatale
De Tentale.
Il cueille une grenade mûre
Et s'assure
Qu'un reste de soleil y luit
Il la tend à Perséphone
Qui s'émerveille et s'étonne
De retrouver dans sa nuit
Un rappel de la lumière
De la terre
Les belles couleurs du plaisir
La voici plus confiante
Et riante
Qui s'abandonne au désir
Saisit la grenade mûre
Y mord...Aussitôt Mercure
S'envole et Pluton sourit.

Le rythme accéléré de la musique, ironique et stridente au
moment où Mercure selon le chant d'Eumolpe, bondit pour
s'emparer de la grenade. Il la tend à Perséphone qui veut
s'en emparer. Le choeur des nymphes s'interpose jusqu'au
moment où Mercure rompt le cercle qu'elles ont formé.Per-
séphone a pris la grenade et y mord. Eclat de rire dans
l'orchestre. Sur les derniers mots d'Eumolpe, le cortège
des heures, Mercure et Pluton se sont retirés. L'on ne voit
plus que Perséphone et le choeur des nymphes.

Example 23

Example 24

7-

PERSÉPHONE

Où suis-je ?.. qu'ai-je fait ?..Quel trouble me saisit ?..
Soutenez-moi, mes soeurs, la grenade mordue
M'a redonné le goût de la terre perdue.

CHOEUR

Si tu contemplais le calice
Du narcisse
Peut-être reverrais-tu
Les prés délaissés et ta mère
Comme il advint quand sur la terre
Le mystère
Du monde infernal t'apparût.

PERSÉPHONE

Entourez-moi, protégez-moi, ombres fidèles,
Cette fleur des prés, la plus belle,
Seul reste du printemps que j'emporte aux enfers,
Si, pour l'interroger, je me penchais sur elle,
que saurait-elle me montrer ?...

CHOEUR

L'hiver.

Perséphone, entourée du choeur des ombres, sur le
devant de la scène a pris la fleur de narcisse
qu'elle gardait à la ceinture et la contemple.

PERSÉPHONE

Où donc avez-vous fui, parfums, chansons, escortes
De l'amour ?.. Je ne vois rien que des feuilles mortes,
Les prés vides de fleurs et les champs sans moissons
Racontent le regret des riantes saisons.
Plus, au penchant des monts, les flûtes bucoliques
N'occupent les bosquets de leurs claires musiques.
De tout semble couler un lent gémissement
Car tout espère en vain le retour du printemps.

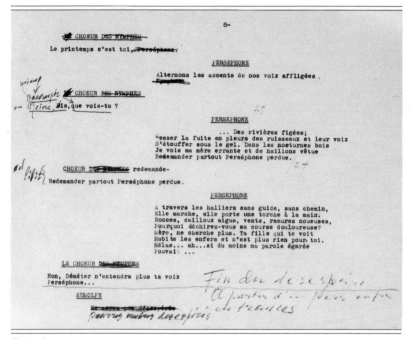

8-

CHŒUR DES NYMPHES

Le printemps c'est toi, ~~Perséphone.~~

PERSÉPHONE

Alternons les accents de nos voix affligées.

CHŒUR DES NYMPHES

Dis, que vois-tu ?

PERSÉPHONE

... Des rivières figées;
Cesser la fuite en pleurs des ruisseaux et leur voix
S'étouffer sous le gel. Dans les nocturnes bois
Je vois ma mère errante et de haillons vêtue
Redemander partout Perséphone perdue.

CHŒUR DES NYMPHES redemande-

Redemander partout Perséphone perdue.

PERSÉPHONE

A travers les halliers sans guide, sans chemin,
Elle marche, elle porte une torche à la main.
Ronces, cailloux aigus, vents, ramures noueuses,
Pourquoi déchirez-vous sa course douloureuse?
Mère, ne cherche plus. Ta fille qui te voit
Habite les enfers et n'est plus rien pour toi.
Hélas... ah...si du moins ma parole égarée
Pouvait ...

LE CHŒUR DES NYMPHES

Non, Déméter n'entendra plus ta voix
Perséphone...

EUMOLPE

Example 25

Example 26

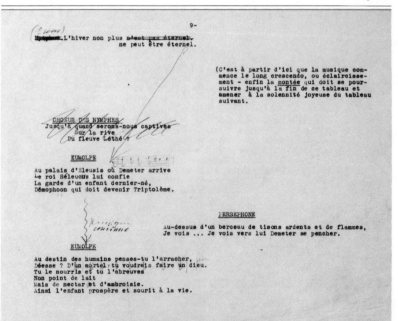

9-

L'hiver non plus ~~n'est pas éternel.~~
ne peut être éternel.

(C'est à partir d'ici que la musique commence le long crescendo, ou éclaircissement - enfin la montée qui doit se poursuivre jusqu'à la fin de ce tableau et
amener à la solennité joyeuse du tableau
suivant.

CHŒUR DES NYMPHES
Jusqu'à quand serons-nous captives
Sur la rive
Du fleuve Léthé

EUMOLPE

Au palais d'Eleusis où Demeter arrive
Le roi Séleucus lui confie
La garde d'un enfant dernier-né,
Démophoon qui doit devenir Triptolème.

PERSÉPHONE

Au-dessus d'un berceau de tisons ardents et de flammes,
Je vois ... Je vois vers lui Demeter se pencher.

EUMOLPE

Au destin des humains penses-tu l'arracher,
Déesse ? D'un mortel, tu voudrais faire un dieu.
Tu le nourris et tu l'abreuves
Non point de lait
Mais de nectar et d'ambroisie.
Ainsi l'enfant prospère et sourit à la vie.

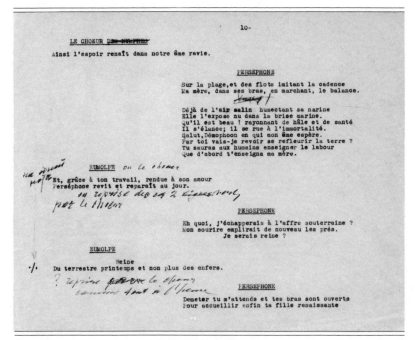

10-

LE CHOEUR DES NYMPHES

Ainsi l'espoir renaît dans notre âme ravie.

PERSÉPHONE

Sur la plage,et des flots imitant la cadence
Ma mère, dans ses bras, en marchant, le balance.

Déjà de l'air salin humectant sa narine
Elle l'expose nu dans la brise marine.
Qu'il est beau ! rayonnant de hâle et de santé
Il s'élance; il se rue à l'immortalité.
Salut,Démophoon en qui mon âme espère.
Par toi vais-je revoir se refleurir la terre ?
Tu sauras aux humains enseigner le labour
Que d'abord t'enseigna ma mère.

EUMOLPE *ou le choeur*

Et, grâce à ton travail, rendue à son amour
Perséphone revit et reparaît au jour.

PERSÉPHONE

Eh quoi, j'échapperais à l'affre souterraine ?
Mon sourire emplirait de nouveau les prés.
Je serais reine ?

EUMOLPE

Reine
Du terrestre printemps et non plus des enfers.

PERSÉPHONE

Demeter tu m'attends et tes bras sont ouverts
Pour accueillir enfin ta fille renaissante

Example 27

Example 28

11-

Au plein soleil qui fait les ombres ravissantes
Venez, Perséphone. Forçons les portes du trépas.
Non, le sombre Pluton ne nous retiendra pas
Nous reverrons bientôt, agités par les vents
Les branchages aux délicats balancements.
O mon terrestre époux, radieux Triptolème
qui m'appelle, j'accours. Je t'appartiens, je t'aime.

Perséphone accompagnée du choeur des
Nymphes s'est dirigée vers le fond de
la scène qui s'illumine, tandis que le
devant de la scène s'obscurcit.

RIDEAU.

-II-

TROISIEME TABLEAU -

Auteuil 29-79 (handwritten)

EUMOLPE - (durant le changement de scène)

C'est ainsi , nous raconte Homère,
Que l'effort de Démophoon
Rendit Perséphone à sa mère,
Et à la terre son printemps.

Le rideau se relève sur un paysage ensoleillé, bleu et or. Au
fond , une colline que domine un temple dorique. Au premier
plan, sur la gauche, un tumulus surmonté de chênes verts, et sur
le flanc duquel, vu de biais par le spectateur, l'entrée d'un
tombeau, fermé d'abord par de lourds vantaux de pierre, à la
manière des tombes étrusques. Devant ce porche funèbre se tient
le génie de la mort, une torche éteinte à la main .

(Le texte ci-après ne pourra être definitivement établi que
d'après la musique et la mise en scène. A étudier .)

Cependant sur la colline
Qui domine
Le présent et l'avenir
Les Grecs ont construit un temple
Pour Déméter qui contemple
Un peuple heureux ~~l'annelie~~ _accourir_
Triptolème est auprès d'elle,
Dont la ~~famille~~ reluit.   _famille_
Et fidèle
Le chœur des nymphes les suit.

prennent le chant d'Eu. (handwritten)

Un chœur d'adolescents, ~~sans doute~~ monte
à la rencontre du chœur des nymphes.

Le chœur des NYMPHES -

Venez à nous, enfants des hommes.

Example 29

Example 30

-I2-

CHŒUR DES ENFANTS - //

Accueillez-nous, filles des dieux .

LES DEUX CHOEURS - _se rejaignaient_ (handwritten)

Nous apportons nos offrandes   _ou: vous apportez vos_
De guirlandes
Lys, safrans, crocus, bleuets   _es (une syllabe)_
Renoncules, anemones.....
Des bouquets pour Perséphone
Des épis pour Deméter
Les blés sont encore verts
Mais les seigles déjà blonds.

CHŒUR DES ENFANTS - //

Deméter reine _de l'été_
Dispensez-nous vôtre sérénité.

LE CHŒUR DES NYMPHES -

Oh ! reviens à nous Perséphone
Brise les portes du tombeau
Archange de la mort rallume ton flambeau.
Deméter t'attend. Triptolème   _t'attend et non t'attens?_
Arrache le manteau de deuil
Qui la couvre encore et parsème
De fleurs l'alentour du cercueil.

LES CHŒURS MÊLES .

Ouvrez-vous, fatales portes.
Flambeaux éteints, flammes mortes
Ravivez-vous. Il est temps.
Il est temps enfin que tu sortes
Des gouffres de la nuit, Printemps.

Les vantaux de pierre roulent sur leurs gonds. Perséphone

-13-

surgit du tombeau.

LE CHOEUR DES NYMPHES -

Encore mal réveillée
Perséphone émerveillée
Sort du sinistre parvis.
Chancelante et comme ivre
De nuit, tu doutes de vivre
Encore, et pourtant tu vis.

CHOEUR DES ENFANTS -

Parle, Perséphone, raconte
Ce que nous cachent les hivers.

LE CHOEUR DES NYMPHES -

Avec toi, quel secret remonte
Du fond des gouffres entrouverts.

LES CHOEURS MÊLÉS -

Dis, qu'as-tu vu dans les Enfers ?

Example 31

Example 32

Encore mal réveillée
Perséphone émerveillée,
Hors du sinistre parvis
bis ou (Tu t'avances et, comme ivre
ter ad (De nuit, tu doutes de vivre
libitum (Encore, et pourtant tu vis.

L'ombre encore t'environne
Chancelante Perséphone
Comme prise en un réseau,
bis ou (Mais partout où ton pied pose
ter ad (S'épanouit une rose
libitum (Et s'élève un chant d'oiseau

(s'épanou-it, ce vers, ainsi
que tous les autres, est de
sept pieds)

Chaque geste te dégage;
Et ta danse est un langage
Qui propage le bonheur;
L'abandon, la confi-ance
Et le rayon se fi-ance
Au pétale de la fleur.

Tout, dans la nature entière,
Rit, s'abreuve de lumière...
Toi, tu bondis vers le jour.
(Mais pourquoi, si sérieuse,
bis ou (Restes-tu silencieuse
ter (Lorsque t'accueille l'amour ?

(La suite, en vers de huit
pieds; et par conséquent,
sur un rythme différent)

Parle, Perséphone, raconte
Ce que nous cachent les hivers.

Avec toi quel secret remonte
Du fond des gouffres entr'ouverts.

Dis, qu'as-tu vu dans les enfers ?

Je n'ai pas besoin d'ordre et me rends de plein gré

Où non point tant la loi que mon amour me mène

Et je vais pas à pas descendre les degrés

Qui conduisent au fond de la détresse humaine.

Perséphone a pris, des mains de
Mercure la torche allumée. Précé-
dée et guidée par Mercure, elle
descend lentement et solennellement
vers la porte tombale qui s'ouvre d
devant elle. Les Nymphes entourent
Déméter et Triptolème. Le choeur des
enfants et Eumolpe restent à flanc
de coteau

EUMOLPE

Ainsi, vers l'ombre souterraine

Tu t'achemines à pas lents,

Porteuse de la torche et reine

Des vastes pays somnolents

Ton lot est d'apporter aux ombres

Un peu de la clarté du jour,

Un répit à leurs maux sans nombre

A leur détresse un peu d'amour.

Il faut, pour qu'un printemps renaisse

Que le grain consente à mourir

Sous terre, afin qu'il reparaisse

En moisson d'or pour l'avenir.

Example 33

Example 1. The rotation is a major second lower than the melody as it appears in the final form, where, also, the choice of the upper interval and the emphasis on the first syllable of "reine" are obvious improvements over the simple repetition.

Example 2. The notations suggest that Stravinsky conceived the rhythm of the chorus before the pitches and established that the piece was to be staccato in character, the words lending themselves to separation into their component syllables. The initial motif—two sixteenths and an eighth followed by an eighth rest and an eighth note—is the same as in the final version.

Example 3. The pitches and rhythms are virtually the same as in the published score, which is also true of Eumolpus's first line and of the rhythms of the next two lines.

Example 4. The $\frac{6}{8}$ meter is surprising, and the notations are remote from the final version. Stravinsky's Russian words next to Gide's parentheses read: "Use this either bis or ter, because the piece could be too long."

Example 5. The Russian may be translated: "During the fermata, or [else] changing chords," but in the final score the declamation takes place during a sustained chord. Stravinsky followed his memo here, that is to repeat the music of the previous chorus from "Tiens" to "sur tes gardes."

Example 6. The page reveals that Persephone's descent to the underworld was conceived as a march; her last phrases are designated "prelude to the 'March.' "

Example 7. The Russian words on the left side of the page may be translated: "A few measures of music before the chorus." Stravinsky does not seem to have had the pitches in mind for Eumolpus's last line, but the rhythm and stresses are the same as in the final score. The notations adjoining the chorus of Nymphs may contain some of the music in embryo, but the melodic contour is not discernible.

Example 8. The music of three of the measures in $\frac{3}{4}$ time is a half-step higher than that of the final version, if this is a sketch for the music of the Berceuse; but the melody of the last measure resembles the chorus "O reviens à nous, Perséphone" in the third part.

Example 9. In the final score, Stravinsky gave three syllables to "envie." In the note in Russian, he suggests that the word "de" could be omitted. The motif and rhythms in the middle of the page are remote from the final version.

Example 10. The Russian following "Pluton" says "a pause after this word." The other Russian phrases may be translated: "Very majestic music, like a psalm," and "[illegible] Persephone's companions."

Example 11. Stravinsky retained the idea of a full chorus loudly calling Mercury and of an antiphonal male chorus singing pianissimo.

Example 12. All of the script on this page is Gide's.

Example 13. Stravinsky's underscoring in red pencil of three of Gide's recommendations for the music express the composer's opinion of the poet's understanding of the art of music.

Example 14. Stravinsky relieved the monotony of the Persephone-Eumolpus dialogue by giving the words "l'hiver" to altos and tenors.

Example 15. Stravinsky shaped Persephone's long speech by dividing it and assigning one of her lines to the chorus.

Example 16. The writing at the bottom of the page shows that Gide has found the last lines of the speech but not the preceding ones.

Example 17. The last lines that Gide marked for Eumolpus, Stravinsky set for the chorus.

Example 18. Stravinsky did not use Eumolpus's first speech here as indicated but saved it for the third scene.

Example 19. As in the first draft of the second scene, Eumolpus's notes are in the tonality of the final version. Here the melodic shape is closer to the final form, but the triplet rhythm and the repeated minor thirds (instead of the full triad) of the final version are more poignant.

Example 20. The musical sketch is remarkably similar to the finished score, in which the addition of the canonic horn part at the distance of an eighth-note is a great improvement.

Example 21. Stravinsky's comments in Russian may be translated: "add music for ½ minute" (left center); "not bad" (the sarcastic words followed by an exclamation point); "Oh these poets, how they would like to spew all of this out is music" (the words in a box); "A pause, after 'Pluto' " (bottom of page). The 40 seconds calculated for Persephone's speech exactly correspond to the music that Stravinsky was to provide, though as yet he apparently had no notational ideas to accompany the speech.

Example 22. In the final score, the infernal sarabande is more in character than the celestial one, if the latter is the middle section of the "da capo" dance that Stravinsky eventually composed.

Example 23. The Russian script to the right may be translated: "Everything that occurs during Eumolpus's aria." The Russian to the lower left says: "What a mentality!" The rhythm of the music for the line "Les belles couleurs" more nearly corresponds (in different note values) to the rhythm of the line "La voici" in the final version.

Example 24. The estimated 40 seconds for Persephone's speech tallies with the duration of the music that was actually composed.

Example 25. Stravinsky's irritation with Gide's Nymphs is evident in his vigorous deletion of the words "des nymphes" and, at the top of the page, "Perséphone."

Example 26. The rhythmic notations in Eumolpus's second line anticipate the final version.

Example 27. The memo in Russian (before the line of Eumolpus and the chorus together) may be translated: "On a single note" (i.e., in unison).

Example 28. The repetition of the word "Venez" is Stravinsky's change, not Gide's.

Example 29. Stravinsky rightly questions his $\frac{4}{4}$ meter. The final score is strikingly superior to these equal eighth-notes. The notation below may be the first idea for the music at 224.

Example 30. The hammering rhythm at the bottom of the page contains the idea developed between 216 and 219.

Example 31. Stravinsky ignored Gide's designations for the choruses but retained the fermatas to slow the pace in preparation for the ending.

Example 32. The $\frac{3}{8}$ meter, the B-flat tonality, and the melodic interval were used in the children's chorus. The rhythm and meter for "s'épanouit une rose" are the same as in the final score. The Russian words (next to the bracket) say: "for the children alone."

Example 33. The melody and the accompaniment rhythm form the nucleus of the final piece.

APPENDIX C

THE RAKE'S PROGRESS: *The Evolution
of the Libretto and the Sketches*

The transcription of the scenario of *The Rake's Progress* published in *Memories
and Commentaries* (New York, 1960) is inaccurate and incomplete. The page
containing the Trio with Chorus, Act III, Scene 1, is missing, probably because
this scene was not drafted during the sessions in Stravinsky's home, and because the page is in the hand of Chester Kallman, for which reason Stravinsky
did not file it under "Auden." Kallman also contributed a "Note on the suggested two-part structure" of this scene. (Part 1 begins with Anne's "He loves
me still," Part 2 with Baba's "I shall go back.") Stravinsky followed the suggestion but added an Introduction (Baba: "You love him") and an Interlude
(Baba: "So find him").

Some of Stravinsky's and Auden's handwritten corrections and additions
are missing from the five pages of the scenario that were published, including
the composer's notation at the end, "Hollywood, Nov. 18/1947," and the poet's
repeated instruction for Shadow to whistle (rather than to laugh) at his exits
and entrances. But obviously the complete scenario must be made available before a satisfactory study of the dramatic conception of the opera can be undertaken.[1] It is in the scenario, after all, that directors have found justification for
dividing Acts II and III into four and two scenes, respectively.

Stravinsky received the libretto in three installments, in January and February 1948—or four, counting the pact between Shadow and Rakewell (not
found in the original, where the text goes directly from Shadow's "All is ready,
sir" to Rakewell's "Dear father Trulove"), which was sent separately on February 9. In Washington, D.C., on March 31, Auden presented the composer with a
substantially revised version of the whole. By this date, however, Stravinsky had
added so many marginal notes and scansion and other marks that the first version was the one from which he composed the opera, in spite of the many
changes and inserts that this required. But more surprising than any of the
changes that he introduced is his retention of Auden's favorite heading, "Orchestral Recitative." Stravinsky kept this even when it did not fit the music.
Thus Shadow's "Fair Lady" aria is called "Recitative and Quartet" in the published score, even though the recitative comes only at the end of the piece, and
"Quartet" is the title of the next one.

Stravinsky's queries in his working copy of the libretto were numerous,
but he erased nearly all of them. The few that remain are characteristically
waspish. After Auden's note "Return of the orchestra," Stravinsky wrote: "It nev-

---

[1] The scenario is included in Edward Mendelson's forthcoming edition of the Auden
and Kallman libretti.

er stopped." And following the stage direction for Baba, "Brushes herself off while the chorus murmurs," Stravinsky penciled in the objection: *"During* her aria or *after it,* not *while."* At one place in Act III, the composer inserted the question: "What is the difference, for the music, between 'chorus' and 'crowd'?"

Most of Stravinsky's comments in the "Washington" libretto are in Russian, probably for the reason that, with Auden watching, the composer was afraid of making mistakes in English. At the end of the Brothel scene, however, Stravinsky did write in English, though at a later date: "What are doing the men and women during Shadow's last lines?" (No stage direction is given after the chorus forms "a lane" for Mother Goose and Rakewell.)

In the revised version of the Cabaletta, the line "Or freed unwanted" had become "Or be rejected," but during the meeting in Washington this was further amended to "Or be forgotten." And whereas in the original the preceding recitative ends with the words "Tom is weak," the revision adds: "And wants the comfort of a helping hand" (soon changed to "And needs the comfort of a faithful hand"). In Washington, or soon after, the line "This engine shall all men excite" was changed to the less risqué "This engine Adam shall excite." On that March 31, too, Auden added prosodic markings on the alternating eight- and six-syllable verse beginning "In youth the panting slave pursues"; decided that the "tea cosy" of the first version and "dust cover" of the second should become "the wig"; and, in response to Stravinsky's criticism of wordiness, wrote "Omit if too much" and "could be cut" next to several passages, including the beautiful quatrain "Defeated, mocked . . ." and the two choral stanzas "In triumph glorious . . ." and "For what is sweeter. . . ?" But Stravinsky set every word, after resolving his doubts about some of them ("o'er," to name only one).

The next major revision, made on Stravinsky's request in October 1949 and sent by Auden before the 24th, was Baba's part in the Terzetto. Her lines in both the original and revised versions had been the same:

> I *believe* I explained that I was waiting . . . *Who* can this
> person be? . . . It could hardly be thought that wedded
> bliss entailed *such* manner of attention . . . I confess that
> I do *not* understand . . . When am I to be helped from this
> infernal box? . . . Should I expire, the world will know whom
> to blame . . . Tell her to go, you have your duties as a
> spouse, you know, and I cannot but feel this is the least
> of them . . . Allah! . . . I'm suffocating . . . Hussy,
> begone, or I shall summon spirits and have you well haunted
> for your presumption . . . A plague upon matrimony . . . My
> love, if you do not wish Baba to be piqued, do see that she
> is not condemned to remain immured in this conveyance forever.

Auden now changed this to the following, marking the stresses as well, and dividing the text into metrical units:

Why this de- | lay? A- | way, *or the* | *crowd will* | . . . . | O!
And | *why, if I* | *may be al-* | *lowed to in-* | *quire, does my* | hus-band de- | sire
To con- | *verse with this* | *per-son?* | Who is it, | pray,
He pre- | fers to his | Ba-ba on their | wed-ding | day?

A | fa-mi-ly | friend? An | an-cient | flame?
A | *bride has* | *sure-ly the* | *pri-or* | *claim*
On the | *bri-dal* | *night!* I'm | quite per- | plexed
And | more, I con- | *fess,* than a | tri-fle | vexed!

E- | nough is e- | nough! | Ba-ba is not | used
To be | so a- | bused. She is | not a- | mused.
Come | here my love. I | hate wai- ting.
I'm | suf-fo-| ca-ting. | Hea-vens a | bove!
Will you per | mit me to | sit in this con-| vey-ance
For | e-ver and | e-ver?

Stravinsky did not set the words indicated here in italics, and the accents and
longs and shorts of the third stanza are much more free and fluent in the music
than in the rhythmic scheme shown here.

   Other changes were made in New York in April 1950. For only two examples, "I wish for nothing else" replaced "Wishful chance, farewell," and "such
a hectic" day was substituted for "such a thrilling" one. But by this time, why
did Auden *not* cut

> Attorneys crouched like gardeners to pay,
> Bowers of paper only seals repair.

which, whatever the lines mean, might make the audience wonder about the
relevance of amphibious mammals? Auden had difficulties with Sellem's lines
beginning "An unknown object draws us near," and he temporarily deleted one
of them, "A block of copal? | Mint of alchemy?" in order to insert the following
line before the last one:

> O you whose houses are in order, hear:

The Washington text, however, introduces two lines after the first one ("An
unknown object draws us, draws us near"), which are even worse:

> They cannot face the future who have fear;
> Who does, beyond the Almanack shall peer.

In the first version of the libretto, Shadow addresses Rakewell in the Graveyard
scene as "thee" and "thy," but in one of the New York meetings, Stravinsky
insisted on "you" and "yours." At first, too, the "Fugal Chorus (Funèbre)," as
Auden called it, consisted of the two lines:

> Mourn for Adonis, ever young, the dear
> Of Venus: weep, tread softly round his bier.

He expanded these later to four stanzas, consisting of lines of five, six, seven, and eight syllables, respectively. Since, apart from a few canons and a brief chaconne, the opera does not employ contrapuntal forms, Stravinsky confined the "fugal" idea to simple three-part imitations at the beginning of the Chorus. Regrettably, he chose the octosyllabic lines, with the unfortunate silent possessive ("Venus' ")—for which he added a syllable ("Venus'(es)") and more music.

August 7, 1958, BBC television transmitted a performance of the "second part" of the opera, with a synopsis of the first part, in rhymed couplets by Auden (and possibly Kallman), to be read by Nick Shadow. The televised portion of the opera apparently began with Act II, Scene 3, since the camera is directed to "pull back" from Shadow at his lines

> So to our play. The wedding-knot is tied,
> And now you'll meet the bridegroom and the bride.

As the librettists' afterview interpretation of their drama, the text, of approximately sixty lines, sheds light on several questions, among them Rakewell's decision to marry Baba. Shadow says to Rakewell:

> Be happy and rejoice,
> Knowing you know no motive for your choice,

and explains to the audience:

>   . . . pride
> Soon won his guilty conscience to my side.

Perhaps the most striking feature of the sketches is that while they differ on every page from the final score, almost all of the first notations for a piece, or passage, are remarkably similar to the ultimate versions. In only one significant instance did Stravinsky alter his original choice of meter, transforming the march rhythm

Lan - ter - loo   my   la - dy

into the $\frac{6}{8}$ dance. Changes of key, or tonality, after the first draft are almost as infrequent. The principal exceptions are "O heart be stronger," of which Stravinsky composed a few measures in C minor before lowering it to B minor; "Venus, mount thy throne"; and the second choral response in the Lullaby, Act III, Scene 3, which was originally in the same key as the first response until Stravinsky discovered the effect of the upward transposition.

Changes in melodic intervals between sketches and final score are numerous but rarely crucial. One important exception is found between the first and final drafts of the music in which Shadow enumerates the means by which Rakewell might choose to die. In the original, the melodic line is confined to seconds; the wide intervals were developed later. Words are sometimes found in purely rhythmic form, without pitches or harmonic "blocking," though these rhythms are often changed from one draft to another. In the sketch of the Act III Lullably, for example, the dotted rhythm in the first measure is continued, while at "[Be thou] insane," the figure ♪♫ occurs on every beat of the measure, including the first; Stravinsky introduced the rests, like the note itself, Shadow's E natural, at a later date.

Not many of the indications for instrumentation, found throughout the sketches, differ significantly from the final score. A trombone makes an appearance in the accompaniment at "The Age of Gold"; horns, rather than trumpets, are indicated at **33** in Act II; and at Baba's "My love, am I to remain in here forever?" Stravinsky's first preference was for English horn and bassoon (instead of two bassoons).

A comparison of the sketch and final score reveals many improvements in pacing. To mention only one, Rakewell's acceptance of Shadow's pact—"A fair offer, 'tis agreed"—was originally followed by a perfect cadence and by some notations for a new piece in F, $\frac{3}{16}$ time. The next draft contains the elision to A minor. Virtually no music was discarded, apart from "ossia" versions of brief phrases. The one exception is found at **46,** in Act III, scene 1. Here Stravinsky wrote, and promptly canceled, a two-measure interlude for flute and clarinet.

Finally, it should be said that on first reading the libretto, Stravinsky was exasperated by Shadow's philosophical asides in the Graveyard scene—"The positive appalls him" and "the simpler the trick." By the time this point had been reached in the composition, however, the composer treasured every word of the libretto, and cut or changed very few of them.

Stravinsky wrote the summary sketch score in pencil on large sheets of Manila paper, drawing all of the staves with his stylus. In comparatively dense passages, such as the quartet in Act I, scene 1, he used blue and red pencil to clarify the part-writing. Many separate sketch pages of different sizes are clipped to the Manila ones or folded within them.

"The Stravinsky *Nachlass:* A Provisional Checklist of Music Manuscripts," by John Shepard, in the June 1984 issue of the Music Library Association *NOTES* purports to be a survey of Stravinsky's collection of his manuscripts and an account of its history but is inadequate in both respects. (Mr. Shepard, a reference librarian in the Music Division of the New York Public Library, was employed in the removal of the manuscripts to the library in late March 1983 pending their final disposition.) As an opening example, Mr. Shepard states that the materials in the collection "give clues" about "the correct musical text of nearly every work [Stravinsky] composed from 1904 to 1966." In actuality, the collection contains nothing of the original versions of *Firebird, Petrushka,* and *Le Sacre du printemps* (one small notation from the Danse sacrale excepted); nothing of *Zvezdoliki,* the Balmont songs (except in the late instrumentations), *Perséphone, Requiem Canticles,* and "The Owl and the Pussycat"; only fragments of *Histoire du soldat;* no sketches for the 1924 Concerto and almost none for the *Dumbarton Oaks* Concerto; nothing of the compositions with opus numbers; no juvenilia except the manuscripts for *How the Mushrooms Prepared for War* (described as "unpublished" despite an excellent 1982 Soviet edition); no source materials for *Le Baiser de la fée,* and only very incomplete ones for *Pulcinella.*

Mr. Shepard states that "after the Library was given custody of the collection in late January, Thor Wood, Chief of the Library's Performing Arts Research Center, and the present writer worked in the Stravinsky apartment checking the music manuscripts against an existing inventory and producing a preliminary inventory of the documentary archives." What he neglects to mention is that at all times, I was present as well, as my signature next to each checked item attests, and that *two* inventories were used, the one he describes, compiled by Sigmund Rothschild, and another, compiled by Andre Marion, Stravinsky's son-in-law. (Rothschild, a certified appraiser, was employed by Arnold Weissberger, Stravinsky's attorney, in January 1970, and the task was completed in three weeks—most inefficiently, partly because Rothschild and the secretary he worked with could read neither music nor any foreign language.) The only complete and accurate inventory was a microfilm, made in 1967–68 in Stravinsky's Hollywood home and in the Beverly Hills bank in which his manuscripts were kept. That Mr. Shepard does not mention this is puzzling: it must have been obvious to him that the only useful survey of the *Nachlass* would have to be based on the microfilm, not on the two inventories; moreover, his Performing Arts Research Center had access to a copy of the microfilm from Stravinsky's children, who had had it for fifteen years and who were responsible for the court order transferring the manuscripts from the Stravinsky apartment to the New York Public Library. The Paul Sacher Foundation purchased the collection not as listed in the Rothschild and Marion inventories but as recorded on the microfilm.

Mr. Shepard gives no account of the background of the collection, yet it is essential to an understanding of Stravinsky's American years to know that his libraries of music, books, manuscripts, and personal and business papers were not in his possession from 1939 to 1949. Before leaving Europe for America in September 1939, he placed most of his full-score manuscripts in a Paris bank vault. Other manuscripts were stored in the cellar of his apartment at 7, rue Antoine-Chantin. During the war, many items from his collection were removed by his younger son, Soulima, according to Mina Svitalski, the Stravinsky children's governess since 1917, who lived at the address and who reported this to a family friend, Olga Sallard, who informed Stravinsky in 1946 or 1947. After the war, Stravinsky's elder son, Theodore, shipped manuscripts, books, the complete collection of family photographs (formerly in the possession of Stravinsky's mother), and furniture (including Stravinsky's Swiss work table and Swiss painted cabinet) from Paris to Geneva. (In the spring of 1950, Stravinsky asked Theodore for an inventory of manuscripts in his possession in Geneva, but no full accounting was ever received.) In 1949 Stravinsky invited me to catalogue the manuscripts that had been sent to him from rue Antoine-Chantin and that he wished to sell. These were kept in closets in his home at 1260 North Wetherly Drive, Hollywood, until 1965, when he moved to 1218 North Wetherly Drive and decided to place the manuscripts in a bank in Andre Marion's name. In October 1969, after moving to New York, Stravinsky asked Marion to send the manuscripts there, and when Marion did not comply, Stravinsky sued for their return. He received them at the end of December 1969.

The manuscripts in the *Nachlass* are not, despite Mr. Shepard's claim, those that Stravinsky "chose to retain." In the late 1940s, after selling a 1910 *Petrushka* sketchbook and the full score of the 1946 *Petrushka*, Stravinsky hoped to dispose of all of his manuscripts no less profitably. This was the raison d'être for the 1949 catalogue, bearing only my name but actually compiled by Stravinsky and myself together: Stravinsky wanted to provide prospective buyers with a descriptive brochure. It was this catalogue, updated to 1954, that was published as an appendix to Eric Walter White's biography of the composer. I regret that Mr. Shepard based his survey on an inventory that is inaccurate, incomplete, and hopelessly out of date.

Future scholars should be made aware of numerous inaccuracies in Mr. Shepard's discussions of individual works. For example, he describes one manuscript as Stravinsky's "realization of a canon by Schoenberg." In fact, the "realization" was published in shorthand form by Schoenberg himself in 1928: I simply wrote it out in score form when I recorded it, while Stravinsky, who admired the piece, made a calligraphic copy of the manuscript. Mr. Shepard also describes a manuscript of the *Double Canon: Raoul Dufy in Memoriam* as the "draft of an episode." As in the case of the Schoenberg canon, the manuscript contains the complete four-part canon in shorthand form.

Mr. Shepard perpetuates a serious misunderstanding by quoting Elliott

Carter's recollections of Stravinsky showing him a book of sketches for *The Flood*. According to Carter, Stravinsky "proceeded to explain how he chose fragments from his sketches, tore them out, shuffled them in different orders until he found one that satisfied him, and then pasted them down. I was genuinely surprised to learn of such an unexpected way of composing. . . ." That Stravinsky never composed in this "unexpected way" should be obvious to anyone who has compared the sketches and the final score. The truth of the matter is that from the time of *The Flood*, Stravinsky sketched on any scrap of paper that came to hand—a sheet from a hotel telephone note pad, a paper napkin, his wife's stationery, the back of an envelope or a telegram—and pasted each lapidary notation in scrapbooks, one of which he showed to Carter. Whatever Carter thought Stravinsky had said about the contents of these pages, the sequence of the sketches was never in doubt in his mind.

Mr. Shepard quotes a description from my 1954 catalogue of a large (12 by 15½ inches) orchestra score of the *Sacre*, remarking that this item has not been traced and was not listed in the Rothschild catalogue (naturally enough, since this does not list any published music), but stating that "plate 4 of a 1978 publication, *Stravinsky in Pictures and Documents*, shows page 48 of this score in full color. . . ." In fact, this plate was photographed, actual size, from a miniature score. The Stravinsky-Ansermet correspondence makes clear that the rubricated corrections in the timpani parts shown in plate 4 date from the summer of 1922 and are those contained in this miniature score.[1] The very different timpani parts in all corrected *large* scores were inserted in 1926, when the work was in demand in several cities simultaneously.[2] The large score mentioned in the 1954 catalogue is partly identified there by a statement that "pages 99, 100, and 101 are almost entirely in [Stravinsky's] blue- and red-pencil manuscript." But in the only large score that Stravinsky had not sold or otherwise disposed of by the 1960s, pages 99–101 are written in sepia and in the hand of a copyist; they do not contain a single mark by Stravinsky. In a letter to Ralph Hawkes of November 6, 1948,[3] Stravinsky says that "a big full score" of the *Sacre* in his possession was used for the "second edition" (1926 version), but "since then I made new changes."

Mr. Shepard erroneously writes: "a draft of the second theme area of the first movement of the *Sonata for Two Pianos* (1943–44) begins with instrumental indications which show that that work was originally planned for orchestra. . . ." The "draft of the second theme area" does have indications for instrumentation, and is even written in short-score form; but this music was intended for a separate and autonomous piece, part of an aborted film score. Only later was the orchestral section incorporated into the Sonata.

A draft of the Etude for Pianola "omits the final score's opening bars," Mr. Shepard reveals. But what had not yet been composed could not be omitted: ob-

---

[1] See *S.S.C.* I, pp. 155–61.

[2] See Appendix D, *"Le Sacre du printemps:* A Chronology of the Revisions," in *S.S.C.* I.

[3] See the letters to Boosey & Hawkes in the present volume.

viously the opening bars were *added,* though when this took place remains to be discovered. According to a letter from Stravinsky to Alfred Cortot, the holograph was sent to Madame Eugenia Errazuriz.[4]

Mr. Shepard's "Checklist" mentions features of the sketches and drafts but too often fails to note the real point of interest. It is not surprising that the volume of sketches for *Oedipus Rex* "opens to reveal Latin text in IS's hand on the left page." But what is to be made of the French translations that sometimes accompany the Latin? That Stravinsky was dependent on them? And how are we to account for the twelve-note series of Schoenberg's Quintet, Op. 26, on a sketch page of Stravinsky's Septet, but in a different hand?

Mr. Shepard's most evident howler is his identical description of forty pages of sketches for the 1931 "Concerto en ré pour violon et orchestre" (Violin Concerto) and the 1946 "Concerto en ré pour orchestre à cordes" (Basler Concerto).

Mr. Shepard says that the Russian text of *Les Noces* is interspersed with numbers that "may" refer to sources in the Afanasiev and Kireyevsky folklore collections. But these sources exist in many libraries, and Theodore Stravinsky has the originals from which his father worked. Further, Mr. Shepard's description of the *Noces* materials is confusing. For instance, he distinguishes two score drafts of the "1st instrumentation for large orchestra." At least three very different early score drafts are found in the collection, one with, and another without, two string "quintuors" (one playing arco, the other pizzicato), the third listing a harpsichord. Since all strings, in all of these scores, are soli, the ensembles cannot qualify as "large" orchestras. Mr. Shepard dates a chart showing Stravinsky's tuning of each string of the cimbalom from the time of the 1919 "2nd instrumentation" of *Les Noces*. But 1915 is a more likely year, since that is when Stravinsky learned to play the instrument and restrung it himself.

Mr. Shepard says that the *Petit Ramusianum harmonique* is unpublished, though Stravinsky's contribution is found on the first page of the volume for which it was solicited, *Hommage à Ramuz,* published in Lausanne in 1937 in an edition of eight hundred. Mr. Shepard also lists as unpublished *Valse des fleurs* and *Lied ohne Name,* both of which have been published in facsimile.[5] Finally, he claims that "Sagesse" (Verlaine), from Two Songs, Op. 9, was never published in the original scoring, yet a Soviet edition exists.

The chronological order of Mr. Shepard's identifications of the lettered sketchbooks is wrong: his A, B, C, D, E, F should be D, A, B, C, F, E.

Referring to a "smaller page" among the sketches for the Three Songs from William Shakespeare, Mr. Shepard says that it contains a "substitute 4-bar passage." What the smaller page actually contains is the missing music for a part of the text that Stravinsky had neglected to set.

---

[4] See Stavinsky's letter to Alfred Cortot of December 18, 1917, in *S.S.C.* II, 182–83, n. 4.

[5] See *A Stravinsky Scrapbook* (London: Thames & Hudson, 1983), pp. 146–47, and *S.S.C.* I, p. 410.

Many dozens of other pieces of misinformation must be overlooked in this brief review. I should mention, however, that in postponing his discussion of the archives for a "future article," Mr. Shepard states that they consist of "manuscript letters and librettos, typescripts, photographs, programs, clippings, royalty statements, posters, and drawings." This omits such extensive categories as publishers' contracts and lawyers' affidavits—this last the largest of all, since Stravinsky never learned the truth of Donne's "If any man will sue thee for thy coat, let him have thy cloak, too, for if thy adversary have it not, thine advocate will."

"Stravinsky: Sein Nachlass, sein Bild," the Basel Kunstmuseum's exhibition (June 6–September 30, 1984), was lavish in both substance and presentation. Of the makers of the age, perhaps only Picasso could fill so much space with so much interest, as the forty-six works by him in this show attest. These include little-known gouaches for *Pulcinella* and sketches for the cover design of *Ragtime,* but his three portraits of the composer brought together on one wall provided a greater surprise. Though known to most of us only in similar-size reproductions, the drawing of Stravinsky seated is actually twice as large as the one in profile and three times larger than the frontal map of his face.

The dimensions of the three J.-E. Blanche portraits also differ greatly and, with his Redonesque *Karsavina as the Firebird,* add to his stature as an artist. Bakst, Benois, and Roerich are fairly represented, Auberjonois in huge disproportion, but justified in that the documentation of *Histoire du soldat* in his graphics and letters was the most thorough for any opus in the exhibition. The Giacometti room was in bleak contrast to that of the Russians and had drawings spread on all sides; this viewer, at least, would have preferred to see the tiny heads closer together. (All of these studies were assigned to 1957, incidentally, though two of them date from May 1965; one other, not shown, and never reproduced or catalogued, was done from a photograph of the composer in his Hollywood studio nearly a year before the artist knew him.)

For an exhibition that emphasizes Swiss artists and collections, some omissions are puzzling. Thus Theo Meier and Steven-Paul Robert are here, but not Boris Solotareff, whose portrait was completed at the same time and place (1918, Lausanne) as the Robert sketches; and Hans Erni, who made an album of drawings of Stravinsky in Zürich in October 1961. Of set and costume designs, the most regrettable absences are Tchelichev's 1942 *Apollo* (or any reproduction of it) and Hockney's *Rake's Progress,* which would have been of greater interest than reproductions of the Hogarth engravings, which Auden's scenario followed only loosely. And is there no maquette or photograph of Pirandello's 1925 Rome *Histoire du soldat?*

Separate rooms were devoted to *Renard, Les Noces,* and other theatre works, each of which was focused on sketches and drafts of the same passages in the music at different stages, supplemented by photographs, letters, other memorabilia, and artwork. The displays for ballets and operas were obviously

more abundant than those for concertos and cantatas, yet *Perséphone,* one of
Stravinsky's few large-scale theatrical creations, was not represented at all. And
the roles in Stravinsky's biography of those evidently not in favor with Theodore
Stravinsky were censored out, most glaringly that of the composer's second
wife, whose image was limited to a single portrait from her pre-Stravinsky years.
(Her designs for *Perséphone,* now in the Stravinsky-Diaghilev Collection in
New York, were greatly admired in Berlin in 1961, when the Santa Fe Opera
staged the work there.)

The *Sacre* exhibit was the most stunning, with eleven colorful costumes
from the original production suspended from the ceiling, and the draft and full
scores beneath—on loan from the Paul Sacher Foundation, the exhibition's
main source. Valentine Gross's pastels of the poussettes, or khorovods, were
there too, further countering the strangely hard-to-kill notion that the 1913
Sacre was black and white, or brown and white, like Nijinska's *Noces.* The music was piped in, in the 4-hand version, a worrying prospect; but the volume was
sub-restaurant level and the keyboard arrangement too unfamiliar to distract.

René Auberjonois emerged from the exhibition as a figure of larger dimension in Stravinsky's life than has hitherto been recognized. The composer often
characterized him as "sharp" and *"méchant,"* but fondly, as a kindred spirit,
and his letters help to explain the adjectives. " 'I squeeze the lemon to the last
drop,' " the painter quotes Stravinsky on his music, and in a 1935 letter, Auberjonois asks his son Fernand, in New York, to try to discover something from
Stravinsky, on tour there, about his adoption of "an intensive, even bigoted, religion," and whether the contradiction between his religious beliefs and his
"extravagantly materialistic mode of life" has had an effect on his work. Not
unexpectedly, Fernand did not succeed in broaching these matters, conversing
with the composer about buffalo hunting instead.

Another Auberjonois letter describes a lunch at Ouchy with Stravinsky
and Ramuz, August 3, 1935: "Stravinsky crossed the Lake at Thonon and returned to the Haute-Savoie in the evening. Little, feisty Igor did not stop eating:
fried foods on the boat; meats, salads, and cheeses at lunch; ice cream back on
the wharf, where we participated in a traveling fair—at the booth of a colossal
woman who asked us to feel her muscles." Fernand noted here: "A drawing in
the margin of the letter admirably contrasts the daring of the great Russian
musician and the reticence of the Swiss painter when confronted by life in the
raw."

The Kunstmuseum's catalogue is indispensable to anyone concerned with
music, ballet, and theatre decors of the period. Though published only nine
months after the transferral of the *Nachlass* from the New York Public Library to Basel, and a still shorter time after the acquisition of such prime exhib-
its as the full score of *Agon* and the 1920 Errazuriz sketchbook (where is the
one, mentioned in correspondence, from 1917?), no signs of haste are apparent
in the production. True, languages are occasionally mixed ("Three Quatrains
for Unaccompanied Voice auf Texte von . . ."); titles are inconsistent (if *Pribaoutki* is given in Russian, why not *Berceuses du chat*?); important

dates are missing (such as when Stravinsky made his copies of Webern's orchestration of Bach and of Schoenberg's canon); performance information is garbled (the Serenade is listed as having been played by Stravinsky months before it was written); and misattributions occur (that the red crayon markings on the envelope shown on page 72 are not Stravinsky's—they are his son-in-law's—is evident in their near obliteration of the composer's signature; also, the rehearsal number on the *Noces* score reproduced on page 89 is not Stravinsky's but Lawrence Morton's. Yet the mystifying identification of one composer as "J. St. Smith"—a latter-day Anglican saint?—could have been an intentional kindness, to protect the perpetrator of the most-played national anthem at the 1984 Olympic Games.

During the last few weeks of the Basel Kunstmuseum's exhibition "Stravinsky: Sein Nachlass, sein Bild," the composer's death mask was displayed for the first time anywhere—a disturbing apparition, since the furrows from the tubes of an oxygen mask are still visible.

Stravinsky's Swiss decade, the natural focus of the show, was his most fertile and varied, encompassing the Second Tableau of *Petrushka,* most of the *Sacre* and *The Nightingale,* all of *Renard, Histoire du Soldat, Pulcinella, Les Noces* (except for the final instrumentation), and numerous songs and instrumental pieces.

Were the rich displays accompanying the music manuscripts of this period achieved at the expense of so important a later work as *Oedipus Rex?* Whatever the answer, the visitor could not have formed a notion of what *Oedipus* might have looked like at any point in its half-century in the theatre, and this though its designers have included Alfred Roller, Ewald Dülberg, Robert Edmond Jones, Cocteau, Manzù, and Hockney. Since Stravinsky considered Dülberg's set design for the Kroll Oper (February 1928) to be "a perfect realization, the decorative sobriety and sensible positioning of the soloists and chorus resulting in a performance that was a logical extension of my score," perhaps this might have been shown along with the other major loans from the Theatre Museum in the Victoria and Albert. Stravinsky did not see the Roller version at the Vienna Staatsoper, which scooped the Berlin stage premiere by three days; but a friend of the composer's described it to him as "a mélange of Louis-Quinze and Hubert Robert." The singing chorus was in the pit, in the tradition of Diaghilev's productions of *The Nightingale* and *Les Noces.*

More has been written about the *Bild* aspect of the exhibition, the iconography and decorative art, than about the *Nachlass,* the manuscripts and archives, though Stravinsky's manuscripts must be regarded as calligraphic art in addition to the musical art that they notate. Yet the sumptuous catalogue devoted more full pages (sixty-eight) to illustrations of music sketches and scores than to portraits and theatre and costume designs (sixty-four). Inks, crayons, and pencils of more than one color are used in most of the manuscripts, and these are faithfully reproduced. The catalogue reader can learn even from a

Excerpts from The Melodist, *an anthology of dances and songs, copied by Stravinsky as models for use in a projected film score for Orson Welles's* Jane Eyre.

single page. Thus, to compare the sketch and published score of the 1924 Sonata is to discover that piano fingerings were a part of the composing process, though Stravinsky might remove them later, as a builder does his scaffolding. (Stravinsky even revised Isidor Philipp's fingerings in his two volumes of exercises, which were part of the composer's daily piano practice.) The reader can also see how a chord has been revoiced, an orchestral balance adjusted, and a serial order or segment deployed. In one remarkable catalogue page, juxtaposing the sketches for the first and last versions of the ending of the second movement of the Violin Concerto, musicians can follow the act of imagination that expanded an unremarkable five bars into six marvelously vaulting ones.

A few errors are noticeable in the catalogue text. First, the score of *Les Noces* shown on page 86 is not a holograph but a blue carbon of one, as the penciled-over chord for woodwind and timpani shows. Second, the florid script on the sketch for *Apollo* on page 114 is not Stravinsky's but Boris Kochno's (a greeting to the composer). Third, performance data are missing for the Tango—inexplicably, since some of it is to be found in Stravinsky's own hand on the verso of one of Picasso's *Ragtime* covers (no. 201 in the catalogue). And, on page 262, the 1965 orchestral Canon is confused with the *Introitus* of the same year.

Whereas some of the art has been borrowed from Britain, France, West Germany, and the United States, the provenance of the music manuscripts (with a single exception from the Picasso Museum in Paris) is unique and local: the Paul Sacher Foundation. No doubt the music will be exhibited in Basel again, in its own new home, and with the benefit of further acquisitions. Stravinsky's source books have not yet been collected, but in the future we may hope to be able to examine the Kireyevsky volumes containing the annotations for *Les Noces,* as well as such curiosa as *The Melodist* (New York, 1820), from which the composer chose model dance pieces to be used in the *Jane Eyre* film score, a project that absorbed him as *Wuthering Heights* did Balthus; Stravinsky copied out dialogue from the novel, kept on the wall of his studio Bramwell Brontë's drawing of himself and his sisters, and read Mrs. Gaskell's life of Charlotte Brontë.

Perhaps at some future exhibition at the Sacher Foundation, Stravinsky's choice of excerpts from *Linda di Chamounix,* for a projected "Donizetti ballet" (1943),[6] might be on view, and his arrangement for piano of the Overture to Weber's *Turandot.* Perhaps, too, the foundation will succeed in acquiring the manuscripts given to Ernest Ansermet (*Pribaoutki* and the *Berceuses du chat*), Giacomo Manzù (*Oedipus Rex*), Alexander Tansman (*Four Norwegian Moods*), John Cage (*Fanfare*), Henry Moore (*Abraham and Isaac*), and Nijinsky (the orchestral draft of the Danse sacrale, missing from the Lifar *Sacre* manuscript now in the private collection of Paul Sacher, and the most important Stravinsky manuscript still in private hands). No doubt a recording library is also being assembled, beginning with Chaliapin's 1910 disc of Stravinsky's instrumentation of Mussorgsky's *Song of the Flea* and including the composer's voice in a message, relayed to Occupied France, on the twenty-fifth anniversary of Debussy's death, as well as the 1945 Montreal radio interview, and the 1935 speech at MGM, in German, to a group of Hollywood refugee composers. The foundation has already acquired the vast Tony Palmer archive of Stravinsky on film.

To classify the photographic record may take several years. Since a representative selection could not be presented, the Kuntsmuseum confined this branch of the *Bild* to portraits by twelve acknowledged artists of the camera. The results are disappointing, Stravinsky having been overposed by Man Ray, Edward Weston, George Platt Lynes, and even Cartier-Bresson, all of whom also, disastrously, avert the composer's eyes. Auerbach, Langdon Coburn, Mili, and Beaton are not here, or Ruth Orkin, whose glimpse of Stravinsky motioning her to leave him alone at a reception after the premiere of the *Rake* recalls a whole vocabulary of his body language.

Picasso's Stravinsky is more real, even literally, than the thousands created by photographers. Otherwise, among the graphic images only a few Cocteau cartoons and Giacometti drawings are worthy of mention. Eugene Berman had more opportunity to observe the composer than any other artist, but Berman was unable to draw faces. He did leave a sketch of Stravinsky seen from an angle behind and below the podium that exactly captures the dome of the head, the large ears, and the hunched shoulders. Marino Marini's two skulls seem small in relation to the death mask, but they convey the qualities that the sculptor describes as having felt for his subject during those two (only!) modeling sessions in April 1950: "*Stravinsky, personaggio così vivo, così nervosa, così apprensivo mi interessava per la sua forza così sensitiva, per cui procurava grandi difficoltà, e mi dava anche gioia.*"

---

[6]See p. 279.

INDEX

A NOTE ON THE TYPE

This book was set in a digitized version of the type face called
Primer, designed by Rudolph Ruzicka (1883–1978). Ruzicka was
earlier responsible for the design of Fairfield and Fairfield
Medium, faces whose virtues have for some time been accorded
wide recognition.
The complete range of sizes of Primer was first made available in
1954, although the pilot of 12-point was ready as early as 1951.
The design of the face makes general reference to Century—long a
serviceable type, totally lacking in manner or frills of any kind—
but brilliantly corrects its characterless quality.

Composition by American–Stratford Graphics Services, Inc.,
Brattleboro, Vermont.
Printing and binding by The Haddon Craftsmen, Inc.,
Scranton, Pennsylvania.
Calligraphy by G. G. Laurens
Design by Betty Andersen